Felix Frankfurter on the Supreme Court

Felix Frankfurter on the Supreme Court

Extrajudicial Essays on the Court and the

Constitution / edited by Philip B. Kurland

The Belknap Press of Harvard University Press

Cambridge, Massachusetts, 1970

Distributed in Great Britain by Oxford University Press, London
Library of Congress Catalog Card Number 70-99518
SBN 674-29835-7
Printed in the United States of America

Frontispiece, portrait of the Justice by Gardner Cox, courtesy of the artist and the Harvard Law School Library.

TO F.F.'S "BELOVED M.J."

Editor's Preface

Between his retirement from the Supreme Court and his death, Mr. Justice Frankfurter planned the publication of three books. The first was produced shortly before his death by Harvard University Press under the title *Of Law and Life and Other Things That Matter. Felix Frankfurter on the Supreme Court* is the second, a selection of his extrajudicial writings about the Supreme Court and the men that perform its function. The third, so far as I know, was never written.

The present collection was not planned as a book for constitutional lawyers, although these, too, can hardly fail to benefit from reading it. One of Felix Frankfurter's roles before he ascended the bench was as interpreter of the work of the Court to the people who ought to care about its business. For, as he says in one of the essays contained herein: "The evolution of our constitutional law is the work of the initiate. But its ultimate sway depends upon its acceptance by the thought of the nation. The meaning of Supreme Court decisions ought not therefore to be shrouded in esoteric mystery. It ought to be possible to make clear to lay understanding the exact scope of constitutional doctrines that underlie [its] decisions." It is in this spirit that this book was compiled.

This volume, like *Of Law and Life*, is Felix Frankfurter's book, not mine. The conception was his; the words are his. I served merely to execute his will and my contribution has been a very limited one. Because so many of these essays were prepared for popular journals of opinion, they did not carry the stigmata of the technical pieces written for law reviews and other scholarly publications: an abundance of footnotes. On the theory, concurred in by the Justice, that the interested public in this more sophisticated day would want the opportunity to see the sources of his quotations and references, I have attempted to supply these omissions. When footnotes are supplied, a statement is added to the source note or the specific notes are followed by [Ed.]. All other notes are in the original articles, although sometimes I have changed the form or cited later editions. I have not, in all instances, succeeded in uncovering all the materials that the Justice, with his catholicity, was able to command. In this search, and more particularly in verifying the references that I have inserted, I have had the able assistance of Leslie Nute and Samuel Clapper, students at The Law School of The University of Chicago. Their work, in turn, was made possible by the generosity of the University in providing resources from Law School funds.

I want here to express publicly my gratitude, in connection with both volumes, to Mrs. Elsie Douglas, so long the Justice's secretary and "right-hand man." Her contributions to these volumes have been so varied and so many that they are not even subject to being catalogued. Mrs. Artie Scott, my own secretary, has handled the manuscripts for these two volumes with the same meticulous care and dedication that she has bestowed on all my writings and editorial efforts for more than a decade. I am, of course, most grateful to her. To Messrs. Max Freedman and Benjamin F. Goldstein I am indebted for information permitting me to check the authenticity of some of the Justice's unsigned publications. Finally, I must point out that the projection of these two volumes—to the extent that someone other than the Justice may be said to be responsible—was as much the conception of Federal Trade Commissioner Philip Elman as of anyone. Certainly the books derived from his conversations with the Justice. And it was he who negotiated the contract on behalf of the Justice for their publication.

For me this work has been a labor of love from which I derived much learning. I regret only that the Justice did not survive to see the volume brought to fruition under the imprint of the University which was so important to him and to which he was so important. My hope is that it will bring some small measure of satisfaction to Mrs. Frankfurter, for whom the world has been such an empty place since February 22, 1965.

Chicago, Illinois — P.B.K.
July 1969

Contents

Contents

Felix Frankfurter on the Supreme Court

The Zeitgeist and the Judiciary

I am sure that none of us will ever again enjoy the divine feeling of being one of the potentates of the profession that the editorship of the *Review* afforded. No, not even were we to sit on the Supreme Bench. For it was our frequent and joyous duty to reverse even that tribunal in an infallible judgment of 165 words. Representing those to whom that luxury is still a green memory, I suppose I am to give expression to the ardor of youth, still untempered by responsibility, and not yet disillusioned by experience.

Last August, the American Bar Association with solemnity adopted vigorous resolutions condemning the recall of judges. I was one of those who favored the resolution, and I should vote for it again. But as I left the meeting, I had a conviction that the action was inadequate, that the American Bar Association fell short of its responsibility in not going beyond negative criticism and inquiring into the cause of the ferment that partly expresses itself in the ill-conceived proposal of the judicial recall. The fallacy of a specific remedy may be crushingly exposed, but we cannot whistle down the wind a widespread, insistent, and well-vouched feeling of dissatisfaction.

The tremendous economic and social changes of the last fifty years have inevitably reacted upon the functions of the state. More and more government is conceived as the biggest organized social effort for dealing with social problems. Our whole evolutionary thinking leads to the conclusion that economic independence lies at the very foundation of social and moral well-being. Growing democratic sympathies, justified by the social message of modern scientists, demand to be translated into legislation for economic betterment, based upon the conviction that laws can make men better by affecting the conditions of living. We are persuaded that evils are not inevitable, and that it is the business of statesmanship to tackle them step by step, tentatively, experimentally, not demanding

This speech, delivered at the twenty-fifth anniversary dinner of the *Harvard Law Review*, was first published in *Survey* magazine for January 1913. Footnotes supplied by editor.

perfection from social reforms any more than from any other human efforts.

This movement, this hopeful experiment, is world-wide, but in this country it encounters a unique factor—in the United States, social legislation must pass challenge in the courts, it must have the visé of our judiciary. Having regard to things and not words, the fate of social legislation in this country rests ultimately with our judges.

The existence of this power is so elementary a feature of our constitutional system that until recently we little considered the true nature of the problems involved in the exercise of the power. Social legislation concerns itself with economic and social conditions, and aims at their conscious readjustments, for social legislation deals with the stuff of life. And, insofar as they have the last word on this legislation, our courts, of necessity, are concerned with economic and social questions, which can be rightfully solved only by a due regard to the facts which induced the legislation. For instance, in passing upon the constitutionality of an eight-hour law for bakers,[1] just what principles of jurisprudence are to be resorted to for guidance? Questions of hygiene, of health, of the present conditions of the industry, the occasion for protecting this particular class against its employers, and the public against both employer and employee—these are the considerations, it would seem, which ought to be vitally in the minds of the judges. Is it really to be doubted that in passing upon the validity of a workmen's compensation act, a court cannot get at the heart of the question without concerning itself, whether avowedly or implicitly, with economic and social questions? It involves a consideration of the vital changes produced by modern industrialism, the bearing of such legislation on the fairer adjustments of the inevitable risks of modern industry, the promotion of harmonious relations between capital and labor and the resulting peace to the community—in a word, its promotion of the social welfare. When the Supreme Court sustained the validity of legislation restricting the hours of work for women,[2] it invoked no legal principles, it resorted

1. See Lochner v. New York, 198 U.S. 45 (1905).
2. Muller v. Oregon, 208 U.S. 412 (1908).

to no lawbooks for guidance, but considered the facts of life—marshaled with overwhelming force by Mr. Brandeis—drawn from medical data, industrial reports, and the experience of the world. And so, when the minimum-wage bills, the first of which is now before the Massachusetts legislature, will, without doubt, soon come up for judicial determination, will not the decisive consideration that will inevitably confront the courts be the facts of the particular industries and the right of the community to insist upon a social wage as the first condition of human welfare over against the claim of the individual unrestricted industrial enterprise? Must not, of necessity, facts, not general principles or well-worn phrases, be the determinants?

This, which may now have the sound of heterodoxy, will, one is warranted in hoping, before long enjoy the respectability of the commonplace. For the viewpoint here urged has, fortunately, during the last few years, received the tremendous authority of, and increasing application from, the Supreme Court of the United States. Far in advance of any State court, our Supreme Bench recently has come to realize time's change of emphasis, that new conditions bring new problems and press for new solutions. Social legislation, under our constitutional system, must rest upon the exercise of the police power. Only the other day the Supreme Court told us that: "In a sense the police power is but another name for the power of government," and that it "extends to so dealing with the conditions which exist in the State as to bring out of them the greatest welfare of its people."[3] But "the power of the government is a living power, constantly changing and developing to meet new conditions and accomplish new purposes." And the conception of the people's welfare varies, according to the dominant opinion, with time and place. Of necessity, therefore, the police power, as the power of government, is no more stable than the conditions which induce its exercise. If facts are changing, law cannot be static. So-called immutable principles must accommodate themselves to facts of life, for facts are stubborn and will not yield. In

3. Mutual Loan Co. v. Martell, 222 U.S. 225, 233 (1911).

truth, what are now deemed immutable principles once, themselves, grew out of living conditions. Thus, the notion of unrestrained liberty of contract arose at a time when industrial conditions were shackled by restrictive legislation and the slogan of the hour was unrestricted industrial enterprise. The conditions of life have changed; the shibboleths remain. There is an increasing conviction of the need of collective responsibility and a demand of governmental intervention for fairer social adjustment. More and more we realize that there is no greater inequality than the equality of unequals. And, happily, the Supreme Court, unlike some of the State courts, realizes that the Fourteenth Amendment does not, in the words of Justice Holmes, interfere with legislation by creating "a factitious equality without regard to practical differences."[4] In a word, may not one venture the suggestion that constitutional law, in its relation to social legislation, is not at all a science, but applied politics, using the word in its noble sense?

It is important to recognize this not only abstractly, as an intellectual proposition, but to make it a dynamic part of our professional equipment of the legal habits of thought.

> The felt necessities of the time, the prevalent moral and political theories, intuitions of public policy, avowed or unconscious, even the prejudices which judges share with their fellow-men, have had a good deal more to do than the syllogism in determining the rules by which men should be governed.[5]

Thus wrote Mr. Holmes more than thirty years ago. And because he has so vitally felt this, Justice Holmes has been a powerful influence in the changed attitude of the Supreme Court. Again and again, we find him yielding to the social expression of the day, with which, if one should make a guess, as an individual, he was probably not in sympathy. Speaking of the English bench, Professor Dicey, a distinguished conservative, says while the judges

4. Standard Oil Co. v. Tennessee, 217 U.S. 413, 420 (1910).
5. Holmes, *The Common Law* 5 (Howe ed. 1963).

> are swayed by the prevailing beliefs of a particular time, they are also guided by professional opinions and ways of thinking which are, to a certain extent, independent of and possibly opposed to the general tone of public opinion. The judges are the heads of the legal profession. They have acquired the intellectual and moral tone of English lawyers. They are men advanced in life. They are for the most part persons of a conservative disposition.[6]

It is because of this natural tendency of our profession, and because of the far-reaching power enjoyed by the bench in this country, that it is essential that a correct appreciation of the problems raised by social legislation should become a vital part of our professional thinking. It is not only a delicate but an infinitely difficult human function that our courts discharge in passing upon the limits of their own power. Insofar as these questions are necessarily questions of fact, dealing with actual conditions of life and current dominant public opinion, it is essential that the stream of the Zeitgeist must be allowed to flood the sympathies and the intelligence of our judges. This is necessary, not only for the well-being of the state and the social order, but for the unimpaired continuance of our judicial system. Until social and economic legislation came before the courts, they did not touch the people at large. But dealing with such legislation, involving as they do the vital interests of life of a vast body of the community, the courts necessarily are brought in direct contact with the public needs, and their work has intimate public significance. Hence the importance of recognizing the true character of the questions that come before them. If this is done, it is safe to say that courts generally will reach the conclusion which one may gather from the recent Supreme Court decisions: namely, that which is reasonably defensible on economic or social grounds, whether or not it accords with our individual notion of economics, cannot be offensive on constitutional grounds. Otherwise, it necessarily follows that the Constitution definitively incorporated an economic theory prevalent

6. Dicey, *Law and Opinion in England* 364 (2d ed. 1914).

over a hundred years ago that may well be inadequate and unsuited to modern conditions, whereas, in truth, "a constitution is not intended to embody a particular economic theory . . . It is made for people of fundamentally differing views."[7]

One of the great leaders of the bar, and a distinguished statesman, seeking for a deeper explanation for the present widespread unrest than one generally hears, attributes it to our failure, as yet, to make through our legislation and constitutions the readjustments demanded by the new conditions incident to the extraordinary industrial development of the last half century. One ventures the suggestion that it is demonstrable, as Professor Roscoe Pound has shown, that one of the prime factors contributing to the dissatisfaction is the fact that judges have thwarted legislative efforts at such readjustments, not because of any coercion of the Constitution, but by reason of their constitutional conservatism. Therefore, as to legislation of this character, the suggestion of constitutional amendments does not meet the situation, for back of the constitutional amendment is the construing power of the courts. Unless our profession, from whose ranks the courts are recruited, has the right attitude of approach to these questions, human ingenuity cannot frame language specific enough, even if desirable, to meet the situation. Mere words cannot induce insight and right sympathies or appreciative interpretation. On the other hand, if our courts, generally, will have the attitude that the Supreme Court now has, it is safe to say that all social legislation which has the commanding facts of life behind it will be allowed to justify itself by experience.

The standards here suggested in dealing with the constitutionality of this class of legislation are broad, but not indefinite. The limits of the life of a people cannot be charted by easy rules of thumb. We are dealing with considerations as flexible and complex as the public welfare. The constitutional limitation upon the lawmaking power is as definite, but not more so, as a reasonably possible view of the public welfare. This leaves us still unimpaired

7. Lochner v. New York, 198 U.S. at 75, 76.

the benefits of the reviewing power of the judiciary in our governmental system, for the reflex action of the *existence* of this power on the part of the courts to set aside legislation restrains unwise legislative action and induces the scientific attitude of basing legislation only upon adequately ascertained facts. On the other hand, it does not make of the Constitution a mere charter of negation upon the power of the state. The courts should be a restraining, but not a hampering, force. Doubtless, grave mistakes in legislation will thus go unchallenged through the courts, but legislation is essentially empirical, experimental, and the Constitution was not intended to limit this field of experimentation. Think of the gain of having experience demonstrate the fallacy of a law after the Supreme Court has sustained its constitutionality! For, as a wise man has truly said, to fail and learn by failure is one of the sacred rights of a democracy.

Hours of Labor and Realism in Constitutional Law

The Massachusetts Supreme Court was called upon recently to consider the constitutionality of the following statute:

> Employees in and about steam railroad stations in this Commonwealth designated as baggage men, laborers, crossing tenders and the like, shall not be employed for more than nine working hours in ten hours' time; the additional hour to be allowed as a lay off.

The increasing demand for shorter hours of labor throughout the industrial world, the likelihood that such demand will receive legislative recognition, the nationwide importance of the attitude of the judiciary toward such legislation; conversely, the attitude of public opinion upon the continued exercise by the courts of their traditional power under the American constitutional system—all these considerations, and more, justify a constant critique within the profession of the point of view, no less than the explicit factors, which control judicial decisions upon social and industrial legislation.[1]

The question before the Massachusetts Supreme Court was not a new question. Necessarily, therefore, the court had to consider the applicable precedents, and the legal

Excerpt from Felix Frankfurter's first signed law review article, 29 *Harv. L. Rev.* 353 (1916). Copyright 1916 by the Harvard Law Review Association. The portion of the article omitted here consists of synopses of the cases cited in note 3 *infra* which was added by the editor.

1. Valuable contributions have been made in recent years which will be referred to later, particularly the admirable papers of Professor Ernst Freund, "Limitation of Hours of Labor and the Federal Supreme Court," 17 *Green Bag* 411 (1905); Judge Learned Hand, "Due Process of Law and the Eight Hour Day," 21 *Harv. L. Rev.* 495 (1908); and Professor Roscoe Pound, "Liberty of Contract," 18 *Yale L.J.* 454 (1909).

thinking which was embodied therein.[2] What then was the legal background?

A study of the opinions[3] indicates a change not only in the decisions but in the groundwork of the decisions. We find a shift in the point of emphasis, a modification of the factors that seem relevant, a different statement of the issues involved, and a difference in the technique by which they are to be solved. The turning point comes in 1908 with *Muller v. Oregon*.[4] While lone voices of wisdom had been heard for almost two decades,[5] and the tendency

2. This paper will concern itself wholly with the validity of the regulation of hours of labor as a problem in what Mr. Justice Holmes calls the "apologetics of the police power." Therefore, objections to the specific statute under consideration because (1) it fails to make provision for emergencies, (2) it is a denial of the equal protection of the laws by reason of arbitrary classification, and (3) it interferes with a field taken over by Congress in the Hours of Service Act of March 4, 1907, or special arguments in its favor, based (a) on the power to amend corporate charters and (b) on the fact that a special obligation may be imposed on public-service companies, are all put on one side.

3. (a) Regulation of labor of women and children: Commonwealth v. Hamilton Mfg. Co., 120 Mass. 383 (1876); Ritchie v. People, 155 Ill. 98 (1895); Wenham v. State, 65 Neb. 394 (1902); State v. Buchanan, 29 Wash. 602 (1902); People v. Williams, 189 N.Y. 131 (1907); Burcher v. People, 41 Colo. 495 (1907); Muller v. Oregon, 208 U.S. 412 (1908); Ritchie & Co. v. Wayman, 244 Ill. 509 (1910); Sturges v. Beauchamp, 231 U.S. 320 (1914); Riley v. Massachusetts, 232 U.S. 671 (1914); Hawley v. Walker, 232 U.S. 718 (1914); Miller v. Wilson, 236 U.S. 373 (1915); Bosley v. McLaughlin, 236 U.S. 385 (1915); People v. Schweinler Press, 214 N.Y. 395 (1915).

(b) Regulation of labor in dangerous employment: Holden v. Hardy, 169 U.S. 366 (1898); In re Morgan, 26 Colo. 415 (1899); Re Ten Hour Law for Street Railway Companies, 24 R.I. 603 (1902); Ex parte Boyce, 27 Nev. 299 (1904); Ex parte Kair, 28 Nev. 127 (1904), 28 Nev. 425 (1905); State v. Cantwell, 179 Mo. 245 (1904); Baltimore & Ohio R.R. v. I.C.C., 221 U.S. 612 (1911).

(c) Regulation of hours of labor in general: Low v. Rees Printing Co., 41 Neb. 127 (1894); Lochner v. New York, 198 U.S. 45 (1905); State v. Miksicek, 225 Mo. 561 (1909); State v. Lumber Co., 102 Miss. 802 (1912); State v. Barba, 132 La. 768 (1913); State v. Bunting, 71 Ore. 259 (1914), [aff'd, 243 U.S. 426 (1917) (F.F. of counsel.) Ed.]; People v. Klinck Packing Co., 214 N.Y. 121 (1915).

4. 208 U.S. 412.

5. See the dissenting opinion of Mr. Justice Holmes in Commonwealth v. Perry, 155 Mass. 117, 123 (1891); Thayer, *Legal Essays* 1 (1908).

was clearly in its direction, yet this case marks the culmination.

Prior to 1908 the decisions disclose certain marked common characteristics:

(1) Despite disavowal that the policy of legislation is not the courts' concern, there is an unmistakable dread of the class of legislation under discussion.[6] Intense feeling against the policy of the legislation must inevitably have influenced the result in the decisions. In truth this presents the point of greatest stress in our constitutional system, for it requires minds of unusual intellectual disinterestedness, detachment, and imagination to escape from the too easy tendency to find lack of power where one is convinced of lack of wisdom.

(2) Legislation is sustained as part of the prevailing philosophy of individualism, as an exceptional protection to certain individuals as such, and not as a recognition of a general social interest. Thus legislation is supported either because women and children are wards of the state, are not sui juris, or to relieve certain needy individuals in the community from coercion.[7] The underlying assumption was, of course, that industry presented only contract relations between individuals. That industry is part of society, the relation of business to the community, was naturally enough lost sight of in the days of pioneer development and free land.[8]

(3) The courts here deal with statutes seeking to affect in a very concrete fashion the sternest actualities of modern life: the conduct of industry and the labor of human

6. "The tendency of legislatures, in the form of regulatory measures, to interfere with the lawful pursuits of citizens, is becoming a marked one in this country, and it behooves the courts, firmly and fearlessly, to interpose the barriers of their judgments, when invoked to protest against legislative acts plainly transcending the powers conferred by the Constitution upon the legislative body." People v. Williams, 189 N.Y. 131, 135 (1907).

"This interference on the part of the legislatures of the several states with the ordinary trades and occupations of the people seems to be on the increase." Lochner v. New York, 198 U.S. 45, 63 (1905).

7. Holden v. Hardy, 169 U.S. 366, 397 (1898).

8. See the stimulating paper, Adler, "Labor, Capital, and Business at Common Law," 29 *Harv. L. Rev.* 241, particularly 262–274 (1916).

beings therein engaged. Yet the cases are decided, in the main, on abstract issues, on tenacious theories of economic and political philosophy. There is lack of scientific method either in sustaining or attacking legislation. Legislation is sustained or attacked on vague humanitarianism, on pressure of immediate suffering, or "common understanding." This is not the fault of the courts. It was characteristic of our legislative processes, as well as of the judicial proceedings which called them into question. It was true, substantially, of the social legislation of the nineteenth century.[9]

The courts decided these issues on a priori theories, on abstract assumptions, because scientific data were not available or at least had not been made available for the use of courts. But all this time scientific data had been accumulating. Organized observation, investigation, and experimentation produced facts, and science could at last speak with rational if tentative authority. There was a growing body of the world's experience and the validated opinions of those competent to have opinions. Instead of depending on a priori controversies raging around jejune catchwords like "individualism" and "collectivism," it became increasingly demonstrable what the effect of modern industry on human beings was and what the reasonable likelihood to society of the effects of fixing certain minimum standards of life.

The *Muller* case, in 1908, was the first case presented to our courts on the basis of authoritative data. For the first time the arguments and briefs breathed the air of reality. The response of the court on this method of presenting the case is significant.

> In patent cases counsel are apt to open the argument with a discussion of the state of the art. It may not be amiss, in the present case, before examining the constitutional question, to notice the course of legislation as

9. The earliest Factory Act was the "work of benevolent Tories." Dicey, *Law and Opinion in England* 110, and Lecture VII, particularly pp. 220 et seq., 228, 229 (2d ed. 1914); Goldmark, *Fatigue and Efficiency* ch. 1 (1912).

well as expressions of opinion from other than judicial sources. In the brief filed by Mr. Louis D. Brandeis, for the defendant in error, is a very copious collection of all these matters . . .[10]

The legislation and opinions referred to in the margin may not be, technically speaking, authorities, and in them is little or no discussion of the constitutional question presented to us for determination, yet they are significant of a widespread belief that woman's physical structure, and the functions she performs in consequence thereof, justify special legislation restricting or qualifying the conditions under which she should be permitted to toil. Constitutional questions, it is true, are not settled by even a consensus of present public opinion, for it is the peculiar value of a written constitution that it places in unchanging form limitations upon legislative action, and thus gives a permanence and stability to popular government which otherwise would be lacking. At the same time, *when a question of fact is debated and debatable, and the extent to which a special constitutional limitation goes is affected by the truth in respect to that fact,* a widespread and long continued belief concerning it is worthy of consideration.[11]

10. Muller v. Oregon, 208 U.S. 412, 419 (1907). The great mass of data contained in the brief is epitomized in the margin of the Court's opinion. Miss Josephine Goldmark, Publication Secretary of National Consumers' League, collaborated with Mr. Brandeis in the preparation of this and subsequent briefs, which are now available in part II of Miss Goldmark's book, *Fatigue and Efficiency.*

The present-day demand for scientific ascertainment of facts for legislation and administration is strikingly illustrated by Miss Lathrop in her *Third Annual Report as Chief of the United States Children's Bureau* 23–24 (1915): "The whole field of child labor is thus far singularly barren of scientific study . . . Full and intelligent protection of the physique and mental powers of the youthful workers in this country requires costly and laborious studies in laboratory and in workshop . . . The Children's Bureau now desires to call attention to these studies and to submit the reasonableness of spending money to make them. It proposes a later presentation of carefully considered plans for which certain preparatory studies are now going forward. The more rapidly the restrictive child labor legislation becomes uniform, the more evident must be the need of studying the welfare of the young worker within the occupation, so that we may secure just standards for the use of labor, as new standards for material are being developed."

11. 208 U.S. at 420–421. (Emphasis added by Frankfurter [Ed.]).

That upon such showing the Supreme Court should sustain the contested statute was inevitable. But the *Muller* case is "epoch making," not because of its decision, but because of the authoritative recognition by the Supreme Court that the way in which Mr. Brandeis presented the case—the support of legislation by an array of facts which established the reasonableness of the legislative action, however it may be with its wisdom—laid down a new technique for counsel charged with the responsibility of arguing such constitutional questions, and an obligation upon courts to insist upon such method of argument before deciding the issue, surely, at least, before deciding the issue adversely to the legislature. For there can be no denial that the technique of the brief in the *Muller* case has established itself through a series of decisions within the last few years, which have caused not only change in decisions, but the much more vital change of method of approach to constitutional questions.[12]

The most striking illustration is the attitude of the New York Court of Appeals in *People* v. *Schweinler Press*.[13] In that case, the court courageously overruled *People* v. *Williams*,[14] and sustained a statute prohibiting night work for women. We find a careful ascertainment of facts by the legislature as the basis of its action, and thereafter a careful presentation of facts before the court to support the legislative reason. Not only was there a presentation of facts in 1915 such as counsel failed to make in 1907, but there was a presentation of new facts acquired since 1907. If the point of view laid down in this case be sedulously observed in the argument and disposition of constitutional cases, it is safe to say that no statute which has any claim to life will be struck down by the courts.

While theoretically we may have been able to take judicial notice of some of the facts and of some of the

12. See briefs in Ritchie & Co. v. Wayman, 244 Ill. 509 (1910); Hawley v. Walker, 232 U.S. 718 (1914); Miller v. Wilson, 236 U.S. 373 (1915); Bosley v. McLaughlin, 236 U.S. 385 (1915); Stettler v. O'Hara, 69 Ore. 519 (1914) [aff'd, 243 U.S. 629 (1917) (F.F. of counsel). Ed.]; People v. Schweinler Press, 214 N.Y. 395 (1915).

13. 214 N.Y. 395 (1915).

14. 189 N.Y. 131 (1907).

> legislation now called to our attention as sustaining the belief and opinion that night work in factories is widely and substantially injurious to the health of women, actually very few of these facts were called to our attention, and the argument to uphold the law on that ground was brief and inconsequential.
>
> There is no reason why we should be reluctant to give effect to new and additional knowledge upon such a subject as this even if it did lead us to take a different view of such a vastly important question as that of public health or disease than formerly prevailed. Particularly do I feel that we should give serious consideration and great weight to the fact that the present legislation is based upon and sustained by an investigation by the legislature deliberately and carefully made through an agency of its own creation, the present factory investigating commission.[15]

These recent cases, dealing with regulation of the hours of labor, do not stand apart but illustrate two dominant tendencies in current constitutional decisions:

(1) Courts, with increasing measure, deal with legislation affecting industry in the light of a realistic study of the industrial conditions affected.[16]

(2) The emphasis is shifted to community interests, the affirmative enhancement of the human values of the whole community—not merely society conceived of as independent individuals dealing at arms' length with one another, in which legislation may only seek to protect individuals under disabilities, or prevent individual aggression in the interest of a countervailing individual freedom.[17]

As a result, we find that recent decisions have modified the basis on which legislation limiting the hours of labor is supported. As science has demonstrated that there is no sharp difference in kind as to the effect of labor on men

15. 214 N.Y. at 411, 412–413.

16. McLean v. Arkansas, 211 U.S. 539, 549–550 (1908) (it is significant that Mr. Justice Brewer and Mr. Justice Peckham dissented); Baltimore & Ohio R.R. v. I.C.C., 221 U.S. 612, 619 (1911).

17. People v. Klinck Packing Co., 214 N.Y. 121, 128 (1915).

and women, courts recently have followed the guidance of science and refused to be controlled by outworn ignorance. And so we find the Supreme Court of Oregon, in sustaining the ten-hour law for men, observing that "legislative regulation of the hours of labor of men and that of women differ only in the degree of necessity therefor."[18] True enough, we are not out of the woods of difficulty by saying the question is a matter of difference of degree. But once that is recognized, once we cease to look upon the regulation of women in industry as exceptional, as the law's graciousness to a disabled class, and shift the emphasis from the fact that they are *women* to the fact that it is *industry* and relation of industry to the community which is regulated, the whole problem is seen from a totally different aspect. Once admit it is a question of degree, there follows the recognition—and the conscious recognition is important—that we are balancing interests, that we are exercising judgment, and that the exercise of this judgment, unless so clear as to be undebatable, is solely for the legislature.[19]

What, then, are the common factors in the labor of men and women that would make a limitation of the hours of labor, in employments not dangerous or inherently unhealthy, to ten hours or nine hours an exercise of legislative discretion not beyond the pale of reasonable argument, and therefore to be respected by the courts? They are:

(1) "The common physiological phenomenon, fatigue," and the need of rest to repair the waste of the toxin.[20] Can the point where the line is to be drawn possibly be drawn a priori? Or, at the least, in the light of modern physiology is any layman entitled to say that a limitation of routine manual labor of masses of men to nine hours is a capricious and wilful oppression, without sustaining reason?[21]

(2) An enlarged conception of leisure and the tendency to regard not only its relation to the immediate effects

18. State v. Bunting, 71 Ore. 259, 271 (1914).
19. Price v. Illinois, 238 U.S. 446, 452 (1915).
20. See Goldmark, *supra* note 9, at ch. 2.
21. Price v. Illinois, 238 U.S. 446, 452 (1915).

upon animal health but also its bearing on the industrial output and the demands of citizenship.[22]

(3) Experience, based upon adequate trial, with the gradual reduction of labor and the slow increase of hours of leisure encouragingly demonstrates that such limitation of labor and increase of leisure have been put to fruitful uses. The tried measures of curtailing manual labor have added to the sum total of that by which we measure the civilized aspects of life.[23]

This then was the "state of the art" which confronted the Massachusetts Supreme Court in passing upon the constitutionality of the nine-hour law in question. One would suppose that in the light of all this it would be an easy matter for the court to hold that a nine-hour day is not "so extravagant and unreasonable, so disconnected with the probable promotion of health and welfare that its enactment is beyond the jurisdiction of the legislature,"[24] or, at the very least, that, since the subject is "debatable, the legislature is entitled to its own judgment."[25]

Quite the contrary. The court held that the statute "is an unwarrantable interference with individual liberty and an interference with property rights, and therefore contrary to constitutions which secure these fundamental rights."[26]

How could such a result have been reached?

(1) The case was inadequately presented. The court was not called upon to pass on the validity of the statute as such, but upon an agreed statement of facts under the statute to the effect that there is nothing inherently unhealthy about the work which the employee did, as it was half performed in the open air and was not arduous.[27]

22. See, e.g., Hobson, *Work and Health,* particularly chapters XIV and XV (1914); Taussig, *Inventors and Money Makers* 63, 65 et seq., 71 et seq. (1915); Meeker, "The Work of the Federal Bureau of Labor Statistics," 63 *Annals* 262, 267 (1916).

23. See Goldmark, *supra* note 9, at 279.

24. People v. Klinck Packing Co., 214 N.Y. 121, 127 (1915).

25. Price v. Illinois, 238 U.S. 446, 452 (1915).

26. Commonwealth v. Boston & M.R.R., 222 Mass. 206 (1915).

27. Ibid.

The assumption back of such a statement is that where work is not inherently unhealthy it is immaterial how long such work is pursued. Thus a wholly unscientific concession of fact was made, and therefore a wholly unscientific issue was presented to the court. But even such an issue was not supported by the available body of scientific facts. No attempt was made to bring to the attention of the court a detailed, painstaking, thoroughly marshaled array of facts to explain and to fortify the experience and theory back of labor legislation. In other words, the case was not argued in the way in which the decisions in the *Muller* case, the second *Ritchie* case, the *Hawley* case, the *Miller* case, the *Bosley* case, and the *Schweinler* case demanded that it should be argued.[28]

(2) One can therefore understand why the court found the case "governed" by the *Lochner* case. Nevertheless, one is compelled to conclude that the illumination that has been cast upon the *Lochner* case during the past decade does not leave to that case any principle which ipso facto controls the validity of specific measures regulating hours of labor. The principle of the *Lochner* case is simple enough: that arbitrary restriction of men's activities, unrelated in reason to the "public welfare," offends the Fourteenth Amendment. As to the principle, there is no dispute. But the principle is the beginning and not the end of the inquiry. The field of contention is in its application. The *Lochner* case, judged by its history and by more recent decisions of the Supreme Court, does not in itself furnish the yardstick for its application.

(a) It is now clearly enough recognized that each case presents a distinct issue; that each case must be determined by the facts relevant to it; that we are dealing, in truth, not with a question of law but the application of an undisputed formula to a constantly changing and growing variety of economic and social facts.[29] Each case, there-

28. See *supra* note 3.

29. See People v. Schweinler Press, 214 N.Y. 395, 411–412 (1915); Bosley v. McLaughlin, 236 U.S. 385, 392 et seq. (1915); Miller v. Wilson, 236 U.S. 373, 382 (1915); McLean v. Arkansas, 211 U.S. 539, 549–550 (1908).

fore, calls for a new and distinct consideration, not only of the general facts of industry but the specific facts in regard to the employment in question and the specific exigencies which called for the specific statute.

(b) The groundwork of the *Lochner* case has by this time been cut from under. The majority opinion was based upon "a common understanding" as to the effect of work in bakeshops upon the public and upon those engaged in it. "Common understanding" has ceased to be the reliance in matters calling for essentially scientific determination. "Has not the progress of sanitary science shown," Professor Freund pertinently inquires, "that common understanding is often equivalent to popular ignorance and fallacy?"[30] On the particular issue involved in the *Lochner* case "study of the facts has shown that the legislature was right and the court was wrong."[31] Either because matters as to which the court of its own knowledge cannot know, or, because not knowing, it cannot assume the nonexistence of facts, contested legislative action should be resolved in favor of rationality rather than capricious oppression. Happily the fundamental constitutional doctrine of the assumption of rightness of legislative conduct, where the court is uninformed, is again rigorously being enforced by the United States Supreme Court.[32]

(c) So far as the general flavor of the *Lochner* opinion goes, it surely is no longer "controlling." If the body of professional opinion counts for anything in the appraisal

30. 17 *Green Bag* at 416.

31. Pound, *supra* note 1, at 480, and n. 123.

32. Thus, in one of its latest opinions, the Supreme Court refused to upset a "police measure" with the following language:

"Petitioner makes his contention depend upon disputable considerations of classification and upon a comparison of conditions of which there is no means of judicial determination and upon which nevertheless we are expected to reverse legislative action . . ." Hadacheck v. Sebastian, 239 U.S. 394, 413 (1915).

Here, as elsewhere in the law, Mr. Justice Holmes long ago put the matter with acute finality: "I cannot pronounce the legislation [prohibiting fines against weavers for defective workmanship] void, as based on a false assumption, since I know nothing about the matter one way or the other." Commonwealth v. Perry, 155 Mass. 117, 124–125 (1891). As to the reasonableness of the legislature's belief that a system of fines affords dangerous temptations for oppressive use, see Tawney, *Minimum Rates in the Tailoring Industry* 60, 95 (1915).

of authority of a decision (itself decided by a divided court, and since departed from in effect in an important series of cases), it has been impressively arrayed against this decision. If ever an opinion has been subjected to the weightiest professional criticism it is the opinion in the *Lochner* case. Judge Andrew Bruce, Professor Ernst Freund, Judge Learned Hand, Professor Roscoe Pound—to mention no others—surely speak with high competence upon this subject. Nevertheless, the body of persuasive authority which their writings present was not brought to the court's attention and failed to be considered in the disposition of the case.[33]

The circumstances which resulted in this decision reveal anew a situation of far-reaching importance. For it affects the very bases on which constitutional decisions are reached and, therefore, affects vitally the most sensitive point of contact between the courts and the people. The statute under discussion may well have been of no particular social import. The decision which nullified it, one may be sure, offers no intrinsic obstruction to needed legislation, and in itself has merely ephemeral vitality. But, unfortunately, the evil that decisions do lives after them. Such a decision deeply impairs that public confidence upon which the healthy exercise of judicial power must rest.

Under the present-day stress of judicial work it is inevitable that courts, on the whole, can only decide specific cases as presented to them.[34] In other words, the substan-

33. Bruce, "The Illinois Ten Hour Labor Law for Women," 8 *Mich. L. Rev.* 1 (1909); Corwin, "The Supreme Court and the Fourteenth Amendment," 7 *Mich. L. Rev.* 643 (1909); Freund, *supra* note 1; Freund, "Constitutional Limitations and Labor Legislation," 4 *Ill. L. Rev.* 609 (1910); Greeley, "The Changing Attitude of the Courts toward Social Legislation," 5 *Ill. L. Rev.* 222 (1910); Hand, *supra* note 1; Pollock, "The New York Labor Law and the Fourteenth Amendment," 21 *L.Q. Rev.* 211 (1905); Pound, *supra* note 1. Cf. Wigmore, "The Qualities of Current Judicial Decisions," 9 *Ill. L. Rev.* 529, 530–531 (1914).

But see Atkins v. Grey Eagle Coal Co., 84 S.E. 906 (1915), where the Court of Appeals of West Virginia sustained a truck act, in effect overruling the decision in State v. Goodwill, 33 W. Va. 179 (1889), and cited among its authorities Professor Pound's article, "Liberty of Contract."

34. See Swayze, "The Growing Law," 20 *Yale L.J.* 1, 18–19 (1910); People v. Schweinler Press, 214 N.Y. 395, 411 (1915).

tial dependence upon the facts and briefs presented by counsel throws the decision of the courts largely upon those chances which determine the selection of counsel. These are, of course, necessary human drawbacks, and the practice works out well enough in controversies where purely individual interests are represented by counsel. This is not the situation in cases such as the one before the Massachusetts court. The issue submitted to the court in fact was the issue as determined by the district attorney of Worcester and counsel for the Boston and Maine Railroad. In truth, the issue was between the court and the legislature. In such a case either the legislative judgment should be sustained if there is "no means of judicial determination" that the legislature is indisputably wrong,[35] or the court should demand that the legislative judgment be supported by available proof.[36] It would seem clear that courts have inherent power to accomplish this by indicating the kind of argument needed to reach a just result; or even by calling for argument from members of the bar—officers of the court—of particular equipment to assist in a given problem.[37] If legislation be necessary New York furnishes an example in its recent enactment authorizing the courts to request the attendance of the attorney general in support of an act of the legislature when its constitutionality is brought into question.[38]

These, after all, are only expedients. Fundamental is the need that the profession realize the true nature of the issues involved in these constitutional questions and the limited scope of the reviewing power of the courts.[39] With the recognition that these questions raise, substantially, disputed questions of fact must come the invention of some machinery by which knowledge of the facts, which are the foundation of the legal judgment, may be

35. Hadacheck v. Sebastian, 239 U.S. 394, 413 (1915); Price v. Illinois, 238 U.S. 446, 452 (1915).

36. Freund, *supra* note 33.

37. It is interesting to note that the chief arguments in the series of cases beginning with the *Muller* case were made by an *amicus curiae*, Mr. Louis D. Brandeis, in behalf of the National Consumers' League.

38. New York Laws, 1913, ch. 442, p. 919.

39. See 28 *Harv. L. Rev.* 790 (1915).

at the service of the courts as a regular form of the judicial process. This need has been voiced alike by jurists and judges.[40] Once the need shall be felt as the common longing of the profession the inventive powers of our law will find the means for its satisfaction.

40. Pound, "Legislation as a Social Function," 7 *Pub. Am. Sociol. Soc.* 148, 161 (1912): "In the immediate past the social facts required for the exercise of the judicial function of law-making have been arrived at by means which may fairly be called mechanical. It is not one of the least problems of the sociological jurist to discover a rational mode of advising the court of facts of which it is supposed to take judicial notice." So (in dealing with a somewhat similar problem) Judge Learned Hand, in Parke Davis & Co. v. Mulford & Co., 189 Fed. 95, 115 (C.C.S.D.N.Y. 1911): "How long we shall continue to blunder along without the aid of unpartisan and authoritative scientific assistance in the administration of justice, no one knows; but all fair persons not conventionalized by provincial legal habits of mind ought, I should think, unite to effect some such advance." Cf. also, Steenerson v. Great Northern Ry., 69 Minn. 353, 377 (1897).

The Constitutional Opinions of Mr. Justice Holmes

Called upon late in life to teach constitutional law, a great teacher of property law, after a brief trial, gave it up in despair on the ground that constitutional law "was not law at all, but politics." John Chipman Gray was right— if his norm of law was the rule against perpetuities; not, however, if we concede it to be the law's province also to settle controversies that involve more complex interests, permitting of flexibility in application to make the necessary accommodation to the diversities and changes in the facts of life. We find a growing extension of this sphere of law, a gradual displacement of force by law, bringing not only the peaceful settlement of controversies as isolated instances, each on its own bottom, but settlement based on certain common considerations beyond the mere avoidance of force.[1] Undoubtedly, such a field of law by the very nature of the issues sought to be settled, by reason of the interests sought to be enforced, leaves wider scope and calls for the exercise of a broader experience than the familiar domains of the common law. Such, in effect, has been that body of decisions contained in the 240 volumes of *United States Reports* which we call American Constitutional Law. To be sure we are in the field of greatest flexibility. Undoubtedly the Constitution is what the Supreme Court interprets it to be—and constitutional interpretation inescapably opens a Pandora's box of difficulties. But there are differences between this body of constitutional decisions and the judgments of a Kadi or the foreign policies of a Secretary of State. Just these differences entitle the decisions to be called law. But the necessary flexibility makes the personality of the justices so much more important in their decisions on constitutional law than in questions of property or corporation law.

There is thus marked opportunity for individual influence in the collective judgment which a Marshall exer-

Reprinted from 29 *Harv. L. Rev.* 683 (1916).

1. See, for instance, the line of thought opened up by Mr. Justice Higgins, in "A New Province for Law and Order," 29 *Harv. L. Rev.* 13 (1915).

cised. Of course he did not attain single-handed, and we know that among his associates were probably two men of more commanding equipment as common law lawyers. But it is to Marshall that we owe the foundations of our national power as they were laid. From Marshall's days, except for an occasional flurry, there is a comparatively quiescent period in constitutional law until the acute, and growingly acute, issues of the last thirty years reflected themselves more intensely in legislation. This brought sharp contests before the Supreme Court. Two issues mainly concerned the Court: the scope of the power of Congress over commerce, and the new limitations placed upon the States by the Fourteenth Amendment. The commerce clause had been largely a slumbering power until the Interstate Commerce Act and the Sherman Law, and, more particularly, the legislation since 1906, brought its intensive application into constant question and resistance. In a series of important litigations there was pressed for decision, not only invalidity of State legislation as an encroachment upon the federal power, but, even more, the affirmative exercise of the federal power, rendered significant and detailed because of the pervasive aspect of modern commerce. The second class of cases involved the whole brood of questions arising from the new power of negation of the federal Constitution over State action.

Mr. Justice Holmes came to the Supreme Court at this period of legislative exuberance, marking a broad extension of governmental activities both in nation and States. There was thus presented to the Court in greater volume and with unparalleled intensity, the determination of the powers of the nation and of the State, and a delimitation of the field between them—questions whose decision probably touched the public at once more widely and more immediately than any issues at any previous stage of the Court's history. On both these two basic problems of constitutional law—the power of the States and the power of the nation—Mr. Justice Holmes's influence has been steady and consistent and growing. His opinions form a coherent body of constitutional law, and their effect upon the development of the law is the outstanding characteristic of constitutional history in the last decade.

In our days, as in Marshall's, the issues before the Court have necessitated not merely an interpretation of this or that specific clause of the Constitution, but an inquiry into the fundamental attitude toward the Constitution and a conscious realization of the function of the Court as its interpreter. Marshall's great major premise was that "it is a *constitution* we are expounding." That was the background against which he projected every inquiry as to specific power or specific limitation. With that as a starting point, with the recognition, not as an arid bit of intellectualism but enforced with emotional drive, that the Constitution deals with great governmental powers to be exercised to great public ends, he went far toward erecting the structure within which the national spirit could freely move and flourish. Like all truths, Marshall's great canons had to be revivified by new demands that were made upon them by a new generation. Constant resort to the reviewing power of the Court based on claims that acts of legislatures or Congress transcended constitutional limitations, called again for a major premise as to the scope of the instrument which the Court must construe and the right attitude of the Court in its interpretative function. There always is a starting point in such questions, however inarticulate or even unconscious. What the pressure of new legislation demanded was a conscious reexamination of the starting point, a vigorous realization of the scope and purpose of constitutional law, an analysis of the realistic issues in any given constitutional question. In a time of legislative activity, in a period of especial unrest in the law, signifying an absorption of new facts and changing social conceptions,[2] the starting point must be a conscious one, lest power and policy be unconsciously confused.

2. See Dean Pound's various papers, particularly, "Do We Need a Philosophy of Law?" 5 *Colum. L. Rev.* 339 (1905); "Common Law and Legislation," 21 *Harv. L. Rev.* 383 (1907); "Mechanical Jurisprudence," 8 *Colum. L. Rev.* 605 (1908); "The Scope and Purpose of Sociological Jurisprudence," 24 *Harv. L. Rev.* 591 (1911); 25 id. 489 (1912).

Mr. Justice Holmes has recalled us to the traditions of Marshall, that it *is* a Constitution we are expounding, and not a detached document inviting scholastic dialectics. To him the Constitution is a means of ordering the life of a young nation, having its roots in the past—"continuity with the past is not a duty but a necessity"—and intended for the unknown future. Intentionally, therefore, it was bounded with outlines not sharp and contemporary, but permitting of increasing definiteness through experience.

> The provisions of the Constitution are not mathematical formulas having their essence in their form; they are organic living institutions transplanted from English soil. Their significance is vital not formal; it is to be gathered not simply by taking the words and a dictionary, but by considering their origin and the line of their growth.[3]

He has ever been keenly conscious of the delicacy involved in reviewing other men's judgment not as to its wisdom but as to their right to entertain the reasonableness of its wisdom. We touch here the most sensitive spot in our constitutional system: that its successful working calls for minds of extraordinary intellectual disinterestedness and penetration lest limitations in personal experience and imagination be interpreted, however conscientiously or unconsciously, as constitutional limitations. When regard is had to the complexities of modern society and the necessary specialization and narrowness of individual experience, the need for tolerance and objectivity in realizing, and then respecting, the validity of the experience and beliefs of others becomes one of the most dynamic factors in the actual disposition of concrete cases.

> Great constitutional provisions must be administered with caution. Some play must be allowed for the joints of the machine, and it must be remembered that legis-

3. Gompers v. United States, 233 U.S. 604, 610 (1914).

latures are ultimate guardians of the liberties and welfare of the people in quite as great a degree as the courts.[4]

While the courts must exercise a judgment of their own, it by no means is true that every law is void which may seem to the judges who pass upon it excessive, unsuited to its ostensible end, or based upon conceptions of morality with which they disagree. Considerable latitude must be allowed for differences of view as well as for possible peculiar conditions which this court can know but imperfectly, if at all. Otherwise a constitution, instead of embodying only fundamental rules of right, as generally understood by all English-speaking communities, would become the partisan of a particular set of ethical or economical opinions, which by no means are held *semper ubique et ab omnibus*.[5]

Therefore, except in the case of a few specific constitutional prohibitions (for that very reason rarely called into question), we are at once in a different atmosphere of approach from the rigid and the absolute. We are in a field where general principles are recognized but settle few controversies. Claim or denial of governmental power, of "individual rights," reveal themselves not as logical antitheses, but as demands of clashing "rights," of matters of more or less, of questions of degree.

General propositions do not decide concrete cases. The decisions will depend on a judgment or intuition more subtle than any articulate major premise.[6]

As in other cases where a broad distinction is admitted, it ultimately becomes necessary to draw a line, and the determination of the precise place for that line in

4. Missouri, Texas & Kansas Ry. v. May, 194 U.S. 267, 270 (1904).
5. Otis v. Parker, 187 U.S. 606, 608–609 (1903).
6. Lochner v. New York, 198 U.S. 45, 76 (1905).

> nice cases always seems somewhat technical, but still the line must be drawn.[7]

This by no means implies a crude empiricism. True, judgment, conscious or inert, enters. Choice must be exercised. The choice is not, however, capricious; it involves judgment between defined claims, each of recognized validity, each with a pedigree of its own, but all of which necessarily cannot be satisfied completely.

> All rights tend to declare themselves absolute to their logical extreme. Yet all in fact are limited by the neighborhood of principles of policy which are other than those on which the particular right is founded, and which become strong enough to hold their own when a certain point is reached. The limits set to property by other public interests present themselves as a branch of what is called the police power of the State. The boundary at which the conflicting interests balance cannot be determined by any general formula in advance, but points in the line, or helping to establish it, are fixed by decisions that this or that concrete case falls on the nearer or farther side. For instance, the police power may limit the height of buildings, in a city, without compensation. To that extent it cuts down what otherwise would be the rights of property. But if it should attempt to limit the height so far as to make an ordinary building lot wholly useless, the rights of property would prevail over the other public interest, and the police power

7. Ellis v. United States, 206 U.S. 246, 260 (1907).

The recognition of differences of degree in the whole development of the law is most luminously put in the following passage: "I do not think we need trouble ourselves with the thought that my view depends upon differences of degree. The whole law does so as soon as it is civilized. See Nash v. United States 229 U.S. 373, 376, 377. Negligence is all degree—that of the defendant here degree of the nicest sort; and between the variations according to distance that I suppose to exist and the simple universality of the rules in the Twelve Tables or the Leges Barbarorum, there lies the culture of two thousand years." LeRoy Fibre Co. v. Chicago, Milwaukee & St. Paul Ry., 232 U.S. 340, 354 (1914).

would fail. To set such a limit would need compensation and the power of eminent domain.[8]

Thus, while Mr. Justice Holmes has expounded the philosophy of differences of degree and applied it in a variety of cases, he has been alert to demand a telling difference upon which a distinction can be predicated. A neat instance is his dissenting opinion in *Haddock* v. *Haddock.*

> I am the last man in the world to quarrel with a distinction simply because it is one of degree. Most distinctions, in my opinion, are of that sort, and none are the worse for it. But the line which is drawn must be justified by the fact that it is a little nearer than the nearest opposing case to one pole of an admitted antithesis. When a crime is made burglary by the fact that it was committed thirty seconds after one hour after sunset, ascertained according to mean time in the place of the act, to take an example from Massachusetts (R.L. c. 219, sec. 10), the act is a little nearer to midnight than if it had been committed one minute earlier, and no one denies that there is a difference between night and day. The fixing of a point when day ends is made inevitable by the admission of that difference. But I can find no basis for giving a greater jurisdiction to the courts of the husband's domicil when the married pair happens to have resided there a month, even if with intent to make it a permanent abode, than if they had not lived there at all.[9]

This, in brief, is the attitude in which and the technique with which Mr. Justice Holmes approaches the solution of specific questions in the two great active fields of constitutional law: the commerce clause and the Fourteenth Amendment.

Just as the needs of commerce among the several States furnished the great centripetal force in the establishment of the nation, so the commerce clause has now become the

8. Hudson County Water Co. v. McCarter, 209 U.S. 349, 355–356 (1908).
9. Haddock v. Haddock, 201 U.S. 562, 631–632 (1906).

most important nationalizing agency of the federal government. Mr. Justice Holmes has at once applied this power with unimpaired depth and breadth, and affirmed the true basis of its need today no less than in 1789.

> I do not think the United States would come to an end if we lost our power to declare an Act of Congress void. I do think the Union would be imperiled if we could not make that declaration as to the laws of the several States. For one in my place sees how often a local policy prevails with those who are not trained to national views, and how often action is taken that embodies what the Commerce Clause was meant to end.[10]

He has sought to enforce the power of commerce among the States with depth and breadth because to him such "commerce is not a technical legal conception, but a practical one drawn from the course of business."[11] That interstate commerce is a practical conception he recognizes in its practical implications. Thus, commerce means, not only transportation, not only control over the instrumentalities of transportation, but the human relations involved in commerce. They present some of the acutest problems of commerce. Therefore, insisting in himself as he does in others on the need "to think things instead of words," in one of his memorable opinions, against the majority of the Court, he asserted the power of Congress to legislate in regard to the industrial relations on interstate railroads as a means of securing industrial peace.

> It cannot be doubted that to prevent strikes, and, so far as possible, to foster its scheme of arbitration, it might be deemed by Congress an important point of policy, and I think it impossible to say that Congress might not reasonably think that the provision in question would help a good deal to carry its policy along. But suppose the only effect really were to tend to bring about the complete unionizing of such railroad laborers as

10. *Occasional Speeches of Justice Oliver Wendell Holmes* 172 (Howe ed. 1962).

11. Swift & Co. v. United States, 196 U.S. 375, 398 (1905).

> Congress can deal with, I think that object alone would justify the act. I quite agree that the question what and how much good labor unions do, is one on which intelligent people may differ—I think that laboring men sometimes attribute to them advantages, as many attribute to combinations of capital disadvantages, that really are due to economic conditions of a far wider and deeper kind—but I could not pronounce it unwarranted if Congress should decide that to foster a strong union was for the best interest, not only of the men, but of the railroads and the country at large.[12]

The extension of interstate commerce through modern inventions, the overwhelming field which it has absorbed, are obvious. Logically, there is no limit to the interrelation of national commerce and the activities of men in the separate States. But the main ends of our dual system of States and nation here, too, call for adjustment, and logic cannot hold sterile sway.

> In modern societies every part is related so organically to every other, that what affects any portion must be felt more or less by all the rest. Therefore, unless everything is to be forbidden and legislation is to come to a stop, it is not enough to show that, in the working of a statute, there is some tendency, logically discernible, to interfere with commerce or existing contracts.[13]

Therefore distinctions have to be made and "even nice distinctions are to be expected."[14] But the federal power must be dominantly left unimpaired and a State cannot defeat the withdrawal of national commerce from State tampering "by simply invoking the convenient apologetics of the police power."[15]

Thus far as to the great federal power which indirectly limits State activity. In its negative prohibitions the Constitution is a denial of State action as such. When the

12. Adair v. United States, 208 U.S. 161, 191–192. Cf. *supra* note 1, at 23ff.

13. Diamond Glue Co. v. United States Glue Co., 187 U.S. 611, 616 (1903).

14. Galveston, etc. Ry. v. Texas, 210 U.S. 217, 225 (1908).

15. Kansas Southern Ry. v. Kaw Valley Dist., 233 U.S. 75, 79 (1914).

Fourteenth Amendment first came before the Court in the *Slaughterhouse Cases*,[16] the four dissenting justices, under the lead of Mr. Justice Field, sought to pour into the general words of the due process clause the eighteenth-century "law of nature" philosophy. This attempt gradually prevailed and Mr. Justice Field's dissent in effect established itself as the prevailing opinion of the Supreme Court.[17] In *Allgeyer* v. *Louisiana*,[18] we reach the crest of the wave. The break comes with the *Lochner* case.[19] Mr. Justice Holmes has given us the explanation for this attempt to make a permanent prohibition of a temporary theory.

> It is a misfortune if a judge reads his conscious or unconscious sympathy with one side or the other prematurely into the law, and forgets that what seem to him to be first principles are believed by half his fellow men to be wrong. I think that we have suffered from this misfortune, in State courts at least, and that this is another and very important truth to be extracted from the popular discontent. When twenty years ago a vague terror went over the earth and the word socialism began to be heard, I thought and still think that fear[20] was translated into doctrines that had no proper place in the Con-

16. 16 Wall. 36 (1873).
17. See Pound, "Liberty of Contract," 18 *Yale L.J.* 454, 470 (1909).
18. 165 U.S. 578 (1875).
19. 198 U.S. 45 (1905).
20. That this fear has been an unconscious factor he has told us elsewhere: "When socialism first began to be talked about, the comfortable classes of the community were a good deal frightened. I suspect that this fear has influenced judicial action both here and in England, yet it is certain that it is not a conscious factor in the decisions to which I refer. I think that something similar has led people who no longer hope to control the legislatures to look to the courts as expounders of the Constitutions, and that in some courts new principles have been discovered outside the bodies of those instruments, which may be generalized into acceptance of the economic doctrines which prevailed about fifty years ago, and a wholesale prohibition of what a tribunal of lawyers does not think about right. I cannot but believe that if the training of lawyers led them habitually to consider more definitely and explicitly the social advantage on which the rule they lay down must be justified, they sometimes would hesitate where now they are confident, and see that really they were taking sides upon debatable and often burning questions." "The Path of the Law," 10 *Harv. L. Rev.* 457, 467 (1897).

> stitution or the common law. Judges are apt to be naif, simple-minded men, and they need something of Mephistopheles. We too need education in the obvious—to learn our own convictions and to leave room for much that we hold dear to be done away with short of revolution by the orderly change of law.[21]

Against this subtle danger of the unconscious identification of personal views with constitutional sanction he has battled incessantly. Enough is said if it is noted that the tide has turned. The turning point is the dissent in the *Lochner* case. It still needs to be quoted.

> The Fourteenth Amendment does not enact Mr. Herbert Spencer's Social Statics . . . Some of these laws embody convictions or prejudices which judges are likely to share. Some may not. But a constitution is not intended to embody a particular economic theory, whether of paternalism and the organic relation of the citizen to the State or of *laissez faire*. It is made for people of fundamentally differing views, and the accident of our finding certain opinions natural and familiar or novel and even shocking ought not to conclude our judgment upon the questions whether statutes embodying them conflict with the Constitution of the United States.[22]

His general attitude towards the Fourteenth Amendment at once reflects his whole point of view towards constitutional interpretation and is a clue to the hundreds of opinions in which it is applied. In all the variety of cases the opinions of Mr. Justice Holmes show the same realism, the same refusal to defeat life by formal logic, the same regard for local needs and local habits, the same deference to local knowledge. He recognizes that government necessarily means experimentation; and while the very essence of constitutional limitations is to confine the area of experimentation, the limitations are not self-defining, and they were intended to permit government. Necessar-

21. *Supra* note 10, at 171–172.
22. Lochner v. New York, 198 U.S. 45, 75–76 (1905).

ily, therefore, the door was not meant to be closed to trial and error. "Constitutional law, like any other mortal contrivance, has to take some chances."[23] The ascertainment of the limitations must be, as recently put by Mr. Justice McKenna, through "a judgment from experience as against a judgment from speculation."[24] That means that opportunity must be allowed for vindicating reasonable belief by experience.

> In answering that question we must be cautious about pressing the broad words of the Fourteenth Amendment to a drily logical extreme. Many laws which it would be vain to ask the court to overthrow could be shown, easily enough to transgress a scholastic interpretation of one or another of the great guarantees in the Bill of Rights. They more or less limit the liberty of the individual or they diminish property to a certain extent. We have few scientifically certain criteria of legislation, and as it often is difficult to mark the line where what is called the police power of the States is limited by the Constitution of the United States, judges should be slow to read into the latter a *nolumus mutare* as against the law-making power.[25]

> Again we cannot wholly neglect the long settled law and common understanding of a particular state in considering the plaintiff's rights. We are bound to be very cautious in coming to the conclusion that the Fourteenth Amendment has upset what thus has been established and accepted for a long time. Even the incidents of ownership may be cut down by the peculiar laws and usages of a state.[26]

> Obviously the question so stated is one of local experience on which this court ought to be very slow to declare that the State Legislature was wrong in its facts. *Adams* v. *Milwaukee,* 228 U.S. 572, 583. If we might trust popular speech in some States it was right—but it is enough

23. Blinn v. Nelson, 222 U.S. 1, 7 (1911).
24. Tanner v. Little, 240 U.S. 369 (1916).
25. Noble State Bank v. Haskell, 219 U.S. 104, 110 (1911).
26. Otis Co. v. Ludlow Co., 201 U.S. 140, 154 (1906).

> that this court has no such knowledge of local conditions as to be able to say that it was manifestly wrong.[27]
>
> If the Fourteenth Amendment is not to be a greater hamper upon the established practices of the States in common with other governments than I think was intended, they must be allowed a certain latitude in the minor adjustments of life, even though by their action the burdens of a part of the community are somewhat increased. The traditions and habits of centuries were not intended to be overthrown when that amendment was passed.[28]

The application of the Fourteenth Amendment, as thus approached, falls, broadly speaking, into four great classes of cases: legislation called forth by the modern industrial system, regulation of utilities, eminent domain, and taxation. As to each of these classes an illustration or two will have to suffice.[29] To discuss Mr. Justice Holmes's opinions is to string pearls.

27. Patsone v. Pennsylvania, 232 U.S. 138, 144–145 (1914).
28. Interstate Ry. Co. v. Massachusetts, 207 U.S. 79, 87 (1907).
29. Since his accession to the Supreme Court in 1902, Mr. Justice Holmes has written about five hundred opinions; of these, about two hundred involve constitutional law. In view of the increase of work before the Court in recent years, Mr. Justice Holmes has already participated in decisions extending considerably over one-fifth in volume of the decisions of the Court since 1789. One is reminded of his remarks at a dinner given him by the Boston Bar when he became Chief Justice of the Massachusetts Supreme Court: "I look into my book in which I keep a docket of the decisions of the full court which fall to me to write, and find about a thousand cases. A thousand cases, many of them upon trifling or transitory matters, to represent nearly half a lifetime! A thousand cases, when one would have liked to study to the bottom and to say his say on every question which the law ever has presented, and then to go on and invent new problems which should be the test of doctrine, and then to generalize it all and write it in continuous, logical, philosophic exposition, setting forth the whole corpus with its roots in history and its justifications of expedience real or supposed!

"Alas, gentlemen, that is life. I often imagine Shakespeare or Napoleon summing himself up and thinking: 'Yes, I have written five thousand lines of solid gold and a good deal of padding—I, who would have covered the milky way with words which outshone the stars!' 'Yes, I beat the Austrians in Italy and elsewhere: I made a few brilliant campaigns, and I ended in middle life in a *cul-de-sac*—I, who had dreamed of a world monarchy and Asiatic power!' We cannot live our dreams. We are lucky enough if we can give a sample of our best, and if in our hearts we can feel that it has been nobly done." *Supra* note 10, at 123–124.

In industrial and social legislation the fighting, of course, has been around the conception of "liberty." Mr. Justice Holmes has been unswerving in his resistance to any doctrinaire interpretation. The effectiveness of his fight lies mostly in the acuteness with which he has disclosed when a claim is doctrinaire. Perception of the forces of modern society and persistent study of economics have enabled him to translate large words in terms of the realities of existence.

> If Montana deems it advisable to put a lighter burden upon women than upon men with regard to an employment that our people commonly regard as more appropriate for the former, the Fourteenth Amendment does not interfere by creating a fictitious equality where there is a real difference. The particular points at which that difference shall be emphasized by legislation are largely in the power of the state.[30]

> In present conditions a workman not unnaturally may believe that only by belonging to a union can he secure a contract that shall be fair to him. *Holden* v. *Hardy*, 169 U.S. 366, 397; *Chicago, Burlington & Quincy R.* v. *McGuire*, 219 U.S. 549, 570. If that belief, whether right or wrong, may be held by a reasonable man, it seems to me that it may be enforced by law in order to establish the equality of position between the parties in which liberty of contract begins. Whether in the long run it is wise for the workingmen to enact legislation of this sort is not my concern, but I am strongly of opinion that there is nothing in the Constitution of the United States to prevent it, and that *Adair* v. *United States*, 208 U.S. 161, and *Lochner* v. *New York*, 198 U.S. 45, should be overruled.[31]

> If the legislature shares the now prevailing belief as to what is public policy and finds that a particular instrument of trade war is being used against that policy in certain cases, it may direct its law against what it

30. Quong Wing v. Kirkendall, 223 U.S. 59, 63 (1912).
31. Coppage v. Kansas, 236 U.S. 1, 26–27 (1915).

> deems the evil as it actually exists without covering the whole field of possible abuses, and it may do so none the less that the forbidden act does not differ in kind from those that are allowed . . .
>
> It might have been argued to the legislature with more force than it can be to us that recoupment in one place of losses in another is merely an instance of financial ability to compete. If the legislature thought that that particular manifestation of ability usually came from great corporations whose power it deemed excessive and for that reason did more harm than good in their State, and that there was no other case of frequent occurrence where the same could be said, we cannot review their economics or their facts.[32]

What makes these opinions significant beyond their immediate expression is that they come from a man who, as a judge, enforces statutes based upon economic theories which he does not share, and of whose efficacy in action he is sceptical.[33] The judicial function here finds its highest exercise.

In the regulation of utilities we have an excellent illustration of the need of balancing interests and the delicacy of the task. Mr. Justice Holmes has both laid down the general considerations and illustrated their application.

> An adjustment of this sort under a power to regulate rates has to steer between Scylla and Charybdis. On the one side if the franchise is taken to mean that the most profitable return that could be got, free from competition, is protected by the Fourteenth Amendment, then the power to regulate is null. On the other hand if the power to regulate withdraws the protection of the Amendment altogether, then the property is naught. This is not a matter of economic theory, but of fair inter-

32. Central Lumber Co. v. South Dakota, 226 U.S. 157, 160–161 (1912).

33. See, e.g., Dr. Miles Medical Co. v. Park & Sons, 220 U.S. 373, 411–412 (1911).

> pretation of a bargain. Neither extreme can have been meant. A midway between them must be hit.[34]

> We express no opinion whether to cut this telephone company down to six per cent by legislation would or would not be confiscatory. But when it is remembered what clear evidence the court requires before it declares legislation otherwise valid void on this ground, and when it is considered how speculative every figure is that we have set down with delusive exactness, we are of opinion that the result is too near the dividing line not to make actual experiment necessary. The Master thought that the probable net income for the year that would suffer the greatest decrease would be 8.6 per cent on the values estimated by him. The Judge on assumptions to which we have stated our disagreement makes the present earnings $5\frac{10}{17}$ per cent with a reduction by the ordinance to $3\frac{6}{17}$ per cent. The whole question is too much in the air for us to feel authorized to let the injunction stand.[35]

The cases arising under the power of eminent domain furnish a striking illustration of the element of relativity in constitutional law. It is settled that a State can take private property for "public purposes." What is "a public purpose"? The Supreme Court has refused to allow the States to be fettered by formula on this subject. Time and place and local need as determined by the local legislature must govern. Mr. Justice Holmes the other day again gave point to these considerations in sustaining the growing control by States over water power.

> In the organic relation of modern society it may sometimes be hard to draw the line that is supposed to limit the authority of the legislature to exercise or delegate the power of eminent domain. But to gather the streams from waste and to draw from them energy, labor with-

34. Cedar Rapids Gas Co. v. Cedar Rapids, 223 U.S. 655, 669 (1912).
35. Louisville v. Cumberland Tel. & Tel. Co., 225 U.S. 430, 436 (1912).

> out brains, and so to save mankind from toil that it can be spared, is to supply what, next to intellect, is the very foundation of all our achievements and all our welfare. If that purpose is not public we should be at a loss to say what is. The inadequacy of use by the general public as a universal test is established.[36]

One would expect Mr. Justice Holmes to allow no finicky or textual arguments to interpose the Constitution as a barrier to the States' taxing power. In his opinions on taxation matters there is an amiable appreciation of the tantalizing difficulty of statesmen to make taxation in any form palatable.

> In the first place it is said to be an arbitrary discrimination. This objection to a tax must be approached with the greatest caution. The general expression of the Amendment must not be allowed to upset familiar and long established methods and processes by a formal elaboration of rules which its words do not import. . . . The inequality of the tax, so far as actual values are concerned, is manifest. But, here again equality in this sense has to yield to practical considerations and usage. There must be a fixed and indisputable mode of ascertaining a stamp tax. In another sense, moreover, there is equality. When the taxes on two sales are equal the same number of shares is sold in each case; that is to say, the same privilege is used to the same extent. Valuation is not the only thing to be considered. As was pointed out by the Court of Appeals, the familiar stamp tax of two cents on checks, irrespective of amount, the poll tax of a fixed sum, irrespective of income or earning capacity, and many others, illustrate the necessity and practice of sometimes substituting count for weight.[37]

> There is a look of logic when it is said that special assessments are founded on special benefits and that a law which makes it possible to assess beyond the

36. Mt. Vernon Cotton Co. v. Alabama Power Co., 240 U.S. 30, 32 (1916).
37. Hatch v. Reardon, 204 U.S. 152, 158, 159–160 (1907).

> amount of the special benefit attempts to rise above its source. But that mode of argument assumes an exactness in the premises which does not exist. The foundation of this familiar form of taxation is a question of theory. The amount of benefit which an improvement will confer upon particular land, indeed whether it is a benefit at all, is a matter of forecast and estimate. In its general aspects at least it is peculiarly a thing to be decided by those who make the law. The result of the supposed constitutional principle is simply to shift the burden to a somewhat large taxing district, the municipality, and to disguise rather than to answer the theoretic doubt. It is dangerous to tie down legislatures too closely by judicial constructions not necessarily arising from the words of the Constitution. Particularly, as was intimated in *Spencer* v. *Merchant,* 125 U.S. 345, it is more important for this court to avoid extracting from the very general language of the Fourteenth Amendment a system of delusive exactness in order to destroy methods of taxation which were well known when that Amendment was adopted and which it is safe to say that no one then supposed would be disturbed.[38]

Throughout, these opinions recognize the pressure of diverse interests of the State, the problems that confront the effort to compose those interests, and the fruitful recognition that the Constitution was not meant to thwart such obligations of statesmanship. It is just this perception of statesmanship that is dominant. So, when the very foundation of the life of a State is challenged, when the

38. Louisville v. Barber Asphalt Co., 197 U.S. 430, 433–434 (1905). "Accidental inequality is one thing, intentional and systematic discrimination another." First National Bank v. Albright, 208 U.S. 548, 552 (1908).

This leads him also to scrutinize shrewdly a contract of exemption from taxation:

"The construction of the statute by the Court of Appeals although not conclusive upon its meaning as a contract is entitled to great deference and respect. As a literal interpretation it is undeniably correct, and we should not feel warranted in overruling it because of a certain perfume of general exemption." Interborough Transit Co. v. Sohmer, 237 U.S. 276, 284 (1915).

trusteeship of the State in its natural resources is involved, we get at once an eloquent and profound support of such trusteeship.

> It appears to us that few public interests are more obvious, indisputable, and independent of particular theory than the interest of the public of a state to maintain the rivers that are wholly within it substantially undiminished, except by such drafts upon them as the guardian of the public welfare may permit for the purpose of turning them to a more perfect use. This public interest is omnipresent wherever there is a state, and grows more pressing as population grows. It is fundamental, and we are of opinion that the private property of riparian proprietors cannot be supposed to have deeper roots. Whether it be said that such an interest justifies the cutting down by statute without compensation, in the exercise of police power, of what otherwise would be private rights of property, or that apart from statute those rights do not go to the height of what the defendant seeks to do, the result is the same. But we agree with the New Jersey courts, and think it quite beyond any rational view of riparian rights that an agreement, of no matter what private owners, could sanction the diversion of an important stream outside the boundaries of the state in which it flows. The private right to appropriate is subject not only to the rights of lower owners but to the initial limitation that it may not substantially diminish one of the great foundations of public welfare and health.
>
> We are of opinion, further, that the constitutional power of the state to insist that its natural advantages shall remain unimpaired by its citizens is not dependent upon any nice estimate of the extent of present use or speculation as to future needs. The legal conception of the necessary is apt to be confined to somewhat rudimentary wants, and there are benefits from a great river that might escape a lawyer's view. But the state is not to submit even to an aesthetic analysis. Any analysis may be inadequate. It finds itself in possession of what all

admit to be a great public good, and what it has it may keep and give no one a reason for its will.[39]

Only the shallow would attempt to put Mr. Justice Holmes in the shallow pigeonholes of classification. He has been imaginatively regardful of the sensibilities of the States, particularly in State controversies, and he has shown every deference, even as a matter of "equitable fitness or propriety,"[40] to agencies of the States. In thus manifesting every rightful regard for self-reliant individual States, he to that extent only the more sought to maintain, so far as the judiciary plays a part, the full vigor of our dual system. From his opinions there emerges a conception of a nation adequate to its great national duties and consisting of confederate States, in their turn possessed of dignity and power available for the diverse uses of civilized people.

In their impact and sweep and fertile freshness, the opinions have been a superbly harmonious vehicle for the views which they embody. It all seems so easy—brilliant birds pulled from the magician's sleeve. It is the delusive ease of great effort and great art. He has told us that in deciding cases "one has to try to strike the jugular," and his aim is sure. He has attained it, as only superlative work, no matter how great the genius, can be attained. "The eternal effort of art, even the art of writing legal decisions, is to omit all but the essentials. 'The point of contact' is the formula, the place where the boy got his finger pinched; the rest of the machinery doesn't matter." So we see nothing of the detailed draughtsmanship. We get, like Corot's pictures, "magisterial summaries."

We get more: we get the man. Law ever has been for him one of the forces of life, a part of it and contributing to it. Back of his approach to an obscure statute from Oklahoma or Maine we catch a glimpse of his approach to life. That glimpse each must get and treasure for his own. For me, another artist unaware has expressed the clue:

39. Hudson County Water Co. v. McCarter, 209 U.S. 349, 356–357 (1908).

40. Prentiss v. Atlantic Coast Line Co., 211 U.S. 210, 228 (1908).

Why is there a limited authority in institutions? Why are compromise and partial cooperation practicable in society? Why is there sometimes a right to revolution? Why is there sometimes a duty to loyalty? Because the whole transcendental philosophy, if made ultimate, is false, and nothing but a selfish perspective hypostasized; because the will is absolute neither in the individual nor in humanity; because nature is not a product of the mind, but on the contrary there is an external world, ages prior to any *a priori* idea of it, which the mind recognizes and feeds upon; because there is a steady human nature within us, which our moods and passions may wrong, but cannot annul; because there is no absolute imperative, but only the operation of instincts and interests more or less subject to discipline and mutual adjustment; and finally because life is a compromise, an incipient loose harmony between the passions of the soul and the forces of nature, forces which likewise generate and protect the souls of other creatures, endowing them with powers of expression and self-assertion comparable to our own and with aims not less sweet and worthy in their own eyes; so that the quick and honest mind can not but practise courtesy in the universe, exercising its will without vehemence or forced assurance, judging with serenity, and in everything discarding the word absolute as the most false and the most odious of words.[41]

41. Santayana, "German Philosophy and Politics," 12 *J. Phil., Psych., etc.*, 645, 649 (1915).

The Nomination of Mr. Justice Brandeis

One public benefit has already accrued from the nomination of Mr. Brandeis. It has started discussion of what the Supreme Court means in American life. From much of the comment since Mr. Brandeis's nomination it would seem that multitudes of Americans seriously believe that the nine Justices embody pure reason, that they are set apart from the concerns of the community, regardless of time, place, and circumstances, to become the interpreter of sacred words with meaning fixed forever and ascertainable by a process of ineluctable reasoning. Yet the notion not only runs counter to all we know of human nature; it betrays either ignorance or false knowledge of the actual work of the Supreme Court as disclosed by 239 volumes of *United States Reports*. It assumes what is not now and never was the function of the Supreme Court.

The significant matters which come before the Supreme Court are not the ordinary legal questions of the rights of *Smith* v. *Jones*. If they were, the choosing of a Supreme Court Justice would be of professional rather than of public interest. In our system of government the Supreme Court is the final authority in the relationship of the individual to the State, of the individual to the United States, of forty-eight States to one another, and of each with the United States. In a word, the Court deals primarily with problems of government, and that is why its personnel is of such nation-wide importance. But though the Court has to decide political questions, it escapes the rough-and-tumble of politics, because it does not exercise power for the affirmative ends of the State. What it does is to define limitations of power. It marks the boundaries between State and national action. It determines the allowable sphere of legislative and executive conduct.

These are delicate and tremendous questions, not to be answered by mechanical magic distilled within the four corners of the Constitution, not to be solved automatically in the Constitution "by taking the words and a diction-

Reprinted from an unsigned editorial in the *New Republic*, February 5, 1916, with permission. Footnotes supplied by editor.

ary."[1] Except in a few very rigid and very unimportant specific provisions, such as those providing for geographic uniformity or prohibiting the enactment of bills of attainder, the Justices have to bring to the issues some creative power. They have to make great choices which are determined in the end by their breadth of understanding, imagination, sense of personal limitation, and insight into governmental problems. It is a commonplace of constitutional law, insisted upon by students like James Bradley Thayer, a commonplace to be kept vigilantly in mind, that Justices of the Supreme Court must be lawyers, of course, but above all, lawyers who are statesmen.

To generalize about periods and tendencies in the history of the Supreme Court is to omit many details and qualifications, but that the great problems of statesmanship have determined the character of the Court at different periods in our history there can be no doubt. In the first period, barring a negligible opening decade, the Court under Marshall's great leadership dealt with the structure of government. It gave legal expression to the forces of nationality. Marshall also laid down what may be called the great canon of constitutional criticism by insisting that "it is a *constitution* we are expounding,"[2] a great charter of government with all the implications that dynamic government means. After Marshall the ever-present conflict of State and national power absorbed attention until the Civil War. Then followed a third period in which national power was ascendant, a period of railroad and industrial development, of free lands and apparently unlimited resources, a period in which the prevailing philosophy was naturally enough laissez-faire. It was a period of luxuriant individualism. The Fourteenth Amendment was made the vehicle of its expression; the quality of the Court was exemplified in the sturdy personalities of Justices like Brewer and Peckham. "Liberty of contract" flourished, social legislation was feared, except during the sound but brief leadership in the opposite direction by Chief Justice Waite.

1. Gompers v. United States, 233 U.S. 604, 610 (1914) (Holmes, J.).
2. McCulloch v. Maryland, 4 Wheat. 316, 407 (1819).

The period of individualism and fear is over. Occasionally there is a relapse, but on the whole we have entered definitely upon an epoch in which Justice Holmes has been the most consistent and dominating force, and to which Justices Day and Hughes have been great contributing factors. It is the period of self-consciousness as to the true nature of the issues before the Court. It is the period of realization that basically the questions are not abstractions to be determined by empty formula, that contemporary convictions of expediency as to property and contract must not be passed off as basic principles of right. It is this new spirit which led Justice Holmes to say that it was the Court's duty "to learn to transcend our own convictions and to leave room for much that we hold dear to be done away with short of revolution by the orderly change of law."[3]

At present the important field of judicial interpretation is practically restricted to two provisions of the Constitution: the commerce clause and the Fourteenth Amendment. Around these center the contending forces of State and national action. The Fourteenth Amendment in a word involves an application of the "police power," which extends to all the great public needs.[4] And so it covers the whole domain of economic and social and industrial facts and the State's response to these facts. The principle of law—that the State cannot exercise arbitrary or unwarranted power—is undisputed. The difficulty is with the application of the principle, and the application involves grasp and imagination and contact with the realities of a modern industrial democracy. Under the commerce clause we are dealing not with abstract legal questions but the pervasive facts of life, for, as the Supreme Court itself has said, "commerce among the States is not a technical legal conception, but a practical one, drawn from the course of business."[5]

To the consideration of these very questions Mr. Brandeis has given his whole life. To their understanding he

3. Holmes, *Speeches* 98, 102 (1934).
4. See Freund, *The Police Power* (1904).
5. Swift & Co. v. United States, 196 U.S. 375, 398 (1905).

brings a mind of extraordinary power and insight. He has amassed experience enjoyed by hardly another lawyer to the same depth and richness and detail, for it is the very condition of his mind to know all there is to be known of a subject with which he grapples. Thus he is a first-handed authority in the field of insurance, of industrial efficiency, of public franchises, of conservation, of the transportation problem, of the interrelations of modern business and modern life.

But his approach is that of the true lawyer, because he seeks to tame isolated instances to as large a general rule as possible, and thereby to make the great reconciliation between order and justice. Mr. Brandeis would extend the domain of law, as he only very recently put it before the Chicago Bar Association,[6] by absorbing the facts of life, just as Mansfield in his day absorbed the law merchant into the common law. This craving for authentic facts on which law alone can be founded leads him always to insist on establishing the machinery by which they can be ascertained. It is this which has led him to create practically a new technique in the presentation of constitutional questions. Until his famous argument on the Oregon ten-hour law for women,[7] social legislation was argued before our courts practically *in vacuo*, as an abstract question unrelated to a world of factories and child labor and trade unions and steel trusts. In the *Oregon* case for the first time there were marshaled before the Supreme Court the facts of modern industry which reasonably called for legislation limiting hours of labor. This marked an epoch in the argument and decision of constitutional cases, and resulted not only in reversal of prior decisions, but in giving to the courts a wholly new approach to this most important class of present-day constitutional issues. As advocate Mr. Brandeis has secured the approval of every constitutional case which he has argued—argued always for the public—not only from the Supreme Court of the United States but from the courts of New York, Illinois, and Oregon.

6. *Business—A Profession* 344 (2d ed. 1925).
7. Muller v. Oregon, 208 U.S. 412 (1908).

We may be perfectly certain, then, that Mr. Brandeis is no doctrinaire. He does not allow formulae to do service for facts. He has remained scrupulously flexible. While, for example, he has made us realize that there may be a limit to the efficiency of combination, yet he has insisted that the issue must be settled by authoritative data, that such data must be gathered by a permanent nonpartisan commission. So Mr. Brandeis helped to give us the Federal Trade Commission. He sees equally clearly that there are limits to the uses of competition, and no man has spoken more effectively against the competition that kills or more vigorously for the morality of price maintenance.

The very processes of his mind are deliberate and judicial—if we mean by deliberation and judicial-mindedness a full survey of all relevant factors of a problem and courageous action upon it. He has an almost unerring genius for accuracy, because his conclusion is the result of a slow mastery of the problem. Events have rarely failed to support his judgments. In the New Haven situation,[8] for instance, the conclusions which Mr. Brandeis had reached and for which he sought quiet acceptance a decade ago were finally vindicated. So of all his public activities—the adoption of a sliding scale in franchise returns, the adoption of a savings-bank insurance, the settlement of industrial disputes, the regulation of conditions of labor, the conservation of our natural resources—in each problem there have been three stages: thorough investigation by and with experts; education of the public to the results of such investigation; and then political action with informed public opinion behind it, either by legislation for the government or by changes in the structure of one of the great groups of the state, such as the trade union or employers' organizations.

Mr. Brandeis says of himself: "I have no rigid social philosophy; I have been too intent on concrete problems

8. Brandeis led a battle against the Morgan interests that controlled the New Haven railroad when they attempted a monopolization of the New England railroads. The story is a complex one in which Brandeis was the subject of much vituperation but from which he emerged triumphant. The tale is summarized in Todd, *Justice on Trial: The Case of Louis D. Brandeis* (1964).

of practical justice."[9] A study of his work verifies this analysis. It is true he has a passion for justice and a passion for democracy, but justice and democracy enlist a common fealty. It is by his insistence on translating these beliefs into life, by his fruitful intellectual inventiveness in devising the means for such translation, that Mr. Brandeis is distinguished. One who has brought the agency of a vitalizing peace to the most anarchistic of all industries, the garment trades, and has done it not by magic but by turning contending forces into cooperative forces, has that balance of head and heart and will which constitutes real judicial-mindedness.

It is said of him that he is often not amiable in a fight. There is truth in the statement. The law has not been a game to him; the issues he has dealt with have been great moral questions. He has often fought with great severity. He has rarely lost. His great fights have been undertaken in the public interest. In the course of his career he has made enemies, some of whom were malicious, others honestly convinced that he had wronged them. A number of charges have been made against him, no one of which has been proved, though no one can question that Mr. Brandeis's enemies have spared no pains to prove them. His friends who are in a position to know the details of his career believe in him passionately. They are delighted that so able a committee of the Senate should have undertaken the work of running down every insinuation. They believe that no man's career can stand as much scrutiny as his. They want the insinuations crystallized, examined, and disposed of, so that the nation may begin to employ this man who has at once the passion of public service and the genius for it.

9. Cf. quotation of Brandeis by Hutchins Hapgood, New York *Globe*, January 8, 1912.

Taft and the Supreme Court

> Mr. Wilson is in favor of a latitudinarian construction of the Constitution of the United States to weaken the protection it should afford against socialist raids upon property rights . . .
>
> He has made three appointments to the Supreme Court. He is understood to be greatly disappointed in the attitude of the first of these [Mr. Justice McReynolds] upon such questions. The other two [Mr. Justice Brandeis and Mr. Justice Clarke] represent a new school of constitutional construction, which if allowed to prevail will greatly impair our fundamental law. Four of the incumbent Justices are beyond the retiring age of seventy, and the next President will probably be called upon to appoint their successors. There is no greater domestic issue in this election than the maintenance of the Supreme Court as the bulwark to enforce the guaranty that no man shall be deprived of his property without due process of law . . .[1]

These are the views of ex-President Taft, reputedly one of our greatest authorities in constitutional law. The lay reader of his article in the October *Yale Review* might naturally assume that Justices Brandeis and Clarke are a pair of firebrands who, as members of the Supreme Court, have enunciated novel and revolutionary doctrines. If Mr. Taft's words mean anything they mean that a study of the opinions of the Supreme Court will show that Brandeis and Clarke form a group apart from the other members of the Court, and, particularly, that in cases involving the due process clause these two Justices have gone off on frolics of their own—frolics strange and disruptive.

Suppose, however, some lay reader, with a curiosity exceeding his respect for Mr. Taft's weighty *ipse dixit,* retained some responsible lawyer to analyze the constitutional attitude of Brandeis and Clarke as revealed by the

Reprinted from three unsigned editorials in the *New Republic,* October 27, 1920, January 18, 1922, and January 25, 1922, with permission. Footnotes supplied by editor.

1. Taft, "Mr. Wilson and the Campaign," 10 *Yale Review* 1, 19–20 (1920).

recorded decisions. Such a lawyer would at once put Mr. Justice Clarke on one side without a detailed examination. He would say that Clarke's sober and conventional attitude is sufficiently attested by the fact that on the gravest issue which has recently divided the Supreme Court—the protection of freedom of speech when invoked by so-called radicals—he was the Court's spokesman of views pleasing even to Attorney General Palmer.[2] But what of Brandeis? A careful lawyer would report that at the bar Brandeis achieved distinction, not as the propounder of new constitutional doctrines, but as the inventor of a new technique in the application of settled constitutional law—an innovation of *method* which received the unanimous approval of a Supreme Court containing lawyers of such unquestionable orthodoxy as Fuller, Brewer, and Peckham. And what is Brandeis's record as Justice? That means a study of his dissents, for only in these can we discover "the new school" which, according to Mr. Taft, he represents. For Mr. Taft can hardly mean that Brandeis could have corrupted the constitutional views of appointees of Cleveland, McKinley, Roosevelt, and Taft.

Brandeis dissented alone in only four cases, he and Clarke alone in six more—in all other cases Brandeis was associated with one or more of the senior Justices. And what were the ten cases? Of the four exclusive Brandeis dissents one involved a novel question of equity jurisdiction,[3] one a claim against the government in which Brandeis held for a railroad against the government,[4] two involved a delimitation between federal and State power and Brandeis took a rather conservative "States' rights" point of view;[5] of the six Brandeis–Clarke dissents

2. See Abrams v. United States, 250 U.S. 616 (1919).

3. International News Service Inc. v. Associated Press, 248 U.S. 215, 248 (1918).

4. New York, N.H. & H.R. Co. v. United States, 251 U.S. 123, 127 (1919).

5. These are two series of cases rather than two cases, and, in fact, Mr. Justice Clarke joined Brandeis in the first of them: New York Central R.R. Co. v. Winfield, 244 U.S. 147, 154 (1917); Erie R.R. Co. v. Winfield, 244 U.S. 170, 174 (1917); Dakota Central Tel. Co. v. South Dakota, 250 U.S. 163, 188 (1919); Kansas v. Burleson, 250 U.S. 188, 190 (1919); Burleson v. Dempcy, 250 U.S. 191, 194 (1919); MacLeod v. New England Tel. Co., 250 U.S. 195, 199 (1919).

two involved questions of procedure[6] and four concerned interpretation of franchises[7]—issues as to which courts everywhere and always show differences of opinion. Not one of these ten cases involved the questions which particularly trouble Mr. Taft—the due process clause—not one of them involved any novel constitutional construction, not one of them was among the cases raising great public issues. Ten negligible dissents—out of a total of over seventeen hundred decisions! The utter disregard for accuracy in Mr. Taft's accusation shows that Professor Taft—teacher of Constitutional Law at Yale—does not control the irresponsibility of politician Taft.

But, after all, so much heat in Mr. Taft must have some provocation. Brandeis is the easy target, but what Mr. Taft really means is not that Brandeis brought new views to the Court, but that he brought new strength to an old conflict—the conflict between the liberals and the hidebound. The Supreme Court is hopelessly split, in constant throes of clash on vital issues. Social and economic questions divide the Justices according to the largeness of view with which they are able to dissociate the requirements of the Constitution from their personal bias. The last few years have shown many such divisions and the future is not likely to lessen them. What does Mr. Taft mean by his general language about "Socialist raids upon property rights"? Does he mean that he agrees with the nullification of the federal child labor law,[8] that he agrees with the "school of constitutional construction" which invalidated the stock dividend tax[9] and upheld the espionage convictions in the *Abrams*,[10] *Schaefer*,[11] and *Pierce*[12] cases? Does Mr. Taft, who avows belief in the necessity

6. Ex parte Abdu, 247 U.S. 27, 31 (1918); Peters v. Veasey, 251 U.S. 121, 123 (1919).

7. Owensboro v. Owensboro Water Works Co., 243 U.S. 166, 174 (1917); Cincinnati v. Cincinnati & H. Trac. Co., 245 U.S. 446, 455 (1918); Northern Ohio Trac. Co. v. Ohio, 245 U.S. 574, 585 (1918); Covington v. South Covington St. Ry. Co., 246 U.S. 413, 419 (1918).

8. Hammer v. Dagenhart, 247 U.S. 251 (1918).

9. Eisner v. Macomber, 252 U.S. 189 (1920).

10. *Supra* note 2.

11. Schaefer v. United States, 251 U.S. 466 (1920).

12. Pierce v. United States, 252 U.S. 239 (1920).

of trade unions in the abstract, support the *Hitchman* case,[13] which throws all the weight of the injunction against unionization in the concrete? On these and kindred issues Mr. Taft will be called upon to act, and perhaps cast a deciding vote, should President Harding make him Mr. Justice Taft.

And we are entitled to know the answers to these specific questions *now*. For Mr. Taft justly says there is no greater domestic issue in this election than the personnel of the Supreme Court in the coming years. Mr. Taft deserves our gratitude for his candor in recognizing that the Supreme Court involves political issues to be discussed like other political issues. In 1912, Mr. Taft was shocked that Roosevelt should dare drag the Court into the political arena. But now Mr. Taft warns us that no issue is more important than the views of the candidates as to future Justices. Of course that means we must study past decisions, the line-up of the Justices, their attitude towards economic ("property") questions, the attitude of likely appointees towards such questions. Not only may specific decisions be popularly considered, but the justification of the whole function of final law-making or unmaking exercised by the Supreme Court can hardly escape scrutiny. Mr. Taft has now made respectable what was heretofore tabooed. The door to the Holy of Holies has been opened. Others will follow where Mr. Taft's profanation leads.

II

The press greets Mr. Taft's appointment with almost universal acclaim . . . The *New Republic* does not begrudge Mr. Taft this outpour of good-will. But the Chief Justiceship . . . is not a subject for mere good-nature . . . Cases involving the social control allowed the states under the Fourteenth Amendment . . . will soon again call forth a clash of differing conceptions of policy and of the proper scope of the Court's ultimate veto power. Mr. Taft, even before he was one of its members, has

13. Hitchman Coal & Coke Co. v. Mitchell, 245 U.S. 229 (1917).

> been rather obsessed by the notion that the Supreme Court is a sacred priesthood immune from profane criticism. He is not likely to be more hospitable to criticism as the presiding Justice of the Court. But the *New Republic* cannot emphasize too often that the only safeguard against the terrible powers vested in the Supreme Court lies in continuous, informed and responsible criticism of the work of the Court. Only thus will it be able to function as a living organ of the national will and not as an obstructive force of scholastic legislation. (*New Republic*, July 27, 1921)

Arizona became a State in 1912. Its first legislature was confronted with the task of formulating a civil code properly adapted to the needs of the people of Arizona. One of the most insistent and delicate problems was the just and effective settlement of industrial controversies. In case of a conflict between employer and employees what "legal rights" may be asserted and how should those rights be enforced? How much should be left to the pressure of public opinion, to enlightened self-interest, to the competition of economic forces, and how much should be dealt with by law, and what machinery should the law utilize within the field of its authority? These were and are very complicated questions, as to which differences of opinion are acute because experience has as yet not brought decisive answers. This, if anything can, affords peculiarly a field for the exercise of legislative discretion; if there can be any justification at all for having legislatures, a stronger case for determining the State's policy by the responsible judgment of its legislature can hardly be imagined. Nor was Arizona facing this problem in the abstract. Labor difficulties were not unknown in the past, and their recurrence was certainly a fact near the horizon of the lawmakers of the State.

Charged with the duty of devising rules for the future conduct of labor litigation the Arizona legislature could hardly escape the necessity of some pronouncement upon the most contentious issue which presented itself in American labor law, to wit, the use of the injunction against picketing and the boycott, particularly where no violence was used and the claim of destruction of property was merely colorable. The highest courts of the country, acting solely upon their own lawmaking function, were hopelessly divided. Thus Massachusetts, California, Michigan, and New Jersey outlawed peaceful picketing while the courts of Ohio, Minnesota, Montana, New York, Oklahoma, and New Hampshire sanctioned it. The conviction of an impressive body of opinion, which had accumulated at the time the Arizona legislature was considering this problem, has thus been summarized by Mr. Justice Brandeis:

> The equitable remedy, although applied in accordance with established practice, involved incidents which, it was asserted, endangered the personal liberty of wage-earners. The acts enjoined were frequently, perhaps usually, acts which were already crimes at common law or had been made so by statutes . . . The effect of the proceeding upon the individual was substantially the same as if he had been successfully prosecuted for a crime; but he was denied, in the course of the equity proceedings, those rights which by the Constitution are commonly secured to persons charged with a crime.
>
> It was asserted that in these proceedings an alleged danger to property, always incidental and at times insignificant, was often laid hold of to enable the penalties of the criminal law to be enforced expeditiously without that protection to the liberty of the individual which the Bill of Rights was designed to afford; that through such proceedings a single judge often usurped the functions not only of the jury but of the police department; that, in prescribing the conditions under which strikes were permissible and how they might be carried out, he usurped also the powers of the legislature; and that incidentally he abridged the constitutional rights of individuals to free speech, to a free press and to peaceful assembly.

> It was urged that the real motive in seeking the injunction was not ordinarily to prevent property from being injured nor to protect the owner in its use, but to endow property with active, militant power which would make it dominant over men. In other words, that, under the guise of protecting property rights, the employer was seeking sovereign power. And many disinterested men, solicitous only for the public welfare, believed that the law of property was not appropriate for dealing with the forces beneath social unrest; that in this vast struggle it was unwise to throw the power of the State on one side or the other according to principles deduced from that law; that the problem of the control and conduct of industry demanded a solution of its own; and that, pending the ascertainment of new principles to govern industry, it was wiser for the state not to interfere in industrial struggles by the issuance of an injunction.[14]

With this as a background, the Arizona legislature yielded to the experience of England and several American States, by prohibiting interference, through extraordinary relief by injunction, between employer and employees in any case growing out of a dispute concerning terms of conditions of employment, unless injury through violence was at stake. In all other cases of industrial conflict it left the rights of the parties to be protected through the criminal law and ordinary suits for damages. This act was passed in 1913, has remained untouched since then, and has passed challenge in the Arizona courts.

But the Supreme Court of the United States now says otherwise.[15] Eight years after the law has been in force the Supreme Court holds that Arizona has laid impious hands upon the Ark of the Covenant as enshrined in the Fourteenth Amendment. To a mere layman this result must appear as incredible as the process by which it is reached

14. Brandeis, J., dissenting in Truax v. Corrigan, 257 U.S. 312, 366–368 (1921).

15. Truax v. Corrigan, *supra* note 14.

is mysterious—although the decision immediately affects some thirty million lay men and women, who earn their livelihood in industry, and it no less affects the whole hundred million lay population of this country, insofar as it involves the power of the Supreme Court of the United States to translate its views of social policy into the law of each of the forty-eight States. Nor will the layman's bewilderment be lessened by the fact that this appalling result is reached by the votes of five men as against the votes of four men. The Chief Justice helps neither an understanding of the decision nor respect for the law in asserting that "It does not seem possible to escape the conclusion"[16] that the Arizona act is unconstitutional when in fact four of his associates—Justices Holmes, Pitney, Brandeis, and Clarke—find not the slightest difficulty in escaping that conclusion and in emphatically dissenting from it. Judged by its point of view and its significance for the future this decision of the Supreme Court is, in our judgment, fraught with more evil than any which it has rendered in a generation. It challenges the whole scope of judicial review under the Fifth and Fourteenth Amendments. We know of no problem in the institutional life of this country which calls for a more courageous searching and fundamental scrutiny than the nature of the power which the majority of the Court exercises in the Arizona case and the manner in which that power is wielded.

Let us recall the words of the Fourteenth Amendment to see the exact terms of the limitations by which the States are circumscribed in determining for themselves, in the language of Mr. Justice Pitney, "their respective conditions of law and order, and what kind of civilization they shall have as a result."[17]

> . . . nor shall any State deprive any person of life, liberty, or property without due process of law; nor deny to any person within its jurisdiction the equal protection of the laws.

16. 257 U.S. at 334.
17. Id. at 349.

Chief Justice Taft finds that the denial in labor cases of extraordinary relief by injunction deprives the owner of a business of "property" without "due process of law," and that in selecting the class of employers and employees for special treatment, though dealing with both sides alike, Arizona is guilty of a denial of "the equal protection of the laws." Whence does the Court derive this result? Surely not from the *words* of the Fourteenth Amendment. That amendment, to be sure, imposes limitations upon State action, but it does not define them. "Due process of law" and "the equal protection of the laws" are not self-defining. Their content is derived from without. "The Constitution was intended, "says the Chief Justice, "to prevent experimentation with the fundamental rights of the individual."[18] Of course. But what "rights" are "fundamental" is *the* question to be answered. For Chief Justice Taft the beginning of the problem is the end. "When fundamental rights are thus attempted to be taken away,"[19] he says in speaking of the Arizona statute, and thus blithely indulges in a schoolboy's begging of the question. The very problem at issue is whether the use of the injunction in labor cases *is* a "fundamental right." It does not bring us one whit nearer solution to be told repeatedly that the Constitution safeguards "fundamental rights." The central problem is evaded by an effortless repetition of phrases.

The content of the Fourteenth Amendment is to be derived, the Supreme Court has told us, by a judicial process of inclusion and exclusion. The Court has been at this process for fifty years. Sedulously avoiding definition, the Court has insisted that the Fourteenth Amendment does not alter the basic nature of our federal system. It still leaves each State free to choose its own mode of life, so long as the "immutable principles of justice which inhere in the very idea of free government"[20] are respected. The Fourteenth Amendment embodies "broad and general

18. Id. at 338.
19. Ibid.
20. Holden v. Hardy, 169 U.S. 366, 389 (1898).

maxims of liberty and justice . . . founded on the essential nature of law."[21]

Moreover, the Court has recognized that "while the cardinal principles of justice are immutable, the methods by which justice is administered are subject to constant fluctuation,"[22] and "The power of the people of the States to make and alter their laws at pleasure is the greatest security for liberty and justice."[23] The Fourteenth Amendment, so the Supreme Court has told us again and again, is not the arbiter of policy. Only "immutable principles" are in its keeping.

Is it really possible for anyone living in the present day to insist that the restriction of the use of the injunction in labor cases is the denial of "a fundamental principle of liberty and justice which inheres in the very idea of free government and is the inalienable right of a citizen of such a government"? No wonder Mr. Justice Pitney, dealing with the issue in the concrete, writes: "I cannot believe that the use of the injunction in such cases—however important—is so essential to the right of acquiring, possessing and enjoying property that its restriction or elimination amounts to a deprivation of liberty or property without due process of law, within the meaning of the Fourteenth Amendment."[24]

Equally incredible and ominous is an application of the requirement of the equal protection of the laws which excludes differentiating treatment of such a distinct problem as a labor controversy, compared with other types of litigation. Again let members of the Court speak. "I think further," writes Mr. Justice Holmes, "that the selection of the class of employers and employees for special treatment, dealing with both sides alike, is beyond criticism on principles often asserted by this Court. And especially I think that without legalizing the conduct complained of, the extraordinary relief by injunction may be denied to the class. Legislation may begin where an evil begins.

21. Hurtado v. California, 110 U.S. 516, 532 (1884).
22. 169 U.S. at 387.
23. Twining v. New Jersey, 211 U.S. 78, 106 (1908).
24. 257 U.S. at 349.

If, as many intelligent people believe, there is more danger that injunctions will be abused in labor cases than elsewhere I can feel no doubt of the power of the legislature to deny it in such cases."[25]

How is one to account for such a decision by the majority, and for this opinion by Chief Justice Taft? We venture the following analysis:

1. Chief Justice Taft deals with abstractions and not with the work-a-day world, its men, and its struggles. To him, also, words are things and not the symbols of things. The jejune logomachy of his judicial process is thus exposed by Mr. Justice Holmes:

> The dangers of a delusive exactness in the application of the Fourteenth Amendment have been adverted to before now . . . By calling a business "property" you make it seem like land, and lead up to the conclusion that a statute cannot substantially cut down the advantages of ownership existing before the statute was passed. An established business no doubt may have pecuniary value and commonly is protected by law against unjustified injuries. But you cannot give it definiteness of contour by calling it a thing. It is a course of conduct and like other conduct is subject to substantial modification according to time and circumstances both in itself and in regard to what shall justify doing it a harm. I cannot understand the notion that it would be unconstitutional to authorize boycotts and the like in aid of the employees' or the employers' interest by statute when the same result has been reached constitutionally without statute by Courts with whom I agree.[26]

For all the regard that the Chief Justice of the United States pays to the facts of industrial life, he might as well have written this opinion as Chief Justice of the Fiji Islands. Mr. Taft, as a member of the War Labor Board, came in contact with not a little that must have informed his mind as to the industrial struggle, and law's relation

25. Id. at 343.
26. Id. at 342–343.

to it. But all those crude and sordid and unsymmetrical facts have no place in the mind of Chief Justice Taft. From reading his opinion the historian of the future would have to assume that the Arizona legislature withdrew injunctive relief in labor cases out of sheer malevolence or in a spirit of reckless oppression.

2. "What we call necessary institutions," says de Tocqueville, "are often no more than institutions to which we have grown accustomed." The Chief Justice, we venture to suggest, is a victim of this process of self-delusion. For him there never was a time when injunctive relief was not the law of nature. For him the world never was without it, and therefore the foundations of the world are involved in its withdrawal. And yet, 1888 marks the first recorded opinion of an injunction in labor litigation,[27] and in 1896, the Chief Justice of Massachusetts still speaks of injunctions in such cases as "a practice of very recent origin."[28] By 1921, the right to an injunction has become "an immutable principle of liberty and justice," world without end! The result is that while the due process clause does not guarantee trial by jury as at common law even in criminal cases, the due process clause *does* guarantee the right to trial *without jury*—for the nub of the matter is that the resort to equity for an injunction in labor disputes is due to a "greater probability of a conviction for contempt by a judge alone . . . than of conviction by a jury likely to sympathize in some degree with the offender."

3. As a result of both these tendencies—abstract reasoning and canonizing the familiar into the eternal—the judge's limitations are stereotyped into limitations of the Constitution. The danger has been voiced by one of the most discerning of recent judges, the late Mr. Justice Moody:

> Under the guise of interpreting the Constitution we must take care that we do not import into the discussion our own personal views of what would be wise, just and

27. Sherry v. Perkins, 147 Mass. 212 (1888).
28. Field, C.J., in Vegelahn v. Guntner, 167 Mass. 92, 100 (1896).

> fitting rules of government to be adopted by a free people and confound them with constitutional limitations.[29]

This is precisely what Chief Justice Taft has done, and that too in the most sensitive field of social policy and legal control.

III

Senator Beveridge, in his *Life of John Marshall*, has shown with new vividness that the Constitution of the United States is not a document whose text was divinely inspired, and whose meaning is to be proclaimed by an anointed priesthood removed from knowledge of the stress of life. It was born of the practical needs of government; it was intended for men in their temporal relations. The deepest significance of Marshall's magistracy is his recognition of the Constitution as a living framework within which the nation and the States could freely move through the inevitable growth and changes to be wrought by time and the great inventions.

But it requires the insight of a Marshall to be unflaggingly on the alert against perverting a great instrument of government into mere mystic words of a dead scholasticism.

Mr. Taft, before his accession to the Supreme Court, had shown impatience not merely with those who regard the Constitution as a document of human origin and directed to human ends, but even towards critics who ventured to suggest the human fallibility of those who construed the Constitution. To his mind, it seemed, the very words of the Constitution assured automatic infallibility to the interpretation of five men—if only those five men happened to have the "right" views and happened to be Justices of the Supreme Court. Therefore, the *New Republic* made Mr. Taft's appointment as Chief Justice the occasion for expressing anew its conviction that a steady stream of enlightened criticism must play upon the work of the Supreme Court, if its transcendent function in exercising a

29. 211 U.S. at 106–107.

vital veto-power over national and State action is to be saved from destructive obscurantism.

Last week we briefly analyzed the meaning of the Chief Justice's opinion in holding that the right to an injunction is one of those "immutable principles of liberty and justice" which have been forever enshrined in the Constitution. By this decision and still more by the opinion sustaining it, Chief Justice Taft has justified the worst fears about him more quickly than the sturdiest sceptic was entitled to fear. But in what is presaged for the future by Chief Justice Taft in *Truax* v. *Corrigan*—the name of this case is destined to become even more classic than the *Lochner* case[30]—a challenge is offered to all who find intolerable authoritarian rule by five men in contested fields of social policy, and that, too, of social policy which is the concern not of the entire nation but of the varying needs and purposes of each of the forty-eight States. The gravity of the issues thus raised compels us to repeat that the nature of the power which the majority of the Court exercised in *Truax* v. *Corrigan*, and the manner in which that power is wielded, call for fundamental scrutiny.

1. In any consideration of the power of the Supreme Court to nullify legislation, important distinctions between different spheres of its action must be observed. Some organ of government must maintain the equilibrium between the States and the nation. "For one in my place," Mr. Justice Holmes has told us, "sees how often a local policy prevails with those who are not trained to national views and how often action is taken that embodies what the Commerce Clause was meant to end. But I am not aware that there is any serious desire to limit the Court's power in this regard."[31] But even this power is not exercised by distilling the meaning of mystic words of the Constitution. The decisions under the commerce clause, either allowing or confining State action, are at bottom acts of statesmanship. A noted professor of constitutional law in Columbia University thus summarizes these cases

30. Lochner v. New York, 198 U.S. 45 (1905).

31. Holmes, "Law and the Court," in *Collected Legal Papers* 296 (1920).

under the commerce clause: "The court has drawn its lines where it has drawn them because it has thought it wise to draw them there. The wisdom of its wisdom depends upon a judgment about practical matters and not upon a knowledge of the Constitution."[32]

When we deal with the "due process" and the "equal protection of the law" clauses of the Fifth and the Fourteenth Amendments, we are in a totally different domain of judicial action. Those amendments do not concern the delimitation between federal and State jurisdictions. They do not embody specific guarantees or limitations, such as the prohibition against ex post facto laws or State taxation of exports, which are relatively easy of application and allow comparatively meager play for individual judgment as to policy. In these general "guarantees" and "limitations" upon federal and State action, we have the enunciation, as we have seen, of "immutable principles of liberty and justice." They embody "broad counsels of moderation . . . intended to protect the individual against extravagant or invidious discrimination." Clearly, these open the door to the widest differences of opinion. Judgment upon them is bound to be determined by the experience, the environment, the imagination, the hopes, and the fears of those who sit in judgment.

Should such power, affecting the intimate life of nation as well as States, be entrusted to five men? For that is the lowest common denominator of the problem. Its justification has been eloquently put by a great judge, who himself exercises this power with the utmost humility.

> The great ideals of liberty and equality are preserved against the assaults of opportunism, the expediency of the passing hour, the erosion of small encroachments, the scorn and derision of those who have no patience with general principles, by enshrining them in constitutions, and consecrating to the task of their protection a body of defenders . . . The restraining power of the judiciary does not manifest its chief worth in the few

32. Powell, "Supreme Court Decisions on the Commerce Clause and State Police Power, 1910–14 II," 22 *Colum. L. Rev.* 28, 48 (1922).

> cases in which the legislature has gone beyond the lines that mark the limits of discretion. Rather shall we find its chief worth in making vocal and audible the ideals that might otherwise be silenced, in giving them continuity of life and of expression, in guiding and directing choice within the limits where choice ranges. This function should preserve to the courts the power that now belongs to them, if only the power is exercised with insight into social values, and with suppleness of adaptation to changing social needs.[33]

Has not the time come when an objective study, so far as that is possible, should be made of the actual operation of the power by which the Court cuts down Congressional and State legislation as offensive to the due process clause? Is it not necessary to make an appraisal of this judicial power in action, as revealed by such a series of decisions as the *Lochner* case,[34] the *Adair* case,[35] the *Coppage* case,[36] *Adams* v. *Tanner*,[37] and, now, the culminating *Truax* v. *Corrigan*? Can it fairly be said that this power of the Supreme Court is exercised "with insight into social values and with suppleness of adaptation to changing social needs?" Is the price of this power worth its cost? Is the invasion of "immutable principles of liberty and justice" by legislatures a sufficiently lively danger, in the light of experience, to call for this extraordinary trust of power to five men? We have the testimony of so conservative a student of constitutional law as Professor Freund (himself a supporter of the existing power of the courts) that "It is unlikely that a legislature will otherwise than through inadvertence violate the most obvious and cardinal dictates of justice; gross miscarriages of justice are probably less frequent in legislation than they are in the judicial determination of controversies."[38]

33. Cardozo, *The Nature of the Judicial Process* 92–94 (1921).
34. *Supra* note 30.
35. Adair v. United States, 208 U.S. 161 (1908).
36. Coppage v. Kansas, 236 U.S. 1 (1915).
37. 244 U.S. 590 (1917).
38. Freund, *Standards of American Legislation* 213 (1917).

Over against the influence of judicial review as a restraining power upon unjust legislation is the power of paralysis upon just and needed legislation, because of fear of the judicial veto. Minimum wage legislation was ventured by some of the States more than ten years ago. Its constitutional fate is still in doubt, with the result that the utilization of this tried social instrument has been largely retarded through fear of the overhanging judicial sword of Damocles. Moreover, if the exercise of this power has resulted in a series of indefensible decisions, calamitous in their immediate effects, and still more in their deeper consequences, has not the time come to ask if the nature of our legal education, the basis of judicial selections, and the conditions of judicial life are reasonably calculated to assure a handful of statesmanlike judges, capable of exercising such power "with insight into social values and with suppleness of adaptation to changing social needs"?

2. Granted this power of judicial review is to be retained, its true nature should be frankly recognized by the public, and frankly avowed by the courts. The simple fact of the matter is that in a decision like *Truax* v. *Corrigan,* the Court, under the guise of legal form, exercises political control. That the courts are especially fitted to be the ultimate arbiters of policy is an intelligent and a tenable doctrine. But let them and us face the fact that five Justices of the Supreme Court *are* conscious molders of policy instead of the impersonal vehicles of revealed truth.

3. Such appreciation of the true function of the Supreme Court, in the aspects of the Constitution here considered, will at least make for a needed revision of attitude towards their qualifications and the public's responsibility in their selection. It will then be recognized that "the Constitution" which they profess to interpret is to no small degree the interpretation of *their* own experience and *their* "judgment about practical matters." Therefore, their background, their experience, their ability to transcend their experience—all are pertinent matters of inquiry before putting a man for a lifetime upon the Supreme Bench. For the part played by unconscious partiality is tremendous. Lord Justice Scrutton, one of the

powerful and conservative present-day English judges, has penetratingly expressed it. "The habits you are trained in, the people with whom you mix, lead to your having a certain class of ideas of such a nature that, when you have to deal with other ideas, you do not give as sound and accurate judgment as you would wish. This is one of the great difficulties at present with Labour. Labour says: 'Where are your impartial Judges? They all move in the same circle as the employers, and they are all educated and nursed in the same ideas as the employers. How can a labour man or a trade unionist get impartial justice?' It is very difficult sometimes to be sure that you have put yourself into a thoroughly impartial position between two disputants, one of your own class and one not of your class."[39]

This psychological fact is, of course, of infinitely greater significance with us than in England. There an *Osborne* judgment may promptly be corrected by Parliament;[40] here *Truax* v. *Corrigan* becomes forever a strait-jacket for a free people until and unless the Supreme Court some day sees fit to change its mind. And this terrific veto-power over legislation may be exerted over the ordinances of every Gopher Prairie, and is potent against the local life of the individual States. The harm to our federalism resulting from the frustration of the free life of the individual States in their local affairs has been memorably emphasized by Mr. Justice Holmes:

> There is nothing that I more deprecate than the use of the Fourteenth Amendment beyond the absolute compulsion of its words to prevent the making of social experiments that an important part of the community desires, in the insulated chambers afforded by the several States, even though the experiments may seem futile or even noxious to me and to those whose judgment I most respect.[41]

39. Scrutton, "The Work of the Commercial Court," 1 *Camb. L.J.* 6, 8 (1821).

40. See Osborne v. Amalgamated Society of Railway Servants [1909], 1 Ch. 139; Trade Union Act of 1913.

41. 257 U.S. at 344.

Surely the men who wield this power of life and death over legislation should be subjected to the most vigorous scrutiny before being given that power. In theory it is the people's power that they are wielding. In practice the people should determine whether they should be entrusted with this power. At the very least public opinion and the confirming authority of the Senate should be alive to an understanding of what the appointment of a Supreme Court Justice means.

The "Law" and Labor

On October 15th, 1914, President Wilson signed the Clayton Act and commemorated labor's great interest in the historic occasion by presenting to Mr. Gompers the pen which brought the act into being. "This pen with which the President signed the Clayton bill," wrote Gompers, "has been added to the collection of famous pens at the A. F. of L. headquarters—trophies of humanitarian legislation secured by the workers of America. This last pen will be given the place of greatest honor—it is symbolic of the most comprehensive and most fundamental legislation in behalf of human liberties that has been enacted anywhere in the world." And now, the pen of a majority of the Supreme Court has unwritten what Mr. Gompers believed the President's pen to have written.

The Supreme Court's decision in the *Duplex* case[1] has naturally aroused the passions of partisanship. Execration or jubilation marks the tone of current comment. What to Mr. Gompers is "a blow at human freedom," is interpreted by Tory papers as "the Supreme Court rebukes the class struggle." We, too, deem the decision of great significance. Here was a statute upon which, as Mr. Gompers' eloquence attests, the highest hopes were based. It behooves us to try to understand on what these hopes were founded, and why they have been frustrated.

Ever since industrial conflicts became persistently acute in this country—that is for over twenty years—organized labor has been struggling, so far at least as the federal courts were concerned, against two drastic legal weapons, the injunction and the Sherman Law. Disinterested opinion increasingly supported labor's complaint against the abusive exercise of injunctions as a mode of interfering in the industrial conflict by prohibiting specific labor tactics which alone render effective the abstract rights to organize and to strike. Similarly, the potential danger that the Sherman Law might be invoked against

Reprinted from an unsigned article in the *New Republic*, January 26, 1921, with permission. Footnotes supplied by editor.

1. Duplex Co. v. Deering, 254 U.S. 443 (1921).

trade unions was constantly flashed as a sword before labor. This threat was realized in the minds of labor by the decision in the *Danbury Hatters' Case* in 1908.[2] But the case as a matter of fact involved liability for acts done, not for *being* a trade union. Yet labor, not unnaturally, feared in the existing legal atmosphere the threat of proceedings for dissolution of the American Federation of Labor itself, precisely as the French government recently proceeded against the Confédération Générale du Travail. The *Danbury Hatters' Case* undoubtedly added fresh impetus to the gathering momentum for relief. Labor, now supported by the progressive tide, had two objectives; one, to remove all possible doubt as to the legality of trade unions as such, and to withdraw their activities from the scope of the Sherman Law; the other, to prohibit the use of injunctions against the conventional tactics of labor.

The Clayton Act was intended to translate these objectives into law. Section 6 dealt with the first aim, Section 20 with the second. As a matter of fact, Section 6 is words and nothing else. What labor wanted and thought it got was the exemption of all labor controversies from the operation of the Sherman Law. All Section 6 did was to declare that the Sherman Law did not forbid the existence and operation of labor organizations—which the Sherman Law never did, but merely applies to certain conduct in the course of its operations; and to permit their members to *lawfully* carry out their *legitimate* objects—which is another way of saying what is lawful shall be lawful! But Section 20 grappled in detail with the problem of legalizing specific acts which theretofore had run afoul of federal injunctions. It provided that the following familiar tactics of labor shall not be deemed violations "of any law of the United States":

> Terminating any relation of employment, or
> Ceasing to perform any work or labor, or
> Recommending, advising, or persuading others by peaceful means to do so, or

2. Loewe v. Lawlor, 208 U.S. 274 (1908).

> Attending at any place where such person or persons may lawfully be, for the purpose of obtaining or communicating information, or
>
> Peacefully persuading any person to work or to abstain from working, or
>
> Ceasing to patronize or employ any party to such dispute, or
>
> Recommending, advising, or persuading others by peaceful and lawful means so to do, or
>
> Paying or giving to, or withholding from, any person engaged in such dispute any strike benefits or other moneys or things of value.

These acts having frequently been the basis of injunctions, Congress provided that thereafter they shall not be prohibited by injunction "in any case between an employer and employees, or between employers and employees involving or growing out of a dispute concerning terms or conditions of employment."

Against this background of the terms and the history of the Clayton Act the facts of the *Duplex* case must be projected. What are the facts? There are in the United States only four manufacturers of printing presses; and they are in active competition. Between 1909 and 1913 the machinists' union induced three of them to recognize and deal with the union, to grant the eight-hour day, to establish a minimum wage scale, and to comply with other union requirements. The fourth, the Duplex Company of Battle Creek, Michigan, refused to recognize the union; insisted upon conducting its factory on the "open shop" principle; refused to introduce the eight-hour day and operated, for the most part, ten hours a day; refused to establish a minimum wage scale; and disregarded other union standards. Thereupon two of the three manufacturers who had assented to union conditions, notified the union that they should be obliged to terminate their agreements with it unless their competitor, the Duplex Company, also entered into the agreement with the union, which, in giving more favorable terms to labor, imposed correspondingly greater burdens upon the employer.

Because the Duplex Company refused to enter into such an agreement and in order to induce it to do so, the machinists' union declared a strike at its factory, and in aid of that strike instructed its members and the members of affiliated unions not to work on the installation of presses which the Duplex Company had delivered in New York. In a word the machinists supported the strike at the Duplex factory by a strike against its product in New York because of the common interests of the members of the machinists' union to resist an attack upon the standard of living secured for them by the union and maintainable, as they believed, only through the union. The Duplex Company thereupon sought to enjoin the officials of the machinists' union in New York from inducing their members not to work for the company or its customers in connection with the installation of its presses.

Here is a case, one would suppose, within the plain tenor of the act of Congress—if Congress meant its words to have any efficacy at all. But the majority of the Court found no restraint in Section 20 against an injunction in this case. Clearly the acts enjoined are among the acts enumerated in Section 20 as not "held to be violations of any law of the United States." But the Supreme Court now decides that the effort of the New York machinists, by not working on Duplex presses, to secure union conditions for their fellow machinists in the Duplex Company's plant and thereby to maintain their own union conditions elsewhere is not a case "growing out of a dispute concerning terms or conditions of employment." Furthermore the Court holds the act does not apply to a case arising between an employer in Michigan and workers in New York not in its employ, but affected immediately by the conditions of employment in Michigan, because the immunity of the Clayton Act is restricted to cases "between an employer and employees or between employers and employees." In other words, the Court reads this language as though Congress had written "between an employer and employees *in his employ.*"

The upshot of the decision, in the naïve but honest language of one judge, is that the Clayton Act has legalized lawful strikes. The law is what it was before. Verily, the mountains labored and brought forth a dead mouse—except that now an employer can get an injunction against unions under the Sherman Law, while formerly he had to be content with treble damages. Surely the layman will be puzzled. It must seem strange to him that language should so completely conceal thought, as the Supreme Court now finds Section 20 to have concealed it. It will seem incredible to anyone whose curiosity is stronger than his prejudices that an elaborate effort to *change* the law should turn out to be merely a reaffirmation of it. And surely lawyers would be as much puzzled as laymen—if this statute dealt with a noncontentious issue. It is an elementary principle of statutory construction that *some* effect must be given to legislation—all effect, in fact, that the traffic of the language will bear. This is a particularly binding rule when the history of the legislation shows that there were evils in the existing law and the legislature sought to remedy them. This is peculiarly the case of the Clayton Act. As the dissent points out:

> This statute was the fruit of unceasing agitation, which extended over more than twenty years and was designed to equalize before the law the position of workingmen and employer as industrial combatants . . . It was objected that, due largely to environment, the social and economic ideas of judges, which thus became translated into law, were prejudicial to a position of equality between workingmen and employer; that due to this dependence upon the individual opinion of judges, great confusion existed as to what purposes were lawful and what unlawful; and that in any event Congress, not the judges, was the body which should declare what public policy in regard to the industrial struggle demands.
>
> By 1914 the ideas of the advocates of legislation had fairly crystallized upon the manner in which the inequalities and uncertainty of the law should be removed. It was to be done by expressly legalizing certain acts regardless of the effects produced by them upon other persons . . . In other words, the Clayton Act sub-

> stituted the opinion of Congress as to the propriety of the purpose for that of differing judges; and thereby it declared that the relations between employers of labor and workingmen were competitive relations, that organized competition was not harmful, and that it justified injuries necessarily inflicted in its course.[3]

How came it then that six Justices of the Supreme Court have decided that Congress wrote words without meaning? It will not do to say "economic determinism." That still leaves open the question how "economic determinism" operates through judicial logic, and how it finds its opportunities for operation. We venture this analysis of the factors which underlie the opinion of Mr. Justice Pitney:

1. Facts are considered abstractly, and not as they are imbedded in the matrix of the industrial struggle. If one were to read only the opinion of the Court one would be left with the impression that the machinists' union of some 60,000 ruthlessly sought to interfere with the business of the Duplex Company. In fact we are in the presence of a contest between employer and workers in which the employer's conduct not only affected the conditions of his own workers, but necessarily, in view of the competition of the industry, threatened the basic standards of life which the union had procured for its men elsewhere. Not a word of all this in the majority opinion, although the trial judge who was able to estimate the facts at first hand wrote: "a careful reading of the entire record leads to the conclusion that, if men have a right to strike and to endeavor to prevail upon others to fail to work for the employer this is such a case as exemplifies careful, prudent, and lawful conduct on the part of the employés."[4]

2. Loose language in legislation dealing with matters of social policy enables judges to pour into the mold of ambiguity their own beliefs and hopes and fears, in a word, *their* social policy. Deceived by the process of logic and the language of law, judges fail to pierce the quivering

3. 254 U.S. at 484–486.
4. 247 Fed. 192, 198.

and conflicting social issues underneath the thick phraseology of their prejudices. "The training of lawyers," wrote Mr. Justice Holmes long ago, "is a training in logic. The processes of analogy, discrimination and deduction are those in which they are most at home. The language of judicial decision is mainly the language of logic. And the logical method and form flatter that longing for certainty and for repose which is in every human mind. But certainty generally is illusion, and repose is not the destiny of man. Behind the logical form lies a judgment as to the relative worth and importance of competing legislative grounds, often an inarticulate and unconscious judgment, it is true, and yet the very root and nerve of the whole proceeding."[5]

3. Therefore where the "law" is a process of judicial analogizing, or legislation is so drawn as to leave ample play for judicial "construction," the limits of the judge's experience with the actualities of life and the range of his imagination, which determine his conception of social policy, will determine the "law." In a word, unless legislation is most carefully drawn to accomplish a definitely conceived legislative policy the judges are the "law"—as they ultimately are as to all legislation, in this country, in view of their power to declare unconstitutional the most carefully devised legislation. Here again, more than twenty-five years ago, Mr. Justice Holmes called attention "to the very serious legislative considerations which have to be weighed . . . To measure them justly needs not only the highest powers of a judge and a training which the practice of the law does not insure, but also a freedom from prepossessions which is very hard to attain. It seems to me desirable that the work should be done with express recognition of its nature. The time has gone by when law is only an unconscious embodiment of the common will. It has become a conscious reaction upon itself of organized society knowingly seeking to determine its own destinies."[6]

5. Holmes, *Collected Legal Papers* 181 (1920).
6. Id. at 129–130.

If this explains, at least in part, the wherefore of the *Duplex* decision, what practical consequences are to be drawn?

1. It is safe to say, this is not the last of decisions adverse to labor's combative resources in the industrial struggle. Public opinion is likely to reflect the attitude of courts in restricting trial by combat. There is a very significant closing paragraph in Mr. Justice Brandeis's opinion:

> Because I have come to the conclusion that both the common law of a State and a statute of the United States declare the right of industrial combatants to push their struggle to the limits of the justification of self-interest, I do not wish to be understood as attaching any constitutional or moral sanction to that right. All rights are derived from the purposes of the society in which they exist; above all rights arises duty to the community. The conditions developed in industry may be such that those engaged in it cannot continue their struggle without danger to the community. But it is not for judges to determine whether such conditions exist, nor is it their function to set the limits of permissible contest and to declare the duties which the new situation demands. This is the function of the legislature which, while limiting individual and group rights of aggression and defense, may substitute processes of justice for the more primitive method of trial by combat.[7]

In a word, organized labor must seek a new, or rather, a wider orientation than that which it has heretofore pursued. Through an intensive program of education, through the development of the cooperative movement, through a grappling with the basic problems of waste and disorganization of industry, through methods of industrial government, a wider basis for labor's position in the state will be established and increasing strength will be attained.

2. The *Duplex* decision demonstrates anew labor's need for expert assistance. If the American Federation of Labor

7. 254 U.S. at 488.

had been equipped with highly trained counsel, such a shabbily drawn piece of legislation as the Clayton Act could not have been put on the statute books—at least not without Mr. Gompers knowing that he was being offered a gold brick. Careful counsel certainly would have guarded against the very contingency upon which the act has now shipwrecked. Instead of leaving to ambiguity the question whether the immunity against injunctions should be restricted to litigation between an employer and workmen in *his* employ, or is also to apply to cases where the "parties are generically the hired and the hirer," a careful draftsman would have insisted on some such safeguarding provision as is contained in the British Trades Disputes Act of 1906, which specifically applies to workers "whether or not in the employment of the employer with whom a trade dispute arises." We hope that Mr. Gompers's recent consultations with Mr. Hoover and his engineers are significant of the recognition of the leaders of the A. F. of L. of the necessity for bringing the resources of science in every direction to labor's cause. There is need of a general staff to do continuous thinking for labor, trained writers and speakers to interpret the needs and the methods of labor to the general public, and, finally, skilled technicians dealing with special problems. Mr. Gompers will learn that "intellectuals" may have as deep a social sympathy and understanding as men who work at crafts. American labor leaders will learn, as English labor is steadily learning, that one of the banes of our civilization is the cleavage between labor by hand and labor by brain. What the Webbs, R. H. Tawney, Arthur Greenwood, Norman Angell, have brought to the labor movement of England is a contribution and a comradeship that American labor will not very much longer disdain.

3. Through these so-called "intellectuals," working as collaborators with trade unionists, the bridge will be thrown for others to cross. Steadily labor will cease to be essentially a "class" movement of hand workers, and will make its broad appeal to the liberal forces of the country.

4. Adverse judicial decisions energized the Labor party of England. The *Duplex* case and like decisions may ac-

complish a similar good for this country. Despite his protests Mr. Gompers always has been in politics. But he has been content to be dependent on legislators who are either indifferent to or ignorant of the fundamental significance of the labor movement. A little more experience with Clayton acts and *Duplex* decisions may persuade Mr. Gompers that he has been too trusting. Labor *is* in politics of necessity, because industry means politics; industry is the center of gravity of the modern state. But labor's participation in politics must be continuous and comprehensive, not innocent and impotent.

The Berger Decision

A gentle and generous philosopher noted the other day a growing "intuition" on the part of the masses that all judges, in lively controversies, are "more or less prejudiced." But between that "more or less" lies the whole kingdom of the mind; the differences between the "more or less" are the triumphs of disinterestedness, they are the aspirations we call justice. And the very consciousness by judges of potential prejudice, an alertness against its dominance, is in itself a potent corrective against the sway of prejudice. The basic consideration in the vitality of any system of law is confidence in this proximate purity of its process. Corruption from venality is hardly more damaging than a widespread belief of corrosion through partisanship.

Our judicial system is absolutely dependent upon a popular belief that it is as untainted in its workings as the finite limitations of disciplined human minds and feelings make possible. It is inevitable that (in the disposition of industrial and social controversies that come before them) our judges be limited by their own experience and environment and imagination. Against that the only safeguards are a healthy scepticism about their own beliefs, and a vigorous, informed, and continuous critique from without of the judicial process. But there can be no justification for the cruder emotional and class prejudices; far better frankly enthrone force than use the forms of law as the instruments of lawlessness. Whoever shares in such perversion of "justice," or connives in its exercise, truly undermines the basis of the existing order. Consciousness of the gravity of this issue leads the *New York Tribune* to say: "The case of Mooney is important because it involves the honor of our judicial system. Never must there be given even plausibility to the radical charge that our courts are respecters of persons and amenable to improper influences."

Reprinted from an unsigned editorial in the *New Republic*, February 23, 1921, with permission. Footnotes supplied by editor.

This was the real issue of the *Berger* case before the Supreme Court.[1] The decision did not call for a determination of Berger's guilt or innocence, his liability under the dragnet scope of the Espionage acts. The issue was the more fundamental one, whether Berger was tried according to law or by the lynch-law of war passions. Whatever be the contributing causes—the subsidence of fearsome feelings, the growing demonstration of lawless tyrannies and constitutional infractions all in the name of "law" and "patriotism," the growing articulation of the old faith in freedom—the Supreme Court in the *Berger* case has spoken with clarion clearness. As a result the atmosphere of the country seems less stifling and law bears less the mien of hypocrisy.

Professional comment has been inclined to whittle the decision down to a "technical" point of statutory construction, just as loose "radical" opinion has narrowed the decision to one of only personal significance. The *New Republic* believes that all decisions, particularly those of the United States Supreme Court, involving public issues must be quickened into widespread public understanding, and not be allowed to be buried in their technical cerements. To be sure, a technical point of procedure, in the jargon of the lawyers, *was* the issue in the *Berger* case. But behind that technical point and behind Section 21 of the Federal Judicial Code lie issues that concern every citizen of a democracy.

Section 21 of the Judicial Code provides that:

> Whenever a party to any action . . . shall make . . . an affidavit that the judge before whom the action . . . is to be tried . . . has a personal bias or prejudice . . . against him . . . such judge shall proceed no further therein, but another judge shall be designated . . . Every such affidavit shall state the facts and the reasons for the belief that such bias or prejudice exists . . . No party shall be

1. Berger v. United States, 255 U.S. 22 (1921). Victor L. Berger was the editor of the Socialist newspaper, the Milwaukee *Leader*. He was elected to the 66th Congress as a Socialist, but the House refused to permit him to take the oath of office.

entitled in any case to file more than one such affidavit; and no such affidavit shall be filed unless accompanied by a certificate of counsel of record that such affidavit and application are made in good faith.[2]

Congressman Berger having been indicted, in effect, for obstructing the prosecution of our war against Germany, invoked Section 21 against Judge Landis, who was to preside at his trial. Berger set forth alleged utterances by Judge Landis, intemperate and unrestrained, showing virulent hatred of Germans ("if anybody has said anything worse about the Germans than I have, I would like to know it so I can use it") and of German-Americans ("one must have a very judicial mind indeed not to be prejudiced against the German-Americans in this country. Their hearts are reeking with disloyalty" etc.). On the basis of these utterances, Berger charged Judge Kenesaw Mountain Landis with prejudice unfitting him for a fair trial of the case. The affidavit was accompanied by certificate of counsel vouching for its good faith.

Judge Landis denied his disqualification, denied the motion for the assignment of another judge, and the case proceeded to conviction, resulting in sentences of twenty years imprisonment to Berger and his associates. An appeal was thereupon taken to the Circuit Court of Appeals of the Seventh Circuit, but that court, being in doubt upon the question which went to the very heart of the conviction, namely, whether in view of the affidavit against him Judge Landis was legally authorized to conduct the trial, certified this question to the Supreme Court.[3]

The legal question as formulated by the Supreme Court was whether under Section 21 the filing of an affidavit of prejudice against a judge "compels his retirement from the case or whether he can exercise a judgment upon the facts affirmed and determine his qualification against them and the belief based upon them."[4] In other words,

2. See 28 U.S.C. §144.
3. 255 U.S. at 30.
4. Ibid.

where the facts and reasons in support of a claim of prejudice "are not frivolous or fanciful but substantial and formidable"[5] may a judge charged with prejudice himself determine the truth or tenacity of his prejudices, or does such a charge automatically operate to make it his duty "to proceed no further" in the case?

The Supreme Court decisively answered the question put to it (and has thereby established the practice of the federal courts), by holding that an affidavit of prejudice, substantial in its allegations and duly supported by counsel's certificate of good faith, automatically disqualifies a judge whose fairness is thus impugned from presiding at a trial.

Here, as elsewhere, it is important to cut below the cuticle of the Court's opinion to reach the living tissues. On the surface the decision merely involves a detached effort to ascertain the meaning of Congressional expression and enforce it. But this objective—the interpretation of the will of Congress—is not the same thing as merely interpreting the English of Congress. Something more is involved than the distillation of the meanings of words. A choice from among different meanings attaching to the same collocation of words depends necessarily upon a choice of contesting considerations of policy. And Mr. Justice McKenna's forthright opinion reveals the ground of policy. In answering the alarms of dreadful consequences that the Court's decision will entail, Mr. Justice McKenna lets the cat of "policy" out of the bag of "law" by adding "but, we may say, that its [Congress's] solicitude is that the tribunals of the country shall not only be impartial in the controversies submitted to them, but shall give assurance that they are impartial."[6] Or as Lord Chancellor Herschell long ago put it, "important as it is that people should get justice, it is even more important that they should be made to feel and see that they are getting it."

The dissenting Justices would admit this policy—as a general proposition. How comes it then that Justices Day

5. Id. at 34.
6. Id. at 35–36.

and Pitney reach a different result in its application? Why do they allow the challenged judge to pass upon the truth of the prejudice charged against him? They do so, for one thing, because they are more impressed with the need of protecting federal judges against "imposition" than with the social importance of assuring impartiality: popular confidence in the fairness of our courts is not as urgent a policy to them as the rather remote danger, through an abuse of Section 21, "to the independent discharge of duties by federal judges." The second reason for the difference in the interpretations placed upon Section 21 by Mr. Justice McKenna and Mr. Justice Day is a difference in valuation of the psychologic factor in the judicial process. Justices Day and Pitney assume objectivity of judgment by judges, unswerved by unconscious emotional undertows. Mr. Justice McKenna, and this time, fortunately, the majority of the Court, are in a real sense humanists:

> To commit to the judge a decision upon the truth of the facts gives chance for the evil against which the Section is directed. The remedy by appeal is inadequate. It comes after the trial and if prejudice exist, it has worked its evil, and a judgment of it in a reviewing tribunal is precarious. It goes there fortified by presumptions, and nothing can be more elusive of estimate or decision than a disposition of a mind in which there is a personal ingredient.[7]

Even the minority opinion of Justices Day and Pitney twice admits that the offending language of Judge Landis "might have been more temperate."[8] Not so Mr. Justice McReynolds! To him Judge Landis was the normal patriot, and one who did not share the bilious hatred of Kenesaw Mountain Landis "was simply unfit for his place."[9] We leave Mr. Justice McReynolds to his pitiable isolation and to the judgment of his associates.

7. Id. at 36.
8. Id. at 41.
9. Id. at 43.

Press Censorship by Judicial Construction

If people truly acted according to self-interest, it has been observed, this would be a very different world. The dictum finds striking confirmation in the attitude of the press towards the recent decision of the Supreme Court in the Milwaukee *Leader* case.[1] With few exceptions, newspapers have either approved or have been indifferent to a decision which immediately affects only a despised Socialist sheet, but which involves nothing less than the control of the press.

As the Milwaukee *Leader* had for weeks systematically carried matter which the Postmaster General deemed nonmailable, in September 1917 he denied second-class postal rates to all future issues of the *Leader*. To deny mail service to a newspaper except at six times the usual cost of the service furnished to papers is normally, of course, to make its circulation impossible. The Supreme Court has now sustained this power of suppression in the Postmaster General. Our government, we are constantly told, is "a government of laws and not of men"; whence, then, is this power derived? Since the offending matter in the *Leader* was obstructive to the conduct of the war, was the power to deny second-class rates found in the Espionage Act? No; Congress did not confer such power upon the Postmaster General even in that drastic war legislation. Was the Supreme Court, then, able to point to any general statute giving the Postmaster General discretionary authority over the life and death of a paper by denying it second-class rates in the future because of infractions of the postal laws in the past? No; there is no such statute. How then does the Supreme Court give the action of the Postmaster General the color of law? It does so by making two parallel lines of law meet. Let us trace this freak of legal geometry.

Congress from time to time by specific statutes has forbidden the deposit in the mails of certain printed matter.

Reprinted from an unsigned editorial in the *New Republic*, March 30, 1921, with permission. Footnotes supplied by editor.

1. Milwaukee Publishing Co. v. Burleson, 255 U.S. 407 (1921).

It seeks by this means to keep the mails free from publications offensive to decency or otherwise counter to the policy of the law, as for instance matter violative of the copyright law or information concerning abortion. This legislation makes the use of the mails for transmission of papers carrying nonmailable matter criminal and also authorizes the Postmaster General to refuse to carry papers containing the nonmailable matter. But there is no law which, either by way of punishment or prevention, authorizes the Postmaster General to order that future issues of a past offender shall be refused transmission. The Espionage Act enlarged the class of nonmailable matter; it did not enlarge the power of the Postmaster General in dealing with it. Violations of the Espionage Act through the newspapers could be dealt with only as violations of Section 211 of the Federal Criminal Code, prohibiting obscenities, can be dealt with, namely, by criminal prosecution and by refusal to transmit the issues containing the nonmailable matter. In other words—and it cannot be emphasized too often—Congress trusted to criminal prosecution with all its constitutional safeguards, and to a denial of the mails to the offending *thing,* but not to the offender.

Alongside of this exercise by Congress of its power to police the mails is legislation dealing with the cost of the mail service. Since 1879 a tariff of postal rates has been in force, graduating according to the nature of the mail matter. The second-class mail rate is confined to newspapers and other periodicals which possess the qualifications and comply with the conditions prescribed by Congress. The rate is very low and noncompensatory. "The justification for this non-compensatory service lies in the belief that education in its broad sense—intellectual activity fostered through the dissemination of information and of ideas—is essential to the life of a free, self-governing and striving people."[2] Undoubtedly the Postmaster General, subject to a limited review by the courts, must determine whether or not a publication satisfies the con-

2. Id. at 433, n. 1 (Brandeis, J., dissenting).

ditions for second-class prescribed by Congress. Does, for instance, the *Tip Top Weekly,* each issue carrying a story complete in itself, or the *Riverside Literary Series,* meet the definitions of a newspaper laid down by the law? He must answer such questions; but there is not a scintilla of a suggestion in the Mail Classification Act which makes the rating as second-class matter by the Postmaster General contingent upon the Postmaster General's verdict as to the legality either of the past or of the future issues of a newspaper. In other words, the low newspaper rate was not used as a means of policing the mails. "The question of the rate has nothing to do with the question whether the matter is mailable."[3] A newspaper is a newspaper even though a Victor Berger edit it.

The Mail Classification Act provides that a newspaper to be mailable at the second-class rate "must be regularly issued at stated intervals as frequently as four times a year," and that it must be "originated and published for the dissemination of information of a public character." Postmaster General Burleson held that if any issue of the paper contained matter violative of the Espionage Act, the paper is "no longer regularly issued," and that it has likewise ceased to be a paper "published for the dissemination of information of public character." Mr. Burleson certainly deserves high rank as a sophist. No wonder Mr. Justice Holmes makes short shrift of this contention by calling it "a quibble."[4] The Classification Act empowers the Postmaster General to determine whether a publication is a newspaper; it does not make him a censor of the press nor qualify him to distinguish good newspapers from bad.

The majority of the Court sustains Mr. Burleson's order on a somewhat less specious claim. Inasmuch as the *Leader* was found by the Postmaster General to have violated the Espionage Act in the past, "it is a reasonable presumption" that the character of the publication will continue and, therefore, will continue to violate the act in the future. Nor would it be "practicable to examine

3. Id. at 437 (Holmes, J., dissenting).
4. Ibid.

each issue of a newspaper" to determine whether the issue is offending. "Government is a practical institution, adapted to the practical conduct of public affairs."[5] The menacing implications of the "practical" powers thus conferred by the Supreme Court need not be labored. Without warrant of express grant of authority to the Postmaster General the Supreme Court derives this terrific power solely through administrative necessity. The want of justification for this implication, Mr. Justice Brandeis effectively answered:

> In respect to newspapers mailed by a publisher at second-class rates there is clearly no occasion to imply this drastic power. For a publisher must deposit with the local postmaster, before the first mailing of every issue, a copy of the publication which is now examined for matter subject to a higher rate and in order to determine the portion devoted to advertising . . . If there is illegal material in the newspaper, here is ample opportunity to discover it and remove the paper from the mail. Indeed, of the four classes of mail, it is the second alone which affords to the postal official full opportunity of ascertaining, before deposit in the mail, whether that which it is proposed to transmit is mailable matter.[6]

And Mr. Justice Holmes with a few strokes of his pen brought down the house of cards of the majority opinion:

> When I observe that the only powers expressly given to the Postmaster General to prevent the carriage of unlawful matter of the present kind are to stop and to return papers already existing and posted, when I notice that the conditions expressly attached to the second-class rate look only to wholly different matters, and when I consider the ease with which the power claimed by the Postmaster could be used to interfere with very sacred rights, I am of opinion that the refusal to allow the relator the rate to which it was entitled whenever its

5. Id. at 416.
6. Id. at 429.

newspaper was carried, on the ground that the paper ought not to be carried at all, was unjustified by statute and was a serious attack upon liberties that not even the war induced Congress to infringe.[7]

It will not do to say that this issue concerns only the Milwaukee *Leader*, or the New York *Call*. Newspapers of high respectability not only may, but have, run afoul of the postal laws. The decision reveals a lethal remedy against their misbehavior—or rather the Postmaster General's finding of their misbehavior, for *there* is the rub. The Postmaster General, without court or jury, may find that newspapers are nonmailable. The old New York *Herald*, for instance, was convicted by a jury for sending systematically obscene matter through the mail in its "personal" columns. The *Burleson* decision would have justified "a reasonable presumption" by the Postmaster General that the character of the publication will continue and second-class rates might have been denied to the New York *Herald*. The New York *World* was prosecuted for libel by Mr. Roosevelt's administration. To be sure, this prosecution failed. But if Mr. Roosevelt's Attorney General had not denied the very power which the Supreme Court has now sanctioned, there is little doubt that President Roosevelt would have ordered the withdrawal of second-class rates to the *World*. It is a fact worth noting that the *World* is one of the few papers which has pointed out the sinister significance of this decision.

For the present, the Espionage Act of 1918 has been repealed. But there is no guarantee that it may not be revived in peacetime and again forbid the publication of "any language intended to bring the form of the government of the United States or the Constitution of the United States ... into contempt, scorn, contumely, or disrepute." An attack of Mr. Gomper's *Federationist*, or of Mr. Bryan's *Commoner*, upon the power of the Supreme Court to nullify legislation may easily be the basis of a finding by the Postmaster General that they are publica-

7. Id. at 438.

tions bringing the form of the government of the Constitution of the United States "into disrepute," resulting in denial of second-class rates and consequent guillotining of those papers. Or Colonel Harvey, upon his return from the Court of St. James's, may resume his bizarre editing, and find a Democratic Postmaster General denying him second-class rates for publishing another offending cartoon. Little evidence is necessary to justify the administrative finding, particularly where the finding involves offenses depending on opinion. Administrative partisanship and bigotry are poisons too subtle for detection by the process of appeal. It is for this reason that Mr. Justice Brandeis interprets the power which the Supreme Court has now conferred upon the Postmaster General as one making him "the universal censor of publications."[8]

But there is an even deeper significance, if possible, to this decision than the control which it sanctions over the sources of public opinion. More perhaps than any of the decisions which the war has engendered, it shakes confidence in the judicial process. Again and again behind so-called questions of "statutory construction"—what has Congress said, and what does its language mean, in terms of power?—lurk great issues of policy. Instead of exercising a detached and distinterested calm, the Supreme Court seems to have been torn from its judicial moorings by the passions of the time. For the real basis of the decision apparently is that "a government competent to wage war against its foreign enemies" is not "powerless against its insidious foes at home."[9] "Government" is a large abstraction for a little Burleson.

Against these fallibilities of the Court there is no simple panacea. We must look to a broader and more conscious legal education. "I cannot believe," Mr. Justice Holmes has told us, "that if the training of lawyers led them habitually to consider more definitely and explicitly social advantage on which the rule they lay down must be justified, they sometimes would hesitate where they now are confident, and see that really they were taking sides upon

8. Id. at 423.
9. Id. at 416.

debatable and often burning questions."[10] Above all, a sustained and informed public opinion must exercise a continuous critique of the decisions of the courts. Roosevelt's "recall of judicial decisions" was an inadequate mechanical recognition of the truth that the Supreme Court is not apart from, but a part of, our national life. The extent of the public understanding of what the Supreme Court does, and how the Court does it, will largely determine the Supreme Court's responsiveness to the best traditions and the deepest needs of the country.

10. Holmes, *Collected Legal Papers* 184 (1920).

Child Labor and the Court

The recent decision of the Supreme Court,[1] invalidating the Federal Child Labor Tax Law, raises two wholly different questions, each of very serious public importance. The first involves judgment upon the Supreme Court's action, and to that extent is part of a process of continuing critique of the functioning of the Supreme Court in our national life. A totally different, and immediately practical, issue is presented by the consequences of the Supreme Court's decision; in other words, what are we going to do about child labor?

Is it just to claim, as its critics do claim, that the Supreme Court's decision is "unjust and inhumane"? So to maintain is to imply that the Supreme Court either approves of, or, at least, is indifferent to the horrors of child labor. Such an accusation is absurd. Four of the Justices have heretofore expressed themselves in no uncertain terms about the evils of stunted childhood, and in the present case the Chief Justice, speaking for the Court, characterized the Federal Child Labor Tax Law as "legislation designed to promote the highest good."[2] It is appropriate also not to forget the services which the Chief Justice, while President, rendered in behalf of child welfare. To call the decision "unjust" implies that the Supreme Court, within the bounds of its duty, should have sustained the federal measure. But such a conclusion cannot be reached out of hand. "Humanity" is not the test of constitutionality. Recognition that a law enacted by Congress seeks to redress monstrous wrongs and to promote the highest good does not dispose of the Supreme Court's duty when the validity of such a law is challenged. So long as we are governed by a written Constitution, distributing different powers of government between the federal government and the States, with the Supreme

Reprinted from the *New Republic,* July 26, 1922, with permission. Footnotes supplied by editor.

1. Child Labor Tax Case (Bailey v. Drexel Furniture Co.), 259 U.S. 20 (1922).
2. Id. at 37.

Court as arbiter of a conflict between them, just so long will there be occasions, from time to time, when a good law will not be a "just" law, because it will violate the bond of union. We must pay a price for federalism—at one time the impotence of the federal government to correct glaring evils unheeded by some of the States, at other times the impotence of States to correct glaring evils unheeded by the federal government.

Let us see how the matter stands with the recent Federal Child Labor Tax Law. In 1918 the Supreme Court, in *Hammer* v. *Dagenhart*,[3] invalidated an act of Congress which prohibited transportation in interstate commerce to child-labor products. This unfortunate decision was rendered by a divided Court, and the dissenting opinion of Mr. Justice Holmes, on behalf of four of the Justices, has never been answered. Congress at once set about to circumvent *Hammer* v. *Dagenhart*. It did so by levying a tax of 10 percent on the net profits, for a year, of any mill or mine employing children below the prohibited age. The scope of this act is thus accurately described by the Chief Justice:

> It provides a heavy exaction for a departure from a detailed and specified course of conduct in business. That course of business is that employers shall employ in mines and quarries, children of an age greater than sixteen years; in mills and factories, children of an age greater than fourteen years, and shall prevent children of less than sixteen years in mills and factories from working more than eight hours a day or six days in the week. If an employer departs from this prescribed course of business, he is to pay to the Government one-tenth of his entire net income in the business for a full year. The amount is not to be proportioned in any degree to the extent or frequency of the departures, but is to be paid by the employer in full measure whether he employs five hundred children for a year, or employs only one for a day. Moreover, if he does not know the child is within the named age limit he is not to pay; that

3. 247 U.S. 251 (1918).

> is to say, it is only where he knowingly departs from the prescribed course that payment is to be exacted.
>
> Scienter is associated with penalties not with taxes. The employer's factory is to be subject to inspection at any time not only by the taxing officers of the Treasury, the Department normally charged with the collection of taxes, but also by the Secretary of Labor and his subordinates whose normal function is the advancement and protection of the welfare of the workers.[4]

It was inevitable that the Court should draw the obvious conclusion as to the aim of this act and its real field of operation:

> In the light of these features of the act, a court must be blind not to see that the so-called tax is imposed to stop the employment of children within the age limits prescribed. Its prohibitory and regulatory effect and purpose are palpable. All others can see and understand this. How can we properly shut our minds to it?[5]

Clearly this was not the usual case involving social legislation before the Supreme Court, where invalidity is based on meanings read into the vague "counsels of moderation" embodied in the "due process" clauses. In such decisions—like the *Lochner* and the *Coppage*[6] cases, and the recent *Truax* v. *Corrigan*[7]—there is no question of conflicting jurisdiction between States and nation, but a nullification of State action based on eighteenth-century conceptions of "liberty" and "equality." In the present cases, however, the questions before the Court were (1) the dishonest use of the taxing power, and (2) the distribution of power between national and State governments.

These are vital questions, and their disposition could not be evaded by the Court. Whatever a man's social out-

4. 259 U.S. at 36–37.
5. Id. at 37.
6. Lochner v. New York, 198 U.S. 45 (1905); Coppage v. Kansas, 236 U.S. 1 (1915).
7. 257 U.S. 312 (1921).

look, be he standpatter or liberal, as a member of the Supreme Court his freedom of action is limited, in good conscience, within the federal framework of the Constitution. Passion for the abolition of child labor burns, probably, as strongly in some, at least, of the Justices, as it does in Samuel Gompers. Only the former happen to be on the Supreme Court and could hardly escape the force of the following conclusion:

> Grant the validity of this law, and all that Congress would need to do, hereafter, in seeking to take over its control any one of the great number of subjects of public interest, jurisdiction of which the States have never parted with, and which are reserved to them by the Tenth Amendment, would be to enact a detailed measure of complete regulation of the subject and enforce it by a so-called tax upon departures from it. To give such magic to the word "tax" would be to break down all constitutional limitation of the powers of Congress and completely wipe out the sovereignty of the States.[8]

To be sure, the Court had heretofore used weighty language in support of the idea that any measure of federal social control will be sustained if cast in the form of a tax, however much the substance may be beyond federal power. During the Civil War State circulating notes were taxed out of existence. That such was the purpose of this heavy tax on State issues was notorious; and yet the Court sustained the federal enactment.[9] But, while there was some general language as to the uncontrolled scope of the taxing power, the case easily rests on the power of Congress to secure a national currency and, as a consequence, the power to restrain the circulation of notes, as money, not issued under its authority.

A more difficult precedent to explain away is the *McCray* case,[10] which sustained the validity of a federal tax of ten cents per pound on yellow oleomargarine. The distinc-

8. 259 U.S. at 38.
9. Veazie Bank v. Fenno, 8 Wall. 533 (1870).
10. McCray v. United States, 195 U.S. 27 (1904).

tion was taken that in this instance an oppressive tax may have been involved, destructive in its tendency, yet not, on its face, "the detailed specifications of a regulation of a state concern and business with a heavy exaction to promote the efficacy of such regulation."[11]

To my taste the distinction thus made between the *Oleomargarine* and the *Child Labor Taxes* is not only a fine one—it's too fine. Certainly some of the language used in, and the lead of, the earlier case have been repudiated, and respect for law would not have suffered if the repudiation had been made more explicitly. It is not healthy that the broad issues involved in delimiting the proper scope of federal and State powers should rest on grounds so subtle that intelligent lawyers, no less than laymen, cannot readily grasp them. This decision will doubtless check further sham use of the taxing power—always excepting the tariff!—by Congress; in any event we may expect, in the future, should new instances arise, increasing frankness from the Supreme Court. All this presupposes, of course, continuance of the established structure of federal government and States, and the established scope of judicial review.

The door to the federal action having now been twice shut, what are we to do about child labor, particularly in the stubborn black spots of the South? In my judgment further federal legislation, under the existing Constitution, is unavailing and any such proposal as requiring the products of child labor to be branded as a means of notice to the consumer, before acceptance for interstate shipment, would be as futile as, under *Hammer* v. *Dagenhart,* it is clearly unconstitutional. Naturally, therefore, in and out of Congress, the friends of the child labor movement are pressing for a constitutional amendment. But a whole brood of questions at once demands attention as to the form of such an amendment. Should the amendment deal with children alone, or should Congress be given power to deal with industrial relations? If the amendment concerns itself wholly with the prohibition of child labor what

11. 259 U.S. at 42.

means of enforcement should be provided—what power or what duty of enforcement should be lodged in the States? Prohibition of child labor presents different elements from prohibition of liquor; nevertheless, the Eighteenth Amendment has taught us something as to the limits of effective federal enforcement. At least it has taught us that there *are* limits. These are questions that call for the most mature consideration, and should enlist, for their wise solution, not merely devoted humanitarians, but legal specialists equally zealous to abolish the plague spots of child labor, but also alive to the delicacies of American constitutional law and to the inherent difficulties of law enforcement.

One even ventures to express serious doubt of the wisdom of a constitutional amendment, rather than, as Secretary Hoover urges, a renewed energetic movement to rouse the States to action. Such an attitude, I am well aware, will be received with impatience and disdain by those who see nothing but the cruel evils of child labor to the exclusion of all else. But the method of dealing with this ancient enemy does present difficulties perhaps as important as the evil itself. Nothing less seems to be involved than the fashioning of responsible citizenship. It is too easy to look to Washington and a centralized administration for the correction of all our national shortcomings. I do not speak from any regard for traditional States' rights, nor as the exponent of any theory of political science, but as one with some knowledge of the functioning of the federal machinery and its power further to absorb and discharge effectively nation-wide duties, especially duties of intimate local concern, affected by local conditions of great variety throughout the country.

Of course child labor is of national concern, and some benefits will accrue from national action. But this is true of many other fields which we have not turned over to Washington, because such concentration would be self-defeating in its execution and make for a corresponding paralysis of local responsibility.

Withdrawing children from shop and mine is not enough, unless provision is made to put the children into schools. Today no State can plead financial want or the need for aid to discharge these duties. If these rudimentary tasks are not fulfilled by the States the fact shows that there is not enough civic understanding and will, among a sufficiently large number of people, to bring to pass a decent level of citizenship. The deeper statesmanship may well be not to attempt removal from the remote center of this or that glaring evil, but to awaken the community to the need of its removal, for only by such vigorous civic education will an informed public opinion, essential to the enforcement of decent standards, be secured and sustained. Only thus will the national aspirations be translated from mere negative prohibitions into affirmatively good lives of men and women. The mere fact that progress through the States in the past has been slow—which, naturally, tries the devotion of such noble champions of children's lives as Mrs. Florence Kelley —need be no measure of future progress. For a new political instrument is now available—the women's vote. Why should not the League of Women Voters in every State make it the order of the day to put a wise child labor law upon the statute books of every State and—what is almost everywhere forgotten—an adequate and efficient corps of inspectors for enforcement? What possible competition for the women's interest *in action* can there be to that of securing a wholesome and just child life? If it be said that the women are least organized in those States where the evil of child labor is the most flagrant the simple answer is that nothing will furnish such a stimulant to the cohesive organization of women, for the exercise of their political power, as the procurement of fit lives for children. If the women will it, not only would child labor be prohibited by paper legislation but the enforcement of such laws, and an environment fit for children to be born into and to grow up in, will quickly become the possession of every State in the Union. Indeed, the States would furnish competition not in child labor, but in child welfare.

The Coronado Case

The enormous verdict of $600,000 was rendered by a jury, after a month's trial, against the United Mine Workers of America for an alleged violation of the Sherman Law. Judgment for that amount (to which was added a counsel fee of $25,000 and interest) was affirmed by the United States Circuit Court of Appeals for the Eighth Circuit. The unanimous reversal by the Supreme Court of the two lower federal courts, in sustaining the jury's verdict, is so rare an occurrence in such a case that to a lawyer's mind, at least, it is the most dramatic fact about the decision in the *Coronado Case*.[1] If the Supreme Court had reversed a $600,000 verdict against a powerful coal operators' association, the dominant exploitation of such a decision would surely have been "Operators Win." The Mine Workers, through their counsel and their journal, have treated the decision as a victory for the union. But by labor generally, despite the startling reversal of a drastic verdict against the Mine Workers, the *Coronado Case* is interpreted as a great set-back for labor.

Let us see what the *Coronado Case* involved, and what the Supreme Court decided.

First. The controversy had its origin in a conflict, variously called a "strike" or a "lock-out," depending upon one's point of view, for the maintenance of union conditions in coal mines controlled by one Bache in Sebastian County, on the west border of Arkansas. The tactics of the conflict were directed by District No. 21, one of the thirty districts into which the United Mine Workers are divided. The International, however, had cognizance of the conflict: the then president approvingly reported the progress of the fight to the International, spurred on the fight, and the International had some share in the pardoning of one of the union miners in prison for contempt of court. Throughout all the conflict, culminating in murders and arson, the International office did not exercise its power

Reprinted from the *New Republic,* August 16, 1922, with permission. Footnotes supplied by editor.

1. United Mine Workers v. Coronado Coal Co., 259 U.S. 344 (1922).

of discipline, secured to it under the union's constitution, over any of the miners affiliated with the local or district organizations. In the light of all these facts, taken in connection with the cardinal influence of the maintenance of union conditions in one district upon the achievement of the Mine Workers' nation-wide aims, it was held by the two lower courts that the responsibility of the International for the acts of the local unions and of the district was an issue of fact for jury determination, and that such responsibility by the International having been established by the jury's verdict could not be upset by the court. The Supreme Court, however, despite the great presumption that adheres to the concurrence by two courts in a jury's verdict, held that there was no evidence from which the jury could infer "actual agency" by District No. 21, and that without such "actual agency" by the district in carrying out the authority of the International the latter is not chargeable for the autonomous actions of the district.

The great gain to labor of this ruling can best be measured by contemplating the consequences of the reverse. If the decisions of the lower court had been allowed by the Supreme Court to stand, every local strike conducted by workers affiliated with a national or international union, and in furtherance of a common purpose, would subject the International to liability for money damages or—still worse—to injunction. On the contrary, by its decision the Supreme Court leaves large freedom of action to local unions, if in fact they act as local unions in a predominantly local controversy and not as the immediate instruments of their central organization.

Second. But the Supreme Court did not merely absolve from liability the Mine Workers of America; it likewise upset the jury's verdict, and judgment thereon, by the two lower courts, against District No. 21 and the various local unions. It did so on the ground that the fight was a local fight to maintain certain standards of living in that locality, and not a conspiracy in restraint of interstate commerce. Here, again, it was urged that three quarters of the coal produced by the Bache mines went out of Arkansas, and thus directly interstate commerce was obstructed; moreover, that while the locus of the strike was Arkansas, its consequences were nation-wide in that the strike was part and parcel of the Mine Workers' policy of maintaining scale agreements everywhere, for the protection of the great central competitive coal fields of Ohio, Indiana, and Illinois. This argument did in fact prevail with the jury, the District Court, and the Circuit Court of Appeals. The Supreme Court swept away not only the argument but the support which it derived from the sanction given to it by a jury and two federal courts; it held that the alleged restraint of interstate commerce, either by reason of obstruction to the shipment of the Bache coal, or the relation of the Arkansas fight to the national strategy of the United Mine Workers, was too remote to justify the submission of the case to the jury, and that the local nature of the controversy was so clear as to call for the direction of a verdict in favor of the coal unions and the individual defendants. In a word it held that there was no federal wrong.

On this aspect of the case too, a contrary result would have been disastrous to union effort for the maintenance or the attainment of decent standards of living in local industrial controversies. The so-called "right to strike" would have become an empty phrase. A Damocles sword of treble damages in a suit under the Sherman Law in the federal courts would have hung over every effort of workers to enforce standards of living in every case where either the products of the industry went into interstate commerce, or where the local union was affiliated with a national organization. Practically, jurisdiction over every strike would thus have been sought to be drawn into the federal courts. And yet, in view of the record of the *Coronado Case* and the general background of labor litigation, it should be a source of deep satisfaction to labor, and to the country at large, that the Supreme Court not merely reversed the lower courts in the *Coronado Case*, but unanimously reversed them. It would have been easy, at least for a portion of the Court, to vindicate its feelings which the record must have aroused in them—for the situation was similar to the recent Herrin tragedy[2]—by relying on the jury's verdict. In the light of this provocation, we know of no more reassuring manifestation of self-restraint and the governance of law than the unanimous action of the Supreme Court in reversing the *Coronado* judgment.

Third. Why then the great perturbation on the part of some spokesmen for labor? Because, while relieving both the International and the local unions from liability under the facts of the case, the Court ruled that no mere procedural difficulty prevented suit against the union as such, instead of suit of its individual members. This presents a technical problem which calls for elucidation.

Lay critics have assumed that, until this ruling in the *Coronado Case*, the unincorporated associations of men united for common action and acting as a unit which we know as trade unions enjoyed a special immunity before the law, as compared with other associations, because of the humanitarian aims of trade unions. This view springs from an unfamiliarity with our law and our legal history. It involves a confusion between the recognition by courts of entities acting as such, and legislative policy, within the limits of the Constitution, in subjecting conduct varying in its purpose and in its consequences to a different measure of legal responsibility. No one would dispute for a moment that if the United Mine Workers Union incurs debts, either for money borrowed or for a printer's bill, it is amenable to law for the payment of such debts. But bring into question the amenability of the Mine Workers to suit for money damages or to injunction for picketing in the course of a strike, and a clash of opinions is at once produced. But it is the same United Mine Workers. If the union can be brought into court as an entity to pay a printer's bill, by the same procedure the union can be haled into court to respond to a claim for damages unlawfully caused by it in the course of a strike. The objection to this

2. On June 22, 1922, during a nation-wide coal miners' strike, several hundred striking union miners forced nonunion workers at a Herrin, Illinois mine to leave the mine. The nonstrikers were marched to a point near Herrin and then ordered to run for their lives. They were fired upon as they ran and more than twenty were killed in what came to be known as the "Herrin massacre."

latter liability does not lie in the nature of the union, but in the nature of the conduct for which suit is brought. The question is not whether the union should be responsible for a wrong, but whether certain acts complained of constitute a wrong.

The common law has had difficulties, wholly apart from economic conflicts, in dealing with any "entity" except an individual and a corporation. By all kinds of compromises and exceptions, the law has been seeking to adjust itself to the recognition of collective entities—aggregations of human beings acting as a unit—that are not corporations. That law is a laggard in facing reality is the constant complaint of lay critics. Just such an adjustment to reality is the issue involved in this aspect of the *Coronado Case*. And as the decisions have been progressively recognizing as entities associations acting as units, for instance, social clubs, but not partaking of the corporate form, it would have been a distinct departure from reality for the Supreme Court solemnly to hold that that which is an entity for all the affairs of life, the law, for some mystical reasons of its own, cannot so recognize. The Supreme Court has held the contrary—that there is no technical procedural reason why a trade union, like any other association, should not sue or be sued.

This ruling, too, it is ventured, will be a source of gain to labor. Contemplate its significance by assuming, again, a contrary result. To have held, categorically, that a trade union has no legal standing and no legal responsibility, would, in the very nature of things, have brought very serious consequences to its leaders and its rank and file, no less than to the public. Complete immunity for all conduct is too dangerous an immunity to confer upon any group. Psychologically, such a victory would have wreaked its vengeance upon the union and its leaders; and it would have been found so intolerable to the feeling of the general public that in seeking to withdraw the immunity public opinion would have gone beyond the dictates of reason, to the injury of common interest in labor's cause.

The real rub is the substantive law—under what circumstances and for what conduct can a particular association be sued? In the *Coronado Case* it was held that a trade union cannot be sued under the Sherman Law unless it actively directs conduct aimed primarily to restrain interstate commerce. Of course, the liability of a trade union to suit subjects it to the uncertainties of litigation. That is a risk which every one runs. The danger is intensified when the law is as uncertain as it is in regard to torts arising out of industrial conflicts—conduct, that is, which retrospectively courts and juries may find without legal justification. That risk, however, works far greater harm to trade unions in the abusive issuance of injunctions, from which labor has suffered most, and which have, to no small degree, been unfairly indulged in by judges against trade unions, because it was deemed at one time that they were not liable to money damages for those acts which it was the purpose of injunctions to forestall. In seeking to forestall these acts courts too frequently have taken sides, and against labor.

The real problem, then, is not to deny the fact that a trade union *is*, but to work out the legal scope of its activities. Thus, in the *Coronado Case*, the record established conclusively the commission of murder and arson. But these horrors did not arise capriciously. They were the terrible end of an industrial controversy that ought not to occur as frequently as it does in a country which styles itself civilized. The Chief Justice thus recited the familiar story, without justifying "in the slightest the lawlessness and outrages committed":

> Bache's breach of his contract with the District No. 21 in employing non-union men three months before it expired, his attempt to evade his obligation by a manipulation of his numerous corporations, his advertised anticipation of trespass and violence by warning notices, by enclosing his mining premises with a cable and stationing guards with guns to defend them, all these in the heart of a territory that had been completely unionized for years were calculated to arouse a bitterness of spirit entirely local among the union miners against a policy that brought in strangers and excluded themselves or

> their union colleagues from the houses they had occupied and the wages they had enjoyed. In the letter which Bache dictated in favor of operating the mines on a non-union basis, he said, "To do this means a bitter fight but in my opinion it can be accomplished by proper organization." Bache also testified that he was entering into a matter he knew was perilous and dangerous to his companies because in that section there was only one other mine running on a non-union basis.[3]

How to deal with the causes underlying these conflicts is the real question confronting law no less than labor, and not the recognition by law of the reality of the existence of trade unions.

3. Id. at 411-412.

Labor Injunctions Must Go

Never in American history has an appeal by the government to the courts, ostensibly on behalf of "law and order," been received with such widespread condemnation as the injunction granted to Attorney General Daugherty at Chicago.[1] Criticism does not abate with time nor with reflection. And never, to such an extent, have conservative organs like the *New York Times* and the *Journal of Commerce* joined in the outcry. That so powerful and responsible a paper as the *New York World* should deem Mr. Daugherty's conduct plausible ground for urging his impeachment is a measure of the depth to which the Attorney General has outraged American feeling. When it comes to criticism of its own, the legal profession, so far at least as represented by "the leaders of the bar," is a reticent priesthood. But so far as legal opinion has become articulate, it supports the popular condemnation. Senator Borah, himself a distinguished lawyer, voices publicly volumes of private legal protest. We have little doubt but that if the president of the American Bar Association, Mr. John W. Davis, were to take the public into his confidence, we should hear some pretty plain speaking.

Such wide and powerful condemnation, obviously, must be deeply grounded. No mere technical differences of opinion, no merely doubtful exercise of discretion can so fiercely and so abidingly stir public and professional feeling. The *New York Times* is very moderate when it declares that certain parts of the Daugherty injunction "are apparently not warranted by federal law or are in conflict with it," and other "provisions . . . whether legally justified or not, are manifestly absurd and incapable of execution." The *New York Evening Post* thus briefly characterizes Mr. Daugherty's performance:

Reprinted from an unsigned editorial in the *New Republic,* September 27, 1922, with permission. Footnotes supplied by editor.

1. Attorney General Harry M. Daugherty had secured an injunction in the federal court in Chicago against a strike by the railroad shopmen's union. The conduct banned and the persons enjoined were extraordinarily broad. Daugherty purported to rely on the injunction in the *Debs* case as authority for his action. See In re Debs, 158 U.S. 564 (1895).

> The terms of the injunction give it the unfortunate appearance of a blow below the belt. If it were designed merely to give the Federal Government power to deal with violence and threats, it would be much less a shock to labor and the public. But the year 1922 is too late a date for an injunction that stops all the normal and innocent activities of a union and forbids the elementary rights of free speech.

"The criticism in Congress and in the press rose to such a pitch" (in the language of the *Literary Digest*, after a survey of the newspaper comments of the country) that the Attorney General himself sought to make a verbal retreat by announcing that the injunction would not be used to infringe upon anyone's constitutional rights—though the terms of the injunction, with all the menace of overhanging contempt proceedings for their violations, remain.

It is utterly absurd to claim the *Debs* case as a precedent.[2] Nothing like the following prohibition in the Daugherty injunction was contained in the decree against Debs:

> Attempting to induce by the use of . . . entreaties, argument, persuasions, rewards or otherwise . . . any person to abandon the employment of said railway companies . . .
>
> Assembling . . . numbers of the members of said federated shop crafts . . . in proximity of said railway companies . . . and by . . . persuasion . . . entreaties or arguments or in any other way attempt to prevent any of the employees of the said railway companies . . . from entering upon . . . their duties.
>
> In any manner by letters . . . word of mouth . . . oral persuasion or suggestion . . . or otherwise in any manner whatsoever . . . encouraging any person . . . to abandon the employment of said railway companies.[3]

2. See note 1, *supra*. The injunction referred to was issued by Judge James H. Wilkerson in a suit to enjoin a strike of railroad shopmen. See Frankfurter and Landis, "Power to Regulate Contempts," 37 *Harv. L. Rev.* 1010, 1101 (1924), in which the injunction is set out in its entirety.

3. Id. at 1101 et seq.

The plain meaning and intent of such prohibitions is the denial of those means of association and activities which are a trade union. To say that trade unions have received "affirmative legal recognition of their existence and usefulness and provisions for their protection"[4]—as the Supreme Court of the United States, speaking through Chief Justice Taft, held last June—and at the same time deny them the very means of life, is to make a hypocrite of law, and an enslaving hypocrite.

The simple truth is that Harry M. Daugherty, Attorney General by grace of political friendship, with the complicity of Judge Wilkerson, has set himself above the Constitution, and by his own fiat has prohibited conduct which Congress deliberately refused to declare illegal. The effort to prohibit peaceful, though concerted, abandonment of "the employment of said railway companies," and concerted refusal to reenter such employment, was tried, under the leadership of Senator Cummins and others, when the Transportation Act of 1920 went through Congress. That effort, as every lawyer knows, failed. Mr. Daugherty goes beyond even this attempted failure. It is certainly questionable whether Congress itself, in view of the First Amendment of the federal Constitution, could put such curbs on "freedom of speech" as Mr. Daugherty jauntily asked for and Judge Wilkerson obeisantly granted. What's the Constitution between friends!—even though one of them happens to be the Attorney General of the United States and the other a federal judge.

The personal elements of the situation are items of aggravation. There is probably agreement by informed professional opinion that in the history of this country there never has been a more unlearned and professionally less equipped Attorney General than Harry M. Daugherty. The spectacle of this man, unrestrained by the statesman's wisdom or the lawyer's tradition from attempting to write his economic prejudices into the law of the land, has a touch of humor which alone saves it from tragedy. The tragic farce was completed by a compliant judge,

4. United Mine Workers v. Coronado Co., 259 U.S. 344, 385–386 (1922).

who had only a few weeks before been appointed by the President, doubtless upon the usual recommendation of his Minister of Justice. And so we read that Judge Wilkerson at once, without careful scrutiny of what he was signing, granted the prayer of the Attorney General, conveyed in a voluminous document of some fifty pages!

These, we say, are merely elements of aggravation. The vice is inherent in the use of injunctions by the government or by employers in labor controversies. Unwittingly the Attorney General and Judge Wilkerson may have rendered great service by dramatizing the excesses which such injunctions necessarily involve.

For more than thirty years the injunction has been used as a familiar weapon in American industrial conflicts. It does not work. It neither mines coal, nor moves trains, nor makes clothing. As an adjustor of industrial conflict the injunction has been an utter failure. It has been used as a shortcut—but it has not cut anything, except to cut off labor from confidence in the rule of law and of the courts, as its impartial organs. No disinterested student of American industry, or of American law, can have the slightest doubt that, beginning with the *Debs* case, the use of labor injunctions has, predominately, been a cumulative influence for discord in our national life. Mounting embitterment in masses of men and women has generated the growing conviction that the powers of the government are perverted by and in aid of the employers, and that the courts are the instruments of this partisan policy. Such has been the price we have paid for this use of the injunction—and the industrial conflict is uglier than ever.

And this result is inevitable so long as this use of the injunction persists. For the acts which injunctions seek to restrain necessarily involve disputed questions of fact, and disputed questions of fact touching men's feelings and motives and opinions. The traditional Anglo-American method for ascertaining such facts is a jury. The social justification of the jury system lies precisely in its element of popular cooperation in the enforcement of law. In labor controversies, if anywhere, one would suppose, this popular vindication of the law would be resorted to. From the point of view of revivifying respect for law and gaining order, no less than from any attempt towards decent industrial relations, it is of the essence that the curb upon trade union action should be administered by courts only through proceedings in which disputed facts are determined by jury.

And there is no reason whatever in so-called expediency for continuing the disastrous shortcut of the injunction. The responsibility of the union, as such, for wrongful acts has now been established. Civil redress by the employer can now be had and should be had only through action for damages. So far as acts of violence are concerned, the resources of the state are ample in the criminal law—if it be made effective. If trade unions are convicted of wrongful acts by their own representatives—the jury of the vicinage—belief in the fairness of law and the impartiality of courts may be restored.

The abandonment of "settling" labor difficulties by injunctions and confronting these difficulties on their merits raises social and economic questions to which the *New Republic* will advert from time to time. For the moment we know of no more pressing need for the country's well-being than the restoration of confidence in our courts and respect for law through the abandonment of the abuses of the injunction. And the abuse of injunctions in labor cases can be discontinued only by the discontinuance of their use.

Mr. Justice Holmes

On December 15, 1882, Oliver Wendell Holmes, Jr., became an Associate Justice of the Supreme Judicial Court of Massachusetts. Twenty years later, on December 8, 1902, he took his seat on the United States Supreme Court. The soldier's faith, the faith he lived in war and lives in peace, he has described as "having known great things, to be content with silence."[1] But for us, for whom the "great things" are still being wrought by the Justice—we cannot be content with silence. And so the *New Republic* also wishes to mark the anniversary of forty years of judicial service, and twenty years of Mr. Justice Holmes with rejoicing and with gratitude. "We live by symbols";[2] and the judicial work of Mr. Justice Holmes is the symbol at once of the promise and the fulfillment of the American judiciary.

With myriad variations his great juristic patterns have been woven. "The life of the law has not been logic; it has been experience."[3] The Constitution "is an experiment, as all life is an experiment."[4] In these aperçus, we have the clues to his two thousand odd opinions, "samples of his best," long since acclaimed by the world's juristic masters as work done in the grand manner and nobly done. The conflict between the nation and the States, between liberty and authority—these are the themes that have solicited his judgment. He has been vigilant for the Union, for which he fought at Ball's Bluff and Antietam and Fredericksburg; and equally watchful of needed scope for the States, upon which the Union rests. His opinion in the first *Child Labor* case[5] vindicates the basis of federal power as only his eloquence can illuminate,

Reprinted from an unsigned article in the *New Republic*, December 20, 1922, with permission. Footnotes supplied by editor.

1. *Occasional Speeches of Justice Oliver Wendell Holmes* 83 (Howe ed. 1962).
2. Id. at 134.
3. *The Common Law* 5 (Howe ed. 1963).
4. Abrams v. United States, 250 U.S. 616, 630 (1919).
5. Hammer v. Dagenhart, 247 U.S. 251, 277 (1918).

while his brief opinion in *Truax* v. *Corrigan*[6] is a massive warning against strait-jacketing the States, in dealing with their local problems, through pedantic and partisan reading of the Fourteenth Amendment. To be sure, these are dissenting opinions, as are some of his greatest utterances—but they are dissents that shape history and record prophecy.

He has found the Constitution equal to the needs of a great nation at war and devoid of obstacles to beneficent treaties with other nations. But, according to the same Constitution, the individual must not be sacrificed to the Moloch of fear; there is a sanctuary in law even for those outlawed by prevalent opinion:

> When men have realized that time has upset many fighting faiths, they may come to believe even more than they believe the very foundation of their own conduct that the ultimate good desired is better reached by free trade in ideas—that the best test of truth is the power of the thought to get itself accepted in the competition of the market, and that truth is the only ground upon which their wishes can safely be carried out.[7]

Serenely dwelling above the passing shibboleths, he has steadfastly refused to lower his ear so as to catch the murmur of the moment. But he is too much compounded of humility and humor to regard even the highest tribunal as a Grand Lama. The Supreme Court, too, like all human institutions, must earn reverence through the test of truth.

To Mr. Justice Holmes it is literally true that "law is a seamless web," for him the "web" is life. His gallantry and gaiety, his faith and doubt, his passionate dream of spiritual reign, the solitude of the thinker, the bounty and the splendor of his tenderness—of all these and of his very self his opinions, however "formal" the appearance and "technical" the question, are the vehicles. Occasionally he has allowed us to share his intimate glimpses. Behind the sceptic is invincible faith:

6. Truax v. Corrigan, 257 U.S. 312, 342 (1921).
7. Abrams v. United States, 250 U.S. 616, 630 (1919).

And so beyond the vision of battling races and an impoverished earth I catch a dreaming glimpse of peace.

The other day my dream was pictured to my mind. It was evening. I was walking homeward on Pennsylvania Avenue near the Treasury, and as I looked beyond Sherman's statue to the west the sky was aflame with scarlet and crimson from the setting sun. But, like the note of downfall in Wagner's opera, below the skyline there came from little globes the pallid discord of the electric lights, and I thought to myself the Götterdämmerung will end, and from those globes clustered like evil eggs will come the new masters of the sky. It is like the time in which we live. But then I remembered the faith that I partly have expressed, faith in a universe not measured by our fears, a universe that has thought and more than thought inside of it, and as I gazed, after the sunset and above the electric lights there shone the stars.[8]

And ours still the glory of his labor, still ours the music of his dream.

8. *Collected Legal Papers* 296–297 (1920).

Twenty Years of Mr. Justice Holmes's Constitutional Opinions

When Mr. Taft was appointed Chief Justice, a great New York paper, after referring to his "tact and good humor," gave utterance to a wide-spread public feeling by remarking, "with Justice Taft as moderator, it is probable that not a few asperities that mar the harmony of the celestial chamber, the consulting room, will be softened, and that not quite so often in the future will the Court divide five to four." Such a view attributes at once too much and too little, in the shaping of the Supreme Court's decisions, to transient personalities. It exaggerates absurdly the power of camaraderie, to the neglect of the deeper influences behind constitutional adjudications. Of course, the editorial expressed the nation's regard for the contagious urbanity of the Chief Justice, which doubtless radiates significant bonhomie in that "celestial chamber, the consulting room," whither the lawyer dare not follow the editor, even in imagination. But the divisions of the Court in decisive issues are not attributable to want of "tact and good humor" in the "moderator," nor is unanimity, or even substantial accord, secured through genial and irenic personalities. Such naïveté as this betrays disregard of the Court's history. A more lubricating humor and a more accommodating mind probably never presided over the Supreme Court than during the incumbency of Chief Justice Fuller. Yet divided opinions in cases raising crucial public issues were plentiful during his time, as they were during the time of Chief Justice White, as they have been, and will continue to be, during the successive terms of Chief Justice Taft. The key to an understanding of this drastic division of opinion on issues of great public concern must be looked for not in the temperamental felicities of the Chief Justice and his associates, but in a candid analysis of "the nature of the judicial process" in constitutional cases. The latter alone profoundly matter in the work of the Court; at all events they alone are our present concern.

Only informed, responsible belief in the preservation of the power which the Supreme Court exercises in the nation's life can secure the necessary public support for the maintenance by the Supreme Court of its essential place in our federal system. This requires a frank recognition of the nature of the Supreme Court's function and of the necessary equipment for its exercise. A steady stream of enlightened and disinterested professional criticism must play upon the work of the Supreme Court if its transcendent function, in exercising a virtual veto power over national and State action, is to be saved from destructive obscurantism.

The significant issues which come before the Court are not the ordinary legal questions in the multitudinous lawsuits of *Doe* v. *Roe*. That the single term "law" should cover the Rule against Perpetuities as well as the result of a controversy under the commerce clause is a prolific source of confusion. It is a great pity that the differences in the content of the material, the intellectual approach, and the technique of adjudication between the two types of cases are not indicated at least by recognizing the broad classification of "private law" and "public law." It ought to be a platitude to say that there are many kinds of "law" as administered by the courts, but, unfortunately, it is not. I do not mean to venture upon the heavy sea of philosophic inquiry as to the nature of "law." I am solely concerned with such rigorously practical differences in the exercise of judicial power as are involved, for instance, in construing the "restraint of princes" clause of a bill of lading,[1] and the "due process" clause of the Fourteenth Amendment by the same Justices at the same term of Court.[2]

The Supreme Court is the final authority in adjusting the relationship of the individual to the separate States, of the individual to the United States, of the forty-eight States to one another, and of each, some, or all the States to the United States. The substance and form by which this authority is exercised we call, compendiously, "constitutional law." Plainly this "law" concerns itself primarily with problems of government; no less plainly the mem-

1. The Kronprinzessin Cecillie, 244 U.S. 12 (1917).
2. Adams v. Tanner, 244 U.S. 590 (1916).

bers of the Court move in the field of statesmanship. But though the Court thus exercises a political[3] function, it escapes the rough and tumble of politics partly through the restraints of traditional mental habits and the scrutiny of professional judgment, intermittently effective; but largely because it does not directly exercise its powers to promote or deny affirmative ends of the state. What it does is to define limitations of power. It marks the boundaries between State and national action. It mediates between the individual and government.

These are delicate and tremendous questions, not to be answered by mechanical magic distilled from the four corners of the Constitution, nor self-revealed in the Constitution "by taking the words and a dictionary."[4] The Justices are not passive interpreters of ready-made "law." For the most part and in the decisive cases they exercise creative power. They have to make great choices, which are determined in the end by their breadth of understanding, experience in affairs, imagination, intellectual humility, and insight into governmental problems.

These, to be sure, are platitudes; but of nothing is it more true than of constitutional law that "at this time we need education in the obvious more than investigation of the obscure."[5] To an extraordinary degree the assumption is prevalent that the nine Justices embody pure reason, that they are set apart from the concerns of the community, regardless of time, place, and circumstances, to become the interpreters of self-determining words with fixed content, yielding their meaning to a process of inexorable reasoning.

Freed of its enveloping fog, constitutional law is neither mystery nor metaphysics—nor revelation. It is safe to say

3. I am, of course, aware of the small and ill-defined class of cases, usually raising issues that are contentiously prickly or that affect foreign relations, which the Supreme Court characterizes as "political" and over which, therefore, it denies itself jurisdiction. E.g., Luther v. Borden, 7 How. 1 (1849), and Pacific States T. & T. Co. v. Oregon, 223 U.S. 118 (1911). That the lines between such cases and cases in which jurisdiction is assumed are not drawn merely by process of reasoning hardly admits of doubt.

4. Gompers v. United States, 233 U.S. 604, 610 (1913).

5. Holmes, *Collected Legal Papers* 292, 293 (1920).

that none of the large branches of private law is simpler to state in terms of legal formula than constitutional law. The peculiar confusions to which constitutional law gives rise are due to its very simplicity qua law. The formulated precepts of judgment are few; the factual instances which call for their application are as shifting and as variegated as the complexities of modern society.

Broadly speaking, two sets of constitutional provisions come before the Court:

First. Provisions making specific prohibitions, based upon the history of a specific political grievance, or embodying a specific limitation of power in the division of government between States and nation.

Second. General standards of "fair play" and broad divisions of power between States and nation.

These involve two different types of adjudication, because they rest upon different sources of material and provoke differences in mental outlook.

First. The definiteness of the terms of these specific provisions, the definiteness of their history, the definiteness of their aims, all combine to canalize within narrow limits the scope of judicial review in the rare instances when their meaning is called into question. Only occasionally there is a flurry as to whether "a fact tried by a jury" has been "reexamined in any Court of the United States" otherwise than "according to the rules of the common law,"[6] or whether a tax is "laid upon Articles exported from any State,"[7] or whether a crime is "infamous,"[8] or whether the prohibition against "unreasonable searches and seizure" is violated.[9] Here, in other words, is a part of constitutional law relatively easy of application because it allows comparatively meager play for individual judgment as to policy.

Second. When we come to the broad, undefined clauses of the Constitution we are in a decisively different realm

6. Slocum v. New York Life Insurance Co., 228 U.S. 364 (1912).

7. United States v. Hvoslef, 237 U.S. 1 (1914), and Thames & Mersey Marine Ins. Co., Ltd., v. United States, 237 U.S. 19 (1915).

8. United States v. Moreland, 258 U.S. 433 (1922).

9. Boyd v. United States, 116 U.S. 616 (1885); Gouled v. United States, 255 U.S. 298 (1920).

of judicial action. The scope of application is relatively unrestricted, and the room for play of individual judgment as to policy correspondingly wide. A few simple terms like "liberty" and "property," phrases like "regulate Commerce . . . among the several States" and "without due process of law" call for endless "interpretation." These are the terms invoked in judgment upon the appalling domain of economic, social, and industrial facts. But phrases like "due process of law" are, as Judge Hough has reminded us, phrases of "convenient vagueness."[10] Their content is derived from without, not revealed within the Constitution. To such words a favorite quotation of John Chipman Gray, a sentence of Bishop Hoadly, is peculiarly pertinent: "Whoever hath an *absolute authority to interpret* any written or spoken laws, it is *he* who is truly the *Law-Giver* to all intents and purposes, and not the person who first wrote or spoke them."[11] When dealing with this second and most vital type of constitutional issues the Justices are cartographers who give temporary definiteness but not definitiveness to the undefined and shifting boundaries between State and national power, between individual freedom and governmental authority.

But even in considering the application of these broad powers, important distinctions between different spheres of the Court's action must be taken. In a federated nation, particularly one as vast in its territory and varied in its interests as ours, some organ of government must maintain the equilibrium between States and nation. "I do not think," Mr. Justice Holmes has said, "the United States would come to an end if we lost our power to declare an Act of Congress void. I do think the Union would be imperiled if we could not make that declaration as to the laws of the several States. For one in my place sees how often a local policy prevails with those who are not trained to national views and how often action is taken that embodies what the Commerce Clause was meant to end."[12] But it is sheer illusion to assume that this power is exer-

10. Hough, "Due Process of Law—Today," 32 *Harv. L. Rev.* 218 (1919).

11. Gray, *Nature and Sources of the Law* 102, 125, 172 (2d ed. 1921).

12. Holmes, *supra* note 5, at 295–296.

cised by drawing meaning out of the words of the Constitution. The decisions under the commerce clause, whether allowing or confining state action, whether sanctioning or denying federal power, are in any true perspective acts of statesmanship. The pith and marrow of these decisions has been put with fine precision by their ablest commentator: "The Court has drawn its lines where it has drawn them because it has thought it wise to draw them there. The wisdom of its wisdom depends upon a judgment about practical matters and not upon a knowledge of the Constitution."[13]

The "due process of law" and the "equal protection of the laws" clauses present very different problems of statecraft. Such provisions do not concern a necessary adjustment in the distribution of powers in a federated nation. These broad "guarantees" in favor of the individual, with resulting limitations upon both federal and State governments, seek to embody "immutable principles of liberty and justice."[14] Clearly they open the door to the widest differences of opinion. The words of these provisions are so unrestrained, either by their intrinsic meaning, or by their history,[15] or by tradition, that they leave the individual Justice free, if, indeed, they do not actually compel him, to fill in the vacuum with his own controlling conceptions, which are bound to be determined by his experience, environment, imagination, his hopes and fears—his "idealized political picture of the existing social order."[16]

13. Powell, "The Commerce Clause and State Police Power," 22 *Colum. L. Rev.* 28, 48 (1922).

14. Hurtado v. California, 110 U.S. 516, 535 (1884).

15. See Shattuck, "Meaning of the Term 'Liberty,'" 4 *Harv. L. Rev.* 364 (1891); Pound, "Liberty of Contract," 18 *Yale L.J.* 454 (1909); Reeder, "The Due Process Clause and the Substance of Individual Rights," 58 *U. of Pa. L. Rev.* 192 (1910); Hazeltine, "The Influence of Magna Carta on American Constitutional Development," in *Magna Carta Commemoration Essays* 180 (Malden ed. 1917).

16. Pound, "The Theory of Judicial Decision," 36 *Harv. L. Rev.* 641, 651 et seq. (1923); compare Lippman, *Public Opinion* ch. 1 (1922), and Mill, quoted by Lord Acton, in his *Lectures on Modern History* 884 n. 27 (1906): "Improvement consists in bringing our opinions into nearer agreements with facts; and we shall not be likely to do this while we look at facts only through glasses colored by those very opinions."

Should such power, affecting the intimate life of nation and States, be entrusted, ultimately, to five men? The justification has been eloquently put by a distinguished judge who, with insight and humility, exercises like power within the limited confines of a great State:

> The great ideals of liberty and equality are preserved against the assaults of opportunism, the expediency of the passing hour, the erosion of small encroachments, the scorn and derision of those who have no patience with general principles, by enshrining them in constitutions, and consecrating to the task of their protection a body of defenders. By conscious or subconscious influence, the presence of this restraining power, aloof in the background, but none the less always in reserve, tends to stabilize and rationalize the legislative judgment, to infuse it with the glow of principle, to hold the standard aloft and visible for those who must run the race and keep the faith. I do not mean to deny that there have been times when the possibility of judicial review has worked the other way. Legislatures have sometimes disregarded their own responsibility, and passed it on to the courts. Such dangers must be balanced against those of independence from all restraint, independence on the part of public officers elected for brief terms, without the guiding force of a continuous tradition. On the whole, I believe the latter dangers to be the more formidable of the two. Great maxims, if they may be violated with impunity, are honored often with lip-service, which passes easily into irreverence. The restraining power of the judiciary does not manifest its chief worth in the few cases in which the legislature has gone beyond the lines that mark the limits of discretion. Rather shall we find its chief worth in making vocal and audible the ideals that might otherwise be silenced, in giving them continuity of life and of expression, in guiding and directing choice within the limits where choice ranges. This function should preserve to the courts the power that now belongs to them, if only the power is exercised

with insight into social values, and with suppleness of adaptation to changing social needs.[17]

The beauty of Judge Cardozo's utterance must make any coda sound discordant, and yet one ventures to ask whether the time has not come for a scientific, intensive study of the actual exercise of the power by which the Court cuts down federal and State legislation as offensive to the "due process" clause. Is it not wise and even necessary to make an appraisal of this judicial function in action, in order to determine whether it *is* wielded "with insight into social values, and with suppleness of adaptation to changing social needs?" If the exercise of this power has in fact resulted in a series of decisions which have evoked overwhelming criticism of informed professional opinion,[18] is it not time to inquire if the nature of our legal education, the professional ideals and atmosphere, the basis of judicial selections, and the conditions of judicial life are reasonably calculated to assure statesmanlike Justices, capable of exercising such authority "with insight into social values, and with suppleness of adaptation to changing social needs?"

Granted that the power of judicial review in this widest field of social policy is to be retained, its true nature should be frankly recognized. Since the nine Justices are molders

17. Cardozo, *The Nature of the Judicial Process* 92–94 (1921).

18. See, for instance, criticisms of (i) Lochner v. New York, 198 U.S. 45 (1905), in Bruce, "The Illinois Ten Hour Labor Law for Women," 8 *Mich. L. Rev.* 1 (1909); Corwin, "The Supreme Court and the Fourteenth Amendment," 7 *Mich. L. Rev.* 643 (1909); Freund, "Limitation of Hours of Labor and the Federal Supreme Court," 17 *Green Bag* 411 (1905); "Constitutional Limitations and Labor Legislation," 4 *Ill. L. Rev.* 609 (1910); Greeley, "The Changing Attitude of the Courts toward Social Legislation," 5 *Ill. L. Rev.* 222 (1910); Hand, "Due Process of Law and the Eight Hour Day," 21 *Harv. L. Rev.* 495 (1908); Pollock, "The New York Labor Law and the Fourteenth Amendment," 21 *L.Q. Rev.* 211 (1905); Pound, *supra* note 15; (ii) Adair v. United States, 208 U.S. 161 1908, in Olney, "Discrimination Against Union Labor—Legal?" 42 *Am. L. Rev.* 161 (1908), and Pound, *supra* note 15, at 481; (iii) Truax v. Corrigan, 257 U.S. 312 (1921), in 10 *Calif. L. Rev.* 237 (1924); 7 *Cornell L.Q.* 251 (1922); 22 *Colum. L. Rev.* 252 (1922); 20 *Mich. L. Rev.* 657 (1922); 66 *N.Y.L.J.* 1756 (1922); 28 *W. Va. L.Q.* 144 (1922); 31 *Yale L.J.* 408 (1922); cf. contra, Wheeler, 8 *A.B.A.J.* 506 (1922) and 8 *Va. L. Rev.* 374 (1922).

of policy instead of impersonal vehicles of revealed truth,[19] the security of the powers which they exercise demands that, in this realm of law, the most sensitive field of social policy and legal control, the judicial process should become a *conscious* process. The Justices will then recognize that the "Constitution" which they "interpret" is to a large measure the interpretation of *their own experience*, their "judgment about practical matters,"[20] their "ideal pictures of the social order."[21]

This inevitably calls for a revision of attitude toward the qualifications indispensable for membership on the Court. Of course a Justice should be an outstanding lawyer in the ordinary professional acceptance of the term, but that is the merest beginning. Once recognize the true nature of the judicial process in these constitutional cases, and the determining factors in the qualifications of a Justice become his background, the range of his experience, and his ability to transcend his experience. For the part played by the familiar and unconscious is tremendous. Lord Justice Scrutton, one of the powerful and conservative present-day English judges, has penetratingly expressed it:

> The habits you are trained in, the people with whom you mix, lead to your having a certain class of ideas of such a nature that, when you have to deal with other ideas, you do not give as sound and accurate a judgment as you would wish. This is one of the great difficulties at present with Labour. Labour says: "Where are your impartial Judges? They all move in the same circle as the employers, and they are all educated and nursed in the same ideas as the employers. How can a labour man or a trade unionist get impartial justice?" It is very difficult sometimes to be sure that you have put yourself into a thoroughly impartial position between two disputants, one of your own class and one not of your class.[22]

19. Kales, "The Inarticulate Major Premise," 26 *Yale L.J.* 527 (1917).
20. Powell, note 13 *supra*.
21. Pound, note 16 *supra*.
22. Scrutton, "The Work of the Commercial Courts," 1 *Camb. L.J.* 6, 8 (1921).

This psychological factor is, of course, of infinitely greater significance where a court possesses the power of our Supreme Court.

With the great men of the Court constitutional adjudication has always been statecraft. The deepest significance of Marshall's magistracy is his recognition of the practical needs of government, to be realized by treating the Constitution as the living framework within which the nation and the States could freely move through the inevitable changes wrought by time and inventions. Those of his successors whose labors history has validated have been men who brought to their task insight into the problems of their generation. Taney's statesmanship on the Bench has unfortunately been obscured by the tragic dicta of the *Dred Scott* case. Mr. Henderson[23] and Mr. Warren[24] have rendered notable service by bringing into perspective the constructive achievements of Taney in guiding the corporate and industrial expansion of the country during his incumbency. Taney's decision in the *Charles River Bridge* case[25] shows the statesman; Story's dissent proves that even vast erudition is no substitute for creative imagination.[26] Though Chief Justice Waite be not on the calendar of our great names, is there any doubt today that on crucial issues such as were raised by *Munn* v. *Illinois*[27] Waite gave effect to prophetic insight, while Field, despite his powerful mind, was mastered by the philosophy and experience of a frontier community?[28] Not anointed priests, removed from knowledge of the stress of life, but men with proved grasp of affairs who have developed

23. Henderson, *The Position of Foreign Corporations in American Constitutional Law,* passim, particularly ch. 10 (1918).

24. Warren, *The Supreme Court in United States History,* chs. 22 and 24 (1926). Taney and his times still await an adequate history.

25. 11 Pet. 420 (1837).

26. Of course, Story powerfully influenced American legal development, but his great talents found special scope in commercial law. See Pound, "The Place of Judge Story in the Making of American Law," 7 *Proc. Cambridge Hist. Soc.* 33 (1914); 48 *Am. L. Rev.* 676 (1914); and the comments on Story of that shrewd judge of men, Gray, *supra* note 11, at 129, 253.

27. 94 U.S. 113 (1876).

28. See Pound, *supra* note 15, at 470.

resilience and vigor of mind through seasoned and diversified experience in a work-a-day world are the judges who have wrought abidingly on the Supreme Court.[29]

Mr. Justice Holmes is the great exception. A résumé of his constitutional opinions, with his outlook and technique, was ventured in this *Review* on the occasion of his seventy-fifth birthday.[30] The present Term marks twenty years of his service on the Court, and it is pertinent to add what is necessary to a summary of those twenty years.[31]

Assuredly Mr. Justice Holmes did not bring to the Court the gifts of a lawyer who had been immersed in great affairs, and yet his work is in the school of statesmanship. He is philosopher become king. Where others are guided through experience of life he is led by the humility of the philosopher and the imagination of the poet.

With myriad variations and ever-new detail his juristic patterns have been woven:

> The life of the law has not been logic; it has been experience.[32]

29. See the very significant observations of Chief Justice Taft, in his response to the resolutions of the Bar in commemoration of the late Chief Justice: "The Interstate Commerce Commission was authorized to exercise powers the conferring of which by Congress would have been, perhaps, thought in the earlier years of the Republic to violate the rule that no legislative power can be delegated. But the inevitable progress and exigencies of government and the utter inability of Congress to give the time and attention indispensable to the exercise of these powers in detail forced the modification of the rule. Similar necessity caused Congress to create other bodies with analogous relations to the existing legislative, executive, and judicial machinery of the Federal Government, and these in due course came under the examination of this court. Here was a new field of administrative law which needed a knowledge of government and an experienced understanding of our institutions safely to define and declare. The pioneer work of Chief Justice White in this field entitles him to the gratitude of his countrymen." 257 U.S. xxv–vi.

30. 29 *Harv. L. Rev.* 683. [See "Constitutional Opinions of Mr. Justice Holmes," *supra.* Ed.]

31. "Oliver Wendell Holmes, Associate Justice, appointed in place of Horace Gray, Associate Justice, . . . took his seat December 8, 1902," 187 U.S. iii. The opinions here under review are confined to cases actually decided during Mr. Justice Holmes's twenty years' incumbency. Therefore no opinions are considered in decisions rendered after December 8, 1922.

32. Holmes, *The Common Law* 5 (Howe ed. 1963).

> [The Constitution] is an experiment, as all life is an experiment.[33]

> Great Constitutional provisions must be administered with caution. Some play must be allowed for the joints of the machine, and it must be remembered that legislatures are ultimate guardians of the liberty and welfare of the people in quite as great a degree as the courts.[34]

> The word "right" is one of the most deceptive of pitfalls; it is so easy to slip from a qualified meaning in the premise to an unqualified one in the conclusion. Most rights are qualified.[35]

> I am the last man in the world to quarrel with a distinction simply because it is one of degree. Most distinctions, in my opinion, are of that sort, and none are the worse for it. But the line which is drawn must be justified by the fact that it is a little nearer than the nearest opposing case to one pole of an admitted antithesis.[36]

> It is a misfortune if a judge reads his conscious or unconscious sympathy with one side or the other prematurely into the law, and forgets that what seem to him to be first principles are believed by half his fellow men to be wrong . . . We too need education in the obvious—to learn to transcend our own convictions and to leave room for much that we hold dear to be done away with short of revolution by the orderly change of law.[37]

These aperçus give the clues to his two thousand opinions. With these as guides he has fashioned a resolute and harmonious whole out of the isolated instances which involve the eternal conflicts between nation and States, between liberty and authority. He has been vigilant for the Union, for which he fought at Ball's Bluff and Antie-

33. Abrams v. United States, 250 U.S. 616, 630 (1919).
34. Missouri, Texas & Kansas Ry. v. May, 194. U.S. 267, 270 (1904).
35. Amer. Bank & Trust Co. v. Federal Bank, 256 U.S. 350, 358 (1921).
36. Haddock v. Haddock, 201 U.S. 562, 631, 632 (1906).
37. Holmes, *supra* note 5, at 295.

tam and Fredericksburg; he has been equally watchful to assure the scope for the States upon which the Union rests. Federal power over commerce beyond State lines is not paralyzed by sterile abstractions; nor are the States, in dealing with their local problems, confined through a partisan or provincial picture of the Fourteenth Amendment. He has found the Constitution equal to the needs of a great nation at war. But according to the same Constitution the individual must not be sacrificed to the Moloch of fear. To be sure, some of his weightiest utterances applying these views are merely dissenting opinions —but they are dissents that shape history and record prophecy.

In the large and undefined field of constitutional law it is preeminently true that exercise of judgment is screened by formal "principles." That is the significance of Mr. Justice Holmes's aphorism, "general propositions do not decide concrete cases."[38] But the intensity with which "general propositions" are felt, the flexibility with which they are applied, the recognition, that is, of competing "general propositions," and of the necessity of mediating between them or of leaving the field of accommodation to the legislature, *do* decide concrete cases. In law, also, the emphasis makes the song. It makes all the difference in the world whether the Constitution is treated primarily as a text for interpretation or as an instrument of government. This will determine whether the conception of the document is derived essentially from itself, or from one's conception of the country, its developments, its needs, its place in a civilized world:

> It is said that a treaty cannot be valid if it infringes the Constitution, that there are limits, therefore, to the treaty-making power, and that one such limit is that what an act of Congress could not do unaided, in derogation of the powers reserved to the States, a treaty cannot do . . . We do not mean to imply that there are no qualifications to the treaty-making power; but they must be

38. Lochner v. New York, 198 U.S. 45, 76 (1905).

ascertained in a different way . . . We are not yet discussing the particular case before us but only are considering the validity of the test proposed . . . When we are dealing with words that also are a constituent act, like the Constitution of the United States, we must realize that they have called into life a being the development of which could not have been foreseen completely by the most gifted of its begetters. It was enough for them to realize or to hope that they had created an organism; it has taken a century and has cost their successors much sweat and blood to prove that they created a nation. The case before us must be considered in the light of our whole experience and not merely in that of what was said a hundred years ago. The treaty in question [protecting migratory birds] does not contravene any prohibitory words to be found in the Constitution. The only question is whether it is forbidden by some invisible radiation from the general terms of the Tenth Amendment.

Here a national interest of very nearly the first magnitude is involved. It can be protected only by a national action in concert with that of another power. The subject-matter is only transitorily within the State and has no permanent habitat therein. But for the treaty and the statute there soon might be no birds for any powers to deal with. We see nothing in the Constitution that compels the Government to sit by while a food supply is cut off and the protectors of our forests and our crops are destroyed. It is not sufficient to rely upon the States. The reliance is vain, and were it otherwise, the question is whether the United States is forbidden to act. We are of opinion that the treaty and statute must be upheld.[39]

As the United States is a nation in its dealings with other nations so this country is a single nation in the activities of commerce which project themselves beyond the lines of the individual States. The legislative exertion of this federal power raises some of the most difficult

39. Missouri v. Holland, 252 U.S. 416, 432–435 (1920).

issues of practical wisdom that confront a federal government which rules a continent. The power itself is not to be denied or mutilated by distinctions which rest neither in reason nor in the actualities of industrial life:

> The objection urged against the power [to prohibit the shipment in interstate commerce of the products of cotton mills employing child labor] is that the States have exclusive control over their methods of production and that Congress cannot meddle with them, and taking the proposition in the sense of direct intermeddling I agree to it and suppose that no one denies it. But if an act is within the powers specifically conferred upon Congress, it seems to me that it is not made any less constitutional because of the indirect effects that it may have, however obvious it may be that it will have those effects, and that we are not at liberty upon such grounds to hold it void . . . I should have thought that that matter had been disposed of so fully as to leave no room for doubt. I should have thought that the most conspicuous decisions of this Court had made it clear that the power to regulate commerce and other constitutional powers could not be cut down or qualified by the fact that it might interfere with the carrying out of the domestic policy of any State.
>
> The notion that prohibition is any less prohibition when applied to things now thought evil I do not understand. But if there is any matter upon which civilized countries have agreed—far more unanimously than they have with regard to intoxicants and some other matters over which this country is now emotionally aroused—it is the evil of premature and excessive child labor. I should have thought that if we were to introduce our own moral conceptions where in my opinion they do not belong, this was preeminently a case for upholding the exercise of all its powers by the United States.
>
> But I had thought that the propriety of the exercise of a power admitted to exist in some cases was for the consideration of Congress alone and that this Court

always had disavowed the right to intrude its judgment upon questions of policy or morals. It is not for this Court to pronounce when prohibition is necessary to regulation if it ever may be necessary—to say that it is permissible as against strong drink but not as against the product of ruined lives.

The act does not meddle with anything belonging to the States. They may regulate their internal affairs and their domestic commerce as they like. But when they seek to send their products across the State line they are no longer within their rights. If there were no Constitution and no Congress their power to cross the line would depend upon their neighbors. Under the Constitution such commerce belongs not to the States but to Congress to regulate. It may carry out its views of public policy whatever indirect effect they may have upon the activities of the States. Instead of being encountered by a prohibitive tariff at her boundaries the State encounters the public policy of the United States which it is for Congress to express. The public policy of the United States is shaped with a view to the benefit of the nation as a whole. If, as has been the case within the memory of men still living, a State should take a different view of the propriety of sustaining a lottery from that which generally prevails, I cannot believe that the fact would require a different decision from that reached in *Champion* v. *Ames*. Yet in that case it would be said with quite as much force as in this that Congress was attempting to intermeddle with the State's domestic affairs. The national welfare as understood by Congress may require a different attitude within its sphere from that of some self-seeking State. It seems to me entirely constitutional for Congress to enforce its understanding by all the means at its command.[40]

The nation that was called into being by the Constitution was thus endowed adequately to meet growth and change and to maintain its dignity and its interest in the com-

40. Hammer v. Dagenhart, 247 U.S. 251, 277–281 (1918).

mon interests of the world. But the Constitution was also the product of great historic conflicts, and sought specifically to guard against the recurrence of historic grievances by preferring the risks of tolerance to the dangers of tyranny. Mr. Justice Holmes's dissenting opinion in the *Abrams* case will live as long as the august majesty of English prose has power to thrill:

> I do not doubt for a moment that by the same reasoning that would justify punishing persuasion to murder, the United States constitutionally may punish speech that produces or is intended to produce a clear and imminent danger that it will bring about forthwith certain substantive evils that the United States constitutionally may seek to prevent. The power undoubtedly is greater in time of war than in time of peace because war opens dangers that do not exist at other times.
>
> But as against dangers peculiar to war, as against others, the principle of the right to free speech is always the same. It is only the present danger of immediate evil or an intent to bring it about that warrants Congress in setting a limit to the expression of opinion where private rights are not concerned. Congress certainly cannot forbid all effort to change the mind of the country.
>
> In this case sentences of twenty years imprisonment have been imposed for the publishing of two leaflets that I believe the defendants had as much right to publish as the Government has to publish the Constitution of the United States now vainly invoked by them. Even if I am technically wrong and enough can be squeezed from these poor and puny anonymities to turn the color of legal litmus paper; I will add, even if what I think the the necessary intent were shown; the most nominal punishment seems to me all that possibly could be inflicted, unless the defendants are made to suffer not for what the indictment alleges but for the creed that they avow—a creed that I believe to be the creed of ignorance and immaturity when honestly held, as I see no reason to doubt that it was held here, but which, although made

the subject of examination at the trial, no one has a right to consider in dealing with the charges before the Court.

Persecution for the expression of opinions seems to me perfectly logical. If you have no doubt of your premises or your power and want a certain result with all your heart you naturally express your wishes in law and sweep away all opposition. To allow opposition by speech seems to indicate that you think the speech impotent, as when a man says that he has squared the circle, or that you do not care whole-heartedly for the result, or that you doubt either your power or your premises. But when men have realized that time has upset many fighting faiths, they may come to believe even more than they believe the very foundations of their own conduct that the ultimate good desired is better reached by free trade in ideas—that the best test of truth is the power of the thought to get itself accepted in the competition of the market, and that truth is the only ground upon which their wishes safely can be carried out. That at any rate is the theory of our Constitution. It is an experiment, as all life is an experiment. Every year if not every day we have to wager our salvation upon some prophecy based upon imperfect knowledge. While that experiment is part of our system I think that we should be eternally vigilant against attempt to check the expression of opinions that we loathe and believe to be fraught with death, unless they so imminently threaten immediate interference with the lawful and pressing purposes of the law that an immediate check is required to save the country. I wholly disagree with the argument of the Government that the First Amendment left the common law as to seditious libel in force. History seems to me against the notion. I had conceived that the United States through many years had shown its repentance for the Sedition Act of 1798, by repaying fines that it imposed. Only the emergency that makes it immediately dangerous to leave the correction of evil counsels to time warrants making any exception to the sweeping command, "Congress shall make no

> law . . . abridging the freedom of speech." Of course I am speaking only of expressions of opinion and exhortations, which were all that were uttered here, but I regret that I cannot put into more impressive words my belief that in their conviction upon this indictment the defendants were deprived of their rights under the Constitution of the United States.[41]

His statesmanship is nowhere more manifest than in his lively realization that in domestic affairs the nation is a union of States. He has sturdily resisted every tendency of the Court to translate its views or assumptions as to social policy into the law of each of the forty-eight States. With him the conception of federalism, with its flexible resources for compromising the requirements of national uniformity with the needs of local diversities and effective local action, is not frustrated in application:

> There is nothing that I more deprecate than the use of the Fourteenth Amendment beyond the absolute compulsion of its words to prevent the making of social experiments that an important part of the community desires, in the insulated chambers afforded by the several States, even though the experiments may seem futile or even noxious to me and to those whose judgment I most respect.[42]

> The Fourteenth Amendment, itself a historical product, did not destroy history for the States and substitute mechanical compartments of law all exactly alike.[43]

And so in all the varieties of State action evoked by a complex industrial civilization, he permits the States

41. Abrams v. United States, 250 U.S. 616, 627–631 (1919). For a discussion of Mr. Justice Holmes's treatment of the First Amendment, in a series of cases, see Chafee, *Freedom of Speech*, ch. 2 (1920), and the comments upon the *Abrams* case by Sir Frederick Pollock, in 36 *L.Q. Rev.* 334 (1920).
42. Truax v. Corrigan, 257 U.S. 312, 344 (1921).
43. Jackman v. Rosenbaum Co., 260 U.S. 22, 31 (1922).

ample scope to solve their problems with energy and individuality:

> The dangers of a delusive exactness in the application of the Fourteenth Amendment have been adverted to before now . . . I cannot understand the notion that it would be unconstitutional to authorize boycotts and the like in aid of the employees' or the employers' interest by statute when the same result has been reached constitutionally without statute by Courts with whom I agree.[44]

> I think further that the selection of the class of employers, and employees for special treatment, dealing with both sides alike, is beyond criticism on principles often asserted by this Court. And especially I think that without legalizing the conduct complained of the extraordinary relief by injunction may be denied to the class. Legislation may begin where an evil begins. If, as many intelligent people believe, there is more danger that the injunction will be abused in labor cases than elsewhere, I can feel no doubt of the power of the legislature to deny it in such cases.[45]

Thus in regard to the most sensitive field of State legislation. Equally adequate is the scope permitted the States in devising ways and means for paying the bills of society or using taxation as an instrument of social policy:

> The objection to the taxation as double may be laid on one side. That is a matter of State law alone. The Fourteenth Amendment no more forbids double taxation than it does doubling the amount of a tax; short of confiscation or proceedings unconstitutional on other grounds . . . We are of opinion that it is also within the power of a State, so far as the Constitution of the United States is concerned, to tax its own corporations in re-

44. Truax v. Corrigan, 257 U.S. 312, 342, 343 (1921).
45. Id. at 343.

> spect of the stock held by them in other domestic corporations, although unincorporated stockholders are exempt. A State may have a policy in taxation. *Quong Wing* v. *Kirkendall,* 223 U.S. 59, 63. If the State of Arkansas wished to discourage but not to forbid the holding of stock in one corporation by another and sought to attain the result by this tax, or if it simply saw fit to make corporations pay for the privilege, there would be nothing in the Constitution to hinder. A discrimination between corporations and individuals with regard to a tax like this cannot be pronounced arbitrary, although we may not know the precise ground of policy that led the State to insert the distinction in the law.[46]

The difficulties of adjusting the contesting claims arising from congested communities, railroads, and the hazards to life are sufficiently baffling without being cast into the mold of rigid constitutional categories:

> Grade crossings call for a necessary adjustment of two conflicting interests—that of the public using the streets and that of the railroads and the public using them. Generically the streets represent the more important interest of the two. There can be no doubt that they did when these railroads were laid out, or that the advent of automobiles has given them an additional claim to consideration . . . Being places to which the public is invited and that it necessarily frequents, the State, in the care of which this interest is and from which, ultimately, the railroads derive their right to occupy the land, has a constitutional right to insist that they shall not be made dangerous to the public, whatever may be the cost to the parties introducing the danger . . . It is said that if the same requirements were made for the other grade crossings of the road it would soon be bankrupt. That the States might be so foolish as to kill a goose that lays golden eggs for them, has no

46. Ft. Smith Lumber Co. v. Arkansas, 251 U.S. 532, 533, 534 (1920).

> bearing on their constitutional rights. If it reasonably can be said that safety requires the change it is for them to say whether they will insist upon it, and neither prospective bankruptcy nor engagement in interstate commerce can take away this fundamental right of the sovereign of the soil ... Intelligent self-interest should lead to a careful consideration of what the road is able to do without ruin, but this is not a constitutional duty.[47]

In many instances and in various forms he has repelled efforts to spell pedantic perfection into the Fourteenth Amendment. Again and again he has recognized the necessity for allowing play to the joints of the crude machine of government:

> [W]hen the power of the Court in all other respects is established, what acts of the defendant shall be deemed a submission to its power is a matter on which States may differ. If a statute should provide that filing a plea in abatement, or taking the question to a higher court should have that effect, it could not be said to deny due process of law ... It can be no otherwise when a court so decides as to proceedings in another State. It may be mistaken upon what to it is matter of fact, the law of the other State. But a mere mistake of that kind is not a denial of due process of law ... Whenever a wrong judgment is entered against a defendant his property is taken when it should not have been, but whatever the ground may be, if the mistake is not so gross as to be impossible in a rational administration of justice, it is no more than the imperfection of man, not a denial of constitutional rights.[48]

But there are limits to State action—the limits derived from the fact of union and from the rudimentary decencies of fair play. The difficulties of adjusting the powers of taxation of the States and the nation in common sources of revenue, like a great transcontinental railroad

47. Erie R.R. v. Public Util. Commrs., 254 U.S. 394, 410, 411 (1920).
48. Chicago Life Ins. Co. v. Cherry, 244 U.S. 25, 29, 30 (1917).

system, will not be allowed to defeat an obvious attempt of the State to project itself beyond State lines at the expense of the organic whole:

> As the law is administered, the tax commissioner fixes the value of the total property of each railroad by the total value of its stocks and bonds and assesses the proportion of this value that the main track mileage in North Dakota bears to the main track of the whole line. But on the allegations of the bill, which is all that we have before us, the circumstances are such as to make that mode of assessment indefensible. North Dakota is a State of plains, very different from the other States, and the cost of the roads there was much less than it was in mountainous regions that the roads had to traverse. The State is mainly agricultural. Its markets are outside its boundaries and most of the distributing centers from which it purchases also are outside. It naturally follows that the great and very valuable terminals of the roads are in other States. So looking only to the physical track the injustice of assuming the value to be evenly distributed according to main track mileage is plain. But that is not all.
>
> The only reason for allowing a State to look beyond its borders when it taxes the property of foreign corporations is that it may get the true value of the things within it, when they are part of an organic system of wide extent, that gives them a value above what they otherwise would possess. The purpose is not to expose the heel of the system to a mortal dart—not, in other words, to open to taxation what is not within the State.[49]

The problems raised by "big business" baffled the wisdom and courage of a [Theodore] Roosevelt. Their intricacies and urgencies have only increased with time. The widest scope must be permitted to the inventions of

49. Wallace v. Hines, 253 U.S. 66, 69 (1920).

statesmanship, the experimentation and bunglings of legislatures. Only they must not outrage common decency and disregard those procedural safeguards which are so largely the assurance of political liberty:

> The statute bristles with severities that touch the plaintiff alone, and raises many questions that would have to be answered before it could be sustained. We deem it sufficient to refer to those that were mentioned by the District Court; a classification which, if it does not confine itself to the American Sugar Refinery, at least is arbitrary beyond possible justice—and a creation of presumptions and special powers against it that can have no foundation except the intent to destroy . . .
>
> As to the presumptions, of course the legislature may go a good way in raising one or in changing the burden of proof, but there are limits . . . The presumption created here has no relation in experience to general facts. It has no foundation except with tacit reference to the plaintiff. But it is not within the province of a legislature to declare an individual guilty or presumptively guilty of a crime.[50]

Mr. Justice Holmes's insistence, in all his writings, on intellectual rigor is vindicated in his constitutional opinions. He bids us, steadily, to think things and not words. At the core of his legal opinions is the realization that words are but symbols of things and relations. And so his constitutional opinions are but applications of his candid insight into the realities of lawmaking and the share that courts have in its process. For him jurisdiction rests ultimately on power, and law is the voice of some defined organ of the state:

> The foundation of jurisdiction is physical power, although in civilized times it is not necessary to main-

50. McFarland v. Amer. Sugar Co., 241 U.S. 79, 86 (1916).

tain that power throughout proceedings properly begun, and although submission to the jurisdiction by appearance may take the place of service upon the person. *Michigan Trust Co.* v. *Ferry,* 228 U.S. 346, 353. *Pennsylvania Fire Insurance Co.* v. *Gold Issue Mining & Milling Co.,* [243 U.S.] 93. No doubt there may be some extension of the means of acquiring jurisdiction beyond service or appearance, but the foundation should be borne in mind . . . And in States bound together by a Constitution and subject to the Fourteenth Amendment, great care should be used not to let fiction deny the fair play that can be secured only by a pretty close adhesion to fact.[51]

The common law is not a brooding omnipresence in the sky but the articulate voice of some sovereign or quasi-sovereign that can be identified; although some decisions with which I have disagreed seem to me to have forgotten the fact. It always is the law of some State, and if the District Courts adopt the common law of torts, as they have shown a tendency to do, they thereby assume that a law not of maritime origin and deriving its authority in that territory only from some particular State of this Union also governs maritime torts in that territory—and if the common law, the statute law has at least equal force, as the discussion in *The Osceola* assumes. On the other hand the refusal of the District Courts to give remedies coextensive with the common law would prove no more than that they regarded their jurisdiction as limited by the ancient lines—not that they doubted that the common law might and would be enforced in the courts of the States as it always has been.[52]

I do not suppose that anyone would say that the words, "The judicial power shall extend . . . to all cases of ad-

51. McDonald v. Mabee, 243 U.S. 90, 91 (1917). Cf. Flexner v. Farson, 248 U.S. 289 (1919), and its discussion by Scott, "Business Jurisdiction over Non-Residents," 32 *Harv. L. Rev.* 871, 877, 889 et seq. (1919).

52. Southern Pacific Co. v. Jensen, 244 U.S. 205, 222 (1917).

miralty and maritime jurisdiction," Const. Art. III, §3, by implication enacted a whole code for master and servant at sea, that could be modified only by a constitutional amendment. But somehow or other the ordinary common-law rules of liability as between master and servant have come to be applied to a considerable extent in the admiralty. If my explanation, that the source is the common law of the several States, is not accepted, I can only say I do not know how, unless by the fiat of the judges. But surely the power that imposed the liability can change it, and I suppose that Congress can do as much as the judges who introduced the rules. For we know that they were introduced and cannot have been elicited by logic alone from the mediaeval sea laws.[53]

He does not delude himself with phrases, and to that extent helps us to avoid verbal mirages:

Such words as "right" are a constant solicitation to fallacy.[54]

Delusive exactness is a source of fallacy throughout the law. By calling a business "property" you make it seem like land, and lead up to the conclusion that a statute cannot substantially cut down the advantages of ownership existing before the statute was passed. An established business no doubt may have pecuniary value and commonly is protected by law against various unjustified injuries. But you cannot give it definiteness of contour by calling it a thing. It is a course of conduct and like other conduct is subject to substantial modification according to time and circumstances both in

53. Knickerbocker Ice Co. v. Stewart, 253 U.S. 149, 167 (1920). As to the application of Mr. Justice Holmes's conception of the admiralty jurisdiction of the United States, see Palfrey, "The Common Law Courts and the Law of the Sea," 36 *Harv. L. Rev.* 777 (1923).

54. Jackman v. Rosenbaum Co., 260 U.S. 22, 31 (1922).

itself and in regard to what shall justify doing it a harm.[55]

The eternal struggle in the law between constancy and change[56] is largely a struggle between the forces of history and the forces of reason, between past reason and present needs. The valid claims of both, but with varying weight in different aspects of legal control, find frequent expression in Mr. Justice Holmes's opinions. The essential difficulty of these adjustments lies in the impossibility of making quantitative determinations. Specific cases gradually work out the approximate directions. The wise application of the claims of history and of reason was strikingly indicated by two opinions rendered the same day. In determining the present attitude of the law towards a man standing his ground when attacked with a deadly weapon, ancient history has very little pertinence:

It is useless to go into the developments of the law from the time when a man who had killed another no matter how innocently had to get his pardon, whether

55. Truax v. Corrigan, 257 U.S. 312, 342, 343 (1921). The reports are rampant with illustrations of the confusion between human claims of diverse interests and their legal recognition and enforcement. To this confusion are traceable serious divisions in the Supreme Court in cases of large public importance. See, for instance, Hitchman Coal & Coke Co. v. Mitchell, 245 U.S. 229, 251, 270, 271 (1917); Denver v. Denver Union Water Co., 246 U.S. 178, 196–198 (1918); Internat'l News Serv. v. Assoc. Press, 248 U.S. 215, 234, 235, 246–248, 250, 262–267 (1918). Mr. Justice Holmes has deemed it necessary to remind us that it "is true and not quite as tautologous as it seems, that the law knows nothing but legal rights," Denver v. Denver Union Water Co., *supra*. The underlying philosophic considerations to be kept in mind by judges in their process of lawmaking, particularly with the increasing complexity of modern society, he has also set forth:

"As law embodies beliefs that have triumphed in the battle of ideals and then have translated themselves into action, while there still is doubt, while opposite convictions still keep a battle front against each other, the time for law has not come; the notion destined to prevail is not yet entitled to the field. It is a misfortune if a judge reads his conscious or unconscious sympathy with one side or the other prematurely into the law, and forgets that what seem to him to be first principles are believed by half his fellow-men to be wrong." Holmes, *supra* note 5, at 294, 295.

56. Pound, *Interpretations of Legal History* ch. I (1913).

> of grace or of course. Concrete cases or illustrations stated in the early law in conditions very different from the present, like the reference to retreat in Coke, Third Inst. 55, and elsewhere, have had a tendency to ossify into specific rules without much regard to reason . . . The law has grown, and even if historical mistakes have contributed to its growth it has tended in the direction of rules consistent with human nature.[57]

But when the technical restriction of the Constitution as to laying a "direct tax" is invoked against the modern device of succession taxes, "a page of history is worth a volume of logic."[58]

Serenely dwelling above the sound of passing shibboleths, Mr. Justice Holmes has steadfastly refused to lower his ear to catch the murmur of the moment. But his humor and humility are too strong to make him regard even the highest tribunal as a Grand Lama. The Supreme Court, like all human institutions, must earn reverence through the test of truth.[59] He has built himself into the structure of our national life. He has written himself into the slender volume of the literature of all times.

57. Brown v. United States, 256 U.S. 335, 343 (1921).

58. New York Trust Co. v. Eisner, 256 U.S. 345, 349 (1921).

59. See the Lincoln Day, 1898, address of Mr. Justice Brewer, "Government by Injunction," in 15 *Nat. Corp. Rep.* 848, 849 (1898): "It is a mistake to suppose that the Supreme Court is either honored or helped by being spoken of as beyond criticism. On the contrary, the life and character of its justices should be the objects of constant watchfulness by all, and its judgments subject to the freest criticism. The time is past in the history of the world when any living man or body of men can be set on a pedestal and decorated with a halo. True, many criticisms may be, like their authors, devoid of good taste, but better all sorts of criticism than no criticism at all. The moving waters are full of life and health; only in the still waters is stagnation and death."

Exit the Kansas Court

The Kansas Court of Industrial Relations is dead. That great achievement of the middle western "law and order" movement is killed by the Supreme Law of the land. Not all the eloquence of Governor Allen can blow the breath of life into it again. For, while in the recent *Wolff Packing Company* case[1] the Supreme Court invalidated only that part of the Industrial Court Act which permitted the fixing of wages in a packing house as a means of avoiding a strike, the scope of the decision drags down with it the whole structure of the act. It is inconceivable that if any attempt were made to enforce the anti-strike features of the Kansas law, the Supreme Court would sustain it. The opinion of the Chief Justice clearly recognizes that "joint compulsion"—"compelling the employer to pay the adjudged wages and forbidding the employees to combine against working and receiving them"—is the underlying theory of the act.[2] The Supreme Court thus treated the case before it as a clear issue of compulsory arbitration, and decided that no State can attempt to solve its industrial relations by resorting to compulsory arbitration, except, probably, in a restricted class of public utilities. Thus fails another social experiment, not because it has been tried and found wanting, but because it has been tried and found unconstitutional.

A decision which is acclaimed by both Mr. Gompers and the Counsel of the National Manufacturers' Association satisfies, at least, the combatants in the industrial conflict. But issues are raised by this decision, as by other recent decisions of the Court, calling into question the scope of the Court's veto power over the social policies of the individual States. The *New Republic* is opposed to the idea which underlay the Kansas Industrial Court. We believe that compulsory arbitration is not the road to solu-

Reprinted from an unsigned editorial in the *New Republic*, June 27, 1923, with permission. Footnotes supplied by editor.

1. Wolff Packing Co. v. Court of Industrial Relations, 262 U.S. 522 (1923).
2. Id. at 541.

tion of our industrial difficulties, in the present stage of American industry. We believe that compulsory arbitration is ineffective and unjust so long as trade unionism is not frankly and widely accepted, and there is no recognized body of industrial standards capable of application by industrial courts adequately equipped to apply such standards. We therefore disbelieve in compulsory arbitration as a social policy; but we do not disbelieve in Kansas or any other State venturing a trial of the experiment. The Supreme Court now holds that the Constitution, unless amended, presents a permanent barrier against such a venture. This obstruction is again found in the "due process" clause. The plain fact is that the Court puts this meaning into the phrase "due process" and then finds it there. We too rejoice with Messrs. Gompers and Emery over the death of the Kansas Industrial Court; but it was for the legislature of Kansas, and not for the Supreme Court, to kill it.

The satisfaction of Mr. Gompers and Mr. Emery is the satisfaction of combatants who are allowed to fight. The Supreme Court says, in effect, "Go to it!" Industrial warfare is legalized; its compulsory arbitrament forbidden. Mr. Gompers in his happy escape is, for the moment, indifferent to the legal handicaps which other Supreme Court decisions have imposed against organized labor. The right to strike, generally, is in the *Wolff Packing Company* case recognized as a constitutional right, but in view of the legal restrictions against it it is largely a paper right. By means of the "yellow dog" contracts, sanctioned in the *Hitchman* case,[3] employers may resort to equity against threatened interference with their "property" rights through attempted unionization. The injunction as a favorite strike-breaker, though not strike-curer, is constantly doing a flourishing business. Not only has the Supreme Court emasculated the effort of Congress to restrict the use of the injunction in labor controversies in the federal courts;[4] it has denied a State the right to with-

3. Hitchman Coal & Coke Co. v. Mitchell, 245 U.S. 229 (1917).
4. See Duplex Co. v. Deering, 254 U.S. 443 (1921).

draw the injunction altogether from labor controversies.[5] Thus the Supreme Court's contribution to the solution of the industrial conflict consists largely of outworn dicta of the political economists of the nineteenth century, and practical partisanship, however fairly intended, with the employers' side of the controversy.

For ourselves we are convinced that peace and order cannot come to American industry until the balance which now in fact operates against labor is redressed. Redress by law is for the present barred by some of the Court's constitutional decisions. But it is still as true as when Mr. Dooley first said it, that the "Supreme Coorth follows th' iliction returns." Public opinion, if sufficiently sustained and sufficiently strong, seeps into Supreme Court decisions. The Kansas decision bars the door to one experiment. It challenges all the more insistently well-directed effort at solutions dependent upon negotiation and cooperation. Such solutions, however, presuppose a definite attitude in the public mind towards unions. It is idle to recognize the abstract right of unions and even abstractly to recognize that a healthy social order demands unions, while in practice fighting their existence. Unions must wholeheartedly be admitted into our social scheme. Correspondingly they must be subjected to social and legal responsibility. But the injunction in labor disputes must go. Criminal prosecutions and civil suits, with the safeguard of jury trial, are the only tolerable means of vindicating the law. Once freely admit the indispensable function of the union and change its attitude of suspicion and grievance towards the law by removing the attitude of hostility towards labor generated by the injunction, and the conditions for voluntary negotiation and cooperation will be created. The Kansas decision may help towards this end by throwing the public back upon itself by asserting the compelling power of public opinion. In denying compulsory arbitration, the Supreme Court may have provoked compulsory thinking as the beginning of voluntary action.

5. Truax v. Corrigan, 257 U.S. 312 (1921).

Lèse Majesté Mayer

The history of the New York City traction companies is a long story of corruption, financial hugger-mugger, and maladministration. In due course they found their way, one by one, into the federal court, and more particularly under the paternal care of United States Judge Julius M. Mayer. Receiverships were the method of control, and "friendly suits" were the devices by which the business of running the transit facilities of New York was assumed by the federal court. Now the city of New York had vast interests at stake. Millions of city money were invested in the properties, and it had heavy claims against the roads. Much more important than that, upon the honest and wise management and reorganization of its traction system largely depended the social health of the city's future. Properly to protect these paramount interests, the city sought from Judge Mayer the appointment of Comptroller Craig, the chief fiscal officer of the city, as co-receiver with the court's own appointee, who was presumably agreeable to the interests behind the "friendly suit." Judge Mayer declined the city's petition, although the appointment of two receivers in important cases, even where only private interests are involved, is not a very unusual thing in the federal courts. Months afterwards, Comptroller Craig was invited to attend a conference "of all parties at interest in the transit situation." Mr. Craig refused to attend, in a letter in which he set forth at length the city's ground of opposition to Judge Mayer's denial to the city of "any representation in these receiverships." The letter contained the following paragraph which aroused Judge Mayer's ire, to soothe which he sentenced the comptroller to sixty days in jail:

> Before any such conference can be seriously considered, and as an evidence of good faith on the part of those acting by and under the authority of United States

Reprinted from an unsigned editorial in the *New Republic,* December 12, 1923, with permission. Footnotes supplied by editor.

> District Judge Mayer, there must be a reversal of the policy for which Judge Mayer is responsible of denying to myself and other members of the Board of Estimate and Apportionment any access to original services of information concerning the property and affairs of these various public utility corporations holding franchises to operate in the streets of New York.

This paragraph must be read in its setting. It plainly concerns itself with the denial of the application to appoint a co-receiver. If the comptroller were appointed co-receiver, the city through him would have access to all the original documents as a matter of right. Judge Mayer read the paragraph as charging him with a denial of access as a matter of grace. On this argumentative false charge Judge Mayer based his jail sentence as a contempt of court. Judge Mayer could, of course, have tested his claim of false charges in a libel suit against the comptroller. He preferred to be his own accuser, judge, and jury.

In effect, the Supreme Court, with its familiar division, sustained Judge Mayer.[1] To be sure, the matter is much befogged by pedantic discussions about the scope of the Court's review on habeas corpus. But cutting through the maze of technicalities, the simple fact emerges that the majority of the Court, appropriately led by Mr. Justice McReynolds, decides that a federal judge has power to commit for contempt, on such facts as are presented by the *Craig* case, while Mr. Justice Holmes and Mr. Justice Brandeis unqualifiedly deny this power. "Unless a judge, while sitting, can lay hold of any one who ventures to publish anything that tends to make him unpopular or to belittle him I cannot see what power Judge Mayer had to touch Mr. Craig,"[2] is the downright conclusion of Mr. Justice Holmes. How then does the majority reach its opposite result? By doing violence to an act of Congress and by disregarding cherished traditions of Anglo-American law.

1. Craig v. Hecht, 263 U.S. 255 (1923).
2. Id. at 281.

Nearly a hundred years ago, as a result of its abusive exercise, Congress strictly defined the power of federal courts to punish for contempt. "The said courts," reads the act of Congress, "shall have power . . . to punish . . . contempts of their authority: Provided, That such power to punish contempts shall not be construed to extend to any cases except the misbehavior of any person in their presence, or so near thereto as to obstruct the administration of justice."[3] Surely the plain English of this restricts the exercise of a power that all judges agree to be peculiarly liable to abuse and wilful in its practical operations to conduct that positively interferes with a court at work. A situation like the *Craig* case is wholly outside the conditions of the statute. Only legal legerdemain can bring it within them.

It took two steps to bring about this perversion of law and its consequent disregard of liberty. In June 1918, at the height of the war, the Supreme Court took the first disastrous step. Though it very vitally challenged the freedom of the press, it was unfortunately all too little noticed at the time. In a contempt proceeding against the *Toledo News-Bee,*[4] the Supreme Court construed the authority of the Court to punish misbehavior "in their presence, *or so near thereto* as to obstruct the administration of justice," to mean anything uttered anywhere having a "tendency" to obstruct—a standard vague enough to terrorize the press, considering the summary power to apply the standard. Plainly the words refer to spatial proximity to the Court's work, and not to criticism argumentatively disturbing. This decision is intolerable, for reasons which Mr. Justice Holmes made abundantly clear in his dissent.

> When it is considered how contrary it is to our practice and ways of thinking for the same person to be accuser and sole judge in a matter which, if he be sensitive, may involve strong personal feelings, I should expect the power to be limited by the necessities of the case, "to

3. Act of March 2, 1831, 21st Cong., 2d Sess.
4. Toledo Newspaper Co. v. United States, 247 U.S. 402 (1918).

> insure order and decorum in their presence . . ." And when the words of the statute are read, it seems to me that the limit is too plain to be construed away. To my mind they point and point only to the present protection of the Court from actual interference, and not to postponed retribution for lack of respect for its dignity—not to moving to vindicate its independence after enduring the newspaper's attacks for nearly six months as the Court did in this case.[5]

The Supreme Court has now gone one step further by holding, in the *Craig* case, that there is power to commit for contempt although there is no matter immediately pending before the Court and the publication complained of at worst has merely a general tendency to belittle the Court. Again let Mr. Justice Holmes comment on his colleague:

> This . . . makes a man judge in matters in which he is likely to have keen personal interest and feeling although neither self-protection nor the duty of going on with the work requires him to take such a part. It seems to me that the statute on its face plainly limits the jurisdiction of the judge in this class of cases to those where his personal action is necessary in a strict sense in order to enable him to go on with his work . . .
>
> I think that the sentence from which the petitioner seeks relief was more than an abuse of power. I think it should be found wholly void. I think in the first place that there was no matter pending before the Court in the sense that it must be to make this kind of contempt possible. It is not enough that somebody may hereafter move to have something done. There was nothing then awaiting decision when the petitioner's letter was published . . . But if there had been, and giving the most unfavorable interpretation to all the letter says, I do not see how to misstate past matters of fact of the sort

5. Id. at 423.

> charged here could be said to obstruct the administration of justice.[6]

But the Court's decision seriously obstructs the sense of freedom of expression without which actual freedom of speech and of the press are impossible. These basic considerations were admirably voiced by Judge Learned Hand in dissenting from the opinion in the Circuit Court of Appeals which the Supreme Court has now sustained.

> It is in small encroachments upon the right of free criticism of all the acts of public officials that the real danger lies. If a judge may punish those who directly interfere with possible decisions, remote in time (when the force of the present obloquy has been spent), the line between that and punishment for unseemly or false comment upon past decisions becomes so shadowy as in application to disappear. It will, in effect, be practically impossible to show that the utterer did not have in mind the effect of his words upon similar cases in the future. Especially is this the case if there be added the doctrine that all men are charged with those results of their conduct which are to be reasonably apprehended.[7]

The *Toledo Newspaper* case gave ample warning of the tyrannous power which may be exercised by some 150 federal judicial potentates. But the press and the bar gave little heed. If now the *Craig* case does not rouse us to put an end to an intolerable tyranny cloaking itself behind a perverted application of the power to commit for contempt, the courts will be justified in manifesting their contempt for ancient liberties. The present protest against sending Mr. Craig to jail must not be allowed to spend itself in fulminations. Prompt and ample Congressional relief should follow. A bill should at once be introduced and pressed to passage, intended to accomplish the fol-

6. 263 U.S. at 280–281.
7. 282 Fed. 138, 160 (2d Cir. 1923).

lowing objects couched in language so unequivocal that not even the present majority of the Supreme Court can pervert it:

1. Power of a judge to punish for contempt should be limited exclusively to those cases where "his personal action is necessary in a strict sense in order to enable him to go on with his work."

2. Such a case of contempt should not be heard by the accusing judge but should automatically go before another judge.

The American Judge

The more complicated society the more it depends upon law for its adjustments. That is a truism to which at least lip-service is accorded everywhere. But the application of that truism to the American political system is strangely unappreciated. Ours is necessarily a legalistic country, because our written constitutions, with the history that lies back of them, potentially make of every question, from the affairs of a village to our international relations, not merely difficulties to be adjusted by peaceful processes, which we call law, but legal controversies to be decided by courts. In no other country is the immanence of legal institutions so deep-rooted and so pervasive as with us; correspondingly, in no other country is a critical understanding of legal institutions so indispensable for laymen. Strangely enough, with the exception of Judge Cardozo's exhilarating little volume, *The Nature of the Judicial Process,* and Dean Pound's *Spirit of the Common Law,* this duty of enlightening laymen has hardly been attempted by the profession.

It is to this great end that Judge Andrew A. Bruce addresses himself. "We need to make the law, and especially constitutional law, intelligible to the ordinary intelligent citizen."[1] Especially constitutional law! "The public needs to be informed both as to the nature and the scope and the limitations of the law."[2] Most assuredly! Here is a task, one would suppose, singularly adapted for the rare experience of Judge Bruce. Who better fitted to interpret the legal institutions under which the American democracy is working out its salvation than one who was reared in English institutions, educated in this country, for many years the associate of Jane Addams and Florence Kelley in reconciling law and social needs, a leader among law teachers, the chief justice of a state supreme court? How

Reprinted from a Book Review of Andrew A. Bruce, *The American Judge* (1924) in the *New Republic,* April 23, 1924, with permission. Footnotes supplied by editor.

1. P. 74.
2. P. 171.

then has Judge Bruce, who so clearly discerns the urgency of enlightenment, helped to give the layman understanding of the law?

Laymen think of "law" mostly as it manifests itself in constitutional adjudications, in industrial controversies, and in the administration of criminal justice. The lay emphasis responds to a shrewd instinct. The dominant notes of Judge Bruce's volume confirm the layman's notions as the chief scope of law.

Throughout the book Judge Bruce seeks to convey the impression that "constitutional law" is some authoritative and impersonal deposit of truth which, for all practical purposes, automatically gives answer when acts of legislature or executive are called into question. "Ours is a government of laws and not of men, and the members of the supreme courts are compelled to announce and decide not what they desire but that which the law and the constitution have authorized"[3] is a typical sentence. But no light is shed as to the process by which the courts ascertain what it is that the Constitution has "authorized." The general impression sought to be conveyed puts Judge Bruce's influence behind the mischievous assumption that our judges embody pure reason, that they are set apart from the concerns of the community, regardless of time, place, and circumstances, to become the interpreters of self-determining words with fixed content, yielding their meaning to a process of inexorable reasoning.

Of course Judge Bruce knows better. He knows that judges are not passive interpreters of ready-made "law." He knows that, for the most part and in decisive constitutional cases, they exercise creative power. No attempt is made, however, to enlighten a layman on the complicated process of "interpretation." The judicial process of dealing with words varies with the words dealt with. Some legal words and phrases approach mathematical symbols like π or $\surd$, meaning substantially the same thing to all who have occasion to use them. Other law terms, like "due process" are not symbols, but labels of a complicated process

3. P. 165.

of judgment and choice. There are thus varying degrees of compulsion behind different words, the differences being due to the words themselves, their setting in the text, their history, their relation to other parts of the law, etc., etc. These distinctions, wholly disregarded by Judge Bruce, have profound consequences in decision-making.

Roughly speaking, the Constitution of the United States involved two types of provisions: (1) provisions making specific prohibitions, based on the history of a specific political grievance, or embodying a specific limitation of power in the division of government between States and nation; (2) general standards of fair play and broad divisions of power between States and nation. These two types of constitutional provisions result in two different types of adjudication, because they rest on different sources of material and provoke differences in mental outlook. As to the first class, the definiteness of the terms, the definiteness of their history, the definiteness of their aim, all combine to canalize within narrow limits the scope of judicial review in the rare instances when their meaning is called into question. The result is a part of constitutional law relatively easy of application because it allows comparatively meager play for individual judgment as to policy. But when we come to the second class, to the broad undefined clauses of the Constitution, we are in a decisively different realm of judicial action. The scope of application is largely unrestricted and the room for play of individual judgment as to policy is correspondingly wide. Simple terms of vast content, like "liberty," and phrases like "without due process of law" are the instruments for judgment upon the whole domain of economic, social, and industrial life. The problem is further complicated because we are a federated nation. One set of considerations comes into play when the Supreme Court mediates between the federal government and the States; a totally different set when it sits in judgment upon the social experiments of an individual State.

Surely all this is something that Judge Bruce's "intelligent citizen" ought to be told. Of all this, in his prewar writing, Judge Bruce was not unaware. But his present readers he darkens by fiction and contradiction, tempered with apologetics. We encounter such orthodox casuistry as: "Generally speaking, the courts have not attempted to set statutes aside. They have refused to enforce them."[4] This particular fiction is very respectable. Judge Bruce, after telling us, in effect, that the Supreme Court is the impersonal voice of sovereign law, and really does not "set statutes aside," goes on to tell us that judges sometimes in fact speak for themselves and not for the Constitution but under the guise of the Constitution.

The layman must be puzzled in his effort to understand the mysteries of constitutional law when so readily assured by Judge Bruce that "if the courts have at times exceeded their authority in passing upon the validity of statutes . . . it is doubtful if any lasting harm has come from the unauthorized activity."[5] How long is "lasting" in Judge Bruce's timekeeping? What is "harm" to him, and how does he measure it? One would judge from the general fearsome temper of the book that popular "unrest" is deemed by him a potent "harm." Surely there can be no greater harm than lack of popular confidence in law and in legal institutions; and Judge Bruce himself tells us that it is by this "unauthorized activity" of our courts "that they have created a large measure of the popular distrust which now prevails."[6]

Constitutional issues apart, the most challenged activity of the American judge arises in his use of the injunction in industrial controversies. What light has Judge Bruce here to offer? Just this. The injunction is a "prerogative" which "should never be surrendered or taken away . . . The writ of injunction is the preventive medicine of the law. Surely we are not compelled to stand idly by and see our property demolished and our institutions destroyed. Have not the World War and the failure of Germany to make reparation shown us that an ounce of prevention is worth a pound of cure? Surely it is sometimes wise to prevent the horse from getting out of the barn. Much dis-

4. P. 37.
5. P. 24.
6. P. 57.

cretion is necessary in the exercise of the power to issue the writ of injunction. But the power should certainly be recognized."[7]

Surely, also, Judge Bruce might have told his readers of the experience which lies back of the efforts to restrict the use of injunctions in labor controversies. At least he might have quoted, for instance, the following paragraph from Mr. Justice Brandeis in his famous dissent in the *Arizona Injunction* case:

> It was urged that the real motive in seeking the injunction was not ordinarily to prevent property from being injured nor to protect the owner in its use, but to endow property with active militant power which would make it dominant over men. In other words, that, under the guise of protecting property rights, the employer was seeking sovereign power. And many disinterested men, solicitous only for the public welfare, believed that the law of property was not appropriate for dealing with the forces beneath social unrest; that in this vast struggle it was unwise to throw the power of the state on one side or the other according to principles deduced from that law; that the problem of the control and conduct of industry demanded a solution of its own; and that, pending the ascertainment of new principles to govern industry, it was wiser for the state not to interfere in industrial struggles by the issuance of an injunction.[8]

Judge Bruce writes as though there lay no history of tragic futility between the *Debs* case[9] and the *Wilkerson* injunction.[10] For thirty years, the injunction has been used as a familiar weapon in American industrial conflicts. It does not work. It neither mines coal, nor moves trains, nor makes clothing, nor, above all, does it make for peace. As

7. Pp. 140–141.
8. Truax v. Corrigan, 257 U.S. 312, 368 (1921).
9. In re Debs, 158 U.S. 564 (1895).
10. See Frankfurter and Landis, "Power to Regulate Contempts," 37 *Harv. L. Rev.* 1010, 1101 (1924).

an adjuster of industrial conflicts, the injunction has been a failure. It has been used as a shortcut—but it has not cut anything, except to cut off labor from confidence in the rule of law and of the courts, as its impartial organs. No disinterested student of American industry or of American law can have much doubt that the use of labor injunctions has, predominantly, been a cumulative influence for discord in our national life. Without appeasing, and in fact exacerbating the industrial conflict, judicial intervention in labor controversies through the injunction has planted in the minds of masses of workers, with increasing intensity, the feeling that the courts are the instruments of a partisan policy. This result is inevitable so long as this use of the injunction persists. For the conduct which injunctions in labor cases seek to restrain necessarily involves disputed questions of fact touching men's feelings and motives and opinions. The traditional Anglo-American method for ascertaining such facts is a jury. The social justification of the jury system lies precisely in its utilization of popular cooperation in the enforcement of law. In labor controversy, if anywhere, one would suppose this popular vindication of the law would be resorted to. From the point of view of revivifying a respect for law and regaining order, no less than from any attempt towards decent industrial relations, it is of the essence that the curb upon trade-union action should be administered by the courts only through proceedings in which disputed facts are determined by a jury. Nor is there any just basis in so-called expediency for continuing the disastrous shortcut of the injunction. The direct responsibility of the union for wrongful acts has now been established.[11] Civil redress by the employer can now be had and should be had only through action for damages. So far as acts of violence are concerned, the resources of the State are ample in the criminal law—if it be made effective. Only if trade unions are convicted of wrongful acts not by a single judge but by their fellow citizens—the jury of the vicinage—will it restore belief by the millions of trade-

11. United Mine Workers v. Coronado Co., 259 U.S. 344 (1922).

union workers and their friends in the fairness of law and the impartiality of courts.

This brings us to Judge Bruce's treatment of the administration of criminal justice. In the portions concerning criminal law we have a curious hodge-podge of shallow generalities about social causes of crime, politics, inadequacies of our criminal procedure, and "public opinion," that weary scapegoat for a failure to think clearly and hardily. Not that a good deal of what Judge Bruce says isn't so—if only the reader were made aware of it. But his conclusions, even when sustained by proved analysis, lack perspective, guiding detail, and impact. Here, for instance, is Judge Bruce's summary of the conditions determining law enforcement in this country: "The curse of the American administration of the criminal law, is our system of politics, our spoils system, the fact that the under-world has a vote as well as the upper-world, and above all, the short tenure of office of all our public officials."[12] Let anyone compare this analysis with the following summary by Dean Pound of the defects in our system of criminal justice:

> (1) The transition from rural to urban and thence to metropolitan conditions has been met not by intelligent reconstruction, but by patching and addition of members; (2) lack of continuity in administration; (3) rigidity of organization, making adjustment to the exigencies of rapid growth and exceptional diversity of population impossible; (4) a tendency to perfunctory routine growing out of the foregoing circumstances; (5) division of power and diffused, ill-defined responsibility, making it difficult to hold anyone to account for unsatisfactory results; (6) an assumption of versatility on the part of the officials and subordinates, whereby they are expected to do specialized work offhand, in a system of frequent rotation, without any adequate provision for the specialization involved in the large undertaking of enforcing the criminal law in a modern city; (7) want of

12. Pp. 92–93.

provision for intelligent study of the functioning of administrative machinery, either by those who operate it or by others.[13]

Here we have the kind of diagnosis which is capable of guiding opinion and furnishes blueprints for social construction. Such an analysis of defects suggests the problems for reform, of which the most important are the reshaping of the substantive criminal law, the organization of the administration of justice, adequate provision for petty prosecutions and preventive methods—always remembering, in the words of Mr. Alfred Bettman, "the unescapable influence of the atmosphere, the traditions, the ideals, and the standards of the community itself."[14]

But Judge Bruce is too preoccupied with "selling" the American judge to give a painstaking critique of the problems of present-day law enforcement. The chief aim, apparently, is to clear the courts of all responsibility for the justified discontent with what Senator Root calls "the product" of our judicial system. And so we have an application of most transparent whitewash: "Certain it is that no modern appellate court reverses a judgment unless it is satisfied that a fundamental right has been violated."[15]

In view of his exaltation of our existing system, it is not too surprising, however disheartening, that Judge Bruce "views with alarm" one of the few notable achievements of recent years in procedural reform—the small-claims courts. "Serious dangers are involved in their creation. They are informal and they are presumed to be informal. Being informal they are often arbitrary. They represent and enforce the justice of the beneficent despot rather than that of the established law."[16] Here is a matter vital to the great masses, and vital to continued confidence in law. What is the basis for this condemnation of the actual working of the small-claims courts? The testimony avail-

13. This quotation derives from Pound's 1923 lecture at Brown University, the substance of which later appeared in Pound, *Criminal Justice in America* (1930).

14. *Cleveland Crime Survey* 225 (1922).

15. P. 178.

16. P. 190.

able is all the other way, as evidenced by the reports at last year's meeting of the American Bar Association and in the report now in preparation for the Carnegie Foundation by Reginald H. Smith,[17] bringing down to date his *Justice and the Poor.*

One might go on applying the scientific scalpel to almost every page of this book. It is not a congenial task and would only add cumulative evidence to what must be abundantly clear. The book is neither scholarly nor scientific. An exposition of technical problems for laymen makes a particularly exacting demand on scholarship. The paraphernalia and pomp of learning must be dispensed with; learning must be distilled in draughts at once pure and potent. But rhetoric is not the layman's substitute for technical jargon, and a problem cannot be simplified by expression of its difficulties. Judge Bruce's pages are happily unencumbered by any heavy apparatus of legal learning; unfortunately, they show no traces that scholars have greatly labored in fields from which he brings reports to laymen. If this book were the only witness, Mr. Justice Brandeis, Judge Cardozo, Mr. Justice Holmes, Dean Pound, and Dean Wigmore (to mention but a few) might as well not have written. Much as the flavor and substance of scholarship is wanting, the book is still less infected with the scientific spirit. Fear permeates its pages. The sad truth is that Judge Bruce made for the cyclone cellar after his grievous experience when North Dakota went nonpartisan, and this book was largely written in the cyclone cellar. A fruitful book in social science cannot be written by a pen moved by fear and dipped in a grievance. And so we have a book by two Bruces, the prewar, Hull House Bruce, and the postwar, Red fearing Bruce. Both wrote—but with a very different temper, with a very different outlook. In the present book, these two streams of writing are strangely blended. Two different whiskeys do not make a good cocktail simply because one is bitter. Judge Bruce set out to "save the country" instead of enlightening it to save itself.

17. Smith, *Justice and the Poor* (3d ed. 1924).

The Red Terror of Judicial Reform

It is frequently charged that this tribunal is tyrannical. If the Constitution of the United States be tyranny; if the rule that no one shall be convicted of crime save by a jury of his peers; that no orders of nobility shall be granted; that slavery shall not be permitted to exist in any state or territory; that no one shall be deprived of life, liberty or property without due process of law; if these and many other provisions made by the people be tyranny, then the Supreme Court when it makes decisions in accordance with these principles of our fundamental law is tyrannical. Otherwise it is exercising the power of government for the preservation of liberty. The fact is that the Constitution is the source of our freedom. Maintaining it, interpreting it and declaring it are the only methods by which the Constitution can be preserved and our liberties guaranteed . . .

Some people do not seem to understand fully the purpose of our constitutional guaranties. When this country was set up and the Constitution of the United States was written we gave to the Americans of that day and all who might come after them certain fundamental rights that could never be taken away . . .

If Congress should pass a law tomorrow denying to you, or to the people of this country, freedom of your person, should pass a law tomorrow denying the right of assembly; if it should pass a law tomorrow denying to you the freedom of your person, or visit upon you punishment except as a penalty for crime, you would be entirely within your rights if you disregarded it, and if you were arrested for its violation any judge in all this country who was faithful to his oath would release you . . .

I deny that there is any such thing as despotic power in these United States, in Presidents, or governors, or courts, or congresses, or legislatures. There must be in this country some power to which

Reprinted from an unsigned editorial in the *New Republic,* October 1, 1924, with permission. Footnotes supplied by editor.

pose of our constitutional restraints. They are not protecting the majority, either in or out of the Congress. They can protect themselves with their votes. We have adopted a written Constitution in order that the minority, even down to the most insignificant individual, might have their rights protected.

—President Coolidge, speaking at Baltimore, Md., September 6, 1924.

the American citizen can appeal when these sacred rights of his are invaded.

—Mr. Davis, speaking at Dubuque, Ia., September 5, 1924.

Republican papers are entitled to point out the identity of views between the Republican and Democratic candidates on the issues raised by judicial control over legislation. It is a mere coincidence that the President and Mr. Davis spoke on this subject at the same time; but it is of the deepest significance that they expressed the same beliefs. The two speeches reflected a common mind, and they might have been written by the same pen. What meaning would they convey to a foreign student of our affairs who aimed at a disinterested understanding of vital American problems? If such an inquirer were confined for understanding to the Coolidge and Davis utterances, he would only be told that some precious aspects of human liberty were formulated by the American Constitution and that the Supreme Court of the United States is their vigilant and effective guardian. Nothing more appearing in the explanations of the President of the United States and his contender for the presidency, speaking with the added apparent authority of eminence at the bar, our foreign seeker for truth would be wholly baffled to understand why traditional liberties, or the means of rendering them effective, should find opposition. Naturally he would assume that only malevolence compounded with ignorance can be the enemy. This is, of course, precisely the aim of the Coolidge and Davis speeches.

One expects nothing better on this profoundly important issue from Mr. Coolidge. He doubtless honestly entertains all his fears and phantasies about constitutional law in action. The famous author of "The Reds in Our Colleges" knows no better.[1] But what is one to say of John W. Davis? He cannot be unfamiliar with the judicial record which has kept this issue in American politics, with vigorous insistence, during the last thirty years. Surely he must know that neither William J. Bryan nor Theodore Roosevelt was a malevolent foreigner bent on destroying Americanism; he must know that these two leaders expressed deep grievances in their attacks upon judicial abuses, whatever one may think of the remedies which they proposed. Does Mr. Davis's conscience really permit him to miseducate his hearers, as he did in his Dubuque speech, on a subject so vital to the maintenance of confidence in the essentials of the American Constitution? For it is inconceivable that Mr. Davis is unaware of the fact that by grave omissions in his treatment of the courts and the Constitution he conveyed a mutilated and, therefore, untrue picture.

Of course, our constitutional mechanism requires an independent Supreme Court. In all governments there must be organs for finality of decision. In a federated government like ours, with powers distributed in necessarily broad terms under a written constitution, a free court is the most dependable instrument for adjusting controversies between the constituent States and the nation, and between individual States. It does not, however, follow that the Supreme Court should be the arbiter for all controversies in State and nation. At once, therefore, distinctions must be taken as to the power of the Supreme Court, and the wisdom of the grant of power, in the different classes of cases over which the Court has jurisdiction. Under the commerce clause the Supreme Court maintains the equilibrium between States and nation by determining when a State has sought to project its authority beyond its State lines and when, on the other hand, Congress has interfered with the purely domestic concerns of

1. See Coolidge, "Enemies of the Republic," *Delineator,* p. 4 (June 1921).

the individual States. Here is a power that must be left with the Supreme Court although its exercise is not at all a necessitous deduction of "principles" hidden in the Constitution, to which only the Supreme Court has the code. The simple truth of the matter is that decisions of the Court denying or sanctioning the exercise of federal power, as in the first child labor case,[2] largely involve a judgment about practical matters, and not at all any esoteric knowledge of the Constitution. Therefore it is that the decisions of the Court must be subjected to relentless scrutiny to save them from pedantry and sterility, as the unconscious rationalizations of the economic and social biases of individual Justices. Nevertheless, the power of the Supreme Court to mediate between the States and the nation in interpreting the commerce clause must be left intact.

> I do not think [Mr. Justice Holmes has said] the United States would come to an end if we lost our power to declare an Act of Congress void. I do think the union would be imperiled if we could not make that declaration as to the laws of the several states. For one in my place sees how often a local policy prevails with those who are not trained to national views and how often action is taken that embodies what the Commerce Clause was meant to end.[3]

The next broad class of constitutional provisions which comes before the Court involves specific prohibitions upon the legislative power both of the States and of Congress and is intended to protect individual rights. These guarantees are based upon the history of a specific political grievance, or they embody a specific limitation of power in the formulation of governmental powers which came out of the Philadelphia convention. These are the features of the Constitution that Messrs. Coolidge and Davis disingenuously dwell upon, because, in their judicial construction,

2. Hammer v. Dagenhart, 247 U.S. 251 (1918).
3. Holmes, *Collected Legal Papers* 295–296 (1920).

they give rise to relatively little difficulty. The definiteness of the terms of these specific provisions, the definiteness of their history, the definiteness of their aims, all combine to limit narrowly the scope of judicial review in the rare instances when their meaning is called into question. Only occasionally is doubt raised as to whether "a fact tried by a jury" has been "re-examined in any court of the United States" otherwise than "according to the rules of the common law"; or whether a tax is "laid upon articles exported from any state"; or whether a crime is "infamous"; or whether the prohibition against "unreasonable searches and seizures" is violated. Here, in other words, is a part of constitutional law relatively easy of application because it allows comparatively meager play for individual judgment as to policy. In this field, economic and social conflicts play little or no part. Even here, however, the record of the Supreme Court in interpreting the guarantee of "freedom of speech" shows how, with rare exceptions, passions lay prey even the courts.

But there are two clauses of the Constitution which present very different problems of statecraft—the "due process" clause of the Fifth Amendment, a limitation upon the federal government, and the "due process of law" and the denial of the "equal protection of the laws" clauses of the Fourteenth Amendment, limiting state action and subjecting every local act of every State to the scrutiny of the Supreme Court at Washington. President Coolidge in his innocence assumes that there are settled "principles" and fixed rules by which these provisions are specifically applied, all, as he thinks, "with the sole purpose of protecting the freedom of the individual, of guarding his earnings, his home, his life." Doubtless Mr. Coolidge would say that courts in declaring unconstitutional workmen's compensation laws,[4] the ten-hour law for bakers,[5] laws prohibiting discrimination against trade union workers,[6] the minimum wage law for women,[7] as violative of due process, did so "with the sole purpose of

4. Ives v. South Buffalo Ry. Co., 201 N.Y. 271 (1911).
5. Lochner v. New York, 198 U.S. 45 (1905).
6. Adair v. United States, 208 U.S. 161 (1908).
7. Adkins v. Children's Hospital, 261 U.S. 525 (1923).

protecting the freedom of the individual, of guarding his earnings, his home, his life." Mr. Davis evidently knows better, for he is significantly silent about the "due process" and the "equal protection of the laws" clauses and the actual results of their judicial interpretation. Mr. Davis must know that these broad "guarantees" in favor of the individual are expressed in words so undefined, either by their intrinsic meaning, or by history, or by tradition, that they leave the individual Justice free, if indeed they do not actually compel him, to fill in the vacuum with his own controlling notions of economic, social, and industrial facts with reference to which they are invoked. These judicial judgments are thus bound to be determined by the experience, the environment, the fears, the imagination of the different justices. For it cannot be too often made clear that the meaning of phrases like "due process of law," and of simple terms like "liberty" and "property," is not revealed within the Constitution; their meaning is derived from without. As a great legal scholar has put it, social legislation of the twentieth century is declared unconstitutional by putting eighteenth-century Adam Smith into the Constitution.[8] As an outstanding and candid member of the federal bench, Judge Charles M. Hough, reminds us, due process of law is a phrase of "convenient vagueness."[9] "Convenient" for whom or to what end?

These are the clauses—"due process" and "equal protection of the laws"—which have brought forth the most abundant crop of judicial nullifications, and through which the most effective barrier has been raised against utilizing the inherent flexibilities of our Constitution for the adaptation of our traditional legal system to modern needs. The activity of our courts in bending the "conveniently vague" language of due process to the dominant service of vested property interests is a relatively recent tendency of our constitutional law. The Fourteenth Amendment, "politically intent on the Negro, and with nothing else in mind," afforded the courts the opportunity, about forty years ago, to curb those tendencies towards economic and social readjustments of which the Granger

8. See Pound, "Liberty of Contract," 18 *Yale L.J.* 454 (1909).
9. Hough, "Due Process—Today," 32 *Harv. L. Rev.* 218 (1919).

Movement was the beginning. Until the Fourteenth Amendment was written into the Constitution each State was the exclusive judge of its domestic life. The Fourteenth Amendment, as interpreted by judges fearful of the new economic and social ferment, subjected the detailed local affairs of the forty-eight States to the supervision, ultimately, of five men at Washington.

For nearly a hundred years the due process clause restricting the federal government had lain inactive or strictly confined in the Fifth Amendment. The exuberant application given to the clause in the Fourteenth Amendment was now carried over to the Fifth Amendment, and federal as well as State legislation had to meet the growingly unknown and unknowable terrors of due process. And so we reach, for the present at least, the culmination of a long line of legislative fatalities in the decision striking down the District of Columbia minimum wage law for women which led even Chief Justice Taft in his dissenting opinion to speak out: "But it is not the function of this Court to hold congressional acts invalid simply because they are passed to carry out economic views which the Court believes to be unwise or unsound."[10]

The sophisticated suggestion is sometimes made that the Supreme Court has invalidated only a few laws, compared with the total which has passed muster. It isn't true! A numerical tally of the cases does not tell the tale. In the first place, all laws are not of the same importance. We are here concerned with matters that involve qualitative judgment. Secondly, a single decision may decide the fate of a great body of legislation, as was true of *Coppage* v. *Kansas,*[11] declaring invalid a Kansas law prohibiting discrimination against trade unionists and, more recently, in the District of Columbia minimum wage case. Moreover, the discouragement of legislative efforts in fields related to that involved in a particular adjudication and the general weakening of the sense of legislative responsibility have wrought incalculable harm to the fruitful

10. 261 U.S. at 562.
11. 236 U.S. 1 (1915).

development of American political life. These are the themes upon which the electorate is entitled to hear from a presidential candidate who professes, as does Mr. Davis, progressivism as well as candor in public discussion, and whose past peculiarly charges him with the responsibility of educating the American people to an understanding of the actual workings of our constitutional system. Unfortunately, Mr. Davis on the stump only repeats the conservative platitudes which last year he expressed as president of the American Bar Association.

Angling for Progressive votes Mr. Davis withheld on the stump one illuminating comment which he made as president of the American Bar Association: "Much of the current discontent is caused perhaps by the publication of dissenting opinions which serve to fan the flame of public distrust."[12] Evidently, the real culprits are men like Mr. Justice Hughes, Mr. Justice Holmes, Mr. Justice Brandeis, and occasionally even Chief Justice Taft (as in the minimum wage case), who, from time to time, expressed their objection to the slaughtering of social legislation on the altar of the dogma of "liberty of contract." Criticism of dissents is not to be wondered at in one who emphasizes, as did Mr. Davis in his Labor Day speech, "the right of free contract." It is this doctrine which the Supreme Court has used as a sword with which to slay most important social legislation and to deny the means of freedom to those least free. To invoke it is to indulge in sterile abstractions and cruelly to shut one's eyes to cases like *Lochner* v. *New York*,[13] *Adair* v. *United States*,[14] *Coppage* v. *Kansas*,[15] *Adams* v. *Tanner*,[16] *Hitchman Coal & Coke Company* v. *Mitchell*,[17] *Truax* v. *Corrigan*,[18] *Adkins* v. *Children's Hospital*.[19] Mr. Davis is silent about such decisions, but he cannot be ignorant of them.

12. Davis, "Present Day Problems," 9 *A.B.A.J.* 553, 557 (1923).
13. *Supra* note 5.
14. *Supra* note 6.
15. *Supra* note 11.
16. 244 U.S. 590 (1917).
17. 245 U.S. 229 (1917).
18. 257 U.S. 312 (1921).
19. *Supra* note 7.

The contribution of Senator La Follette and the Progressive platform lies in the ventilation of this grave issue rather than in the specific remedies proposed. In this respect the Progressive campaign is not unlike that of 1912. No student of American constitutional law can have the slightest doubt that Mr. Roosevelt's vigorous challenge of judicial abuses was mainly responsible for a temporary period of liberalism which followed in the interpretation of the due process clauses, however abhorrent the remedy of judicial recall appeared to both bar and bench. The public opinion which the Progressive campaign aroused subtly penetrated the judicial atmosphere. In cases involving social-industrial issues, public opinion, if adequately informed and sufficiently sustained, seeps into Supreme Court decisions. Roosevelt shrewdly observed: "I may not know much about law, but I do know one can put the fear of God into judges." The "Fear of God" was needed to make itself felt on the bench in 1912. The "fear of God" very much needs to make itself felt in 1924. Let any disinterested student of constitutional law read the decision of the Supreme Court last spring invalidating legislation fixing a standard rate for a loaf of bread and deny that we have never had a more irresponsible period in the history of that Court.

But the "fear of God" is too capricious, too intermittent. We need most the wisdom of man. What is needed is a thorough understanding of our constitutional system in action, as a basis of determining what is the proper scope of judicial control, and what conditions are most likely to insure the exercise of this tremendous power by ordinary mortals, to avoid at once the abuses of tyranny and the timidities of dependence. Particularly does it behoove Progressives not to content themselves with mere abuse of abuses, nor to fall back upon mechanical contrivances when dealing with a process where mechanics can play but a very small part. An informed study of the work of the Supreme Court of the United States will probably lead to the conclusion that no nine men are wise enough and good enough to be entrusted with the power which the unlimited provisions of the due process clauses confer. We have had fifty years of experiment with the Fourteenth Amendment, and the centralizing authority lodged with the Supreme Court over the domestic affairs of forty-eight widely different States is an authority which it simply cannot discharge with safety either to itself or to the States. The due process clauses ought to go. It is highly significant that not a single constitution framed for English-speaking countries since the Fourteenth Amendment has embodied its provisions. And one would indeed be lacking in a sense of humor to suggest that life, liberty, or property is not amply protected in Canada, Australia, South Africa. By eliminating this class of cases the Supreme Court would really be relieved of a contentiously political burden. It would free itself to meet more adequately the jurisdiction which would remain and which ought to remain. The Court would still exercise the most delicate and powerful function in our dual system of government. To discharge it wisely, it needs a constant play of informed criticism by the professional as well as the lay press. This, in turn, implies an alertly progressive bar, the product of a lively spirit of legal education at our universities, and a public opinion trustful of the workings of our judiciary because the trust is justified by its exercise.

The Lawless Judge

Many influences, carefully fostered by persistent propaganda, have erected our judges, particularly the federal judiciary, into a sacred priesthood. Public criticism of their conduct, even when it involves obvious public interests and not merely decisions on purely technical questions, has been rendered increasingly difficult by the subservience of the press. An attitude of idolatry which supports the judiciary as the most dependable safeguard of things as they are, regards scrutiny of the courts as attacks on the holy of holies and critics like Roosevelt and La Follette as traitors to the Republic. The press, confining criticisms largely to Congressional activities, has thus largely become atrophied as an adequate commentator on the terrific part the courts play in the nation's affairs. And so we need not wonder that newspapers receive with silence the rebuke of four federal judges by the Supreme Court itself for conduct characterized as "harsh," "unfair," and "oppressive"—the same press that so vociferously applauded the *Craig* decision[1] over a year ago.

The abusive exercise of the tyrannical power to punish for contempt has at last aroused the Supreme Court to check the exuberance of the lower federal courts. The facts are set forth at length in the opinion of the Chief Justice in the case of *Cooke* v. *United States,*[2] decided April 13, speaking for a unanimous Court. Clay Cooke was the attorney of a litigant named Walker, who was defendant in a series of suits before the United States District Court at Fort Worth, Texas. After a heavy verdict against him, while the matter was still before Judge Wilson, Walker by direction of Cooke delivered to Judge Wilson, in the privacy of his chamber, a letter signed by Cooke, in which the latter accused the judge of personal prejudice against Walker and asked Judge Wilson not to

Reprinted from an unsigned editorial in the *New Republic,* May 6, 1925, with permission. Footnotes supplied by editor.

1. Craig v. Hecht, 263 U.S. 255 (1923). See "Lèse Majesté Mayer," *supra.*
2. 267 U.S. 517 (1925).

act in the other cases pending against Walker. This happened on February 15, 1923. Eleven days later Judge Wilson ordered the arrest of Cooke and Walker. After a brutal travesty of a trial, to the facts of which we shall at once return, Judge Wilson, the same day, sentenced both Cooke and Walker to jail for thirty days—having first been admonished by his counsel acting as "friend of the court," against the legality of adding a fine of five hundred dollars included in the original sentences. The Circuit Court of Appeals for the Fifth Circuit, consisting of Judges Walker, Bryan, and Grubb, reversed Walker's sentence, and affirmed that of his lawyer.[3] The Supreme Court now has reversed also Cooke's sentence.

The whole proceedings were initiated in violation of due process of law: "it was harsh under the circumstances to order the arrest" is the ruling of the Supreme Court. A rule to show cause was the orderly procedure. What began in illegality proceeded with brutality. Let Chief Justice Taft summarize the facts:

> After the Court elicited from the petitioner [Cooke] the admission that he had written the letter, the Court refused him time to secure and consult counsel, prepare his defense and call witnesses, and this although the Court itself had taken time to call in counsel as a friend of the Court. The presence of the United States District Attorney was also secured by the Court on the ground that it was a criminal case.
>
> The Court proceeded on the theory that the admission that the petitioner had written the letter foreclosed evidence or argument. In cases like this where the intention with which acts of contempt have been committed must necessarily and properly have an important bearing on the degree of guilt and the penalty which should be imposed, the court can not exclude evidence in mitigation. It is a proper part of the defense. There was a suggestion in one of the remarks of the petitioner to the court that while he had dictated the letter he had not

3. 295 Fed. 292 (5th Cir. 1923).

> read it carefully and that he had trusted to the advice of his partner in sending it, but he was not given a chance to call witnesses or to make a full statement on this point. He was interrupted by the court or the counsel of the court in every attempted explanation. On the other hand, when the court came to pronounce sentence, it commented on the conduct of both the petitioner and his clients in making scandalous charges in the pleadings against officials of the court and charges of a corrupt conspiracy against the trustee and referee in bankruptcy and of employing a detective to shadow jurymen while in charge of the marshal, and afterwards to detect bribery of them, in proof of which the court referred to a sworn statement of the detective in its hands, which had not been submitted to the petitioner or his client. When Walker questioned this, the court directed the marshal to prevent further interruption. It was quite clear that the court considered the facts thus announced as in aggravation of the contempt. Yet no opportunity had been given to the contemnors even to hear these new charges of the court, much less to meet or explain them, before the sentence. We think the procedure pursued was unfair and oppressive to the petitioner.[4]

The issues raised by this case reach far deeper than the misconduct of a single autocratic judge. For one thing Judge Wilson is not the first offender. The last few years have seen several manifestations of arbitrary conduct, cloaking itself behind a perverted exercise of the power to punish for contempt. Moreover, it is an ominous sign that the three appellate judges should have sustained Judge Wilson's behavior which the Supreme Court has now so severely rebuked—thereby rebuking the appellate court. The difficulty is inherent in the power that is vested in a federal judge under the interpretation of existing federal law, to be accuser and judge in his own case, albeit that

4. 267 U.S. at 537–538.

formally the case be not his but his court's, which is equivalent to himself. The Supreme Court has now admonished the federal judges to exercise this dangerous power with what Mr. Dooley calls "gintleminly restraint." We again quote the Chief Justice:

> Another feature of this case seems to call for remark. The power of contempt which a judge must have and exercise in protecting the due and orderly administration of justice and in maintaining the authority and dignity of the court is most important and indispensable. But its exercise is a delicate one and care is needed to avoid arbitrary or oppressive conclusions. This rule of caution is more mandatory where the contempt charged has in it the element of personal criticism or attack upon the judge. The judge must banish the slightest personal impulse to reprisal, but he should not bend backward and injure the authority of the court by too great leniency. The substitution of another judge would avoid either tendency but it is not always possible. Of course where acts of contempt are palpably aggravated by a personal attack upon the judge in order to drive the judge out of the case for ulterior reasons, the scheme should not be permitted to succeed. But attempts of this kind are rare. All of such cases, however, present difficult questions for the judge. All we can say upon the whole matter is that where conditions do not make it impracticable, or where the delay may not injure public or private right, a judge called upon to act in a case of contempt by personal attack upon him, may, without flinching from his duty, properly ask that one of his fellow judges take his place.
>
> The case before us is one in which the issue between the judge and the parties has come to involve marked personal feeling that did not make for an impartial and calm judicial consideration and conclusion, as the statement of the proceedings abundantly shows. We think, therefore, that when this case again reaches the District Court to which it must be remanded, the judge who

> imposed the sentence herein should invite the senior circuit judge of the circuit to assign another judge to sit in the second hearing of the charge against the petitioner.[5]

Undoubtedly the Supreme Court's disposition of the *Cooke* case will bring moderation. The federal courts have been feeling their oats since the decision in the *Toledo News-Bee* case,[6] in 1918, reinforced by the outcome of the *Craig* case. The *Cooke* case marks a turning point. But it does not go far enough. The situation should not be allowed to rest here. Quite the contrary. The *Cooke* case only proves the need for remedial legislation—not the less so when it is recalled that the Supreme Court's review of contempt proceedings is a matter of grace and not of right. The great mischief of the *Toledo News-Bee* decision must be rectified. Nearly a hundred years ago, as a result of judicial abuse, Congress strictly defined the power of federal courts to punish for contempt. "The said courts," reads the act of Congress, "shall have power . . . to punish . . . contempts of their authority: Provided, That such power to punish contempts shall not be construed to extend to any cases except the misbehavior of any person in their presence, or so near thereto as to obstruct the administration of justice."[7] Surely the plain English of this restricts the exercise of a power which the greatest judges agree to be peculiarly liable to abuse and willful in its practical operations to conduct which positively interferes with a court at work.

But in the *Toledo News-Bee* case, rendered at the height of the war, the act of Congress was construed away. The power of courts to punish misbehavior "in their presence, or so near thereto as to obstruct the administration of justice" was held, by a majority, to mean anything uttered anywhere having a "tendency" to obstruct—a standard vague enough to terrorize, considering the power to apply

5. Id. at 539.
6. Toledo Newspaper Co. v. United States, 247 U.S. 402 (1918).
7. Act of March 2, 1831, 21st Cong., 2d Sess.

the standard. This decision is intolerable, for reasons made clear in Mr. Justice Holmes's dissent:

> When it is considered how contrary it is to our practice and ways of thinking for the same person to be accuser and sole judge in a matter which, if he be sensitive, may involve strong personal feeling, I should expect the power to be limited by the necessities of the case to "insure order and decorum in their presence" . . . And when the words of the statute are read it seems to me that the limit is too plain to be construed away. To my mind they point and point only to the present protection of the Court from actual interference, and not to postponed retribution for lack of respect for its dignity . . .[8]

The legislation called for by the *Toledo News–Bee* decision has been too long delayed. Experience has accumulated since 1918 to prove that the accusing judge cannot be left to sit in judgment on the accused contemner. The next Congress should promptly formulate, in effective legal language, a law which will make two indispensable changes in the power of the federal Courts:

1. The authority of a judge to punish for contempt should be strictly limited to cases where "his personal action is necessary in a strict sense in order to enable him to go on with his work."

2. Such a case of contempt should not be disposed of by the accusing judge (who may temporarily order the confinement of a contemner) but should automatically go before another judge. Here is a program for immediate judicial reform which no party can wisely oppose.

8. 247 U.S. at 423.

Can the Supreme Court Guarantee Toleration?

In 1922 Oregon passed an Education Act with "the manifest purpose," in the language of the Supreme Court of the United States, "to compel general attendance at public schools by normal children, between eight and sixteen, who have not completed the eighth grade."[1] The act was to become effective September 1, 1926. Two years before the new dispensation became operative, two private schools—a Catholic institution and a military academy—sought to enjoin the future enforcement of the act. This was the legal machinery by which the Supreme Court was enabled to invalidate the notorious Oregon legislation. Inasmuch as our legal system affords judicial relief only when a plaintiff shows some direct personal grievance, it was necessary to find some present threatened interest of the Society of Sisters and the Hill Military Academy to justify the issuance of an injunction against the enforcement of a law which would not come into being for two years. This it is that led the Supreme Court to find as the immediate basis of the claims of the plaintiffs in the Oregon cases the so-called property interests of the two institutions, now endangered because of the necessity of making long-term contracts. The plaintiffs' property interest gave the court "jurisdiction"; it has also led to an undue emphasis in the reports of, and comments upon, the Oregon decision.

The offense of the law was a much more far-reaching one. It is summed up in the following sentence of Mr. Justice McReynolds' opinion: "The fundamental theory of liberty upon which all governments in this Union repose excludes any general power of the State to standardize its children by forcing them to accept instruction from public teachers only."[2] Thus comes to an end the effort to regiment the mental life of Americans through coerced public school instruction. Two years ago the Supreme

Reprinted from an unsigned editorial in the *New Republic*, June 17, 1925, with permission. Footnotes supplied by editor.

1. Pierce v. Society of Sisters, 268 U.S. 510, 531 (1925).
2. Id. at 535.

Court invalidated legislation ultimately rooted in the same attitude of intolerance,[3] which led Nebraska, Iowa, and Ohio to prohibit the teaching of any other modern language except English in any school, public or private, during the tender years of youth. And perhaps within two years the Supreme Court will exercise its veto against the Bryan movement already embodied in Tennessee law which finds the test of truth in Bible stories.[4]

The Oregon decision, like its Nebraska forerunner, in and of itself, gives just cause for rejoicing. The Supreme Court did immediate service on behalf of the essential spirit of liberalism. It put the quietus on two striking manifestations of postwar obscurantism. But the Oregon case again opens up two wider issues. It raises a new consideration of the Supreme Court's function in the American political scheme. It calls for a more rigorous appraisal of the actual encouragement to liberalism afforded by judicial nullification of anti-liberal legislation.

Great argument is drawn from both the Oregon and the earlier Nebraska case for the beneficent value inhering in the scope of judicial review over the social legislation of the States by the United States Supreme Court. But, of course, the Oregon case alone does not tell the tale. It is only one in a series, which has been spun profusely out of the fateful words of the Fourteenth Amendment. "No state shall . . . deprive any person of life, liberty, or property without due process of law" are the vague words which hold the power of life and death over State action. These words mean what the shifting personnel of the United States Supreme Court from time to time makes them mean. The inclination of a single Justice, the tip of his mind—or his fears—determines the opportunity of a much-needed social experiment to survive, or frustrates, at least for a long time, intelligent attempt to deal with a social evil. Equally, of course, these words may be availed of, as is shown in the Oregon case, to stifle certainly for the moment the recrudescence of intolerance. Before

3. Meyer v. Nebraska, 262 U.S. 390 (1923).

4. The Supreme Court did not "exercise" this "veto" until 1968. See Epperson v. Arkansas, 393 U.S. 97 (1968).

one can find in the Oregon case proof of the social value of the Supreme Court's scope of judicial review a balance must be struck of all the cases that have been decided under the Fourteenth Amendment. In rejoicing over the Nebraska and the Oregon cases, we must not forget that a heavy price has to be paid for these occasional services to liberalism. The New York bakeshop case,[5] the invalidation of anti-trade union laws,[6] the sanctification of the injunction in labor cases,[7] the veto of minimum wage legislation,[8] are not wiped out by the Oregon decision. They weigh heavily in any full accounting of the gains and losses to our national life due to the Supreme Court's control of legislation by the States that does not involve an arbitrant between State and national powers, such as arises when purely State legislation encroaches upon the commerce powers of the federal government. No calculus has yet been invented to make such a precise accounting.

For ourselves, we regard the cost of this power of the Supreme Court on the whole as greater than its gains. After all, the hysteria and chauvinism that forbade the teaching of German in Nebraska schools may subside, and with its subsidence bring repeal of the silly measure; the narrow margin by which the Oregon law was carried in 1922 may, with invigorated effort on the part of the liberal forces, result in its repeal, at least by a narrow margin. But when the Supreme Court strikes down legislation directed against trade unions, or enshrines the labor injunction into the Constitution, or denies to women in industry the meager protection of minimum wage legislation, we are faced with action more far-reaching, because ever so much more durable and authoritative than even the most mischievous of repealable state legislation.

And this brings us to consider the intrinsic promotion of the liberal spirit by the Supreme Court's invalidation

5. Lochner v. New York, 198 U.S. 45 (1905).

6. Adair v. United States, 208 U.S. 161 (1908); Coppage v. Kansas, 236 U.S. 1 (1915).

7. Truax v. Corrigan, 257 U.S. 312 (1921).

8. Adkins v. Children's Hospital, 261 U.S. 525 (1917).

of illiberal legislation. It must never be forgotten that our constant preoccupation with the constitutionality of legislation rather than its wisdom tends to preoccupation of the American mind with a false value. Even the most rampant worshiper of judicial supremacy admits that wisdom and justice are not the tests of constitutionality. Even the extreme right of the Supreme Court occasionally sustain laws which they abominate. But the tendency of focusing attention on constitutionality is to make constitutionality synonymous with propriety; to regard a law as all right so long as it is "constitutional." Such an attitude is a great enemy of liberalism. Particularly in legislation affecting freedom of thought and freedom of speech much that is highly illiberal would be clearly constitutional. Reliance for the most precious interests of civilization, therefore, must be found outside of their vindication under the guarantees of the Constitution— particularly as those guarantees are likely to be construed in the future as they have been in the past. It is not without significance that, much as he undoubtedly disliked the mischievous policy of the laws prohibiting the teaching of foreign languages, Mr. Justice Holmes found it necessary to dissent in the Nebraska school law case. And in the Oregon case the Supreme Court has temptingly indicated to those bent on coercion how much room for mischief there is still left under the aegis of the Constitution:

> No question is raised concerning the power of the State reasonably to regulate all schools, to inspect, supervise and examine them, their teachers and pupils; to require that all children of proper age attend some school, that teachers shall be of good moral character and patriotic disposition, that certain studies plainly essential to good citizenship must be taught, and that nothing be taught which is manifestly inimical to the public welfare.[9]

We need not labor the ambiguities which lurk in such loose phrases as "patriotic disposition" or "studies plainly

9. 268 U.S. at 534.

essential to good citizenship." Here is ample room for the patrioteers to roll in their Trojan horses. And here is ample warning to the liberal forces that the real battles of liberalism are not won in the Supreme Court. To a large extent the Supreme Court, under the guise of constitutional interpretation of words whose contents are derived from the disposition of the Justices, is the reflector of that impalpable but controlling thing, the general drift of public opinion. Only a persistent, positive translation of the liberal faith into the thoughts and acts of the community is the real reliance against the unabated temptation to straightjacket the human mind.

The Case of Anita Whitney

For five years the name of Anita Whitney has intermittently come to the front in news dispatches, as one phase after another of her case was passed, and her entrance into San Quentin Penitentiary approached. On October 19 the United States Supreme Court declined jurisdiction[1] and the last avenue of escape has been closed. There remains nothing between Miss Whitney and a prison term except pardon by the governor of California.

The case of Miss Whitney grew out of the legal terrorism practiced, under cover of the excitement of war and the fear of revolution, against workers who sought to improve their condition. The I.W.W., which had secured notable improvement in the status of labor in the Northwest and on the Pacific coast, was especially the object of repressive measures. Special legislation was passed to outlaw the organization; members were imprisoned; and in some places, as at Tulsa and Centralia, mob violence was let loose against them with the connivance of the authorities. In California a criminal syndicalism act was passed according to which

> Any person who . . . organizes or assists in organizing, or is or knowingly becomes a member of, any organization, society, group or assemblage of persons organized or assembled to advocate, teach or aid and abet criminal syndicalism . . . is guilty of a felony and punishable by imprisonment in the state prison not less than one nor more than fourteen years.[2]

The I.W.W. is held by California courts to be an organization advocating criminal syndicalism within the mean-

Reprinted from an unsigned editorial in the *New Republic,* November 4, 1925, with permission. Footnotes supplied by editor.

1. 269 U.S. 530 (1925). Rehearing was granted on December 14, 1925. 269 U.S. 538 (1925). The judgment was affirmed on the merits in 1927. Whitney v. California, 274 U.S. 357 (1927). Mr. Justice Brandeis's classic statement on freedom of speech is to be found in his concurring opinion in this case. Id. at 372.
2. 274 U.S. at 359–360.

ing of the act. There are at present seventy-two members serving sentences for the crime of merely belonging to the organization. Some of these men were arrested when they confessed membership in order to testify to the true nature and purposes of the I.W.W. at the trial of their fellows. Miss Whitney's membership in the organization came about through her interest in the effort to improve the condition of workers of which the I.W.W. was the most prominent representative on the Pacific coast. It is absurd to imagine that she would have joined that organization or any other for the purpose of "commission of crime, sabotage, or unlawful methods of terrorism as a means of accomplishing a change in industrial ownership or control." Indeed Miss Whitney was known for her outspoken advocacy of political means of securing a change in the social order as opposed to revolutionary or direct action. Her trial on four other counts which charged personal participation in criminal practices failed of conviction. Her only crime was membership in a proscribed organization, a revival, as the American Civil Liberties Union points out, of the medieval doctrine of guilt by association.

It is regrettable that the Supreme Court did not see its way clear to accepting jurisdiction in the case. As it is, the country will be spared the humiliating spectacle of a woman whose whole life has been devoted to the cause of her fellow men being punished by them for actions springing directly out of her self-devotion only if the governor of California grants a pardon. To this end those who believe in a liberal interpretation of civil rights are asked to write to Governor Friend W. Richardson, asking for this action on the ground of humanity and public policy, and to engage the support of organizations and the press to this end.

The Supreme Court as Legislator

In these pages we have frequently called attention to the enormous growth in control over State legislation exercised by the veto power of the Supreme Court. Through its steady expansion of the meaningless meaning of the "due process" clause of the Fourteenth Amendment the Supreme Court is putting constitutional compulsion behind the private judgment of its members upon disputed and difficult questions of social policy. A growing body of decisions, all spun out of the boundless provision "nor shall any state deprive any person of life, liberty or property, without due process of law," is intervening almost at every point of legislative activity by the individual States in matters confessedly of local concern, dealing solely with local situations and expressing remedies derived from local experience.

During the last ten years the Supreme Court has invalidated such local action with increasing ruthlessness, at the same time that it has professed, when dealing with federal legislation like the first Child Labor law,[1] to be peculiarly solicitous of the vital interests of the States in the equilibrium of our federal system. The veto power of the Supreme Court, thus exercised through the due process clause over the social legislation of individual States, is the most vulnerable aspect of undue centralization; it is at once the most destructive and the least responsible. The most destructive, because judicial nullification on grounds of constitutionality stops experimentation at its source; it debars an increase to the fund of social knowledge by scientific tests of trial and error. The least responsible, because it so often turns on the accidents which determine a majority decision of the Supreme Court, and shelters the fallible and remote judgment in the fields of fact and opinion not peculiarly within the special competence of judges behind the impersonal dooms of the Constitution.

Reprinted from an unsigned editorial in the *New Republic*, March 31, 1926, with permission. Footnotes supplied by editor.

1. Hammer v. Dagenhart, 247 U.S. 251 (1918).

The upas-tree growth of this penetrating negation of State action by the Supreme Court has now aroused the concern of the historian of the Supreme Court, Mr. Charles Warren, who, in the *Harvard Law Review*,[2] raises the question as to the value of continuing the due process clause of the Fourteenth Amendment. The *New Republic* has long been convinced that in cramping necessary experimentation by the different States, in sapping the independence of legislatures who gladly "pass the buck" to the courts, in mutilating the educative process of responsibility by a democratic electorate, the costs of the due process clause outweigh its gains.

The Supreme Court has just handed down two decisions which furnish cumulative evidence of this modern process of controlling the intimate life of the States by five or six judges. The first case concerned the very difficult problem of stopping evasion of death duties by distribution of wealth in an owner's lifetime.[3] The second presented a phase of the widespread effort to protect the community from disease through the use of shoddy.[4] In both instances the Court had before it legislation which represented the conscientious response of various States, made in various ways, to pressing problems of industrialized society. In both cases tolerance for legislative discretion was sufficient to carry the day for the legislation. In both cases the majority of the Court disregarded experience and tenable assumptions on which the local legislatures may well have acted, but against which the Supreme Court set its own opinions, its own facts and evaluation of them. In both instances the Supreme Court, in effect, enforced its own judgment of what was fair legislation and what was unfair, but in both instances it identified its own opinion of fairness and reason with "constitutional guaranties."

How dubious these "guaranties," how ambiguous the Delphic oracles of the Constitution, which a majority of

2. "The New 'Liberty' under the Fourteenth Amendment," 39 *Harv. L. Rev.* 431 (1926).
3. Schlesinger v. Wisconsin, 270 U.S. 230 (1926).
4. Weaver v. Palmer Bros. Co., 270 U.S. 402 (1926).

the Court are able to hear so unequivocally, is demonstrated by the two crushing dissenting opinions by Mr. Justice Holmes. In the first case he wrote as follows:

> If the Fourteenth Amendment were now before us for the first time I should think that it ought to be construed more narrowly than it has been construed in the past. But even now it seems to me not too late to urge that in dealing with state legislation upon matters of substantive law we should avoid with great caution attempts to substitute our judgment for that of the body whose business it is in the first place, with regard to questions of domestic policy that fairly are open to debate.
>
> The present seems to me one of those questions. I leave aside the broader issues that might be considered and take the statute as it is written, putting the tax on the ground of an absolute presumption that gifts of a material part of the donor's estate made within six years of his death were made in contemplation of death. If the time were six months instead of six years I hardly think that the power of the State to pass the law would be denied, as the difficulty of proof would warrant making the presumption absolute; and while I should not dream of asking where the line can be drawn, since the great body of the law consists in drawing such lines, yet when you realize that you are dealing with a matter of degree you must realize that reasonable men may differ widely as to the place where the line should fall. I think that our discussion should end if we admit what I certainly believe, that reasonable men might regard six years as not too remote. Of course many gifts will be hit by the tax that were made with no contemplation of death. But the law allows a penumbra to be embraced that goes beyond the outline of its object in order that the object may be secured. A typical instance is the prohibition of the sale of unintoxicating malt liquors in order to make effective a prohibition of the sale of beer. The power "is not to be denied simply because some innocent articles or transactions may be found within the proscribed class" . . .

I am not prepared to say that the legislature of Wisconsin, which is better able to judge than I am, might not believe, as the Supreme Court of the State confidently affirms, that by far the larger proportion of the gifts coming under the statute actually were made in contemplation of death. I am not prepared to say that if the legislature held that belief, it might not extend the tax to gifts made within six years of death in order to make sure that its policy of taxation should not be escaped. I think that with the States as with Congress when the means are not prohibited and are calculated to effect the object we ought not to inquire into the degree of the necessity for resorting to them . . .

It may be worth noticing that the gifts of millions taxed in this case were made from about four years before the death to a little over one year [the last being after the donor had had an attack of angina pectoris, although he is said to have attributed his sufferings to a less serious cause]. The statute is not called upon in its full force in order to justify this tax. If I thought it necessary I should ask myself whether it should not be construed as intending to get as near to six years as it constitutionally could, and whether it would be bad for a year and a month.[5]

A week later in the shoddy case Mr. Justice Holmes again preached his lesson of forbearance and due deference to the legislative discretion:

If the Legislature of Pennsylvania was of opinion that disease is likely to be spread by the use of unsterilized shoddy in comfortables I do not suppose that this Court would pronounce the opinion so manifestly absurd that it could not be acted upon. If we should not, then I think that we ought to assume the opinion to be right for the purpose of testing the law. The Legislature may have been of opinion further that the actual practice of filling comfortables with unsterilized shoddy gathered from

5. 270 U.S. at 241–242. Bracketed phrase was added by Frankfurter.

filthy floors was widespread, and this again we must assume to be true. It is admitted to be impossible to distinguish the innocent from the infected product in any practicable way, when it is made up into the comfortables. On these premises, if the Legislature regarded the danger as very great and inspection and tagging as inadequate remedies, it seems to me that in order to prevent the spread of disease it constitutionally could forbid any use of shoddy for bedding and upholstery . . .

It is said that there was unjustifiable discrimination. A classification is not to be pronounced arbitrary because it goes on practical grounds and attacks only those objects that exhibit or foster an evil on a larger scale. It is not required to be mathematically precise and to embrace every case that theoretically is capable of doing the same harm. "If the law presumably hits the evil where it is most felt, it is not to be overthrown because there are other instances to which it might have been applied."[6]

It only remains to add the encouraging fact that in these two dissents Mr. Justice Holmes had the concurrence of Mr. Justice Stone as well as that of Mr. Justice Brandeis.

6. 270 U.S. at 415–416.

Supreme Court Decisions: "What Stuff 'Tis Made Of"

That its business is of a different order from the common run of litigation has been recognized by the Court in the aids which it has called to its assistance, in the mode of arguments which it entertains, and in the extra-legal authorities upon which it relies. Thus, in the *Employers' Liability Cases,*[1] the litigation was in form between Damselle Howard and the Illinois Central Railroad Company to vindicate the private right of Damselle Howard against her husband's employer for the loss of his life. In essence, however, the right of Congress to legislate about the agents and instruments of interstate commerce was at stake, as well as the appropriate area of authority in the distribution of political power between the federal government and the States. The Court, therefore, did not rely for the elucidation of these governmental issues upon the private litigants, but heard the United States "through the Attorney General as a friend of the court."[2] A still more striking recognition by the Court that at the heart of these constitutional problems is usually a "politico-legal question"[3] is furnished by the recent *Myers* case.[4] In form, this was a suit by a postmaster for the recovery of his back sal-

1. 207 U.S. 463 (1908).

2. Id. at 490. In the Second Employers' Liability Cases, 223 U.S. 1 (1912), where the litigation was again in form between private litigants the attorney general, by leave of Court, again appeared as *amicus curiae* to represent the interest of the United States. In *Ex parte* Grossman, 267 U.S. 87, 108 (1925), involving the power of the President to pardon for criminal contempt, in form a petition for habeas corpus to release the petitioner from confinement despite the pardon, "Special counsel, employed by the Department of Justice, appear for the respondent to uphold the legality of the detention. The Attorney General of the United States, as *amicus curiae,* maintains the validity and effectiveness of the President's action. The petitioner, by his counsel, urges his discharge from imprisonment."

3. Carpenter, J., in United States v. Grossman, 1 F.2d 941, 952 (N.D. Ill. 1924). See "Address of Lawrence Maxwell, Jr.," *1921 Proc. Ky. Bar Assn.* 150, 168.

4. Myers v. United States, 272 U.S. 52 (1926).

ary. In fact, the real issue was the historic contest between President and Congress for control over the tenure of federal officeholders. Here was a problem of statecraft of the first magnitude, and the Court treated it as such. As soon as the original argument disclosed the fact that the real issue was a challenge to the Senate's power, the case was set down for reargument with an invitation by the Court to the Senate to present its position at the bar of the Court.[5] In ordinary controversies, where individual interests are dominantly at stake, courts rely upon counsel for the parties in interest. Decisions are influenced not inconsiderably by those chances which determine the selection of counsel. In the *Myers* case, by calling for argument on behalf of the Senate, the Supreme Court gave weighty evidence of its belief that a practice which works well enough in everyday litigation is inadequate and likely to be disastrous when great issues of state are before the Court.[6]

Since the Court's business is rooted on judgment on materials outside of technical law books, the technique for assuring itself an adequate knowledge and understanding of such data assumes a primary role in the Court's work. With an empiricism characteristic of Anglo-American lawyers, methods for adjudication in these

5. "Apparently, after some review of the arguments in the proceeding, the court became convinced that the rights and prerogatives of the Senate were so deeply involved that the legislative department should be given the right of appearance. Accordingly, a rehearing was ordered and the matter was brought to the attention of Senator Albert B. Cummins, as President of the Senate, who conferred with Chairman George S. Graham, Pennsylvania, of the House Judiciary Committee, with a view to arranging Congressional representation." *N.Y. Times,* Feb. 3, 1925. On Feb. 2, 1925, however, the Chief Justice announced that Senator George Wharton Pepper of Pennsylvania had been invited to appear as a friend of the Court to present upon reargument the right of Congress to impose limitations upon the Executive's powers of removal. Ibid.

6. "Before closing this opinion, we wish to express the obligation of the Court to Mr. Pepper for his able brief and argument as a friend of the Court. Undertaken at our request, our obligation is none the less if we find ourselves obliged to take a view adverse to his. The strong presentation of arguments against the conclusion of the Court is of the utmost value in enabling the Court to satisfy itself that it has fully considered all that can be said." Taft, C.J., in Myers v. United States, 272 U.S. at 176–177.

cases have not been systematically pursued.[7] Constitutional problems are still presented haphazardly, and too much in the atmosphere and with the attitude of conventional appellate arguments. But consciousness of the need for a specialized technique has definitely emerged. In various forms the Court has indicated that these public causes call for difference in treatment by counsel and court from what is appropriate to mere private litigation.

At least five modes of proof have been relied on for the facts relevant to the characteristic business of the Court. The duty of ascertaining the need for corrective legislation is the essential function of legislatures. Deference to the legislative judgment that circumstances exist warranting a change in the policy of law is a postulate of all judicial review when the constitutionality of legislation is assailed.[8] But the mere fact that the legislature has spoken, provided that its opinion is not "manifestly absurd,"[9] ought to, and sometimes does, save legislation.[10] Again, with a view to advising the Court, modern legislation

7. See Pound, "Legislation as a Social Function," 7 *Pub. Am. Sociol. Soc.* 148, 161 (1913); Frankfurter, "Hours of Labor and Realism in Constitutional Law," 29 *Harv. L. Rev.* 353, 364–373 (1916); Biklé Judicial Determination of Questions of Fact Affecting the Constitutional Validity of Legislative Action," 38 *Harv. L. Rev.* 6 (1924).

8. "The judicial function therefore with respect to the invalidation of a legislative act does not consist merely in comparing the determination evinced by such act with that reached by the court and the substitution of the latter for the former whenever they happen to differ. On the contrary, the ultimate judicial question is not whether the court construes the constitution as permitting the act, but whether the constitution permits the court to disregard the act; a question that is not to be conclusively tested by the court's judgment as to the constitutionality of the act, but by its conclusion as to what judgment was permissible to that department of the government to which the constitution has committed the duty of making such judgment." Garrison, J., in Wilson v. McGuinnes, 78 N.J.L. 346, 373 (1910). See Thayer, "The Origin and Scope of the American Doctrine of Constitutional Law," 7 *Harv. L. Rev.* 129 (1893), reprinted in *Legal Essays* 1 (1927).

9. See, Holmes, J., dissenting, in Weaver v. Palmer Bros. Co., 270 U.S. 402, 415 (1926).

10. "I suppose that this act was passed because the operatives, or some of them, thought that they were often cheated out of a part of their wages under a false pretence that the work done by them was imperfect, and persuaded the Legislature that their view was true. If their view was true, I cannot doubt that the Legislature had the right to deprive the employers of an honest tool which they were using for a dishonest purpose, and I cannot pronounce the legislation void, as based on a false

shows some striking illustrations of recitals embodying the considerations for its enactment. These have been relied upon by the Court in upholding laws.[11] More frequently, however, courts support legislative policy by drawing on information based on common knowledge or in books of reference. Courts use such material on their own initiative on the theory of "judicial notice."[12] But this is a tenuous basis for informing the judicial mind. It places an undue burden of independent investigation on judges who are limited in their facilities and still more limited by the pressure of business. Therefore, extra-legal facts which determine constitutionality have in recent years been brought to the Supreme Court's attention in briefs of counsel. Such weighty presentation of the experience which underlies challenged legislation has been welcomed by the Court and relied on in its adjudications.[13]

assumption, since I know nothing about the matter one way or the other." Holmes, J., dissenting, in Commonwealth v. Perry, 155 Mass. 117, 124 (1891). See, e.g., Hadacheck v. Sebastian, 239 U.S. 394, 413 (1915), and Ohio v. Deckebach, 274 U.S. 392 (1927).

11. See Stafford v. Wallace, 258 U.S. 495, 520 (1922); Dayton–Goose Creek Ry. v. United States, 263 U.S. 456, 476 (1924); Buck v. Bell, 274 U.S. 200 (1927). The Court has also on occasion had resort to the report of legislative committees in charge of a measure to discover its purposes. E.g., James Everard's Breweries v. Day, 265 U.S. 545, 561 (1924); Omaechevarria v. Idaho, 246 U.S. 343 (1918).

12. Jacobson v. Massachusetts, 197 U.S. 11 (1905). See, e.g., Brandeis, J., dissenting, in Jay Burns Baking Co. v. Bryan, 264 U.S. 504, 517 (1924), and in Adams v. Tanner, 244 U.S. 590, 597 (1917).

13. The method begins with the brief filed by Louis D. (now Mr. Justice) Brandeis in Muller v. Oregon, 208 U.S. 412 (1908). See Frankfurter, *supra* note 7, at 364. The effect of such a presentation of the issue is shown by the following passage from Mr. Justice Brewer's opinion in Muller v. Oregon, 208 U.S. at 419–421: "It may not be amiss, in the present case, before examining the constitutional question, to notice the course of legislation as well as expressions of opinion from other than judicial sources. In the brief filed by Mr. Louis D. Brandeis, for the defendant in error, is a very copious collection of all these matters, an epitome of which is found in the margin . . . The legislation and opinions referred to in the margin may not be, technically speaking, authorities, and in them is little or no discussion of the constitutional question presented to us for determination, yet they are significant of a widespread belief that woman's physical structure, and the functions she performs in consequence thereof, justify special legislation restricting or qualifying the conditions under which she should be permitted to toil. Constitutional questions, it is true, are not settled by even a consensus of present public opinion, for it is the peculiar value of a written constitution that it places in unchanging form limitations upon legislative action, and thus

Finally, the warrant for legislation has been made an issue for proof to be established by evidence, like matters in ordinary litigation.[14] This method of testimonial proof, calling into formal issue the actual or presumed findings of the legislature, was rejected by the Court in an earlier phase of the development of modern constitutional interpretation.[15] It raises, indeed, far-reaching questions of policy in the accommodation of the respective functions of court and legislature. One thing is clear. The legal profession has not yet put its mind to devising the necessary method and machinery by which knowledge of those facts, which are the foundation of constitutional judgment, may be formally at the service of courts. Here, as elsewhere, the inventive powers of lawyers will have to experiment consciously with different procedures, in order to evolve the technique best adapted to the elucidation of these politico-legal issues, or to formulate a variety of methods appropriate to different situations.

This brings into focus the part played by the bar in constitutional litigation. An adequately equipped professional bar is the mainstay of the Anglo-American legal order, for

gives a permanence and stability to popular government which otherwise would be lacking. At the same time, when a question of fact is debated and debatable, and the extent to which a special constitutional limitation goes is affected by the truth in respect to that fact, a widespread and long continued belief concerning it is worthy of consideration. We take judicial cognizance of all matters of general knowledge." The method has since been followed in Bunting v. Oregon, 243 U.S. 426 (1917); Settler v. O'Hara, 243 U.S. 629 (1917); Adkins v. Children's Hospital, 261 U.S. 525 (1923). Cf. People v. Schweinler Press, 214 N.Y. 395, where the court upon "new and additional knowledge" came to a different conclusion upon a statute regulating night-work of women in factories from its former decision in People v. Williams, 189 N.Y. 131 (1907).

14. Chastleton Corp. v. Sinclair, 264 U.S. 543 (1924), where the Court reversed the case with directions to the lower court to discover whether the exigency necessary for rent regulation still existed. In Buck v. Bell, 274 U.S. 200 (1927), specific findings were made by a State court upon the necessity for compulsory sterilization of mental defectives. As to the determination "either by the court or the jury" of conditions on which constitutional validity of the application of a statute may, under the due process clauses, turn, see concurring opinion of Brandeis, J., in Whitney v. California, 274 U.S. 357 (1927).

15. Jacobson v. Massachusetts, 197 U.S. 11 (1905).

it is a necessary adjunct of our courts. If the bar is to fulfill its duties in this most important domain of law, it must realize the nature of issues raised by constitutional controversies and be capable of assisting courts in their solution. The intellectual direction of the bar will certainly in the future be decided by the law schools. The aims and atmosphere of our law schools, the ideas and philosophy which underlie their curricula, the breadth of scholarship and understanding of their faculties, will determine the quality of our lawyers. With legal education rests the responsibility for training men fitted for constitutional adjudications.

Promising efforts to lift the level of the lawyer's technical training are under way. Undoubtedly the standards of legal education have been notably raised in recent years.[16] As befits our national needs, about a dozen really important centers of legal education are in process of making. Law schools ample in number and adequate in resources for the training of a competent bar will be sustained in their purposes by the increasing imposition of higher professional requirements for admission to the bar.[17] But a bar better trained merely in technical legal learning will not in itself produce fitness for participation in the work of the Supreme Court. The admonition addressed by Elihu Root in 1916 to the American bar is increasingly pertinent:

> To deal with American law as it is, however, is but half the problem. We are in the midst of a process of rapid change in the conditions to which the principles of law are to be applied, and if we are to have a consis-

16. See, e.g., Redlich, *Common Law and the Case Method in American University Law Schools* (Carnegie Foundation for the Advancement of Teaching, Bull. No. 8); *Tendencies in Legal Education,* Annual Report of Dean Harlan F. Stone of Columbia Law School, 1921.

17. See "Proceedings of the National Conference of Bar Associations on Legal Education at Washington, D.C., in Feb. 1922," 8 *A.B.A. Rep.* 137; *In the Matter of Requirements for Admission to the New York Bar,* Report of Committee on Character and Fitness, First Department, 1926; Order of N.Y. Court of Appeals, June 7, 1927, relative to admission to bar (*N.Y. Times,* June 8, 1927, p. 14); "Rules of Colorado Supreme Court," 13 *A.B.A.J.* 423 (1927).

> tent system that change must be met not at haphazard but by constructive development. The industrial and social changes of our time have been too swift for slowly forming custom. Old rules, applied to new conditions never dreamed of when the rules were stated, prove inadequate too suddenly for the courts readily to overtake them with application of the principles out of which the rules grew. We have only just begun to realize the transformation in industrial and social conditions produced by the wonderful inventions and discoveries of the past century.[18]

The form of litigation reveals the forces of this transformation in detached and isolated instances. But the individual case will be given dwarfed and distorted significance unless it is related to the deeper controversies of which it is a part. Mr. Root proceeded to indicate the tasks which now confront the law:

> 192 The vast increase of wealth resulting from the increased power of production is still in the first stages of the inevitable processes of distribution. The power of organization for the application of capital and labor in the broadest sense to production and commerce has materially changed the practical effect of the system of free contract to the protection of which our law has been largely addressed. The interdependence of modern life, extending not merely to the massed city community but to the farm and mine and isolated factory, which depend for their markets and their supplies upon far distant regions and upon complicated processes of transportation and exchange, has deprived the individual largely of his power of self-protection, and has opened new avenues through which, by means unknown to the ancient law, fatal injuries may be inflicted upon his rights, his property, his health, his liberty of action, his life itself. We have not yet worked out the *formulae* through which old principles are to be applied to these new conditions—the new forms perhaps through which

18. Root, *Addresses on Government and Citizenship* 532–533 (1916). Also, Root, "Public Service by the Bar," 41 *A.B.A. Rep.* 355, 366 (1916).

> the law shall continue to render its accustomed service to society.[19]

Unless the lawyer is equipped to penetrate to the core of these issues, to move freely in the world of ideas and knowledge which they imply, his technical training will be either futile or obstructive to the overwhelming enterprise of governing modern society by law. New facts must be able to find a ready access to his mind. "Improvement," Lord Acton quotes from Mill, "consists in bringing our opinions into clearer agreement with facts; and we shall not be likely to do this while we look at facts only through glasses colored by those very opinions."[20] The powers and *esprit* thus demanded of the bar the universities alone can cultivate.

Only a bar so trained will furnish a judiciary with ample horizon. But for a seat on the Supreme Bench still greater qualities are demanded. Throughout its history the Supreme Court has called for statesmanship—the gifts of mind and character fit to rule nations. The capacity to transcend one's own limitations, the imagination to see society as a whole, come, except in the rarest instance, from wide experience. Only the poetic insight of the philosopher can replace seasoned contact with affairs.[21] Lord Haldane's comments on the personnel of the Judicial Committee of the Privy Council reflect the same considerations which have largely determined selection for the Supreme Court:

> It is not always that the King can be safely advised to interfere with what belongs to the constitutions or systems of government of the countries of the Empire, and so the Judges of the Judicial Committee have been selected because of their training, not only in the law, but because in the case of most of them they have had experience elsewhere—in the House of Commons or in the House of Lords as members of it, or as Chancellors

19. Root, *supra* note 18, at 533.
20. Acton, *Lecture on the Study of History* 84, n. 27 (1905).
21. See Frankfurter, "Twenty Years of Mr. Justice Holmes' Constitutional Opinions," 36 *Harv. L. Rev.* 909, 919 (1923), reprinted *supra*.

> or ex-Chancellors, or by training calculated to give what is called the statesmanlike outlook to the Judge—that is to say, the outlook which makes him remember that with a growing Constitution things are always changing and developing, and that you cannot be sure that what was right ten years ago will be right to-day.[22]

Not by chance have the most influential Chief Justices been drawn from the world of affairs. Jay and Marshall and Taney, Chase and White and Taft were summoned to preside over the Court not merely because they were lawyers. The accents of statesmen are the recurring motif of Supreme Court opinions. From the beginning, the Court had to resolve what were essentially political issues—the proper accommodation between the States and the central government. These political problems will persist as long as our federalism endures; and the Supreme Court will remain the ultimate arbitrator between nation and States. Now the still more subtle conflicts of economic forces also press for answers from the nine Justices in Washington. To wisdom in political adjustment, talent for industrial statesmanship must be joined. No graver responsibilities ever confronted a judicial tribunal; no more searching equipment was ever exacted from judges.

22. Haldane, "The Work for the Empire of the Judicial Committee of the Privy Council," 1 *Camb. L.J.* 143, 148 (1922). Mr. John Maynard Keynes's recipe for a master-economist is illuminating, *mutatis mutandis,* for an understanding of the qualities demanded of a great justice of the Supreme Court: "The study of economics does not seem to require any specialised gifts of an unusually high order. Is it not, intellectually regarded, a very easy subject compared with the higher branches of philosophy and pure science? Yet good, or even competent, economists are the rarest of birds. An easy subject, at which very few excel! The paradox finds its explanation, perhaps, in that the master-economist must possess a rare *combination* of gifts. He must reach a high standard in several different directions and must combine talents not often found together. He must be mathematician, historian, statesman, philosopher —in some degree. He must understand symbols and speak in words. He must contemplate the particular in terms of the general, and touch abstract and concrete in the same flight of thought. He must study the present in the light of the past for the purposes of the future. No part of man's nature or his institutions must lie entirely outside his regard. He must be purposeful and disinterested in a simultaneous mood; as aloof and incorruptible as an artist, yet sometimes as near the earth as a politician." Keynes, *Essays in Biography* 140–141 (1951 ed.)

The Judiciary Act of 1925

A survey of the Court's work makes abundantly clear that opinions only in part tell the story of its labors. Nevertheless, the most enduring and interesting activity of the Court is expressed through its opinions. Having noted a diminution in the number of adjudicated cases since the Act of 1925, we are prepared to find a decrease in opinions. Their distribution among the members of the Court is happily not determined by a mechanical rule in their assignment, as is the case in some State courts. Here again considerations of individualization are operative. The complexity and bulk of the record, specialized equipment in certain fields of the law, and the burden of judicial administration are all factors which determine the nature and the volume of cases assigned to individual Justices and account for the differences in the number of opinions rendered by members of the Court.

The expression of dissents began with the first opinion of the Court,[1] and its practice may well be characterized as one of the settled traditions of the Court. Dissenting opinions have been among the most important influences in the development of our constitutional law.[2] Dissents prevent undue or premature generalizations of specific instances into rigid doctrine. The more constitutional adjudications turn upon judgment upon social and economic data, the more will they provoke differences of opinion among members of the Court. The last five terms reflect a rise in dissents and an increase in their expres-

Excerpt from an article by Frankfurter and James M. Landis in 42 *Harv. L. Rev.* 1, 15–24 (1928). Copyright 1928 by The Harvard Law Review Association.

1. Georgia v. Brailsford, 2 Dall. 402 (1792), 2 Dall. 415 (1793).

2. See Hughes, *The Supreme Court of the United States* 67–70 (1928). "I am of the opinion," wrote Mr. Justice Story, in Briscoe v. Bank of Kentucky, 11 Pet. 257, 350 (1837), "that upon Constitutional questions, the public have a right to know the opinion of every judge who dissents from the opinion of the court and the reasons of his dissent." In Rhode Island v. Massachusetts, 12 Pet. 657, 752 (1838), Chief Justice Taney wrote: "It has, I find, been the uniform practice in this Court, for the justices who differed from the Court on constitutional questions, to express their dissent."

sion. Dissents entail as much labor as majority opinions. They constitute a burden in addition to the average quota of opinions written by the individual Justice. A wise determination of the Court's jurisdiction ought to assure its members ample time for adequate expression of dissents, no less than for careful preparation of the Court's opinions.

The history of the Supreme Court since the Civil War shows a steady atrophy of ordinary private litigation and growing preoccupation by the Court with public law. In freeing the Court for litigation of national and public importance, the Act of 1925 furthered that tendency. When the Act of 1925 was passed, common-law controversies constituted about 5 percent of the Court's business,[3] and common-law litigation appears to be stabilizing at that ratio. Although the increased role played by certiorari has greatly enlarged the Court's power of preventing cases without a real public interest from reaching it, in several instances during the last Term the Court assumed jurisdiction in cases where a public or general interest is hardly discernible. Special mention may be made of several cases under the Federal Employers' Liability Act presenting unique circumstances for decision rather than occasions for the formulation of general rules.[4]

Issues of public law, then, constitute the stuff of Supreme Court litigation. But the conflicts which they engender are due far less to differences over abstract principles than to disagreements in the application of recognized doctrine to the complex problems of modern industrial society. Differences of degree become more and more the vital differences. And a perception of these differences depends on familiarity with social and economic details and an understanding of their significance. What led the Supreme Court to sustain the Packers and Stock-

3. Frankfurter and Landis, *The Business of the Supreme Court* 306 (1927).

4. E.g., Atlantic Coast Line R.R. v. Southwell, 275 U.S. 64 (1927); Missouri Pac. R.R. v. Aeby, 275 U.S. 426 (1928); Gulf M. & N. R.R. v. Wells, 275 U.S. 455 (1928); Toledo, St. Louis & Western R.R. v. Allen, 276 U.S. 165 (1928). See also Book Review, 28 *Colum. L. Rev.* 516, n. 4 (1928).

yards Act of 1921 was not any technical interpretation of the commerce clause but a vivid realization of the role played by the stockyards "as great national public utilities to promote the flow of commerce from the ranges and farms of the West to the consumers in the East."[5] And so again, Congress was justified in the novel provisions for the recapture of railroad earnings not by any abstruse legal dialectic but by due regard to the concrete consideration of railroad economics which the experience of the World War wrote into the Transportation Act of 1920.[6] Explicitly or implicitly, considerations of a like nature determine judgment upon legislation affecting economic enterprise through direct limitations upon the conduct of business or its indirect control through taxation. And this is true whether the controversies involve the determination of State powers under the Fourteenth Amendment or the eternal adjustments of authority under the commerce clause between the federal government and the States. In passing upon zoning laws, in sanctioning or disallowing "yellow dog contracts," in formulating the bases for rate fixing, the process of adjudication necessarily implies judgment upon the economic and social considerations from which such policies derive. The validity of the judgment made will therefore depend upon the adequacy and relevance of the extra-legal data upon which it ultimately rests.

A technique which will assure the effective presentation of these determining issues of fact becomes thus a matter of crucial importance in the administration of American public law. Since these adjudications turn so largely on the particularities of fact in individual cases, the specific circumstances should be established decisively by the record before the Court and not be shrouded in ambiguity or left to speculation. Otherwise, the Court will be driven to hypothetical judgments and moot decisions. Adherence to the traditional considerations against intruding into controversies regarding political power, whether as between the different departments of the federal govern-

5. Stafford v. Wallace, 258 U.S. 495, 516 (1922).
6. Dayton-Goose Creek Ry. v. United States, 263 U.S. 456 (1924).

ment or as between the federal government and the States, becomes the more vital since the demarcation of power may depend upon minor variations of fact in individual cases. Unless adequate provision be made for the ascertainment of these controlling details, issues of gravest public concern may be determined in violation of the root principle of American constitutional theory, to wit, that the Supreme Court decides cases and does not announce abstract policy.

The dependence on fact in modern Supreme Court litigation was strikingly illustrated in two cases at the last Term of the Court.[7] They involved perplexing problems of control over motor bus lines. Abstractly, the legal questions concerned limitations imposed by the commerce clause upon the State's power to regulate traffic and promote safety, but the decision turned on the particular traffic conditions and transportation facilities in the city of Hammond, Indiana. The record in these cases, however, failed to furnish the necessary light upon these decisive circumstances. In this state of the record, the Supreme Court found itself unable to decide the legal questions argued before it, and remanded the cases to the lower court for determination of the facts essential to their decision:

> These questions have not, so far as appears, been considered by either of the lower courts. The facts essential to their determination have not been found by either court. And the evidence in the record is not of such a character that findings could now be made with confidence. The answer denied many of the material allegations of the bill. The evidence consists of the pleadings and affidavits. The pleadings are confusing. The affidavits are silent as to some facts of legal significance; lack definiteness as to some matters; and present serious conflicts on issues of facts that may be decisive. For aught that appears, the lower courts may have differed in their decisions solely because they differed as to con-

7. Hammond v. Schappi Bus Line, Inc., 275 U.S. 164 (1927); Hammond v. Farina Bus Line & Co., 275 U.S. 173 (1927).

> clusions of fact. Before any of the questions suggested, which are both novel and of far reaching importance, are passed upon by this Court, the facts essential to their decision should be definitely found by the lower courts upon adequate evidence.[8]

The *Hammond* cases indicate forcibly the burden cast upon the Court in searching the record for proof of facts underlying legal issues. The Supreme Court should be free from such tasks. Lower courts ought to be required to report findings of those facts which determine Supreme Court decisions. Such findings are demanded by the whole range of public law litigation—the review of rate regulation, the respective fields of control over interstate commerce, the various instances of State legislation challenged under the Fourteenth Amendment. It is not for the Supreme Court to disentangle confused testimony, nor for a Court charged with keeping our constitutional system in equilibrium to pass upon disputation over evidence. The credibility of witnesses, the reconciliation of conflicting testimony, the proof of economic data, and the reliability of experts are problems with which, as a rule, the Supreme Court ought not to be inflicted.[9] Carefully framed findings by the lower courts should serve as the foundation for review, leaving for the Supreme Court the ascertainment of principles governing authenticated facts, the accommodation between conflicting principles, and the adaptation of old principles to new situations. The mechanism for review of decisions of the Court of Claims and of common-law actions tried without a jury should be generally adapted to cases coming from the federal courts, whether arising in equity or at law.[10]

The Supreme Court is equally dependent upon the thoroughness with which issues are sifted and explored before they reach the Court. In this process, the opinions below play an important role. They compel analysis and formulation of the issues in a controversy, sharpen responsibility

8. 275 U.S. at 171.
9. Frankfurter and Landis, *supra* note 3, at 290.
10. Id. at 291, notes 134–135.

in adjudication, and advise litigants and the appellate court of the factors that control decision. Only by such a process is the controversy adequately focused for the consideration of the Supreme Court. Opinions by the lower courts are therefore indispensable for the adequate exercise by the Supreme Court of its *reviewing* function. Without them, as the Supreme Court has remarked on several occasions during the last two Terms,[11] "the appellate court is denied an important aid in the consideration of the case; and the defeated party is often unable to determine whether the case presents a question worthy of consideration by the appellate court. Thus, both the litigants and this court are subjected to unnecessary labor."[12]

Furthermore, as the questions coming before the Court are "rooted in history and in the social and economic development of the nation,"[13] the Court requires aid from counsel for a full presentation of the issues in the light of their political and social history.[14] The determination of the scope of the President's power of removal, in the famous *Myers* case,[15] compelled an investigation into practices and opinions since the foundation of our government. The constitutionality of legislation such as the New Jersey Employment Agency Act, considered at the last Term of Court, cannot fairly be determined without regard to the voluminous data set forth in Mr. Justice Stone's dissenting opinion.[16] Their ascertainment, however, involves laborious research which counsel should supply. If the task of independent inquiry is left to the Court, only in relatively few cases will time permit its adequate pursuit. There is thus real danger that constitutional adjudi-

11. Cleveland, etc. Ry. v. United States 275 U.S. 404, 414 (1928); Virginian Ry. v. United States, 272 U.S. 658, 674 (1926). Cf. Lawrence v. St. Louis–San Francisco Ry., 274 U.S. 588 (1927); Arkansas R.R. Comm. v. Chicago R.I. & Pac. R.R., 274 U.S. 597 (1927); Hammond v. Schappi Bus Line Co., Inc., 275 U.S. 164 (1927); Hammond v. Farina Bus Line & Co., 275 U.S. 173 (1927).

12. Cleveland, etc. Ry. v. United States, 275 U.S. 404, 414 (1928).

13. Stone, "Fifty Years Work of the United States Supreme Court," 14 *A.B.A.J.* 428, 435 (1928).

14. Frankfurter and Landis, *supra* note 3, at 312–317.

15. Myers v. United States, 272 U.S. 52 (1926).

16. Ribnik v. McBride, 277 U.S. 350, 359 (1928).

cations will be determined by abstractions or jejune generalizations on obsolete data. No longer does the Supreme Court possess a specialized bar of constitutional lawyers. But the character of its business requires a bar fully equipped to deal with the social and economic implications of the issues presented by modern Supreme Court litigation.

The Paradoxes of Legal Science

We welcome this new little volume by the distinguished Chief Judge of the New York Court of Appeals not as the completion of a trilogy, but as an augury that we shall have from his pen a sheaf of juristic studies every three or four years. *The Nature of the Judicial Process* (1921), *The Growth of the Law* (1924), and now *The Paradoxes of Legal Science*, form an organic whole. The books are important chapters of what we hope some day will be a spacious work entitled, *Reflections on the Art of Adjudication.* Were a Browning to put their substance into verse, he would doubtless entitle it, *Any Judge to Himself.* For in truth, these are judicial self-revelations. But they belong to science rather than to biography, because they describe the conditions and influences which, in varying proportions, determine the labors not of this author-judge but of every judge of a high court.

The contributions to understanding which have endured are not so much systems as insights. Perhaps systems themselves are the result of the elaboration and over-refinement of penetrating glimpses into truth. It is not without significance that the two judges in our day who have given powerful direction to juristic thinking have done so not by heavy treatises on jurisprudence. Mr. Justice Holmes has re-fashioned the assumptions and methods of American legal thinking through essays. The work of philosophic permeation begun by Mr. Justice Holmes more than a half a century ago, and happily still continued in his opinions, is being carried on by Chief Judge Cardozo, and again through the essay form. The task of adjudication is a strong corrective against over-systematization, and a constant admonition against premature generalization. But the judicial function also reveals the bankruptcy and deception of mere empiricism. Decisions are not ad hoc judgments. An individual case is both offspring and parent. After quoting a remark of Ches-

Reprinted from a Book Review of Benjamin N. Cardozo, *The Paradoxes of Legal Science* (1928), in 77 *U. of Pa. L. Rev.* 436 (1929). Copyright by the *University of Pennsylvania Law Review.*

terton's to the effect that the most important thing about a man is his philosophy, Judge Cardozo adds, "The more I reflect about a judge's work, the more I am impressed with the belief that this, if not true for everyone, is true at least for judges."[1] Here is the key to Judge Cardozo's writings and to his opinions, though one must quickly add his qualification, "of course, it is easy to misunderstand such a statement—to press it too far—and to make it an untruth." The essay form is the fit instrument for a thinker whose chief concern is to lay bare the contending claims that seek the mediation and authority of society through law, and to give some indication, at least, of how these processes of mediation in fact operate. For the essay is tentative, reflective, suggestive, contradictory, and incomplete. It mirrors the perversities and complexities of life.

Viewing the judge not as technician but as philosopher, Judge Cardozo, in attempting a candid scrutiny of what confronts the judge, must deal with what confronts the law. In each of his books he is concerned with the enduring problems of State-enforced law, however varying the range of control exercised by State law, however different the modes by which it is asserted, and however shifting the fashions in nomenclature of the guild which administers law. What are the factors entering into an individual pronouncement of law? What are the methods of inquiry to ascertain the norms relevant to judgment upon the particular instance? When should the past exclusively govern, and when must the past be tested by conformity to the standards and feelings of contemporary society? What are the sources for ascertaining the needs of the present, and, in the clash of needs, whose need prevails? These and like questions are not conundrums. They are the daily stuff of the solicitude of every critically minded judged. Of such is not the kingdom of heaven, but this world's jurisprudence.

Upon these themes Judge Cardozo sheds light in each of his three books, but each has its own preoccupation. In *The Nature of the Judicial Process*, he described memorably the known forces and tendencies which are ex-

1. *The Growth of the Law* 59 (1924). [Ed.]

pressed in decisions. In his *Growth of the Law,* the emphasis was on the dynamic conceptions in judging. In the latest book, law is revealed more and more as the comprehension of contradictories, the art of mediating between antitheses. Precedent and justice, stability and progress, the individual and society, liberty and authority —these are life's antinomies and they are the burdens of the law. At once we are out of the realm of the absolute, the dooms of the foreordained. Not the logic of certainties, but the logic of probabilities—and there is no calculus of probabilities! Not yet, certainly; and no early hope of attaining one. One hears an occasional sigh of longing in these pages for such a calculus, the aspiration for certainty, the assurance of the multiplication-table, which from time to time must possess everyone who works with the treacherous and intractable materials of the social sciences. All too often this desire betrays us into the formulation of illusory certainty. It is a natural but an idle quest. Law would gain in candor and wisdom if we exorcised the wish for such a calculus, emphasized the necessary meagerness and evanescence of our data, and concentrated on such assurances of attainable objective norms as we can derive from a recognized procedure of judgment and an unflinching rigor in laying bare the conscious foundations of judgment.

This is merely putting into clumsy language what Judge Cardozo has often expressed so felicitously. In this book he has made still more clear his awareness of the forces in law—and his awareness of his unawareness—the pulls and pressures included in the resultant of the forces that make law, but of which we know neither the sources nor their direction. Only by rigorous and continuous inquiry, analysis, and criticism can we discover these concealed forces or know the strength of those that are patently operative.

Judge Cardozo draws much of his material from the problems of public law. And here a reticence is laid upon the Judge, even in the role of essayist. In graceful and delicate language, Judge Cardozo hints at the peculiar demands made upon the American judge by a candid analysis of the problems of constitutional law and of the materials and methods appropriate to their solution. Humility, painstaking solicitude for the ascertainable feelings and needs of present-day society, the imaginative effort to reconcile contending claims, respect for "the spontaneity and persistence with which groups are established"[2] to conserve a social interest—these are the high qualities of discernment, of tolerance, of wise statecraft without which constitutional law is a system of pernicious abstractions instead of the governance of a teeming continent. Law is seen to be more and more related to the organic processes of life outside of the law. Nothing is more striking, nor more hopeful for a synthetic approach to the problems of society, than the common nature of the problems discussed by Judge Cardozo and those dealt with by professional philosophers, especially philosophers reflecting upon life through the discipline of the sciences, like Whitehead, or of statecraft, like Haldane and Smuts. The necessary adaptation of means to ends, the interplay between organism and environment, the futility of believing that fallible minds can fashion infallible molds for the future—these are themes for the philosopher, but they also have the most concrete possible meaning for all who have a duty towards law, whether as judges, practitioners, or teachers. "It is the first step in sociological wisdom," writes Whitehead, "to recognize that the major advances in civilization are processes which all but wreck the societies in which they occur:—like unto an arrow in the hand of a child. The art of free society consists first in the maintenance of the symbolic code; and secondly in fearlessness of revision, to secure that the code serves those purposes which satisfy an enlightened reason. Those societies which cannot combine reverence to their symbols with freedom of revision, must ultimately decay either from anarchy, or from the slow atrophy of a life stifled by useless shadows."[3]

Through his opinions and his essays, and the contagion of his example, Judge Cardozo is contributing mightily to the penetration of this "sociological wisdom" into the hardened and complacent fabric of the law.

2. P. 133. [Ed.]
3. Whitehead, *Symbolism, Its Meaning and Extent* 88 (1927).

Hughes on the Supreme Court

A dilatory reviewer must expect to find that all the things that should have been said about a book, and even all the things that should not have been said, have been said before him. But sometimes tardiness is not its own punishment. One psychological moment may have passed, but the fates in moments of irrational generosity create other psychological moments. An old book may become if not new at least news. A book may attain new significance because of the new significance of its author.

About this book as an interpretation, particularly for laymen, of the history, the methods, and the achievements of the Supreme Court, all that needs to be said has amply been said, particularly in reviews by Professor Thomas Reed Powell[1] and Professor James M. Landis.[2] The limits which the author imposed upon himself must be borne in mind. He told his audience that his aim was to show the "cross-sections of the jurisprudence of the Supreme Court in order that you may see the grain and growth of the tree."[3] He explicitly disavowed "a critique."[4] Certain it is that this little volume gives the nonspecialist the most compact story of the foundations of the Court and an excellent description of the Court at work. One is more doubtful how much understanding of the nature of the judicial process in constitutional adjudications can be conveyed to the lay reader by an exposition, even at its best, of the formulas in which the results of that judicial process are clothed. Indeed, I have long felt that there is only one truly good course on constitutional law—the discussions at the Saturday [now Friday] conferences of the Supreme Court. But, alas, that course in constitutional law is a strictly confined seminar, open only to the nine members of the Court. All academic courses in constitutional law

Reprinted from a Book Review of Charles Evans Hughes, *The Supreme Court of the United States* (1928), in 16 *A.B.A.J.* 251 (1930), with permission.

1. 41 *Harv. L. Rev.* 1071 (1928).
2. 24 *Ill. L. Rev.* 358 (1929).
3. P. 235.
4. Ibid.

and all writings upon it are only faint speculations as to the content of these Saturday discussions, guided by such hints as break through the discreet reticences of the Court's opinions.

As an ex-Justice, the author of these lectures, naturally enough, wrote in the tradition of the Court's discretion. Nevertheless, on a number of the intellectual issues that concern the work of the Court and the intellectual procedure for meeting them, the lecturer, doubtless with never a thought that he was speaking as the future Chief Justice, significantly revealed his mind. These revelations are matters of prime importance to an understanding of some of the attitudes which the new Chief Justice will bring to the work of the Court. The extent to which his attitude will influence the Court's attitude depends on considerations which he himself has bluntly stated:

> The Chief Justice as the head of the Court has an outstanding position, but in a small body of able men with equal authority in the making of decisions, it is evident that his actual influence will depend upon the strength of his character and the demonstration of his ability in the intimate relations of the judges.[5]
>
> While the Chief Justice has only one vote, the way in which the Court does its work gives him a special opportunity for leadership.[6]

It is idle to scan these lectures for intimations concerning the leanings of the new Chief Justice on matters of substantive law, on his inclinations this way or that regarding specific cases of power and policy that will find their way to the Court during his magistracy. At all events, to look for these needles in the haystack, and mostly needles that are not there, is not my concern. But in his analysis of the true nature of the most vital contests before the Court, and the general intellectual procedure which the wise discharge of the Court's duties requires, Chief Jus-

5. P. 57.
6. P. 58.

tice Hughes made profoundly important observations. Upon a rigorous observance of them, I venture to believe, depends the Court's successful contribution to the statesmanship of the country.

First and foremost, these lectures leave no doubt that the new Chief Justice realizes that the effectiveness of the Court's work does not derive from any language of the Constitution or the compulsions of logic or the mechanical contrivances of its organization. It depends upon the self-denying ordinances of the Justices. He recognizes fully the subtle psychologic difficulties in drawing the line, at times the shadowy line, between questions of mere wisdom or policy and those of power by pointing out that "It is doubtless true that men holding strong convictions as to the unwisdom of legislation may easily pass to the position that it is wholly unreasonable."[7] Or, as Mr. Justice Moody once put it:

> Under the guise of interpreting the Constitution we must take care that we do not import into the discussion our own personal views of what would be wise, just and fitting rules of government to be adopted by a free people and confound them with constitutional limitations.[8]

In his book the new Chief Justice was alive to the fact that this danger is to be avoided only by the self-discipline of the Justices, by working "in an objective spirit."[9] And so he found that:

> The success of the work of the Supreme Court in maintaining the necessary balance between State and Nation, and between individual rights as guaranteed by the Constitution and social interest as expressed in legislation, has been due largely to the deliberate determination of the Court to confine itself to its judicial task, and, while careful to maintain its authority as the interpreter of the Constitution, the Court has not sought to

7. Pp. 37–38.
8. Twining v. New Jersey, 211 U.S. 78, 206–207 (1908).
9. P. 38.

aggrandize itself at the expense of either executive or legislature.[10]

Thus he found that when damage has come to the reputation and usefulness of the Court, it came not through criticism from without but "from self-inflicted wounds."[11] The need for rigorous objectivity, for scrupulous alertness, against confounding personal convictions upon ephemeral policies with enduring principles of right and wrong, becomes all the more manifest when we consider the exact scope of issues that must frequently solicit the judgment of the Court. Again and again the future Chief Justice in these lectures took occasion to point out the narrow controversy regarding fact and experience upon which Supreme Court decisions turn:

> The division in the Court illustrates the vast importance of its function, as, after all, the protection both of the rights of the individual and of those of society rests not so often on formulas, as to which there may be agreement, but on a correct appreciation of social conditions and a true appraisal of the actual effect of conduct.[12]

These are matters on which differences of opinion are common both within the Court and outside it. Because they turn so much on questions of fact and upon the meaning of experience, the utmost tolerance and detachment is demanded in the application of vague constitutional phrases, like that of the due process of law which represents "an American conception of extraordinary pervasiveness."[13]

Such are the issues and such their demands upon rather uncommon gifts of intellectual objectivity. Since it is unavoidable that "judges will have their convictions,"[14]

10. Pp. 40–41.
11. P. 50.
12. Pp. 165–166.
13. P. 185.
14. P. 240.

Chief Justice Hughes regarded it "of the essence of the appropriate exercise of judicial power that these should be independently expressed."[15] Dissenting opinions have for him no terrors. Quite the contrary. He regards them as instruments of truth, as feeders to the stream of reason:

> There are some who think it desirable that dissents should not be disclosed as they detract from the force of the judgment. Undoubtedly, they do. When unanimity can be obtained without sacrifice of conviction, it strongly commends the decision to public confidence. But unanimity which is merely formal, which is recorded at the expense of strong, conflicting views, is not desirable in a court of last resort, whatever may be the effect upon public opinion at the time. This is so because what must ultimately sustain the court in public confidence is the character and independence of the judges.
>
> A dissent in a court of last resort is an appeal to the brooding spirit of the law, to the intelligence of a future day, when a later decision may possibly correct the error into which the dissenting judge believes the court to have been betrayed.
>
> Nor is this appeal always in vain. In a number of cases dissenting opinions have in time become the law.[16]

Thus, the narrator of the Court's history. He now becomes the maker of its history to an extent that may be momentous in the life of the Court and of the country.

15. Ibid.
16. Pp. 67–68.

The Appointment of a Justice

Senate opposition to nominations for the Supreme Bench is no novelty in American history. The Senate has always acted upon the constitutional requirement that the President "shall appoint . . . judges of the Supreme Court" but only "by and with the advice and consent of the Senate." Participation by the Senate in appointments to the Court has been especially active in regard to filling the Chief Justiceship. His own party was ready to reject John Marshall in 1801 if they could have persuaded John Adams to name another. The second greatest Chief Justice—Roger B. Taney—was confirmed by a vote of 29 to 15 in 1836 after a bitter fight of nearly three months against an opposition led by Webster and Clay. Morrison R. Waite became Chief Justice in 1874 only after the Senate had successfully resisted two prior nominations by Grant, and even for the gentle Fuller, in 1888, the vote of confirmation was 41 to 20. The Associate Justices have similarly had to meet the Senate's constitutional duty of approval. Not a few nominations have been actually rejected. The great Taney himself came to the Chief Justiceship after he had previously failed of confirmation as an Associate Justice. Bitter opposition held up President Wilson's nomination of Louis D. Brandeis for four months. By common consent, Mr. Justice Brandeis already belongs to the pre-eminent figures in the Court's history. Historians are agreed that hostility to his nomination was derived from opposition to his economic and social views.

Seldom, indeed, have nominations for the Court been opposed on the score of personal disqualification. Fundamentally, the objections have been political. They have concerned the general outlook of nominees upon the public issues that in different periods of the country's history were likely to come before the Court. By the very nature of its place in the American scheme of government the Supreme Court is in the stream of public affairs, and its decisions thus have entangled the Court in political controversy. Frequently they have led to proposals for constitutional amendments, and twice feeling was intense enough to secure such amendments. The case of *Chisholm v. Georgia*,[1] decided in 1792, led to the Eleventh Amendment barring suits by an individual against a State except by the latter's consent. A hundred years later came the *Income Tax Cases*,[2] in effect denying to the federal government power to levy income taxes. These decisions led to the Sixteenth Amendment. Another decision, the famous *Dred Scott* case,[3] probably helped to promote the Civil War, as it certainly required the Civil War to bury its dicta.

These are striking instances, but the Court has been entangled in political controversy, barring an occasional quiet decade, throughout most of its history. Such is not the experience of courts generally, except on rare occasions. English courts for the last century have been out of the swirl of politics. When taking sides on an acute public issue, however, they, too, occasionally become politically involved. Thus, the development of the British Labor party was considerably fostered by two decisions of the House of Lords affecting the status of trade unions —the *Taff Vale* case[4] in 1901 and the *Osborne* judgment[5] in 1909. When courts deal with political issues there are bound to be political repercussions. In so far as courts deal with ordinary controversies between private litigants, they are outside the current of public affairs and public interest, except in an occasional case of dramatic human appeal. When issues are essentially political, public discussion is inevitable. When feelings strongly divide opinion, when the issues touch intimately the daily concerns of the public, political controversy will sooner or later break out and criticism not infrequently become raucous. To understand the political debates in which the Supreme Court has been involved from time to time, one must

1. 2 Dall. 419 (1792).
2. Pollock v. Farmers' Loan & Trust Co., 157 U.S. 429 (1895), 158 U.S. 601 (1895).
3. Dred Scott v. Sanford, 19 How. 393 (1857).
4. Taff Vale Ry. v. Amalgamated Soc. of Ry. Servants, [1901] A.C. 426.
5. Amalgamated Soc. of Railway Servants v. Osborne, [1910] A.C. 87.

understand the nature of the Court's business. While the Supreme Court has always been arbiter of issues intrinsically political in their consequences, this is preeminently the characteristic of the Court's business in our own day . . .

While all generalizations about history have an illusory definiteness, one may without undue omission of qualifying details, note periods and tendencies in the history of the Supreme Court. After an almost negligible opening decade, the Court, under Marshall's leadership, dealt with the structure of the new government. Through legal doctrines it furthered the forces of nationality. After Marshall, "the irrepressible conflict" between State and national power was the predominant issue, until the Civil War, more effectively than the Constitution, finally made of the States a nation instead of a confederation. Then followed a third period in which national power was ascendant—the period of railroad and industrial development, of the exploitation of free lands and other natural resources. It was the period when laissez faire was the dominant philosophy. The Fourteenth Amendment was made the vehicle of its expression and "liberty of contract" was erected into a dogma. Social legislation emerged but was successfully resisted, except during the very brief leadership in the opposite direction of Chief Justice Waite. Speaking in 1913, Mr. Justice Holmes thus characterized this period: "When twenty years ago a vague terror went over the earth and the word socialism began to be heard, I thought and still think that fear was translated into doctrines that had no proper place in the Constitution or the common law."[6]

Two cases particularly reveal the trend of the Court at this period. In the *Lochner* case[7] a divided Court declared it beyond the power of a State to limit the working hours of bakeshop workers to ten, and in the *Adair* case[8] a majority invalidated the carefully considered efforts of Congress to prevent the recurrence of a Pullman strike by

6. Holmes, *Collected Legal Papers* 295 (1920).
7. Lochner v. New York 198 U.S. 45 (1905).
8. Adair v. United States, 208 U.S. 161 (1910).

prohibiting discrimination against trade unions. These two cases aroused widespread criticism. And not only by the laity. Thus, the *Adair* case was assailed by such conservative leaders of the bar as Richard Olney, Grover Cleveland's attorney general and secretary of state. Such excesses of judicial individualism, resulting in fatal obstruction to needed reforms, finally found an effective voice of protest in Roosevelt. There followed a short period in which the Court was more tolerant toward legislation, less prone to write its own social-economic views into the Constitution. It was during this period that the Court found that "police power" of the States extends "to all the great public needs."

The World War and its aftermath ushered in once again a period dominated by fears—the fear of change, the fear of new ideas—and these fears were written into the Constitution. By a series of decisions, particularly in regard to public utilities, the dictum of President Coolidge that "the business of America is business" was also sought to be written into the Constitution. Thus, the recent Baltimore case[9] which has stirred so much feeling was a holding that a net return of 6.26 percent, calculated upon a most favorable basis of "present value" for a monopolistic street railway in Baltimore, is less than the Constitution requires.

At almost every point of legislative activity the Supreme Court interposed its veto against State action in matters confessedly of local concern, dealing solely with local situations and expressing remedies derived from local experience. Since 1920 the Court has invalidated more legislation than in fifty years preceding. Views that were antiquated twenty-five years ago have been resurrected in decisions nullifying minimum wage laws for women in industry,[10] a standard-weight bread law to protect buyers from short weights and honest bakers from unfair competition,[11] a law fixing the resale price of theater

9. United Railways v. West, 280 U.S. 234 (1930).
10. Adkins v. Children's Hospital, 261 U.S. 525 (1923).
11. Jay Burns Baking Co. v. Bryan, 264 U.S. 504 (1924).

tickets by ticket scalpers in New York,[12] laws controlling exploitation of the unemployed by employment agencies[13] and many tax laws. It is sometimes suggested that the Supreme Court has invalidated only a few laws compared with the total which has passed muster. Since 1921 the Court has held laws invalid in about 30 percent of the cases under the due process clauses. Merely as a matter of arithmetic this is an impressive mortality rate. But a numerical tally of the cases does not tell the tale. In the first place, all laws are not of the same importance. Secondly, a single decision may decide the fate of a great body of legislation. This was true of *Coppage* v. *Kansas*,[14] declaring invalid a Kansas law which prohibited discrimination against trade unionists, and of the decision nullifying the minimum wage law for the District of Columbia.[15] Similarly, a single decision involving utility valuations affects utility valuations in every State and in every city of the union. Moreover, the discouragement of legislative efforts through a particular adverse decision and the general weakening of the sense of legislative responsibility are destructive influences not measurable by statistics.

The crucial criticism of the Court is that it is putting constitutional authority behind the personal opinion of its members in disputed and difficult questions of social policy. The strongest admonitions against this misuse of constitutional power have been uttered by members of the Court themselves. One might call the roll of some of the greatest names in the Court's history in support of the recent protest in the Senate against the Court's tendency to make of the Constitution a vehicle for the private views of Justices upon matters of policy. "Under the guise of interpreting the Constitution," wrote Mr. Justice Moody, "we must take care that we do not import into the discussion our own personal views of what would be wise, just and fitting rules of government to be adopted by a free

12. Tyson & Bros. v. Banton, 273 U.S. 418 (1927).
13. Ribnik v. McBride, 277 U.S. 350 (1928).
14. 236 U.S. 1 (1915).
15. *Supra* note 10.

people and confound them with constitutional limitations."[16]

From time to time remedies have been suggested to guard against such misuse of judicial power. Roosevelt made popular the proposal of a recall of judicial decisions in constitutional matters, as John Marshall himself had apparently once given support to some such proposal. In 1829 Philip P. Barbour, Congressman from Virginia and later one of the Justices of the Court, proposed that no law be invalidated without the concurrence of more than a majority of the Court. The elder La Follette revived this idea in 1924. Such a scheme is in fact in operation in Ohio. But neither of these nor any other mechanical device fits the problem. Such remedies create new difficulties and do not help in the slightest the ultimate requirement for the Court, namely, men adequately equipped for the peculiar tasks committed to it. Everything turns on men.

Unless the President, the Senate, and the country are alert to the qualities that Justices of the Supreme Court ought to possess and insist upon suitable appointees, no mechanics will save us from the evils of narrow prepossessions by members of the Court. Contrariwise, if we are fully alive to the indispensable qualifications for the high work of the Court, and insistent upon measuring appointees accordingly, mechanical devices are superfluous and obstructive. It is because the Supreme Court wields the power that it wields, that appointment to the Court is a matter of general public concern and not merely a question for the profession. In good truth, the Supreme Court *is* the Constitution. Therefore, the most relevant things about an appointee are his breadth of vision, his imagination, his capacity for disinterested judgment, his power to discover and to suppress his prejudices. Judges must learn to transcend their own convictions, says the greatest of living judges. They must leave room for much, continues Mr. Justice Holmes, that they "hold dear to be done away with short of revolution by the orderly change of law."[17]

16. Twining v. New Jersey, 211 U.S. 78, 106–107 (1908).
17. *Supra* note 16, at 295.

For the part played by unconscious partiality is tremendous. The significance of such psychological factors —"the potency of mental prepossessions"—is especially vital in the work of a tribunal exercising the powers possessed by the Supreme Court. Therefore it is that the men who are given this ultimate authority over legislature and executive, whose vote may determine the well-being of millions and affect the country's future, should be subjected to the most vigorous scrutiny before being given that power. In theory, judges wield the people's power. Through the effective exertion of public opinion, the people should determine to whom that power is entrusted. The country's well-being depends upon a far-sighted and statesmanlike Court. And the Court's ultimate dependence is upon the confidence of the people.

The Supreme Court and the Public

"We are very quiet there, but it is the quiet of a storm center, as we all know."[1] So spoke Mr. Justice Holmes about the Supreme Court in 1913, the year after judicial review in constitutional cases had provided a leading issue in a presidential campaign. Theodore Roosevelt did not create the issue; he merely sponsored it. Now again, in 1930, the Supreme Court is a "storm center" which may give rise to even livelier political issues than in 1912. The recent Senate debate upon the confirmation of the new Chief Justice,[2] to writers of headlines, may have appeared as a sudden eruption, but every attentive student of the "social trends" of the Supreme Court during the postwar decade has been aware that a storm was gathering.

Presumably President Hoover's Commission on Social Trends will in due course report on the "social trends" of the Supreme Court since 1920.[3] In the meantime, an understanding of the nature of the cases that come before the Court and how it decides them, will make the recent controversy intelligible. The Court moves in a "very quiet" atmosphere and its work is largely withdrawn from the public gaze. Only occasionally, therefore, are press and public aware of the decisive influence which the Court exercises upon the economic and social development of American civilization. Such awareness is apt to come dramatically and without preparation.

But it is not good, either for the country or the Court, that the part played by the Court in the life of the country should be shrouded in mystery. Some elementary but basic facts must therefore be recalled. For it is well, whenever we are confronted with a recurring political issue, to apply Lincoln's famous recipe: "If we could first know *where* we are, and *whither* we are tending, we could then better judge *what* to do, and *how* to do it."

Reprinted from *The Forum,* June 1930. Footnotes supplied by editor.

1. *Occasional Speeches of Justice Oliver Wendell Holmes* 168 (Howe ed. 1962).
2. See 2 Pusey, *Charles Evans Hughes* ch. 63 (1951).
3. See 2 *Recent Social Trends* 1430 (1933).

The Supreme Court and the Public

Unlike President and Congress, the Supreme Court never takes the initiative. It only acts when it has a case, and the Court must wait till litigants bring cases before it. But there are cases and cases. An appreciation of the differences between cases affords the clue to the political aspects of the Supreme Court compared with the function of courts generally.

A collision between two tugboats, failure to deliver a carload of coal on time, a Paris divorce, the blowing of cinders from hot ashes thrown upon a dump—these and a thousand like situations create controversies between man and man that come in and out of courts without even remotely touching the fringes of politics. Cases like these constitute the bulk of the business of the State courts, the lower federal courts, the English courts. These are not the cases which give rise to Senate debates. At the present time, such cases rarely come before the Supreme Court.

Formally, the cases before the Supreme Court are also between two litigants, but in essence they involve the stuff of politics. To read the opinions of the Supreme Court is to move among city councils, public service commissions, tax boards, governors, State legislatures, Congress, and the President. Every act of national or State government, every law passed by Congress, every treaty ratified by the Senate, every order issued by the Interstate Commerce Commission, every tax attempted to be levied, may have to run the hazards of litigation and encounter the judicial veto of the Supreme Court.

May Gopher Prairie go in for town planning? May New York restrict the avarice of theater ticket scalpers? May the State of Washington establish a public employment agency system and bar exploitation by private agencies, or New Jersey at least limit the fee that such agencies may charge? May Nebraska fix a standard weight for a loaf of bread? Or Arizona decide that the labor injunction has, on the whole, done more harm than good? May the States encourage agricultural cooperatives? May the Senate investigate the corruptive influence of campaign contributions? May Congress regulate stockyards and stockyard agencies? Upon what basis are utilities to figure their return, and should they be allowed a return upon a franchise given them by the State? And how much of a return must they be allowed to earn? Is a net return of 6.26 percent upon the present value, including such franchises, an adequate profit for the transit lines of Baltimore, or is 7.5 or even 8 percent profit necessary for a "street railway enjoying a monopoly in one of the oldest, largest, and richest cities on the Atlantic Seaboard"?[4]

These issues and issues like them are at stake in the bulk of the litigation that comes before the Supreme Court.

The issues which thus are normally decided by the Supreme Court are not the ordinary legal question in the myriad law suits of *Smith* v. *Jones* before other courts. In large measure, Supreme Court litigation concerns the interplay of government and economic enterprise. It was not always thus. Both the volume of litigation before the Court and its nature have changed at different periods in its history.

In 1825 the Court rendered 26 opinions, and of these almost half involved applications of recognized principles of the common law. Fifty years later the Court wrote 193 opinions. But these still predominantly dealt with common law topics or technical legal questions of not wide public concern, while only 17 cases, less than 10 percent, involved questions of constitutionality, taxation, and like issues of public import. At the end of another fifty years, for 1925, the business disposed of is about the same, but the meaning of the litigation has drastically changed. Common law controversies hardly appear. The opinions reveal a steady absorption of the Court's time with questions of control over economic enterprise and kindred public controversies.

The substantial business of the Court today is to pass upon the validity of acts of government. In effect, the Court is the ultimate arbiter of the relations between citizen and government as well as of the relations of the forty-eight States to one another and to the United States.

4. Brandeis, J., dissenting, in United Railway v. West, 280 U.S. 234, 255 (1930).

The Court thus exercises essentially political functions, though it exercises them in a different atmosphere and under different circumstances than those which apply to legislatures and Congress, to governors and President.

To the success of our scheme of government an independent and statesmanlike Supreme Court is vital. In all governments there must be organs for finality of decision. In a union of States like ours, with the respective powers of the States and the union distributed in the Constitution in necessarily broad terms, a detached and strong court is the most dependable mechanism for adjusting controversies between the individual States, and between States and nation.

It does not at all follow, however, that a court must be the arbiter for all controversies that may arise in State and nation. This is not essential to a federal system, even under a written constitution. Canada and Australia prove that national well-being does not necessarily call for the same range of powers that are now exercised by our Supreme Court.

It is important to differentiate sharply, therefore, between the different types of controversies affecting public or political issues that come before the Supreme Court. There *are* different issues which vary in the scope that they afford the Justices for expressing their personal predilections.

Under the commerce clause of the Constitution, the Supreme Court maintains the balance between States and nation by determining when a State has attempted to project its authority beyond its State lines, and when, on the other hand, Congress has interfered with the purely domestic concerns of the individual State. Here is an area of conflict within which peace must be preserved by the Supreme Court. But here, too, merely as a matter of form, the Supreme Court deduces "principles" hidden in the Constitution to which only the Supreme Court has the code.

The decision under the commerce clause, whether allowing or confining State action, whether sanctioning or denying the exercise of federal power, as in the first child labor case, involve judgment on facts and policies, and not at all on an esoteric knowledge of the Constitution. The Stockyard Act, the Grain Futures Act, the West Virginia Natural Gas Act, the recapture clause of the Transportation Act, the first child labor law, and numerous tax measures of the States, all involved "interpretation" of the commerce clause. But the fate of these laws depended on adequate information before the Court on the economic and industrial facts behind this legislation and judgment on these facts by the Court.

Professor Thomas Reed Powell has thus summed up the cases under the commerce clause. "The Court has drawn its lines where it has drawn them because it has thought it wise to draw them there. The wisdom of its wisdom depends upon a judgment about practical matters and not upon a knowledge of the Constitution."[5] In other words, these decisions are at bottom acts of statesmanship. Therefore it is that the decisions of the Court must be subjected to constant scrutiny to save them from pedantry and sterility, as the unconscious rationalizations of the economic and social biases of the individual Justices. But the power of the Supreme Court to mediate between the States and the nation in interpreting the commerce clause must be left intact.

Another class of constitutional provision which comes before the Supreme Court involves specific restrictions upon the legislative power both of the States and of Congress. These are guarantees of individual rights and are based upon the history of specific political grievances or embody some specific limitation of power in the adjustment of our federal system. They are features of the Constitution which give rise to relatively little difficulty in their judicial construction. For the definiteness of the history and aims of these provisions tends to limit rather narrowly the scope of judicial review. Only occasionally is doubt raised as to whether "a fact tried by jury" has been "re-examined in any court of the United States" otherwise than "according to the rules of the common law," or whether a crime is "infamous," or whether a tax

5. "Supreme Court Decisions on the Commerce Clause and State Police Power, 1910–14 II," 22 *Colum. L. Rev.* 28, 48 (1922).

is "laid upon articles exported from any State," or even whether the protection against "unreasonable searches and seizures" is violated.

In this field economic and social conflicts play a relatively negligible part. Even here, however, in their interpretation of the guaranty of "freedom of speech," the decisions prove that the Supreme Court is not immune to temporary fears and passions.

But there are two clauses of the Constitution which present very different problems of statecraft: the "due process" clause of the Fifth Amendment, a limitation upon the federal government; and the provisions of the Fourteenth Amendment guaranteeing "due process of law" and the "equal protection of the laws," whereby every local act of every State must, under challenge, meet the approval of the Supreme Court at Washington.

These amendments do not concern the delimitation between federal and State power. They do not embody technical conceptions nor specific guarantees based upon specific historic experience. The power of States to safeguard natural resources, to assure a living wage for women workers, to limit the rents that landlords may exact, to fix standard weights for bread, to prohibit the use of shoddy, to prescribe building zones, to require the sterilization of mental defectives—these needs of modern society and needs like them can be fulfilled only by leave of the Supreme Court. And the Supreme Court's whole power to deal with these matters is derived from its reading of the "due process" clauses.

But the meaning of "due process" and the content of terms like "liberty" are not revealed by the Constitution. It is the Justices who make the meaning. They read into the neutral language of the Constitution their own economic and social views. It is in reference to these matters that Chief Justice Hughes, while governor of New York, said, "We are under a Constitution, but the Constitution is what the judges say it is.[6]

These are the clauses—"due process" and "equal protection of the laws"—which have brought forth the most

6. Hughes, *Addresses* 139 (1908).

abundant crop of judicial vetoes and through which the most effective barrier has been raised against utilizing the inherent flexibilities of our Constitution to meet modern needs. Until the Fourteenth Amendment was written into the Constitution, following the Civil War, each State was substantially the exclusive judge of its domestic life. The Fourteenth Amendment, as interpreted by judges fearful of new economic and social forces, subjected the detailed local affairs of the forty-eight States to the ultimate supervision of five men at Washington. For nearly a hundred years the "due process" clause restricting the federal government had lain largely inactive in the Fifth Amendment. The exuberant application given to the same clause in the Fourteenth Amendment was then carried over to the Fifth Amendment, so that federal as well as State legislation now has to meet the increasingly unknown and unknowable terrors of "due process."

How little of law, in the ordinary meaning of that term, there is in these decisions, and how much of politics, was revealed by Chief Justice Taft in protesting against the decision of five of the Justices in overturning the District of Columbia minimum wage law for women, and thereby the minimum wage laws of a dozen states. It "is not the function of this Court to hold Congressional Acts invalid simply because they are passed to carry out economic views which the Court believes to be unwise or unsound."[7]

The Court has been particularly active since the World War in striking down legislation, both State and federal. One might have supposed that the limit of intolerance was reached in the famous *Lochner* case,[8] whereby a ten-hour law for workers in bakeshops was declared unconstitutional. This case was Theodore Roosevelt's constant text against judicial unreasonableness. For a period after the outcries against that decision, the Court pursued a more liberal attitude. But since 1920 there have been decisions even less defensible than the *Lochner* case.

The story is best told, however, by the aggregate tendencies of the Court's work in this field. A study of all its decisions up to 1927 has been made by Professor Ray A.

7. Adkins v. Children's Hospital, 261 U.S. 525, 562 (1923).
8. Lochner v. New York, 198 U.S. 45 (1905).

Brown of the University of Wisconsin Law School.[9] From his analysis it appears that up to 1912 the Court had decided, under the "due process" clause, ninety-eight cases involving social and economic legislation. In only six of these did the Court hold the legislation unconstitutional. From 1913 to 1920 the Court decided ninety-seven cases of this type and held seven laws invalid. But since 1920, out of fifty-three cases the Court has held against the legislation in fifteen.

"Phrased in percentages this means that from 1868 to 1912 the Court held against the legislation in a very little more than six percent of the cases; from 1913 to 1920 in a little more than seven percent of the cases; while since 1920 the Court has held against the legislature in twenty-eight percent of the cases. And if we go behind the decisions and look at the votes of the individual judges in each case, we will find the same startling increase in the number of opinions adverse to the validity of legislation under the due process clauses. In the period up to 1921 the judicial vote was cast approximately ninety percent in favor of the various statutes considered, and only ten percent against. Since then, however, the favorable vote has shrunk to about sixty-nine percent and the adverse vote grown to thirty-one percent."[10] This destructive tendency of the Court, it need only be added, has continued its activity during the last few years.

The harm to our federalism thus resulting from the frustration of the free life of the individual States in their local affairs has been memorably emphasized by Mr. Justice Holmes: "There is nothing that I more deprecate than the use of the Fourteenth Amendment beyond the absolute compulsion of its words to prevent the making of social experiments that an important part of the community desires, in the insulated chambers afforded by the several states, even though the experiments may seem futile or even noxious to me and to those whose judgment I most respect."[11]

9. Brown, "Due Process of Law, Police Power, and the Supreme Court," 40 *Harv. L. Rev.* 943 (1927).

10. Id. at 944–945.

11. Truax v. Corrigan, 257 U.S. 312, 344 (1921).

No wonder that Mr. Charles Warren, the historian of the Supreme Court, has raised the basic question as to the wisdom of continuing the "due process" clause.[12] He has thus expressed doubts increasingly felt by conservative judges and students of constitutional law. In any event, so long as this power of judicial review exists, its true nature should be frankly recognized by the public and by the Court. The simple fact is that in these matters the Court, under the guise of legal form, exercises political and economic control. This is the bottom meaning of the decisions on utility valuations. That the Supreme Court is especially fitted to be the ultimate arbiter of policy, is an intelligent and tenable doctrine. But let us face the fact that five Justices of the Supreme Court *are* molders of policy, rather than impersonal vehicles of revealed truth.

Such an appreciation of the true function of the Supreme Court, in the aspects of the Constitution here considered, will help to revise our attitude toward the qualifications of its judges and the public's responsibility in their selection. Roosevelt shrewdly observed: "I may not know much about law, but I do know one can put the fear of God into judges." And in 1912 he proceeded to put the "fear of God" into them. But the "fear of God" is too intermittent and at best not a wise instrument for wisdom. What is needed is a thorough understanding of our constitutional system in action, as a basis for determining the proper scope of judicial control and the condition most likely to insure the exercise of this tremendous power by ordinary mortals, so as to avoid at once the abuses of tyranny and the timidities of dependence.

It is idle merely to abuse abuses, and equally futile to fall back upon mechanical contrivances when dealing with a process where mechanics can play but a very small part. The remedy does not lie in panaceas like the recall of judicial decisions or the requirement that more than a majority of the Court should declare legislation unconstitutional. The ultimate determinant is the quality of the Justices. Once it is candidly recognized that their whole

12. Warren, "The New 'Liberty' under the Fourteenth Amendment," 39 *Harv. L. Rev.* 431 (1926).

outlook on life, their freedom from fear, their experience and their capacity to transcend their experience, determine their decisions, it follows inevitably that these qualities will become pertinent matters of inquiry before a man is put on the Supreme Bench for life.

It is noteworthy that Presidents so unlike as Lincoln and Roosevelt should have deemed relevant the general direction of mind of prospective members of the Court toward public issues. Surely the men who wield the power of life and death over the political decisions of legislatures and executives should be subjected to the most vigorous scrutiny before being given that power. Public opinion, the President, and the Senate should all have a lively understanding of what the appointment of a Supreme Court Justice means. To discharge its powers wisely, the Court needs a constant play of informed criticism by the professional as well as the lay press.

In memorable words, one of the great men of the Court, Mr. Justice Brewer, has told of the Court's own dependence upon criticism: "It is a mistake to suppose that the Supreme Court is either honored or helped by being spoken of as beyond criticism. On the contrary, the life and character of its justices should be the object of constant watchfulness by all, and its judgments subject to the freest criticism. The time is past in the history of the world when any living man or body of men can be set on a pedestal and decorated with a halo. True, many criticisms may be, like their authors, devoid of good taste, but better all sorts of criticism than no criticism at all. The moving waters are full of life and health; only in the still waters is stagnation and death."[13]

This in turn implies a high-spirited and disinterested bar—the product of farsighted legal education at our universities—and a public opinion trustful of the workings of our judiciary because the judiciary is worthy of the trust.

13. Brewer, "Government by Injunction," 15 *Nat. Corp. Rep.* 848, 849 (1898).

The Supreme Court and the Interstate Commerce Commission

The Supreme Court under Taft had reached the zenith of reaction, and so any change in its personnel was bound to be ameliorating. Moreover, there was good reason to hope that the new Chief Justice would revert to his more liberal proclivities when first on the Bench; and the new Associate Justice, Owen J. Roberts, had, as special prosecutor in the oil scandals, given signs of understanding the excesses of the profit motive. Yet, nothing is more characteristic of the optimism of American political thought than the uncritical hosannas which greeted two or three liberal decisions in the early days of the reconstituted Court. At once it was assumed that the minority of Holmes, Brandeis, and Stone (now unhappily still further reduced by the resignation of Mr. Justice Holmes) had become overnight a permanent majority.

The Court's approval, after condemnation by the Interstate Commerce Commission, of the banker-lawyer trick in the St. Paul reorganization[1] should have given pause regarding the Court's "liberality," at least in the profoundly important domain of railroad regulation. Despite the powerful opposition of financial interests, no government agency has displayed more courage and competence in dealing with the mysteries and machinations of modern finance than the Interstate Commerce Commission. Against it were arrayed all the elements of antediluvian laissez-faire philosophy as well as the more practical exploiters of private profit in public callings. In the *St. Paul* decision the Supreme Court aligned itself with those who seek to curb the Commission's alert watchfulness of the public interest in the management of railroad properties.

Two recent decisions of the Court more than justify the anxiety which the *St. Paul* decision aroused. In the

Reprinted from the *New Republic,* January 20, 1932, with permission. Footnotes supplied by editor.

1. See United States v. Chicago, M., St. P. & P. R.R., 282 U.S. 311 (1931), discussed below in "Social Issues Before the Supreme Court."

St. Paul decision the Chief Justice did not participate. In these recent cases the Chief Justice helped to constitute the majority. Since cases do not merely decide a concrete controversy but also indicate a tendency, we must record a definite drift by a majority of the Court, consisting of the remnant of the old Taft majority reenforced by Chief Justice Hughes and Mr. Justice Roberts, to curb the Interstate Commerce Commission in the effective exercise of its powers.

Let us summarize the two recent decisions which occasion these remarks. In the *Hoboken Manufacturers' Railroad* case,[2] a small railroad and some of the trunk lines quarreled over the basis of dividing between themselves a joint rate for a through haul. The small line claimed that the big ones were taking, as sometimes happens, too fat a share and the Commission decided for the Hoboken road. Upon appeal, the Supreme Court, without considering the fairness of the Commission's ruling, upset the Commission's order on what must appear to a layman as the shabbiest of technicalities.

If we are incapable of understanding the reason for the Court's action, we have the comforting assurance of Mr. Justice Stone, writing for the dissenters, that the objection which the majority found would not "occur to anyone unfamiliar with legal niceties."[3] It appears that orders of the Commission can take effect only thirty days after issuance. In the *Hoboken* case, the Commission had ruled that the small road was entitled to a larger share of the division in the joint rate both before and subsequent to its order. But after this order, the Supreme Court decided that the Commission was without authority to order a division of rates as to the past, but did possess the power to order divisions for the future. Because the Commission, in the *Hoboken* case, did not specifically name a date when its order should become effective, the majority held the order invalid in its entirety.

No wonder that Mr. Justice Stone, speaking for himself as well as for Mr. Justice Holmes and Mr. Justice Bran-

2. United States v. Baltimore & O. R.R., 284 U.S. 195 (1931).
3. Id. at 205.

deis, evinced feeling against such hair-splitting—feeling which breaks through even the icy style of a judicial opinion. Congress had made no technical requirement that the Commission must name a specific date in its order, but merely curtailed "the power of the Commission to make its order effective within thirty days."[4] Its orders nominally go into effect thirty days after they are made. But even on the majority's own premise, argued the minority, if it be necessary to specify the time of operation of an order, the Commission had plainly intended that its order should become effective at the earliest date permitted by law. Yet, to the majority, the Interstate Commerce Commission seemed to be engaged in the witless game of emitting meaningless words, although the Commission said it was putting a stop to an injustice that big fellows were inflicting upon a little fellow.

The second case also involved a controversy between trunk lines and short lines.[5] It concerned the use of freight cars which travel beyond the owner's lines. Partly to compensate the car-owning railroad for the use of its equipment, partly to penalize the undue detention of cars by a nonowning carrier, the latter is required to pay the former for the car's use. Originally the trunk lines based this charge on mileage. Later, to penalize more effectively, the trunk lines charged a dollar a day per car. The Commission sanctioned the fairness of this per diem rule. The Commission, after a nation-wide investigation, found that such a rule would be unfair to short lines, engaged in time-consuming terminal and originating services. To save the penalty rule of the trunk roads and yet be fair to the short lines, the Commission effected a compromise. An initial period was removed from the per diem charge against short-line roads. This exempt period was made the same as the two days' "free time" allowed to shippers to load or unload cars which the short line receives from, and returns to, its long-haul connections.

According to Mr. Justice Stone, who again spoke also for Holmes and Brandeis, the facts justified this practical

4. Ibid.
5. Chicago, R.I. & P. R. R. v. United States, 284 U.S. 80 (1931).

solution of a practical problem. The majority of the Court did not deny this. It admitted that a "reasonable degree of latitude must be allowed for the exercise of its [the Commission's] judgment. The mere fact that . . . mathematical accuracy . . . may not be attained is not enough to put upon the Commission's order the stamp of invalidity."[6] But the majority refused to act upon the evidence before the Commission in order to determine whether the Commission had exercised a "reasonable degree of latitude." Inasmuch as the Commission had ruled that a charge of a dollar a day is fair, so ran the Court's reasoning, the exception made by the Commission was in contradiction of the Commission's own general rule. In vain did Mr. Justice Stone urge that the Commission obviously could not have intended any self-contradiction; in vain did his powerful dissenting opinion marshal the evidence that the general rule without the Commission's exception would be unjust.

In both cases the majority of the Court was really disdainful of facts. One would suppose that the task of the Interstate Commerce Commission was not that of regulating the workaday difficulties of a national railroad system, but that of playing a highly sterile and tenuous game of finesse. Certainly, the Supreme Court opinions reflect concerns as remote from the hard realities of trunk lines and short lines and their relationships as did the daily accounts of the Culbertson-Lenz match. Even though the Commission could have had no other purpose than to give the promptest effect to the correction of an injustice, its failure explicitly to mention a date deprives a small railroad of its rights for years. Even though the Commission attached a just exception to a general rule, the exception to the general rule by the Commission proved to the Supreme Court the Commission's intention to deny any such exception.

Whatever may be the wider implications of such obscurantism on the part of the Court, and whether or no they indicate a determined attitude on the part of the

6. Id. at 95.

majority to rein in the Interstate Commerce Commission, there can be no doubt that these decisions come as an important help to influences which have been seeking to discredit and obstruct governmental railroad control. Under cover of the confusion incident to the depression, many such attempts are afoot. The administration bill for a "reconstruction finance corporation" has sought to cast off the long established Commission control over government loans to carriers. When recently railroad executives and bankers preferred to let the Wabash and Ann Arbor roads go into receivership rather than accept the Commission's proposal for a railroad pool which might have averted receivership, the Pennsylvania put the blame on the Commission. The press eagerly took up the cry, and even the usually sedate financial editor of the *New York Times* directed sneers against the Commission.

Happily it seems rather late in the day to try to undermine an agency which for forty-four years has amply justified itself as an instrument of public protection, and never more so than in its recent history. During the postwar era of speculative orgies, the Commission has held fast to sound financial policy. By its decisions, whenever it had jurisdiction, and by warnings, whenever railroad bankers and lawyers found a loophole in the law, it sought to prevent the financial excesses by which the railroads also were sucked into the whirlpool of financial madness. In the *Nickel Plate* case,[7] some years ago, and more recently in the *St. Paul* reorganization, bankers and railroad chiefs have been too often opposed to the requirements of sound railroading, and the Commission was the protagonist of conservatism. In our day the conflict has not been so much between railroad and shippers as between the financial controllers of railroads and the great body of investors in railroad securities.

The days ahead will increase and not diminish the need for a strong Commission, whose initiative and independence ought not to be enfeebled by fear of Supreme Court reversals. On the horizon are such vast projects as

7. Nickel Plate Unification, 105 I.C.C. 425 (1926).

the Eastern Rail Consolidation applications. In terms of cold cash, some eight billion dollars are at stake. What this implies in the social and industrial life of the country is beyond figures to tell. The Commission should be free to take such action as the meaning of the facts and its own responsible insight may dictate. Not only should the Commission be free, it should feel free. Among every group of men, no matter how high-minded and able, there are always some who are unduly deferential to what is called higher authority. And nothing is more conducive to timidity than the awing authority of the Supreme Court of the United States. Men become weary of fighting, particularly when the opponent comes panoplied in the majesty of Law. Surely the Charles E. Hughes who, in 1907, put the public-service commission law on the statute books of New York, cannot be unmindful of the imponderables that are involved in recent decisions which, strangely enough, received his concurrence.

The Early Writings of O. W. Holmes, Jr.

Our times may well come to be named, by future dealers in half-truths, the Tired Age. Disillusionment is a mood of fashion as much as a form of ennui after the war's great effort. Whatever the cause, our politics are devoid of ardor and social reform has lost its romance. Such being the mental climate, one would expect jurisprudence to be in the doldrums and to earn its title as the dreary science. Alas for these generalizations about the main currents of thought! The waters of law are unwontedly alive. New winds are blowing on old doctrines, the critical spirit infiltrates traditional formulas, philosophic inquiry is pursued without apology as it becomes clearer that decisions are functions of some juristic philosophy.

New situations, the offspring of technology and changing social conceptions, make new demands upon law. The absorption of new facts and the reconcilement of new conflicts entail a re-examination of the *fundamenta* of the legal order. What are the sources of law, and what its sanctions? What do judges do when they "decide"? What are the wise bounds of *stare decisis* and when is the judicial process free from its own past? What is appropriate to the fluid empiricism of case-law, and when is codification desirable? What is the proper area of lawmaking by courts and what should be left to legislation? These are issues of moment to society. Happily, they are the dominant concern of contemporary legal scholarship on the bench, at the bar, in law schools. And these problems are now seen, not in isolation, but as aspects of the function of reason and the art of thinking. Science and philosophy illumine the interplay of form and substance in legal history, and the logic of law draws sustenance from the laws of logic.

In grappling with these issues, the youngest and most daring thinkers salute as leader him who was born when William Henry Harrison was President. It is a favorite

Reprinted from 44 *Harv. L. Rev.* 717 (1931), where it is one of the articles celebrating the ninetieth birthday of Mr. Justice Holmes.

aperçu of Mr. Justice Holmes's that the ideas of an earlier generation are absorbed but its writings die. The Justice, however, escapes his own verdict. *The Common Law* and half a dozen essays have given the most powerful direction to modern legal science. But they are classic not merely in their influence. They belong to our day.

The Common Law is already fifty years old. Its philosophic underpinning is even older. Ten years before he gave the famous Lowell Lectures, O. W. Holmes, Jr., became editor of the *American Law Review*. Beginning with Volume V (October 1870) and through Volume VII (July 1873), the *American Law Review* printed six essays and at least sixty reviews and comments which, though unsigned, bear the unmistakable *imprimatur* of its editor's thought and style. These earliest of his legal writings canvass all the juristic issues with which the air is now rife. To be sure, the current jargon had not been invented, and so his muscular and luminous English is not outmoded. In his analysis of judicial psychology, Holmes was conscious of the role of the unconscious a generation before Freud began to reorient modern psychology. Though another half-century was to elapse before the appearance of Ogden and Richards's *The Meaning of Meaning,* exploration of the meaning of the meaning of law was Holmes's pioneer enterprise.

Later, after he ceased to be editor, he published over his own signature five more essays in the *American Law Review*: "Primitive Notions in Modern Law" (Pts. I and II),[1] "Possession,"[2] "Common Carriers and the Common Law,"[3] "Trespass and Negligence."[4] All these papers were drawn upon for his *Common Law,* but simply as raw material for the finished product. "I have made," he tells us in its Preface, "such use as I thought fit of my articles in the [*American*] *Law Review,* but much of what has been taken from that source has been rearranged, rewritten, and enlarged, and the greater part of the work is

1. 10 *Am. L. Rev.* 422 (1876); 11 *Am. L. Rev.* 641 (1877). [Ed.]
2. 12 *Am. L. Rev.* 688 (1878). [Ed.]
3. 13 *Am. L. Rev.* 609 (1879). [Ed.]
4. 14 *Am. L. Rev.* 1 (1880). [Ed.]

new."[5] Only one as rich as he could so lavishly discard what he had previously written. Thus, in his "Common Carriers and the Common Law," he reveals the imaginative gift which in a great scientist reconstructs an extinct species from a single vertebra. In Holmes, it takes the form of drawing a profound lesson for the whole story of law from the particular instance of the development of the carriers' liability. His analysis deserves wider currency than the seared pages of the *American Law Review* now gives it. For it epitomizes much of what is most significant in recent jurisprudence:

> The little piece of history above very well illustrates the paradox of form and substance in the development of law. In form its growth is logical. The official theory is that each new decision follows syllogistically from existing precedents. But as precedents survive like the clavicle in the cat, long after the use they once served is at an end and the reason for them has been forgotten, the result of following them must often be failure and confusion from the merely logical point of view. It is easy for the scholar to show that reasons have been misapprehended and precedents misapplied.
>
> On the other hand, in substance the growth of the law is legislative. And this in a deeper sense than that which the courts declare to have always been the law is in fact new. It is legislative in its grounds. The very considerations which the courts most rarely mention, and always with an apology, are the secret root from which the law draws all the juices of life. We mean, of course, considerations of what is expedient for the community concerned. Every important principle which is developed by litigation is in fact and at bottom the result of more or less definitely understood views of public policy; most generally, to be sure, under our practice and traditions, the unconscious result of instinctive preferences and inarticulate convictions, but none the less traceable to public policy in the last analysis. And as

5. *The Common Law* 5 (Howe ed. 1963). [Ed.]

the law is administered by able and experienced men, who know too much to sacrifice good sense to a syllogism, it will be found that when ancient rules maintain themselves in this way, new reasons more fitted to the time have been found for them, and that they gradually receive a new content and at last a new form from the grounds to which they have been transplanted. The importance of tracing the process lies in the fact that it is unconscious, and involves the attempt to follow precedents, as well as to give a good reason for them, and that hence, if it can be shown that one half of the effort has failed, we are at liberty to consider the question of policy with a freedom that was not possible before.

What has been said will explain the failure of all theories which consider the law only from its formal side, whether they attempt to deduce the *corpus* from *a priori* postulates or fall into the humbler error of supposing the science of the law to reside in the *elegantia juris,* or logical cohesion of part with part. The truth is, that law hitherto has been, and it would seem by the necessity of its being is always, approaching and never reaching consistency. It is forever adopting new principles from life at one end, and it always retains old ones from history at the other which have not yet been absorbed or sloughed off. It will become entirely consistent only when it ceases to grow.[6]

Of the unsigned essays, four dealt explicitly with major problems of jurisprudence: "Codes, and the Arrangement of the Law"[7] (two papers). "The Theory of Torts,"[8] "Misunderstandings of the Civil Law,"[9] and two are penetrating inquiries into what were then new perplexities of the substantive law: "*Ultra Vires.* How Far Are Corporations Liable for Acts Not Authorized by Their Charters,"[10] and

6. 13 *Am. L. Rev.* at 630–631; cf. *The Common Law* 31–32 (Howe ed. 1963).
7. 5 *Am. L. Rev.* 1 (1870), reprinted 44 *Harv. L. Rev.* 725 (1931). [Ed.]
8. 7 *Am. L. Rev.* 46 (1872), reprinted 44 *Harv. L. Rev.* 773 (1931). [Ed.]
9. 6 *Am. L. Rev.* 37 (1871), reprinted 44 *Harv. L. Rev.* 759 (1931). [Ed.]
10. 5 *Am. L. Rev.* 272 (1872). [Ed.]

"Grain Elevators. On the Title to Grain in Public Warehouses."[11] In his reviews and comments, Holmes ranged the gamut of the legal literature of his day; he made his own the entire kingdom of law. Reports, digests, casebooks, fresh editions of old texts, new treatises, inaugural lectures, essays—all were judged by his learning and in turn enriched it.

These early pieces should be collected into a volume—even those that are no longer as intrinsically relevant as they were when written. For all of us, truth is born when we discover it. But intellectual genealogy is important. The history of ideas is essential to culture; thereby we are saved from being intellectually *nouveaux riches*. For the present, however, it must suffice to make more available only a portion of Holmes's anonymous writings. The four essays now reprinted[12] pose juristic issues still, or, more accurately, again in controversy. The shorter commentaries furnish samples of his reviewing, whetted, appropriately enough, on the writings of Dicey, Pollock, and Fitzjames Stephen. They give, as well, compact formulations of Holmes's theory of legislation—beside which most talk about legislation sounds hollow and partisan—and foreshadow an outlook which, thirty years later, he was to apply on the Supreme Bench by his forbearance in exercising the power of judicial review.

The masters of art and science are their own best commentators. I shall attempt no gloss upon these Holmesiana. But they insistently raise one question: How is one to account for them? In the basic problems which preoccupied them, in the way they conceived law and its judicial unfolding, they are so out of the legal current of their time. "The study of English law," Mr. Justice Holmes told us, in welcoming Holdsworth's *History*, "has been slow to feel the impulse of science."[13] And later, when he gave his blessing to the Continental Legal Historical Series, he indicated the legal environment in which, strangely enough, his own work flowered:

11. 6 *Am. L. Rev.* 450 (1872). [Ed.]
12. See notes 7, 8, and 9 *supra*. [Ed.]
13. Holmes, *Collected Legal Papers* 285 (1920).

> I can but envy the felicity of the generation to whom it is made so easy to see their subject as a whole. When I began, the law presented itself as a ragbag of details. The best approach that I found to general views on the historical side was the first volume of Spence's *Equitable Jurisdiction,* and, on the practical, Walker's *American Law.* The only philosophy within reach was Austin's *Jurisprudence.* It was not without anguish that one asked oneself whether the subject was worthy of the interest of an intelligent man. One saw people whom one respected and admired leaving the study because they thought it narrowed the mind; for which they had the authority of Burke. It required blind faith—faith that could not yet find the formula of justification for itself.[14]

Happily, he was thrown back upon the deep impulses of his own nature. He was born invincibly to ask the meaning of things and to cut beneath the skin of formulas, however respectable. His mind had commerce, not with ragbag-minded lawyers, but with impractical philosophers like William James and Charles S. Peirce; his pastime was not courtroom gossip, but "twisting the tail of the cosmos." Native predilection was reinforced by the experience of the Civil War. "Polite conversation" did not satisfy Captain Holmes; he was driven to deeper questioning.

There were other personal attributes not at all peculiar to unique creative powers. Holmes mastered the materials of his profession, such as they were. "I should think Wendell worked too hard," wrote William James in 1869.[15] He has never made a fetish of long hours, but he worked—and works—with intensity. He soaked himself in the details of the law, and his imagination saw organic connection between discrete instances. The magistral summaries of his later opinions were the concentrations of his vast and accurate reading in the apprentice years. Not the

14. 1 *Continental Legal History Series: General Survey* xlvii (1912). [Ed.]

15. 1 Perry, *William James* 307 (1935). [Ed.]

least characteristic note in his book reviews is Holmes's insistence on accuracy—accuracy to the utmost nicety.

But the *Zeitgeist* moved also through O. W. Holmes, Jr. He came to maturity when Darwin had upset men's most ancient beliefs. The evolutionary doctrines worked as ferment beyond their immediate scope. If Genesis had to be "reinterpreted," the texts of the law could hardly claim sanctity. To their contemporaries, great men inevitably appear as sports, for they mark revolutions in ideas. We now see the kinship of Whitman and Melville and Holmes. All three express man's passionate effort in the face of the illimitable mystery of the universe—Whitman and Melville as artists, Holmes as thinker.

Forty years ago, an enviable group of young men were vouchsafed glimpses into the inner life of the thinker—his tortures and triumph: "I say to you in all sadness of conviction, that to think great thoughts you must be heroes as well as idealists. Only when you have worked alone—when you have felt around you a black gulf of solitude more isolating than that which surrounds the dying man, and in hope and in despair have trusted to your own unshaken will—then only will you have achieved. Thus only can you gain the secret isolated joy of the thinker, who knows that, a hundred years after he is dead and forgotten, men who never heard of him will be moving to the measure of his thought."[16] To Mr. Justice Holmes, who thus spoke to youth for all time, has been granted the crowning gift of witnessing himself, the sway of his mind over men's thought and action. And this response has come as the victories of the mind always come—by its inner force and worth. For Mr. Justice Holmes has lived his chosen life unflinchingly and without worldly compromise—the life of the thinker under fire, applying the philosopher's temper to the passions of men and the conflicts of society.

His insights have become part of the common stock of our culture. Wherever law is known, he is known. Whatever name classifiers may give to the variants of the legal

16. *Collected Legal Papers* 32 (1920). [Ed.]

order in different parts of the world, the contribution of Mr. Justice Holmes is universally acknowledged—in China and Japan, in South Africa and Australia, by the civilians on the Continent, in the home of the Common Law. He, above all others, has given the directions of contemporary jurisprudence. He wields such a powerful influence upon us today because his deep knowledge of yesterday enables him to extricate the present from meaningless entanglements with the past and yet to see events in the perspective of history.

Since his mind is scrupulously skeptical, he has escaped sterile dogma and romantic impressionism. Only the methods of reason, unsubordinated by ephemeral episodes, can unite coherence with vitality. To this life of reason he has passionately adhered in responding to the most exacting demand that is made upon judges—to compose clashing interests of an empire by appeal to law. The philosopher's stone which Mr. Justice Holmes has constantly employed for arbitrament is the conviction that our constitutional system rests upon tolerance and that its greatest enemy is the Absolute.

In a thousand instances, he has been loyal to his philosophy. Thereby he has resolved into comprehending larger truths the conflicting claims of State and nation, of liberty and authority, of individual and society. The composer of strife, Mr. Justice Holmes has wrought with serene detachment. His deepest allegiance is to civilization—a civilization neither parochial nor utopian, but groping for realization on the stage of the new world as part of the whole world.

When Judge Cardozo Writes

To laymen, the dichotomy between law and literature is merely one aspect of the conflict between law and life. A feeling so widely and deeply held by even the most cultivated outside the law cannot be nurtured wholly upon untruth. And yet it conceals a fine covey of paradoxes which would have been fair game for a Hazlitt, though for all I know he himself shared the feeling or put to flight at least some of its paradoxes. That nothing which is human is alien to him, is truer of the lawyer than even of doctor or priest. For the lawyer's office is frequently a confessional, and long before psychiatry had its name wise lawyers had to practice its arts. The work of courts is in essence the composition of human rivalries, the arbitrament of conflicting human desires. Something of its human origin ought therefore to be secreted in the records of the law; at least an occasional heartbeat ought to be found within law-sheep binding. And the adventurous-minded, the sophisticated who do not like to slumber too easily on the dogma that law is outside of life or that life is without law, would be rewarded more richly than they suspect by those records of the variegated human scene we call the law reports. Thus, in a single pamphlet of recent opinions may be found an exciting analysis of the originality, if any, of the dramatic qualities of "Abie's Irish Rose"[1] and disclosures regarding the practice of birth control in the United States,[2] the more revealing because set forth with calculated sobriety. If it be true, as Robert Louis Stevenson said, that the writer who knew what to omit could turn a daily paper into an Odyssey, then, as the lawyers would say, it is a fortiori true of the law reports.

But I am afraid that even with these few remarks I have added further proof that of the many mansions in the house of literature, law is not one. Incurably subdued by

Reprinted from a Book Review of Benjamin N. Cardozo, *Law and Literature* (1931), in the *New Republic*, April 8, 1931, with permission. Footnotes supplied by editor.

1. Nichols v. Universal Pictures Corp., 45 F.2d 119 (2d Cir. 1930).
2. Youngs Rubber Corporation v. C. I. Lee & Co., 45 F.2d 103 (2d Cir. 1930).

the materials of my profession, I seemingly cannot write a paragraph without "if anys" and a fortioris. Here is the inevitable lawyer's writing—the dull qualifications and circumlocutions that sink any literary barque or even freighter, the lifeless tags and rags that preclude grace and stifle spontaneity. In good measure one may admit the charge, without implying that the limits of one of her votaries are the law's limits. It will not do to press the claims of law upon literature by denying that the law has its own great preoccupation distinct from that of literature. Once and for all, Mr. Justice Holmes has put our case, with colors flying and without arrogance: "Of course the law is not the place for the artist or the poet. The law is the calling of thinkers."[3] Literature is not the goal of lawyers, though they occasionally attain it. With more explicitness to the matter in hand, though wholly free from didacticism, Chief Judge Cardozo in this volume of essays makes clear why the artist's search for beauty cannot be the lawyer's prime concern. For the judge, with us the ultimate spokesman of the law, must be "historian and prophet all in one." The law must be declared "not only as the past has shaped it in judgments already rendered, but as the future ought to shape it in cases yet to come. Those of us whose lives have been spent on the bench and at the bar have learned caution and reticence, perhaps even in excess. We know the value of the veiled phrase, the blurred edge, the uncertain line."[4] Here we have the source of the antinomy between law and literature. "Caution and reticence" are not the wellsprings of literature, but they are indispensable to wisdom in law, certainly to wisdom in adjudication. Since judges must be prophets, in other words since judges not merely register the past but direct the future, they had best not presume too much upon a wisdom that was denied the Delphic oracles. By a strange inconsistency, those who chafe most against the governance of the present by the edicts of the past too frequently want the present to pronounce against the future, forgetting that for the future the present will be the past.

3. Holmes, *Collected Legal Papers* 29–30 (1920).
4. P. 137.

Law, then, is not part of belles lettres. But within the limits of its responsibility and its themes, law has not come empty-handed to the altars of literature. A comprehensive account of English literature, as the expression of English thought, could hardly omit Mansfield, Stowell, and Bowen, to mention only modern judges, and Maitland's genius shows with what imagination and charm the story of the law can be invested.

> When I think thus of the law, I see a princess mightier than she who once wrought at Bayeux, eternally weaving into her web dim figures of the ever lengthening past—figures too dim to be noticed by the idle, too symbolic to be interpreted except by her pupils, but to the discerning eye disclosing every painful step and every world-shaking contest by which mankind has worked and fought its way from savage isolation to organic social life.[5]

244 So wrote an American judge, Mr. Justice Holmes, who among judges has the supreme place in any adequate anthology of English prose. But there are other judges who wrote with the memorable uniqueness of expression that is style. There is of course John Marshall, whom Judge Cardozo, in the exhilarating essay which gives its name to this volume, selects for the "type magisterial or imperative" in his critical and playful analysis of the varieties of judicial opinions. "We hear the voice of the law speaking by its consecrated ministers with the calmness and assurance that are born of a sense of mastery and power. Thus Marshall seemed to judge, and a hush falls upon us even now as we listen to his words. Those organ tones of his were meant to fill cathedrals."[6] There is not space to follow Judge Cardozo in his serio-humorous categories of opinions and their exemplars. I have, besides, my own favorite. Who among nonlawyers writes as Judge Charles M. Hough wrote, and as Judge Learned Hand now

5. *Occasional Speeches of Justice Oliver Wendell Holmes* 22 (Howe ed. 1962).
6. Pp. 10–11.

writes? One might also be tempted to intrude on Judge Cardozo's gentle silences about the versatile forms of judicial stuffiness. Unlike the new Earl Russell, judges are prone to "regard solemnity as a means of attaining truth."

Deference for the well-known shyness of the author has held this review much too long in check. If Judge Cardozo will publish, he must suffer the pains of public appreciation. Who better than he has demonstrated that law is stunted and undernourished by life, if it falls below the dignity of literature? The bar reads his opinions for pleasure, and even a disappointed litigant must feel, when Judge Cardozo writes, that a cause greater than his private interest prevailed. And so it has come to pass that the court over which Judge Cardozo presides enjoys an eminence second only to that of the Supreme Court of the United States. Its Chief must be included in the first half-dozen judges of the English-speaking world.

This volume gives the lay reader a taste of Judge Cardozo's qualities—grace in the service of solidity, sensitiveness directing judgment, awareness of the limits of reason and of the subtle guises of self-deception. Judge Cardozo elsewhere has quoted Chesterton's remark that the most important thing about a man is his philosophy.[7] And this distillate of Judge Cardozo's reflections is inevitably judicial self-revelation. These seven papers were born of distinct occasions; formally they have no common theme. And yet they have the unity of their common source, drawn as they are from the same deep brooding over law's meanings and methods.

The enduring contributions of thinkers, maintains one of the acutest, are not systems but insights. Indeed, systems are apt to be overrefined elaborations of penetrating glimpses into truth. At all events, the two judges who in our day have given powerful direction to juristic thinking have done so not by heavy treatises on jurisprudence. Mr. Justice Holmes has gradually refashioned the whole outlook and methods of American legal thought through his

7. *Growth of the Law* 59 (1924).

essays no less than his opinions. The work of philosophic permeation begun by his master sixty years ago (and happily still continued in his opinions) is being carried on by New York's Chief Judge, and again by essays. What is now set before the general reader, from a hint or suggestive phrase, to students ("The Game of the Law") or to doctors ("What Medicine Can Do for the Law"), with all the seeming casualness of a luncheon ("The Comradeship of the Law"), or at a housewarming ("The Home of the Law"), is the stuff, also, of three small but not slight earlier volumes of essays—"The Nature of the Judicial Process" (1921), "The Growth of the Law" (1924), and "The Paradoxes of Legal Science" (1928). Their common theme is the task that confronts the judge. But a candid scrutiny of what confronts the judge must include what confronts the law. The essay form is the fit instrument for a thinker whose concern is to lay bare the contending claims that seek the mediation of law, and to give some indication of how these processes of mediation in fact operate. For the essay is tentative, suggestive, contradictory, and incomplete. It mirrors the perversities and zests and complexities of life.

"It is the first step in sociological wisdom," according to Whitehead, "to recognize that the major advances in civilization are processes which all but wreck the societies in which they occur—like unto an arrow in the hand of a child. The art of free society consists first in the maintenance of the symbolic code; and secondly in fearlessness of revision, to secure that the code serves those purposes which satisfy an enlightened reason."[8] In the service of this "sociological wisdom" no one is more deeply enlisted than the author of these essays.

8. Whitehead, *Symbolism, Its Meaning and Effect* 88 (1927).

Mr. Justice Brandeis and the Constitution

A definitive history of great political events may challenge the fecundity of historians, but of necessity escapes them. Even an adequate history of the Supreme Court awaits writing, to say which is no failure of gratitude to Mr. Charles Warren, who did not purport to paint a full canvas. He attempted only an essay on "The Supreme Court in United States History." To write the history of the Court presupposes an adequate social history of the United States, which, as yet, we lack. Much brave scholarship is now enlisted to give a critical understanding of our past. And the illuminating chapters of the Beards and of Parrington, together with the *History of American Life,* edited by Professors Schlesinger and Fox, bring nearer the day of a comprehensive history of our civilization.

Moreover, the work of the Supreme Court is the history of relatively few personalities. However much they may have represented or resisted their *Zeitgeist,* symbolized forces outside their own individualities, they were also individuals. The fact that they were *"there"*[1] and that others were not, surely made decisive differences. To understand what manner of men they were is crucial to an understanding of the Court. Yet how much real insight have we about the seventy-five men who constitute the Supreme Court's roll of judges? How much is known about the inner forces that directed their action and

Excerpt from the article that appeared in 45 *Harv. L. Rev.* 33 (1931), and in *Mr. Justice Brandeis* 49 (Frankfurter ed. 1932). The occasion celebrated was Mr. Justice Brandeis's seventy-fifth birthday. Copyright 1931 by The Harvard Law Review Association. The original article contained many lengthy quotations from Brandeis's opinions that have been omitted here.

1. "A great man represents a great ganglion in the nerves of society, or, to vary the figure, a strategic point in the campaign of history, and part of his greatness consists in his being *there.* I no more can separate John Marshall from the fortunate circumstances that the appointment of Chief Justice fell to John Adams, instead of to Jefferson a month later, and so gave it to a Federalist and loose constructionist to start the working of the Constitution, than I can separate the black line through which he sent his electric fire at Fort Wagner from Colonel Shaw." Holmes, "John Marshall," in *Speeches* 88 (1913); *Collected Legal Papers* 268 (1920).

stamped the impress of their unique influence upon the Court? Only of Marshall have we an adequate biography;[2] Story's revealing correspondence takes us behind his scholarly exterior;[3] very recently not a little light has been shed on the circumstances and associations that helped to mold Field's outlook.[4] About most of the Justices we have only mortuary estimates.

However little we may know about the personal and social influences in which the Court's history is enmeshed, we know enough to know that the essential history of the United States is mirrored in the controversies before the Court. The thrust of the American empire against the hostility to extension, the eternal conflict between creditor and debtor classes and between rich and poor, the push toward economic concentration and the resistance of individual enterprise, the struggles between *étatisme* and libertarianism, between racial homogeneity and diversity of strains, the conflict between the attachments of localism and the march of centralization—all the contending forces in our society, throughout our national life, lie buried within the interstices of the 283 volumes of *United States Reports,* ready to be quickened into life by the artist's magic touch.

2. Beveridge, *Life of John Marshall* (1916–1920).
3. Story, *Life and Letters of Joseph Story* (1851).
4. Swisher, *Stephen J. Field: Craftsman of the Law* (1930), and see Walter Nelles's review of Swisher's *Field* in 40 *Yale L.J.* 998 (1931). The following books furnish additional serious biographical or autobiographical material concerning some of the Justices: Black and Smith, *Stephen J. Field as a Legislator, State Judge and Judge of the Supreme Court of the United States* (1881–1895); Bradley, *Miscellaneous Writings* (1902); Brown, *The Life of Oliver Ellsworth* (1905); Clark, *The Constitutional Doctrines of Justice Harlan* (1915); Clifford, *Nathan Clifford, Democrat* (1922); Connor, *John Archibald Campbell* (1920); Curtis, *Memoir of Benjamin Robbins Curtis* (1879); Delaplaine, *Life of Thomas Johnson* (1927); Flanders, *Lives and Times of the Chief Justices* (rev. ed. 1897); Gregory, *Samuel Freeman Miller* (1907); Hart, *Salmon Portland Chase* (1909); Jay, *Life of John Jay* (1873); Kent, *Memoir of Henry Billings Brown* (1915); Lamar, *The Life of Joseph Rucker Lamar* (1926); Macree, *Life and Correspondence of James Iredell* (1857–1858); Mayes, *Lucius Q. C. Lamar; His Life, Times and Speeches* (1896); Shuckers, *Life and Public Services of Salmon Portland Chase* (1874); Steiner, *Life of Roger Brooke Taney* (1922); Tyler, *Memorial of Roger B. Taney* (1872); Whitelock, *Life and Times of John Jay* (1887).

Of spontaneous generation there is little in history. Epochal changes germinate slowly, and dates in history are deluding. They mark fruition rather than beginning. Yet "every schoolboy knows," though without the omniscience which Macaulay attributed to him, that the Great War ushered in a new era. While the forces which burst upon the world in a cataclysmic war had long been burrowing underground, the debacle of three mighty empires, the Russian Revolution and its violent break with the past, the intensification of technological processes induced by the war, loosed economic and social forces far more upsetting to the pre-existing equilibrium than the changes wrought by the French Revolution and the Napoleonic wars. All these conflicts and confusions of recent history also are registered in the recent history of the Supreme Court. Mr. Justice Brandeis came to the Supreme Court at the threshold of this new epoch.[5]

Time is an almost indispensable condition for weaving the impress of distinction upon the work of the Court.[6] Mr. Justice Brandeis has now entered upon his sixteenth Term and written 415 opinions. These reveal an organic

5. "On January 28, 1916, President Wilson nominated Louis D. Brandeis of Massachusetts to succeed Mr. Justice Lamar deceased: he was confirmed by the Senate on June 1, 1916, his commission was dated June 1, 1916, and he took his seat upon the bench June 5, 1916." 241 U.S. iii. The reporter thus veils one of the most stirring occurrences in the Court's history. This is not the occasion to explore the meaning of the contest that resulted in the confirmation of the nomination of Mr. Brandeis. See *Hearings and Report on Nomination of Louis D. Brandeis,* Sen. Doc. No. 409, 64th Cong., 1st Sess. [See Todd, *Justice on Trial* (1964). Ed.]

6. Selection of the dozen judges who have left the greatest mark upon the Court is largely a matter of personal choice. Of those no longer living, my twelve, with their respective years of service, follow: Marshall (34), William Johnson (30), Story (34), Taney (28), Curtis (6), Miller (28), Field (34), Chase (9), Bradley (22), Brewer (21), White (27), Moody (3). It will be noted that the minimum length of service of all but three was twenty-one Terms. Chase had too dominant a share in constitutional and international issues following the Civil War to be omitted. I avouch for Curtis's claims, *inter alia,* Cooley v. Board of Wardens of Philadelphia, 12 How. 299 (1851), and Murray's Lessee v. Hoboken Land and Improvement Co., 18 How. 272 (1856); for Moody's, *inter alia,* Employers' Liability Cases, 207 U.S. 463, 504 (1908) (dissent), and Twining v. New Jersey, 211 U.S. 78 (1908).

constitutional philosophy, which expresses his response to the deepest issues of society. Other Justices have brought to the Court the matured outlook of a lifetime's brooding. But probably no other man has come to the Court with his mind dyed, as it were, in the very issues which became his chief judicial concern. Indeed, his work as Justice may accurately be described as a continuation of devotion to the solution of those social and economic problems of American society with which he was preoccupied for nearly a generation before his judicial career. Some years before going on the Court he had practically withdrawn from private practice and given unique meaning to what Senator Root has called the "public profession" of the law. Whenever some particularly pressing or difficult issue absorbed his interest and his energy, his passion for law and his mastery of its processes were engaged on behalf of the community; the community which he served was increasingly as wide as the nation. And he gave himself to public affairs as a private citizen. He is one of the very few men who became a Justice without having held prior judicial or political office,[7] except for his service as special counsel for the Interstate Commerce Commission in the proceedings for general rate increases in 1913–14.[8] Even this inquiry he conducted not as a partisan but in a judicial spirit, to see "that all sides and angles of the case are presented of record, without advocating any particular theory for its disposition."[9]

Thus for years Mr. Justice Brandeis had been immersed in the intricacies which modern industry and finance have created for society and in the conflicts engendered by them. Hardly another lawyer had amassed experience over so wide a range and with so firm a grip on the details that matter. The intricacies of large affairs, railroading,

7. Apparently, only Bradley (who merely headed the electoral ticket of Grant, in New Jersey, in 1868) and Miller had never held public office before their accession to the Supreme Court. For ascertaining these facts and for other help I am indebted to Mr. Paul A. Freund, Research Fellow, Harvard Law School.

8. The Five Per Cent Case, 31 I.C.C. 351 (1914); 32 I.C.C. 325 (1914).

9. *Hearings and Report on Nomination of Louis D. Brandeis*, Sen Doc. No. 409, 64th Cong. 1st Sess., p. 26.

finance, insurance, the public utilities, and the conservation of our natural resources, had yielded to him their meaning. In all these fields the impact of the concrete instance started his inquiries, but it is of the very nature of his mind to explore a subject with which he is grappling until he sees it in all its social bearing.[10]

But his approach to these problems was always that of the lawyer-statesman, seeking to tame isolated instances to the largest possible general rule and to make thereby the difficult reconciliation between order and justice. At a time when our constitutional law was becoming dangerously unresponsive to drastic social changes, when sterile clichés instead of facts were deciding cases, he insisted, as the great men of law have always insisted, that law must be sensitive to life. And he preached the doctrine by works more than by faith.[11] By a series of arguments and briefs he created a new technique in the presentation of constitutional questions. Until his famous brief in *Muller* v. *Oregon*,[12] social legislation was supported before the courts largely *in vacuo*—as an abstract dialectic between "liberty" and "police power," unrelated to a world of trusts and unions, of large-scale industry and all its implications.

10. See, for instance, the following published by the Justice while at the bar: *Financial Condition of the New York, New Haven and Hartford Railroad Company* (1907); Testimony before the Senate Committee on Interstate Commerce in considering Sen. Doc. No. 2941 "A Bill to Create an Interstate Trade Commission," *Hearings before the Interstate Commerce Commission pursuant to Sen. Res. 98*, 62d Cong., Dec. 14, 15 and 16, 1911, pp. 1146 et seq.; *Other People's Money* (1914); *Business—A Profession* (1914, 1925).

11. Shortly before his appointment to the Court, he delivered an address before the Chicago Bar Association in which he analyzed why law, particularly public law, was then finding itself in heavy waters. "The Living Law," 10 *Ill. L. Rev.* 461 (1916); *Business—A Profession* 344 (1925). His "true remedy" for making law and courts adequate "to meet contemporary economic and social demands" is in striking contrast to the usual mechanical panaceas that, from time to time, are offered:

"We are powerless to restore the general practitioner and general participation in public life. Intense specialization must continue. But we can correct its distorting effects by broader education—by study undertaken preparatory to practice—and continued by lawyer and judge throughout life: study of economics and sociology and politics which embody the facts and present the problems of today." Id. at 362.

12. 208 U.S. 412 (1908).

In the *Oregon* case, the facts of modern industry which provoke regulatory legislation were, for the first time, adequately marshaled before the Court. It marks an epoch in the disposition of cases presenting the most important present-day constitutional issues.[13]

Never was there an easier transition from forum to bench than when Mr. Brandeis became Mr. Justice Brandeis. Since the significant cases before the Supreme Court always involve large public issues and are not just cases between two litigants, the general outlook of the Justices largely determines their views and votes in doubtful cases. Thus the divisions on the Court run not at all along party lines. They reflect not past political attachments, but the philosophy of the judges about government and our Government, their conception of the Constitution and of their own function as its interpreter.

Rich experience at the bar confirmed the teachings which Mr. Brandeis had received from James Bradley Thayer, the great master of constitutional law, that the Constitution had ample resources within itself to meet the changing needs of successive generations. The Constitution provided for the future partly by not forecasting it and partly by the generality of its language. The ambiguities and lacunae of the document left ample scope for the unfolding of life. If the Court, aided by the bar, has access to the facts and heeds them, the Constitution, as he had shown, is flexible enough to respond to the demands of modern society. The work of Mr. Justice Brandeis is in the tradition of Marshall, for, underlying his opinions, is the realization "that it is a *constitution* we are expounding."[14] In essence, the Constitution is not a literary composition

13. The unusual reference by Mr. Justice Brewer, for the Court, to the argument by Mr. Brandeis bears repetition:

"In patent cases counsel are apt to open the argument with a discussion of the state of the art. It may not be amiss, in the present case, before examining the constitutional question, to notice the course of legislation as well as expressions of opinion from other than judicial sources. In the brief filed by Mr. Louis D. Brandeis, for the defendant in error, is a very copious collection of all these matters, an epitome of which is found in the margin." 208 U.S. 412, 419 (1908).

14. McCulloch v. Maryland, 4 Wheat. 315, 407 (1819).

but a way of ordering society, adequate for imaginative statesmanship, if judges have imagination for statesmanship.[15]

This general point of view has led Mr. Justice Brandeis to give free play to the States and the nation within their respective spheres.

For him, the Constitution affords the country, whether at war or peace, the powers necessary to the life of a great nation. It is amply equipped for the conduct of war. It has the widest discretion in raising the fighting services;[16] to strengthen these, it may also mobilize the social and moral forces of the nation.[17] Whether to wage war or to enforce its revenue laws, the United States, like other nations, has all the rights of the high seas recognized by international law.[18]

Taxation has always been the most sensitive nerve of government. The enormous increase in the cost of society and the extent to which wealth is represented by intangibles are putting public finance to its severest tests. To balance budgets, to pay for the cost of progressively civilized social standards, to safeguard the future and to divide these burdens with substantial fairness to the different interests in the community, strains to the utmost the ingenuity of statesmen. They must constantly explore new sources of revenue and find means to prevent the circumvention of their discovery. Subject as they are, in English-speaking countries, to popular control, they must be allowed the widest latitude of power. No finicky limitation upon their discretion nor jejune formula of equality should circumscribe the necessarily empirical process of tapping new revenue or stopping new devices for its evasion. To these needs Mr. Justice Brandeis has been imaginatively alive. He has consistently refused to accentuate the fiscal difficulties of government by injecting into the Constitution his own notions of fiscal policy. In

15. See United States v. Moreland, 258 U.S. 433, 451 (1922) (dissent); Olmstead v. United States, 277 U.S. 438, 472 (1928) (dissent).

16. See Gilbert v. Minnesota, 254 U.S. 325, 336–337 (1920) (dissent).

17. See Jacob Ruppert v. Caffey, 251 U.S. 264, 299–300 (1920).

18. See Maul v. United States, 274 U.S. 501, 524-525 (1927)(concurrence).

the "vague contours of the Fifth Amendment"[19] he reads no restriction upon historic methods of taxation.[20] Nor has he found in the Constitution compulsion to grant additional immunity or benefit to taxpayers merely because they already hold tax-exempt securities.[21]

For the States, within their ambit, Mr. Justice Brandeis also finds ample scope in the Constitution. He feels profoundly the complexities of their problems. Adequate opportunity for experimentation should not, he believes, be denied to them by a static conception of the Constitution. Here, again, the general intimations of fairness and reason in the due process clause were not intended to shut off remedies, however tentative, for the moral and economic waste, the friction of classes, urban congestion, the relaxation of individual responsibility, the subtler forms of corruption, and the abuses of power which have followed in the wake of a highly developed laissez faire industrialism.[22]

19. Mr. Justice Holmes, dissenting, in Adkins v. Children's Hospital, 261 U.S. 525, 568 (1923).

Judge Learned Hand has also put the matter in telling language. The provisions of the Fifth Amendment "represent a mood rather than a command, that sense of moderation, of fair play, of mutual forebearance, without which states become the prey of faction. They are not the rules of a game; their meaning is lost when they are treated as though they were." Daniel Reeves, Inc. v. Anderson, 43 F.2d 679, 682 (C.A.2d, 1930).

20. See Untermeyer v. Anderson, 276 U.S. 440, 447, 450–452 (1928) (dissent).

21. See National Life Ins. Co. v. United States, 277 U.S. 508, 527–528, 533 (1928)(dissent).

22. See Adams v. Tanner, 244 U.S. 590, 613–615 (1917)(dissent); Pennsylvania Coal Co. v. Mahon, 260 U.S. 393, 416–417, 419, 422 (1922) (dissent); Jay Burns Baking Co. v. Bryan, 264 U.S. 504, 519–520, 533–534 (1924)(dissent); Missouri Pac. R.R. v. Western Crawford Road Improv. Dist., 266 U.S. 187, 190 (1924); Truax v. Corrigan, 257 U.S. 312, 355–357 (1921)(dissent).

Dissenting opinions are apt to express in ampler form than views voiced for the Court the constitutional philosophy of the Justices. Mr. Justice Brandeis is not, quantitatively speaking, a dissenting Justice. As to the duty to utter dissents, see Mr. Justice Story, in Briscoe v. Bank of Kentucky, 11 Pet. 257, 349–350 (1837); Mr. Chief Justice Taney, in Rhode Island v. Massachusetts, 12 Pet. 657, 752 (1838); Mr. Justice Moody, in Employers' Liability Cases, 207 U.S. 463, 505 (1908). And see (Mr. Justice) Brown, "The Dissenting Opinions of Mr. Justice Harlan," 46 *Am. L. Rev.* 321, 350–352 (1912).

Particularly, the States should not be hampered in dealing with evils at their points of pressure. Legislation is essentially ad hoc. To expect uniformity in law where there is diversity in fact is to bar effective legislation. An extremely complicated society inevitably entails special treatment for distinctive social phenomena. If legislation is to deal with realities, it must address itself to important variations in the needs, opportunities, and coercive power of the different elements in the State. The States must be left wide latitude in devising ways and means for paying the bills of society and in using taxation as an instrument of social policy. Taxation is never palatable. Its essential fairness must not be tested by pedantic arguments derived from hollow abstractions. Even more dangers than have been revealed by the due process clause may lurk in the requirement of "the equal protection of the laws," if that provision of the Fourteenth Amendment is to be applied with "delusive exactness."[23] That tendency, often revealed during the postwar period, Mr. Justice Brandeis has steadily resisted.[24]

Even though the corporation has become a common form of doing business, differences between corporate and individual enterprise persist. The differences are sufficiently significant legitimately to be reflected in the taxing systems of States.[25] Again, the cooperative movement has far-reaching social implications, and the State ought to be allowed to promote it by differentiating, in a variety of ways, between cooperative and ordinary profit-seeking enterprise, even though cooperatives be formally incorporated.[26]

The veto power of the Supreme Court over the social-economic legislation of the States, when exercised by a

23. Mr. Justice Holmes, dissenting, in Truax v. Corrigan, 257 U.S. 312, 342 (1921).

24. See Royster Guano Co. v. Virginia, 253 U.S. 412, 417–418 (1920) (dissent); Truax v. Corrigan, 257 U.S. 312, 374–375 (1921)(dissent); Louisville Gas & Elec. Co. v. Coleman, 277 U.S. 32, 50–52 (1928)(dissent).

25. See Quaker City Cab Co. v. Pennsylvania, 277 U.S. 389, 403–404, 405–406, 410–411 (1928)(dissent).

26. See Frost v. Corporation Comm., 278 U.S. 515, 531, 533–538, 547–548 (1929)(dissent).

narrow conception of the due process and equal protection of the law clauses, presents undue centralization in its most destructive and least responsible form. The most destructive, because it stops experiment at its source, preventing an increase of social knowledge by the only scientific method available, namely, the test of trial and error. The least responsible, because it so often turns on the fortuitous circumstances which determine a majority decision, and shelters the fallible judgment of individual Justices, in matters of fact and opinion not peculiarly within the special competence of judges, behind the impersonal authority of the Constitution. The inclination of a single Justice, the buoyancy of his hopes or the intensity of his fears, may determine the opportunity of a much-needed social experiment to survive, or may frustrate for a long time intelligent attempts to deal with a social evil. Against these dangers the only safeguards are judges thoroughly awake to the problems of their day and open-minded to the facts which may justify legislation. His wide experience, his appetite for fact, his instinct for the concrete and his distrust of generalities, equip Mr. Justice Brandeis with unique gifts for the discharge of the Court's most difficult and delicate tasks.

No aspect of State intervention in the conduct of private enterprise forms a more settled policy of American public law than the regulation of the social services furnished by "public utilities." Comprehensive utility control initiated a quarter of a century ago by the elder La Follette in Wisconsin,[27] and Governor Hughes in New York,[28] is now part of the governmental machinery of every State. Its rationale is public protection through administrative regulation capable of matching in power and technical resources the power and resources of the utilities. The judicial control of this regulatory system has given rise to the severest conflicts in our time between courts and popular opinion, between the Supreme Court and the States.

The heart of the difficulty has been the Court's attitude, during the period of postwar inflation, regarding the

27. Wis. Laws 1907, c. 499.
28. N.Y. Laws 1907, c. 429; Hughes, *Addresses* 139 (1908).

profits to which utility investors are constitutionally entitled and the rates which may be exacted from the consuming public. Economic questions were transmuted into unreal legal conceptions, for the ascertainment of the rate base and the determination of utility rates are essentially economic problems. It took nearly a generation to settle the share which the Court now exercises in these economic adjudications.[29] But the intrinsic nature of the problem was not changed by the change in forum, from legislature to commission, from commission to court. And the source of the Court's authority in this domain of litigation still remains the general admonitions of fair dealing of the Fourteenth Amendment. However verbally screened, the independent judgment of the Court in valuation matters is not an adjudication governed by technical legal principles. It is an exercise of judgment on economic facts and opinion. Through the generality of language in *Smyth* v. *Ames*,[30] an empiric device for preventing swollen returns on fictitious values during a period of falling prices, was in course of time, during a period of rising prices, in a series of cases beginning in 1923, turned into a most luxuriant means for creating fictitious values. For this economic legerdemain constitutional sanction was sought, and in part, for a time at least, largely gained.

Leadership against that tendency fell to Mr. Justice Brandeis. His series of massive opinions, drawn from his intimate railroad experiences and reinforced by elaborate research constitutes a treatise on the major issues of railroad economics. The late Allyn A. Young, most sagacious of economists, characterized the dissent of Mr. Justice Brandeis in *Southwestern Bell Tel. Co.* v. *Public Serv. Comm.*[31] as the ablest critique of the economics of utility valuation.

29. See Munn v. Illinois, 94 U.S. 113, 134 (1876); Railroad Commission Cases, 116 U.S. 307, 331 (1886); Chicago, etc. Ry. v. Minnesota, 134 U.S. 418 (1890); Ohio Valley Co. v. Ben Avon Borough, 253 U.S. 287 (1920).

30. 169 U.S. 466 (1898). See Frankfurter, *The Public and Its Government* (1930).

31. 262 U.S. 276, 289, 290–292, 308–310 (1922). See also Groesbeck v. Duluth S.S. & A. Ry., 250 U.S. 607 (1919); Georgia Ry. v. Railroad Comm., 262 U.S. 625 (1923); McCardle v. Indianapolis Water Co., 272 U.S. 400, 421 (1926)(dissent).

Exact analysis and a comprehending view of large affairs mark the opinions by Mr. Justice Brandeis which deal with business. In utility cases, he illuminates the known factors, and, in view of the obscurity which still envelops the economic process, is unwilling to substitute judicial judgment for administrative judgment.[32] And he reveals the opportunities of legal science for social invention in the solution of subtle problems like those of depreciation.[33]

Events have clearly vindicated the analysis made by Mr. Justice Brandeis of the reproduction-cost-minus-depreciation doctrine and have underscored his criticisms. His objection to the doctrine on the score both of economic unreality and social waste has been reinforced by the reports upon the workings of the public service laws of New York[34] and Massachusetts,[35] the continued uncertainty and costliness of rate litigation,[36] and the growing anxiety of utility leaders over a situation supposedly favorable to their interests.[37] The present drastic drop in commodity prices should conclude the argument.[38] Changing condi-

32. See Pacific Gas & Elec. Co. v. San Francisco, 265 U.S. 403, 422–425 (1924)(dissent).

33. See United Railways v. West, 280 U.S. 234, 277–280 (1930)(dissent); St. Louis & O'Fallon Ry. v. United States, 279 U.S. 461, 488 (1929) (dissent).

34. *Report of Commission on Revision of the Public Service Commissions Law,* N.Y. Legis. Doc. No. 75 (1930).

35. *Report of the Special Commission on Control and Conduct of Public Utilities,* House Doc. No. 1200 (1930).

36. See Frankfurter, *The Public and Its Government* 95 et seq. (1930), and the tortuous litigation in Smith v. Illinois Bell Tel. Co., 282 U.S. 133 (1930), which is still in process before the District Court for the Northern District of Illinois. [The case was finally disposed of by another Supreme Court decision. Lindheimer v. Illinois Bell Telephone Co., 292 U.S. 131 (1934). Ed.]

37. See, e.g., testimony of Mr. Owen D. Young before the Senate Committee on Interstate Commerce, as quoted by Joseph B. Eastman on behalf of the Interstate Commerce Commission in a letter dated January 20, 1930, to Chairman Couzens of the Senate Committee on Interstate Commerce.

38. The decision of the majority in Southwestern Bell Tel. Co. v. Public Service Comm., 262 U.S. 276 (1923), must surely have been influenced by the then common belief in the permanence of a "new plateau of prices." This assumption Mr. Justice Brandeis did not share; indeed he believed the contrary. It is characteristic of his prophetic insight into

tions will lead a changed Supreme Court to emphasize other factors than those that have heretofore played a decisive part. The very grab-bag nature of the formula in *Smyth* v. *Ames*[39] will enable the Court to pick some things from the bag and neglect others. The familiar process of accommodating general language to new facts will, one ventures to believe, lead the Court in fact, if not in form, to adopt the "prudent investment" doctrine in the protection of those very interests which in recent years, by resort to the reproduction theory, it had overprotected.

Thus far we have considered action by the States within their reserved spheres, limited merely by the negations of the Fourteenth Amendment and never in direct competition with the affirmative powers of the federal government. Where the States and nation touch a field of legislation wherein both may move, fertile opportunities for conflict arise. The commerce clause gives controlling authority to the nation. But how these conflicts are to be resolved—when the commerce clause becomes operative and the States have to stand aside, when the States are still free despite the commerce clause or because Congress has not seen fit to invoke its authority—depends ultimately upon the philosophy of the Justices regarding our federalism.

Mr. Justice Brandeis's regard for the States is no mere lip service. He is greatly tolerant of their powers because he believes intensely in the opportunities which they afford for decentralization. And he believes in decentralization not because of any persisting habit of political allegiance or through loyalty to an anachronistic theory of States' rights. His views are founded on deep convictions regarding the manageable size for the effective conduct of human affairs and the most favorable conditions for the exercise of wise judgment.

---

economic causes and their effects that in 1923 he should have been bold enough to prophesy, in one of his succulent footnotes, that "the present price level may fall to that of 1914 within a decade; and that, later, it may fall much lower." 262 U.S. at 303, n. 16.

39. 169 U.S. 466 (1898).

In the practical adjustments between national rule and local diversities, he is keenly mindful that the nation spans a continent and that, despite the unifying forces of technology, the States for many purposes remain distinctive communities. As to matters not obviously of common national concern, thereby calling for a centralized system of control, the States have a localized knowledge of details, a concreteness of interest and varieties of social policy, which ought to be allowed tolerant scope.

And so he has closely scrutinized objections to State action based merely on remote or hypothetical encroachments upon that national uniformity which is the concern of the commerce clause. The ultimate organic nature of society is not a decree of constitutional centralization. Just because the national government will necessarily absorb more and more power, the States ought to be allowed to manage those activities which bear an essential State emphasis. Even though an enterprise is part of the concatenation that makes up interstate and foreign commerce, its local abuses should be removable by local remedies.[40] The protection which States afford to industries within their borders may properly give rise to the States' taxing power, regardless of a nexus of that industry with interstate business.[41]

Similar issues are raised by the implied immunity from State taxation enjoyed by federal instrumentalities. The simple doctrine by which States and the nation are forbidden to hamper one another's agencies of government has steadily been tortured beyond its original purpose. The practical result of inflating this doctrine has been the contraction of the allowable area of State taxation, without any compensating gain to the strength or resources of the federal government. Here again

40. See DiSanto v. Pennsylvania, 273 U.S. 34, 37–39 (1927)(dissent); Public Utility Comm. v. Attleboro Co., 273 U.S. 83, 91–92 (1927)(dissent).

41. See Texas Transport & Terminal Co. v. New Orleans, 264 U.S. 150, 155, 157 (1924)(dissent); Cudahy Packing Co. v. Hinkle, 278 U.S. 460, 467–468, 470 (1929)(dissent).

the influence of Mr. Justice Brandeis has been on the side of the States.[42]

In the domain of interstate commerce, the States of course must yield the field to Congress when Congress has occupied it. But these familiar phrases are, after all, figures of speech, and figures of speech are dangerous instruments for constitutional law. Whether Congress has occupied the field is not a problem in mensuration. Too often, it is an exercise of judgment about practical affairs; it calls for accommodation between State and national interests in the interacting areas of State and national power. Mr. Justice Brandeis, here also, eschews loose generalities and catchwords. He subjects federal enactment and its challenged State analogue to sharp, precise, and comprehensive examination to ascertain whether both may survive or the national law alone can prevail.[43]

Safeguarding peculiar State interests is one thing; to discriminate against the common national interest is quite another. Through intimate acquaintance with the managerial and financial difficulties of railroads, Mr. Justice Brandeis is firm to check the imposition of gratuitous burdens.[44] And behind the semblance of local regulation he is quick to detect a selfish attempt merely to obstruct interstate commerce.[45]

But whether State action unduly impinges upon interstate commerce depends more and more upon the particularities of fact in individual cases. If the Court is to adhere to tradition in the administration of constitutional law and avoid hypothetical decisions or abstract pronouncements, the record must contain the

42. See Jaybird Mining Co. v. Weir, 271 U.S. 609, 615, 617–619 (1926) (dissent).

43. See N.Y. Cent. R.R. v. Winfield, 244 U.S. 147, 168–170 (1917) (dissent); Napier v. Atlantic Coast Line R.R., 272 U.S. 605, 612–613 (1926).

44. See Davis v. Farmers' Co-operative Co., 262 U.S. 312, 315–316, 317 (1923).

45. See Buck v. Kuykendall, 267 U.S. 307, 315–316 (1925); Lawrence v. St. Louis–San Francisco Ry., 278 U.S. 228, 233–234 (1929).

details which control the application of general doctrine or the Court must secure their ascertainment.[46]

Marshall could draw with large and bold strokes the boundaries of State and national power; today most crucial issues involve the concrete application of settled, general doctrines. The fate of vast interests and hopeful reforms, the traditional contest between centralization and local rule, now turn on questions of more or less, on matters of degree, on drawing lines, sometimes very fine lines. Decisions therefore depend more and more on precise formulation of the issues embedded in litigation, and on alertness regarding the exact scope of past decisions in the light of their present significance. The Court's conception of its own function and awareness of its processes in constitutional adjudication, determine the Constitution in action.

In his whole temperament, Mr. Justice Brandeis is poles apart from the attitude of the technically-minded lawyer. Yet no member of the Court invokes more rigorously the traditional limits of its jurisdiction.[47] In view of our federalism and the Court's peculiar function, questions of jurisdiction in constitutional adjudications

46. See Hammond v. Schappi Bus Line, 275 U.S. 164, 170–172 (1927).

47. The following criteria have guided him:

"It [the Court] has no jurisdiction to pronounce any statute, either of a State or of the United States, void, because irreconcilable with the Constitution, except as it is called upon to adjudge the legal rights of litigants in actual controversies. In the exercise of that jurisdiction, it is bound by two rules, to which it has rigidly adhered, one, never to anticipate a question of constitutional law in advance of the necessity of deciding it; the other never to formulate a rule of constitutional law broader than is required by the precise facts to which it is to be applied. These rules are safe guides to sound judgment. It is the dictate of wisdom to follow them closely and carefully." Steamship Co. v. Emigration Commissioners, 113 U.S. 33, 39 (1885).

"Whenever, in pursuance of an honest and actual antagonistic assertion of rights by one individual against another, there is presented a question involving the validity of any act of any legislature, State or Federal, and the decision necessarily rests on the competency of the legislature to so enact, the court must, in the exercise of its solemn duties, determine whether the act be constitutional or not; but such an exercise of power is the ultimate and supreme function of courts. It is legitimate only in the last resort, and as a necessity in the determination of real, earnest and vital controversy between individuals." Chicago, etc. Ry. v. Wellman, 143 U.S. 339, 345 (1892).

imply questions of political power. The history of the Court and the nature of its business admonish against needless or premature decisions. It has no greater duty than the duty not to decide, or not to decide beyond its circumscribed authority. And so Mr. Justice Brandeis will decide only if the record presents a *case*—a live, concrete, present controversy between litigants.[48] When the record does present a case and judgment must be rendered, constitutional determination must be avoided if a nonconstitutional ground disposes of the immediate litigation.[49]

Moreover, the duty to abstain from adjudicating, particularly in the field of public law, may arise from the restricted nature of the judicial process. The specific claim before the Court may be enmeshed in larger public issues beyond the Court's reach of investigation, or a suitable remedy may exceed judicial resources.[50] Such a situation, even though formally disguised as a case, eludes adjudication. To forego judgment under such circumstances is not abdication of judicial power, but recognition of rational limits to its competence. Law is only partly in the keeping of courts; much must be left to legislation and administration. Nor does the absence of legislation create a vacuum to be occupied by judicial action.

Even though the abstract conditions for judicial competence exist, the Supreme Court may not be the fittest tribunal for its exercise. When cases depend on subtle appreciation of complicated local arrangements or the interpretation of State enactments not yet interpreted by State courts nor yielding their meaning merely to

48. See Arizona v. California, 283 U.S. 423, 463–464 (1931); Swift Co. v. Hocking Valley Ry., 243 U.S. 281 (1917); Bilby v. Stewart, 246 U.S. 255 (1918); Sugarman v. United States, 249 U.S. 182 (1919); Barbour v. Georgia, 249 U.S. 454 (1919); Collins v. Miller, 252 U.S. 364 (1920); Terrance v. Thompson, 263 U.S. 197 (1923); Oliver Co. v. Mexico, 264 U.S. 440 (1924); Willing v. Chicago Auditorium, 277 U.S. 274 (1928).

49. See Chastleton Corp. v. Sinclair, 264 U.S. 543, 549 (1924)(concurring in part).

50. See International News Service v. Associated Press, 248 U.S. 215, 263–264, 267 (1918)(dissent); Pennsylvania v. West Virginia, 262 U.S. 553, 621–623 (1923)(dissent).

a reading of English, original interpretations by the Supreme Court are likely to be *in vacuo*. The local court, whether State or federal, has judicial antennae for local situations seldom vouchsafed to the tribunal at Washington. The Supreme Court should draw on the experience and judgment of the local courts before giving ultimate judgment upon local law.[51]

And when, finally, a constitutional decision is rendered, not the language in explanation of it, but the terms of the controversy which called it forth alone determine the extent of its sway. This is merely the common-law lawyer's general disrespect for dicta; but in constitutional adjudications dicta are peculiarly pernicious usurpers. To let even accumulated dicta govern, is to give the future no hearing. And immortality does not inhere even in constitutional decisions. The Constitution owes its continuity to a continuous process of revivifying changes. "The Constitution can not make itself; some body made it, not at once but at several times. It is alterable; and by that draweth nearer Perfection; and without suiting itself to differing Times and Circumstances, it could not live. Its Life is prolonged by changing seasonably the several Parts of it at several times."[52] So wrote the shrewd Lord Halifax, and it is as true of our written Constitution as of that strange medley of imponderables which is the British constitution. A ready and delicate sense of the need for alteration is perhaps the most precious talent required of the Supreme Court. Upon it depends the vitality of the Constitution as a vehicle for life.[53]

A philosophy of intellectual humility determines Mr. Justice Brandeis's conception of the Supreme Court's function: an instinct against the tyranny of dogma and

51. See Railroad Comm. v. Los Angeles, 280 U.S. 145, 163–166 (1929) (dissent). As to his general desire to confine the volume of the Supreme Court's business to limits consonant with excellence of judicial output, see King Mfg. Co. v. Augusta, 277 U.S. 100, 115 (1928)(dissent).

52. *The Works of George Saville, First Marquess of Halifax* 211 (Raleigh ed. 1921).

53. See Jaybird Mining Co. v. Weir, 271 U.S. 609, 619 (1926)(dissent); Washington v. Dawson & Co., 264 U.S. 219, 235–239 (1924)(dissent); Di Santo v. Pennsylvania, 273 U.S. 34, 42–43 (1927)(dissent).

skepticism regarding the perdurance of any man's wisdom, though he be judge. No one knows better than he how slender a reed is reason—how recent its emergence in man, how powerful the countervailing instincts and passions, how treacherous the whole rational process. But just because the efforts of reason are tenuous, a constant process of critical scrutiny of the tentative claims of reason is essential to the very progress of reason. Truth and knowledge can function and flourish only if error may freely be exposed. And error will go unchallenged if dogma, no matter how widely accepted or dearly held, may not be questioned. Man must be allowed to challenge it by speech or by pen, not merely by silent thought. Thought, like other instincts, will atrophy unless formally exercised. If men cannot speak or write freely, they will soon cease to think freely. Limits there are, of course, even to this essential condition of a free society. But they do not go beyond the minimum requirements of an imminent and substantial threat to the very society which makes individual freedom significant.[54] Together with his colleagues, Mr. Justice Brandeis has refused to make freedom of speech an absolute. But the test of freedom of speech is readiness "to allow it to men whose opinions seem to you wrong and even dangerous."[55]

Freedom of speech and freedom of assembly are empty phrases if their exercise must yield to unreasonable fear. Great social convulsions like the Russian Revolution are bound to have their repercussion of panic among the timid and humorless, particularly panic stimulated by all the modern incitements to mass feeling. Such times present the decisive occasions for a stern enforcement of the right to air grievances, however baseless, and to propose remedies even more cruel than the grievances.[56]

Utterance also has responsibility. To misrepresent fact is to corrupt the source of opinion. No compensating so-

54. See Schaefer v. United States, 251 U.S. 466, 482–483 (1920)(dissent); Pierce v. United States, 252 U.S. 239, 272–273 (1920)(dissent); Gilbert v. Minnesota, 254 U.S. 325, 343 (1920)(dissent).

55. Scrutton, L.J., in Rex v. Secretary of State for Home Affairs, [1923] 2 K.B. 361, 382.

56. See Whitney v. California, 274 U.S. 357, 374–377 (1927)(concurrence).

cial gain demands the right to such misrepresentation. But the free exchange of opinion upon complicated issues must not be turned into crime by treating the prevailing view as a fact and proscribing unpopular dissent.[57]

The press is the most important vehicle for the dissemination of opinion. The Constitution precludes its censorship. Equally inadmissible should be all oblique methods to censor the press. Particularly offensive is the coercive power of unregulated administrative control.[58]

His deep consciousness of the imperfections of reason leads Mr. Justice Brandeis to observe rigorously the conditions which alone assure the fair working of even disinterested judgment. Truth may be beyond mortals, but law should at least satisfy the requirements for truth-seeking. Laymen, and even lawyers who are not historically-minded, are too apt to identify procedure with obstructive technicalities.[59] But there are technicalities and technicalities. The fundamental aspects of judicial procedure have the support of enduring human interests.

English criminal justice rightly serves as a shining contrast to our own. Yet those features in our Bill of Rights which it is now fashionable to regard as unduly favorable to the accused, are even more securely embedded in the texture of English feeling than they are secured through the written words in our Constitution. Here the third degree is widely practiced and too often condoned.[60] In

57. See Pierce v. United States, 252 U.S. 239, 266–267 (1920)(dissent).

58. See Milwaukee Pub. Co. v. Burleson, 255 U.S. 407, 417, 436 (1921) (dissent).

59. "The judge may enlighten the understanding of the jury and thereby influence their judgment; but he may not use undue influence. He may advise; he may persuade; but he may not command or coerce. He does coerce when without convincing the judgment he overcomes the will by the weight of his authority . . .

"It is said that if the defendant suffered any wrong it was purely formal . . . Whether a defendant is found guilty by a jury or is declared to be so by a judge is not, under the Federal Constitution, a mere formality. . . . The offence here in question is punishable by imprisonment. Congress would have been powerless to provide for imposing the punishment except upon the verdict of the jury." Horning v. District of Columbia, 254 U.S. 135, 139–140 (1920).

60. See "Report on the Third Degree" by Chafee, Pollak, and Stern, in *IV Reports, National Commission on Law Observance and Enforcement* 13 (1931).

England the suggestion that Scotland Yard applied the third degree aroused the condemnation of all the parties in the House of Commons.[61] Mr. Justice Brandeis has been true to the civilized standards of the British tradition.[62]

Anxiety over the deep shadows which crime casts upon the American scene should not tempt relaxation of the moral restraints which painful history has prescribed for law officers. Our own days furnish solemn reminders that police and prosecutors and occasionally even judges will, if allowed, employ illegality and yield to passion, with the same justification of furthering the public weal as their predecessors relied upon for the brutalities of the seventeenth and eighteenth centuries.

The possession of political power assumes subtler forms of temptation than its vulgar abuse. The love of power grows by what it feeds on. To Mr. Justice Brandeis, as to Lincoln, concentration of power is a standing threat to liberty; and to him liberty is a greater good than efficiency. So it was to the Age of Reason, and the Constitution is a product of that age. It is in the light of his prejudice for liberty that Mr. Justice Brandeis construes the Constitution.[63]

Passionate convictions are too often in the service of the doctrinaire. In Mr. Justice Brandeis they are the off-spring of an extraordinarily penetrating mind and intense devotion to the commonweal. He never flinches from stubborn reality. Facts, not catchwords, are his sovereigns. Of course, a life-long study of history and deep immersion in affairs have bent him to certain preferences. And since cases are not just cases, but imply alternative social policies, his predilections may decide cases. But Mr. Justice Brandeis is the very negation of a dogmatist. He has remained scrupulously flexible, constantly subjecting experience to the test of wider experience. All men have

61. See 220 Hans. Deb. (Commons), cols. 5, 805 et seq. (July 20, 1928); Inquiry in regard to the Interrogation by the Police of Miss Savidge (Cmd. 3147, 1928).

62. See Wan v. United States, 266 U.S. 1, 14–17 (1924).

63. See Burdeau v. McDowell, 256 U.S. 465, 476–477 (1921)(dissent); Casey v. United States, 276 U.S. 413, 423 (1928)(dissent); Olmstead v. United States, 277 U.S. 438, 483–484, 485 (1928)(dissent).

some ultimate postulates by which they wrest a private world of order from the chaos of the world. The essential postulate of Mr. Justice Brandeis is effective and generous opportunity for the unflagging operation of reason. He is not theory-ridden himself and would not impose theories on others.

And so his opinions reveal consciousness of a world for which no absolute is adequate. It is a world of more or less, of give and take, of live and let live. Interests clash, but no single one must yield. Self-willed power must be guarded against, but government cannot be paralyzed. And even liberty has its bounds.

Knowledge of the facts of industry has made him realize that centralization in the organization of workingmen is a necessary counterpoise to centralization in the control of business. And in the contests between them, the courts ought not to be partisan. But thereby the right of combat is not introduced into the constitutional structure. Society may evolve an adjustment comprehending the specialized interests of both sides.[64]

Mr. Justice Brandeis does not regard all concentration of economic power as a decree of nature, nor even as the inevitable consequence of modern technology. Some of its phases, according to his analysis, are the results of socially inimical practices. These excesses are "a curse of bigness."[65] But recognition of a limit to the economic and social advantages of combination does not lead him to read the Sherman Law as a policy of anarchic laissez faire. One who was the first to espouse business as a profession[66] naturally found no legal obstacles to the efforts of business to rationalize its processes.[67]

Every judicial proceeding, however preliminary its determination, must observe the essential requirements

64. See Myers v. United States, 272 U.S. 52, 291–295 (1926)(dissent).

65. See Bedford Cut Stone Co. v. Stone Cutters Ass'n., 274 U.S. 37, 64–65 (1927)(dissent); Duplex Printing Press Co. v. Deering, 254 U.S. 443, 488 (1921)(dissent). See also Dorchy v. Kansas, 272 U.S. 306 (1926). See Brandeis, *Other People's Money* 162 (1914).

66. In an address delivered at Brown University Commencement Day, 1912; Brandeis, *Business—A Profession* (1914, 1925).

67. See American Column Co. v. United States, 257 U.S. 377, 415, 416, 417–418 (1921)(dissent).

of a fair hearing. This safeguard courts can assure. But the protection of individual liberty, due to oppressive enforcement of the criminal law, does not lie wholly within the power of courts.[68]

The extensive governmental control now so widely exercised by administrative agencies over business and professions is giving rise to a new system of law. Mr. Justice Brandeis has been very hospitable to the necessity for this new development. His opinions in this field are helping to evolve a coherent body of administrative law. He recognizes the informality of procedure which these agencies must be allowed to adopt, and accords deference to the findings of experts.[69] But even experts cannot disregard evidence or dispense with the logic of relevance.[70]

To quote from Mr. Justice Brandeis's opinions is not to pick plums from a pudding but to pull threads from a pattern. He achieves not by epigrammatic thrust but through powerful exposition. His aim is not merely to articulate the grounds of his judgment, but to reach the mind even of the disappointed suitor, deeming it essential for defeated interests to know that their claims have adequately entered the judicial process. His opinions march step by step toward demonstration, with all the auxiliary reinforcement of detailed proof. The documentation of his opinions is one aspect of his reliance on reason. To sever text from accompanying footnotes is therefore to dismember an organic whole.[71]

68. Hughes v. Gault, 271 U.S. 142, 152 (1926)(dissent); Collins v. Loisel, 262 U.S. 426, 429–430 (1923).

69. See, e.g., Bilokumsky v. Tod, 263 U.S. 149 (1923); Tisi v. Tod, 264 U.S. 131 (1924); Williamsport Co. v. United States, 277 U.S. 551 (1928); Tagg Bros. v. United States, 280 U.S. 420, 443–445 (1930); Campbell v. Galeno Chemical Co., 281 U.S. 599 (1930).

70. See Douglas v. Noble, 261 U.S. 165, 169–170 (1923); Northern Pacific Ry. v. Department of Public Works, 268 U.S. 39, 42–45 (1925).

71. See, among others, the following cases in which the heavily documented footnotes in the opinions of Mr. Justice Brandeis are largely the result of his independent research: Truax v. Corrigan, 257 U.S. 312 (1921)(dissent); Southwestern Bell Tel. Co. v. Public Serv. Comm., 262 U.S. 276 (1923)(dissent); Jay Burns Baking Co. v. Bryan, 264 U.S. 504 (1924)(dissent); Myers v. United States 272 U.S. 52 (1926)(dissent); Frost v. Corp. Comm., 278 U.S. 515 (1929)(dissent); St. Louis & O'Fallon Ry. v. United States, 279 U.S. 461 (1929)(dissent); United Rys. v. West, 280 U.S. 234 (1939)(dissent).

The style of his opinions befits their aim. The dominant note is Doric simplicity. Occasionally, as in the terrible case of Ziang Sun Wan,[72] his restraint attains austerity. And sometimes the majesty of his theme stirs him to eloquence. When the issue is freedom of speech, he gives noble utterance to his faith and to the meaning of our institutions as the embodiment of that faith.

In truth, Mr. Justice Brandeis is a moral teacher, who follows Socrates in the belief that virtue is the pursuit of enlightened purpose. His long years of intimate connection with the history of the Harvard Law School symbolize his dominant impulse. Problems, for him, are never solved. Civilization is a sequence of new tasks. Hence his insistence on the extreme difficulty of government and its dependence on sustained interest and effort, on the need for constant alertness to the fact that the introduction of new forces is accompanied by new difficulties. This, in turn, makes him mindful of the limited range of human foresight, and leads him to practice humility in attempting to preclude the freedom of action of those who are to follow.

The Justice himself, while at the bar, disavowed allegiance to any general system of thought or hope. "I have no rigid social philosophy; I have been too intent on concrete problems of practical justice." Devotion to justice is widely professed. By Mr. Justice Brandeis it has been given concrete expression in a long effort toward making the life of the commonplace individual more significant. His zest for giving significance to life is not sentimentality; it arises from a keen sensitiveness to quality. He not only evokes the best qualities in others; he exacts the best in himself. Stern self-discipline of a mind preternaturally rich and deep has fashioned a judge who, by common consent, is a great and abiding figure of the world's most powerful court.

72. Wan v. United States, 266 U.S. 1 (1924).

Legislative History

The plethora of tax litigation vividly reveals the extent to which the Supreme Court is concerned with the intricacies of the legislative process. It discloses no less how inadequate is the traditional technique of the ordinary appellate litigation for the chief work of the Supreme Court. Argument from general principles, applications and refinements of prior decisions, the significance of human testimony—these constitute the training of lawyers and the resources which they bring to the aid of courts. But legislation is specific and concrete, grows out of individual circumstances and relates to definite ends, howsoever much it may be derived from a broader philosophy or be expressive of a new orientation. Indispensable to judicial construction and review of legislation is an exploration of all that is relevant to a full comprehension of that dynamic process of which the language of a statute is merely the surface formulation. Therefore it becomes necessary to seek light from all the elaborate stages which 271
precede the formal enactment of a measure—the occasions which stimulated legislative proposals, the recommendations in which the need for legislation was urged, the technical legislative process from the introduction of a bill to its final passage, with all the windings in committee, on the floor and in conference. But a statute may also be merely one in a related series of enactments[1] or part of a legislative movement transcending the bounds of a particular jurisdiction.[2] Its genealogy is thus often essential for discovering the meaning of a law or weighing its constitutionality. These are not new considerations in the judicial attitude toward legislation. They have been relevant ever since the famous resolutions of Lord Coke's

Excerpt from Frankfurter and James M. Landis, "The Business of the Supreme Court at October Term, 1930," 45 *Harv. L. Rev.* 271 (1931).

1. Cf. Prussian v. United States, 282 U.S. 675 (1931); Interstate Transit, Inc. v. Lindsey, 283 U.S. 183 (1931).

2. Cf. Milliken v. United States, 283 U.S. 15, 22 (1931); Missouri Pac. R.R. v. Norwood, 283 U.S. 249, 256 (1931).

day.[3] But the general hostility toward legislation in the nineteenth century attenuated their application, and substituted a sterile mechanical technique of interpretation.[4]

The heavy volume of legislation now coming to the Supreme Court has again engendered realization that a statute is an organism which derives life from its appropriate environment. Since legislation dealing with modern economic enterprise is so complicated in its details, the statutory aids to which resort must be had are much more subtle and extensive than seventeenth-century legislation demanded. As to tax cases, it is plain that meaning and validity depend upon an elaborate exegesis of the legislative process which formulated the contested provisions. Revenue measures, it becomes relevant to remember, are the product of expert draftsmanship.[5] While modified from year to year, they are bits of a complicated mosaic,

3. "And it was resolved by them [the Barons of the Exchequer], that for the sure and true interpretation of all statutes in general (be they penal or beneficial, restrictive or enlarging of the common law), four things are to be discerned and considered:—

1st. What was the common law before the making of the act.

2nd. What was the mischief and defect for which the common law did not provide.

3rd. What remedy the parliament hath resolved and appointed to cure the disease of the commonwealth.

And, 4th. The true reason and remedy; and then the office of all the judges is always to make such construction as shall repress the mischief, and advance the remedy, and to suppress subtle inventions and evasions for continuance of the mischief, and *pro privato commodo,* and to add force and life to the cure and remedy, according to the true intent of the makers of the act *pro bono publico.*" Heydon's Case, 3 Co. 7b (1584).

4. See Pound, "Common Law and Legislation," 21 *Harv. L. Rev.* 383 (1908).

5. The Court in tax cases places considerable emphasis upon changes made in the evolution of a measure from its introduction to final passage. Cf. Graham & Foster v. Goodcell, 282 U.S. 409, 418, n. 6 (1931); Gambrinus Brewery Co. v. Anderson, 282 U.S. 638, 643–644 (1931); cf. Jewell-LaSalle Realty Co. v. Buck, 283 U.S. 202, 207, n. 5 (1931). The Court also regards the failure of Congress to amend the law in accordance with Treasury recommendations as significant in establishing a Congressional intent that interpretations given to the existing legislation should control. Poe v. Seaborn, 282 U.S. 101, 114–115 (1930); cf. Buck v. Jewell-LaSalle Realty Co., 283 U.S. 191, 199, n. 6, 201, n. 10 (1931); Jewell-LaSalle Realty Co. v. Buck, *supra*, at 208, n. 6. The adoption of a judicial interpretation by Congress in one situation and its failure to adopt it in

and the parts must be fitted within the whole. In Treasury statements, committee reports, and Congressional debates, must be found the meaning of formulas that are embedded in the language of the statute for accommodating the conflicting interests, but which do not yield their meaning to a surface reading.[6] Moreover, new legislation may implicate old administration. And so, construction of statutes or judgment upon their validity involves a close scrutiny of their administrative history as well. Treasury rulings and regulations and decisions of the United States Board of Tax Appeals often constitute the why of legislation.[7] Again they may help to resolve ambiguities and sometimes even to control interpretation.[8] Similar considerations govern the Supreme Court's review of orders under legislation like the Interstate Commerce Acts, where the primary task of statutory construction is committed to important administrative agencies.[9]

another parallel situation, carries a suggestion of intentional differentiation of the two situations. Burnet v. Thompson Oil & Gas Co., 283 U.S. 301, 307 (1931). See Lee, "The Office of the Legislative Counsel," 29 *Colum. L. Rev.* 381 (1929).

6. References to Treasury statements, committee and conference reports, statements made by committee chairmen upon the floor of the House or Senate abound in tax cases. The material is employed to illustrate the purpose of particular provisions, or assumptions as to the nature and incidence of a tax, or to illustrate that the interpretation adopted does not run counter to specific aims of proponents of the statute. Aluminum Castings Co. v. Routzahn, 282 U.S. 92, 98 (1930); Brown & Sons v. Burnet, 282 U.S. 283, 289, n. 7 (1931); Graham & Foster v. Goodcell, *supra* note 5; United States v. Michel, 282 U.S. 656, 659 (1931); Nash-Breyer Motor Co. v. Burnet, 283 U.S. 483, 486 (1931); Indian Motorcycle Co. v. United States, 283 U.S. 570, 574 (1931); Phillips v. Commissioner, 283 U.S. 589, 594 (1931); cf. McCaughn v. Hershey Chocolate Co., 283 U.S. 488, 493 (1931); Arizona v. California, 283 U.S. 423, 454 (1931).

7. See Graham & Foster v. Goodcell, 282 U.S. 409, 417 (1931).

8. Gambrinus Brewery Co. v. Anderson, 282 U.S. 638, 644 (1931); Indian Motorcycle Co. v. United States, 283 U.S. 570, 574 (1931).

9. Cf. Louisville & Nashville R.R. v. United States, 282 U.S. 740 (1931); and Grand Trunk Western Ry. v. United States, 252 U.S. 112 (1920). And see United States v. Midwest Oil Co., 236 U.S. 459, 472 (1915).

The Packers v. The Government

Recalcitrancy to law has been a dominant characteristic of the packers for more than a generation. Efforts to confine their greed and curb their aggressions began in Roosevelt's administration, and the latest chapter in the long story has just been written by Mr. Justice Cardozo on behalf of the majority of the Supreme Court.[1] Investigations by Congressional committees, reports of the Commissioner of Corporations and of the Federal Trade Commission, presidential messages, enforcement of old laws and the enactment of new ones, administrative control, prosecutions, court decrees, decisions by the lower courts and half a dozen decisions by the Supreme Court—all the resources open to government have at one time or another been employed in the thirty years' war of the United States against the packers. Monopoly for private profit in meat and other foods has been the stake for which the packers fought.

Early in his first administration, Roosevelt moved against the beef trust. Dissolution of the Standard Oil, the tobacco, and the beef trusts was the chief objective of Roosevelt's trust-busting. All three had attained their "evil eminence" by the crude and ruthless methods of the pioneer days of big business. The refinements of pyramiding and affiliates were not yet in vogue. Suppression of competition both in the purchase of livestock and in the sale of dressed meat, control of stockyards and terminal railroads, the indispensable instrumentalities for such a combination, unduly favorable traffic arrangements with carriers—by such methods was a monopolistic position in the industry largely attained and a challenge to its power by any foolish individualism successfully resisted. A suit for the dissolution of the combine was instituted by Roosevelt's attorney general; and criminal prosecutions for rebating were brought. The practical results of these proceedings were meager. Soon the World War intervened,

Reprinted from an unsigned editorial in the *New Republic*, May 23, 1932, with permission. Footnotes supplied by editor.

1. United States v. Swift & Co., 286 U.S. 106 (1932).

and a steady flow of meat shipments abroad seemed much more important than a little thing like aggrandized economic power in the hands of a few, whatever might be its future effect upon livestock breeders, independent dealers, and the American consumer. These were matters to which one could turn when peace came, and turn to them the government did. In the meantime its resources against the power of combination had been strengthened by the Clayton Act of 1914.

And so, in 1920, the government took action to dissolve the packers' combination. The charge was monopoly achieved by means thus summarized in Justice Cardozo's opinion:

> They had attained this evil eminence through agreements apportioning the percentages of live stock to which the members of the combinations were severally entitled; through the acquisition and control of stockyards and stockyard terminal railroads; through the purchase of trade papers and journals whereby cattle raisers were deprived of accurate and unbiased reports of the demand for live stock; and through other devices directed to unified control. "Having eliminated competition in the meat products, the defendants next took cognizance of the competition which might be expected" from what was characterized as "substitute foods." To that end, so it was charged, they had set about controlling the supply of "fish, vegetables, either fresh or canned, fruits, cereals, milk, poultry, butter, eggs, cheese and other substitute foods ordinarily handled by wholesale grocers or produce dealers." Through their ownership of refrigerator cars and branch houses as well as other facilities, they were in a position to distribute "substitute foods and other unrelated commodities" with substantially no increase of overhead. Whenever these advantages were inadequate, they had recourse to the expedient of fixing prices so low over temporary periods of time as to eliminate competition by rivals less favorably situated. Through these and other devices

there came about in the view of the Government an unlawful monopoly of a large part of the food supply of the nation.[2]

Although asserting "their innocence of any violation of law in fact or intent," but "desiring to avoid every appearance of placing themselves in a position of antagonism to the government," the patriotic packers consented to an injunction subjecting them to restraints which were justified only if the government's charges were true. What the lawyers call a consent decree was entered, sugar-coated by the phrase that such decree shall not "be considered an adjudication that the defendants or any of them have in fact violated any law of the United States."[3] The diplomats have a name for such a formula: they call it face-saving. By this device an especially offensive combination was dismembered. But more was necessary. Remedies to be effective must forestall their circumvention. The past performances of the packers demanded not only dismemberment of the combination but safeguards against future oppressive tactics by the powerful component units. They were therefore enjoined "from (1) holding any interest in public stockyard companies, stockyard terminal railroads or market newspapers, (2) engaging in, or holding any interest in, the business of manufacturing, selling or transporting any of the 114 enumerated food products (principally fish, vegetables, fruit and groceries), . . . (3) using or permitting others to use their distributive facilities for the handling of any of these enumerated articles, (4) selling meat at retail, (5) holding any interest in any public coldstorage plant, and (6) selling fresh milk or cream."[4]

The desire of the packers "to avoid every appearance of placing themselves in a position of antagonism to the government" was not long-lived. To forgo money-making opportunities in the piping days of Harding normalcy was too quixotic. And so, in 1922, the packers began a series

2. Id. at 110.
3. Id. at 111.
4. Ibid.

of efforts to get from under the decree to which they had consented. First, they used the California Canneries as their cat's-paw. The Canneries asked to have the decree set aside, claiming that it interfered with performance by Armour of a contract to buy large quantities of California canned fruit. After the Coolidge election, with big business triumphantly in the saddle, the packers launched a direct attack on the consent decree. The decree to which they consented was beyond the court's jurisdiction, insisted the packers. But this was too bald an attempt to make an ass of the law, and in March 1928 was unanimously rejected by the Supreme Court.[5] In the meantime, however, at the instance of the California Canneries, the operation of the 1920 decree was suspended by the courts of the District of Columbia and not until May 1929 did the Supreme Court remove the obstacles to its obedience by the packers.[6]

But packers are greedy and lawyers imaginative. Confronted at last with the apparent necessity of obeying restraints, nine years after they so unctuously consented to them, Swift and Armour in April 1930 sought to modify the consent decree "and to adapt its restraints to the needs of a new day."[7]

The lower court modified the decree and gave the packers permission to deal at wholesale in groceries and other commodities. This decision the Supreme Court has just reversed. A majority of the Court refused to undo the consent decree and held the packers to the restraints to which they assented in 1920. Three of the judges were disqualified—the Chief Justice and Mr. Justice Sutherland had been of counsel for the packers in the earlier stages of the litigation, Mr. Justice Stone was attorney general during a prior phase of the case. Mr. Justice Butler, with the concurrence of Mr. Justice Van Devanter, dissented, welcoming the packers as competitors against wholesale grocers. Reading his opinion, one would suppose that the packers had no history.

5. Swift & Co. v. United States, 276 U.S. 311 (1928).
6. United States v. California Canneries, 279 U.S. 553 (1929).
7. 286 U.S. at 113.

Mr. Justice Cardozo placed the new desire of the packers in the perspective of their past conduct:

> Size and past aggressions induced the fear in 1920 that the defendants, if permitted to deal in groceries, would drive their rivals to the wall. Size and past aggressions leave the fear unmoved today. Changes there have been that reduce the likelihood of a monopoly in the business of the sale of meats, but none that bear significantly upon the old-time abuses in the sale of other foods. The question is not whether a modification as to groceries can be made without prejudice to the interests of producers of cattle on the hoof. The question is whether it can be made without prejudice to the interests of the classes whom this particular restraint was intended to protect.[8]

Nor has the rise of chain stores affected the coercive power of the packers. These stores increase rather than curtail the dangers of monopolistic control. Reminding that "size carries with it an opportunity for abuse that is not to be ignored when the opportunity is proved to have been utilized in the past,"[9] the Court thus keeps the packers within the bounds dictated by experience:

> The defendants, the largest packers in the country, will thus hold a post of vantage, as compared with other wholesale grocers, in their dealings with the chains. They will hold a post of vantage in their dealings with others outside the chains. When they add groceries to meats, they will do so, they assure us, with substantially no increase of the existing overhead. Thus in the race of competition they will be able by their own admission to lay a handicap on rivals overweighted at the start. The opportunity will be theirs to renew the war of extermination that they waged in years gone by.
>
> Sporadic instances of unfair practices even in the meat business are stated in the findings to have oc-

8. Id. at 117–118.
9. Id. at 116.

> curred since the monopoly was broken, practices as to which the defendants' officers disclaim responsibility or knowledge. It is easy to make such excuses with plausibility when a business is so huge. They become less plausible when the size of the business is moderate. Responsibility is then centered in a few.[10]

Here is a Supreme Court opinion that deals with economic issues in terms of economic realities. Central control, plus savings in overhead and ability to reduce prices, would be desirable if exercised in the public interest. But the whole story of the efforts to curb the packers sheds a searchlight on the anarchic character of our acquisitive society. For our food, we are largely dependent on the wise pursuit of the money motive by very few men. How naïve of us to expect it of them! In the case of the packers, the Supreme Court for a generation has been alert to the public interest. But adequate regulation of such a basic industry through intermittent lawsuits is to ask of courts what they cannot give.

10. Id. at 118.

The Scottsboro Case

The rags and tags of cases that excite public interest usually draw the headlines. But even lay comment upon the *Scottsboro* decision was alive to a significance that went beyond a respite from death for seven illiterate Negro boys. In truth, the Supreme Court last Monday wrote a notable chapter in the history of liberty, emphasized perhaps in importance because it was conveyed through the sober language of a judicial opinion.[1] The evolution of our constitutional law is the work of the initiate. But its ultimate sway depends upon its acceptance by the thought of the nation. The meaning of Supreme Court decisions ought not therefore to be shrouded in esoteric mystery. It ought to be possible to make clear to lay understanding the exact scope of constitutional doctrines that underlie decisions like the *Scottsboro* case.

The seven vagrant Negro youths involved in the *Scottsboro* case were convicted of the crime most abhorrent of all others to the community in which they found themselves. The conviction was sustained by the Supreme Court of Alabama, but over the vigorous dissent of the chief justice of the State. Thereafter leave was asked and granted for a review of the case by the Supreme Court of the United States. There the denial by the Alabama courts of fundamental rights under the federal Constitution was urged.

Specifically, it was claimed that: "(1) they were not given a fair, impartial and deliberate trial; (2) they were denied the right of counsel, and the accustomed incidents of consultation and opportunity of preparation for trial; and (3) they were tried before juries from which qualified members of their own race were systematically excluded."[2] The Court, through Mr. Justice Sutherland,

Reprinted from "The Supreme Court Writes a Chapter on Man's Rights," editorial page of the *New York Times*, November 13, 1932. Footnotes supplied by editor.

1. Powell v. Alabama, 287 U.S. 45 (1932).
2. Id. at 50.

without considering the first and third claims, sustained the second, reversed the judgment of the Alabama court, and ordered a new trial, in which the denied safeguard would have to be assured.

A rapid summary of the circumstances of the trial, as given by Mr. Justice Sutherland, is a necessary preliminary to the discussion of the legal issues. The defendants were nonresidents of Alabama, riding through the State in an open freight car on which were also several white boys and two white girls. A fight ensued in which the white boys were thrown off the train. Upon the complaint of these boys the train was stopped at a station down the line. There the girls accused the Negroes of assault. They were arrested and taken to Scottsboro, the county seat, where a large crowd had already gathered. Six days later indictments were returned. In six days more—the defendants, without families or friends in the State, having meanwhile been closely confined under military guard—the trial began.

"No one answered for the defendants or appeared to represent or defend them."[3] The trial judge stated that he had designated generally the entire local bar for the purpose of arraigning the defendants, "and then, of course, I anticipated them to continue to help them if no counsel appears."[4] A Tennessee lawyer, acting at the suggestion of unnamed "persons interested" but not in their employ, addressed the court; he stated that he had not had opportunity to prepare the case and was unfamiliar with local practice, but offered to appear with such local counsel as the court might appoint. An attorney expressed his willingness to serve under those conditions: "I will go ahead and help, do anything I can do." "The Court: All right."[5]

"And in this casual fashion," writes Mr. Justice Sutherland, "the matter of counsel in a capital case was disposed of."[6] "The defendants, young, ignorant, illiterate, sur-

3. Id. at 53.
4. Ibid.
5. Id. at 56.
6. Ibid.

rounded by hostile sentiment, haled back and forth under guard of soldiers, charged with an atrocious crime regarded with especial horror in the community where they were to be tried, were thus put in peril of their lives within a few moments after counsel for the first time charged with any degree of responsibility began to represent them."[7] "We think the failure of the trial court to give them reasonable time and opportunity to secure counsel was a clear denial of due process . . . we are of opinion that . . . the necessity of counsel was so vital and imperative that the failure of the trial court to make an effective appointment of counsel was likewise a denial of due process within the meaning of the Fourteenth Amendment."[8]

From this conclusion only Mr. Justice Butler and Mr. Justice McReynolds dissented.

The stock offenses of American criminal law, it must be remembered—murder, arson, rape, theft—are violations of State law and prosecuted solely through the State courts. As a generality, these are matters wholly outside the concern of the federal judiciary. Understanding of this division of function as to criminal matters between the States and the nation is essential to an appreciation of the *Scottsboro* decision. It is no part of the Supreme Court's duty to protect errors inevitable to every administration of criminal justice. Erroneous applications of law, the admission of prejudicial evidence, disregard of the conventional niceties of procedure—all these infringements of common rights, if they are to be remedied at all, must be remedied in the highest courts of the States. The *Scottsboro* decision works no impairment of these fundamental assumptions of our constitutional system.

But upon the freedom of all State action the federal Constitution imposes a broad limitation, applicable to criminal as well as to civil proceedings, to judicial as well as to legislative acts. This is accomplished by the Fourteenth Amendment, which provides that no State

7. Id. at 57–58.
8. Id. at 71.

shall "deprive any person of life, liberty, or property without due process of law." The assertion of that limitation is a duty of the federal judiciary, and a right of defendants under the federal Constitution. In its application of this prohibition in the review of the conduct of a State criminal trial, the significance of the *Scottsboro* decision resides.

The words of the amendment are words of "convenient vagueness,"[9] definable only by the cumulative process of judicial inclusion and exclusion. In matters affecting property rights, and notably the regulation of economic enterprise, they have come to be the foundation of a large body of doctrine often interposing irksome barriers to restrictive legislation. Only last Term they served Mr. Justice Sutherland in the famous Oklahoma ice case[10] as a touchstone for the invalidity of a statute which authorized the State Corporation Commission to deny to any person the right to enter the business of manufacturing ice in a community where in its opinion the existing facilities made such entrance injurious to the public. Now, in the hands of the same Justice, they return to their more immediate purpose of protecting black men from oppressive and unequal treatment by whites.

In the illuminating phrase of Judge Learned Hand, due process "represents a mood rather than a command."[11] The mood of the Supreme Court in subjecting the conduct of State criminal trials to the measure of the Fourteenth Amendment has been insistently cautious. Properly so, for the amendment is not the basis of a uniform code of criminal procedure federally imposed. Alternative modes of arriving at truth are not—they must not be—forever frozen. There is room for growth and vitality, for adaptation to shifting necessities, for wide differences of reasonable convenience in method.

Thus it was long ago settled that proceedings in State criminal actions need not be initiated by indictment of a grand jury, albeit the common law so required. Trial by a

9. Hough, "Due Process of Law—Today," 32 *Harv. L. Rev.* 218 (1919).
10. New State Ice Co. v. Liebmann, 285 U.S. 262 (1932).
11. Daniel Reeves, Inc. v. Anderson, 43 F. 2d 679, 682 (2d Cir. 1930).

jury of twelve is not imperative in state courts. The administration of local justice knows no such rigid federal fetters. Here, too, freedom must be left for new, perhaps improved, methods "in the insulated chambers afforded by the several States."[12]

But—and this is of the essence—certain things are basic to the integrity of the judicial process. One of them is a proper tribunal, impartial and uncoerced. In the memorable case of *Moore* v. *Dempsey,*[13] concerning, like the *Scottsboro* case, the trial of a Negro in a Southern community inflamed by racial hysteria, it was held that a court surrounded by a howling mob threatening vengeance if a conviction were not returned was no court at all, and the case was remanded for retrial under conditions more likely to conduce to the substantial ends of justice. Until the *Scottsboro* case, this decision stood virtually alone. Counsel for the Scottsboro defendants sought to bring their case within its authority. But the Court, instead of reviewing the circumstances of the trial and finding that in substance there was no trial because reason was barred, seized upon a different aspect of the case and enunciated another fundamental requisite of the judicial process.

Not only must there be a court free from coercion, but the accused must be furnished with means of presenting his defense. For this the assistance of counsel is essential. Time for investigation and for the production of evidence is imperative. Especially is this true in a capital case. The more heinous the charge the more important the safeguards which the experience of centuries has shown to be essential to the ascertainment of even fallible truth. Never is it more so than in a case of rape, turning heavily upon the testimony of the alleged victim and requiring to be defended largely by evidence of circumstance and character.

The *Scottsboro* case announces the doctrine that to every defendant must be assured the minimum condi-

12. Truax v. Corrigan, 257 U.S. 312, 344 (1921) (Holmes, J., dissenting).

13. 261 U.S. 86 (1923).

tions for an ordered and reasoned investigation of the charges against him—a proper and a heartening guarantee of fundamental law. The history of liberty, Mr. Justice Brandeis has reminded us, cannot be dissociated from the history of procedural observances. In no sense is the Supreme Court a general tribunal for the correction of criminal errors, such as the Court of Criminal Appeal in England. On a continent peopled by 120,000,000 that would be an impossible task; in a federal system it would be a function debilitating to the responsibility of State and local agencies. But the Court, though it will continue to act with hesitation, will not suffer, in its own scathing phrase, "judicial murder."[14] Here lies perhaps the deepest significance of the case.

Thus the judgment of the Court transcends the fate of the seven pitiful defendants concerned. It leaves the fate ultimately untouched. Upon the question of guilt or innocence it bears not even remotely. That question remains to be determined in normal course by the constituted tribunals of Alabama. The Supreme Court has declared only that the determination must be made with due observance of the decencies of civilized procedure.

14. 287 U.S. at 72.

Social Issues Before the Supreme Court

In this the fourth winter of our discontent it is no longer temerarious or ignorant to believe that this depression has a significance very different from prior economic stresses in our national history. The more things change the more they remain the same is an epigram of comfortable cynicism. There are new periods in history, and we are in the midst of one of them. Not that the new era has come overnight. Epochal changes germinate slowly, and dates in history are deluding. They mark end as much as beginning. To say that even the World War ushered in a new era is to foreshorten events. To be sure, the debacle of three mighty empires, the Russian Revolution and its violent break with the past, the dislocation of a world economy, the emergence and resurgence of nationalism, the intensification of technological processes induced by the war, all loosed economic and social forces far more upsetting to the pre-existing equilibrium than the changes wrought by the French Revolution and the Napoleonic wars. But these powerful solvents only reinforced major influences operating in our national economy. The absorption of free land, the steady drift from rural to a predominantly urban society, with economic consequences of changes in both the distribution of population and the significant decline in the rate of its growth, the attainment of the saturation point in railroad construction—itself an index of the general shift from the winning of a new country to its maintenance—the implications of technological advances both in industry and agriculture, the enormous extension of leisure among the mass of people, the new areas of foreign industrial and agricultural competition, the vast burden of public and private indebtedness—these have for some time been powerfully at work in the making of a new American economic society.

Unfortunately, these new forces left substantially untouched the direction of our political action. We assumed a continuing validity for the economic theories of pioneer

Reprinted from the *Yale Review*, Spring 1933, copyright Yale University Press. Footnotes supplied by editor.

America while fact was insidiously undermining theory. Recognition was lacking of the need for adequate social control of our transforming material development. To realize that there is a new economic order and to realize it passionately, is the central equipment for modern statesmanship.

> The world [writes Sir Arthur Salter] is now at one of the great crossroads of history. The system, usually termed capitalist but I think better termed competitive, under which the Western world has made its astonishing progress of the last century and a half, has developed deep-seated defects which will threaten its existence unless they can be cured. We need to reform, and in larger measure to transform, this system. We need so to improve the framework of law, of institutions, of customs and of public direction and control, that the otherwise free activities and competitive enterprises of man, instead of destroying each other, will insure to the general good. In the organization of industry, of credit, and of money, we need to supplement the automatic processes of adjustment by deliberate planning. This is the specific task of our age. If we fail, the only alternatives are chaos or the substitution of a different system inconsistent with political and personal liberty, perhaps after an intervening period of collapse and anarchy.[1]

In our scheme of government, readjustment to great social changes means juristic readjustment. Our basic problems—whether of industry, agriculture, or finance—sooner or later appear in the guise of legal problems. Professor John R. Commons is therefore justified in characterizing the Supreme Court of the United States as the authoritative faculty of economics. The foundation for its economic encyclicals is the Constitution. Plainly, however, constitutional provisions are not economic dogmas and certainly not obsolete economic dogmas. A classic admonition of Mr. Justice Holmes cannot be

1. Salter, "The Future of Economic Nationalism," 11 *Foreign Affairs* 8 (1932).

recalled too often—a "constitution is not intended to embody a particular theory, whether of paternalism and the organic relation of the citizen to the State or of *laissez faire*. It is made for people of fundamentally differing views, and the accident of our finding certain opinions natural and familiar or novel and even shocking ought not to conclude our judgment upon the question whether statutes embodying them conflict with the Constitution of the United States."[2]

By its very conception the Constitution has ample resources within itself to meet the changing needs of successive generations. For it was "intended to endure for ages to come, and, consequently to be adapted to the various *crises* of human affairs."[3] Through the generality of its language the Constitution provided for the future partly by not forecasting it. If the Court, aided by the bar, has access to the facts and heeds them, the Constitution is flexible enough to respond to the demands of modern society.

And so American constitutional law is not a fixed body of truth but a model of social adjustment. Indeed, the Constitution owes its continuity to an uninterrupted process of change. "The Constitution can not make itself; some body made it, not at once but at several times. It is alterable; and by that draweth nearer Perfection; and without suiting itself to differing Times and Circumstances, it could not live. Its Life is prolonged by changing seasonably the several Parts of it at several times."[4] So wrote the shrewd Lord Halifax, and his words are as true of our written Constitution as of that strange medley of imponderables, the British constitution. A ready sense of the need for alteration is perhaps the most precious talent required of the Supreme Court. Upon it depends the vitality of our Constitution as a vehicle for life.

Public life is thus a most potent instrument of public policy. The significant cases before the Supreme Court are not just controversies between two litigants. They in-

2. Lochner v. New York, 198 U.S. 45, 75–76 (1905).
3. M'Culloch v. Maryland, 4 Wheat. 316, 415 (1819).
4. See *Works of George Savile* 211 (Raleigh ed. 1912).

volve large public issues, and the general outlook of the Justices gives direction to their judicial views. In law also, where one ends, depends much on one's starting point.

The Supreme Court's right and wrong are drawn most frequently from broad and undefined clauses of the Constitution. A few simple-seeming terms like "liberty" and "property," undeterminate phrases like "regulate Commerce . . . among the several States" and "without due process of law," are invoked in judgment upon the shifting circumstances of a dynamic society. Phrases like "due process of law" are of "convenient vagueness."[5] Necessarily their content is derived from without, not revealed within the Constitution. The gloss that is put upon them controls the nation's efforts to meet its tasks. The capacity of States to control or mitigate unemployment, to assure a living wage for the workers, to clear slums and provide decent housing, to make city planning effective, to distribute fairly the burdens of taxation—these and like functions of modern government hinge on the Supreme Court's reading of the due process clause. The various attempts, in the past, to subject great economic instrumentalities to social responsibility—the Stockyard Act, the Grain Futures Act, the Transportation Act, the Child Labor law—depended upon what the lawyers call interpretation of the commerce clause. But what is interpreted depends on who interprets. The fate of such laws turned on facts and assumptions which underlie the social valuations of the judges. Again, the thorny controversies affecting business combinations and trade unions are also described as interpretations of the Sherman Law and the Clayton Act. But the results were determined by the Court's view of our industrial scene. So also the opinions of the Justices regarding the activities of trade associations and cooperatives vary with the general context in which different Justices place the economic data deemed relevant to judgment. The sharp conflicts to which control of the railroads and other public utilities gives rise derive not from variant readings of the same English text. They are nurtured in different economic

5. Hough, "Due Process of Law—Today," 32 *Harv. L. Rev.* 218 (1919).

cultures; they are the concrete expressions of different social philosophies.

The Justices of the Supreme Court are arbiters of social policy because their duties make them so. For the words of the Constitution which invoke the legal judgment are usually so unrestrained by their intrinsic meaning or by their history or by prior decisions that they leave the individual Justice free, if indeed they do not compel him, to gather meaning not from reading the Constitution but from reading life. Only an alert and self-critical awareness of the true nature of the judicial process in these public controversies will avert the translation of discredited assumption or unconscious bias into national policy.

In a period of rapid change like ours, the pace of social adjustments must be quickened. Poignant experience has made us realize the public implications of interests heretofore treated as private. Such interests must be stripped of many of their past immunities and subjected to appropriate responsibility. Courts will thus be called upon to make and to sustain extensive readjustments.

For example, the law must become more sophisticated in its conception of trustees' obligations. It must sharpen and extend the duties incident to the fiduciary relations of corporate directors and officers. The whole process of corporate salaries disproportionate to services rendered must be fearlessly faced, but especially the abuse of agreement for swollen contingent compensation. The Bethlehem Steel bonus system is a notorious example. Another instance, recently before the courts, merits recital. The directors of the American Tobacco Company in 1912 initiated a by-law authorizing six senior officers to divide among themselves 10 percent of any annual profits in excess of those earned by the company in 1910. Since 1921, $10,000,000 has been thus distributed. In addition to his regular salary of $168,000 and "special cash credits" of $273,000, the president of the company in 1930 received a bonus of $840,000. Even these rewards, apparently, did not provide sufficient incentive. The directors therefore adopted an Employee Stock Subscription Plan, which resulted in the sale to themselves, as officer-employees, of 32,000 shares of stock at $25 a share when the market price was $112. The millions which the president and vice-president of the American Tobacco Company thus received appeared to a majority of the United States Circuit Court of Appeals,[6] in New York, only reasonable compensation for making Lucky Strike the most popular cigarette in the world. That Court seemed impressed by the fact that both schemes were approved by the stockholders. To which Judge Thomas W. Swan, with real insight into the actualities of corporate management, suggested, in his dissent, that the shareholders when they adopted the by-law in 1912 could hardly have anticipated that they were conferring upon their president in 1930 a bonus five times his salary, or that through the Employee Stock Subscription Plan three-fifths of the stock would be allotted to directors by themselves. Equally unreal seems the court's failure to explore whether the conventional assent by proxies really signifies considered approval.

An effort to secure a reversal of this decision in the Supreme Court unfortunately failed.[7] On technical considerations which cannot here be canvassed, that Court (Mr. Justice Roberts not sitting) invoked a doctrine of convenience against consideration of the case by the federal courts, and left the matter to the New Jersey courts because the American Tobacco Company was organized under New Jersey law. Against this disposition, three of the Justices—Brandeis, Stone, and Cardozo—protested. They found that "a breach of the fiduciary duties of the directors is a legitimate inference from the allegations," and therefore they could not agree that a "proper exercise of discretion" required them "to deny to the petitioner the relief to which he is so clearly entitled."[8] Mr. Justice Stone admirably expressed the far-reaching objections to the considerations of parochialism to which the Supreme Court, most surprisingly in the light

6. Rogers v. Guaranty Trust Co., 60 F.2d 114 (2d Cir. 1932).
7. Rogers v. Guaranty Trust Co., 288 U.S. 123 (1933).
8. Id. at 144.

of precedents, deferred in this case: "Extension of corporate activities, distribution of corporate personnel, stockholders and directors through many states, and the diffusion of corporate ownership, separated from corporate management, make the integrity of the conduct of large business corporations increasingly a matter of national rather than local concern, . . . to which the federal courts should be quick to respond, when their jurisdiction is rightly invoked."[9]

The case furnishes an illuminating glimpse into the traditional operations of big business and its opportunities for socially indefensible profit to the insiders. The law cannot long continue to give such unbridled rein to the acquisition motive. Our social health cannot afford it.

Disastrous defects have been exposed in our financial institutions; tighter controls must be devised. Secretary Mills calls for legislation that will "remedy the fundamental weakness of our banking structure." Schemes have been adumbrated for a unified national banking system which raise intricate questions of policy and administration as well as of constitutionality. All these will call for judicial understanding of banking and finance, their relation to government and industry and agriculture. But surely legislatures and courts must also address themselves to the disclosed tendency of banks to confound three functions which ought to be kept fastidiously segregated:

1. Savings banks. It is the obligation of the savings bank to take practically no risk. Safety is the prime objective.

2. Commercial banking. The financial needs of merchants and manufacturers make it necessary to take business risks. Banks should not avoid these risks but should know whom to trust and when.

3. Security banking—the buying and selling of securities. This involves not only knowledge of fundamental merits but also knowledge of markets, of social and political movements and the like.

9. Id. 149–150.

By combining these three functions, our banking men have not only dulled and confused their banking wits; they have sometimes also confused the funds of the three departments of banking and thereby disregarded trust obligations. The Glass bill in part addresses itself to some of these abuses. The development and enforcement of effective legal standards for the promotion of sound banking require insight into financial facts, a sympathetic understanding of legislative proposals, and the application of exigent public policy, all too frequently forgotten.

Cutting across all our problems are the manifest aspects of taxation. The enormous increase in the cost of society and the subtle forms which modern wealth so largely takes are putting public finance to its severest test. To balance budgets, to pay for the cost of progressively civilized social standards, to safeguard the future and to divide these burdens with substantial fairness to the different interests in the community—these endeavors present problems more grueling than were ever faced by Colbert or Hamilton. Financial statesmanship must constantly explore new sources of revenue and find means to prevent the circumvention of their discovery. Such a task is bound to fail without wide latitude for experimentation, within the most promising areas of trial, in devising and executing fiscal measures. No finicky limitation upon the discretion of those charged with the duty of providing revenue, nor jejune conceptions about formal equality, should circumscribe the necessarily empirical process of tapping new revenue or stopping new devices for its evasion. The fiscal difficulties of government at best are hard and thorny. They ought not to be made insuperable by reading into the Constitution private notions of social policy. Too often, talk about scientific taxation is only a verbal screen for distributing the incidence of taxation according to traditional notions. Judgments of fairness in taxation, as in other activities of government, are functions of their time. Governing ideas of taxation of the eighteenth century, or even of the nineteenth century, were not permanently frozen into the Constitution.

Indeed, we must recognize the profound shift in the very purposes of taxation. Senator Root once reminded the American bar that:"The vast increase of wealth resulting from the increased power of production is still in the first stages of the inevitable processes of distribution."[10] Mr. Root was himself a member of an administration which employed the taxing power as one of the instruments for such distribution. Theodore Roosevelt was the first President avowedly to use the taxing power as a direct agency of social policy. More and more, it is bound to serve as a powerful means for directing the modern flow of wealth to social uses. The historical ambitions of American democracy and fiscal necessities alike demand it.

> The true principle of a free and popular government would seem to be so to construct it as to give to all, or at least to a very great majority, an interest in its preservation; to found it, as other things are founded, on men's interest . . . The freest government, if it could exist, would not be long acceptable, if the tendency of the laws were to create a rapid accumulation of property in few hands, and to render the great mass of the population dependent and penniless . . . Universal suffrage, for example, could not long exist in a community where there was great inequality of property.[11]

So wrote Daniel Webster in his famous oration celebrating the bicentennial of the Pilgrms' landing. A hundred years later, "great inequality of property" is characteristic of our national economy. Perhaps its most devastating consequence is the permeation of American life with material preoccupations. Even a President of the United States could say that the business of America is business, without realizing that he was uttering words of condemnation. The federal statistics of income dryly tell the tale only in part, as figures do. For a representative year before the depression, out of 6,787,481 who filed income tax returns

10. Root, "Public Service by the Bar," 41 *A.B.A. Repts.* 355, 367 (1916).
11. 1 *The Works of Daniel Webster* 38 (1851).

5,003,155 reported incomes below $3,000, and 6,193,270 incomes below $5,000; while 4,031 had incomes above $100,000; 1,860 had above $150,000; 537, above $300,000; 228, above $500,000; and 67, above $1,000,000 a year. Beneath such quiet figures lie, perhaps, the most pulsating problems of American society.

The law's concern with taxation covers a very wide front, and it must extensively modify its precedents and its predispositions. Much new legislation is indispensable; effective investigation must precede legislation; sympathetic judicial insight will have to support the legislation. Leaks must be stopped; skillful avoidances and evasions must be circumvented. In part, this will involve a correction of detail, a reversal of rulings and decisions both of the taxing agencies and of the courts. More drastic changes will also be required. Professional skill and imagination, if directed to increase of revenue and not to protection of heavy taxpayers, will be able to overcome strained interpretations of the Supreme Court and to limit the baneful effects of some of its holdings of unconstitutionality. Thereby, without a doubt, vast sums will be reached which have been withdrawn from their fair share of taxation.

These are only a few of the new paths to be explored if we are to work ourselves out of the morass. Lawyers have a special responsibility in breaking these new paths and allowing free travel upon them. In this country, theirs is probably the greatest power for good or evil. High technical competence is, of course, demanded in formulating the complicated adjustments necessary for our complicated society. But technical power can thwart as well as promote necessary social invention. The times demand new methods adapted to new problems, the removal of what is obstructive and wasteful in old principles or old applications.

The Supreme Court is indispensable to the effective workings of our federal government. If it did not exist, we should have to create it. I know of no other peaceful method for making the adjustments necessary to a society like ours—for maintaining the equilibrium between State and federal power, for settling the eternal conflicts between liberty and authority—than through a court of great traditions free from the tensions and temptations of party strife, detached from the fleeting interests of the moment. But because, inextricably, the Supreme Court is also an organ of statesmanship and the most powerful organ, it must have a seasoned understanding of affairs, the imagination to see the organic relations of society, above all, the humility not to set up its own judgment against the conscientious efforts of those whose primary duty it is to govern. So wise and temperate a scholar as the late Ernst Freund expressed this judgment after a lifetime's study of our government: "It is unlikely that a legislature will otherwise than through inadvertence violate the most obvious and cardinal dictates of justice; gross miscarriages of justice are probably less frequent in legislation than they are in the judicial determination of controversies."[12] And the Supreme Court itself has told us that "it must be remembered that legislatures are ultimate guardians of the liberties and welfare of the people in quite as great a degree as the courts."[13]

Unfortunately, the Supreme Court forgets at times to remember its own wisdom. In view of the tasks in hand, the price of judicial obscurantism is too great. Let me give two or three instances, reflecting controversies neither minor in character nor resurrected from the dim past, but dealing with the liveliest issues of our day.

The reorganization of the St. Paul has implications far beyond the receivership even of an important railroad. In one form or another, whether through administrative action or legislation or voluntary arrangement, or a combination of these, we must contract the capital structures, certainly of some of the railroads. This process will entail the interplay of financial and moral considerations and will demand the best thought of our regulatory agencies. The recent decision of the Supreme Court in the *St. Paul* case[14] thus affects railroad credit, the financial burdens

12. Freund, *Standards of American Legislation* 213 (1917).
13. Missouri, Kansas, & Tex. R. Co. v. May, 194 U.S. 267, 270 (1904).
14. United States v. Chicago, M. & St. P. R. Co., 282 U.S. 311 (1931).

incident to railroad consolidation, the effective powers of the Interstate Commerce Commission to protect the public interest, and, not least, the standards of fiduciary obligation of investment bankers.

According to Mr. Justice Stone, the question before the Supreme Court was "whether the salutary provisions"[15] of the Interstate Commerce Act can be avoided. Can "an issue of securities . . . to defray excessive reorganization expenses [be] withdrawn from the control of the [Interstate Commerce] Commission?"[16] The majority of the Court decided that by astuteness in the drafting of documents the bankers' lawyers had deprived the Commission of power to enforce necessary public safeguards. As a result, the reorganization managers of the St. Paul secured for themselves over a million dollars, and half a dozen New York law firms, an amount estimated by one of the managers to be between two-thirds of a million and a million.

The minority opinion, representing the views of Justices Stone, Holmes, and Brandeis, characterizes the methods by which the bankers and lawyers were able to get these fees without Commission regulation as a "failure to conform to those elementary standards of fairness and good conscience which equity may always demand."[17] The St. Paul reorganization plan was placed before the Commission in order to obtain its approval of the securities to be issued. A majority of the Commission granted approval, but subject to the condition that testimony be taken as to the fairness of the fees, and subject to such order as the Commission might make on that point. As appears from Mr. Justice Stone's statement of the facts, neither the bankers nor their lawyers disclosed an intention to take advantage of the Commission's approval in order later to deny the validity of the conditions attached to such permission.

The formal party in these proceedings was the reorganized company, which the bankers "created and con-

15. Id. at 333.
16. Ibid.
17. Id. at 342.

trolled."[18] They caused it to go before the federal district court which had charge of the receivership and which had ruled that the properties could not be transferred to the new company until the reorganization securities were approved by the Commission. The bankers caused the new company to display the Commission's order to the court, but withheld their plan "to repudiate the condition upon which the order was founded."[19] After the reorganization was thus consummated and nothing remained but settlement of the fees, the new company applied to the federal courts for immunity against the Interstate Commerce Commission's interference with private arrangement for such fees. The lower court said that the prior moves in the game constituted "a representation" that the new company "had accepted the order and expected to comply with the condition"[20] This was the view adopted by the minority members of the Supreme Court.

But the majority held that the Commission did not have jurisdiction, since the fees were fixed by a "contract between private persons to which the carrier was not a party."[21] Therefore, it was treated as though it were merely a contract between the reorganization managers, the committees, and the stockholders. Mr. Justice Stone and his colleagues felt that these were "technical distinctions" which "ought not to affect the authority of the Commission."[22] He dealt with realities. "No one," he wrote, "familiar with the financial and corporate history of this country could say, I think, that railroad credit and the marketability of railroad securities have not been profoundly affected, for long periods of time, if not continuously, by the numerous railroad reorganizations, in the course of which junior security holders have found it impossible to save more than a remnant of their investment, and that only by the assumption of a heavy burden of expense, too often the result of wasteful and extravagant methods of reorganization."[23]

18. Id. at 334.
19. Id. at 341.
20. Ibid.
21. Id. at 326.
22. Id. at 334.
23. Id. at 337.

Proposed railroad consolidations will involve issues similar to those in the *St. Paul* case. For instance, among the men who will guide the Eastern roads in these consolidations are lawyers and bankers who successfully denied that the Interstate Commerce Commission had jurisdiction over their St. Paul fees. Those fees will probably appear petty in amount when compared with the bankers' and lawyers' charges for consolidating the Eastern roads. If these should prove to be excessive, the losers will be the railroads, and thus the investors and the public. If the Interstate Commerce Commission attempts to determine whether the charges are reasonable or not, its authority to do so may again be put in question. These methods for avoiding control may also be employed in other phases of railroad affairs. In the past, the public has relied on the Interstate Commerce Commission to regulate the railroads in the public interest. That feeling of security is disturbed by the *St. Paul* decision.

Foreigners are fond of calling this the land of paradoxes. Our public finances certainly justify that characterization. The richest country in the world has been the most dilatory in balancing its budget and appears the most distracted and embarrassed in its accomplishment. I venture to believe that a major explanation is the systematically inculcated hostility to the taxation of wealth. For a decade the press has sedulously repeated the Mellon doctrine that the immunity of the rich from taxation is a blessing for the poor. In times of prosperity taxes on bloated incomes will discourage enterprise; in days of adversity there are no bloated incomes—such was the governing philosophy.

It ought not to be too surprising that this deep-seated sentiment against the taxation of wealth should be shared by members of our Supreme Court. How easily private notions of economic or social policy are transmuted into constitutional dogma is amply proved by the *United States Reports* since the war. Enormous wealth has been withdrawn from the taxing power of the nation and the States on the gossamer claim that otherwise governmental instrumentalities would be defeated. The history of taxation is, to no small extent, a battle of wits between skill in devising taxes and astuteness in evading them. By creating constitutional obstructions to safeguards against evasion, the Supreme Court has put the Constitution at the disposal of the evaders. A few years ago the Supreme Court sheltered great wealth by interposing the benevolent "due process" clause on behalf of rich donors who made gifts in anticipation of tax measures especially designed for them.[24] One might suppose the Supreme Court would at least be friendly to the effective enforcement of the inheritance tax. The social justification of that tax has become an accepted postulate even of our individualistic society. But the other day the Court, again under the blessed versatility of "due process," nullified the attempt of Congress, in response to the compelling experience of the Treasury Department, to prevent gross evasions of the inheritance tax.[25]

From the original enactment of the estate tax law in 1916, it was realized that a single tax on estates could be too easily avoided by well-timed and astute disposition of property before death. To check such practices, the act of 1916 contained two safeguards. Gifts made "in contemplation of death," and those in which the donor retained a joint interest during his lifetime, were taxed as part of his estate at death. But other means remained by which property might be withdrawn from the operation of the tax and yet remain within the effective control of the donor: he might, for example, place it in trust with a power of revocation or control reserved in himself. The possibility of escape by this device was materially reduced by legislation, which taxed gifts, by way of trust, taking effect "in possession or enjoyment" at the time of the donor's death. The courts threatened the effectiveness of much of this legislation by technical and sterile definitions of "possession or enjoyment,"[26] and in 1931 Congress was forced to close a broad avenue of escape from the estate tax by making specific provision for the inclusion of property which is transferred in trust for another but from

24. Untermyer v. Anderson, 276 U.S. 440 (1928).
25. Heiner v. Donnan, 285 U.S. 312 (1932).
26. Klein v. United States, 283 U.S. 231 (1931).

which the income is reserved for the donor during his life.

Meanwhile, the tax authorities were beset by difficulties growing out of the vague phrase, "in contemplation of death." In what degree the donor must have apprehended his end, and how to prove that apprehension, were questions which made the collection of a tax precarious at best. The devil himself, the lawyers are fond of quoting, knoweth not the mind of man; and even if he did, the devil's advocate might experience considerable difficulty in proving it to a court of law. Realizing that the limited omniscience of the taxing authorities was finding it impossible to isolate successfully those gifts that were made "in contemplation of death," Congress in 1924 imposed a tax on all gifts, irrespective of date or motive, at rates equal to those under the estate tax. This general gift tax was upheld by the Supreme Court.[27] In addition, the tax on gifts made in contemplation of death was retained, giving the government a second string to its bow, although, of course, credit was allowed where a gift tax had already been paid on the transfer.

The arm of the government was strengthened, moreover, by requiring the representatives of the estate to prove, where the gift was within two years of death, that it was not in contemplation thereof. But this shift of the burden of proof was of little value to the government in a contest against an elderly man of wealth contemplating death with one eye and the tax law with the other. The gift tax itself promised better results, but in 1926 it was repealed. (By the Revenue Act of 1932 it has been restored.)

Congress was alive to the need of conserving the gain which the gift tax had made in the enforcement of the estate tax. Ten years' experience in administering the revenue acts had taught its lesson. Congress provided that gifts made within two years of death should be "deemed to have been made in contemplation of death," and so might be assessed under the estate tax. "The inclusion of this provision," reported the Ways and Means

27. Bromley v. McCaughn, 280 U.S. 124 (1929).

Committee of the House, "will prevent most of the evasion, and is the only way in which it can be prevented."[28] This is the provision which the Supreme Court declared unconstitutional. Again "due process" worked its charm on behalf of wealth.[29]

In thus setting at naught the considered effort of Congress to obtain a really effective tax on decedents' estates, a majority of the Court found the provision arbitrary and unreasonable because it might apply to gifts made with no thought of death or taxes. "The young man in abounding health," writes Mr. Justice Sutherland, "bereft of life by a stroke of lightning within two years after making a gift, is conclusively presumed to have acted under the inducement of the thought of death, equally with the old and ailing who already stands in the shadow of the inevitable."[30] The pity aroused by this affecting apparition of the benevolent young plutocrat is somewhat mollified by the fact that if the property had not been given to kith and kin—gifts to charity being exempted—so shortly before the donor's end, it would in all likelihood have passed by will and been taxed accordingly.

The apparition fades completely before the picture drawn by Mr. Justice Stone in a dissenting opinion, in which he was joined by Mr. Justice Brandeis. (Mr. Justice Cardozo did not sit in the case.) This opinion reveals graphically by whom these gifts are made, and with what effect on the operation of the taxing system. Mr. Justice Stone analyzes 102 cases in which the government and the decedent's estate engaged in litigation over the question whether a gift had been made "in contemplation of death," under the law as it existed before the 1926 provision. He writes:

> In 20 cases involving gifts of approximately $4,250,000, the government was successful. In three it was partially successful; and in seventy-eight involving gifts largely in excess of $120,000,000, it was unsuc-

28. H.R. Rep. No. 1, 69th Cong., 1st Sess., p. 15 (1925).
29. Heiner v. Donnan, 285 U.S. 312 (1932).
30. Id. at 327.

> cessful. In another the jury disagreed. In fifty-six of the total of seventy-eight cases decided against the government, the gifts were made within two years of death. In this group of fifty-six donors, two were more than ninety years of age at the time of death; ten were between eighty and ninety; twenty-seven were between seventy and eighty; six were between sixty and seventy; six were between fifty and sixty; and only one was younger than fifty. There was one gift of $46,000,000 made within two months of death by a donor seventy-one years of age at death; one of $36,790,000 made by a donor over eighty, who consulted a tax expert before making the gift; one of over $10,400,000 made by a donor aged seventy-six, six months before death; and one by a donor aged seventy-five at death, in which the tax assessed was over $1,000,000. There was one other in excess of $2,000,000; five others largely in excess of $1,000,000; four others in excess of $500,000; thirteen in excess of $250,000; and fourteen in excess of $100,000. The value of the gifts was not shown definitely in three cases; twelve involved gifts totaling less than $100,000. In the remaining twenty-two cases the gifts were made more than two years before the death of the donor.[31]

This decision does not touch technical issues that are in the special province of learned judges. How taxes are evaded and how fine a net must be woven to keep big fish from escaping, what the experience of a decade of federal estates administration indicated and what means are adapted to prevent wholesale evasion—these are matters which tax administrators, members of the Ways and Means Committee, students of public finance, are as competent to understand as Mr. Justice Sutherland and his brethren. Is it not the plain truth that Mr. Justice Stone's powerful opinion deals with actualities and demolishes the hollow fabric of unreality erected by the majority? And if it be the truth, the Supreme Court has its duty towards a balanced budget—it ought not to sanc-

31. Id. at 343–346.

tify gross tax evasion or call the word-spinning by which it does so, the Constitution.

Finally, what of the Supreme Court's attitude towards the most inclusive of all our problems, namely, how to subdue our anarchic competitive economy to reason, how to correct the disharmonies between production and consumption? This issue was raised last spring in the now famous Oklahoma ice case.[32] On the basis of watchful scrutiny of the actual operation of the ice industry in Oklahoma, the legislature of that State, acting upon the recommendation of its Corporation Commission, availed itself of a well-tested instrument of public control—the device of a certificate of public convenience and necessity—to subject the ice business to a regulated instead of a wildcat economy. By this means, Oklahoma, within the limited area of the ice industry, endeavored to avoid excessive equipment and the demoralization of deflation and unemployment, and thereby promote stability. But the majority of the Court struck down this very modest essay in regulated economy. It denied Oklahoma's right to act upon its own experience, and, for a time at least, unbridled competition was given the sanction of the United States Constitution.

Against such an attitude, Mr. Justice Brandeis raised his magistral voice. It is not hazardous prophecy to believe that Mr. Justice Brandeis's opinion (concurred in by Mr. Justice Stone, Mr. Justice Cardozo taking no part in the decision) merely anticipates history, even the history of future opinions of the Court. The closing observations of this memorable dissent deserve quotation:

> To stay experimentation in things social and economic is a grave responsibility. Denial of the right to experiment may be fraught with serious consequences to the Nation. It is one of the happy incidents of the federal system that a single courageous State may, if its citizens choose, serve as a laboratory; and try novel social and economic experiments without risk to the rest of the country. This Court has the power to prevent an

32. New State Ice Co. v. Liebmann, 285 U.S. 262 (1932).

> experiment. We may strike down the statute which embodies it on the ground that, in our opinion, the measure is arbitrary, capricious or unreasonable. We have power to do this, because the due process clause has been held by the Court applicable to matters of substantive law as well as to matters of procedure. But in the exercise of this high power, we must be ever on our guard, lest we erect our prejudices into legal principles. If we would guide by the light of reason, we must let our minds be bold.[33]

The faith and enterprise which built this nation are unimpaired. Our intrinsic resources are greater than ever. We have also the unparalleled advantage of a fluid society. Under the guidance of a Supreme Court responsive to the potentialities of the Constitution to meet the needs of our society, it would now lie within our power to have an enduring diffusion of the goods of civilization to an extent never before attainable.

33. Id. at 311.

Judge Manton and the Supreme Court

For a judge of an inferior court to thumb his nose at the Supreme Court is hardly an edifying spectacle, though whether it represents courage or arrogance, we must leave the Supreme Court to determine. We refer, in the present instance, to Martin T. Manton, the presiding judge of the Circuit Court of Appeals for the Second Circuit in New York. The bone of contention between him and the Supreme Court is the control of the transit lines of New York City, with their vast financial and social implications. Through receivers, these lines are now in the hands of the federal court in New York. The Supreme Court has indicated they should be in hands other than those of Judge Manton,[1] and the worthy judge thinks very much better of his own opinion than he does of those of the Supreme Court.

This is not the first time that the Supreme Court and Judge Manton have had serious differences of opinion regarding public policy and judicial propriety. Once before Judge Manton assumed to know what was best for the public good in the administration of New York's transit system. In the bitter controversy between New York City and the Interborough over the five-cent fare, Judge Manton, in 1928, threw the authority of the federal courts on the side of the Interborough. Although applications for an increased fare were still pending before the New York Transit Commission, which is the State tribunal especially charged with problems of utility regulation in New York City, and suits were in progress in the State courts to interpret the complicated series of five-cent contracts between the Interborough and the city, Judge Manton (this time, to be sure, with the concurrence of two colleagues) issued an injunction forbidding State and city authorities to interfere with the Interborough's proposed seven-cent fare.[2] Judge Manton cavalierly

Reprinted from an unsigned editorial in the *New Republic,* July 19, 1933. Footnotes supplied by editor.

1. Johnson v. Manhattan Ry. Co., 289 U.S. 479 (1933).
2. Gilchrist v. Interborough Co., 26 F.2d 912 (S.D.N.Y. 1928).

brushed aside the applicability of the five-cent contracts, entertained no doubt of their invalidity and was equally sure of the constitutional right of the Interborough to a seven-cent fare. But the Supreme Court found not even "fair certainty" of the validity of these conclusions, and was certain only of the impropriety of Judge Manton's action in depriving the State courts of an opportunity to pass upon questions of State law peculiarly meet for their decision. And so Judge Manton's "improvidential" injunction was set aside as beyond the "proper discretion of the court."[3] The Court of Appeals of New York was allowed to rule, as it did, that Judge Manton was wholly wrong and that the five-cent contracts were controlling.[4]

Judge Manton was equally certain of his law when a courageous stockholder of the American Tobacco Company complained of the outrageous cash bonuses and stock preferences, running into millions, which officers and directors of the company had awarded themselves.[5] The Judge apparently did not even see any humor in the fact that the fat wads of stock which President Hill and the other rulers of the American Tobacco Company had awarded themselves were justified as "employee profit-sharing" under the New Jersey corporation law. The enormous cash bonuses, which apart from other "extras" yielded President Hill $843,507.72, received Judge Manton's official blessing. President Hill himself could not have been more righteous in his accents of approval, or more deferential to the great captains of industry, than was Judge Manton in sanctioning these luscious windfalls of the American Tobacco Company.

Not so contiguous to the world of great affairs in New York as was Judge Manton, the Supreme Court viewed these tobacco bonuses with a less tolerant judgment.[6] A majority of the Supreme Court, instead of upholding the

3. Gilchrist v. Interborough Co., 279 U.S. 159 (1929).

4. City of New York v. Interborough Rapid Transit Co., 257 N.Y. 20 (1930).

5. Rogers v. Guaranty Trust Co., 60 F.2d 114 (2d Cir. 1932).

6. Rogers v. Guaranty Trust Co., 288 U.S. 123 (1933). Manton was subsequently convicted of taking a bribe in the tobacco case. For the whole miserable story, see Borkin, *The Corrupt Judge* 23–93 (1962).

stock preferences, thought that the courts of the home state of the tobacco company, New Jersey, should pass on their legality; while Mr. Justice Stone (speaking also for Mr. Justice Brandeis, and joined in a separate opinion by Mr. Justice Cardozo) so severely castigated the whole transaction that President George Washington Hill of the American Tobacco Company announced the surrender of his heavy stock allotment. As for the cash bonuses, the Supreme Court unanimously reversed Judge Manton and approved the dissent of his colleague, Judge Swan. The reprimand of Judge Manton's view of corporate morality, as practiced by the American Tobacco Company, was all the more decisive in that it was pronounced by Mr. Justice Butler, the most uncompromising conservative on the Court.

In the recent Interborough receivership case, Judge Manton acted to forestall an appeal to the district judge before whom applications for receivership would normally come in the orderly distribution of judicial business in the Southern District of New York. He exercised the authority of a senior circuit judge to assign a circuit judge to sit in the district court "when the public interest requires." And Judge Manton assigned himself. By devices reminiscent of Gilbert and Sullivan's Lord Chancellor, he enabled himself to entertain, on August 26, 1932, an application for the appointment of receivers for the Interborough; on the same day he assented to the application and entertained an order appointing receivers and designating their counsel. Judge Manton's action was the culmination of what the Supreme Court characterized as "an acute controversy between the Senior Circuit Judge of the Second Circuit and the District Judges of the Southern District of New York."[7] The dispute concerned the disposition of judicial patronage. Fundamentally, nothing less was involved than the considerations that should govern the orderly administration of justice and the means for assuring the public's respect for the federal courts. It is not too surprising that Judge Woolsey, before whom Judge Manton's action was challenged, was led

7. 289 U.S. at 483.

to conclude that Judge Manton's conduct constituted "acts which involved usurpation of power and . . . consequently, were . . . wholly void and of no effect."[8]

Technically, the Supreme Court reversed Judge Woolsey; morally, they sustained him. The Supreme Court ruled that Judge Manton's assumption of jurisdiction in the Interborough receivership was not "usurpation of power." But the "possession of power is one thing; the propriety of its exercise in particular circumstances is quite a different thing."[9] The Supreme Court rebuked Judge Manton and asked him to mend his ways. At a time when the conduct of federal judges in receivership proceedings have been seriously questioned before Congress and the Supreme Court, and when the whole system of federal receiverships is about to be subjected to a congressional investigation, the observations of the Supreme Court upon Judge Manton's behavior in the *Interborough* case become doubly important. They are at once a warning to the inferior courts throughout the land and a reassurance to the public that the Supreme Court, at all events, will not tolerate judicial shenanigan. We need not apologize, therefore, for quoting extensively from the opinion of Mr. Justice Van Devanter, speaking for the Supreme Court in the *Interborough* case:

> A receivership is not grantable as of course, but only for reasons strongly appealing to the judge to whom the application is made. When large properties are involved a receivership usually involves widely conflicting interests and presents questions fraught with difficulty and exceptional delicacy. This was true of the receivership here in question. It involved properties, estimated to approximate $500,000,000 in value, which were held and used by a public carrier employing thousands of persons in its work and carrying hundreds of thousands of passengers each day. The carrier was in greatly embarrassed condition, had thousands of creditors whose interests were divergent, and was

8. Johnson v. Manhattan Ry., 1 F.Supp. 809 (S.D.N.Y. 1932).
9. 289 U.S. at 504.

> confronted with possible forfeiture of some of its franchises. All this shows that the situation was one in which the assignment of a judge to take charge of the receivership, if one was to be assigned, was a task which needed to be performed upon careful consideration and with the utmost impartiality. The difference of opinion, between the Senior Circuit Judge and the District Judges, respecting the relative fitness of individuals and trust companies as equity receivers, was not a proper ground for taking the cause away from the District Judge before whom it ordinarily would come, and bringing it before the assigning Senior Circuit Judge. Granting that the latter was most sincere in what he did, there was yet no compelling reason for assigning himself. Had he reflected he probably would not have made such an assignment; but he acted hastily and evidently with questionable wisdom. This action has embarrassed and is embarrassing the receivership. If he were now to withdraw from further participation in the receivership proceedings the embarrassment would be relieved; and the belief is ventured here that, on further reflection, he will recognize the propriety of so doing and, by withdrawing, will open the way for another judge with appropriate authority to conduct the further proceedings.[10]

The unusualness of such stern remarks emanating from the Supreme Court re-enforces its admonition. One would suppose that even the least sensitive of judges would heed it. Indeed, on the day that the opinion was handed down, Judge Manton announced his submission to it. Somewhat pharisaically he stated, on May 29, "It has been my intention right along to withdraw, once my original authority was established."[11] But now a month later, he thinks better of it. After full consideration of the Supreme Court's opinion, he concludes, as correctly paraphrased by the *New York Herald Tribune,* "that the Supreme Court did not know what it was talking about."

10. Id. at 504–505.
11. *New York Herald Tribune,* May 30, 1933, p. 1.

And so, in the light of "profound convictions," he announces, "I cannot for the present bring myself voluntarily to withdraw from this case."[12] It is not for us to suggest the means that are at the Supreme Court's disposal to enlighten still further the moral obtuseness of Judge Manton. But we cannot believe that his refusal "voluntarily" to terminate a situation which has received the opprobrium of the Supreme Court and the condemnation of the New York press will be allowed to rest unchallenged. What is at stake is public confidence in the federal judiciary and the Supreme Court's capacity to vindicate it.

12. *New York Herald Tribune*, June 29, 1933, pp. 1, 14.

The Certiorari Process

Certiorari as a mode of review was first introduced into the appellate practice of the Supreme Court by the Circuit Court of Appeals Act of 1891.[1] The purpose and provisions of that act give the clue to the intended function of the writ. The Supreme Court's appellate docket had become intolerably swollen.[2] Accordingly a system of intermediate appellate tribunals was erected to assume a large share of the burdens of review. In defined classes of cases the judgments of the new courts were declared to be final; certiorari in such cases was a device, for use only in exceptional circumstances, to enable the Supreme Court to maintain uniformity of decision among the circuits and to exercise a measure of supervisory control.[3] Holding closely to this conception of its function, the Court from the beginning was chary in allowance of the writ.[4]

The new device was successful; it commended itself to Court and Congress. Persistence of the same conditions which originally had brought it forth steadily

Excerpt from Frankfurter and Henry M. Hart, Jr., "The Business of the Supreme Court at October Term, 1933," 48 *Harv. L. Rev.* 238, 260–276 (1934).

1. Act of March 3, 1891, 26 Stat. 826, 828.

2. See Frankfurter and Landis, *The Business of the Supreme Court* 93–102 (1927).

3. See Lau Ow Bew, Petitioner, 141 U.S. 583 (1891); In re Woods, 143 U.S. 202 (1892); American Const. Co. v. Jacksonville, Tampa & Key West Ry., 148 U.S. 372, 382–383 (1893).

4. The scope of certiorari to the circuit court of appeals appears at first to have been regarded as no more extensive than that of certificate. Cf. Curtis, *Jurisdiction of the United States Courts* 77–78 (2d ed. 1896). In 1893 the Court, in an opinion reviewing the grounds upon which the writ would issue, observed that only two applications had thus far been granted. American Const. Co. v. Jacksonville, Tampa & Key West Ry., 148 U.S. 372, 383 (1893). The number of petitions, however, increased rapidly, and certiorari soon established itself as the normal method of review of circuit court of appeals decisions. At the 1896 Term, 52 petitions were filed, of which the extraordinarily large number of 21, or 40 percent, were granted. At the 1905 Term, only 23 out of 142 applications, or 16 percent, were successful; and this approximate proportion has since maintained itself.

prompted its extension.[5] In 1915 the scope of certiorari to the circuit courts of appeals was broadened;[6] in 1916 certiorari was substituted for writ of error in a wide class of cases from the State courts.[7] In 1925 the general post-war increase in litigation led to still more decisive action. Certiorari was made for practical purposes virtually the sole mode of review of decisions of the circuit courts of appeals,[8] and the jurisdiction of those tribunals was itself broadened by sharp contraction in the scope of direct appeals from the district courts to the Supreme Court.[9] In addition, certiorari was extended in its application to review of State court decisions,[10] and in the important group of cases from the Court of Claims[11] and the Court of Appeals of the District of Columbia[12] it displaced appeal and writ of error almost entirely.[13]

Statistics of the number of petitions filed reflect the progress of legislation and the growing judicial business of the country. There were 52 petitions at the 1896 Term. At the 1905 Term this number had risen to 142; ten years later it was only 154.[14] Then followed a rapid rise. At the 1923 Term there were 389 petitions; at the 1925 Term, 535. In 1930 there were 726 petitions; and at the last Term the total reached the record figure of 880.

This steady broadening of the Supreme Court's jurisdiction upon certiorari and the marked increase in the num-

5. The first extension of the use of certiorari was by way of enlargement of the Supreme Court's appellate jurisdiction rather than its contraction. In the Act of Dec. 23, 1914, 38 Stat. 790, 28 U.S.C.A. § 344 (1928), Congress utilized the certiorari device when for the first time it provided for review of State court decisions sustaining claims of federal right. See Frankfurter and Landis, *supra* note 2, at 190–198.

6. Act of Jan. 28, 1915, 38 Stat. 803.

7. Act of Sept. 6, 1916, 39 Stat. 726.

8. Act of Feb. 13, 1925, §1, 43 Stat. 936, 939.

9. Id. at 938.

10. Id. at 937, 938.

11. Id. at 939.

12. Id. at 938, 939.

13. See Frankfurter and Hart, "The Business of the Supreme Court at October Term, 1932," 47 *Harv. L. Rev.* 245, 256 nn. 16, 18 (1933).

14. See Mr. Justice McReynolds, in Furness, Withy & Co. v. Yang-Tsze Ins. Ass'n., 242 U.S. 430, 434 (1917).

ber of petitions filed have been accompanied, however, by no corresponding gain in understanding at the bar concerning the nature and function of the writ. The accumulations of petitions are for the most part accumulations of petitions denied; the overwhelming majority are petitions which ought never to have been filed at all. "Our experience," said Mr. Chief Justice Taft eleven years ago, "shows that eighty percent of those who petition for certiorari do not appreciate . . . [the] necessary limitations upon our issue of the writ."[15] Last spring, in an address before the American Law Institute, Mr. Chief Justice Hughes elaborated upon the same theme:

> The cooperation we need must be found in the self-imposed restraint which will prevent lawyers from presenting applications which are devoid of merit. I recognize that in many cases the question whether certiorari should be granted is a matter permitting of debate . . . But we find that a very large proportion of the applications are without substantial grounds. Yet the papers submitted must be examined, although on examination the futility of the application is disclosed. For example, we have many applications where the questions raised are those relating to particular contracts or transactions and turn upon the facts of the particular case, and there is no controversy of importance with respect to legal principles. Applications are numerous in which there appears to be no conflict of decision between the Circuit Courts of Appeals, or between Federal and State courts in cases where the latter should be controlling, and no real conflict with the decisions of the Supreme Court, and there is an utter absence of any good reason for asking our review. That review, we must emphasize, is in the interest of the law, not in the interest of particular parties. It is not the importance of the parties or the amount involved that is controlling, but the need of securing harmony of decision and the appropriate settlement of questions of general importance so that the system of federal jus-

15. Magnum Co. v. Coty, 262 U.S. 159, 163 (1923).

tice may be appropriately administered. I commend to the Bar the provisions of Rule 38 of the Rules of the Supreme Court which deal comprehensively with the subject.[16]

Its central purposes certiorari has undoubtedly well served. Application of the principle of discretionary review has made possible the Court's extraordinary achievement of the last four years in keeping abreast of its docket. It has done much more than that. It has enabled the Court, in a society increasingly complex, at the head of a judicial system enormously busier, to maintain its distinctive character—without undue burden and without alteration in its traditional composition, to continue to resolve those critical issues of federalism and constitutionalism which no other tribunal is adequate to determine. These accomplishments can scarcely fail to be impaired by continuing increase in the number of petitions filed. The burden of futile examination of "a very large proportion" of 880 petitions is already sufficiently grave; the burden of examining any considerably greater number would be intolerable.

The effort to secure intelligent, effective participation by lawyers in the certiorari process is hampered by several factors. No cohesive, specially trained Supreme Court bar exists. Save for the law officers of the Government, most of the lawyers who file petitions do so only a few times in the course of a professional lifetime. Many, no doubt, regard the experience largely as an adventure, or as a professional opportunity; others, advising clients in all disinterestedness, advise them badly. An attitude of professional responsibility to the Court, as well as to clients, is far to seek. Perhaps the underlying factor is persisting failure on the part of most of the profession to grasp and accept the conception of the Court's peculiar function which circumstances have compelled, which legislation has recognized, and which the Court itself for many years has steadily enforced. The romantic notion that the Supreme Court sits "to do justice" in every case

16. 20 *A.B.A.J.* 341 (1934).

potentially within its jurisdiction dies hard. Thus, petition after petition continues to be filed seeking a hearing on grounds which, if valid, would require each year thousands of other cases likewise to be heard. The mechanics of certiorari, it must also be recognized, are unfamiliar. Certiorari as a process of decision without avowed reasons is foreign to the main traditions of Anglo-American law and so also to the understanding of lawyers who come into only occasional contact with it. Practitioners not steeped in the philosophy of the Court's special functions and devoid of experience with its practice are not unnaturally at a loss.

These considerations point the special importance, for the guidance of lawyers, of the published rules of the Court. In the absence of detailed, informing studies of certiorari,[17] such rules together with the Court's own infrequent explanations of its policy constitute inexpert counsel's sole reliance. Judged by such standards, it may be questioned whether Rule 38[18] which governs petitions for certiorari is as explicit as it might be. As to the general function of certiorari, it is less explicit, for example, than the Chief Justice's own statement to the American Law Institute last spring.[19] There are, indeed, similar expressions in certain of the cases cited in the rule,[20] but these are lacking in comprehensiveness, and are so placed

17. Reference should be made to 8 Hughes, *Federal Practice Jurisdiction & Procedure* chs. 100–102 (1931).

18. 286 U.S. 622 (1932), as amended, Sup. Ct. J. 250-251 (1933).

19. See text at note 16, *supra*. Rule 38(5) says, "A review on writ of certiorari is not a matter of right, but of sound judicial discretion, and will be granted only where there are special and important reasons therefor. The following, while neither controlling nor fully measuring the court's discretion indicate the character of reasons which will be considered," listing the reasons discussed, in part, *infra*.

20. "The jurisdiction to bring up cases by certiorari from the Circuit Courts of Appeals was given for two purposes, first to secure uniformity of decision between those courts in the nine circuits, and second, to bring up cases involving questions of importance which it is in the public interest to have decided by this Court of last resort. The jurisdiction was not conferred upon this Court merely to give the defeated party in the Circuit Court of Appeals another hearing." Taft, C.J., in Magnum Import Co. v. Coty, 262 U.S. 159, 163 (1923). See also Layne & Bowler Corp. v. Western Well Works, 261 U.S. 387 (1923).

within the rule as to appear to have reference rather to requirements of brevity and form.[21] Either by express statement or more illuminating citation the rule might well explain more fully the philosophy of certiorari.

Nor does Rule 38 unambiguously prescribe the requisites of a proper petition. The major recurrent vice of petitions, apparent from the most casual examination of a representative sampling, is the failure to perceive the elementary distinction between an extended argument on the merits (obviously inappropriate until the merits are before the Court) and an argument on the issue whether certiorari should or should not be granted. Only in exceptional cases is any but cursory discussion of the merits appropriate in the petition at all. Paragraph (2) of the rule does state, "The petition shall contain only a summary and short statement of the matter involved and the reasons relied on for the allowance of the writ." But it adds, "A supporting brief [which must be direct, concise, and in conformity with Rules 26 and 27] may be included."[22] To hundreds of lawyers each year "a supporting brief" means only one thing—a preliminary brief, perhaps somewhat condensed, on the merits. It would be

21. The cases are cited, not after the first sentence in paragraph (5) of Rule 38, *supra* note 19, but after the following statement in paragraph (2): "The petition shall contain only a summary and short statement of the matter involved and the reasons relied on for the allowance of the writ. A supporting brief may be included in the petition, but, whether so included or presented separately, it must be direct, concise and in conformity with Rules 26 and 27. A failure to comply with these requirements will be a sufficient reason for denying the petition." Four cases are then cited, in addition to those in note 20, *supra,* all of which illustrate grounds upon which writs of certiorari, once issued, may be dismissed as improvidently granted: United States v. Rimer, 220 U.S. 547 (1911) (failure of record to raise important questions suggested in petition); Furness, Withy & Co. v. Yang-Tsze Ins. Ass'n, 242 U.S. 430 (1917) (failure of petition to disclose that final decree below rested upon compromise agreement); Houston Oil Co. v. Goodrich, 245 U.S. 440 (1918) (controversy found to depend "essentially upon an appreciation of the evidence"); Southern Power Co. v. North Carolina Public Service Co., 263 U.S. 508, 509 (1924) ("grave question of vital importance to the public" asserted in petition; question of evidence which proved critical at argument "is not the ground upon which we granted the petition and if sufficiently developed would not have moved us thereto.")

22. See note 21, *supra.*

helpful if the rule made clear that the brief must be not only direct and concise but likewise confined to argument upon "the reasons relied on for the allowance of the writ." In this connection reference may be made to the Government's recent practice of filing only a petition, without supporting brief.[23] The omission is obviously sensible; yet Rule 38 as now framed not only fails to make clear that it is proper and to be encouraged, but permits the inference that it is improper. Modification of the rule in this respect, by discouraging useless repetition and extended argument, would serve the double ends of convenience to the Court and economy to the parties.

These matters, however, lie only at the periphery of the problem. The heart of it is a wider, more accurate perception of the canons which ultimately move the Court to action. The governing canon was stated by the Chief Justice: the "settlement of questions of general importance so that the system of federal justice may be appropriately administered."[24] But "general importance" by itself is an inadequate guide; it yields meaning only if broken down into particulars. The Supreme Court performs a different function in different aspects of its jurisdiction; importance with reference to one type of case is not the same as importance with reference to another. Here enters the everyday necessity for trained insight by lawyers into the various aspects of the Court's jurisdiction and its responsibility for the appropriate administration of the federal justice. The importance of such insight can be readily demonstrated by a survey of the varying types of cases coming to the Court and the varying reasons which guide its action.

Paragraph (5) of Rule 38 enumerates "the character of reasons which will be considered" in the grant of cer-

23. Illustrative of the practice of the Government is the petition in Helvering v. Powers, granted May 14, 1934, 292 U.S. 620, and now pending on the merits before the Court. The petition itself is only fourteen pages in length, to which are joined twelve pages of appendices setting forth the applicable statutes. Slightly more than three pages suffice to state the case. Eight pages of argument under the heading "reasons for granting the writ" at once serve the purpose of a supporting brief and satisfy the requirements of a proper petition.

24. See text at note 16, *supra*.

tiorari. It will be sufficient to refer only to those, six in number, relating to cases from the circuit courts of appeals.[25] As the review of decisions from these courts was the original field of certiorari, so that has continued to be its primary function. The number of such cases in recent years has shown a steady increase, both absolutely and proportionately. At the 1927 Term, for example, 397 petitions came from the circuit courts of appeals. or 65 percent of all those filed. At the last term there were 660 such petitions, or 75 percent of the total.

(1) "Where a circuit court of appeals has rendered a decision in conflict with the decision of another circuit court of appeals on the same matter." The necessity of securing uniformity of decision among the circuits was the prime reason for reserving to the Supreme Court in the act of 1891 the power of review by certiorari, and it remains by far the most frequent ground for granting the writ.[26] Of the issues of relatively slight significance which come before the Court each year, the bulk are there for this reason. For let it be noted: the rule does not speak of

25. The discussion that follows is based upon a study of the cases on certiorari from the circuit courts of appeals which were decided at the last Term by full opinion. There were ninety-nine such cases, in which seventy-eight majority opinions were written (two or more cases often involving the same question). Cases in which certiorari was granted at the last Term but which were not reached for hearing on the merits, together with those disposed of by per curiam orders, have been excluded from consideration on account of exigencies of space. It is of course possible in most instances to do no more than surmise the reason which induced the Court to issue the writ; the judgments which have been ventured are based on examination of the papers submitted on both sides at the time the writ was applied for, as well as the opinions ultimately written.

26. The existence of a conflict appears to have accounted, or helped to account, for the grant of certiorari in more than half of the cases which have been studied. In ten cases (in which nine opinions were written) the Court said expressly that it had issued the writ for this reason. [Citations omitted. Ed.] In twenty-eight other cases (in which twenty opinions were written) the grant can with scarcely less confidence be attributed to the same reason. [Citations omitted. Ed.] To these can probably be safely added seven others (in which four opinions were written). [Citations omitted. Ed.] Related are cases in which there was general confusion or contrariety of opinion among the circuits but, because of the peculiarity of the facts of each case, no specific conflict. The Court doubtless acts more hesitantly under such circumstances, and with less predictability. [Citations omitted. Ed.]

conflicts as to matters of importance; the element of importance lies in the fact of conflict rather than the nature of the issue. The existence of a square conflict is the surest ground for applying for the writ; whatever other reason may be influential, this one will be decisive. What constitutes a "conflict"? The answer to this question, of course, imports into the matter the whole of the lawyer's traditional technique of analysis and distinguishing of cases. The concept is not an exact one. One point may be stressed: the Court is interested in conflicts which impair uniformity of decision where uniformity is significant,[27] conflicts which its decision in the particular case will remove.[28] This rules out, of course, hosts of particularistic applications of general rules turning upon the analysis of special states of fact.[29] But many questions of degree inevitably remain. Two or more grounds of action may combine.[30] So, the intrinsic importance of an issue, though insufficient to warrant certiorari in the absence of all conflict,

27. In a number of cases presenting questions of the technical sufficiency of indictments in minor respects, the Court has denied certiorari, despite the admission of conflict by the Government, where the only effect of lack of uniformity was to require district attorneys in certain circuits, in drafting indictments, to add a few words not elsewhere necessary. E.g., Carnahan v. United States, 281 U.S. 723 (1930); Capo v. United States, 281 U.S. 769 (1930); Malinow v. United States, 282 U.S. 875 (1930).

28. The frequent hardship of this scheme of appellate review is apparent. The later decision which gave rise to the conflict may be affirmed, but the losing party in the first case who was unable to obtain certiorari because of the absence of conflict will be unable to profit by the ultimate decision in his favor, may indeed be foreclosed by the doctrine of *res judicata* from asserting it in subsequent litigation. E.g., Crooks v. Harrelson, 282 U.S. 55 (1930); Helvering v. New York Trust Co., 292 U.S. 455 (1934).

29. Especially is the Court wary of spurious conflicts, loose allegations of conflict, conflicts depending upon the petitioning counsel's peculiar view of the facts. Multiplication of asserted conflicts is not only ineffective, but may be damaging; ten or twenty distinguishable cases have been known to bury one which is indistinguishable.

30. For example, in Minnich v. Gardner, 292 U.S. 48 (1934), a bankruptcy case, there was involved in addition to an asserted conflict, what was ultimately held to have been a clear misapplication of local law, reason two. Cf. Ormsby v. Chase, 290 U.S. 387 (1933), *infra*. This latter case, together with Miller v. Union Pac. R.R., 290 U.S. 227 (1933), was also a decision on a question of general law "in conflict with the weight of authority," reason three; and both were in addition in conflict with applicable decisions of the Supreme Court, reason five.

may lead the Court to be less astute to decide that cases in apparent conflict are narrowly distinguishable.[31]

(2) "Or has decided an important question of local law in a way probably in conflict with applicable local decisions." Federal court decisions of questions of State law often raise fundamental issues of division of power between State and nation, issues of public importance as profound as any which the Supreme Court adjudicates. Of this character are federal injunctions tying the hands of State officials on the strength of a view of State law which the State courts may or may not share. Such cases, however, rarely come to the Supreme Court upon certiorari. For the most part the "important questions of local law" urged by petitioners are questions as to the law of master and servant in negligence cases, and the like. Diversity of citizenship jurisdiction is the great feeder of such controversies. For the bulk of ordinary private litigation arising from that jurisdiction the circuit courts of appeals are, and must be, courts of last resort, tribunals of final authority as to the law of States which lie within 321
their circuit. This is not to say that the correct decision of such cases is not important; it is only to say that the importance is of a different quality. The Supreme Court cannot undertake to see that every case in a federal court is decided as a State court would have decided it. At best it must confine its interposition to cases in which a circuit court of appeals has announced a rule, potentially governing a substantial number of other cases, in conflict with a rule announced by authoritative State court decisions. Again, it acts only where it can remove such a conflict. Few grants of certiorari at the last Term, among the cases examined, were attributable to this reason.[32]

31. E.g., Freuler v. Helvering, 291 U.S. 35 (1934); Ilfeld Co. v. Hernandez, 292 U.S. 62 (1934).

32. The only clear case appears to be Stringfellow v. Atlantic Coast Line R.R., 290 U.S. 322 (1933) (two cases), in which the Court found a patent misapplication of the Florida statute governing negligence actions against railroads. The finding of misapplication was premised, however, not upon the Florida decisions but upon the inconsistency of the two holdings under review, and the Court contented itself with reversing both judgments with directions to the circuit court of appeals to determine which one was justified by the evidence. [Citations omitted. Ed.] Other cases presenting in various aspects questions of local law,

(3) "Or has decided an important question of general law in a way probably untenable or in conflict with the weight of authority." This aspect of the Supreme Court's jurisdiction upon certiorari is a consequence of *Swift* v. *Tyson*,[33] and discretion in its exercise can scarcely fail to be colored by basic attitudes toward the doctrine of that decision. Whatever its historical origin, the essential premise of the doctrine today is the desirability and possibility of nation-wide uniformity of decision, at least in the federal courts, upon matters of so-called "general jurisprudence."[34] Whether or not this task is a proper one for the Supreme Court, it is clear that the Court has many other more exigent tasks. Increasingly it has been compelled to remit to the circuit courts of appeals the primary responsibility for uniformity in the "federal common law," and to confine its own interposition to the resolution of conflicts after they arise. It may be seriously questioned whether the inclusion of this reason, as distinct from the first reason respecting conflict between circuits,[35] serves any other purpose than to mislead counsel. Certainly it is one of the most fertile breeders of those futile applications which the Chief Justice deplored. No grants of certiorari at the last Term can be definitely attributed to it.

(4) "Or has decided an important question of federal law which has not been, but should be, settled by this court." This reason, like the preceding one, has also to be

raised also the important federal question as to whether the local law or "general law" was applicable. Swift v. Tyson, 16 Pet. 1 (1842). On this issue, or else on the substantive rule of general law itself, there was conflict.

33. 16 Pet. 1 (1842).

34. See A.N. Hand, J., in Cole v. Pennsylvania R.R., 43 F.2d 953, 956 (2d Cir., 1930); Note, 43 *Harv. L. Rev.* 926 (1930).

35. The fifth reason, respecting the decision of "a federal question in a way probably in conflict with applicable decisions of" the Supreme Court, seems also to be relevant. It is not clear whether the Court treats a question of "general law," on which the federal courts take a peculiar view, as a "federal question." If it is not such a question, nothing in Rule 38 applies to circuit courts of appeals decisions on such matters which are in conflict with applicable Supreme Court decisions. No granted certiorari at the last Term appears to have raised the point directly. All the issues of "general law" before the Court were sufficiently explained by the fact of conflict among the circuits; and it is not possible to estimate the importance of the added circumstance, in some cases, of apparent conflict with the Supreme Court.

considered in connection with the first. The crux of its meaning is in the word "important." This much again is clear: less important questions are to be reviewed only where there is a showing of conflict, more important ones regardless of such a showing. But "importance" in questions of federal law is obviously quite a different matter from "importance" in questions of general law; and it is not surprising that many more cases are taken up under the fourth reason than under the third. The Supreme Court has seldom discussed explicitly its canons in this regard. Useful thinking concerning its practice, one may suggest, depends upon segregation of particular types of cases: cases involving constitutional questions, tax cases, criminal cases, cases concerning the jurisdiction of the federal courts, and the like. Patent cases furnish a notable illustration: almost never is certiorari granted when there is not a conflict of decision. In other types of cases the practice of course is different, because the considerations for or against immediate settlement of the issue by the Court are also different. Generalization under these circumstances is treacherous. But plainly, in view of the heavy demands upon the Court's time made by the routine task of resolving conflicts, it can be no mean standard of importance which will induce the Court to act in advance of conflict. With one or two possible exceptions, the grants of certiorari apparently attributable to this reason at the last Term show consistent adherence to a canon of genuine, intrinsic public significance.

(5) "Or has decided a federal question in a way probably in conflict with applicable decisions of this court." The omission of the word "important" in this reason immediately strikes the eye. The elucidation of its own decisions is of course an indispensable aspect of the Supreme Court's function. If a circuit court of appeals has failed to apply, or has plainly misinterpreted, an authoritative Supreme Court decision, certiorari will issue with small regard to the public importance of the point involved.[36]

36. In this respect, of course, the fifth reason commonly overlaps the first, dealing with conflict between the circuits; if a Supreme Court decision has been apparently misapplied, there is usually to be found a conflicting decision of a circuit court of appeals.

Applications of decisions to peculiar and debatable sets of fact; insistence that the facts are otherwise than the lower courts found them to be—these are the recurrent characteristics of unsuccessful petitions. Such observations, of course, fit only the easier cases. Difficulty centers on the growing edges of the law. The line between an unsettled question and possible misapplication of prior decisions is shadowy, and nothing is more common than to find lawyers appealing to both grounds for the grant of the writ. It is of course impossible for the Court to interfere in every instance of analogical extension of old precedents to fit new problems. If the problem is similar but different, its action is likely to be influenced both by its view of the importance of the particular problem and of the validity of the apparent extension.[37] Inevitably the lines are blurred between cases in which the grant of certiorari is appropriate under the fifth reason or under the fourth, and those in which it will be delayed until it is appropriate under the first. Least predictable of all are cases in which the Court grants certiorari in order to qualify or overrule a decision which has been faithfully followed, or to clarify one which has induced general contrariety of opinion, if not specific conflict, under varying instances of a common category.

(6) "Or has so far departed from the accepted and usual course of judicial proceedings, or so far sanctioned such a departure by a lower court, as to call for an exercise of this court's power of supervision." The ratio of successful to attempted invocations of this reason is smaller than that of any other. To scores of petitioners each year any asserted error in the decision of a case, however minute and of whatever character, is such a departure "from the accepted and usual course of judicial proceedings" as to call for an exercise of the Supreme Court's power of supervision. Of course, the reason refers neither to errors of law nor to minor departures from customary practice. It

37. See, e.g., Hanson v. Haff, 291 U.S. 559 (1934), a deportation case, in which a prior decision that "prostitution or for any other immoral purpose" includes a concubine was held to have been erroneously extended to condemn one whose sexual irregularities, so the Court found, had fallen short of concubinage.

refers to matters of major concern to the integrity of the federal judicial process. How rarely the Supreme Court regards as necessary any intervention on this ground appears from the fact that no single grant of certiorari last Term was attributable to it.

Generalizations of the sort here ventured are, of course, of limited value. At best they serve only to narrow the area of doubt, to indicate directions of profitable inquiry. But the striking fact is how large a proportion of petitions yield to so elementary an analysis. One need not underestimate the complexity of the certiorari process to feel confident that its more detailed study would make that process more intelligible and, perchance, more predictable.

The suggestion has repeatedly been made that the Court in denying certiorari should append a brief statement of reasons for its denial.[38] In rare instances the Court has so expressed its reasons.[39] The proposal to extend the practice to all petitions, despite its surface attractions, is open to grave objections. Extended statements applicable to the facts of the particular case would require such an expenditure of effort as to defeat the very purpose of certiorari. Brief, formalized reasons such as the Court now appends in dismissing appeals upon the jurisdictional statement would be largely meaningless, for the purpose of rendering the grounds of its action discoverable and predictable. Of far greater value would be occasional full opinions upon denial of petitions, where explanation of reasons for denial would illuminate large numbers of cases. Soon after the passage of the act of 1891, the Court, elucidating a new mode of review, did deliver several such opinions.[40] Since then it has con-

38. See, e.g., Moore, "Right of Review by Certiorari to the Supreme Court," 17 *Geo. L.J.* 307 (1929); Handler, Book Review, 28 *Colum. L. Rev.* 515, 517, 518 (1928).

39. Reasons or citations of authority or both were given in four cases at the last Term. [Citations omitted. Ed.]

40. In re Woods, 143 U.S. 202 (1892) (stating that case does not fall "within the category of questions of such gravity and general importance as to require" review); Chicago & N.W. Ry. v. Osborne, 146 U.S. 354 (1892) (per curiam denial, for want of final judgment, preceded by reporter's statement of facts); American Const. Co. v. Jacksonville, Tampa & Key West Ry., 148 U.S. 372 (1893).

sciously abstained from such a practice,[41] except, on occasion, when dismissing writs of certiorari as improvidently granted.[42]

Still other opportunities to give reasons are available in cases in which certiorari is granted, and an opinion written. Commonly the opinions in such cases refer to the grant of certiorari, but seldom do they mention the reasons for it. Virtually all the desiderata urged for statements of reasons for denials would be attained by statements of

41. In Gaines v. Washington, 277 U.S. 81 (1928), the Court, discovering that a writ of error had been improvidently allowed, dismissed it, and entered a rule against the plaintiff in error to show cause why, treating the writ of error as a petition for certiorari, certiorari should not be denied for lack of a substantial federal question. The return having been filed, the petition was denied by full opinion, Mr. Chief Justice Taft stating in explanation, "It has not been the practice of the Court to write opinions and state its reasons for denying writs of certiorari, and this opinion is not to be regarded as indicating an intention to adopt that practice, but in view of the fact that the Court has deemed it wise to initiate a practice for speedily disposing of criminal cases in which there is no real basis for jurisdiction in this Court, it was thought proper to make an exception here, not to be repeated, and write an opinion." Id. at 87. In a case at the last Term the Court requested oral argument "upon the questions presented by the petition for writ of certiorari." Boynton v. Hutchinson Gas Co., Sup. Ct. J. 137, 155, 161 (1933). After argument, certiorari was granted, without explanation. 291 U.S. 656 (1934). Thereupon the case was argued on the merits. Sup. Ct. J. 199, 200 (1933). A week later the writ of certiorari was dismissed per curiam "for the lack of showing of service of summons and severance upon those appellees in the state court who are not parties to the proceedings in this Court." 292 U.S. 601 (1934).

42. In such an opinion in Layne & Bowler Corp. v. Western Well Works, 261 U.S. 387, 393 (1923), Mr. Chief Justice Taft concluded by saying, "If it be suggested that as much effort and time as we have given to the consideration of the alleged conflict would have enabled us to dispose of the case before us on the merits, the answer is that it is very important that we be consistent in not granting the writ of certiorari except in cases involving principles the settlement of which is of importance to the public as distinguished from that of the parties, and in cases where there is a real and embarrassing conflict of opinion and authority between the circuit courts of appeal. The present case certainly comes under neither head." Compare Mr. Justice Stone, dissenting, Washington Fid. Nat. Ins. Co. v. Burton, 287 U.S. 97, 100 (1932). For other opinions written upon the dismissal of improvidently granted writs, see Tyrrell v. District of Columbia, 243 U.S. 1 (1917); Missouri Pac. R.R. v. Hanna, 266 U.S. 184 (1924); Erie R.R. v. Kirkendall, 266 U.S. 185 (1924). The Court's more recent habit has been to dismiss writs of certiorari improvidently granted by per curiam opinion, without explanation of reasons.

reasons for grants; nor in the context of a full statement of the case would brevity be inconsistent with illumination. Accumulated explanations would make familiar the canons which guide the Court; and an essential aspect of its processes would be driven in, as it should be driven in, upon the consciousness of the bar.

One might hope also for other and no less important gains from such a practice. Disturbing instances recur in which the Court's action in granting certiorari appears irreconcilable either with its own professed grounds or with any general canons which can independently be formulated. Usually such doubts vanish upon examination of the papers; an unmentioned conflict between circuits, or failure to follow an authoritative Supreme Court decision, furnishes the explanation. Sometimes the doubts remain. In either case the desirability of a statement by the Court itself is evident. Futile applications are as much encouraged by an apparent as by an actual departure from the Court's ordinary grounds of action. In a process so extraordinary, entailing so wide a range of power, the Court itself must be especially anxious to appear, as well as actually to be, guided in the exercise of its discretion by standards intelligible to the profession as consistent solely with its responsibilities as the Supreme Court of the nation.

The Pressure of Business

The very functions of the Court in our governmental scheme impose limits for their realization. The Constitution itself makes sharp restrictions in confining closely opportunities for originating litigation before the Court. By leaving the great bulk of the Court's business to be defined by Congressional discretion, the Constitution, with characteristic forethought, devises a flexible mechanism to be adjusted according to the practical dictates of government. But even jurisdictional acts are not so detailed and explicit as to sterilize the Court's own resourcefulness in suiting its ways of doing business to the kind and volume of its business. Indeed, the great wisdom of Congress in its more recent legislation governing the Supreme Court has been to rely more and more on the Supreme Court's wisdom in the conduct of the Court's business. And the Court has denied the ancient saw that it is a wise judge who enlarges his jurisdiction. Rather it has found truer insight in Goethe's dictum, *In der Beschränkung beweist sich der Meister*. The Court of last resort for a nation of 120 millions must constantly be mindful of the impossibility of discharging its powers adequately in more than a relatively small number of cases each year.[1] Rules of law and procedure, and judicial conventions, all have to be shaped for administration by a tribunal, which, no matter how distinguished its membership, can annually write not many more than two hundred opinions, if the deliberative process which precedes an opinion and the process of opinion-writing are to partake of those psychologic and intellectual conditions which alone can produce the best judicial product. Concretely, the task of ruling upon statements as to jurisdiction and petitions for certiorari is bound to compete with opinion-

Excerpt from Frankfurter and Henry M. Hart, Jr., "The Business of the Supreme Court at October Term, 1933," 48 *Harv. L. Rev.* 238, 277–281 (1934).

1. Compare the recent legislation in England substituting discretionary for obligatory review in the House of Lords. 24 & 25 Geo. V, c. 40, §1 (1934).

writing in its demands upon the Justices. If the Court is limited in the number of cases it can decide, no less is it limited in the number it can decide not to decide. Increase in the latter burden is the emergent problem of the act of 1925.

Save for the brief respite under the acts of 1891 and 1925, the continuous trend in the Court's history has been one of pressure from increasing business. To expect reversal of this trend for the years that lie ahead is to rely on improbability. Factors making for steady growth in the judicial business of the country abound. No doubt unusual causes were responsible for the abrupt increase in the number of cases in the last Term. Not a few controversies arose out of business failures. Claims of all kinds are pressed under the spur of a depression, and the needs of the Treasury call for particular alertness in the administration of tax laws, by far the most fruitful of litigation for the Court. But whatever the causes, the bumper crop of legislation, State and federal, of the last few years was not among them. Only four cases during the Term, decided by full opinion, presented questions of the validity of depression lawmaking by the States. Cases involving federal statutes were no more frequent. The influx of such litigation is still to come.

A mere recital of the more important recent Congressional measures suffices for intimations of the multitudinous litigation which this legislation has enacted. The first session of the Seventy-Third Congress put on the statute books, *inter alia,* the Emergency Banking Act of 1933, the Economy Act of 1933, the Agricultural Adjustment Act, the Tennessee Valley Authority Act, the Securities Act, the Joint Resolution of June 5, 1933, relating to gold clauses, the Home Owners' Loan Act, the Banking Act of 1933, the National Industrial Recovery Act, the Emergency Railroad Transportation Act, and the Farm Credit Act of 1933. Of the many questions embedded in this mass of legislation, only few, and those few not involving the most contentious issues, faced the Court during the 1933 Term. None of the legislation at the second session of the same Congress came into issue: the Gold

Reserve Act, the Federal Farm Mortgage Corporation Act, the Bankhead Cotton Control Act, the Securities Exchange Act, the Communications Act of 1934, the Federal Credit Union Act, the National Housing Act, the Tobacco Control Act, the Railroad Retirement Act, the important amendments to the Bankruptcy Act, and the numerous extensions of federal control over interstate crime. Some of these enactments will lapse with time; others, repeal will terminate. But most of the new legislation, it is safe to assume, will constitute additions to the permanent structure of federal law. As to such statutes the Court's task transcends the initial determination of basic issues of validity. Neither careful draftsmanship nor conscientious administration can avert the steady and difficult process of judicial distillation of the meaning of complicated new legislation.

These new measures of social and economic policy are not the only breeders of new business for the Court. The Seventy-Third Congress also passed several important acts touching the federal judiciary. And, unless all past history is a false guide, new laws governing the jurisdiction and procedure of the federal courts inevitably imply a long term of judicial clarification. By withdrawing from the district courts power to enjoin the enforcement of State public utility rate orders, Congress may well have relieved one of the tensions between the State and federal authorities. But in diverting the route by which such controversies come to the Supreme Court it has raised novel issues for the Court in the application of the reform. The act conferring upon the Supreme Court the rulemaking power in common-law actions has composed a controversy which has long divided the American bar. But in doing so Congress has imposed upon the Court not only the onerous responsibility of formulating such rules; it has started the extended unfolding by judicial construction of a new code of adjective law. Finally, the Declaratory Judgment Act makes available in the federal courts a form of relief which, despite the light of experience in State and British jurisdictions, cannot fail to raise, in the context of federal constitutional law, many difficult issues for Supreme Court adjudication.[2]

Moreover, the tasks that lie ahead for the Court derive not merely from the prospective sources of new business and the extent and novelty of the questions presented by new legislation. Particularly in the sphere of constitutional adjudication there is need as much of re-examining old starting points as of fixing new ones. The Supreme Court is the vehicle of life latent in the letter of the Constitution. This implies the traditional process of extracting new meaning from old cases, of seeing beneath words to things. Plainly we are in the midst of another great creative period in the Court's history when ultimate issues of society will for a time steadily solicit its judgment. To meet these issues with the learning, wisdom, and largeness of vision appropriate to their majesty, the Court must have that serenity and spacious feeling of detachment which an effective control over its business alone can afford. Only a Court thus freed from undue external pressures will be equal to those demands of judicial statesmanship to which the times summon it.[3]

As it [the Constitution] survives fierce controversies from age to age, it is forever silently bearing witness to the wisdom that went into its composition, by showing itself suited to the purposes of a great people under circumstances that no one of its makers could have foreseen. Men have found, as they are finding now, when new and unlooked-for situations have presented themselves, that they were left with liberty to handle them. Of this quality in the Constitution people sometimes foolishly talk as if it meant that the great barriers of this instrument have been set at naught, and may be set at naught, in great exigencies; as if it were always ready to give way under pressure; and as if statesmen were always standing ready to violate it when important enough occasion arose. What generally happens, however, on these occasions, is that the little-

2. See Note, 45 *Harv. L. Rev.* 1089 (1932); Borchard, *Declaratory Judgments* (1934).

3. Thayer, *Legal Essays* 159 (1927).

ness and the looseness of men's interpretation of the Constitution are revealed, and that this great instrument shows itself wiser and more far-looking than men had thought. It is forever dwarfing its commentators, both statesmen and judges, by disclosing its own greatness. In the entire list of the judges of our highest court, past and present, in the business of interpreting the Constitution, few indeed are the men who have not, now and again, signally failed to appreciate the large scope of this great charter of our national life. Petty judicial interpretations have always been, are now, and always will be, a very serious danger to the country.

Mr. Justice Holmes
8 March 1841 – 6 March 1935

To explore the enduring significance of a life is to ask whether without it the history of thought or action would have been decisively different. Such appraisal, we are often told, must await the verdict of time. A powerful contemporary thinker partly determines our criteria for judgment. That in itself is a great achievement. But Mr. Justice Holmes was not our contemporary. In reviewing a life so complete and venerable as his, we are already dealing with history.

Some things, surely, are outside the realm of rational debate. Suppose that Holmes's *The Common Law* and his occasional essays had never been written, that the Massachusetts Supreme Judicial Court had never known him, and that the Supreme Court of the United States had been without him. Only an eccentric or uninformed judgment would deny that through *The Common Law* the United States has made the single most original contribution thus far to legal scholarship, that through the essays a more rational direction, a healthier tone, was given to legal science. Mr. Justice Holmes's greatness as scholar and philosopher is the more dazzling because it was achieved by such concentration of effort—a maximum of thought and a minimum of words. Nor can there be more doubt about his place in the calendar of judges. For the Massachusetts Court Holmes's name will be coupled with Shaw's, and for the Supreme Bench he is Marshall's closet compeer, however unlike their endowment and services. What a difference it would have made if that capricious bullet, more than seventy years ago, had been sent by a surer aim or at a mark less fairy-favored than Captain O. W. Holmes.

The ultimate accomplishment of a thinker is found not in his books nor in his opinions but in the minds of men. *The Common Law*, the *Collected Legal Papers*, the thousand opinions in the *Massachusetts Reports*, and the six

Reprinted from 48 *Harv. L. Rev.* 1279 (1935). Copyright 1935 by The Harvard Law Review Association. Footnotes supplied by editor.

hundred in the *United States Reports* have been most powerful generators of fresh thinking in the necessary adaptations of the legal tradition to new demands upon it. By his own example, enhanced by his great judicial prestige, Mr. Justice Holmes made legal scholarship at once exciting and respectable. The labors of Langdell and Gray, of Ames and Thayer, of Maitland and Holdsworth stirred his admiration and encouragement. When most needed, he gave a strong impetus to the academic study of law. Though he occupied a chair at the Harvard Law School for only a very brief period, indirectly he remained for the next fifty years probably the most influential law teacher in the land.

For decades throughout the English-speaking world major legal issues have been discussed at the universities and at the bar, and with increasing frequency decided by the courts, in the perspective of Holmes's formulation. The considerations of preference and policy, usually inarticulate and too often unconscious, especially in constitutional controversies, were by him given explicitness and thereby an outlook of tolerance essential to the maintenance of our constitutional system. And both analysis and insight he expressed in language at once phosphorescent and permanent.

All this dry lawyer's talk. "To live is to function,"[1] and Oliver Wendell Holmes functioned as thinker and judge. But the whole of a very rich and imaginative nature poured itself into that task of judging between man and man, between man and the state. For centuries men to whom he will be among the great and "men who never heard of him will be moving to the measure of his thought."[2] Romantic legends doubtless will gather round his name. But men will no longer feel his passionate and poetic temperament nor experience his charm and gaiety and wit. They will not be exhilarated by his sparkling talk and humbled by his deep humility.

1. *Justice Oliver Wendell Holmes: His Book Notices and Uncollected Letters & Papers* 142 (Shriver ed. 1936).
2. Holmes, *Collected Legal Papers* 32 (1920).

The A.A.A. Case

By an interesting coincidence, what was intended to be a calm intellectual inquiry, to be sure of a very momentous aspect of our national system, has been dramatically sharpened by the Court's disposition of this afternoon of A.A.A.[1] No lawyer of any self-respect will discuss a decision without having read and adequately considered the full text of the opinions in a case and I have thus far seen only the mutilated extracts in tonight's paper. But in the light of the briefs and the arguments submitted in the case, these contain sufficient to illustrate factors in the analysis of our problems. Especially does the division in the Court help to pose what is at stake, from the point of view of intellectual analysis in constitutional adjudications. The Court divided six to three in applying some of the provisions of the Constitution of the United States. That in itself tells much. Take the writers of the two opinions. Mr. Justice Roberts and Mr. Justice Stone are about the same age, they had more or less the same cultural antecedents, they are both Republicans (Stone was President Coolidge's Attorney General), they listened to the same arguments, they read the same briefs, they read the very same clauses in the Constitution and the prior decisions of the Courts, all of which were the raw materials for their result. And yet, out of the same legal training and presumably the same presuppositions and from the same data, they reached diametrically opposite conclusions. What emphasizes the divergence is the quality of the two Justices who shared Mr. Justice Stone's opinion. Certainly, no informed, disinterested student of the history of

An epitome of the speech delivered at The Examiner Club of Boston on January 6, 1936. It appears here through the courtesy of Mr. Frank Buxton and Mr. Milton E. Lord, secretary of The Examiner Club.

1. United States v. Butler, 297 U.S. 1 (1936). The Agricultural Adjustment Act was a New Deal statute providing machinery that, it was hoped, would restore the purchasing power to the farm community that it had held prior to World War I. The statute would accomplish this end by payment of a subsidy for voluntary limitation of crop production. The funds for the subsidy were to be secured by a tax levied on the processers of agricultural products. In *Butler,* the Supreme Court held it invalid to tax the processers for the direct payments to the farmers. [Ed.]

the Supreme Court will say that Brandeis, Stone, and Cardozo are not as able a trio as any in the history of the Court and are not as likely fifty years hence to rank as high as any three of the majority of the Court. And such a division, frequently with the ablest members of the Court in the dissent, is not a rare exception. Quite the contrary. In the lifetime of the members of this Club, the great public controversies that eventually came for adjudication before the Supreme Court, almost always led to a five to four or a six to three decision, and usually the most distinguished members of the Court were dissenters.

Another thing to note is that acclaim of the Court in the lay press corresponds rather closely with the favor with which a particular newspaper views the practical or political result of an adjudication. Tomorrow morning, doubtless, the *Herald-Tribune*, the *Sun*, the *Times*, the *Boston Herald* and the *Chicago Tribune* and such like papers will sing paeans of praise over the Supreme Court's invalidation of the processing tax. Yet the columns of these same papers record almost vituperative disapproval of a five to four decision of the Supreme Court, some seventy years ago, which undid some of the reconstruction legislation of the then Radicals in Congress, namely, the Northern Republicans who sought to impose all sorts of restrictive loyalty tests upon the South.

These divisions in the Court and in public opinions are almost inevitable in view of the nature of the issues in Constitutional controversies such as the A.A.A. and T.V.A. raise. The Constitution contains a few provisions that are defined either by the technical nature of the terms used or canalized by their history. About such provisions, there is relatively little controversy. But there are other provisions, with vague phrases like "due process" or undefined concepts like "commerce among the States," or still broader assumptions underlying the whole document like the doctrine of the separation of powers and the whole conception of our federalism. It is when such vague or purposely ambiguous or large dynamic conceptions appear for arbitrament before the Court, that questions of more-or-less, of matters of degree and appraisals of policy necessarily come into play and control the controversy. Usually the precedents are sufficiently open or sufficiently conflicting to permit the Court to choose either one series or the other as the starting point. And the choice of premise usually predetermines the conclusion.

Thus, in construing the Constitution in these vital controversies, the Supreme Court does not go to a dark room and by a process of nature develop the constitutional photographic negative into the picture of its decision. The Court is engaged in a creative act—it must exercise judgment. And into the totality of its judgment enters the whole of the experience, the imagination, the forecast of the future, the fears and hopes, of the members of the Court. This explains the divisions on vital issues. It also poses the real problems of judicial review, and especially the educational problem, both professional and cultural, in the production and selection of men truly qualified to exercise the powers which the Supreme Court wields.

The Orbit of Judicial Power

If it be true that substantive common law was "gradually secreted in the interstices of procedure"[1] it is no less true that procedure, in large measure, has determined the course of American constitutional law. To utilize the technical forms of litigation devised originally for relatively narrow controversies between man and man in the adjustment of great public issues is one of the most creative achievements of lawyers. The transference of ordinary legal procedures and modes of thought to such politico-legal controversies could not have been accomplished, and certainly could not have maintained itself, but for procedural safeguards devised partly by the Supreme Court itself and partly by Congress, by which the course of constitutional adjudication was to be confined. With full consciousness of the terrific implications of the power of judicial review over legislation, particularly in view of the silences and spacious phrasing of the Constitution, the Supreme Court evolved criteria and practices for the exercise of its "delicate" function. And so it has come to pass that the history of substantive constitutional law is intertwined with professions and practices delimiting the controversies which the Court will take, as well as the scope of its decision when it takes them.

Despite the most tempting appeals of patriotism, the Supreme Court at the very outset of its career declined the role of adviser even on legal aspects of policy, and defined its function strictly as that of a court of law. In 1793 the first Chief Justice, on behalf of himself and his Associates, in graceful Addisonian language, abstained from advising Washington "extra-judicially," "being judges of

Excerpt from Frankfurter and Adrian S. Fisher, "The Business of the Supreme Court at October Terms, 1935 and 1936, 51 *Harv. L. Rev.* 577 (1938).

1. See Maine, *Early Law and Custom* 389 (1883), quoted in Maitland, *Equity* 295 (1909).

a court in the last resort."[2] Nor could its opinion be solicited merely because invited through the formalities of a legal proceeding. Before their reply to Washington, the Justices individually, in matters coming before them on circuit, had refused to share in the enforcement of an act of Congress which did not leave them finality of adjudication.[3]

"Judicial power," however large, has an orbit more or less strictly defined by well-recognized presuppositions regarding the kind of business that properly belongs to courts. Their business is adjudication, not speculation. They are concerned with actual, living controversies, and not abstract disputation.[4] While adjudication has phases of lawmaking, legislatures not courts are policy-makers in the large meaning of the term.[5] Courts, therefore, act within relatively narrow bounds of discretion. Their jurisdiction is contingent upon the means of illumination and the resources for judgment to which the technique of an

2. 3 Johnston, *Correspondence and Public Papers of John Jay* 486 (1891). The Court might easily have "slipped into the adoption of a precedent that would have engrafted the English usage upon our system." Thayer, *Legal Essays* 53–54 (1908); cf. Frankfurter, "Advisory Opinions," 1 *Encyc. Soc. Sciences* 475 (1930). In at least two instances, both affecting Monroe, the Court departed from this principle. 1 Miller, *Treaties and Other International Acts* 178 (1931); 1 Warren, *The Supreme Court in United States History* 595–597 (rev. ed. 1926).

3. Hayburn's Case, 2 Dall. 409, 410n (1792).

4. United States v. Ferreira, 13 How. 40 (1851); Gordon v. United States, 2 Wall. 561 (1864), 117 U.S. 697 (1864); Pelham v. Rose, 9 Wall. 103 (1869); Singer Manufacturing Co. v. Wright, 141 U.S. 696 (1891); Muskrat v. United States, 219 U.S. 346 (1911); Willing v. Chicago Auditorium Ass'n, 277 U.S. 274 (1928). There must be an actual adverse interest between the litigants. Lord v. Veazie, 8 How. 251 (1850); Chicago & Grand Trunk Ry. v. Wellman, 143 U.S. 339 (1892); South Spring Hill Gold Min. Co. v. Amador Medean Gold Min. Co., 145 U.S. 300 (1892); see Atherton Mills v. Johnston, 259 U.S. 13, 15 (1922).

5. See Gray, *Nature and Sources of the Law* 211–230, 495–512 (1909); Holmes, J., dissenting, in Southern Pacific Co. v. Jensen, 244 U.S. 205, 221 (1917). "I recognize without hesitation that judges do and must legislate, but they can do so only interstitially; they are confined from molar to molecular motions. A common-law judge could not say I think the doctrine of consideration a bit of historical nonsense and shall not enforce it in my court."

Anglo-American litigation limits them.[6] To be sure, these are the historic deposits of the operations of courts in the English-speaking world for centuries. That is precisely the strength of the doctrines of judicial self-limitation. But these considerations, rooted as they are in the profound empiricism of the common law, have special significance when applied to the peculiar function of the Supreme Court in our federal scheme.

It is true enough, as a matter of doctrine, that the Supreme Court, like every other Anglo-American court, only adjudicates the rights of litigants, even though a particular litigation may implicate a constitutional issue. But howsoever inescapable the duty cast upon the Court,[7] the consequences of invalidating legislation necessarily involve a clash within the different organs of government.[8]

6. See Taney, C. J., dissenting, in Pennsylvania v. Wheeling & Belmont Bridge Co., 13 How. 518, 592 (1851); Brandeis, J., dissenting, in International News Service v. Associated Press, 248 U.S. 215, 264–267 (1918); Brandeis, J., dissenting, in Pennsylvania v. West Virginia, 262 U.S. 553, 618–624 (1923).

7. Beard, *The Supreme Court and the Constitution* (1912); Thayer, *Cases on Constitutional Law* 48 et seq. (1895).

8. In an address as president of the American Bar Association, John W. Davis, Esq., said: "But august as are the functions of the court, surely they do not go one step beyond the administration of justice in individual litigants . . . Shall we say that when an American stands before the court demanding rights given him by the supreme law of the land, the court shall be deaf to his appeal? Shall wrongs visited upon him by the illegal excesses of Congresses or legislatures be less open to redress than those which he may suffer from courts, or sheriffs, or military tyrants or civilian enemies? If this be so, if in any such case the ears of the court are to be closed against him, it is not the power of the court that has been reduced but the dearly-bought right of the citizen that is taken away." Davis, "Present Day Problems," 48 *A.B.A. Rep.* 193, 204 (1923).

Upon these comments by Mr. Davis, Lord Birkenhead made the following observations: "Your constitution is expressed and defined in documents which can be pronounced upon by the Supreme Court. In this sense your judges are the master of your executive. Your constitution is a cast-iron document. It falls to be construed by the Supreme Court with the same sense of easy and admitted mastery as any ordinary contract. This circumstance provides a breakwater of enormous value against ill-considered and revolutionary change. Whether if the forces behind revolutionary change become menacing and strong enough the breakwater will serve must be left for the future to determine. But an outsider must fully and absolutely admit that up to the present its strength has seemed extremely adequate. Your President is one for whom intellectually I have

The legislature of a State or its governor, the Congress or the President, has affirmed and the Supreme Court has denied: that is the essence of an adjudication of unconstitutionality. This makes the decisive difference between litigation enmeshed in affairs of state and the staple business of adjudicating ordinary private rights. To observe the traditional conditions binding Anglo-American courts in the exercise of their jurisdiction has, in constitutional controversies, the added and vital sanction of avoiding undue political conflicts. To this end the common-law attitude of judicial empiricism has expressed itself in procedural doctrines more sharply relevant to constitutional cases. In myriad instances the Supreme Court has announced rules of self-limitation to avoid entering unduly into an area of political conflict or enlarging that area needlessly.

The Court is not the forum for a chivalrous or disinterested defense of the Constitution. Its business is with self-regarding, immediate, secular claims. Legislation will not be struck down except to vindicate a legally protected interest;[9] damage alone is insufficient.[10] But an

a great admiration; and personally a deep affection. His masterly address today carried me entirely with him. But surely one refinement was a little subtle. He said that the Supreme Court had not the right *in abstracto* to construe your fundamental constitutional document; but only in relation to the issues presented by an individual litigation. But is this in ultimate analysis a very serious derogation? When an issue challenged by an individual raises the question whether a law is constitutional or not, the decision of the Supreme Court decides this question for all time; and if the decision is against the legislature, the attempted law is stripped of its attempted authority." Birkenhead, "The Development of the British Constitution in the Last Fifty Years," 48 *A.B.A. Rep.* 224, 226 (1923).

9. Stearns v. Wood, 236 U.S. 75 (1915); Fairchild v. Hughes, 258 U.S. 126 (1922); Massachusetts State Grange v. Benton, 272 U.S. 525 (1926). A merely official interest is not enough. Smith v. Indiana, 191 U.S. 138 (1903); Braxton County Court v. West Virginia, 208 U.S. 192 (1908); cf. Texas v. Interstate Commerce Commission, 258 U.S. 158 (1922). Neither is the interest of a federal taxpayer in funds in the federal Treasury sufficient. Frothingham v. Mellon, 262 U.S. 447 (1923); cf. Crampton v. Zabriskie, 101 U.S. 601 (1879).

10. Marye v. Parsons, 114 U.S. 325 (1884); Alabama Power Co. v. Ickes, 302 U.S. 464 (1938); cf. Truax v. Raich, 239 U.S. 33 (1915); Pierce v. Society of Sisters, 268 U.S. 510 (1925).

assailant of legislation can only urge his interest, not another's.[11] One cannot object to a State tax as an infringement of the commerce clause when the taxed transactions are outside the bounds of interstate commerce. To be sure, this oversimplified generalization smothers subtleties presented by a statute which apparently covers both intrastate and interstate dealings in a single, unseparated provision.[12] These subtleties explain the confusion and fluctuation in applying the generality.[13]

Just as equity, at common law, created its own jurisdictional problems with special reference to the avoidance of friction between two tribunals, so resort to equity for invalidating legislation generates its special problems, if needless friction between the judiciary and other branches of government is to be avoided. The evasion of the requirement for damage that cannot be compensated has a pungency of consequences in these public law controversies which strikingly underlines traditional equity practice. Public interest, however, exerts contradictory pressures. Considerations for abstention from decision, unless technical equity requirements are satisfied, are

11. Austin v. The Aldermen, 7 Wall. 694 (1867); Tyler v. Judges of the Court of Registration, 179 U.S. 405 (1900); New York *ex rel.* Hatch v. Reardon, 204 U.S. 152 (1907).

12. There are two main aspects of the problem. The first arises where a party affected by a statute argues that in a different situation the same statutory language would be unconstitutional. The second arises when the party argues that in the particular situation in which the statute is being applied it is unconstitutional as to some third person. This was dealt with in Holden v. Hardy, 169 U.S. 366, 397 (1898): "It may not be improper to suggest in this connection that although the prosecution in this case was against the employer of labor, who apparently under the statute is the only one liable, his defence is not so much that his right to contract has been infringed upon, but that the act works a peculiar hardship to his employés, whose right to labor as long as they please is alleged to be thereby violated. The argument would certainly come with better grace and greater cogency from the latter class."

13. Compare People *ex rel.* Hatch v. Reardon, 204 U.S. 152 (1907), with Liggett Co. v. Lee, 288 U.S. 517 (1933); compare Tyler v. Judges of the Court of Registration, 179 U.S. 405 (1900), with Wuchter v. Pizzutti, 276 U.S. 13 (1928); compare Cronin v. Adams, 192 U.S. 108 (1904), with Pierce v. Society of Sisters, 268 U.S. 510 (1925). See also, Stern, "Separability and Separability Clauses in the Supreme Court," 51 *Harv. L. Rev.* 76, 82–106 (1937). The question arose during the 1935 Term in Premier-Pabst Sales Co. v. Grosscup, 298 U.S. 226 (1936).

met with the temptation to make use of the flexible facilities of equity for prompt allaying of uncertainty. And so the cases reflect an oscillation between a very strict and a very easy-going attitude toward taking equity jurisdiction to decide constitutionality.[14] Even where Congress for obvious fiscal reasons has withdrawn power to enjoin the collection of federal taxes, the Supreme Court has grafted exceptions upon the statute.[15]

The fecund possibilities of equity have been skillfully utilized in proceedings which introduce distorting elements when employed for a constitutional adjudication. The ordinary stockholder's suit invented for the adjustment of internal corporate difficulties, operates in an environment very different from its common-law habitat as the offspring of a friendly procedure to have legislation declared unconstitutional. The time-honored right of a receiver to ask instructions from his judge is invoked in a wholly different context when he asks his court to pass on the validity of an intricate and far-reaching statute which may affect the estate.[16] Plainly in these situations

14. Moor v. Texas & New Orleans R.R., 297 U.S. 101 (1936), represents a healthy limitation upon the scope of injunctive relief in constitutional cases. A cotton grower sought a mandatory injunction to compel a railroad to accept for shipment cotton which lacked the bale tags required by the Bankhead Cotton Control Act. There was no showing that the plaintiff was unable to move the remaining cotton; his main embarrassment was that if he moved it by the cheapest method, by buying exemption certificates from private persons, he would be unable to recover what he had paid in the event that the act was subsequently declared unconstitutional. The Supreme Court upheld the decision of the lower courts that there was an adequate remedy at law and refused to consider the constitutionality of the statute.

15. See Miller v. Standard Nut Margarine Co., 284 U.S. 498 (1932); see Note, 49 *Harv. L. Rev.* 109 (1935).

16. In Burco, Inc. v. Whitworth, 81 F.2d 721 4th Cir., 1936), *cert. denied,* 297 U.S. 724 (1936), a petition for instructions as to the constitutionality of the Public Utility Holding Company Act of 1935 was filed for the avowed purpose of determining whether the trustee should register under the act and whether any of the proposed plans of reorganization would be feasible. The Government, not a party to the proceeding, felt that it challenged the validity of vital legislation on wholly speculative assumption presented by an inadequate and specious record. One ground upon which the Government opposed certiorari, in a statement filed as *amicus curiae,* was that no justiciable controversy over the constitutionality of the act was presented. The Government denied that the

the deciding factors have been views on the deeper problems of jurisdiction. Intensity of conviction concerning the Court's duty to abstain from constitutional adjudication until decision is really unavoidable, rather than knowledge of recondite equity learning, has determined the fate of these modern equitable devices for securing constitutional review.

The Court has not merely been alert against the use of common-law procedural forms when they are ill-adapted for constitutional adjudications. It has also built up a body of precepts derived from its general postulate of avoiding constitutional adjudication unless the case compels. That means an adequate disclosure in the record of facts which make the constitutional issue an exigent and not a hypothetical problem,[17] as well as absence in the record of a legal ground other than constitutional on which a claim may rest.[18]

The Court's general doctrine of avoidance of constitutional adjudication brought in its train special canons of statutory construction. Needless clash with the legislature is avoided by construing statutes so as to save them, if it can be done without doing violence to the habits of En-

act compelled registration by the trustee or foreclosed the possibility of reorganization, and further stated that the only effect of a decision upon the constitutionality would be to serve as an advisory opinion for the benefit of one of the opposing groups which were jockeying for strategic positions in the ultimate disposition of the estate. Even this effect, it was urged, would be minimized by the fact that the financial condition of the corporation was such that any reorganization would be merely temporary and would probably result in dissolution before the more vital provisions of the act had become operative.

17. Liverpool, N.Y. & P. S.S. Co. v. Commissioners of Emigration, 113 U.S. 33 (1885); Hammond v. Schappi Bus Line, Inc., 275 U.S. 164 (1927); Abrams v. Van Schaick, 293 U.S. 188 (1934); Wilshire Oil Co. v. United States, 295 U.S. 100 (1935); Villa v. Van Schaick, 299 U.S. 152 (1936); cf. Borden's Farm Products Co. v. Baldwin, 293 U.S. 194 (1934), Note, 49 *Harv. L. Rev.* 641 (1936); Honeyman v. Hanan, 300 U.S. 14 (1937).

18. Siler v. Louisville & Nash. R.R., 213 U.S. 175 (1909); Light v. United States, 220 U.S. 523 (1911); Tennessee Publishing Co. v. American Nat. Bank, 299 U.S. 18 (1936); cf. Berea College v. Kentucky, 211 U.S. 45 (1908); Fox Film Corp. v. Muller, 296 U.S. 207 (1935). But cf. Thompson v. Consolidated Gas Utilities Corp., 300 U.S. 55 (1937).

glish speech.[19] Indeed, so wary has the Court been at times of entering the domain of constitutional discussion that it has given constricted meaning to legislation.[20] When a constitutional issue must be faced, the common-law hostility against dicta, against deciding more than has to be decided, is reinforced by admonitions of the highest statesmanship against seeking to foreclose the future.[21] Finally, of course, there is the overriding doctrine of judicial review in constitutional controversies derived from the "delicate" nature of this power and its inevitable political consequences. Marshall gave it its magistral formulation,[22] and James Bradley Thayer, in his classic essay "The Origin and Scope of the American Doctrine of Constitutional Law,"[23] its most luminous exposition.

But the course of constitutional law does not run smooth, either as to procedure or substance. Fluctuations from period to period in the application of unquestioned doctrines, or divisions regarding their incidence within the same Court, affecting the scope of the commerce clause or the "silence of Congress" or due process, have their analogues in the application of procedural doctrines of abstention. The business of the last two Terms was rich in opportunities for observance of adjective rules

19. See Holmes, J., dissenting, in First Employers' Liability Cases, 207 U.S. 463, 541 (1908). "I must admit that I think there are strong reasons in favor of the interpretation of the statute adopted by a majority of the court. But, as it is possible to read the words in such a way as to save the constitutionality of the act, I think they should be taken in that narrower sense. The phrase 'every common carrier engaged in trade or commerce' may be construed to mean 'while engaged in trade or commerce' without violence to the habits of English speech, and to govern all that follows." Compare Holmes, J., in Towne v. Eisner, 245 U.S. 418 (1918), with Holmes, J., dissenting, in Eisner v. Macomber, 252 U.S. 189, 219 (1920).

20. E.g., United States v. Delaware & Hudson Co., 213 U.S. 366 (1909).

21. Compare Myers v. United States, 272 U.S. 52, 135, 171–172 (1926), with Humphrey's Executor v. United States, 295 U.S. 602 (1935); compare *Ex parte* Bakelite Corp., 279 U.S. 438, 450 (1929), with O'Donoghue v. United States, 289 U.S. 516 (1933); see Cohens v. Virginia, 6 Wheat. 264, 399 (1821); Hughes, C.J., dissenting, in Railroad Retirement Board v. Alton R.R., 295 U.S. 330, 375 (1935).

22. See Fletcher v. Peck, 6 Cranch. 87, 128 (1810).

23. 7 *Harv. L. Rev.* 130 (1893), reprinted in Thayer, *Legal Essays* (1908).

of constitutional law but also in departures from them. Numerous cases added new strength to old reasons for finding them outside the periphery of immediate, unambiguous constitutional controversies. Either the record was dubious regarding the adequate presentation of an issue, or the right of a particular party to urge it, or the judgment below could amply be supported on a nonconstitutional ground.

In the whole history of the Court there are few more striking examples of the interplay between explosive political issues and intricate technicalities of procedure than several cases at the last two terms. To the general public and to party leaders the *Ashwander* case[24] challenged the T.V.A. program and derivatively, the entire national power policy. For the student of federal jurisdiction it presented a threshold inquiry quite removed from the tensions of politics and the hopes of a social program. The right of George Ashwander, a preferred stockholder in the Alabama Power Company, to question a bona fide business arrangement between the company and the United States was a hurdle which had to be cleared before the road was open to inquiry into the scope of national power immanent in a national waterway system. Again, to the general understanding, the *Carter* case[25] brought before the Supreme Court a scheme of Congress, enacted after years of agitation and investigation, for dealing with the chronic difficulties of the bituminous coal industry. But consideration of the diverse legal problems with which the Congressional solution was entangled was dependent on the answer to the preliminary inquiry whether the Carter Coal Company could raise them in the specific litigation before the Supreme Court.

In both litigations the Court found jurisdiction. In one case it sustained legislation and thereby avoided conflict with Congressional policy; in the other it frustrated Congressional policy by denying its legality. But, if rules of procedure are modes for assuring the wise exercise of

24. Ashwander v. Tennessee Valley Authority, 297 U.S. 288 (1936).
25. Carter v. Carter Coal Co., 298 U.S. 238 (1936).

the deliberative process and are independent of the desirability of what is decided on the merits in a particular case, the procedural issues in the *Ashwander* and *Carter* cases must be isolated from the fate of the legislation on which they passed. They must be subjected to a critique based on the Court's procedural professions regarding complainants situated as were Ashwander and the Carter Coal Company, but in cases which were unembarrassed by grave political or economic consequences.

Since a single vote decided the jurisdictional issue in both cases,[26] presumably they permitted differentiation from controlling precedents. Where the procedural issue is so delicately balanced it would not be without historic warrant to conclude that the scales were turned in favor of taking jurisdiction by the imponderable pressures of the public importance of the statutes under review.

The *Ashwander* case is the latest in a series of cases showing the penetrating influence of the corporate form of enterprise even upon the procedural phases of law. One of the most interesting chapters in the history of the federal judiciary is the successive enlargement of its jurisdiction through imaginative use of the stockholder's suit. It was first employed as a means of creating diversity of citizenship.[27] After a while, the Supreme Court curbed the excesses of this circumvention of State courts to avoid undue burdens on federal courts and to mitigate the hostility of local communities.[28] Gradually, the stockholder's suit emerged as a conventional instrument of litigation in wider fields of controversy than ordinary corporate squabbles.[29] In the development of this procedure the Supreme Court at times showed a tendency toward its re-

26. In the *Ashwander* case, Brandeis, Stone, Roberts, and Cardozo, JJ., joined in dissent on the jurisdictional point. Hughes, C.J., and Brandeis, Stone, and Cardozo, JJ., dissented on procedural grounds in the *Carter* case.

27. Dodge v. Woolsey, 18 How. 331 (1855).

28. Equity Rule 94, 104 U.S. ix (1882); Equity Rule 27, 226 U.S. 656 (1913).

29. Greenwood v. Freight Co., 105 U.S. 13 (1882); Smyth v. Ames, 169 U.S. 466 (1898); Cotting v. Kansas City Stock Yards Co., 183 U.S. 79 (1901); Chicago v. Mills, 204 U.S. 321 (1907).

striction by requiring a serious breach of director's duty which the stockholder, threatened with serious loss, was powerless otherwise to prevent.[30] However, in assuming jurisdiction in the *Pollock* case, the Supreme Court gave powerful momentum to the modern practice of contesting the validity of regulatory and revenue statutes through a stockholder's suit although the directors, as a matter of fair business judgment, preferred obedience to the statute.[31] While jurisdiction cannot be conferred by consent, it would be surprising if the Government's desire for a decision on the merits of the income tax was without influence upon the Court's sanction of the practice in the *Pollock* case.[32]

The *Pollock* case is clearly a relaxation of some of the rigorous doctrines of the Court against constitutional adjudication except, as it were, *in extremis*.[33] It thus introduces the opportunity for considerable management in bringing constitutional conflicts to a judicial issue. If it be suggested that the practice is merely a mode of accel-

erating the test of the validity of a statute that sooner or later will be tested, the Court's whole history of avowals against anticipating adjudication and the profound conceptions of government on which they are based, give conclusive answer.

But in *Smith* v. *Kansas City Title & Trust Co.*,[34] decided in 1921, the Supreme Court passed on constitutionality in a stockholder's suit when the likelihood of the issue otherwise coming before it was much more doubtful than in

30. Hawes v. Oakland, 104 U.S. 450 (1881); Huntington v. Palmer, 104 U.S. 482 (1881); Detroit v. Dean, 106 U.S. 537 (1882); Corbus v. Alaska Treadwell Gold Mining Co., 187 U.S. 455 (1903).

31. Pollock v. Farmers' Loan & Trust Co., 157 U.S. 429 (1895); Brushaber v. Union Pacific R.R., 240 U.S. 1 (1916); Hill v. Wallace, 259 U.S. 44 (1922). These cases, by widening the area between action by the directors sufficient to justify a stockholder's suit and action so unreasonable as to show that it was not bona fide, have naturally increased the difficulty of discovering collusive suits.

32. See 157 U.S. at 554.

33. The interests of the stockholders could have been sufficiently protected by a decree prohibiting the payment of the tax voluntarily and thus, under the then statute, barring recovery.

34. 255 U.S. 180 (1921).

the *Pollock* case. As a measure for agricultural relief, the Federal Farm Loan Act[35] sought to reduce interest on agricultural loans through a system of Federal and Joint Stock Land Banks. In brief, tax exempt bonds were to be issued against farm mortgages. Claiming that the act was invalid and that, therefore, the bonds were worthless, Smith brought a stockholder's suit against the trust company to enjoin it from buying these bonds.[36] It would appear that an eventual determination of the invalidity of the bonds—were that issue ever to get before the Court in some other proceeding—would not necessarily eliminate the value of the underlying mortgages. Therefore, the claim of threatened loss to the stockholder was a preliminary question which should have been canvassed. Instead, the Court sustained the statute on its merits. Here again considerations extrinsic to the procedural analysis of the case encouraged a disregard of jurisdictional austerity. The bonds could not be successfully marketed with a cloud overhanging their validity. Moreover, all parties assumed the claim of the stockholder that the invalidity of the statute was decisive upon his interest.[37] It is in the context of these qualifications that the assumption of jurisdiction in the *Smith* case must be placed, and they attenuate the force of its authority.

These qualifications were disregarded by the majority in the *Ashwander* case and the scope of the *Smith* case was extended. The Alabama Power Company contracted to sell property to the Tennessee Valley Authority, and arranged for an interchange of power and a division of territory between them for the sale of power. In response to a protest from a group of preferred stockholders, the directors of the company, although expressing belief in the validity of the Tennessee Valley Authority Act, relied upon the difficulties of successful litigation to support the

35. 39 Stat. 360 (1916), *amended,* 40 Stat. 431 (1918).

36. The statement of the stockholder that "The tax exemption question is the real issue sought to be settled here" casts light upon the true nature of the attack. Brief for Appellant, p. 2.

37. See 255 U.S. at 199, 201; Brief for Joint Stock Land Bank of Chicago, Intervenor-Appellee, p. 11.

contract as a wise business adjustment. Thereupon Ashwander and his group brought suit against the company and the Tennessee Valley Authority to enjoin enforcement of the contract and for a declaration of invalidity against the Tennessee Valley Authority Act. Speaking for himself and four of the Justices, the Chief Justice found jurisdiction. Ashwander was allowed to sue, not because of any threatened acts of his corporation; it was sufficient that he challenged the lawfulness of the authority of those with whom the corporation was proposing to deal.[38]

The Chief Justice relied heavily upon *Smith* v. *Kansas City Title & Trust Co.*[39] But whatever impairment of the common stockholder's interest was threatened in the *Smith* case by his company's investment in $20,000 worth of bonds of possible invalidity, the preferred stockholder of the Alabama Power Company could show no such danger through consummation of his company's contract.[40] Moreover, in all previous stockholder's suits to test constitutionality, with the exception of the *Smith* case, the stockholder was merely insisting on a constitutional right belonging to the corporation. The stockholder was pressing a derivative claim. In the *Ashwander* case the Court assumed jurisdiction at the behest of a preferred stockholder although at best it was extremely doubtful whether the company itself could disaffirm its contract.[41]

38. See 297 U.S. at 319.

39. See id. at 320, 322.

40. The effect of the transaction upon the margin of safety of the preferred stockholders was negligible. The Court stated that there was a possibility of injury to the corporation in that, if the Tennessee Valley Authority Act was unconstitutional, the corporation would have no remedy on the contract against the Authority. Even if such a risk to the corporation could threaten injury to the preferred stockholders, it was eliminated by the cash terms of the contract.

41. It is difficult to see how the Alabama Power Company could rescind the contract as *ultra vires* the T.V.A. without proving any likelihood that the T.V.A. would not live up to its obligations. Since the Alabama Power Company had been purchasing power from Muscle Shoals since 1925, it is even more difficult to see how it could claim rescission on the ground that the Government was without authority to manufacture this power. Cf. Great Falls Mfg. Co. v. Attorney General, 124 U.S. 581 (1888); Wall v. Parrot Silver & Copper Co., 244 U.S. 407 (1917); St. Louis Co. v. Prendergast Co., 260 U.S. 469 (1925). The provisions in

Against this conclusion Mr. Justice Brandeis, Mr. Justice Stone, Mr. Justice Roberts, and Mr. Justice Cardozo vigorously protested. In what is perhaps the most notable opinion expounding the rationale of jurisdiction in constitutional controversies, Mr. Justice Brandeis found infringement of those rules of judicial self-limitation which alone gave coherence to the great body of precedents which he passed under review.

In *Carter v. Carter Coal Co.* the Court had before it suits on behalf of coal operators to enjoin the regime established by the Guffey Coal Act[42] for the rationalization of the bituminous coal industry. Of the companies for which relief was sought one sold 75 percent of its total output in interstate commerce, the rest not less than 96 percent. Part I of the Guffey Act formulated a code of fair practice and price stabilization; Part II outlawed unfair labor practices and provided that collective labor agreements regarding wages and hours entered into between operators

---

the contract restricting the areas which the T.V.A. and the power company could serve indicate a conclusive answer to any claim that the power company could test the constitutionality by a suit to enjoin competition, as was done in Tennessee Electric Power Co. v. Tennessee Valley Authority, 306 U.S. 118 (1939). But cf. Alabama Power Co. v. Ickes, 302 U.S. 464 (1938).

The *Ashwander* case was not the last pronouncement by the Supreme Court on the use of stockholder's suits in constitutional litigation. In Carter v. Carter Coal Co., 298 U.S. 238 (1936), the Court apparently abandoned the requirement of a breach of discretion by the directors by upholding one stockholder's suit brought to enjoin the directors of a corporation from accepting the Bituminous Coal Code and another brought to enjoin the directors of a second corporation from not accepting it. Compare Carter v. Carter Coal Co., 63 Wash. L. Rep. 986 (Sup. Ct. D.C. 1935), with Clark v. R. C. Tway Coal Co., 12 F.Supp. 570 (W.D.Ky. 1935). In Helvering v. Davis, 301 U.S. 619 (1937), the Court, by a five to four decision, in an opinion delivered by one of the dissenters, held that the validity of the taxes imposed by Title VII of the Social Security Act for Old Age Benefits was raised by a stockholder's suit to enjoin their payment although the directors had four years in which to sue for refund. The Court relied upon the fact that the Government waived, so far as was within its power, all procedural defects. Mr. Justice Cardozo referred with respect to the opinion of Judge A. N. Hand in Norman v. Consolidated Edison Co., 89 F.2d 619 (2d Cir. 1937), which reached an opposite result on similar facts where the method of raising the question was challenged by the Government.

42. 49 Stat. 991 (1935).

and men under defined conditions should be binding on all code members. The device of a coal tax with a drawback of 90 percent in favor of those who accepted the code was employed for the enforcement of the regime.

In the posture of the litigation before the Court, the only immediately operative features of the act were the provisions dealing with unfair trade competition and price fixing. There was no showing that the operators were affected by the code provisions defining unfair labor practices and the Court found no agreement touching hours or wages, or the threat of any, which would adversely affect the operators. Furthermore by the express terms of the statute, operators were not estopped from contesting in the future the validity of the labor provisions by present acceptance of the code. But a majority of the Court, finding that the labor provisions exceeded the power of Congress, invalidated the whole act. Four members of the Court dissented. Mr. Justice Brandeis, Mr. Justice Stone, and Mr. Justice Cardozo observed the jurisdictional proprieties. Finding the price-fixing provisions valid and not dependent upon the labor provisions, they refused to consider the validity of the latter, until a concrete dispute should come before the Court. The Chief Justice agreed with the majority concerning the invalidity of Part II but agreed with the other three Justices concerning the validity of Part I and its separability.

The assumption of the majority that Congress would not have enacted Part I dissevered from Part II, despite the amplest separability clause, was promptly disproved by the re-enactment, in substance, of Part I as an independent statute.[43] But even on its own assumption, the majority included very disparate situations within the single concept of inseparability. To enforce a valid portion of a statute after a more or less closely connected portion has been found invalid is one thing. To refuse to enforce a

43. Shortly after the decision in the *Carter* case, the House of Representatives passed a statute containing the price-fixing provisions of the Guffey bill. The bill was reported favorable by the Senate Committee on Interstate Commerce but, due to a filibuster, the Senate adjourned before its passage. Substantially the same statute was promptly re-enacted during the first session of the Seventy-Fifth Congress.

valid portion of a statute before any judicial necessity has arisen for passing on the constitutionality of the remainder, quite another. Precisely on such distinctions depends observance of the Court's canons for constitutional jurisdiction.

Of the numerous cases during the last two terms which will pass into history, *Morehead* v. *New York* ex rel. *Tipaldo*[44] represents the most striking fusion of public explosiveness and procedural technicalities. In that case the majority employed jurisdictional restraints not as means for avoiding conflict with legislative policy but as a self-created disability against the removal of such conflict. The Court had granted certiorari without restriction[45] to review a decision of the New York Court of Appeals[46] invalidating a minimum wage law drawn specifically to meet the opinion in the *Adkins* case.[47] Despite the changes in the language of the statute, the New York Court of Appeals deemed itself controlled by the ruling in the *Adkins* case.[48] The Supreme Court invoked two procedural considerations in affirming the Court of Appeals. According to correct appellate practice, so ruled the majority, the only issue before the Court was whether the case at bar could be distinguished from the *Adkins* case.[49]

44. 298 U.S. 587 (1936).
45. 297 U.S. 702 (1936).
46. People *ex rel.* Tipaldo v. Morehead, 270 N.Y. 233 (1936).
47. Adkins v. Children's Hospital, 261 U.S. 525 (1923).
48. See 270 N.Y. at 236–239.
49. See 298 U.S. at 604–605. A rule of practice limits review upon certiorari to the scope of the petition. Gunning v. Cooley, 281 U.S. 90 (1930); New York v. Irving Trust Co., 288 U.S. 329 (1933); Helvering v. Taylor, 293 U.S. 507 (1935); see Robertson and Kirkham, *Jurisdiction of the Supreme Court of the United States* § 389 (1937). The considerations underlying the rule are the same as those which require an assignment of errors on appeal. Opposing counsel and Court should be informed of the issues to be reviewed so that the adjudicatory process may be properly canalized. The discretionary nature of review by certiorari intensifies the importance of this practice. See Frankfurter and Hart, "Business of the Supreme Court," 47 *Harv. L. Rev.* at 245, 284–285 (1933). In all prior cases in which the rule had been applied the conception of a legal issue was derived from the reasons underlying its formulation. E.g., Alice State Bank v. Houston Pasture Co., 247 U.S. 240 (1918) (title as opposed to statute of limitations); Steele v. Drummond, 275 U.S. 199 (1927) (illegality of a contract as opposed to its discharge). In the

And that issue was substantially foreclosed because the Supreme Court interpreted the decision below to establish an identity between the New York statute and the statute in the *Adkins* case and thereby to bar an examination by the Supreme Court of the fact of identity.[50] But, despite these iron-clad procedural confinements,[51] the Court deduced from the *Adkins* case the constitutional invalidity of any minimum wage regulation. The *Adkins* case was then approved, and the New York act, and with it all minimum wage legislation, necessarily held outside constitutional bounds.

The Chief Justice challenged neither the limited scope of review nor the *Adkins* decision. But he denied the majority's construction of the State court's construction of the State statute.[52] Free to differentiate the *Adkins* case, he did not find it controlling and sustained the new statute. In his dissent the Chief Justice had the concurrence of Mr. Justice Brandeis, Mr. Justice Stone, and Mr. Justice Cardozo. But these three Justices, speaking through a

---

Tipaldo case, however, the Court's view implies that counsel must set forth not the legal issue which would give adequate notice to the Court and opposing counsel but the range of argument in their support. The issue in the *Tipaldo* case was whether the statute was such a limitation on the "freedom of contract" as to violate the Fourteenth Amendment.

An examination of the contents of the petition for certiorari affords a conclusive answer to the views of the majority. It shows that the petitioner took the broad position that the statute was constitutional irrespective of anything decided in the *Adkins* case. And such statements as the sixth reason relied upon for the allowance of the writ, that "The circumstances prevailing under which the New York law was enacted call for a reconsideration of the Adkins case in light of the New York Act and conditions deemed to be remedied thereby," raised the argumentative claim that the *Adkins* case should no longer be followed, expressed as euphemistically as the tactful language of advocacy would naturally convey it. For an illuminating analysis of this ruling, see a letter of Mr. Edward F. Prichard, Jr., in the *Boston Herald,* March 31, 1937, reprinted in 81 Cong. Rec. App. 729 (1937).

50. See 298 U.S. at 607–609.

51. The majority stated that the State court "held the Act repugnant to the due process clauses of the state and federal constitutions." See 298 U.S. 603. This statement was passed over in silence by the dissenting Justices. But if it was true, the Court would have been without jurisdiction to review the action of the State court. Lynch v. New York *ex rel.* Pierson, 293 U.S. 52 (1934).

52. See 298 U.S. at 621–622.

trenchant opinion by Mr. Justice Stone, denied the existence of any limitation of appellate practice which imprisoned the Court within its own ruling in the *Adkins* case.[53] Having found that case, on full consideration, to be without reasonable foundation, they desired it overruled.[54]

That a Justice who found technical barriers of appellate practice against even considering whether the specific objections to minimum wage legislation made by the *Adkins* case had been met by a later statute should, within less than a year, make the majority necessary for overruling the *Adkins* case, cannot have many parallels in the history of the Supreme Court. But, within less than a year, the *Adkins* case was overruled.[55]

A veritable Nemesis seems to have pursued the litigation to test minimum wage laws. And the vicissitudes of procedure have played no inconsiderable role in the drama. *Stettler* v. *O'Hara,* the first minimum wage case, was argued on December 16 and 17, 1914. While the case was under advisement important changes in the composition of the Court had occurred, and, on June 12, 1916, it was restored to the docket for reargument. It was reargued on June 18 and 19, 1917, and on April 9, 1917, affirmed by an equally divided Court.[56] Minimum wage legislation in some dozen states was thus given a precarious lease on life. On June 6, 1921, a majority of the Court of Appeals of the District of Columbia sustained a Congressional minimum wage statute for the District.[57] But on July 1, 1921, by a strange rearrangement in the personnel of the Court of Appeals, a rehearing was granted. On November 6, 1922, a new majority of the Court of Appeals invalidated

53. See id. at 636.

54. The mystic doctrine whereby the House of Lords is disabled from overruling itself (London Street Transit Co. v. London County Council, [1898] A.C. 375) has never had the slightest tolerance in the Supreme Court of the United States. The history of the Supreme Court of the United States in no small measure is a process of doctrinal rejuvenation through explicit overruling of decisions which have lost the validity of reason. See Burnet v. Coronado Oil & Gas Co., 285 U.S. 393, 405 (1932).

55. West Coast Hotel Co. v. Parrish, 300 U.S. 379 (1937).

56. 243 U.S. 629 (1917).

57. See 284 Fed. 613, 623 (App. D.C. 1921).

the legislation.[58] In the year intervening between these last two decisions, the membership of the Supreme Court had again greatly changed. On April 9, 1923, the new majority of the Court affirmed the Court of Appeals;[59] Mr. Chief Justice Taft, Mr. Justice Holmes, and Mr. Justice Sanford dissented; Mr. Justice Brandeis took no part.

Thus the span between the first argument on minimum wage laws in the Supreme Court and their sanction covers nearly a quarter century. This is only a partial accounting. For surely history will not gainsay the opinion of Mr. Justice Taft that *Muller* v. *Oregon*[60] really controlled the validity of minimum wage legislation.[61] And the *Parrish* case came nearly thirty years after the then Mr. Louis D. Brandeis had, in the *Muller* case, won the Supreme Court to his view of the appropriate constitutional attitude toward industrial legislation. The end crowns all. But surely it would require the author of *Bleak House* to do justice to a course of litigation whereby it took thirty years for the States to be allowed to deal through minimum wage legislation with some of the deep social problems created by the entry of women in large numbers into industry.

The Court has written its own comment on the wisdom behind its doctrines of abstention from needless expression of constitutional views. Less than a year after the *Carter* case the Chief Justice and Mr. Justice Roberts supported decisions sustaining the Wagner Act hardly reconcilable with some of the views they sponsored regarding the invalidity of the labor provisions under the Guffey Act.[62] The circumstances which entered into a change of

58. See 284 Fed. 613.

59. 261 U.S. 525 (1923). See Powell, "The Judiciality of Minimum-Wage Legislation," 37 *Harv. L. Rev.* 545 (1924).

60. 208 U.S. 412 (1908).

61. See 261 U.S. at 566.

62. N.L.R.B. v. Jones & Laughlin Steel Corp., 301 U.S. 1 (1937); N.L.R.B. v. Fruehauf Trailer Co., 301 U.S. 49 (1937); N.L.R.B. v. Friedman–Harry Marks Clothing Co., 301 U.S. 58 (1937). For the effect of the *Carter* case on the judges in the lower federal courts, see N.L.R.B. v. Jones & Laughlin Steel Corp., 83 F.2d 998 (5th Cir. 1936); N.L.R.B. v. Friedman–Harry Marks Clothing Co., 85 F.2d 1 (2d Cir. 1936); Foster Bros. Mfg. Co. v. N.L.R.B., 85 F.2d 984 (4th Cir. 1936); Eagle Pitcher Lead Co. v. Madden, 15 F.Supp. 407 (N.D. Okla., 1936).

the Court's outlook and of its specific rulings between the 1935 and the 1936 Terms are among the arcana of history. But one thing is patent to every informed reader of the Court's opinions. A disregard of settled doctrines of constitutional procedure dangerously borrows trouble. It adds excessive friction to the complicated workings of our government; it weakens the responsibility of Congress in shaping policy; it undermines vital confidence in the disinterested continuity of the judicial process.

Congressional Control Over the Business of the Supreme Court

Just twenty-five years ago, Mr. Justice Holmes had occasion to say of his Court: "We are very quiet there, but it is the quiet of a storm center."[1] The Supreme Court has come within the purview of the general historian of the United States only for the intermittent periods when the Court was the country's storm center. There are about half a dozen such periods, dating from the beginning of Marshall's magistracy. These explosive chapters in the life of the Court synchronized with periods of intense economic and political conflicts, and were invariably manifestations of controversy between the Court and other branches of the government. Last Term wrote another such chapter. Like all the previous entanglements of the Court in the turbulent currents of politics, the controversy through which the country and the Court have just passed was not an instance of spontaneous combustion but the culmination of a long maturing process.[2]

These dramatic issues are not the immediate concern of the papers in this series.[3] The substantive doctrines of constitutional law are not under scrutiny here but the pro-

Excerpt from Frankfurter and Adrian S. Fisher, "The Business of the Supreme Court at October Terms, 1935 and 1936," 51 *Harv. L. Rev.* 577 (1938).

1. Holmes, "Law and the Courts," in *Collected Legal Papers* 292 (1920).

2. See, e.g., the views of former President Wilson in a letter, just published, to John H. Clarke on the occasion of the latter's resignation, in September 1922, as an Associate Justice of the Supreme Court. "Like thousands of other liberals throughout the country, I have been counting on the influence of you and Justice Brandeis to restrain the Court in some measure from the extreme reactionary course which it seems inclined to follow . . . The most obvious and immediate danger to which we are exposed is that the courts will more and more outrage the common people's sense of justice and cause a revulsion against judicial authority which may seriously disturb the equilibrium of our institutions, and I see nothing which can save us from this danger if the Supreme Court is to repudiate liberal courses of thought and action." 6 Baker, *Woodrow Wilson* 117 (1937).

3. Frankfurter and Landis, "The Supreme Court Under the Judiciary Act of 1925," 42 *Harv. L. Rev.* 1 (1928); "The Business of the Supreme Court," 43 id. 33 (1929); 44 id. 1 (1930); 45 id. 271 (1931); 46 id. 226 (1932); Frankfurter and Hart, 47 id. 245 (1933); 48 id. 238 (1934); 49 id. 68 (1935).

cedure by which the Court speaks—or abstains from speaking—as the ultimate voice of the Constitution. This is a study not of product, but of form and function. To be sure, procedure and substance are interacting forces, especially when the forms and formalities of a technical lawsuit serve as vehicles for adjudicating great public issues. Powerful tensions without are not devoid of influence, however imperceptible, within the judicial process. Procedure is sensitive to these tensions insofar as procedural hurdles must be cleared to reach substantive goals. During the Terms under review, the stresses and strains within the political society, of which the Court is so pervasive a part, have not failed to leave their mark in those more recondite phases of the Court's labors which interest the professional student much more than the general historian.

These influences and their judicial repercussions are hardly the stuff of statistics, though even in this elusive territory an occasional statistical vein is revealed which deserves refined exploration. But no less important is a quantitative appraisal of the Court's total business. It furnishes leads to inquiry which illumine the judicial habits and practices of the Court, the pressures upon time and energy exercised by different categories of litigation, the modes which the Court evolves for dealing with them, and the exactions which it makes upon bar and lower courts. All these factors, if warily pursued, may yield comprehension of the process by which the Supreme Court exercises its functions in the great body of cases which are outside the orbit of popular interest or understanding, but, in their aggregate, profoundly affect the angles of intersection of government and enterprise, of national authority and the localities. Moreover, the disposition of voluminous undramatic cases—their procedural determination and the atmosphere which they generate within the Court—inevitably has its reflex bearing upon the disposition of the dramatic cases.

Inevitably law reflects the forces of economic and social dislocation implied in a great depression and its consequent readjustments. This is true not merely of substantive legal doctrines. A general tendency toward enlarged governmental activity and the centripetal influences within economic enterprise which make for increasing exercise of national authority, have their repercussions in judicial organization and administration. The broader questions of jurisdiction and procedure affecting the federal courts have always presented some of the most delicate problems in the working of our constitutional government. It would indeed be surprising if the recent stresses and strains in our national life had not reflected themselves in the workings of the federal judicial system. All the devices by which procedural changes come to pass have played their part. Rules of the Supreme Court for the conduct of its own business and that of the "inferior courts," resourceful employment of the Court's discretionary powers, fluctuations in the Court's attitude toward its jurisdiction, are all registered in the latest volumes of the *United States Reports*. In addition to these readjustments through judicial self-determination, Congress, during the last Term of Court, deemed it necessary to intervene by redistributing power within the federal judicial system. By modifying, in an important way, the Judiciary Act of 1925, Congress has illustrated the historic truth that every judiciary enactment since the great statute of 1789 is but one of a series, a part of the continuous living process of making the federal courts appropriate instrumentalities for the changing needs of the union.

Ordinary problems of judicial administration make little appeal to the imagination of legislators. The Supreme Court is entangled as much as it is in the political history of the United States because its work is so largely an expression of statecraft and interwoven with the political problems of our national life. Except on the rare occasions when the Court itself needs Congressional relief to master its docket, judiciary legislation invariably is the political answer of Congress to what are believed to be judicial obstructions to needed activities of government. Barring the tariff and land grants, the establishment of the Interstate Commerce Commission, in 1887, was the first major intervention of the federal government in the area of economic enterprise. For the past half century our major domestic issues have been phases of a single central problem, namely, the interplay between enterprise and government. Taxation, utility regulation, control of the security market, banking and finance, industrial relations, agricultural controls, are issues that derive from the circumstances of modern, large-scale, industrialized society, and ultimately turn on conceptions of the relation of individuals one to another in the context of our society. For Congress they present a blend of law and policy; to the Supreme Court, under our Constitution, they come as legal problems. Clashes between courts and Congress affecting the ultimate fate of such legislation often have their origin in procedure. Who may raise legal questions about laws, what tribunals may dispose of them, and when they will be finally adjudicated, are all contingencies of legislation. To effectuate its own policies—as well as those of the States when challenged in the federal courts—Congress has deemed it necessary, from time to time, to modify procedural practices of the federal courts, to exercise its constitutional power to define the authority of the inferior federal courts and to regulate the appellate jurisdiction of the Supreme Court.

Since the intermediate federal appellate tribunals were established in 1891,[4] they have been utilized to relieve the Supreme Court of its obligatory jurisdiction, leaving with the circuit courts of appeals final adjudication in those types of cases for which certiorari was a sufficient safeguard of the national interest. First by the act of 1916[5] and then by the more comprehensive measure of 1925,[6] the flow of cases coming to the Court as of right was greatly dammed. What issues may, as a matter of course, be brought before the Supreme Court is partly a technical, professional matter, but also, by touching the feelings of the general community, becomes a more dominant concern of legislative policy. In placid periods, when the distribution of jurisdiction is pre-eminently a matter of the

4. Act of March 3, 1891, 26 Stat. 826.
5. Act of Sept. 6, 1916, 39 Stat. 726.
6. Act of Feb. 13, 1925, 43 Stat. 936.

internal economy of the judicial system, Congress is naturally responsive to the authoritative wishes of the Court. And so, the adjustments of 1891, 1916, and 1925, to enable the Court to meet adequately the swelling tide of its business, were made by Congress at the Court's own insistence.

On the other hand, for different categories of litigation, Congress had to formulate its own notions of jurisdictional policy to give effect to the social and economic movements which got under way in the administration of Theodore Roosevelt. Orders of the Interstate Commerce Commission often have ramifying economic consequences. Such issues have special claims for prompt, final adjudication, and their complexity, as well as their prior scrutiny by the Commission, requires at *nisi prius* the wisdom and experience of more than a single judge. By the act of February 11, 1903, in cases involving orders of the Interstate Commerce Commission, Congress initiated the device of an original court of three judges and direct review by the Supreme Court.[7] In other spheres, the

7. 32 Stat. 823 (1903), *amended,* 36 Stat. 854 (1910). By this act, suits in equity brought by the United States under the antitrust and interstate commerce laws, when designated by the attorney general as of "general public importance," have precedence and must be tried by a three-judge court. It also provided for a direct appeal to the Supreme Court in all suits in equity brought by the United States under these statutes. For a background of the Expedition Act, see 36 *Cong. Rec.* 1679, 1747, 1871 (1903); 1 Sharfman, *The Interstate Commerce Commission* §2, n. 24 (1931). The Hepburn Act, having provided penalties for disobedience of the orders of the Interstate Commerce Commission, extended the Expedition Act to suits to enjoin the enforcement of Commission orders and gave direct review by the Supreme Court from interlocutory injunctions. 34 Stat. 584, 592 (1906). The Mann–Elkins Act vested jurisdiction of all suits to enjoin the enforcement of the orders of the Commission in the Commerce Court. 36 Stat. 1146, 1149 (1911). When this Court was abolished, the jurisdiction reverted to the three-judge district courts. 38 Stat. 219 (1913). The considerations of public interest which introduced the district court of three judges and direct review by the Supreme Court in litigation arising under the Interstate Commerce Act and the Sherman law were, of course, relevant when Congress fashioned the procedure under the Shipping Act, the Packers and Stockyards Act, the Perishable Agricultural Commodities Act, and the Federal Communications Act. And so, the provisions applicable to orders of the Interstate Commerce Commission were incorporated by reference in each one of these statutes. 39 Stat. 738 (1916), superseded by, 49 Stat. 1987 (1933); 42 Stat. 168 (1921); 46 Stat. 535 (1930); 48 Stat. 1093 (1934).

ignition of public excitement through judicial action deemed adverse to the public interest has led to successive extensions of the Supreme Court's historic scope of review and to a recession from the general tendency to curtail its obligatory jurisdiction.

First, the traditional practice against reviewing rulings in favor of the accused, even where no double jeopardy was at stake,[8] had consequences unknown to the common law when Congress affixed penal sanctions to legislation involving far-reaching issues of policy.[9] The Criminal Appeals Act of 1907 put an end to the power of a single judge to hold up the enforcement of a law for years by invalidating it improperly.[10] Then, the growing range of economic control by the States brought them into conflict with the federal courts. The initial shift from a fundamentally laissez-faire emphasis in government to its modern regulatory activities largely affected public utilities. At first it expressed itself through legislative rate regulation. To federal judges the invalidation of such measures presented only a simple application of conventional doctrines to prevent irreparable damages. To the general public it was nullification of vital State policy by a single federal judge. Congress promptly responded to this feeling,[11] and by the act of 1910[12] applied the safeguards against too irresponsible judicial restraint of the Interstate Commerce Commission to the protection of State laws. Thereafter "no interlocutory injunction suspending or restraining the enforcement, operation or execution of any statute of a state" because of unconstitutionality could be issued except by a three-judge district court, and an appeal could be taken directly to the Supreme Court. That Congress should have used this device only when statutes were called into question, and not for orders of State commissions, is a striking instance of the narrowly empiric nature of the legislative process. For by 1910 it

8. United States v. Sanges, 144 U.S. 310 (1892); cf. United States v. Dickinson 213 U.S. 92 (1909).

9. See Frankfurter and Landis. *The Business of the Supreme Court* 115–117 (1927).

10. 34 Stat. 1246 (1907).

11. See 45 *Cong. Rec.* 7253–7258 (1910).

12. 36 Stat. 557 (1910).

had become abundantly clear that effective utility regulation demanded expert administration, and the movement for the establishment of utility commissions was well under way.[13] But for many judges these new administrative agencies only served to render the trend towards social legislation still more uncongenial. Courts seemed as unaware of the emergence of modern administrative law as an indispensable evolution of the Rule of Law, as the great common-law judges in the days of Coke were unresponsive to the proper role of emerging equity.[14] And so, by the act of March 4, 1913,[15] protection against

13. See Mosher and Crawford, *Public Utility Regulation* 22–26 (1933). The Wisconsin and New York Public Service Commissions were established in 1907.

14. American scholars early called attention to the social-economic phenomena which were bound to give impulse to an Anglo-American administrative law. See Goodnow, *Comparative Administrative Law* (1893); Freund, "The Law of the Administration in America," 9 *Pol. Sci. Q.* 403 (1894), and, some twenty years later, the present Chief Justice and eminent leaders of the bar sounded warning. See Hughes, "Some Aspects of the Development of American Law," 39 *N.Y.B.A. Rep.* 266, 269–270 (1916); Root, "Public Service by the Bar," 41 *A.B.A. Rep.* 355, 368–369 (1916); Sutherland, "Private Rights and Government Control," 42 *A.B.A. Rep.* 197 (1917). The powerful influence of Professor Dicey's *The Law of the Constitution* (but cf. Jennings, *The Law and the Constitution* [1933] passim) tended to obfuscate understanding of the actual development of English law, but Local Gov't Board v. Arlidge, [1915] A.C. 120, compelled Dicey to acknowledge (see Dicey, "The Development of Administrative Law in England," 31 *L.Q. Rev.* 148 [1915], what Maitland, with his usual eye for reality, had been expounding at Cambridge as early as 1887. Maitland, *The Constitutional History of England* 415 et seq. (1908). See *Commonwealth Fund Studies in Administrative Law; Harvard Studies in Administrative Law* (1933); Frankfurter, "The Task of Administrative Law," 75 *U. of Pa. L. Rev.* 614 (1927).

15. 37 Stat. 1013. The act was amended in 1925 to extend the requirement of three judges and the right of appeal to the Supreme Court to the final hearing in such suits. 43 Stat. 938 (1925). The statute does not apply, however, where an interlocutory injunction is not sought. Ex parte Buder, 271 U.S. 461 (1926). The relation between federal courts and State public utility regulation remained a perplexing problem. The statutory proceeding staying proceedings in the federal courts, if, any time before final hearing, a suit is brought in the State court to enforce the order and the order was stayed pending determination, was not adequately utilized by the States. See Pogue, "State Determination of State Law and the Judicial Code," 41 *Harv. L. Rev.* 623 (1928). But hostility to federal curbs on local utility regulation led to still further curtailment of the power of the lower federal courts. The Johnson Act deprived

frustration of State regulation by a single federal judge and direct review by the Supreme Court was extended to administrative as well as legislative action.

Shortly after the amendment of 1913, the general movement of social legislation led to the first extension of the Supreme Court's appellate jurisdiction over State court decisions. Probably no single episode in American judicial history illustrates better the limited relevance of doctrines derived from specialized political preoccupation in legal arrangements when the emphasis of government shifts from politics to economics. The authority of the Supreme Court to review State decisions was, naturally enough, confined by the famous Section 25 of the first Judiciary Act to instances where the State courts denied a federal claim. The assumption that State courts would not find in the federal Constitution a bar tc State laws was valid enough at a time of historic jealousy against national authority. Moreover, the psychological environment in which State court judges move is very different from what it was a hundred years ago, now that economics and law have become more closely interrelated and the vague contours of the Fourteenth Amendment have greatly extended the orbit of judicial discretion. And so, when, in 1911, the New York Court of Appeals temporarily arrested the progress of the now commonplace workmen's compensation legislation,[16] partly by invoking the Fourteenth Amendment, the inability to secure authoritative interpretation of that clause from the Supreme Court inevitably led to legislation. The act of March 23, 1914,[17] sponsored by Senator Elihu Root, extended the

the district courts of jurisdiction in such cases where a "plain, speedy and efficient remedy may be had at law or in equity in the courts of such state." 48 Stat. 775 (1934).

16. Ives v. South Buffalo Ry., 201 N.Y. 271, 94 N.E. 431 (1911). This case was deemed contrary to the implications of the Supreme Court decision in Noble State Bank v. Haskell, 219 U.S. 104, 575 (1911).

17. 38 Stat. 790 (1914). However, since the New York Court of Appeals in the *Ives* case had rested its decision partly on the State constitution, the Supreme Court would have been without jurisdiction to reverse the judgment. Lynch v. New York ex rel. Pierson, 293 U.S. 52 (1934). But cf. Morehead v. New York ex rel. Tipaldo, 298 U.S. 587 (1936). But the incongruity of having State and federal courts give different meaning to

Supreme Court's review to a State court ruling even when it sustained a claim under the United States Constitution. This was accomplished by allowing the use of certiorari to the Supreme Court in such cases.

Although today dramatic ingredients may bulk large, the Judiciary Act of August 24, 1937,[18] will surely take its place as part of the sequence of Congressional adjustments of judicial administration which begot the acts of 1903, 1910, 1913, 1914. That the fate of acts of Congress should depend, even temporarily, upon the view of a single judge; that the United States should have no standing to defend effectively a law of the utmost national importance simply because the canons of legal procedure make the controversy merely a private litigation; that the ultimate validity of a statute may be a long drawn out process depending in part upon the state of the Supreme Court's docket and its notions of exigency,[19] have long been sources of anxiety to students of public law[20] and have occasioned remedial proposals in Congress. To be sure, in a period when legislative energies run strong and the judiciary interposes powerful and persistent restraints, the pace of procedural reform is accelerated. At no time in the country's history did the judiciary play a more permeating part in the affairs of the country. At no time in the country's history was there a more voluminous outpouring of judicial rulings in restraint of acts of

the same concept of "due process" contained in different constitutions eliminated fine shadings in jurisdictional learning as to the availability of such a statute as that of March 23, 1914. As a matter of history, New York immediately adopted a constitutional amendment legalizing workmen's compensation legislation, and a statute passed under this amendment was upheld by the Supreme Court. New York Central R.R. v. White, 243 U.S. 188 (1917). Accord: Arizona Employers' Liability Cases, 250 U.S. 400 (1919).

18. 50 Stat. 811 (1937). See "Legislation," 51 *Harv. L. Rev.* 148 (1937).

19. Delay in settling the constitutionality of important statutes is not confined to the United States. The Canadian Industrial Disputes Investigation Act of 1907 was declared ultra vires the Dominion Parliament by the Privy Council after it had been in operation for eighteen years. Toronto Electric Comm. v. Snider, [1925] A.C. 396.

20. See, e.g., Borchard, *Declaratory Judgments* 301 (1934); Arnold, "Trial by Combat and the New Deal," 47 *Harv. L. Rev.* 913 (1934); Notes, 25 *Geo. L.J.* 967 (1937); 45 *Yale L.J.* 649, 659–661 (1936).

Congress than the body of decisions in which the lower courts, in varying degree, invalidated every measure deemed appropriate by Congress for grappling with the great depression. Friction between Congress and the judiciary was intensified by the atmosphere which enveloped some of the opinions of the lower court judges. There were utterances more appropriate to the hustings than to the bench,[21] reminiscent of political harangues by early Federalist judges which involved the federal judiciary for the first time in the conflict of politics.[22]

As in similar periods when the judiciary interposed obstacles to legislative policies having wide popular support, the traditional scope of judicial review in constitutional controversies came under scrutiny and numerous bills proposing drastic modifications were introduced in both houses of Congress.[23] The past further repeated itself in that narrower measures for reform were urged to remove inadequacies in the existing federal procedure when applied to cases of large public moment.[24] Speedy justice has been the aim of Anglo-American law reformers since Magna Carta, and evils entailed through avoid-

21. See, e.g., Hart Coal Corp. v. Sparks, 7 F.Supp. 16, 28 (W.D.Ky. 1934); Duke Power Co. v. Greenwood County, 10 F.Supp. 854, 865–866 (W.D.S.C. 1935); Stout v. Pratt, 12 F.Supp. 864, 867, 869–870 (W.D.Mo. 1935). But see Bemis Bros. Bag Co. v. Fiedelson, 13 F.Supp. 153, 154–155 (W.D.Tenn. 1936); cf. Industrial Mercantile Marine Co. v. Stranahan, 155 Fed. 428, 430 (S.D.N.Y. 1907).

22. See 3 Beveridge, *Life of Marshall* 30, n. 1 (1919); 2 McRee, *Life of Iredell* 505 (1857); 1 Warren, *The Supreme Court in United States History* 165, 274 (rev. ed. 1926).

23. Several years prior to the President's message on Feb. 5, 1937, concerning reform of the federal judiciary, a large number of bills were proposed to deprive the courts altogether of their power to declare federal statutes unconstitutional. 74th Cong., 1st Sess., H.R. 4534, 8123, H.J. Res. 287, 296, 329; S. 1381; S.J. Res. 147. 74th Cong., 2d Sess., H.R. 10315; H.J. Res. 462, 509, 565. 75th Cong., 1st Sess., H.R. 44, 50, 51, 2265, 3895, 4279. The proposal to require the concurrence of various percentages of the Justices to declare acts of Congress unconstitutional was also revived. 74th Cong., 1st Sess., H.R. 8100, 8123, 8168, H.J. Res. 301. 74th Cong., 2d Sess., H.R. 10102, 10196, 10362; S. 3739. 75th Cong., 1st Sess., S. 1098, 1276.

24. 74th Cong., 1st Sess., H.R. 3433, 8309; H.J. Res. 317, 344, 374; S. 2176, 3211. 74th Cong., 2d Sess., H.R. 9478, 10128, 10839. 75th Cong., 1st Sess., H.R. 2260, 2284, 3593, 3902; S. 1180.

able delay in adjudication were deemed to be especially far-reaching when the operation of economic measures affecting large regions or even the whole nation depended upon judicial validation. The motive power for such reform is usually some concrete experience, close to the interests of a particular legislator. The prosecution of its program by the Tennessee Valley Authority had a strong regional hold on Senator Black of Alabama.[25] The decision of Judge Grubb on November 28, 1934,[26] put at hazard a scheme of public development which, after more than a decade of political struggle, received overwhelming Congressional approval. Clothed as abstract issues of governmental power, the litigation affected vast investments and touched the lives of millions of people. Yet ultimate decision, argued Senator Black, had to take the tortuous path of reaching the Supreme Court through the circuit court of appeals.[27]

By a bill introduced on March 6, 1935, Senator Black addressed himself to the single, narrow purpose of securing prompt, definitive disposition of decrees restraining the operation of federal laws. The crux of his proposal was to eliminate the circuit court of appeals in these cases and to route them from the district court directly to the Supreme Court.[28] The bill was referred to the Senate Com-

25. The fight over Muscle Shoals had been under way for years when Senator Black entered the Senate, in the 70th Congress, 1st Session (1927). During four sessions of Congress, Senator Black was active in support of this legislation. 69 *Cong. Rec.* 2521–2529, 3435–3444, 4087–4094, 4179–4190, 4252–4255, 4310–4334, 4391–4393, 4449–4468, 4510–4534, 4536–4551, 9698, 9823–9824 (1928); 70 *Cong. Rec.* 2312 (1929); 71 *Cong. Rec.* 1962, 2148, 3786, 5591, 5753 (1929); 72 *Cong. Rec.* 584, 6373-6377, 6400–6404, 6427-6440, 6495–6508, 6564, 10849–10852, 10995,11177–11178, 11313, 11672, 11965–11970, 12382–12385 (1930); 74 *Cong. Rec.* 317–318, 1902–1904, 2920, 3276–3304, 3376–3391, 3675, 3691, 5017, 5169–5185, 5710–5715, 7070–7093 (1931).

26. Ashwander v. Tennessee Valley Authority, 8 F.Supp. 893 (N.D. Ala. 1934), 9 F.Supp. 965 (N.D. Ala. 1935), rev'd, 78 F.2d 578 (5th Cir., 1935), aff'd, 297 U.S. 288 (1936).

27. See *Hearings before the Committee on Judiciary on S. 2176*, 74th Cong., 1st Sess., 13 et seq. (1935).

28. S. 2176, 74th Cong., 1st Sess. It provided direct appeal to the Supreme Court from any "restraining order, decree, judgment, or injunction prohibiting any Federal official or employee, or Federal agency or bureau" from carrying out a federal statute.

mittee on Judiciary and the Court invited to express its views. On behalf of the Court, the Chief Justice appeared with two of his colleagues and gave reasons against the enactment of the measure.[29] The public interest with which Senator Black was concerned seemed to the Court sufficiently safeguarded through its power to jump a circuit court of appeals by the discretionary use of certiorari.[30] To open the door to every case that came within the ambit of the Black bill, seemed to the Chief Justice to be an inroad on the philosophy of selective jurisdiction underlying the act of 1925 without compensating advantage.[31] Not to have its docket thrown out of balance was a driving consideration with the Court. Probably, also, it regarded the illumination which serious questions should derive from passing through a circuit court of appeals as valuable to the perspective and thoroughness of the Court's own deliberative process. The bill never emerged from committee.

The fate of acts of Congress in the lower courts and some of the circumstances attending their invalidation were not calculated to allay Congressional concern over procedural inadequacies. The existing scheme of proce-

29. Mr. Justice Van Devanter and Mr. Justice Brandeis appeared with the Chief Justice. Mr. Justice Van Devanter briefly reiterated the views of the Chief Justice; Mr. Justice Brandeis merely expressed concurrence with what had been said by his colleagues.

30. See *Hearings before the Committee on Judiciary on S. 2176*, 74th Cong., 1st Sess., 2–4 (1935). The Chief Justice pointed to the exercise of this power in the Gold Clause and Railroad Retirement Act cases and assured the committee that there was every probability of similar action in future cases involving the constitutionality of important acts of Congress.

31. See id. at 6–8. The Chief Justice also stated that the provision for appeals from restraining orders and interlocutory injunctions would cause the bill to delay decisions upon the constitutionality of statutes. Senator Black controverted the force of all three points made by the Chief Justice. He stated that every case mentioned by the Chief Justice to prove that the bill was unnecessary had taken two or three months before it reached the Supreme Court after decision by the district court, and that under the proposed bill that could be accomplished in ten days. He also denied that the statute would have a dilatory effect or unduly burden the Court, stating that reliance could be placed upon the attorney general to exercise the right of appeal only when an important issue would be presented to the Court. See id. at 13 et seq.

dure did not preclude delay in securing the final word from the Supreme Court. Thereby uncertainty hung over many of the most important activities of government. Moreover, the ability of the government adequately to represent the national interest within the framework of purely private litigation, while an old problem,[32] emerged with new intensity. Chairman Sumners of the House Committee therefore renewed the proposal of the Black bill and widened its scope. His bill provided both for direct review and for participation by the United States in litigation in which, under settled practice, it would have no standing as a party.[33] But attention was diverted from

32. Attempts to meet this problem in the past have been through the device of allowing the United States to appear as *amicus curiae*. E.g., Pollock v. Farmers' Loan & Trust Co., 157 U.S. 429, 469, 499 (1895); First Employers' Liability Cases, 207 U.S. 463, 490 (1908); Ex parte Grossman, 267 U.S. 87, 108 (1925). But the increasing importance of facts in constitutional decisions and the difficulties inherent in the process of establishing them before the appellate tribunal keeps this expedient from being a satisfactory solution. See Frankfurter and Landis, *The Business of the Supreme Court* 310–318 (1927). For a prior statutory provision regarding the appearance of State officers in private suits, see New York Executive Law §68 (1913).

33. H.R. 2260, 75th Cong., 1st Sess. This bill was introduced in the House and referred to the Committee on Judiciary on January 8, 1937. 81 *Cong. Rec.* 139 (1937). The bill did not contain Section 3, but in other respects was similar to the present act. The bill was amended and reported favorably by that committee, debated in Committee of the Whole, reported favorably, and passed by the House on April 7. H.R. Rep. No. 212, 75th Cong., 1st Sess. (1937); 81 *Cong. Rec.* 3273.

In the meantime, on February 5, 1937, President Roosevelt addressed a special message to the Congress recommending the enactment of legislation for judicial reform and attached a draft bill embodying his suggestions. The proposed bill was introduced, as S. 1392, by Senator Ashurst, and was referred to the Committee on Judiciary. After extensive hearings this committee made an adverse report on June 14. *Hearings before Senate Committee on Judiciary on S. 1392*, 75th Cong., 1st Sess. (1937); Sen. Rep. No. 711, 75th Cong., 1st Sess. (1937). On July 6, Senator Robinson introduced an amendment to S. 1392, in the nature of a substitute, which had been proposed by Senator Logan for himself and for Senators Hatch and Ashurst on July 2. After a debate lasting through July 13, a motion to recommit the bill to the Committee on the Judiciary was passed on July 22. 81 *Cong. Rec.* 7375–7381 (1937). A bill similar to S. 1392 was introduced in the House as H.R. 7765, on July 6, and was referred to the Committee on the Judiciary. 81 *Cong. Rec.* 6869 (1937).

On July 28, the Senate Committee on the Judiciary reported out H.R. 2260 with amendments, and recommended that the bill pass. Sen.

these attempts to adapt the ways of private litigation to their serious public implications by the dramatic emergence of the great political controversy to which the President's proposal regarding the Supreme Court gave rise. Only after this issue was no longer before Congress, did the Senate address itself to these seemingly technical aspects of litigation. Their important relation to the whole process of constitutional litigation then became manifest, and the Senate Committee on the Judiciary unanimously reported the Judiciary Act of 1937 in substantially its present form.

In sum, the new act gave matured expression to the combined aims of the Black and Sumners bills. The decision in *In re American States Public Service Co.*[34] vividly demonstrated that the power of the United States to share in the control of litigation, whereby the constitution-

Rep. No. 963, 75th Cong., 1st Sess. (1937). The bill was debated on August 7, amended and passed as amended. 81 *Cong. Rec.* 8515 (1937). On August 9, the House disagreed to the amendments, requested a conference and appointed conferees. 81 *Cong. Rec.* 8557 (1937). The Senate, having insisted on the amendments, appointed conferees the same day. 81 *Cong. Rec.* 8527 (1937). On August 10, the Senate Conference report was made, and was adopted by the Senate. 81 *Cong. Rec.* 8609 (1937). The House conference report, made on the same day, was adopted on August 11 after debate. 81 *Cong. Rec.* 8705 (1937). On August 24, the President approved the bill with an explanatory memorandum. 81 *Cong. Rec.* 9679 (1937).

34. 12 F.Supp. 667 (D.Md. 1935), aff'd *sub nom.* Burco, Inc. v. Whitworth, 81 F.2d 721 (4th Cir. 1936). In this case the lower courts considered the constitutionality of the Public Utility Holding Company Act of 1935 upon a trustee's petition for instructions under 77B. The Government did not receive notice of the proceedings until the petitions had been filed, and the issues joined and largely concluded by admissions of fact and law in the pleadings. Counsel for the Government appeared as *amicus curiae* ten days after the filing of the petitions, but were denied a continuance for the purpose of investigation. The Government was allowed to cross-examine on the issue of jurisdiction but was not allowed to share in building the record of the substantive issues. The district court held the act unconstitutional in its entirety; the circuit court of appeals held the act unconstitutional as applied to the particular company. When certiorari was asked the Government submitted a statement in opposition, fundamentally because under the circumstances of the litigation the record was inadequate for a decision upon the constitutional problem. It was urged that the parties, through collaboration in the pleadings and in the presentation of testimony, had not made an accurate representation of the facts underlying the relation of the act to the reorganization and the constitutionality of the act as applied to the debtor. The Supreme Court denied certiorari. 297 U.S. 724 (1936).

ality of legislation of the profoundest national import would be effectively tested, ought not to be thwarted by the use of subtle legal forms available to a private litigant. Section 1 of the act therefore put the exclusion of the United States from such litigation beyond the power of any judge.[35] Again, the denial by the Supreme Court of a speedy test of the Public Utility Holding Company Act of 1935, sought both by the utility interests and by the Government in the *Electric Bond & Share* case, reinforced the momentum of the proposals for direct review.[36] This is the

35. Whenever the constitutionality of an act of Congress affecting the public interest is drawn into question, the United States is entitled to intervene and become a party for the presentation of evidence and argument upon the constitutionality of the act.

36. A deluge of injunction suits had made it necessary for the Securities & Exchange Commission practically to suspend the operation of the Public Utility Holding Company Act of 1935 until a decision upon its constitutionality could be obtained in an adequate test of the law such as was involved in its suit against the Electric Bond & Share Co. The Supreme Court upheld the staying of suits to enjoin the enforcement of the act until the decision of the district court in that case. Landis v. North American Co., 299 U.S. 248 (1936); see Note, 50 *Harv. L. Rev.* 655 (1937). Upon a stipulated record, the result of a year's negotiation between the parties, Judge Mack upheld the validity of the registration provisions. Securities & Exchange Comm. v. Electric Bond & Share Co., 18 F.Supp. 131 (S.D.N.Y. 1937). An appeal was taken to the Circuit Court of Appeals for the Second Circuit and a petition for certiorari filed in the Supreme Court. The Government joined in a request for certiorari, setting forth the necessity for speedy determination and pointing out that the nature of the record made intermediate review by the circuit court of appeals superfluous. The Supreme Court, however, denied certiorari and postponed by at least six months the earliest possible time at which the act could become effective. 301 U.S. 709 (1937). In Davis v. Boston & Maine R.R., 299 U.S. 614 (1937), there was an attempt to secure certiorari to review the action of a district court upholding the constitutionality of the unemployment provision of the Social Security Act. No questions of fact were involved in the case and it was desirable to have a quick decision upon the constitutionality of the statute, both from the standpoint of the large number of people who had to make returns and pay the tax within six and a half weeks, and from that of the Government, faced as it was with large expenditures in setting up administrative machinery and with the possibility of a multiplicity of suits for want of a speedy decision. Certiorari was, however, denied. The denial of certiorari to the Court of Claims in Continental Mills, Inc. v. United States, 299 U.S. 614 (1936), delayed a decision upon the constitutionality of the provisions of the Revenue Act of 1936 dealing with the recovery of taxes paid under the Agricultural Adjustment Act. Here, too, the Government joined in the request for certiorari.

essence of Section 2 of the act.[37] Finally, the inevitable irritation of Congress at the free-handed way in which judges throughout the country enjoined the enforcement of some of the most vital measures ever enacted, made inevitable the requirement of Section 3 for a court of

---

Certiorari was granted prior to decision by the circuit court of appeals in the cases involving the Gold Clause, the First Railroad Retirement Act, the Bituminous Coal Conservation Act, and the processing tax on Philippine coconut oil. The Government did not seek review prior to decision by the circuit court of appeals in cases involving the validity of the Agricultural Adjustment Act, Titles I and II of the National Industrial Recovery Act, and the Tennessee Valley Authority Act. Cases involving the validity of the National Labor Relations Act and the Silver Purchase Act of 1934 reached the Supreme Court as speedily as possible. The Government did not file memoranda on the question of certiorari in the cases between private persons involving the validity of the Bankhead Cotton Control Act, the first and second Frazier-Lemke Acts, and the Railway Labor Act.

37. Section 2 gives all parties a right to appeal to the Supreme Court from any interlocutory or final judgment or decree involving a decision against the constitutionality of an act of Congress made by any court of the United States in a case to which the United States, any agency, officer, or employee thereof was a party or in which the United States had intervened pursuant to Section 1.

The legislative history of the first two sections of the act is extremely enlightening. The bill which was originally passed by the House was not drafted on the theory that the United States should become a party but gave the United States the right to appear in any proceeding in which it was not already represented in which the constitutionality of a federal statute was drawn into question, provided that the court deemed the question substantial. The right of direct appeal to the Supreme Court of the United States was given to the United States alone, and this right existed whether or not the United States had appeared in the lower court. 81 *Cong. Rec.* 3273 (1937). The fact that the right of direct appeal was given to the United States alone, whether it was a party or even whether it had appeared, raised constitutional difficulties. Muskrat v. United States, 218 U.S. 346 (1911); Columbus & Greenville Ry. v. Miller, 283 U.S. 96 (1931); see "Legislation," 51 *Harv. L. Rev.* 148, 149–151 (1937). Aware of these doubts, the Senate Committee on Judiciary changed the theory of the bill to provide that the United States should become a party, but only on showing that it had a legal interest in the case. The committee stated, however, that the interest was not limited to a pecuniary interest but covered the rights and duties relating to sovereignty. See Sen. Rep. No. 963, 75th Cong., 1st Sess. (1937) 2; cf. Texas v. Interstate Commerce Comm., 258 U.S. 158 (1922); In re Debs, 158 U.S. 564, 584 (1895). The Senate Committee retained the requirement that the lower court find the question substantial, and eliminated many objections to the House bill by putting the section relating to appeals in its present form. Sen. Rep. No. 963, *supra*. The bill was passed by the Senate, after the requirement that the lower court find the

three judges to set aside the will of Congress.[38] This feeling fused with considerations derived from the gravity of the issues presented by such litigation and from the desire

---

question substantial had been eliminated. 81 *Cong. Rec.* 8515 (1937). The conference report, adopted by both houses, retained the theory of the Senate bill that the United States become a party but eliminated the requirement that the United States have a legal or probable interest; it inserted the requirement that the statute involved affect the public interest. 81 *Cong. Rec.* 8527, 8705 (1937).

This compromise eliminated many of the defects of both House and Senate bills. Through its provision that the United States alone could appeal, the House bill rested upon the incorrect assumption that the interest of the United States in a favorable decision as to the constitutionality of a federal statute, in a case to which neither it nor any of its agents is a party, is sufficient to create a case or controversy. By providing that the original party injured by the decision against constitutionality could appeal, the Senate bill made it unnecessary in any case in which this right was exercised to consider the Government as the only party whose interests could sustain a case or controversy. In such cases it would be possible to support the participation of the United States as being merely auxiliary to a controversy already in existence. But the provisions inserted by the Senate Committee which limited the right of the United States to intervene to cases in which it had a legal interest made it possible that, as a matter of construction, the statute was dependent upon the right of the United States to maintain an independent suit. The conference amendment eliminated this difficulty. Under the bill as passed, the right of the United States to participate in a controversy already in existence and the right of the United States to maintain a suit of its own are clearly separated, the latter problem arising only when the United States attempts to appeal by itself.

38. Injunctions by single judges practically forced suspension of the Public Utility Holding Company Act of 1935 and of the construction of power projects under Title II of the National Industrial Recovery Act of 1933 and the Emergency Relief Appropriation Act of 1935. Approximately one quarter of the taxes due under the Agricultural Adjustment Act were impounded by injunctions. There was considerable injunctive interference with the operation of the National Labor Relations Act although there seemed to be no grounds for equitable relief. There was not a great deal of equitable interference with the operation of Title I of the National Industrial Recovery Act of 1933 or with the taxing provisions of the Social Security Act. See *Injunctions in Cases Involving Acts of Congress,* Sen. Doc. No. 42, 75th Cong. 1st Sess. (1937).

Probably the greatest single psychological impression was created by the extremely broad preliminary injunction issued by Judge Gore in Tennessee Electric Power Co. v. Tennessee Valley Authority, 21 F.Supp. 947 (1936), rev'd, 90 F.2d 885 (6th Cir. 1937). It was estimated, in a letter by the chairman of the Authority, that the injunction cost the Authority $1,500,000 in power revenue alone. See *Injunctions in Cases Involving Acts of Congress,* Sen. Doc. No. 42, 75th Cong., 1st Sess. (1937) 7–8. For the feelings which the Gore injunction aroused in

for their thorough exploration before they reached the Supreme Court.[39]

The new Judiciary Act contains inevitable frailties of draftsmanship. Like all its predecessors, it will have to be supplemented by authoritative construction.[40] But the operations of the new procedure, as has been true of all important judiciary acts, will depend mostly on the general environment in which it moves. Thus it becomes sheer speculation to estimate the extent to which clashes between Congress and the judiciary would have differed had the enactment of last August governed constitutional adjudications since March 4, 1933. The materials for prophecy of its future consequences for American constitutional law are no less exiguous. Some obvious factors in the administration of the act will limit the freedom of the federal courts and that of the Government as litigant. The requirement of three judges entails an absorption of judicial resources which may have unexpected repercussions upon judicial efficiency, should there be a plethora of litigation.[41] Again, the course of litigation is not auto-

Congress, see 81 *Cong. Rec.* 235, 248, 480–482, 2142–2143 (1937). Whatever may have been the specific justification as a matter of substantive law of this or that individual decision, the cumulative effect of this barrage of injunctions by single judges on the wide front of governmental activity aroused a sense of disquietude regarding the potentialities of the existing procedural situation.

39. Section 3 provides that interlocutory or permanent injunctions restraining the enforcement or operation of an act of Congress as unconstitutional shall be issued only by three-judge district courts, and that there shall be an appeal to the Supreme Court from any decree granting or denying an interlocutory or permanent injunction in such a case.

40. The relation of the right of appeal to the Supreme Court granted by the new act to the right of appeal to the circuit court of appeals is not explicitly treated. The right of appeal to the Supreme Court from the decision of a single judge under Section 2 probably should not preclude an appeal to the circuit court of appeals. On the other hand an appeal to the circuit court of appeals from a three-judge district court would be futile and would doubtless be found to be precluded by Section 3.

41. The device of a stay order which was used in Landis v. North American Co., 299 U.S. 248 (1936), may be used to prevent the waste of effort involved in simultaneous consideration of the same issue by more than one three-judge court. This may be supplemented by the holding that a plaintiff is not entitled to a three-judge court when the complaint plainly does not state a case. Ex parte Poresky, 290 U.S. 30 (1933). The increase in the obligatory jurisdiction of the Court naturally directs

matic. It depends not a little on the strategy of litigants. To the extent that the new act makes mandatory appeals to the Supreme Court from rulings adverse to the validity of legislation, it circumscribes the discretion of the attorney general. But these are all factors contingent upon larger forces quite outside any judiciary act. They depend upon the future of legislation, its range and volume; they depend on the impregnating political and psychological atmosphere. The Judiciary Act of 1937 is part of a continuous history of interplay between the judiciary and the other branches of the government. Insofar as the act leaves creative scope for the courts, its ultimate significance in that historic process will be determined by the Supreme Court's attitude toward the inarticulate major premises which underlay the enactment of that statute.

---

attention to the effect which it will have upon the docket of the Court in a period of legislative exuberance. An examination of the cases of the last four years suggests that the increase in the number of appeals caused by the act will largely be absorbed by an increase in those disposed of on the jurisdictional statement.

Justice Holmes Defines the Constitution

The history of the Supreme Court would record fewer explosive periods if, from the beginning, there had been a more continuous awareness of the role of the Court in the dynamic process of American society. Lawyers, with rare exceptions, have failed to lay bare that the law of the Supreme Court is enmeshed in the country's history; historians no less have seemed to miss the fact that the country's history is enmeshed in the law of the Supreme Court. Normally historians, much more than lawyers, guide the general understanding of our institutions. But historians have, in the main, allowed only the most spectacular decisions—the *Dred Scott*[1] controversy or the *Legal Tender Cases*[2]—to intrude upon the flow of national development through their voluminous pages. The vital share of the Court in the interplay of the country's political and economic forces has largely escaped their attention. Not unnaturally the Court has been outside the permanent focus of the historian's eye. For the momentum of the Court's influence has been achieved undramatically and imperceptibly, like the gradual growth of a coral reef, as the cumulative product of hundreds of cases, individually unexciting and seemingly even unimportant, but in their total effect powerfully telling in the pulls and pressures of society . . .

We speak of the Court as though it were an abstraction. To be sure the Court is an institution, but individuals, with all their diversities of endowment, experience, and outlook, determine its actions. The history of the Supreme Court is not the history of an abstraction, but the analysis of individuals acting as a Court who make decisions and lay down doctrines, and of other individuals, their successors, who refine, modify, and sometimes even overrule the decisions of their predecessors, reinterpreting and transmuting their doctrines. In law also, men make a dif-

Reprinted from 162 *Atlantic Monthly* 484 (1938). © President and Fellows of Harvard College. Footnotes supplied by editor.

1. Dred Scott v. Sandford, 19 How. 393 (1857).
2. Knox v. Lee, 12 Wall. 457 (1871).

ference. It would deny all meaning to history to believe that the course of events would have been the same if Thomas Jefferson had had the naming of Spencer Roane to the place to which John Adams called John Marshall, or if Roscoe Conkling rather than Morrison R. Waite had headed the Court before which came the Granger legislation.[3] The evolution of finance capital in the United States, and therefore of American history after the Reconstruction period, would hardly have been the same if the views of men like Mr. Justice Miller and Mr. Justice Harlan had dominated the decisions of the Court from the Civil War to Theodore Roosevelt's administration. There is no inevitability in history except as men make it.

II

The United States got under way one hundred and fifty years ago, and only seventy-seven men have shaped its destiny, insofar as law has shaped it. To understand what manner of men they were who have sat on the Supreme Bench is vital for an understanding of the Court and its work. Yet how meager is our insight into all but a very few! A lawyer's life before he becomes a judge, like that of an actor, is largely writ in water unless he has had a rich political career. And legal opinions are not conducive to biographical revelation. On the whole, we have a pitifully inadequate basis for understanding the psychological and cultural influences which may be the roots of judicial opinions. The obvious map to the minds of the Justices—the opinions of the Court—is deceptive precisely because they are the opinions of the Court. They are symphonies, not solos. Inferences from opinions to the distinctive characteristics of individual Justices are treacherous, except insofar as a man's genius breaks through a collective judgment, or his vivid life before he went on the bench serves as commentary, or as he expresses individual views in dissent or through personal writings. Not to speak of the present Court, Mr. Justice Holmes possessed these qualities of personal genius perhaps in richer measure than any member in the Court's history.

3. See, e.g., Munn v. Illinois, 94 U.S. 113 (1877).

The Chief Justice of Massachusetts became Mr. Justice Holmes of the Supreme Court on December 4, 1902, and resigned on January 12, 1932. He was thus a member of the Court for a fifth of its entire active history, and participated in more than a third of its adjudications. More important than these items of duration or volume is the historic significance of the period. Long-maturing social forces which the Civil War released or intensified found powerful political expression just about the time that Mr. Justice Holmes went to Washington. Time did not abate these conflicts. And so it came about that the Court, during his whole thirty years, was sucked into political controversies more continuous and of more immediate popular concern than at any other time in its history.

To the discerning, the burst of capitalistic activity following the victory of the North early revealed that reconciliation of unfettered individual enterprise with social well-being would be the chief issue of politics. A letter by Mr. Justice Miller, written in 1878, which has recently come to light, is a straw showing the way the wind was blowing. Miller, an appointee of Lincoln, and probably the most powerful member of his Court, kept a close watch on events, in Washington as well as from the vantage point of the agricultural Middle West, where he traveled much on circuit:

> I have met with but few things of a character affecting the public good of the whole country that have shaken my faith in human nature as much as the united, vigorous, and selfish effort of the capitalists, the class of men who as a distinct class are but recently known in this country—I mean those who live solely by interest and dividends. Prior to the late war they were not numerous. They had no interest separate from the balance of the community, because they could lend their money safely and at high rates of interest. But one of the effects of the war was greatly to reduce the rate of interest by reason of the great increase in the quantity of the circulating medium. Another was by the creation of a national funded debt, exempt from taxation to provide a means for the investment of surplus capital.

> This resource for investment was quadrupled by the bonds issued by the States, by municipal corporations, and by railroad companies. The result has been the gradual formation of a new kind of wealth in this country, the income of which is the coupons of interest and stock dividends, and of a class whose only interest or stake in the country is the ownership of these bonds and stocks. They engage in no commerce, no trade, no manufacture, no agriculture. They *produce nothing*.[4]

Mr. Justice Miller was here describing early manifestations of the impact of technological science upon society. Finance capital was in its early stages. Its evolution since Mr. Justice Miller wrote has been analyzed in Veblen's writings and in Brandeis's *Other People's Money*; the pungent details are recorded in the massive volumes of the Pujo and the Pecora investigating committees. In brief, technological advances led to large-scale industry, large-scale industries flowered into mergers and monopolies, thereby producing in considerable measure a subordination of industry to finance. On the social side came the shift from a dominantly agricultural to an urbanized society. Big business vigorously stimulated trade-unionism. Since modern politics is largely economics, these conflicting forces soon found political expression. After several abortive attempts, the various agrarian and progressive movements, in combination with organized labor and other less defined groups, three times won the presidency. For the "square deal" of Theodore Roosevelt, the "new freedom" of Woodrow Wilson, and the "new deal" of Franklin D. Roosevelt have a common genealogy. Disregarding for the moment detailed or minor differences, the three eras which these slogans summarize derived from efforts to reconcile modern economic forces with the demands of a popular democracy.

The result of the process of economic concentration in the half century since the Miller letter is luminously con-

4. See Fairman, *Mr. Justice Miller and the Supreme Court* 67 (1939).

veyed by some Treasury figures. I quote from Solicitor General Robert H. Jackson in his recent report on the Sherman Law:

> In 1932, according to the statistics of the Bureau of Internal Revenue, 53 percent of all corporate owned assets in this country was held by 618 corporations, which constitutes only 0.2 of 1 percent of the number of corporations reporting. Five percent of the corporations owned 85 percent of all corporate owned wealth in 1932. More than 50 percent of all the net income enjoyed by corporations in 1932 went to 232 corporations, while the country's manufacturing corporations 1.2 percent of the total number accounted for 63 percent of the aggregate net profits. In 1934 the only group of corporations to earn an aggregate net profit was the group whose assets exceeded $50,000,000. Thus, the process of concentration was continuing.
>
> There was likewise a high degree of concentration in the ownership of these corporations. 1929 was a banner year for stock ownership and in that year the 3.28 percent of the population who filed individual income tax returns accounted for the receipt of more than 83 percent of all dividends paid to individuals. And 78 percent of those dividends reported were received by 0.3 of 1 percent of our population.
>
> The effect of this centralization is reflected at the distribution of national income. In 1933 the Bureau of Internal Revenue statistics show that there were only 1,747,740 taxable individual incomes in the United States and nearly one third of all the property reported as passing by death was found in less than 4 percent of the estates. Brookings Institution's studies of 1929 show that about 6,000,000 families or 21 percent of all families, had incomes of less than $1000 annually, and that 36,000 families in the high income brackets received as much of our national income in that year as 11,000,000 families with lowest income.[5]

5. *Annual Report of the Attorney General of the United States* 36 (1937).

Instead of using dry figures, Mr. Bernard Baruch, who is uniquely equipped to describe it, has portrayed the present economic scene by a few swift strokes:

> In the industrial East, at least, individual initiative had begun to merge into corporate collectivism around the end of the nineteenth century, attaining its fullest effect in the decade following the World War. It has long since replaced the older capitalism as the dominant force in our economic life.
>
> Naturally, there is only one means of controlling this collectivist growth in corporate enterprise. Government regulation must be extended to a direct proportionate degree.
>
> This is a sine qua non which business must accept.[6]

Short of the immediate issues of today, Mr. Justice Holmes's period of service on the Court covered the years of most intense interaction between government and business. Barring the tariff and the National Bank Act, there were only two important measures of economic legislation on the federal statute books when Mr. Justice Holmes came to the Court, and these two, the Interstate Commerce Act of 1887 and the Sherman Law of 1890, had only somnolent vitality. Nor had State legislation, after the flurry of the Granger days, proved itself an effective device for social control over economic circumstance. Theodore Roosevelt's presidency marked the change. Under him the federal government for the first time embarked upon a positive program of social welfare. Through use of the taxing power and by regulatory legislation, not only were abuses to be remedied but benefits to be achieved for the common man. A vast field of hitherto free enterprise was brought under governmental supervision. Regardless of the political complexion of successive administrations, the area of national oversight of business was extended. From 1903 to 1932, an invigorated Interstate Commerce Commission, the Federal Trade

6. Letter, *Springfield Republican,* March 29, 1938, p. 6.

Commission, the Federal Reserve Board, the Farm Loan Board, the Tariff Commission, the Federal Power Commission, the Railroad Labor Board, followed each other in quick succession.

This vigorous legislative movement was partly a reflex of energetic State action and partly stimulated States to action. Wisconsin, under the elder La Follette, and New York, under Charles E. Hughes, took the lead in effective State regulation of utilities. In the decade between 1910 and 1920 all but half a dozen States enacted workmen's compensation laws. Local antitrust laws, shorter hours acts, minimum wage laws, blue-sky laws, banking laws, conservation enactments, illustrate only some of the topics on which laws came from the forty-eight States. Such were the problems that were presented to Mr. Justice Holmes for adjudication.

III

What equipment did Mr. Justice Holmes bring to the Court for dealing with these problems? What qualities did Theodore Roosevelt look for in appointing a Supreme Court Justice at this time? Thanks to Senator Lodge, the elder, to whom President Roosevelt unburdened his mind, we know both the hopes and the doubts that he felt about Mr. Justice Holmes's qualifications for the Supreme Bench at that particular time:

> First of all, I wish to go over the reasons why I am in his favor . . . The labor decisions which have been criticized by some of the big railroad men and other members of large corporations constitute to my mind a strong point in Judge Holmes's favor. The ablest lawyers and the greatest judges are men whose past has naturally brought them into close relationship with the wealthiest and most powerful clients, and I am glad when I can find a judge who has been able to preserve his aloofness of mind so as to keep his broad humanity of feeling and his sympathy for the class from which he has not drawn his clients. I think it eminently desirable that our Supreme Court should show in unmistakable

> fashion their entire sympathy with all proper effort to secure the most favorable possible consideration for the men who most need that consideration . . .
>
> Now a word as to the other side . . . In the ordinary and low sense which we attach to the words "partisan" and "politician," a judge of the Supreme Court should be neither. But in the higher sense, in the proper sense, he is not in my judgment fitted for the position unless he is a party man, a constructive statesman, constantly keeping in mind his adherence to the principles and policies under which this nation has been built up and in accordance with which it must go on; and keeping in mind also his relations with his fellow statesmen who in other branches of the government are striving in cooperation with him to advance the ends of government . . .
>
> . . . the majority of the present Court who have, although without satisfactory unanimity, upheld the policies of President McKinley and the Republican Party in Congress, have rendered a great service to mankind and to this nation. The minority—a minority so large as to lack but one vote of being a majority—have stood for such reactionary folly as would have hampered well-nigh hopelessly this people in doing efficient and honorable work for the national welfare . . .
>
> Now I should like to know that Judge Holmes was in entire sympathy with our views, that is with your views and mine . . . before I would feel justified in appointing him. Judge Gray has been one of the most valuable members of the Court. I should hold myself as guilty of an irreparable wrong to the nation if I should put in his place any man who was not absolutely sane and sound on the great national policies for which we stand in public life.[7]

In taking account of the general philosophy of a prospective member of the Supreme Court towards major public issues likely to come before it, Theodore Roosevelt

7. 1 *Selections from the Correspondence of Theodore Roosevelt and Henry Cabot Lodge* 517–519 (Lodge ed. 1925).

was merely following the example of other Presidents, notably Lincoln in appointing Chase as Chief Justice. The psychological assumptions made by Theodore Roosevelt and Lincoln that the past in which a man is inured may have a powerful effect upon his future decisions are supported by weighty judicial experience.

When judges decide issues that touch the nerve center of economic and social conflict, the danger, in de Tocqueville's phrase, of confounding the familiar with the necessary is especially hazardous. The matter was put with candor by Lord Justice Scrutton, a great English judge:

> The habits you are trained in, the people with whom you mix, lead to your having a certain class of ideas of such a nature that, when you have to deal with other ideas, you do not give as sound and accurate judgements as you would wish. This is one of the great difficulties at present with Labour. Labour says: "Where are your impartial Judges? They all move in the same circle as the employers, and they are all educated and nursed at the same ideas as the employers. How can a labour man or a trade-unionist get impartial justice?" It is very difficult sometimes to be sure that you have put yourself into a thoroughly impartial position between two disputants, one of your own class and one not of your class.[8]

Unlike the great men on the Court before him, Mr. Justice Holmes had been singularly outside the current of public affairs or of interest in them. He was essentially the philosopher who turned to law. Ultimate issues of the destiny of man, not the evanescent events of the day, preoccupied his mind. That he did not read newspapers revealed neither affectation, nor a sense of superiority; it mirrored his worldly innocence. When Senator Lodge tried to induce him to run for governor, with the bait that it would inevitably lead to a seat in the United States Senate, Mr. Justice Holmes blandly replied: "But I don't give a damn about being a Senator." And yet, though he

8. Scrutton, "The Work of the Commercial Court," 1 *Camb. L. J.* 6, 8 (1921).

did not bring to the Court the experience of great affairs, not even Marshall exceeded him in judicial statesmanship. Other great judges have been guided by the wisdom distilled from an active life; Mr. Justice Holmes was led by the divination of the philosopher and the imagination of the poet.

Because he had an organic philosophy, he was not distracted by the infinite diversity of detail in the appearance of the same central issues. No one realized better than he that, while principles gain significance through application, concrete instances are inert except when galvanized into life by a general principle. And so it is perhaps more true of him than of any other judge in the history of the Court that the host of public controversies in which he participated was subdued to reason by relatively few guiding considerations. This was true whether he was called upon to strike a balance between the claims of property and its obligations, or between the rights of individuals and their duties, or between the limits of State action and the authority of the federal government.

What is the role of a judge in making these adjustments between society and the individual, between the States and the nation? The conception which a judge has of his own function, and the fastidiousness with which he follows it, will in large measure determine the most delicate controversies before him. Justices of the Court are not architects of policy. They can nullify the policy of others; they are incapable of fashioning their own solutions for social problems. The use which a judge makes of his power of negation is largely determined by two psychological considerations. It depends first on the judge's philosophy, conscious or implicit, regarding the nature of society; that is, on his theory of the clash of interests. This, in turn, will influence his conception of the place of the judge in the American constitutional system.

Mr. Justice Holmes's view of the play of forces in society hardly differed from that of Madison in his classic statement in *The Federalist:*

> Those who hold, and those who are without property, have ever formed distinct interests in society. Those

who are creditors, and those who are debtors, fall under a like discrimination. A landed interest, a manufacturing interest, a monied interest, with many lesser interests, grow up of necessity in civilized nations, and divide them into different classes, actuated by different sentiments and views. The regulation of these various and interfering interests forms the principal task of modern legislation, and involves the spirit of party and faction in the necessary and ordinary operations of government.[9]

Thirty years before he went on the Supreme Court, Mr. Justice Holmes expressed this view in his own way:

This tacit assumption of the solidarity of the interests of society is very common, but seems to us to be false . . . in the last resort a man rightly prefers his own interest to that of his neighbors. And this is as true in legislation as in any other form of corporate action. All that can be expected from modern improvements is that legislation should easily and quickly, yet not too quickly, modify itself in accordance with the will of the de facto supreme power in the community, and that the spread of an educated sympathy should reduce the sacrifice of minorities to a minimum . . . The objection to class legislation is not that it favors a class, but either that it fails to benefit the legislators, or that it is dangerous to them because a competing class has gained in power, or that it transcends the limits of self-preference which are imposed by sympathy . . . But it is no sufficient condemnation of legislation that it favors one class at the expense of another; for much or all legislation does that; and nonetheless when the bona fide object is the greatest good of the greatest number . . . If the welfare of all future ages is to be considered, legislation may as well be abandoned for the present . . . The fact is that legislation in this country, as well as elsewhere, is empirical. It is necessarily made a means by which

9. *The Federalist* No. 10.

a body, having the power, puts burdens which are disagreeable to them on the shoulders of somebody else.[10]

Mr. Justice Holmes never forgot that the activities of government are continual attempts by peaceful means to adjust these clashes of interest, and he was equally mindful of the fact that the body to whom this task of adjustment is primarily delegated is the legislature. And so he gave complete loyalty in his work as a judge to the major premise of Marshall "that it is a *constitution* we are expounding."[11] He scrupulously treated the Constitution as a broad charter of powers for the internal clashes of society, and did not construe it as though it were a code which prescribed in detail answers for the social problems of all time.

Thus the enduring contribution of Mr. Justice Holmes to American history is his constitutional philosophy. He gave it momentum by the magic with which he expressed it. Great judges are apt to be identified with what lawyers call great cases. Mr. Justice Holmes's specialty was great utterance. "For great cases," he himself has said, "are called great, not by reason of their real importance in shaping the law of the future, but because of some accident of immediate, overwhelming interest which appeals to the feelings and distorts the judgment."[12] He saw the vital in the undramatic; to him, inconspicuous controversies revealed the clash of great social forces. And so the significance of his genius would evaporate in any analysis of his specific decisions. In this case, form and substance were beautifully fused. His conception of the Constitution must become part of the political habits of the country if our constitutional system is to endure; and if we care for our literary treasures the expression of his views must become part of our national culture.

10. "Summary of Great Events, Great Britain," 7 *Am. L. Rev.* 582, 583–584 (1873); see *Justice Oliver Wendell Holmes: His Book Notices and Uncollected Papers* 104, 107–109 (Shriver ed. 1936).

11. McCulloch v. Maryland, 4 Wheat. 316, 407 (1819).

12. Northern Securities Corp. v. United States, 193 U.S. 197, 400 (1903).

IV

The Constitution is, of course, a legal document, but a legal document of a fundamentally different order from an insurance policy or a lease of timberland. For the Justice, the Constitution was not primarily a text for dialectic, but a means of ordering the life of a progressive people. While its roots were in the past, it was projected for the unknown future.

> The provisions of the Constitution are not mathematical formulas having their essence in their form; they are organic living institutions transplanted from English soil. Their significance is vital, not formal; it is to be gathered not simply by taking the words and a dictionary, but by considering their origin and the line of their growth.[13]

> When we are dealing with words that also are a constituent act, like the Constitution of the United States, we must realize that they have called into life a being the development of which could not have been foreseen completely by the most gifted of its begetters. It was enough for them to realize or to hope that they had created an organism; it has taken a century and has cost their successors much sweat and blood to prove that they created a nation. The case before us must be considered in the light of our whole experience and not merely in that of what was said a hundred years ago.[14]

While the Supreme Court is thus in the exacting realm of government, it is itself freed from the terrible burdens of governing. The Court is the brake on other men's actions, the judge of other men's decisions. Responsibility for action rests with legislators. The range of the Court's authority is thus very limited, but its exercise may vitally affect the nation. No wonder John Marshall spoke of this power of the Court as "delicate."[15]

13. Gompers v. United States, 233 U.S. 604, 610 (1914).
14. Missouri v. Holland, 252 U.S. 416, 433 (1920).
15. Fletcher v. Peck, 6 Cranch 87, 128 (1810).

No man who ever sat on the Court has been more keenly or more consistently sensitive than Mr. Justice Holmes to the dangers and difficulties inherent in the power of judges to review legislation. For it is subtle business to decide, not whether legislation is wise, but whether legislators were reasonable in believing it to be wise. In view of the complexities of modern society and the restricted scope of any man's experience, tolerance and humility in passing judgment on the worth of the experience and beliefs of others become crucial faculties in the disposition of cases. The successful exercise of such judicial power calls for rare intellectual disinterestedness and penetration, lest limitations in personal experience and imagination operate as limitations of the Constitution. These insights Mr. Justice Holmes applied in hundreds of cases, and expressed in memorable language:

> It is a misfortune if a judge reads his conscious or unconscious sympathy with one side or the other prematurely into the law, and forgets that what seem to him to be first principles are believed by half his fellow men to be wrong . . . When twenty years ago a vague terror went over the earth and the word socialism began to be heard, I thought and still think that fear was translated into doctrines that had no proper place in the Constitution or the common law.[16]

> While the courts must exercise a judgment of their own, it by no means is true that every law is void which may seem to the judges who pass upon it excessive, unsuited to its ostensible end, or based upon conceptions of morality with which they disagree. Considerable latitude must be allowed for differences of view as well as for possible peculiar conditions which this court can know but imperfectly, if at all. Otherwise a constitution, instead of embodying only relatively fundamental rules of right, as generally understood by all English-speaking communities, would become the

16. Holmes, *Collected Legal Papers* 295 (1920).

partisan of a particular set of ethical or economical opinions, which by no means are held *semper ubique et ab omnibus*.[17]

While in the '80s and '90s our economy was in process of drastic transformation, members of the Supreme Court continued to reflect the economic order in which they grew up. Between the presidencies of Grant and the first Roosevelt, laissez faire was the dominant economic social philosophy, and it was imported into the Constitution. Ephemeral facts were translated into legal absolutes; abstract conceptions concerning "liberty of contract" were erected into constitutional dogmas. Malleable and undefined provisions of the Constitution were applied as barriers against piecemeal efforts of adjustment through legislation to a society permeated by the influence of technology, large-scale industry, progressive urbanization, and the general dependence of the individual on economic forces beyond his control. The due process clauses were especially the destructive rocks on which this legislation foundered. Judge Learned Hand, one of the most eminent of our judges, has said that the requirement of due process is merely an embodiment of the English sporting idea of fair play. In England, particularly from the time of the Campbell-Bannerman government, the same causes that induced American legislative attempts led to a continual Parliamentary modification of the system of private enterprise. The scope of this trend in England is revealed by a few telltale figures. The social services established by this legislation have entailed an increase in expenditure from £0.19.2 per capita in 1900 to £8.16.6 in 1934; and about a third of the national income of Great Britain is now spent through public channels.

Yet, as late as 1905, the Supreme Court held it unconstitutional to limit the working hours of bakers to ten,[18] and as recently as 1936 the Court adhered to its ruling that it was beyond the power both of the States and of the nation to assure minimum wage rates for women workers

17. Otis v. Parker, 187 U.S. 606, 608–609 (1903).
18. Lochner v. New York, 198 U.S. 45 (1905).

obviously incapable of economic self-protection.[19] Every variety of legislative manifestation to subject economic power to social responsibility encountered the judicial veto.

The doctrinal process by which the majority reached such results was thus explained by Mr. Justice Holmes in dissenting from his brethren in the minimum wage case:

> The only objection that can be urged [against a minimum wage law for women for the District of Columbia] is found within the vague contours of the Fifth Amendment, prohibiting the depriving any person of liberty without due process of law. To that I turn.
>
> The earlier decisions upon the same words in the Fourteenth Amendment began within our memory and went no farther than an unpretentious assertion of the liberty to follow the ordinary callings. Later that innocuous generality was expanded into the dogma, Liberty of Contract. Contract is not specially mentioned in the text that we have to construe. It is merely an example of doing what you want to do, embodied in the word liberty. But pretty much all law consists in forbidding men to do some things that they want to do, and contract is no more exempt from law than other acts.[20]

For a short time after the bakeshop case the views of Mr. Justice Holmes were in the ascendant. Chief Justice White was heard to attribute to the influence exerted by President Theodore Roosevelt's messages and speeches no inconsiderable share in the shift of the Court's emphasis. The fact is that for less than a decade, between 1908 and the World War, the Court did allow legislation to prevail which, in various aspects, regulated enterprise with reference to its social consequences and withdrew phases of industrial relations from the area of illusory individual bargaining.

19. Morehead v. New York ex. rel. Tipaldo, 298 U.S. 587 (1936).
20. Adkins v. Children's Hospital, 261 U.S. 525, 568 (1923).

But those who had assumed a permanent change in the Court's outlook were soon disappointed. Changes in the Court's personnel and in the general economic and social climate of the Harding-Coolidge era soon reflected themselves in decisions. Until after the 1936 election, the Court was back to the high tide of judicial negation reached in the *Lochner* case, in 1905. Mr. Justice Holmes's classic dissent in that case will never lose its relevance:

> This case is decided upon an economic theory which a large part of the country does not entertain. If it were a question whether I agreed with that theory, I should desire to study it further and long before making up my mind. But I do not conceive that to be my duty, because I strongly believe that my agreement or disagreement has nothing to do with the right of a majority to embody their opinions in law. It is settled by various decisions of this court that state constitutions and state laws may regulate life in many ways which we as legislators might think as injudicious or if you like as tyrannical as this, and which equally with this interfere with the liberty of contract. Sunday laws and usury laws are ancient examples. A more modern one is the prohibition of lotteries. The liberty of the citizen to do as he likes so long as he does not interfere with the liberty of others to do the same, which has been a shibboleth for some well-known writers, is interfered with by school laws, by the Post Office, by every state or municipal institution which takes his money for purposes thought desirable, whether he likes it or not. The Fourteenth Amendment does not enact Mr. Herbert Spencer's Social Statics . . . Some of these laws embody convictions or prejudices which judges are likely to share. Some may not. But a constitution is not intended to embody a particular economic theory, whether of paternalism and the organic relation of the citizen to the State or of laissez faire. It is made for people of fundamentally differing views, and the accident of our finding certain opinions natural and familiar or novel and even

shocking ought not to conclude our judgment upon the question whether statutes embodying them conflict with the Constitution of the United States.[21]

This was the great theme of his judicial life—the amplitude of the Constitution as against the narrowness of some of its interpreters. And so, having analyzed with brave clarity the governing elements in the modern economic struggle, he did not shrink from giving his analysis judicial recognition. "One of the eternal conflicts out of which life is made up," he wrote, more than forty years ago, "is that between the effort of every man to get the most he can for his services, and that of society, disguised under the name of capital, to get his services for the least possible return. Combination on the one side is patent and powerful. Combination on the other is the necessary and desirable counterpart, if the battle is to be carried on in a fair and equal way."[22] Mr. Justice Holmes therefore found nothing in the Constitution to prevent legislation which sought to remove some of the more obvious inequalities in the distribution of economic power.

Economists and historians are now largely agreed that the resistance to a natural and responsible trade-unionism has been one of the most disturbing factors in our economy. Had the views of Mr. Justice Holmes prevailed, the Constitution would not have been used as an obstruction to the healthy development of trade-unionism. More than thirty years ago he protested when a majority of the Court invalidated an act of Congress against the "yellow dog" contract which was drawn by Richard Olney, as attorney general, and sponsored by President Cleveland.[23] The need for legislation to remove disabilities against the effective right of association by workers became more manifest with time. State after State, therefore, passed laws to assure trade-unions the opportunity which they already had in the rest of the English-speaking world.

21. 198 U.S. at 75–76.
22. Vegelahn v. Guntner, 167 Mass. 92, 108 (1896).
23. Adair v. United States, 208 U.S. 161 (1908).

But a majority of the Court remained obdurate and imposed a doctrinaire view of the Constitution against such legislation. One can only surmise what would have been the gain to social peace and economic security had the dissenting views expressed more than twenty years ago by Mr. Justice Holmes been the Court's views:

> In present conditions a workman not unnaturally may believe that only by belonging to a union can he secure a contract that shall be fair to him . . . If that belief, whether right or wrong, may be held by a reasonable man, it seems to me that it may be enforced by law in order to establish the equality of position between the parties in which liberty of contract begins. Whether in the long run it is wise for the workingmen to enact legislation of this sort is not my concern, but I am strongly of the opinion that there is nothing in the Constitution of the United States to prevent it.[24]

V

Mr. Justice Holmes denied that the Constitution stereotyped any particular distribution of economic power for all time. With the clean precision of a surgeon he uncovered the process by which, under the guise of deductive reasoning, partial claims were given the shelter of the Constitution as comprehensive interests of property:

> Delusive exactness is a source of fallacy throughout the law. By calling a business "property" you make it seem like land, and lead up to the conclusion that a statute cannot substantially cut down the advantages of ownership existing before the statute was passed. An established business no doubt may have pecuniary value and commonly is protected by law against various unjustified injuries. But you cannot give it definiteness of contour by calling it a thing. It is a course of conduct and like other conduct is subject to substantial modification according to time and circumstances both in

24. Coppage v. Kansas, 236 U.S. 1, 26–27 (1915).

itself and in regard to what shall justify doing it a harm."[25]

By a steady extension of doctrines which, to Mr. Justice Holmes, had no justification in the Constitution, a majority of the Court persistently denied exertions of the legislature toward reconciling individual enterprise and social welfare. Abstract conceptions regarding property and "liberty of contract" were the swords with which these measures were struck down. Mr. Justice Holmes was finally roused to an unusual judicial protest. His dissent from the decision of the majority in declaring unconstitutional a New York statute regulating theater-ticket scalping fully reveals his mind. It also gives a glimpse of the importance he attached to art throughout life:

> We fear to grant power and are unwilling to recognize it when it exists . . . when legislatures are held to be authorized to do anything considerably affecting public welfare it is covered by apologetic phrases like the police power, or the statement that the business concerned has been dedicated to a public use. The former expression is convenient, to be sure, to conciliate the mind to something that needs explanation: the fact that the constitutional requirement of compensation when property is taken cannot be pressed to its grammatical extreme; that property rights may be taken for public purposes without pay if you do not take too much; that some play must be allowed to the joints if the machine is to work. But police power often is used in a wide sense to cover and, as I said, to apologize for the general power of the legislature to make a part of the community uncomfortable by a change.
>
> I do not believe in such apologies. I think the proper course is to recognize that a state legislature can do whatever it sees fit to do unless it is restrained by some express prohibition in the Constitution of the United States or of the State, and that Courts should be careful not to extend such prohibitions beyond their obvious

25. Truax v. Corrigan, 257 U.S. 312, 342–343 (1921).

meaning by reading into them conceptions of public policy that the particular Court may happen to entertain. Coming down to the case before us, I think, as I intimated in *Adkins* v. *Children's Hospital*, 261 U.S. 525, 569, that the notion that a business is clothed with a public interest and has been devoted to a public use is little more than a fiction intended to beautify what is disagreeable to the sufferers. The truth seems to me to be that, subject to compensation when compensation is due, that legislature may forbid or restrict any business when it has a sufficient force of public opinion behind it. Lotteries were thought useful adjuncts of the State a century or so ago; now they are believed to be immoral and they have been stopped. Wine has been thought good for man from the time of the Apostles until recent years. But when public opinion changed it did not need the Eighteenth Amendment, notwithstanding the Fourteenth, to enable a State to say that the business should end. *Mugler* v. *Kansas*, 123 U.S. 623. What has happened to lotteries and wine might happen to theatres in some moral storm of the future, not because theatres were devoted to a public use, but because people had come to think that way.

But if we are to yield to fashionable conventions, it seems to me that theatres are as much devoted to public use as anything well can be. We have not that respect for art that is one of the glories of France. But to many people the superfluous is the necessary, and it seems to me that Government does not go beyond its sphere in attempting to make life livable for them. I am far from saying that I think that this particular law is a wise and rational provision. That is not my affair. But if the people of the State of New York speaking by their authorized voice say that they want it, I see nothing in the Constitution of the United States to prevent their having their will.[26]

Taxation is perhaps the severest testing ground for the objectivity and wisdom of a social thinker. The enormous

26. Tyson & Bro. v. Banton, 273 U.S. 418, 445–447 (1927).

increase in the cost of society and the extent to which wealth is now represented by intangibles, the profound change in the relation of the individual to government and the resulting widespread insistence on security, are subjecting public finance to the most exacting demands. To balance budgets, to pay for the costs of progressively civilized social standards, to safeguard the future, and to divide these burdens fairly among different interests in the community, put the utmost strain on the ingenuity of statesmen. They must constantly explore new sources of revenue and find means of preventing the circumvention of their discoveries. Subject as they are, in English-speaking countries, to popular control, they should not be denied adequate latitude of power for their extraordinary difficult tasks.

Mr. Justice Holmes never yielded to finicky limitations or doctrinaire formulas, drawn from the general language of the Constitution, as a means of circumscribing the discretion of legislatures in the necessarily empirical process of tapping new revenue or stopping new devices for evasion. He did not have a curmudgeon's feelings about his own taxes. A secretary who exclaimed "Don't you hate to pay taxes!" was rebuked with the hot response, "No, young feller. I like to pay taxes. With them I buy civilization."[27] And as a judge he consistently refused to accentuate fiscal difficulties of government by injecting into the Constitution his own notions of fiscal policy. Nor did he believe that there was anything in the Constitution to bar even a conscious use of the taxing power for readjusting the social equilibrium. One of the last utterances as a Justice gives the general flavor of his many opinions in tax cases:

> I have not yet adequately expressed the more than anxiety that I feel at the ever increasing scope given to the Fourteenth Amendment in cutting down what I believe to be the constitutional rights of the States. As the decisions now stand, I see hardly any limit but the

27. Cf. Compania Gen. De Tabacos v. Collector, 275 U.S. 87, 100 (1927).

> sky to the invalidating of those rights if they happen to strike a majority of this Court as for any reason undesirable. I cannot believe that the Amendment was intended to give us carte blanche to embody our economic or moral beliefs in its prohibitions. Yet I can think of no narrower reason that seems to me to justify the present and the earlier decisions to which I have referred . . . It seems to me to be exceeding our powers to declare such a tax a denial of due process of law.
>
> And what are the grounds? Simply, so far as I can see, that it is disagreeable to a bondowner to be taxed in two ways. Very probably it might be good policy to restrict taxation to a single place, and perhaps the technical conception of domicil may be the best determinant. But it seems to me that if that result is to be reached it should be reached through understanding among the States, by uniform legislation or otherwise, not by evoking a constitutional prohibition from the void of "due process of law," when logic, tradition and authority have united to declare the right of the State to lay the now prohibited tax.[28]

I have indicated the general direction of Mr. Justice Holmes's judicial mind on the great issues of the constitutional position of property in our society. During most of his thirty years on the Supreme Bench, and especially during the second half of his tenure, his were not the views of a majority of the Court. But the good that men do lives after them. In the spring of 1937 the old views of Mr. Justice Holmes began to be the new constitutional direction of the Court.

His own constitutional outlook was, throughout a long life, free from fluctuations. This was so because it was born of a deeply rooted and coherent philosophy concerning the dynamic character of the American Constitution and of a judge's function in construing it. If he threw the weight of his authority on the side of social readjustments through legislation it was not because of any faith in

28. Baldwin v. Missouri, 281 U.S. 586, 595–596 (1930).

panaceas in general or in measures of social amelioration in particular. He personally "disbelieved all the popular conceptions of socialism,"[29] and came dangerously close to believing in the simplicities of the wage-fund theory. But his skepticism and even hostility, as a matter of private judgment, toward legislation which he was ready to sustain as a judge only serve to add cubits to his judicial stature. For he thereby transcended personal predilections and private notions of social policy, and became truly the impersonal voice of the Constitution.

29. Holmes, *Collected Legal Papers* 307 (1920).

Mr. Justice Cardozo and Public Law

The fairies that presided over Benjamin N. Cardozo's birth were not wholly benign. But they endowed him with one gift of grace far more significant than his rare talents of mind. He was given a contagious goodness which brought to life the goodness in others. In no invidious sense was the New York Court of Appeals, especially during his presidency, Cardozo's court. And the compulsions of Cardozo's spirit upon those with whom he labored were revealed even through the austerity which insulates the Supreme Court from public knowledge of its intimate life. It is not surprising that the persuasiveness of his personality subdued his immediate environment by its sheer unconscious radiations. It is astonishing that so cloistered a spirit should have attained such a hold on popular feeling.

Other judges have had much more influence upon the governing forces of American society than fell to Cardozo's lot. Perhaps a few, but at best a very few, judges had as keen an insight into the peculiar role of the judge in the American scheme. Finally, there was one judge of greater originality and deeper penetration into the intellectual presuppositions of the judicial process. For it was not merely the language of playful deference which made Cardozo always speak of Holmes as "the Master." But the history of the Supreme Court affords no analogue to the unanimity of lay as well as professional opinion that Chief Judge Cardozo was the one man adequate to fill the historic place vacated by Holmes; nor is there a parallel to the deep feeling of the country as a whole that the death of Cardozo was not merely the premature termination of a distinguished judicial career, but the end of the living

Reprinted from an essay in memory of Benjamin Nathan Cardozo published simultaneously by the Harvard, Yale, and Columbia law reviews. 52 *Harv. L. Rev.* 440; 48 *Yale L.J.* 458; 39 *Colum. L. Rev.* 88 (1939).

energy of one of the most powerful moral resources of the nation.

Ordinarily observations like these are properly uncongenial to pages concerned with the discussion of juristic problems. But in the case of Cardozo the main path to his views on public law leads from his character. His conception of the Constitution cannot be severed from his conception of a judge's function in applying it. His views of the judge's function derive from his convictions on philosophic issues which implicate the workings of the judicial mind. Such issues in turn involve a man's notions of his relation to the universe. These are abstractions. They seem far removed, let us say, from No. 180 of the October Term, 1936. But the clarity with which a specific controversy is seen in the context of the larger intellectual issues beneath the formal surface of litigation, and the courage with which such analysis infuses decision and opinions are the ultimate determinants of American public law.

I

That the task of constitutional construction is a function not of mechanics but of imponderables is now known even by Macaulay's omniscient schoolboy. There is, however, no authorized catalogue of the imponderables; still less is there an accepted organon for striking the balance among competing and conflicting values. Partly because of the wise common-law tradition of ad hoc adjudication, partly because of the distinctive temperament and experience of judges, an avowed juristic philosophy of which individual decisions are particular expressions seldom emerges from the opinions of a judge. The formulation of such a philosophy before a judge ascends the Supreme Bench is a still rarer phenomenon. Barring only Holmes, no man had so completely revealed the map of his mind before he went on the Court as had Cardozo. If surprise there was in anything that he wrote as a Justice, it was not for want of disclosure by him as to the way he looked at questions that would come before him.

Ultimately, a particular decision in a realm not obviously foreclosed by authority[1]—the decisive field for the play of a judge's creative powers—is the exercise of a high art, what in the happier phraseology of the seventeenth century was called a "mystery." But it is a most subtle and complicated art, at its best the end of a long ratiocinative process. Scientific discoveries, we are told, come to the prepared mind. So the art of adjudication is most imaginatively exercised by those Judges who know that the ultimate determination of values is not within the power of formula or measurement. Therefore they explore to the uttermost the rational foundations of what they affirm and what they reject, in order to avoid confusion between their private universe and the universe. All of Cardozo's extrajudicial writings, but more particularly *The Nature of the Judicial Process* and *The Paradoxes of Legal Science* are suffused with intimations of what later came from his pen as a Justice, as well as glosses upon what is so shyly expressed in opinions. But his lectures on "The Methods of History" and "Tradition and Sociology,"[2] "The Judge as a Legislator"[3] and "Liberty and Government"[4] convey explicit analysis of the nature of the issues which cases frame in deceptively logical form. They also reveal the extent of the freedom which judges have in dealing with these issues, as well as the limits of that freedom.

Whereas Holmes all his life was much more occupied with his first love, Philosophy, than was Cardozo, he never formulated his philosophy as systematically as did Cardozo except in a short essay or two.[5] Indeed, while Holmes was a conscientious student of all the great systems of

1. "The radiating potencies of a decision may go beyond the actual holding . . . An opinion may be so framed that there is doubt whether the part of it invoked as an authority is to be ranked as a definitive holding or merely a considered dictum." Hawkes v. Hamill, 288 U.S. 52, 58–59 (1933). See Llewellyn, "The Rule of Law in Our Case-Law of Contract," 47 *Yale L.J.* 1243 (1938).
2. *The Nature of the Judicial Process* ch. II (1921).
3. Id., ch. III.
4. *The Paradoxes of Legal Science* chs. 3 and 4 (1928).
5. See "The Path of the Law" and "Law in Science and Science in Law," in Holmes, *Collected Legal Papers* (1920).

philosophy and reread such disparate thinkers as Spinoza and John Dewey again and again, he distrusted system, and inclined to the view that systems are apt to be merely the elegant elaborations of a few profound insights. On the other hand, Holmes often made his opinions the vehicles of his philosophic beliefs. He summarized his own views as to ultimates in the amber of his apothegms. While he was alert to the dangers of what the shrewd Lincoln called "pernicious abstractions," particularly in the business of judging, the flair of his mind was for abstractions. Thus it is that from his opinions may be culled sentences which convey his vision of the Constitution in its relation to the organic process of human society and his conception of the judge as a custodian of that vision.

With Cardozo it was otherwise. Perhaps because he had spelled out his philosophic beliefs and directions in his trilogy,[6] his opinions stuck close to the circumstance of the particular record and indulged sparingly in detachable epigrammatic utterance. But the specific inevitably implicates the general, and in a few instances Cardozo expressed the underlying principles that guided his constitutional function in language and accent not confined to the immediacies of the case.

Indeed the only scope for originality in elucidating the process of constitutional adjudication is the power of putting old truths with freshness. In the abstract, the appropriate ways of looking at the Constitution, when brought within the focus of the judiciary, have been stated in essentially similar terms since Marshall first intoned them in the solemn rhetoric of his day. The sanctions of statesmanship which vindicate this viewpoint were stated with the finality of exquisite scholarship by James Bradley Thayer nearly fifty years ago.[7] Nor have the intermittent

6. *The Nature of the Judicial Process* (1921); *The Growth of the Law* (1924); *The Paradoxes of Legal Science* (1928).

7. "The Origin and Scope of the American Doctrine of Constitutional Law," 7 *Harv. L. Rev.* 129 (1893), reprinted in Thayer, *Legal Essays* 1 (1908); see Frankfurter and Fisher, "The Business of the Supreme Court at the October Terms, 1935 and 1936," 51 *Harv. L. Rev.* 577, 620–637 (1938).

deviations in the applications of Marshall's canons and Thayer's philosophy ever explicitly challenged either canons or philosophy. That the Constitution contains within itself the formulated past but was also designed for the unfolding future; that it is a source of governmental energy no less than of governmental restriction; that in the most difficult areas of adjudication the issues which come before the Court do not primarily present questions as to the meaning of words but invite judgment upon ultimate issues of society which in the now classic language of Mr. Justice Holmes "must be considered in the light of our whole experience and not merely in that of what was said a hundred years ago"[8]—these are generalities to which fealty is never denied.

But the recognition of their relevance to a specific controversy and the fidelity with which they are applied are the turning points of decisions. Difference among judges is not in knowledge of constitutional precepts but in the persistence and insight with which they respect them. Normally, the raw materials of public law controversies are contemporary affairs, and understanding of their significance is seldom achieved on the bench without considerable prior immersion in affairs. Cardozo is a striking exception. The market place was not his milieu. Sociological problems were not the preoccupation of his leisure moments, his spontaneous writings, or his talk. Like Holmes, he was sensitive to social tensions and the conflicts of interest not by the bent of his mind, but because the scholar in him made him realize that to be a good judge he had to become conversant with the processes of government and of industry.

Cardozo realized the essentially empiric character of government and the range of discretion implied by its activities. "Time with its tides," he was aware, "brings new conditions which must be cared for by new laws." The need for legislation, its scope and limits, "in last analysis is one of legislative policy, with a wide margin of discretion conceded to the lawmakers. Only in cases

8. Missouri V. Holland, 252 U.S. 416, 433 (1920).

of plain abuse will there be revision by the courts."[9] But review of another's right to exercise policy without substituting one's own presents the most treacherous judicial difficulties. For it necessitates extraordinary powers of detachment not to confound personal disapproval with an enduring constitutional prohibition, not to translate the rarest gifts of tolerance and a respect for much that is not fully understood. Cardozo recognized that new policies must be perfected or discarded by the test of experience, and must not be judged as though the legislature were a modern Minerva. Except in the limited instances where explicit constitutional restrictions fence in legislative freedom, laws justify themselves before courts if they manifest

> a pursuit of legitimate ends by methods honestly conceived and rationally chosen. More will not be asked by those who have learned from experience and history that government is at best a makeshift, that the attainment of one good may involve the sacrifice of others, and that compromises will be inevitable until the coming of Utopia.[10]

Taxation is the most sensitive area of contemporary government, but the intellectual perspective in which Cardozo placed tax measures induced by social rather than fiscal motives was expressive of his general attitude toward the diverse manifestations of the modern state:

> Systems of taxation are not framed, nor is it possible to frame them, with perfect distribution of benefit and burden. Their authors must be satisfied with a rough

9. Williams v. Mayor, 289 U.S. 36, 46 (1933). See also the observations made more than one hundred years ago by William Johnson, one of the ablest members of the Court: "The science of government is the most abstruse of all sciences; if, indeed, that can be called a science which has but a few fixed principles, and practically consists in little more than the exercise of a sound discretion, applied to the exigencies of the state as they arise. It is the science of experiment." Anderson v. Dunn, 6 Wheat. 204, 226 (1822).

10. Stewart Dry Goods Co. v. Lewis, 294 U.S. 550, 577 (1935) (dissenting).

> and ready form of justice. This is true in special measure while the workings of a novel method are untested by a rich experience. There must be advance by trial and error . . . In discarding as arbitrary symbols the lines that it [the legislature] has chosen, there is danger of forgetting that in social and economic life the grooves of thought and action are not always those of logic, and that symbols may mean as much as conduct has put into them.[11]

Since language is the sword by which the judiciary intervenes in the legislative process, those who wield it must be unremittingly on guard against its hazards:

> A fertile source of perversion in constitutional theory is the tyranny of labels. Out of the vague precepts of the Fourteenth Amendment a court frames a rule which is general in form, though it has been wrought under the pressure of particular situations. Forthwith another situation is placed under the rule because it is fitted to the words, though related faintly, if at all, to the reasons that brought the rule into existence.[12]

II

The main stuff of contemporary Supreme Court litigation is fairly indicated by the fact that both the first and the last opinions written by Mr. Justice Cardozo arose out of the interaction of government and business. Nor does it urge significance unduly to note that in his first opinion[13] Cardozo spoke only for himself, Mr. Justice Brandeis, and Mr. Justice Stone, while his last opinion[14] announced in his absence by the Chief Justice, was on behalf of a majority of the Court. The economic and social context of Cardozo's period of service, the spate of legislation which came from Congress and the States, and the resistances to which it gave rise, are too familiar to call even for summary.

11. Liggett Co. v. Lee, 288 U.S. 517, 586 (1933) (dissenting).
12. Snyder v. Massachusetts, 291 U.S. 97, 114 (1934).
13. Coombes v. Getz, 285 U.S. 434, 448 (1932) (dissenting).
14. Smyth v. United States, 302 U.S. 329 (1937).

Since *Chisholm* v. *Georgia,*[15] Supreme Court decisions have on occasion furnished materials for popular discussion. But never in our history was interest in the Court so continuous nor were its opinions so extensively canvassed in the lay press as during the incumbency of Cardozo. To a very considerable degree, therefore, his opinions have become common property. This is not the place for their detailed review. A conspectus of his attitude toward the subjection of economic legislation to judicial review must suffice.

The radiations of taxation have steadily extended the intrusion of government into economic affairs. The tasks of statesmanship in tapping new sources of revenue without killing the goose that lays the golden eggs have correspondingly multiplied. The enormous diversity in types of business activity, the nice calculations involved in making classifications at once fair and effective, the repercussions of different taxes upon diverse enterprises are among the most exigent but elusive riddles for those charged with governing. Clichés like "scientific taxation" cover up a thousand perplexities not susceptible of solution by procedures and criteria familiar to the natural sciences. It is in this perspective of pervasive fiscal needs and the intractable problems they present to legislators, that tax measures must be seen when brought under the scrutiny of such large phrases as "due process" and "the equal protection of the laws":

> A tax upon the receipts of a business is not invalid as of course because some forms of business are hit and others are exempt. To bring about that result the assailant of the tax must be able to satisfy the court that the classification had its origin in nothing better than whim and fantasy . . . This is the heavy burden that the appellant must sustain. Is it a whimsical and fantastic act to tax foreign fire insurance companies upon all their net receipts, including those derived from casualty premiums, when no such tax is imposed upon the receipts of insurance companies that do a casualty

15. 2 Dall. 419 (1793).

business only? If so, the arbitrary quality of the division must have its origin in the fact that the activities of the one class overlap to some extent the activities of the other. But plainly there is no rule that overlapping classes can never be established in the realm of taxation except at the price of an infringement of the federal constitution. The recognition of such a rule means that a department store may not be taxed on the net receipts of its business unless all the many activities thus brought under a single roof are taxed in the same way when separately conducted . . . There must be a tax on the business of the draper, the jeweler, the shoemaker, the hatter, the carpet dealer and what not. For the same reason the proprietor of a retail market dealing in meats and groceries and vegetables and fruits will then escape, at least proportionately, a tax upon receipts if the statute does not cover the business of the shopkeeper who derives a modest income from the sale of peanuts and bananas. There are few taxes upon earnings that would pass so fine a sieve. The rule, if there is any, against the creation of overlapping classes for the purposes of taxation is manifestly not one of general validity. The range of its application must depend upon the facts.[16]

The rule is elementary that a state in adopting a system of taxation is not confined to a formula of rigid uniformity . . . It may tax some kinds of property at one rate, and others at another, and exempt others altogether . . . It may lay an excise on the operations of a particular kind of business, and exempt some other kind of business closely akin thereto . . . What is true of division into classes according to subject matter must be true of division into classes dependent upon time. The temporal arrangement must have its origin, to be sure, in something more than . . . a tyrannical exhibition of arbitrary power. If that reproach has been avoided, the classification does not fail because the

16. Concordia Ins. Co. v. Illinois, 292 U.S. 535, 554–555 (1934) (dissenting).

> burdens before and after are not always and everywhere in perfect equilibrium.
>
> From all this it follows that a distinction between wills or deeds effective before 1907 and those effective afterwards—the exercise or non-exercise of powers under instruments of the first class giving rise to a succession to be taxed as a bequest from the donee, and the exercise or non-exercise of powers under instruments of the second class to be taxed as a bequest from the donor—is not rooted in caprice. The point of time which separates the classes is not interjected arbitrarily or by an exertion of brute force, but corresponds to the behests of a rational taxonomy . . . A legislature cannot be expected in drafting legislation to think out every conceivable situation in which the members of one class will bear a heavier burden than the members of another . . . Eccentricities of incidence are common, and perhaps inevitable, in every system of taxation. The future would have to be scanned with microscopical powers of vision to foresee and forestall every possible diversity. For present purposes it is enough that the order of events removes the stigma of caprice from a system of classification whereby donees of a power before the passage of the act are treated as grantors, the tax to be laid upon that basis, whereas donors of a power are recognized as the source of the succession in respect of transfers afterwards.[17]

Taxation primarily for revenue can hardly exclude social consequences. The complexities of tax legislation are intensified whenever social policy is its predominant aim. From the day of Hamilton's Report on Manufactures, American statesmen have employed taxation for purposes other than revenue. Beginning with Theodore Roosevelt's administration, taxation has assumed a mounting share in the process of social adjustment. "A motive to build up through legislation the quality of men," Cardozo was allowed to say for a narrow majority of the Court, "may be as creditable in the thought of some as a motive to

17. Binney v. Long, 299 U.S. 280, 297–299 (1936) (dissenting).

magnify the quantity of trade. Courts do not choose between such values in adjudging legislative powers. They put the choice aside as beyond their lawful competence. . . . The tax now assailed may have its roots in an erroneous conception of the ills of the body politic or of the efficacy of such a measure to bring about a cure. We have no thought in anything we have written to declare it expedient or even just, or for that matter to declare the contrary. We deal with power only."[18]

Thus, various forms of exaction have been devised as one response to the problems presented by economic concentration. Whether to differentiate between big and smaller business, and how to do so—these are questions which divide expert as well as lay opinion. It is not disrespectful for a lawyer to suggest that this is a realm of public finance in which the fog of doubt and confusion has not yet been wholly lifted by economists. That nevertheless this is a field into which the State may enter no one will deny. And yet there is no legal litmus to give ready answers when State action is challenged. Again the ultimate canons for constitutional construction must do service. The Constitution does not have preferences between competing theories, and the wide range of discretion which this leaves to the legislative judgment must not be curtailed by judicial intrusion, under the guise of abstract absolutes, into the domain of policy. By Cardozo these generalities were translated into living practice. For he viewed measures of social taxation with a shrewd eye for actuality undiverted by hypothesized unrealities:

> Statistics . . . indicate that there is a definite line of cleavage between chains that serve consumers within a single territorial unit and those framed for larger ends. The business that keeps at home affects the social organism in ways that differ widely from those typical of a business that goes out into the world. It affects the social organism, but also it affects itself. With the lengthening of the chain there are new fields to be exploited. The door is open to opportunities that have

18. Fox v. Standard Oil Co., 294 U.S. 87, 100–101 (1935).

hitherto been closed. Where does the local have an end and the non-local a beginning? The legislature had to draw the line somewhere, and it drew it with the county. Within the range of reasonable discretion its judgment must prevail.

... Lawmakers are not required to legislate with an eye to exceptional conditions. Their search is for probabilities and tendencies of general validity, and these being ascertained, they may frame their rule accordingly. They are not required to legislate with an eye to forms of growth beyond the limits of their own state. In laying a tax upon a Florida chain their concern is with those activities that have social and economic consequences for Florida and her people. The question for them, and so for us, is not how a business might be expected to develop if its forms and lines of growth were to be predicted in the abstract without reference to experience. The question is how it *does* develop in normal or average conditions, and the answer to that question is to be found in life and history.

... It will not do to shut one's eyes to the motive that has led so many legislatures to lay hold of this difference [between integrated and voluntary chains] and turn it into a basis for a new system of taxation. The system has had its origin in the belief that the social utility or inutility of one group is less or greater than that of others, and that the choice of subjects to be taxed should be adjusted to social gains and losses. Courts would be lacking in candor if they were not to concede the presence of such a motive behind this chain store legislation. But a purpose to bear more heavily on one class than another will not avail without more to condemn a tax as void ... We must know why the discrimination is desired, to what end it is directed and the relation between end and means. If the motive is vindictiveness, ensuing in mere oppression, the result may be one thing. If the motive and the end attained are the advancement of the public good, the result may be quite another, unless preference and repression go so far as to outrun the bounds of reason. The legislature

> has determined with the approval of the court that an integrated chain is a taxable class separable from independent dealers and even from chains that are merely cooperative leagues. If these differences suffice to establish a basis for distinction between a tax and none at all, smaller differences may suffice for the graduation of the scale. The legislature has found them in those variations of degree that separate a chain within the territorial unit of the locality from chains that are reaching out for wider fields of power. There is no need to approve or disapprove the concept of utility or inutility reflected in such laws . . . The concept may be right or wrong. At least it corresponds to an intelligible belief, and one widely prevalent today among honest men and women . . . With that our function ends.[19]

The bite of a tax case, as of a tax measure, is in its particular circumstances. Fair-sounding generalities too often shelter concrete evasions of them. And so, only detailed analysis of a tax like that involved in *Stewart Dry Goods Co.* v. *Lewis*[20]—its economic setting, its practical operations, and the hopes and fears that it expressed—could give an adequate critique of the meaning of the decision, of its relation to antecedent authorities, and of the clash of intellectual procedures which, from the same precedents and precepts, drew opposite conclusions. Cardozo's dissent in this case has such organic unity that one can hardly avoid mutilation in brief excerpts:

> The prevailing opinion commits the court to a holding that a tax upon gross sales, if laid upon a graduated basis, is always and inevitably a denial of the equal protection of the laws, no matter how slight the gradient or moderate the tax . . .
>
> The question then is whether there is rationality in the belief that capacity to pay increases, by and large, with an increase of receipts. Certain it is that merchants

19. Liggett Co. v. Lee, 288 U.S. 517, 581–586 (1933) (dissenting).
20. 294 U.S. 550 (1935).

have faith in such a correspondence and act upon that faith . . .

. . . Larger and larger sales are sought for by business and sought for with avidity. They are not the products of whim and fancy. They represent a conception of probabilities and tendencies confirmed by long experience. The conception is no more arbitrary in the brain of a government official than it is in the mind of a company director . . .

The framers of a system of taxation may properly give heed to convenience of administration, and in the search for that good may content themselves with rough and ready compromises. Elaborate machinery, designed to bring about a perfect equilibrium between benefit and burden, may at times defeat its aim through its own elaboration. A crippling result of the decision just announced will be to restrict the choice of means within bounds unreasonably narrow. Hereafter in the taxation of business a legislature will be confined, it seems, to an income or profit tax if it wishes to establish a graduated system proportioning burden to capacity. But profits themselves are not susceptible of ascertainment with certainty and precision except as the result of inquiries too minute to be practicable. The returns of the taxpayer call for an exercise of judgment as well as for a transcript of the figures on his books. They are subject to possible inaccuracies, almost without number. Salaries of superintendents, figuring as expenses, may have been swollen inordinately; appraisals of plant, of merchandise, of patents, of what not, may be erroneous or even fraudulent . . . These difficulties and dangers bear witness to the misfortune of forcing methods of taxation within a Procrustean formula. If the state discerns in business operations uniformities and averages that seem to point the way to a system easier to administer than one based upon a report of profits, and yet likely in the long run to work out approximate equality, it ought not to be denied the power to frame its laws accordingly.

> For answer to all this the thrust will not avail that "it is difficult to be just and easy to be arbitrary." The derogatory epithet assumes the point to be decided. There is nothing arbitrary in rescuing a vast body of taxpayers from the labor and expense of preparing elaborate reports, at best approximately accurate. There is nothing arbitrary in rescuing a government from the labor and expense of setting up the huge and unwieldy machinery of an income tax department with a swarm of investigators and accountants and legal and financial experts. To frame a system of taxation in avoidance of evils such as these is no act of sheer oppression, no abandonment of reason, no exercise of the general will in a perverse or vengeful spirit.[21]

A healthy society is as much dependent upon wise price policies as upon sound systems of taxation. But the puzzles of a proper price mechanism are perhaps even less amenable to unequivocal solutions than are ways for achieving appropriate fiscal measures. The operation of pricing schemes in the market is very different from what it appears to be in economic treatises. Not the least of these perplexities is the influence of governmental intervention in pricing. It is more than sixty years since the Supreme Court gave sanction to price regulation within the limited field of "public callings."[22] Yet even within this circumscribed field confusion and friction, with resulting waste, have been more prominent than agreement on procedure and criteria for fixing values and rates.[23] But in this area of government no less than in that of taxation, legislation cannot wait for accord among economists or general acceptance of their theories. Powerful economic forces produce problems which must be dealt with by legislators with whatever fallible and tentative wisdom they can utilize. The competing claims of consumers and producers, of large producers and small,

21. Id. at 566–577.
22. Munn v. Illinois, 94 U.S. 113 (1877); cf. dissent of Holmes, J., in Tyson & Bro. v. Banton, 273 U.S. 418, 445 (1927).
23. See Frankfurter, *The Public and Its Government* 81 (1930).

of large consumers and small, of producers and distributors, of distributors and consumers, press for adjustment. Fallible wisdom produces fallible legislation. To deny government the right to act except with omniscience and prescience is to deny it the right to act at all.

The right to act is evolving empirically and waveringly.[24] In dealing with these new exertions of governmental power, as where he concerned himself with novel methods of taxation, Cardozo found his bearings in loyal adherence to the classic doctrines for constitutional adjudication. He sharply differentiated the austere responsibility of a judge from the ample discretion of the legislator. He found no barriers to legislative recognition of differences among different industries or among different groups within the same industry; he found no warrant for any doctrine that afforded greater immunity to the price mechanisms of industry than to its other aspects.

That the requirement of due process raises no barrier to price fixing where "the conditions or practices of an industry" justify such a regulatory system was apparently established in *Nebbia's* case.[25] But two years later the provisions of the Guffey Act[26] foundered on the rock of inseparability against the protest of the Chief Justice and that of Brandeis, Stone, and Cardozo, JJ.[27] This impressive minority found the price controls separable from the rest of the act and as such within the doctrine of *Nebbia's* case. That a single decision, reached by a slender majority in a strongly contested field, does not guarantee security for a doctrine, is illustrated by the need which Cardozo felt to argue the legislative power of price fixing under circumstances like those presented by the record in the *Carter* case.

Referring to "the conditions and practices" found in *Nebbia's* case to justify price fixing in the New York milk industry, Cardozo proceeded:

24. See Frankfurter and Fisher, *supra* note 7, at 633–637.

25. Nebbia v. New York, 291 U.S. 502 (1934).

26. The Bituminous Coal Conservation Act of 1935, 49 Stat. 991.

27. Carter v. Carter Coal Co., 298 U.S. 238 (1936). The separate opinion of the Chief Justice appears at 317. Mr. Justice Cardozo spoke for Brandeis and Stone, JJ., as well as for himself, at 324.

All this may be said, and with equal, if not greater force, of the conditions and practices in the bituminous coal industry, not only at the enactment of this statute in August, 1935, but for many years before. Overproduction was at a point where free competition had been degraded into anarchy. Prices had been cut so low that profit had become impossible for all except the lucky handful. Wages came down along with prices and with profits. There were strikes, at times nation-wide in extent, at other times spreading over broad areas and many mines with the accompaniment of violence and bloodshed and misery and bitter feeling. The sordid tale is unfolded in many a document and treatise. During the twenty-three years between 1913 and 1935, there were nineteen investigations or hearings by Congress or by specially created commissions with reference to conditions in the coal mines. The hope of betterment was faint unless the industry could be subjected to the compulsion of a code. In the weeks immediately preceding the passage of this Act the country was threatened once more with a strike of ominous proportions. The plight of the industry was not merely a menace to owners and to mine workers: it was and had long been a menace to the public, deeply concerned in a steady and uniform supply of a fuel so vital to the national economy.

Congress was not condemned to inaction in the face of price wars and wage wars so pregnant with disaster. Commerce had been choked and burdened; its normal flow had been diverted from one state to another; there had been bankruptcy and waste and ruin alike for capital and for labor. The liberty protected by the Fifth Amendment does not include the right to persist in this anarchic riot . . . The free competition so often figured as a social good imports order and moderation and a decent regard for the welfare of the group . . . There is testimony in these records, testimony even by the assailants of the statute, that only through a system of regulated prices can the industry be stabilized and set upon the road of orderly and peaceful progress . . .

> After making every allowance for difference of opinion as to the most efficient cure, the student of the subject is confronted with the indisputable truth that there were ills to be corrected, and ills that had a direct relation to the maintenance of commerce among the states without friction or diversion. An evil existing, and also the power to correct it, the lawmakers were at liberty to use their own discretion in the selection of the means.[28]

Never was judicial utterance more felicitously chosen than when Marshall characterized the power of courts to sit in judgment upon legislatures as a "delicate" function. How fine the threads by which the Supreme Court weaves its share in the texture of government is beautifully illustrated by the series of cases in which the Court passed upon the New York Milk Control Act. In *Nebbia's* case, as we have seen, the Court over vigorous protest found no restraint in the federal Constitution against fixing the selling price of milk. In the same year the Court sustained an order under the New York statute, fixing a minimum price to be paid to producers as well as a minimum resale price, against the claim of a dealer that under this order he would be operating at a loss.[29] "The appellant's grievance amounts to this," wrote Mr. Justice Cardozo for the Court, "that it is operating at a loss, though other dealers more efficient or economical or better known to the public may be operating at a profit."[30] Little indulgence was given to such a grievance. "The Fourteenth Amendment does not protect a business against the hazards of competition." In *Borden's Co.* v. *Ten Eyck*[31] the Court, again dividing as it did in *Nebbia's* case, sustained a subordinate feature of the New York milk control system allowing a differential in the selling price of milk between dealers who had and dealers who did not have well-advertised trade names. The very same day a majority of the Court

28. 298 U.S. at 330–332.
29. Hegeman Farms Corp. v. Baldwin, 293 U.S. 163 (1934).
30. Id. at 170.
31. 297 U.S. 251 (1936).

declared invalid another provision of the New York act discriminating between milk dealers without well-advertised trade names who were in the business before April 10, 1933, and those in that class who entered it later.[32] Against this conclusion Brandeis, Stone, and Cardozo, JJ., entered dissent. How tenuous was the margin of difference between these cases is attested by the robust sentence opening Cardozo's dissenting opinion: "The judgment just announced is irreconcilable in principle with the judgment in *Borden*'s case, *ante*, p. 251, announced a minute or so earlier."[33]

The whole of Cardozo's closely-knit dissent in this case illustrates the treacherous appearance of law given to issues essentially of fact that come before the Court for judgment under the due process clauses. It also illustrates the rigor with which Cardozo pursued the Holmesian tradition of not allowing questions of degree, however close, to be elevated into constitutional principles:

> A minimum price for fluid milk was fixed by law in April, 1933. At that time, "independents" were underselling their competitors, the dealers in well-advertised brands, by approximately a cent a quart. There was reason to believe that unless that differential was preserved, they would be driven out of business. To give them an opportunity to survive, the lawmakers maintained the differential in the City of New York, the field of keenest competition. We have learned from the opinion in *Borden*'s case that this might lawfully be done.
>
> The problem was then forced upon the lawmakers, what were to be the privileges of independents who came upon the scene thereafter? . . .
>
> Hardships, great or little, were inevitable, whether the field of the differential was narrowed or enlarged. The legislature, and not the court, has been charged with the duty of determining their comparative extent. . . . In declaring the equities of newcomers to be not inferior to those of others, the judgment makes a choice

32. Mayflower Farms v. Ten Eyck, 297 U.S. 266 (1936).
33. Id. at 274.

> between competing considerations of policy and fairness, however emphatic its professions that it applies a rule of law.
>
> For the situation was one to tax the wisdom of the wisest. At the very least it was a situation where thoughtful and honest men might see their duty differently . . . It is juggling with words to say that all the independents make up a single "class," and by reason of that fact must be subjected to a single rule. Whether the class is divisible into subclasses is the very question to be answered. There may be division and subdivision unless separation can be found to be so void of rationality as to be the expression of a whim rather than an exercise of judgment . . . On this occasion, happily, the facts are not obscure. Big dealers and little ones, newcomers in the trade and veterans, were clamorously asserting to the legislature their title to its favor. I have not seen the judicial scales so delicately poised and so accurately graduated as to balance and record the subtleties of all these rival equities, and make them ponderable and legible beyond a reasonable doubt.
>
> To say that the statute is not void beyond a reasonable doubt is to say that it is valid.[34]

III

The ample scope which Cardozo thus gave to legislative discretion in devising policy did not make him indifferent to those procedural safeguards in the exercise of governmental powers which give historic basis to "due process."[35] Prices may be fixed and profits limited, certainly for the "public callings," but not without fair inquiry and an adequate canvass of the factors relevant to adjustment between private and public interests:

> The fundamentals of a trial were denied to the appellant when rates previously collected were ordered to be

34. Id. at 275–278.

35. Shattuck, "The True Meaning of the Term 'Liberty' in Those Clauses in the Federal and State Constitutions Which Protect 'Life, Liberty, and Property,'" 4 *Harv. L. Rev.* 365 (1891).

refunded upon the strength of evidential facts not spread upon the record.

> The Commission had given notice that the value of the property would be fixed as of a date certain . . . Without warning or even the hint of warning that the case would be considered or determined upon any other basis than the evidence submitted, the Commission cut down the values for the years after the date certain upon the strength of information secretly collected and never yet disclosed. The company protested. It asked disclosure of the documents indicative of price trends, and an opportunity to examine them, to analyze them, to explain and rebut them. The response was a curt refusal. Upon the strength of these unknown documents refunds have been ordered for sums mounting into millions, the Commission reporting its conclusion, but not the underlying proof. The putative debtor does not know the proofs today. This is not the fair hearing essential to due process. It is condemnation without trial.[36]

The accomplishments of half a century have won for the Interstate Commerce Commission a place in the Supreme Court's esteem not second to that accorded the lower federal courts. Mr. Justice Cardozo gave voice to that esteem:

> The structure of a rate schedule calls in peculiar measure for the use of that enlightened judgment which the Commission by training and experience is qualified to form . . . It is not the province of a court to absorb this function to itself . . . The judicial function is exhausted when there is found to be a rational basis for the conclusions approved by the administrative body. In this instance the care and patience with which the Commission fulfilled its appointed tasks are plain, even to the casual reader, upon the face of its report.[37]

36. Ohio Bell Tel. Co. v. Comm., 301 U.S. 292, 300 (1937).
37. Mississippi Valley Barge Co. v. United States, 292 U.S. 282, 286–287 (1934).

But the very complexity of the technical tasks entrusted to such a commission led to the requirement that it formulate the basis of its determinations. This is the justification for findings, that they serve to illumine and thereby to safeguard the Commission's own procedures. It was not in the spirit of Baron Parke that Cardozo spoke for the Court in vindicating the rationale of findings:

> We would not be understood as saying that there do not lurk in this report phrases or sentences suggestive of a different meaning. One gains at places the impression that the Commission looked upon the proposed reduction as something more than a disruptive tendency; that it found unfairness in the old relation of parity between Brazil and Springfield; and that the new schedule in its judgment would confirm Milwaukee in the enjoyment of an undue proportion of the traffic. The difficulty is that it has not said so with the simplicity and clearness through which a halting impression ripens into reasonable certitude. In the end we are left to spell out, to argue, to choose between conflicting interferences . . . We must know what a decision means before the duty becomes ours to say whether it is right or wrong.[38]

But insistence on procedural regularity was not, for Cardozo, an expression of inhospitality to the process behind the development of administrative law. Nor did he see administrative law as a collection of explicit rules uniformly applicable throughout the domain of what the British call "delegated legislation." Cardozo recognized that the broad concepts of hearing, findings, and judicial review summarized a variety of diversified situations in which the large aims expressed by these concepts were variously achieved:

> We are not unmindful of cases in which the word "hearing" as applied to administrative proceedings has been thought to have a broader meaning. All depends

38. United States v. Chicago, M., St. P. & P. R.R., 294 U.S. 499, 510–511 (1935).

> upon the context . . . The answer will not be found in definitions of a hearing lifted from their setting and then applied to new conditions. The answer will be found in a consideration of the ends to be achieved in the particular conditions that were expected or foreseen. To know what they are, there must be recourse to all the aids available as well as to the dictionary.[39]

Cardozo had, if not Maitland's genius, the latter's perception of the social forces that mold law.[40] He had, to be sure, an enormous fund of technical learning. But he escaped that dangerous narrowness of the mere legal pedant which has been the subject of classic animadversions by Burke[41] and Bagehot.[42] He did so by seeing law as part of our whole cultural history. Cardozo was not imprisoned by the tags and rags of learning, for he was guided by understanding of the circumstances summarized in historic clichés and by philosophic insight into their significance. Thus he never forgot that forms are related to functions; that court procedures not expressive of ultimate liberties are not necessarily norms of universal applicability; that practices of administration may have a momentum of rationality; and that activities of government which are not the immediate province of courts ought not to be circumscribed by formalities historically appropriate to courts.[43] He used his learning in technical law not as the standard for judgment of allowable development in new branches of the law, but as a fertile source for proving that old principles have creative energies for new situations.[44]

39. Norwegian Nitrogen Co. v. United States, 288 U.S. 294, 317 (1933) (dealing with procedure of the Tariff Commission under the Revenue Act of 1922).

40. Cf. Maitland, *Constitutional History of England* 415 et seq. (1913).

41. See "Letter to the Sheriffs of Bristol," 2 Burke, *Works* 196 et seq. (3d ed. 1869).

42. See Bagehot's portrait of Lord Eldon in "The First Edinburgh Reviewers," in 2 Barrington, *Works and Life of Walter Bagehot* 56 et seq. (1915).

43. United States v. Henry Prentiss & Co., 288 U.S. 73 (1933); Bemis Bro. Bag. Co. v. United States, 289 U.S. 28, (1933).

44. See Bemis Bro. Bag. Co. v. United States, 289 U.S. 28, 33 (1933).

Thus viewing administrative law, Cardozo eschewed unreal abstractions[45] and stuck close to the practicalities of government as revealed by history, by legislative ends and administrative responsibilities:

> The opinion of the court reminds us of the dangers that wait upon the abuse of power by officialdom unchained. The warning is so fraught with truth that it can never be untimely. But timely too is the reminder, as a host of impoverished investors would be ready to attest, that there are dangers in untruths and half truths when certificates masquerading as securities pass current in the market. There are dangers in spreading a belief that untruths and half truths, designed to be passed on for the guidance of confiding buyers, are to be ranked as peccadillos, or even perhaps as part of the amenities of business. When wrongs such as these have been committed or attempted, they must be dragged to light and pilloried. To permit an offending registrant to stifle an inquiry by precipitate retreat on the eve of his exposure is to give immunity to guilt; to encourage falsehood and evasion; to invite the cunning and unscrupulous to gamble with detection. If withdrawal without leave may check investigation before securities have been issued, it may do as much thereafter, unless indeed consistency be thrown to the winds, for by the teaching of the decision withdrawal without leave is equivalent to a stop order, with the result that forthwith there is nothing to investigate. The statute and its sanctions became the sport of clever knaves.
>
> Appeal is vaguely made to some constitutional immunity, whether express or implied is not stated with distinctness . . . If the immunity rests upon some express provision of the Constitution, the opinion of the court does not point us to the article or section. If its

45. "Abstraction, though necessary to thought, is liable to be the death of it. It lures the more guileless of its devotees into solemn futilities." R. H. Tawney, Book Review, 16 *The New Statesman and Nation* (N.S.) 880–882 (1938).

source is to be found in some impalpable essence, the spirit of the Constitution or the philosophy of government favored by the Fathers, one may take leave to deny that there is anything in that philosophy or spirit whereby the signer of a statement filed with a regulatory body to induce official action is protected against inquiry into his own purpose to deceive. The argument for immunity lays hold of strange analogies. A Commission which is without coercive powers, which cannot arrest or amerce or imprison though a crime has been uncovered, or even punish for contempt, but can only inquire and report, the propriety of every question in the course of the inquiry being subject to the supervision of the ordinary courts of justice, is likened with denunciatory fervor to the Star Chamber of the Stuarts. Historians may find hyperbole in the sanguinary simile.[46]

IV

In the domain of economic affairs, the penumbral region where law and policy blend, Cardozo walked humbly. But when those ethical precepts which are embodied in the Bill of Rights were invoked, he responded with all the certitude of one whose most constant companion was reason and whose life was rooted in the moral law. Unfortunately, the brevity of his tenure and the contingencies upon which the assignment of opinions depends gave him only limited opportunity in Washington to express with new vitality the claims of civilization expressed by constitutional protection to civil liberties. Doubtless his presence on the Court, particularly in these matters, made itself felt otherwise than through his own opinions. For, while the conferences in Washington could hardly have had for Cardozo the intimate camaraderie which so gladdened his days at Albany, the contagion of his ethical qualities must have affected the currents of his newer associations. To trace such influences upon the actions and opinions of others is, however, too elusive

46. Jones v. SEC, 298 U.S. 1, 32–33 (1936) (dissenting).

a pursuit for one outside the inner mysteries of the Court. We do not therefore have in his Supreme Court opinions such full-bodied expression of his philosophy of spiritual freedom as that which opportunities enabled Holmes to add to our permanent literature.[47] Happily, however, he wrote on the great theme of the freedom of the human mind in perduring language to which not even an opinion could have added intrinsic authority.

> Many an appeal to freedom is the masquerade of privilege or inequality seeking to intrench itself behind the catchword of a principle. There must be give and take at many points, allowance must be made for the play of the machine, or in the clash of jarring rivalries

47. Friendly critics have suggested that Cardozo viewed encroachments upon civil liberties with less deference to the legislative judgment than that which he accorded to economic measures. The same seeming inconsistency has been suggested against Holmes, and the answer made in Holmes's case applies to Cardozo as well:

"The Justice deferred so abundantly to legislative judgment on economic policy because he was profoundly aware of the extent to which social arrangements are conditioned by time and circumstances, and of how fragile, in scientific proof, is the ultimate validity of a particular economic adjustment. He knew that there was no authoritative fund of social wisdom to be drawn upon for answers to the perplexities which vast new material resources had brought. And so he was hesitant to oppose his own opinion to the economic views of the legislature. But history had also taught him that, since social development is a process of trial and error, the fullest possible opportunity for the free play of the human mind was an indispensable prerequisite. Since the history of civilization is in considerable measure the displacement of error which once held sway as official truth by beliefs which in turn have yielded to other truths, the liberty of man to search for truth was of a different order than some economic dogma defined as a sacred right because the temporal nature of its origin had been forgotten. And without freedom of expression, liberty of thought is a mockery. Nor can truth be pursued in an atmosphere hostile to the endeavor or under dangers which only heroes hazard.

"Naturally, therefore, Mr. Justice Holmes attributed very different legal significance to those liberties of the individual which history has attested as the indispensable conditions of a free society from that which he attached to liberties which derived merely from shifting economic arrangements . . . Because these civil liberties were explicitly safeguarded in the Constitution or conceived to be basic to any notion of the liberty guaranteed by the Fourteenth Amendment, Mr. Justice Holmes was far more ready to find legislative invasion in this field than in the area of debatable economic reform." Frankfurter, *Mr. Justice Holmes and the Supreme Court* 50–51 (1938).

> the pretending absolutes will destroy themselves and ordered freedom too. Only in one field is compromise to be excluded, or kept within the narrowest limits. There shall be no compromise of the freedom to think one's thoughts and speak them, except at those extreme borders where thought merges into action. There is to be no compromise here, for thought freely communicated, if I may borrow my own words, is the indispensable condition of intelligent experimentation, the one test of its validity. There is no freedom without choice, and there is no choice without knowledge—or none that is not illusory. Here are goods to be conserved, however great the seeming sacrifice. We may not squander the thought that will be the inheritance of the ages.[48]

In at least one case—the last opinion he delivered in person—he had to consider judicially the scope of the civil liberties protected by the Constitution. He did so in order to discover a "unifying principle," if possible, in those cases in which the Bill of Rights or its embodiment in the Fourteenth Amendment had been invoked. It is a superb example of his strict adherence to the common-law tradition—especially important in constitutional controversies—of dealing with the concrete case, but dealing with it not in the shallow belief that a case is a discrete phenomenon having neither genealogy nor offspring, but in the vivid awareness that the specific inevitably implicates principles and premises:

> The exclusion of these immunities and privileges [in cases cited] from the privileges and immunities protected against the action of the states has not been arbitrary or casual. It has been dictated by a study and appreciation of the meaning, the essential implications, of liberty itself.
>
> We reach a different plane of social and moral values when we pass to the privileges and immunities that have been taken over from the earlier articles of the federal bill of rights and brought within the Fourteenth

48. Cardozo, "Mr. Justice Holmes," 44 *Harv. L. Rev.* 682, 687–688 (1931).

> Amendment by a process of absorption. These in their origin were effective against the federal government alone. If the Fourteenth Amendment has absorbed them, the process of absorption has had its source in the belief that neither liberty nor justice would exist if they were sacrificed . . . This is true, for illustration, of freedom of thought, and speech. Of that freedom one may say that it is the matrix, the indispensable condition, of nearly every other form of freedom. With rare aberrations a pervasive recognition of that truth can be traced in our history, political and legal. So it has come about that the domain of liberty, withdrawn by the Fourteenth Amendment from encroachment by the states, has been enlarged by latter-day judgments to include liberty of the mind as well as liberty of action. The extension became, indeed, a logical imperative when once it was recognized, as long ago it was, that liberty is something more than exemption from physical restraint, and that even in the field of substantive rights and duties the legislative judgment, if oppressive and arbitrary, may be overriden by the courts.[49]

Human interests of such dignity he would not imprison in the subtle meshes of procedural technicality. He was alert against the dangers of concessions in principle but attritions in practice. "A system of procedure is perverted from its proper function when it multiplies impediments to justice without the warrant of clear necessity."[50] Thus he wrote in a little case between man and man. Naturally, therefore, this master of procedure refused to be hobbled by the Court's contrivances for the orderly presentation of appeals, when a vital issue of freedom of speech appeared from the record as clearly and as opportunely as the strange circumstances of the *Herndon* case[51] permitted. Again, no one knew better than he the rational

49. Palko v. Connecticut, 302 U.S. 319, 326–327 (1937).
50. Reed v. Allen, 286 U.S. 191, 209 (1932) (dissenting).
51. "I hold the view that the protection of the Constitution was seasonably invoked and that the court should proceed to an adjudication of the merits. Where the merits lie I do not now consider, for in the view of the majority the merits are irrelevant. My protest is confined to the disclaimer of jurisdiction . . .

limits of our system of evidence, but he also knew the reaches of its utility in protecting life from human caprice and fallibility. Consequently he was alert against the risks of over-refinement in rules to be amplified by the men and women who sit in the jury-box, particularly when life is in the balance.[52]

Civil liberties were for Cardozo not empty slogans but cherished protections of the human spirit. They derived meaning from history and were given pertinence by contemporary society. He was, however, too steeped in the history of the law not to detect quickly meretricious uses of history. By seeing decisions like that in *Bushell's* case in their setting, he adhered to a principle without distorting it to alien purposes.[53] And so he never rested on a for-

---

"What was brought into the case on the motion of rehearing was a standard wholly novel, the expectancy of life to be ascribed to the persuasive power of an idea. The defendant had no opportunity in the state court to prepare his argument accordingly. He had no opportunity to argue from the record that guilt was not a reasonable inference or one permitted by the Constitution, on the basis of that test any more than on the basis of others discarded as unfitting . . . The argument thus shut out is submitted to us now. Will men 'judging in calmness' . . . say of the defendant's conduct as shown forth in the pages of this record that it was an attempt to stir up revolution through the power of his persuasion and within the time when that persuasion might be expected to endure? If men so judging will say yes, will the Constitution of the United States uphold a reading of the statute that will lead to that response? Those are the questions that the defendant lays before us after conviction of a crime punishable by death in the discretion of the jury. I think he should receive an answer." Herndon v. Georgia, 295 U.S. 441, 447, 454–455 (1935) (dissenting).

52. "Discrimination so subtle is a feat beyond the compass of ordinary minds. The reverberating clang of those accusatory words would drown all weaker sounds. It is for ordinary minds, and not for psychoanalysts, that our rules of evidence are framed. They have their source very often in considerations of administrative convenience, of practical expediency, and not in rules of logic. When the risk of confusion is so great as to upset the balance of advantage, the evidence goes out." Shepard v. United States, 290 U.S. 96, 104 (1933).

53. "Nothing in our decision impairs the authority of *Bushell's* case, Vaughan 135, 1670, with its historic vindication of the privilege of jurors to return a verdict freely according to their conscience . . . *Bushell's* case was born of the fear of the Star Chamber and of the tyranny of the Stuarts . . . It stands for a great principle, which is not to be whittled down or sacrificed. On the other hand it is not to be strained and distorted into fanciful extensions. There is a peril of corruption in these days which is surely no less than the peril of coercion." Clark v. United States, 289 U.S. 1, 16–17 (1933).

mula, even one that embodied the most precious victory of reason. Had Cardozo ever been called upon to vindicate the security which the Constitution guarantees to "the free exercise" of religion, he doubtless would have done so in majestic utterance. But when immunity from compulsory instruction in military science in a state university sought the shelter of religious liberty, he rejected the claim sympathetically but robustly:

> The petitioners have not been required to bear arms for any hostile purpose, offensive or defensive, either now or in the future. They have not even been required in any absolute or peremptory way to join in courses of instruction that will fit them to bear arms. If they elect to resort to an institution for higher education maintained with the state's moneys, then and only then they are commanded to follow courses of instruction believed by the state to be vital to its welfare. This may be condemned by some as unwise or illiberal or unfair when there is violence to conscientious scruples, either religious or merely ethical. More must be shown to set the ordinance at naught . . . Instruction in military science is not instruction in the practice or tenets of a religion. Neither directly nor indirectly is government establishing a state religion when it insists upon such training. Instruction in military science, unaccompanied here by any pledge of military service, is not an interference by the state with the free exercise of religion when the liberties of the constitution are read in the light of a century and a half of history during days of peace and war.[54]

V

The constitutional history of our federal system as disclosed in Supreme Court decisions is in no small measure the still unwritten story of the rhythm of emphasis now upon national power, now upon State power. But no period of the Court's life contained such extreme fluctuations of rhythm within so short a span as the less than six Terms during which Cardozo sat.

54. Hamilton v. Regents, 293 U.S. 245, 265–266 (1934) (concurring).

Certainly constitutional dialectic has never been employed to more self-defeating ends than when a narrow majority of the Court invoked State sovereignty against the Municipal Bankruptcy Act as a means of destroying the State's freedom of action. Such a doctrine of impotence, Cardozo protested, was consonant neither with reason nor with the whole "evolutionary process" of our constitutional law:

> The question is not here whether the statute would be valid if it made provision for involuntary bankruptcy, dispensing with the consent of the state and with that of the bankrupt subdivision. For present purposes one may assume that there would be in such conditions a dislocation of that balance between the powers of the states and the powers of the central government which is essential to our federal system . . . The statute now in question does not dislocate the balance. It has been framed with sedulous regard to the structure of the federal system. The governmental units of the state may not act under this statute except through the medium of a voluntary petition which will evince their own consent, their own submission to the judicial power. Even that however is not enough . . . To cap the protective structure, Texas has a statute whereby all municipalities, political subdivisions and taxing districts in the state are empowered to proceed under the challenged Act of Congress, and to do anything appropriate to take advantage of its provisions . . . To hold that this purpose [relief for distressed municipalities] must be thwarted by the courts because of a supposed affront to the dignity of a state, though the state disclaims the affront and is doing all it can to keep the law alive, is to make dignity a doubtful blessing.[55]

This conception of the federal system became the law of the land within two years, for the dissenters in *United States* v. *Bekins*[56] were surely justified in their opinion,

55. Ashton v. Cameron County Dist., 298 U.S. 513, 538–539, 541 (1936).

56. 304 U.S. 27, 54 (1938).

"that the principle approved in *Ashton* v. *Cameron County District*" was controlling in the *Bekins* case if that principle had vitality.

Within a year after the *Ashton* case protected the States from federal collaboration which they sought, Mr. Justice Cardozo was permitted to speak for a majority of the Court in sustaining one of the most ramifying exertions of federal power. For a hundred years the implications of the general welfare clause were debated by publicists and statesmen. The Supreme Court, with wise abstention, avoided this thorny conflict. Excepting only the creative interpretations of Marshall whereby great national powers were breathed into the inert words of the Constitution, probably no other adjudications of the Court initiated such far-reaching recognition of federal authority as that which was given in the Social Security cases.[57] From such powerful and luminous opinions as those which Cardozo rendered there, the choice of short excerpts becomes an invidious necessity:

> Congress may spend money in aid of the "general welfare" . . . The conception of the spending power advocated by Hamilton and strongly reinforced by Story has prevailed over that of Madison, which has not been lacking in adherents. Yet difficulties are left when the power is conceded. The line must still be drawn between one welfare and another, between particular and general. Where this shall be placed cannot be known through a formula in advance of the event. There is a middle ground, or certainly a penumbra in which discretion is at large. The discretion, however, is not confided to the courts. The discretion belongs to Congress, unless the choice is clearly wrong, a display of arbitrary power, not an exercise of judgment . . . Nor is the concept of the general welfare static. Needs that were narrow or parochial a century ago may be interwoven in our day with the well-being of the Nation. What is critical or urgent changes with the times.

57. Steward Machine Co. v. Davis, 301 U.S. 548 (1937); Helvering v. Davis, 301 U.S. 619 (1937).

> The purge of nation-wide calamity that began in 1929 has taught us many lessons. Not the least is the solidarity of interests that may once have seemed to be divided. Unemployment spreads from State to State, the hinterland now settled that in pioneer days gave an avenue of escape . . .
>
> The problem is plainly national in area and dimensions. Moreover, laws of the separate states cannot deal with it effectively. Congress, at least, had a basis for that belief . . . Only a power that is national can serve the interests of all.
>
> Whether wisdom or unwisdom resides in the scheme of benefits set forth in Title II, it is not for us to say. The answer to such inquiries must come from Congress, not the courts. Our concern here, as often, is with power, not with wisdom. Counsel for respondent has recalled to us the virtues of self-reliance and frugality. There is a possibility, he says, that aid from a paternal government may sap those sturdy virtues and breed a race of weaklings. If Massachusetts so believes and shapes her laws in that conviction, must her breed of sons be changed, he asks, because some other philosophy of government finds favor in the halls of Congress. But the answer is not doubtful. One might ask with equal reason whether the system of protective tariffs is to be set aside at will in one state or another whenever local policy prefers the rule of *laissez faire*. The issue is a closed one. It was fought out long ago. When money is spent to promote the general welfare, the concept of welfare or the opposite is shaped by Congress, not the states. So the concept be not arbitrary, the locality must yield.[58]

Cardozo did not deem it necessary to reconcile these cases with the *Butler* case,[59] decided fourteen months earlier, and this is not the place to make the attempt.

In these phases of our federal system Cardozo dealt with relatively novel issues which gave full play to his

58. 301 U.S. at 640–641, 644–645.
59. United States v. Butler, 297 U.S. 1 (1936).

learning, imagination and serene devotion to the ultimate but narrowly confined function of the Court in assessing the validity of legislation. He left his special mark in every case he wrote, but when dealing with the commerce clause he wrote upon a heavily encrusted palimpsest. In view of the illumination which the Chief Justice has shed upon the organic relation of modern industry in his opinions in the *Labor Board Cases*,[60] the earlier exposition by Cardozo of the ramifications of modern industry has become part of the established corpus of the law of the commerce clause:

> To regulate the price for such transactions is to regulate commerce itself, and not alone its antecedent conditions or its ultimate consequences. The very act of sale is limited and governed. Prices in interstate transactions may not be regulated by the states . . . They must therefore be subject to the power of the nation unless they are to be withdrawn altogether from governmental supervision . . .
>
> Regulation of prices being an exercise of the commerce power . . . the question remains whether it comes within that power as applied to intrastate sales where interstate prices are directly or intimately affected . . . Sometimes it is said that the relation must be "direct" to bring that power into play . . . At times, . . . the waves of causation will have radiated so far that their undulatory motion, if discernable at all, will be too faint or obscure, too broken by cross-currents, to be heeded by the law. In such circumstances the holding is not directed at prices or wages considered in the abstract, but at prices or wages in particular conditions . . . Always the setting of the facts is to be viewed if one would know the closeness of the tie . . . The power is as broad as the need that evokes it.[61]

60. NLRB v. Jones & Laughlin Steel Corp., 301 U.S. 1 (1937); NLRB v. Fruehauf Trailer Co., id. at 49; NLRB v. Friedman-Harry Marks Clothing Co., id. at 58; Associated Press v. NLRB, id. at 103; and Washington, Va. & Md. Coach Co. v. NLRB, id. at 142.

61. Carter v. Carter Coal Co., 298 U.S. 238, 324, 326–328 (1936) (dissenting). Cf. Mr. Justice Cardozo's concurring opinion in Schechter Poultry Corp. v. United States, 295 U.S. 495, 551, 554 (1935), where similar views were expressed less explicitly.

If he seemed to throw his weight to the side of national power it was not because of any strong doctrinaire beliefs or political preferences. Thus he decided against New York in one aspect of its milk control legislation, doubtless with special sympathy for the difficulties which confronted the State, because he could not escape the conviction that New York was in effect erecting a barrier where the commerce clause enjoined free trade:

> What is ultimate is the principle that one state in its dealings with another may not place itself in a position of economic isolation. Formulas and catchwords are subordinate to this overmastering requirement. Neither the power to tax nor the police power may be used by the state of destination with the aim and effect of establishing an economic barrier against competition with the products of another state or the labor of its residents. Restrictions so contrived are an unreasonable clog upon the mobility of commerce. They set up what is equivalent to a rampart of customs duties designed to neutralize advantages belonging to the place of origin . . . The form of the packages in such circumstances is immaterial, whether they are original or broken. The importer must be free from imposts framed for the very purpose of suppressing competition from without and leading inescapably to the suppression so intended.[62]

These were not matters that closely touched his private intellectual interests. He decided as he decided and wrote what he wrote because the judicial function as he conceived it and so candidly set forth in his philosophic writings compelled his votes and indicated the direction of his opinions.

62. Baldwin v. Seelig, 294 U.S. 511, 527 (1935) (holding unconstitutional, as a burden on interstate commerce, that portion of the New York Milk Control Act prohibiting the sale of milk imported from another State if the price paid to the producer in the other State was less than the minimum price prescribed by New York for purchases from New York producers). Cf. Mr. Justice Cardozo's opinion in Henneford v. Silas Mason Co., 300 U.S. 577 (1937), upholding the Washington compensating use tax.

To adapt a favorite quotation of his, these extracts are but little fragments of the golden fleece that Cardozo has left upon the hedges of his judicial life. But even the fullest reading of his opinions merely gives intimations of his depth of thought and beauty of character. The permanent influence of this great judge was achieved only partially by his own writings, for the current of his culture permeated in ways more subtle than even his opinions can express. Perhaps his qualities are best defined by saying that Cardozo completely satisfied the requirements of a judge wholly adequate for the Supreme Bench.

> I venture to believe that it is as important to a judge called upon to pass on a question of constitutional law, to have at least a bowing acquaintance with Acton and Maitland, with Thucydides, Gibbon and Caryle, with Homer, Dante, Shakespeare and Milton, with Machiavelli, Montaigne and Rabelais, with Plato, Bacon, Hume and Kant, as with the books which have been specifically written on the subject. For in such matters everything turns upon the spirit in which he approaches the questions before him. The words he must construe are empty vessels into which he can pour nearly anything he will. Men do not gather figs of thistles, nor supple institutions from judges whose outlook is limited by parish or class. They must be aware that there are before them more than verbal problems; more than final solutions cast in generalizations of universal applicability. They must be aware of the changing social tensions in every society which make it an organism; which demand new schemata of adaptation; which will disrupt it, if rigidly confined.[63]

63. Hand, "Sources of Tolerance," 79 *U. of Pa. L. Rev.* 1, 12 (1930).

Chief Justice Stone

It was characteristic of Harlan Stone's zest for life that he made no preparations for death. And the circumstances of his death were characteristic of his good fortune. There was no tapering off; rather was he interrupted in labor which engaged the whole of him and just after he had pronounced the principle which should be the pole star of the Supreme Court as he understood its place in our scheme. "It is not the function of this Court to disregard the will of Congress in the exercise of its constitutional power"[1]—such was the message he uttered from the seat of the Chief Justiceship at the very moment that death summoned him on April 22, 1946.

One may be preoccupied with law professionally in five different ways, as teacher, practitioner, administrator, judge, and philosopher. No one can pursue all these callings at the same time and the name does not readily occur of anyone who has done so in due succession if philosophy of law implies dwelling on the high plateau of original thought worthy of the company of thinkers like Holmes. But Stone followed all the other four callings and in each he achieved the acclaim of his professional compeers.

Little imagination is needed to clothe the bare facts of his life with the meaning and significance of his career. Harlan Fiske Stone, the second child of Frederick L. and Anne Sophia (Butler) Stone, was born on October 11, 1872, in Chesterfield, New Hampshire, one of those very small towns of New England with a shrinking population. He was of English stock, but, while professionally he was rooted in English legal traditions, in him, as in many a Yankee, a critical attitude of British policy could easily assert itself. During his childhood the Stone family moved to Amherst, Massachusetts, where the future Chief Justice attended the district school and Amherst High School. Harlan was destined by his father to become

Reprinted from the biographical memoir in the 1946 *Year Book of the American Philosophical Society*, with permission.

1. Girouard v. United States, 328 U.S. 61, 79 (1946). [Ed.]

a scientific farmer and to that end entered the Massachusetts Agricultural College in 1889. The inscrutable fates evidently had purposes of their own. Harlan's student days at that college, and thereby his paternal predestination as a farmer, were quickly terminated by a row in which blows were said to have been exchanged between the sturdy freshman and a member of the faculty. Harlan went back to the ancestral farm until he entered Amherst the next fall. His college career gave promise of all that followed. Under a strong faculty and in rivalry with contemporaries who subsequently became notable in affairs as well as in the world of scholarship, Harlan was an outstanding man of his time at Amherst, attaining distinction both in the classroom and on the gridiron. On graduation in 1894, he followed a familiar American pattern by teaching for a year at the Newburyport, Massachusetts, High School. He taught science, for which he had a bent that happily stood him in good stead when as a judge he had to decide patent law cases. But science as a dominant strain emerged not in him but in his son, Marshall, a distinguished mathematician.

Harlan's drive was for law. He received this training at the Columbia Law School from men of eminence as scholars and teachers. A year after he was graduated, he returned as a part-time lecturer while he quickly made his way at the bar. From 1905 to 1910, he devoted himself exclusively to practice with his firm, Satterlee, Canfield, & Stone. In 1910 he accepted the call to head his law school. Throughout his deanship, he taught two of the basic courses in the training of lawyers, equity and trusts. These specialities were likewise reflected in his judicial work, for they are aspects of law bringing into play, perhaps more than others, ethical principles and their resourceful adaptation to changing circumstances. Only a man endowed with Stone's great vitality and his disciplined powers of concentration could have successfully led a great law school and at the same time met the demands of a large practice. Whether because the burden finally became too heavy even for him or the allurements of practice, particularly of advocacy, too great, he resigned from Columbia in 1923 to become a member of Sullivan & Cromwell.

Again the fates willed otherwise. Attorney General Harry M. Daugherty's malodorous administration of the Department of Justice had so shocked the public conscience that when he was finally retired, that other Yankee, President Calvin Coolidge, saw clearly enough that the imperative need of the situation was an appointment that would at once restore public confidence in the integrity of the Department of Justice. And so, on April 7, 1924, President Coolidge appointed his Amherst college mate Harlan F. Stone. Thereby, the public disquietude was lifted. This restoration of confidence in the country's ministry of justice was Stone's dominant contribution as attorney general. He was there too short a time for much else. Within a year a vacancy on the Supreme Court fell in, through the retirement of Mr. Justice McKenna. On January 5, 1925, President Coolidge nominated Harlan Fiske Stone to fill the place left vacant, and he took his seat on the Supreme Bench on March 2, 1925. Because of professional association between Stone and a son-in-law of the elder Morgan there was opposition to his confirmation in the Senate, led by Senator George W. Norris. This is worth noting because of its sequel. When, upon the retirement of Chief Justice Hughes in 1941, Mr. Justice Stone was nominated by President Roosevelt to be Chief Justice, he was promptly confirmed and Senator Norris in the handsomest way recanted his opposition of 1925. This episode in the too uncommon chapter of candor in American politics did credit alike to Senator Norris and Mr. Justice Stone.

Stone's career divides into two major epochs: for twenty years he was a teacher, for twenty years he was a judge. For him these were not disparate callings. One was the logical fruition of the other. His academic career deeply infused his judicial work. As teacher he was concerned with the place of law and lawyers in society. As a judge he made heavy drafts upon the intellectual capital he had laid up in his own career as an academician, and he continued to draw freely upon the common property of scholarship.

As academician he helped to promote the movement of the study of law, primarily not as occupational training but as a branch of the social sciences. He recognized that a shift in economic and social forces demanded a corresponding shift in the training and the functions of the bar. The history and the technique of law were related to its social purposes and its study required to be pursued by application to working hypotheses, constantly subjected to re-examination, of those standards of accuracy and thoroughness which are the essentials of the scientific method. He was hospitable to new ideas, responsive to critical reconsideration of methods of teaching and student examination as well as of the validity of particular institutions for contemporary needs, no matter what historical title deeds they might have.[2] There are ample reflections in his opinions of his regard for learning as the path to understanding and as indispensable to wise adjudication.

While recognizing necessary adaptations to changes in economic fact, he insisted, in his utterances, on the perdurance of the conditions essential for a free society, no matter how much direction or control comes increasingly from the center. Indeed, because of the almost inevitable extension and concentration of governmental authority, those conditions become more and not less necessary. He believed in freedom of utterance to the extent that he was ready to face the hazards of thought, even of murky or reckless thought.

His years on the Court, interestingly enough, made him feel more rather than less the importance of the law teacher in the circumstances of our time. Partly because of the influence of specialization and undue identification with interests of clients that are less than those of society,

2. See "The Public Influence of the Bar," 48 *Harv. L. Rev.* 1 (1934); "The Common Law in the United States," 50 *Harv. L. Rev.* 4 (1936). These two papers are the ones, perhaps, by which he would most want to be judged.

active practitioners have not the opportunity nor do they form the habit of seeing law as a historic process, or of helping to fashion it as a fair social instrument. The law teachers are set apart, as it were, for these services to law. Indeed, the life of a law teacher was probably the most congenial to him, if one is to judge from his memorial writings of colleagues in teaching. Almost invariably he speaks of "the durable satisfactions" of a law teacher's life.

His experience on the Court had an expanding influence on his mind, partly because of the intimacy that it gave him with Holmes and Brandeis, and, for too few years, with Cardozo, but partly no less because the nature of the issues that come before the Supreme Tribunal made him plow deeper into his own mind than the demands of his life in New York had permitted. It made him realize not merely how profoundly right Holmes was in insisting that we need more theory and not less, but that no judge is fit for his task, certainly on the highest court, unless he be truly cultivated. Stone had always had an interest in the arts. He had visited the best of the European museums and he took full advantage of the opportunities that Washington afforded. When as Chief Justice he became ex officio chairman of the Board of Trustees of the National Gallery of Art and chancellor of the Smithsonian Institution, and, as a distinguished son of Amherst, chairman of the Folger Shakespeare Library, he brought zeal to these offices and drew enrichment from them.

During his twenty years on the Court, Stone wrote either for the Court or in dissent some five hundred opinions. This constitutes a comprehensive body of views on the major legal issues of our time. What is no less important, perhaps even more important, such a body of opinions inevitably discloses the author's philosophy regarding a judge's function in our society, whether explicitly avowed or to be read between the lines. To these opinions, spread through sixty-one volumes of the Reports (268–328 U.S.), the curious and the learned alike must be referred.

Stone was totally devoid of side, instinctively friendly alike with his colleagues, with his law clerks, and with the world at large. He was a great believer in dispatching promptly the business of the Court, knowing that justice unduly delayed is justice denied. He sought to maintain the standards set by his predecessors, particularly those of the Chief Justice whom he succeeded. It was his endeavor to dispose of the business of the Court with all deliberate speed, but only after the freest discussion by every Justice preceding decision and with due regard for the deliberative process of opinion writing.

As is true in every calling, men vary greatly in the temperaments they bring to judging. Some decide without great inner turmoil and others suffer anguish in the process. Some are serene once the inner debate is concluded; with some the throes of conflict linger long and are easily revived. Some are painfully slow workers, trace and retrace their steps; others swiftly strike at the jugular of a case and are done. Stone's writing is deceptive. It does not give the impression of fluency. He was a quick writer. He was not, however, a quick decider. His was not the temperament that decided without much inner contest, or even rested securely after decending from the fence. A friendly wag of a colleague at Columbia once introduced him at a law school function as a person who turned neither to partiality on the one hand, nor to impartiality on the other.

He had his share in the "historic shift of emphasis in constitutional interpretation" which, he said, marked the magistracy of Chief Justice Hughes. But the shift had been made by the time he became Chief Justice. His work as such must be left for the judgment of the scholars of the future. Certainly it cannot now be attempted by one who served with him. Suffice it to say, he came to the great succession qualified by a national outlook, nor the worse, for having been rooted in New England, by an extraordinary diversified professional experience, and with full appreciation of the demands that the business of the Court makes on legal learning.

He had a strong historic sense and naturally enough was concerned with his place in history. Chief Justices of the United States are rarer than Presidents. A Chief Justice cannot escape history.

The "Administrative Side" of Chief Justice Hughes

It is often said of a contemporary figure destined for historical survival that it is too early to pass judgment on his work. The assumption is that the future will pass a definitive judgment. But there never is a definitive appraisal. Each generation places its own valuations; reputations grow and recede, only to grow again and recede. Even majestic figures—Shakespeare and Washington—have fluctuating recognition. No doubt the future attenuates merely personal bias, but it gives no assurance of freedom from partisanship. In any event, contemporary judgment may contribute the impact of vividness and immediacy, which only the most imaginative artist can later create. The limitations of contemporary judgment derive not so much from its closeness to the subject; they are due to the fragmentary materials on which judgment is based. Though history cannot be written solely out of documents, it cannot be written without relevant but as yet inaccessible documents.

This is peculiarly true of the appraisal of contributions made by members of the Supreme Court to the stream of thought which courses through its decisions. The Court's opinions often disclose merely the surface of the judicial process. The compromises that an opinion may embody, the collaborative effort that it may represent, the inarticulate considerations that may have influenced the grounds on which the case went off, the shifts in position that may precede final adjudication—these and like factors cannot, contemporaneously at all events, be brought to the surface.

It is true of opinions as of other compositions that those who are steeped in them, whose ears are sensitive to literary nuances, whose antennae record subtle silences, can gather from their contents meaning beyond the words. All this presupposes, of course, a grasp of the nature of the Supreme Court's functions—the scope and limits of its

Reprinted from 63 *Harv. L. Rev.* 1 (1949), an issue honoring the memory of the late Chief Justice.

constitutional authority—and often, as well, familiarity with the record and briefs of a particular case whose opinion is under scrutiny. Even the most professionally equipped critic possessed of the faculties of a creative artist would be severely handicapped, however, in attempting a balanced estimate of the work of a Chief Justice of the United States if he were restricted to what is found in the *United States Reports*. And no fellow member of the Court may contemporaneously add to what those *Reports* tell.

But he may speak of the Chief Justice as head of the Court. Even of that not all can be told contemporaneously. The relations of a Chief Justice with his colleagues and with the officials of the Court affect the conduct of the Court's business. The influence of a tough-minded Chief Justice in encouraging, if not prodding, a temperamentally indecisive judge to make up his mind may have important consequences in the development of our law. But these are matters that call for exact knowledge that can only become available, if at all, when disclosure is justifiable. Such exact knowledge cannot be conveyed through the distorting and often falsifying medium of surmise and gossip.

For me the qualities of Charles Evans Hughes, as Chief Justice, are conveyed strikingly by Mr. Justice Holmes in speaking of Chief Justice Fuller:

> Of course the function of the Chief Justice differs from that of the other judges only on the administrative side, but on that I think he was extraordinary. He had the business of the Court at his fingers' ends, he was perfectly courageous, prompt, decided. He turned off the matters that daily called for action easily, swiftly, with the least possible friction, with inestimable good humor and with a humor that relieved any tension with a laugh.[1]

Chief Justice Hughes brought to this "administrative side" uncommon powers of concentration, wide relevant

1. King, *Melville Weston Fuller* 334–335 (1950). [Ed.]

experience, a high sense of responsibility, complete absorption in the work of the Court, fidelity to its best traditions not as worship of the past but as a stimulus toward promoting the most fruitful administration of justice.

He knew that the manner of conducting the business of the Court affects the matter. This realization guided him in the watchful exercise of the power the Congress has vested in the Court to control its business. He tried to avoid a swollen docket which precludes the brooding process indispensable for wise adjudication. In Court and in conference he struck the pitch, as it were, for the orchestra. He guided discussion by opening up the lines for it to travel, focusing on essentials, evoking candid exchange on subtle and complex issues, and avoiding redundant talk. He never checked free debate, but the atmosphere which he created, the moral authority which he exerted, inhibited irrelevance, repetition, and fruitless discussion. He was a master of timing: he knew when discussion should be deferred and when brought to an issue. He also showed uncommon resourcefulness in drawing elements of agreement out of differences and thereby narrowing, if not always escaping, conflicts. He knew when a case was over; he had no lingering afterthoughts born of a feeling of defeat, and thereby avoided the fostering of cleavages. Intellectual issues were dealt with by him as such. As a result, differences in opinion did not arouse personal sensitiveness. Partly a disciplined mind, partly long experience at the bar, made him treat a case that was over as over, whether victory or defeat fell to his views. This capacity for detachment also reflected his keen sense of humor, which it often pleased him to conceal; partly such detachment must be ascribed to great conservation of energy that saved him from crying over spilt milk.

Perhaps no aspect of the "administrative side" that is vested in the Chief Justice is more important than the duty to assign the writing of the Court's opinion. In its discharge, Chief Justice Hughes was like a general deploying his army. His governing consideration was what was best for the Court as to the particular case in the particular situation. That meant disregard of self but not of the importance of the Chief Justiceship as a symbol. For there are occasions when an opinion should carry the extra weight which pronouncement by the Chief Justice gives. Selection of the Court's voice also calls for resourcefulness, so that the Court should not be denied the persuasiveness of a particular Justice, though himself procedurally in dissent, in speaking for the Court on the merits.[2] The grounds for assignment may not always be obvious to the outsider. Indeed, they are not always so to the members of the Court; the reasons normally remain within the breast of the Chief Justice. But these involve, if the duty is wisely discharged, perhaps the most delicate judgment demanded of the Chief Justice.

Chief Justice Hughes was an administrator of distinction: he brought things to pass effectively and without friction. But while he gave creative guidance to the Conference of Senior Circuit Judges and the Administrative Office of the United States Courts in making the federal judiciary more responsive to the tasks of a civilized legal system, he avoided the temptations of a strong executive. He realized fully that elaboration of administrative machinery is deadening to the judicial process, that the individual excellence of the judges, not paper efficiency, matters most.

By the very nature of the functions of the Supreme Court, each member of it is subject only to his own sense of the trusteeship of what are perhaps the most revered traditions in our national system. In such a brotherhood, the ultimate undefinable test of leadership is intrinsic authority. No one who served with him is likely to gainsay that Chief Justice Hughes possessed that quality to a conspicuous degree. In open court he exerted authority by the artistic mastery with which he presided. He radiated authority in the conference room. He did not rely upon his position, he fulfilled it. The Supreme Court is a student's life and Chief Justice Hughes could tear the heart out of books because all his life he had been a student. He was

2. See Mr. Justice Cardozo's opinion in Helvering v. Davis, 301 U.S. 619, 639–640 (1937).

also uncomprising with the Court's austere demands. He knew that these austerities promote dignity, that dignity makes for an atmosphere of respect, and that only in such an atmosphere can reason thrive. And without reason, law is merely a screen of words expressing will in the service of desire.

The Supreme Court

The legislative history of the United States Senate began with a bill to implement Article III of the federal Constitution, providing for the establishment of "one Supreme Court" and "such inferior courts as the Congress may from time to time ordain and establish." The scheme for a federal judicial establishment of which the chief architect was Oliver Ellsworth, himself a future Chief Justice, became law on September 24, 1789. There were many contenders for the Chief Justiceship and the five Associates for which the first Judiciary Act provided, and not until February 1, 1790, was the day set for the organization of the Court. Even then a majority of the Court were not able to reach New York and the first formal session of the Court could not be held until the following day. From then on for a period of more than a century and a half the Supreme Court has maintained unbroken its very special relation to the constitutional scheme of American society, although during the first three years practically no business came before the Court. The Supreme Court mediates between citizen and Government; it marks the boundaries between State and national authority. This tribunal is the ultimate organ—short of direct popular action—for adjusting the relationship of the individual to the separate States, of the individual to the United States, of the forty-eight States to one another, of the States to the union, and of the three departments of government to one another.

A tribunal having such stupendous powers inevitably stimulates romantic interpretation. Men of learning on both sides of the Atlantic have characterized the Supreme Court as the great political invention of the framers of the Constitution and have appraised it as their most successful contrivance. The most successful it is, but the claim of originality must be denied. Certainly neither the

The original of this essay was published in 1934 in the *Encyclopedia of the Social Sciences*. This version was prepared by Mr. Justice Frankfurter for publication in the Hansard Society's *Aspects of American Government* (1950), reprinted with permission.

presidency nor the Congress has better withstood the fluctuating winds of popular opinion than the Supreme Court. Despite intermittent popular movements against it the Court is more securely lodged in the confidence of the people than the other two branches of the Government. But the establishment of the Court was not a fruit of the creative intelligence of the Federal Constitutional Convention. It was a continuation of means for adjustment which the colonies first and then the thirteen sovereign States and finally the Confederation had evolved. The various controversies, most of them regarding boundaries between different colonies, had to be settled, and partly they were settled by the Privy Council. After independence these controversies did not cease. To them were later added difficulties between the States and the Confederation. At first the Continental Congress tried to adjust these conflicts, but eventually it became necessary to set up a technical judicial tribunal, the Court of Appeal. Not merely the recognition of the need for a body to compose the difference between the States *inter se* and between the States and a central government but the practical response to that need evolved by the predecessor of the United States dictated the necessity and furnished the materials for the Supreme Court which the Constitution outlined and the First Congress established. At least one litigation that began during the Confederation before its Court of Appeal had its final stage before the Supreme Court.[1] In effect the Supreme Court constituted not the invention of a new institution but the perpetuation and perfection of an old one.

Indeed some mechanism for adjusting conflicts between the center and the constituent units is indispensable to a federal form of government. Such adjustments might be left to the federal legislature, as in part and ineffectively they were under the Confederation. But where the powers in a federal government between the center and the circumference are distributed by a legal document, certainly in any political society where the ideas of public law derive from the common law, it is natural

1. United States v. Peters, 5 Cranch 115 (1809), [Ed.]

that conflict regarding this distribution of power should become legal issues to be resolved by a judicial and not a political tribunal. Canada and Australia represent two different forms of federalism. In each the distribution of governmental authority as between center and circumference is different. In each a court with functions similar to the American Supreme Court is part of the scheme, not in imitation of the American Supreme Court but as an inevitable mechanism of a federal state. To be sure the scope of authority of this adjusting mechanism may vary and is itself defined either explicitly or by the implications imported into constitutions in the document distributing powers in a federal government. That the Supreme Court should have been given all the powers it has is of course not a matter of natural law. But if any federal government is to endure, it must provide for some check rein on the constituent units, and the history of the American colonies and States made it inevitable that that check rein should be a court and not Congress. "I do not think," wrote Justice Holmes, "the United States would come to an end if we lost our power to declare an Act of Congress void. I do think the Union would be imperiled if we could not make that declaration as to the laws of the several States. For one in my place sees how often a local policy prevails with those who are not trained to national views and how often action is taken that embodies what the Commerce Clause was meant to end."[2]

But judicial adjustments in the English-speaking world operate within traditional limitations. By confining the power of the Supreme Court to the disposition of "cases" and "controversies," the Constitution in effect imposed on a tribunal having ultimate power over legislative and executive acts the historic restrictions governing adjudications in common-law courts. Most of the problems of modern society, whether of industry, agriculture, or finance, of racial interactions or the eternal conflict between liberty and authority, become in the United States sooner or later legal problems for ultimate solution by the Supreme

2. Holmes, "Law and the Court," in *Occasional Speeches of Justice Oliver Wendell Holmes* 172 (Howe ed. 1962). [Ed.]

Court. They come before the Court, however, not directly as matters of politics or policy or in the form of principles and abstractions. The Court can only deal with concrete litigation. Its judgment upon a constitutional issue can be invoked only when inextricably entangled with a living and ripe lawsuit. In lawyer's language the Court merely enforces a legal right.

In thus passing on issues only when presented in concrete cases the Supreme Court is true to the empiric process of Anglo-American law. But the attitude of pragmatism which evolved the scope and methods of English judicature and subsequently its American versions was powerfully reinforced by considerations of statecraft in defining the sphere of authority for a tribunal of ultimate constitutional adjustments. For in the case of the Supreme Court of the United States questions of jurisdiction are inevitably questions of power as between the several States and the nation or between the Court and the Executive and Congress. Every decision of constitutionality is the assertion of some constitutional barrier. However much a judgment of the House of Lords may offend opinion, Parliament can promptly change the law so declared. But a decision of constitutionality by the Supreme Court either blocks some attempted exercise of power or releases the cumbersome procedure of changes of fundamental law. Therefore the Supreme Court, and very early, evolved canons of judicial self-restraint. Thus it would avoid decisions on constitutionality not merely by observing common-law conventions. The Court very early in its history refused to give merely advisory opinions. Partly this was an assertion of its independence, a refusal of the role of subordination either to Legislature or Executive. The Court withholds utterance unless a controversy is so molded as to give the Court the last word. Partly also this is a manifestation of the psychology underlying the development of English law, which has special pertinence to the unfolding of American constitutional law. To refuse to give advisory opinions, to refuse to speak at large or indeed until litigation compels, is to rely more on the impact of reality than on abstract unfolding. In the workings of a constitution designed for a dynamic society this means a preference for a "judgment from experience as against a judgment from speculation."[3] To pass on legislation *in abstracto* or still worse in advance of enactment would too often be an exercise in sterile dialectic and as a practical matter would close the door to new experience. But the Court has improved upon the common-law tradition and evolved rules of judicial administration especially designed to postpone constitutional adjudications and therefore constitutional conflicts until they are judicially unavoidable. The Court will avoid decision on grounds of constitutionality if a case may go off on some other ground, as, for instance, statutory construction. So far has this doctrine been carried that at times the Court will give an interpretation to a statute much more restrictive than its text or the intention of Congress apparently indicated. Again, in order to avoid the projection of a conflict between State and federal authority the Court, in reviewing State court decisions, is alert to find that the State court merely enforced some State law which the Supreme Court is bound to respect and thereby to deny the existence of a federal controversy.

The Court has thus evolved elaborate and often technical doctrines for postponing if not avoiding constitutional adjudication. In one famous controversy, involving a conflict between Congress and the President, the Supreme Court was able until comparatively recently to avoid decision of a question that arose in the first Congress. Such a system inevitably introduces accidental factors in decision making. So much depends on how a question is raised and when it is raised. For the composition of the Court decisively affects its decisions in the application of constitutional provisions and doctrines which by their vagueness not only permit but invite conflicting constitutional views on the part of the Justices. But time is the decisive element in phases of government, as in war. The cost of uncertainty in result due to changes in the personnel of the Court, through postponing constitutional adjudication until such a decision is unavoidable, is more easily ab-

3. Tanner v. Little, 240 U.S. 369, 386 (1916).

sorbed than would be the mischief of premature judicial intervention in the multitudinous political conflicts arising in a vast federal society like the United States. Political harmony would not be furthered and the Court's prestige within its proper sphere would be inevitably impaired. And so it is as important for the Court not to decide when a constitutional issue is not appropriately and unavoidably before it as it is to decide when its duty leaves no choice.

Some claims of unconstitutionality, however much they may be wrapped in the form of a conventional litigation, the Court will never adjudicate. Such issues are deemed beyond the province of a Court and are compendiously characterized as political questions. Thus although according to the Constitution "The United States shall guarantee to every state in this union a republican form of government," the Supreme Court cannot be called upon to decide whether a particular State government is "republican,"[4] This and like questions are not suited for settlement by the training and technique and the body of judicial experience which guide a court. What such questions are and what they are not do not lend themselves to enumeration. In these, as in other matters, the wisdom of the Court defines its boundaries.

To be sure judicial doctrine is one thing, practice another. The pressure of so-called great cases is sometimes too much for judicial self-restraint, and the Supreme Court from time to time in its history has forgotten its own doctrines when they should have been most remembered. On the whole the Court has had to weather few popular storms. Even these few could have been avoided by a more careful regard for its own canons of judicial administration. The avoidable political conflicts which the Supreme Court has aroused by transgressing its own technical doctrines of jurisdiction demonstrate the large considerations of policy in which those doctrines are founded.

In the same soil of policy is rooted the canon of constitutional construction to which the Supreme Court throughout its history has avowed scrupulous adherence. The

4. Luther v. Borden, 7 How. 1 (1849). [Ed.]

Court will avoid if possible passing on constitutionality; but if the issues cannot be burked, if it must face its responsibility as the arbiter between contending political forces, it will indulge every presumption of validity on behalf of challenged powers. This is not merely the wisdom of caution but the insight of statesmanship. For the cases involving conflicts between the States and the nation or between Congress and the Executive that touch the sensitive public nerves usually turn on such ambiguous language or such vague restrictions of the Constitution as to afford a spacious area of choice on the part of the primary political agencies of government. And the Supreme Court, being a court even in these matters affecting closely the nation's political life, has enunciated again and again the doctrine that the Court cannot enforce its notions of expediency or wisdom but may interpose its veto only when there is no reasonable doubt about the constitutional transgressions. Here, too, the Supreme Court has sinned against its own rules. Especially in construing such vague generalities as "due process" and "equal protection of the laws" it has overlooked their significance and failed to observe that they express "moods" and not "commands."[5] Cases like *Lochner* v. *New York*[6] and *Adkins* v. *Children's Hospital*[7] illustrate what Chief Justice Hughes has characterized as "self-inflicted wounds,"[8] because the deep resentment they aroused was due essentially to the Court's departure from its own postulates.

A rhythm, even though not reducible to law, is manifest in the history of Supreme Court adjudication. Manifold and largely undiscerned factors determine general tendencies of the Court, much too simplified by phrases like "the centralization" of Marshall or "the States' Rights" of Taney. Thus there are periods when the Court seems to forget its doctrine against declarations of unconstitutionality so long as there is room for reasonable doubt. Thus

5. Daniel Reeves, Inc. v. Anderson, 43 F.2d 679, 682 (2d Cir. 1930); see Hand, *The Spirit of Liberty* 73, 160 (Dilliard ed. 1952). [Ed.]
6. 198 U.S. 45 (1904).
7. 261 U.S. 525 (1923). [Ed.]
8. Hughes, *The Supreme Court of the United States* 50 (1928). [Ed.]

the liberality of the Waite period was followed by the dominance of the strict views of Justice Field, in turn yielding to the reaction which made the Holmes outlook prevail. After the first World War, during the decade when William H. Taft was Chief Justice, the Court again veered toward a narrow conception of the Constitution, although Taft himself, especially in a classic dissent, admonished against this tendency.[9] Between 1920 and 1930 the Supreme Court invalidated more State legislation than during the fifty years preceding. Merely as a matter of statistics this is an impressive mortality rate, and it is no answer to point to the far larger number of laws which went through the Court unscathed. All laws are not of the same importance, and a single decision may decide the fate of a great body of legislation. Moreover the discouragement of legislative effort through an adverse decision and a general weakening of the sense of legislative responsibility are influences not measurable by statistics.

Other factors than personnel explain much of the Court's history. Thus on a long view what the Court does and how depends much on the amount and the nature of its litigation. And these largely turn on the sources of its business. Few suits begin in the Supreme Court. Only the United States or a State or a diplomat can become an original suitor. All other litigants reach the Supreme Court by way of appeal from some other court. While boundary controversies or other contests between States (as, for instance, the litigation arising out of Chicago's attempted use of the waters of the Great Lakes) involve sharp conflicts and invoke one of the most important functions of the Supreme Court, they are relatively few in number. The chief work of the Supreme Court is furnished by appellate business, and that business comes from the highest courts of the forty-eight States as well as from inferior federal courts. The last fact is of profound importance in the history of the Court. Unlike its analogues in Canada and Australia, the Supreme Court is the head of a hierarchy of federal courts. Waiving negligible exceptions, the Supreme Court of Canada and the High Court of Australia

9. See "Taft and the Supreme Court," *supra*. [Ed.]

have before them only constitutional and federal questions coming for review respectively from decisions of the provincial and state courts. Similarly in cases coming to the Supreme Court from the State courts only questions involving the federal Constitution or controlling federal legislation arise. But through the federal courts there reaches the Supreme Court a stream of litigation having nothing to do with the federal Constitution and federal legislation but involving the myriad problems that arise under the common law and under State law and State constitutions.

The Constitution empowered the establishment of inferior federal courts not merely for the enforcement of federal law but also to provide tribunals of impartiality to which nonresident suitors may resort. Congress acted upon this authority, established a nation-wide system of federal courts, and not only entrusted them with the enforcement of federal laws but also conferred upon them the so-called diversity jurisdiction; that is, cases between citizens of different States. Thus instead of setting the Supreme Court apart as a court for adjustments of legal conflicts within the federal system the first Judiciary Act and its successors also gave the Supreme Court a vast budget of common-law business. Indeed down to 1875 the Supreme Court was concerned much more with common law than with issues of federal public law. In that year the power of the lower courts over federal matters was widened and consequently a stronger federal content was given to the cases coming before the Supreme Court. This enlargement of jurisdiction of the lower courts and the increase generally of litigation because of the country's expansion in size, population, and enterprise produced an amount of business which was beyond the physical powers of the Court. It took from three to four years for a case to reach argument after an appeal was perfected. Such delays plainly were denials of justice.

Nor could the Court give itself up completely to grappling with its appellate docket. The federal judicial system as originally established was patterned on the English judicature in including the system of circuit riding. Circuit courts were established, but no circuit judges were created. The members of the Supreme Court were also made circuit justices with *nisi prius* duties in their respective circuits. In plain English, they had to sit as judges in the lower courts and later as a collective body hear appeals from their judgments on circuit. As the Court's appellate work steadily mounted, the Justices had either to neglect their circuit work, especially in view of the difficulties of travel in early days, or their Supreme Court work. In fact the administration of justice suffered both in the Supreme Court and on the circuits. Only partly was the pressure eased by the creation in 1869 of circuit judges in collaboration with circuit justices for circuit work. The obvious remedy was to relieve the judges of the duty of circuit riding. This was urged as early as 1790 by Edmund Randolph, Washington's attorney general, in reporting to the House of Representatives on the workings of the new federal judicial system. But circuit riding was an obstinate institution. Tradition and provincial attachments no less than the desire to promote national sentiment through the peregrinations of the Supreme Court Justices maintained the circuit riding system until 1891. Since then it has fallen into desuetude.

Indeed all efforts to enable the Supreme Court adequately to discharge its essential function foundered on the circuit court system. Instead of the obvious remedy, various mechanical devices for keeping abreast of the Supreme Court docket were urged. With a too frequent misconception as to the nature of the judicial business and the conditions for its wise disposition, it was assumed that more business calls for more judges. The first Judiciary Act provided for a Supreme Court of six members, which was increased to seven in 1807 and to nine in 1837. Subject to short fluctuations from a tribunal of ten to one of seven between the years 1863 to 1869, this has remained the size of the Court.

Variants of the proposal to increase the membership of the Court for dealing with the increase of business have been recurrently urged. Thus a large membership of the Court has been proposed, ranging from fifteen to twenty-four so as to permit shifts in the sittings of the Court or work by standing divisions. England and France were cited as examples of such schemes of judicial organization, and their experience has been drawn upon by some of the States of the United States. But either of these devices would be fatal for the special functions of the Supreme Court. A contemporaneous shifting personnel would disastrously accentuate the personal factor in constitutional adjudications, and divisional courts within the Supreme Court would require a mechanism for adjusting conflicts among the divisions. Not till 1891 did Congress pass the requisite legislation. Instead of increasing the size of the Court, it decreased its business.

This was accomplished by establishing intermediate courts of appeal for each of the nine circuits (in 1929 increased to ten). These were given final authority over a large field of appeals which theretofore had gone to the Supreme Court, leaving the latter Court discretionary power to resolve conflicts among the intermediate courts or, when an important national interest otherwise required finality of determination, by the Supreme Court itself. By thus giving to the Supreme Court obligatory appellate jurisdiction over a restricted type of litigation and for the rest letting the Supreme Court decide whether to review, the Congress enabled the Court to keep abreast of its docket. It did more. It introduced a principle of procedure capable of progressive application, which saved the Court for the discharge of duties peculiarly its own in maintaining the constitutional system. When after the Spanish-American War and the first World War the vast expansion in economic enterprise and the resulting governmental regulation of business again produced a volume of judicial business beyond the Court's powers, Congress in 1925 came to the Court's rescue at its own request, by still further withdrawing the types of cases which can be taken to the Supreme Court as a matter of right and extending the area of litigation in which an appeal can be had in the Supreme Court only by its leave.

The Supreme Court has thus ceased to be a common-law court. The stuff of its business is what on the Continent is formally known as public law and not the ordinary legal questions involved in the multitudinous lawsuits of *Doe* v. *Roe* of other courts. The construction of important federal legislation and of the Constitution is now the staple business of the Supreme Court.

Constitutional interpretation is most frequently invoked by the broad and undefined clauses of the Constitution. Their scope of application is relatively unrestricted and the room for play of individual judgment as to policy correspondingly broad. A few simple terms like "liberty" and "property," phrases like "regulate Commerce . . . among the several States" and "without due process of law" are invoked in judgment upon the engulfing mass of economic, social, and industrial facts. Phrases like "due process of law," as Judge Hough reminded us, are of "convenient vagueness."[10] Their content is derived from without, not revealed within the Constitution. The power of States to enact legislation restricting an owner's use of natural resources, providing a living wage for women workers, limiting the rents chargeable by landlords, fixing standard weights for bread, prescribing building zones, requiring the sterilization of mental defectives, fixing the price of milk and other commodities—these powers hinge on the Court's reading of the "due process" clause of the Fourteenth Amendment. The Stockyards Act, the Grain Futures Act, the West Virginia Natural Gas Act, the recapture clause of the Transportation Act, the First Child Labor Law, all involved interpretation of the commerce clause; but the fate of these laws depended on adequate information before the Court on the economic and industrial data which underlay this legislation, and judgment on these facts by the Court. Again, the *Steel Trust Case*,[11] the *Shoe Machinery Case*,[12] the *Duplex Case*,[13] the *Bedford Cut Stone Case*,[14] all involved interpretation

10. Hough, "Due Process of Law—Today," 32 *Harv. L. Rev.* 218 (1919). [Ed.]
11. United States v. United States Steel Corp., 251 U.S. 417 (1919).
12. United States v. United Shoe Machinery Co., 247 U.S. 32 (1918).
13. Duplex Printing Press Co. v. Deering, 254 U.S. 443 (1921).
14. Bedford Cut Stone Co. v. Journeymen Stone Cutters' Ass'n, 274 U.S. 37 (1927).

of anti-trust acts. But the interpretation of this legislation was decided by the facts of industrial life as seen by the Court. The conflicting opinions of the Justices in cases involving the activities of trade associations were not due to any differences in their reading of the Sherman law *in vacuo*. The differences were attributable to the economic data which they deemed relevant to judgment and the use which they made of them. What constitutes a "spur track," when public convenience justifies a railroad extension or abandonment, under what conditions one railroad must permit use of its facilities by a rival, how far the requirement of a State for the abolition of grade crossings depends on approval by the Interstate Commerce Commission—these and like questions cannot be answered by the most alert reading of the Transportation Act. Their solution implies a wide knowledge of railroad economics, of railroad practices and the history of transportation, as well as a political philosophy concerning the respective roles of national control and State authority.

 These are tremendous and delicate problems. But the words of the Constitution on which their solution is based are so unrestricted by their intrinsic meaning or by their history or by tradition or by prior decisions that they leave the individual Justice free, if indeed they do not compel him, to gather meaning not from reading the Constitution but from reading life. It is most revealing that members of the Court are frequently admonished by their associates not to read their economic and social views into the neutral language of the Constitution. But the process of constitutional interpretation compels the translation of policy into judgment, and the controlling conceptions of the Justices are their "idealized political picture" of the existing social order. Only the conscious recognition of the nature of this exercise of the judicial process will protect policy from being narrowly construed as the reflex of discredited assumptions or the abstract formulation of unconscious bias.

Thus the most important manifestations of our political and economic life may ultimately come for judgment before the Supreme Court, and the influence of the Court permeates even beyond its technical jurisdiction. That a tribunal exercising such power and beyond the reach of popular control should from time to time arouse popular resentment is far less surprising than the infrequency of such hostility and the perdurance of the institution. No political party has been consistent in its support or its hostility to the Court. Every American political party at some time has sheltered itself behind the Supreme Court and at others has found in the Court's decisions obstructions to its purposes. This is a reflection of the fact that the Court throughout its history has not been the organ of any party or registered merely party differences. Clashes of views, and very serious ones, there have been on the Court almost from the beginning, but these judicial differences have cut deeper than any differences as to old party allegiances; they involve differences of fundamental outlook regarding the Constitution and the judge's role in construing it.

Whenever Supreme Court decisions have especially offended some deep popular sentiment, movements have become rife to curb the Court's power. In Marshall's days such efforts were invoked by decisions promoting centralization and subordinating the States. In more recent times invalidation of social legislation, both State and federal, has aroused popular disfavor. In the earlier period we find proposals for repealing the famous Section 25 of the Judiciary Act of 1789, whereby the Supreme Court had power to review decisions of State courts denying some federal right. A brake upon a finding of unconstitutionality was also proposed by requiring the concurrence of seven justices and not a mere majority. The latter safeguard was revived by Senator La Follette in 1924,[15] while in an earlier stage of the Progressive movement, in 1912, Theodore Roosevelt proposed a recall by popular referendum of decisions nullifying State but not Congressional legislation.[16] But no proposal for curtailment of the Supreme Court's power over legislation has ever been adopted. The wise exercise of this power, it has shrewdly been discerned, can-

15. See "The Red Terror of Judicial Reform," *supra.* [Ed.]
16. See "The Zeitgeist and the Judiciary," *supra.* [Ed.]

not be assured by any mechanical device. The only reliance rests in the quality of the judges and the temper and training of the bar, for no graver responsibilities have ever confronted a judicial tribunal, no more searching equipment was ever required of judges. The spirit and culture and insight which should be the possessions of a Justice of the Supreme Court have been stated by Judge Learned Hand:

> I venture to believe that it is as important to a judge called upon to pass on a question of constitutional law, to have at least a bowing acquaintance with Acton and Maitland, with Thucydides, Gibbon and Carlyle, with Homer, Dante, Shakespeare and Milton, with Machiavelli, Montaigne and Rabelais, with Plato, Bacon, Hume and Kant, as with the books which have been specifically written on the subject. For in such matters everything turns upon the spirit in which he approaches the questions before him. The words he must construe are empty vessels into which he can pour nearly anything he will. Men do not gather figs of thistles, nor supply institutions from judges whose outlook is limited by parish or class. They must be aware that there are before them more than verbal problems; more than final solutions cast in generalizations of universal applicability. They must be aware of the changing social tensions in every society which make it an organism; which demand new schemata of adaptation; which will disrupt it, if rigidly confined.[17]

All told, eighty-five judges have sat on the Supreme Court. A goodly number of them have been men of intellectual distinction. But hardly a half dozen are towering figures: Marshall, the creative statesman; Story, a scholar of vast learning; Taney, who adapted the Constitution to the emerging forces of modern economic society; Holmes, the philosopher become king; Brandeis, the master of fact as the basis of social insight. Confidence in the competence of the Court has not been won by the presence of

17. Hand, *supra* note 4, at 81. [Ed.]

a rare man of genius. The explanation lies rather in the capacity of the Court to dispose adequately of the tasks committed to it. The effective conditions for insuring the quality of judicial output of the Supreme Court have in the long run been maintained. Human limitations have been respected. While in response to the country's phenomenal increase in population and wealth and the resulting extension of governmental activities duties have been placed upon Congress, the executive departments, various federal administrative agencies and the lower federal courts which disregarded their strength and capacity, the duties of the Supreme Court have on the whole been kept within the capacities of nine judges who are not supermen.

The Supreme Court's internal procedure moreover has been an important factor in the achievement of its high standards of judicial administration. In its disposition of cases, in the rules and practices which determine argument, deliberation, and opinion writing, the Supreme Court operates under the following conditions, indispensable to a seasoned, collective judicial judgment: (1) Encouragement of oral argument; discouragement of oratory. The Socratic method is applied; questioning, in which the whole Court freely engage, clarifies the minds of the Justices as to the issues and guides the course of argument through real difficulties. (2) Consideration of every matter, be it an important case or merely a minor motion, by every Justice before conference and action at fixed, frequent, and long conferences of the Court. This assures responsible deliberation and decision by the whole Court. (3) Assignment by the Chief Justice of cases for opinion writing to the different Justices after discussion and vote at conference. Flexible use is thus made of the talents and energies of the Justices, and the writer of the opinion enters upon the task not only with knowledge of the conclusions of his associates but with the benefit of their suggestions made at conference. (4) Distribution of draft opinions in print, for consideration by the individual Justices in advance of the conference, followed by their discussion at subsequent conferences. Ample time is thus furnished for care in formulation of the result, for recirculation of revised opinions if necessary, and for writing dissents. This practice makes for team play and encourages individual inquiry instead of subservient unanimity. (5) Discouragement of rehearings. Thoroughness in the process of adjudication excludes the debilitating habit of some State courts of being too prodigal with rehearing. (6) To these specific procedural habits must be added the traditions of the Court, the public scrutiny which it enjoys, and the long tenure of the justices. The inspiration that comes from a great past is reinforced by sensitiveness to healthy criticism. Continuity and experience in adjudication are secured through length of service as distinguished from the method of selection of judges.

These factors probably play a larger part in the effective work of the Supreme Court than elevation of station, high responsibility, and the greater ability of the Justices, drawn as they are from the whole country, as compared with State court judges.

The Impact of Charles Evans Hughes

A reviewer opens with misgivings the Life of a contemporary public character with whom he worked intimately. Not that a current attempt to convey such a figure is undesirable, for though time may bring to light documents and disclosures not within reach of our uninhibited and indiscreet era, time also dims. About some aspects of a man, his contemporaries are the best witnesses. The true face even of a public man is his private face. That can be seen only off stage, in the manner in which he pursues his tasks, day by day, when only those in close association see and hear and feel what he is doing. But a dominant figure is bound to be controversial, and a contemporary biography too readily invites hagiography or debunking.

Let it be said at once that Merlo J. Pusey wholly escapes both temptations. Every biography reflects a viewpoint. The account and appraisal of another man's life are distilled in the alembic of the biographer's judgment. But it makes all the difference in the world whether the judgment is romantic, whether it imposes a preconceived view or passionate feeling upon objectively ascertainable materials, or whether judgment derives from those materials.

During the years that Hughes frequently argued cases before him in the New York Court of Appeals, Judge Cardozo purposefully kept his mind in suspense for twenty-four hours after the conclusion of Hughes's argument. Cardozo said he did so after he came to realize the impact upon him of Hughes's personality. Pusey has felt that impact. No one who was actively associated with Hughes could fail to feel it, unless he were imperviously insignificant or self-consumed. The detached Balfour and the powerful Brandeis were equally impressed. Without reflecting this impact, Pusey could not fairly convey Hughes. But he is not subordinated by it in his search for the truth about Hughes's purposes and performance.

Reprinted from a Book Review of Merlo J. Pusey's Pulitzer-Prize winning biography of Charles Evans Hughes in the *New York Times*, November 18, 1951. © 1951 by The New York Times Company. Reprinted by permission. Footnotes supplied by editor.

After finishing these eight hundred pages, at least one reader wishes that a pen as incisive as Walter Bagehot's or as tart as Lytton Strachey's could write a biographical essay in order to contribute to the understanding of a towering personality, even when economizing truth. But it is fortunate that Chief Justice Hughes entrusted his papers to so conscientious and responsible a digger into materials as Pusey for his authorized Life. The impact of Hughes has not only evoked in Pusey an admiring estimate of Hughes's great services to his country as well as of the power and charm of his personality; Hughes has also infected his biographer with his own judicial standards. Pusey faces the controversial aspects of Hughes—of his policies as well as of his personal conduct. It is unimportant how he strikes the balance. What matters is that he does not blink at what may fairly be brought against Hughes's position, and Pusey himself freely expresses criticism that is not mealy-mouthed.

The Life of Hughes has to be woven on the loom of a half century of our political-judicial history. With a due sense of proportion, Pusey gives us Hughes in that context without losing him in it. Through Pusey's lucid and measured narrative, Hughes emerges as the clearheaded, impressive, self-disciplined, resourceful, witty, companionable, energizing, exacting, and considerate person that all who worked with him in the various roles of his long life will recognize through their own experience. And his lifelong romance with Mrs. Hughes should not go without mention.

Those of us who lived through the exciting days of the relentless but wholly fair investigator, through the Albany years with the moral and intellectual standards in government heightened not as precepts but in practice, through that day of dramatic leadership at the Washington Conference with its justifiable hopes of a disarming world, not the less significant because thereafter cruelly subverted, through the years of Hughes's occupancy of John Marshall's seat, will have the memories of those great days revivified by this account of them by Pusey. And the younger generation, whose participation in history comes through the printed page, should find in Pusey a reliable guide.

Major controversies, to which Hughes as governor of New York and as secretary of state gave rise, are bound to remain legacies for history. This is not the occasion, and I certainly am not the person, to indulge in the critical discussion of them or of their treatment by Pusey. Suffice it to say, as already indicated, Pusey does not flinch facing them and he strikes a fine note of temperateness for future disputants. History may alter Pusey's perspective or shift his emphasis, not merely because new documentation may come to the surface but also because from time to time historians reflect a change of mood or of interest in the past.

But one event in Hughes's life is bound to remain as much a matter of individual judgment, certainly within the legal profession, as it was a torturing issue for him—his resignation from the Supreme Court to accept the nomination for the presidency. Of one thing there cannot be a shadow of doubt—that he did not lift a finger to secure the nomination and that he sorrowfully acted out of a sense of duty in a situation which was not of his making nor even of his encouragement. But the question will not down, futile as such doubts of retrospective wisdom are, whether at the end of his life he would not have preferred the rule of conduct he formulated in 1912, when he declined to be drafted, to the exception he made in 1916: "The highest service that I can render in this difficult situation is to do all in my power to have it firmly established that a Justice of the Supreme Court is not available for political candidacy. The Supreme Court must be kept out of politics."[1]

On matters that lie in the domain of judgment, no book can have the last word. But a basic misconception concerning the manner of man Charles Evans Hughes was surely will not survive Pusey's Life. How the notion of Hughes as a cold, unfeeling, mental machine gained currency deserves a good chapter in any history of the dissemination of error. No doubt he was a man of terrific

1. 1 Pusey, *Charles Evans Hughes* 301 (1951).

concentration and of the most disciplined intellectual habits. His work took possession of him—whether in his masterly examination of witnesses in the insurance investigation, or in his devastating campaign against Hearst, or in carrying to the people his policies as governor, or in his various official appearances as secretary of state, or in the Supreme Court, alike when arguing before it or presiding over it.

In short, he was seized by his task precisely as a poet by his inspiration. And since he had, as he once said of himself, "a positive genius for privacy," there was conveyed to the public, on the basis of his intense attention to public duties, this image of an unfeeling and humorless mere brain. His mode of life on the bench confirmed this caricature. He acted on the realization that aloofness is indispensable to the effective discharge of the Supreme Court's functions.

What a caricature! He was genial though not promiscuous, full of fun and whimsy, a delightful tease and sparkling storyteller, a responsive listener and stimulating talker, drawing without show or pedantry on the culture of a man of wide interests and catholic reading. If he made others feel his moral superiority, they merely felt a fact. He was self-critical rather than self-righteous, extremely tolerant toward views he did not share and even deemed mischievous, impressed as he was, on reflecting a half century's experience since leaving college, "first, that there was so much that we did not learn, and second, that we learned so many things that were not so."[2] When Hughes left the Court in 1916, Holmes, who was not drawn to the solemn and arid, wrote his friend Pollock: "I shall miss him consumedly, for he is not only a good fellow, experienced and wise, but funny, and with doubts that open vistas through the wall of a non-conformist conscience."[3]

But when Hughes put himself on paper the style is not the man. Except on rare occasions, he seemed consciously to exclude from his writing the qualities of his talk—

2. Id. at 62.
3. 1 *Holmes-Pollock Letters* 237 (Howe ed. 1946).

apposite yarns, gay quotations, quiet irony, the wit of a tentative and skeptical outlook. The quality of his writing, particularly on the Court, is sober, rather lapidary, doubtless to conform to his notion of what an opinion should be, as a sonnet has its fourteen lines.

But the opinions of Supreme Court judges do not tell the tale of their significance. It is fair prophecy that it is as Chief Justice that Hughes will become an enduring figure. He was, in fact, the head of two courts, so different in its composition was the Supreme Bench in the two periods of the decade during which Hughes presided over it. However sharp the conflict on the issues that came before the Court, all who served with him recognized the extraordinary combination of qualities possessed by the Chief Justice—subordination of all else to the work of the Court, complete disinterestedness in its service, humor that saves differences from becoming discord, and the translation into daily practice of the precepts of tolerance and reason and bracing good will.

The nine men on the Court are coequals. Each in his work is a law unto himself, except for an overriding sense that he is the trustee of the most important traditions in our national system. The test of leadership in such a body is intrinsic authority. No one who served with him would gainsay that Chief Justice Hughes possessed it to a conspicuous degree. In open court he exerted this authority by the mastery and distinction with which he presided. He radiated this authority in the conference room. There was nothing meretricious or assertive about him. Chief Justice Hughes did not rely upon his position; he fulfilled it.

The legal system of every living society, even when embodied in a written constitution, must itself be alive. Such a constitution does not merely enshrine the past. It is designed to give full scope to the future. Of all the forms of a national community, a federal system is the most complicated. It demands the greatest flexibility and imagination to harmonize national and local interests. The Constitution of the United States is thus not a historic parchment in a glass case. It is a continuous process of delicate governmental adjustments. And its judicial application is not a mechanical exercise, but a profound task of statecraft exercised by judges set apart from the turbulence of politics.

The verdict of history will not be hurried. Nearly a century elapsed before we had an adequate account of the judicial labors of Chief Justice Marshall. But to anticipate history's verdict in some instances is neither folly nor arrogance. We can say with confidence that Chief Justice Hughes will join the enduring architects of the federal structure within which our nation lives and moves and has its being.

Barring only the narrow margin by which he missed the presidency (which he himself came to regard a stroke of fortune), Hughes's life is a story of triumph, remembering Burke's reminder, as the Lord Chief Justice of England once reminded Hughes, that "calumny and abuse are essential parts of triumph."[4]

What is the meaning of such a career as Hughes's in the life of the nation? Let me borrow the words of Judge Learned Hand to define it. "If any society is to prosper, it must be staffed with servants of such stuff; indeed, if any society is to endure, it must not be without them. Sure-footed time will tread out the lesser figures of our day; but, if our heritage does not perish, the work of this man and his example will remain a visible memorial of one who helped to keep alive and pass on that ordered freedom without which mankind must lapse into savagery, and repeat its slow and bitter ascent to even that level of mutual forbearance and good-will which it has now attained. We who knew him can do no better than to record our gratitude for a life to which we have owed so much."[5]

4. 2 Pusey, *supra* note 1, at 642.

5. Hand, "Charles Evans Hughes," in *The Spirit of Liberty* 222 (Dilliard ed. 1952).

Chief Justices I Have Known

I'm told you can't teach an old dog new tricks, but my problem tonight is not to try to indulge in new tricks but to see if I can recall an old trick—talking to a group of people. I must see if I can do what I used to do for twenty-five years—sit in a room and talk with students, fellow students, the difference between whom and myself was merely that I had traveled the road once, or several times, before they did.

Here I am without a note, and therefore we'll just have a chat. This room is larger than the one in which I used to meet with students at the Harvard Law School, but we'll contract the walls and imagine we are sitting around that room, where for twenty-five years I received such stimulus and delight as only the young can give to a teacher. It's about as pleasurable a thing as can come to a man in a lifetime.

I've been told to talk to you about Chief Justices I've known, and I'll talk just as it lies in my mind.

It is 164 years since the Supreme Court of the United States was established by an act of Congress. During those years there have been, including Fred M. Vinson, the present incumbent, thirteen Chief Justices. The term of office of Chief Justices, if nature is kind, as happily it has been to some of the greatest of them, is longer than that of any other official in our government. It seems almost incredible, old as I am, that I've known six of them.

I shall speak to you about five of the Chief Justices. I shall not say anything, of course, of the Chief Justice whom I've known longest in service, the present occupant of the seat. But I shall speak of one—Fuller—whom I knew only rather remotely, somewhat platonically as it were, because I never had any personal relations with him. But I saw him on and off, first when I was a student at the Harvard Law School, and eventually when I appeared before him in that wonderful old courtroom in the

An informal talk, delivered without notes, on May 12, 1953, to the students of the University of Virginia Law School, reprinted from 39 Va. L. Rev. 883 (1953), with permission.

Capitol, which I think it was almost a desecration of tradition to leave.

The five Chief Justices of whom I will speak are Fuller, White, Taft, Hughes, and Stone. But, of course, in order that what I say may have something more than merely episodic significance, a few preliminary remarks ought to be made.

The one judicial figure whom even the least informed knows of in the history of the United States is the great Chief Justice John Marshall, of your Commonwealth. It is an interesting fact that although, for essential purposes, the history of our constitutional law almost begins with him, and the significant history of the Supreme Court of the United States begins with him, he was the fourth Chief Justice. His three predecessors all had very short tenure.

The first was a great man, John Jay. It is not without significance in attempting to understand the then position of the Chief Justice of the United States, that John Jay resigned the chief justiceship to become governor of New York—not that I underrate the importance of the governorship of New York, either then or now. But it is certainly true that since Marshall's time only a madman would resign the chief justiceship to become governor, let me say, even of Virginia.

Jay's successor, John Rutledge of South Carolina, had the singular distinction of serving only a few months as Chief Justice by interim appointment. He was rejected by the Senate of the United States, and therefore was not able to continue to occupy the post.

The third Chief Justice was another eminent man in our history, Oliver Ellsworth, who was the architect of the act that created the federal judicial system. His structure remained, for all practical purposes, unaltered from 1789 to 1869. He was Chief Justice for only four years. Ill health put an end to his service.

Then came John Marshall. I should say the three greatest Chief Justices we've had were John Marshall, Roger Taney, and Charles E. Hughes. It is an interesting fact that the first two of these, between them and in immediate succession, served for almost one half of the 164 years the Court has been in existence. Marshall from 1801 to 1835, and Taney from 1836 to 1864. I emphasize the duration of their service because the length of time during which a Chief Justice presides over the Court has, of course, a great deal to do with his place in history. Time is one of the most important factors in the realization of a man's potentialities.

Coming to the Chief Justices whom I have seen in action, about whom professionally I may be allowed to have some judgment, let me come down to 1888 when Grover Cleveland appointed a man who was not known generally to the country at all. I suppose Melville Weston Fuller was a man about whom there was nothing in what newspapermen call the morgues of the leading newspapers in the country. He had no record to speak of, except a professional one. His appointment is a striking illustration of the contingencies of life. And I think he—and I shall speak of others—illustrates the importance of not having a fixed, specific ambition in life. The chances of realizing a specific ambition are so much against you that, if I may say so, I do not think any of you should harbor an ambition to become Chief Justice of the United States. The likelihood that you will realize it—I do not know what the mathematicians, if there be any in this audience, would say—is worth nothing, and the likelihood that you will have an embittered life is very considerable. The thing to do is to have ambition in a certain direction but not to fix it on a point of arrival, an ambition going to general purpose in life and not to the particular form in which that purpose is to be realized.

When Chief Justice Waite died, if a poll had been taken among lawyers and judges to determine the choice of a successor, I suppose that not a single vote would have been cast for Melville W. Fuller outside Chicago. Indeed, he was not Grover Cleveland's first choice. It was widely believed that a man named Edward J. Phelps of Vermont would become Chief Justice. He was a leader of the bar. He was a well-known man. He had been minister to Great Britain. But 1888 was a time when the so-called Irish vote mattered more than it has seemed to matter in recent years. Edward J. Phelps, as has been true of other ministers and ambassadors to Great Britain, had made some speeches in England in which he said some nice things about the British people. Patrick Collins, a Democratic leader, then an influential member of the House of Representatives and later mayor of Boston, felt that that wouldn't do. He evidently thought that a man who says nice things about the British couldn't possibly make a good Chief Justice of the United States. And since Patrick Collins was a powerful influence in the Democratic party, he advised President Cleveland that if he sent Phelps's name to the Senate, the chances of confirmation might not be very bright. Phelp's name was not sent to the Senate.

Melville Fuller was born in Maine, educated at Bowdoin, and the Harvard Law School. As a young man, after a little political activity in Augusta, Maine, he tried his luck in the beckoning West. He went to Chicago, where he

was active as a Democrat. In that way it chanced that Grover Cleveland came to know and respect him. After some maneuvering, Cleveland named Fuller to the great surprise of the press of the country and even of the profession. Fuller was confirmed, but with a very large vote in opposition. One of the opponents of confirmation was Senator Hoar of Massachusetts, then on the powerful Judiciary Committee, who afterward did the handsome thing by saying how wrong he had been, just as in our day Senator Norris, who had opposed the confirmation of Harlan F. Stone, later publicly expressed his regret.

The point about Fuller was, or rather is, that he was a practicing lawyer, and a lawyer only. I need hardly tell this audience that to me being a lawyer, with the full implications of responsibility and opportunity that the word carries, in a society like ours, in a government of laws under a written Constitution, is a calling second to none. Melville Fuller had held no public office of any kind, unless you call being a member of a constitutional convention public office. He was fifty-five years old when he was appointed to the Supreme Court, and he had not only had no judicial experience, he had had, as I have said, no official experience of any kind. I think Fuller was the only man, with the exception of his immediate predecessor, who came to the chief justiceship so wholly without a record in official public life.

When you deal with a number as small as that of the Chief Justices of the United States, any inference from one or more cases is statistically not of much validity. I merely point out, parenthetically, that five Chief Justices came to the office without having had prior judicial experience. I do not want you to draw any inference from that fact which you cannot rationally defend. There is much to be said, and I have not time to say it now, on the general question of the relevance of prior judicial experience as a qualification for membership on the Supreme Court. Perhaps, parenthetically again, I can sum up my own views by saying that prior judicial experience should be neither an essential qualification nor, of course, a disqualification. I think that when the President of the United States comes to select someone to fill a vacancy on the Supreme Court, no single factor should be the starting point in his deliberation. He should not say, "I want a man who has had experience as a judge," or, "I want a man who hasn't had experience as a judge," I shall say more about this in a moment, but to me it is important that if you blot out the names of those who came to the Supreme Court without any prior judicial experience, you blot out, in my judgment, barring only two, the greatest names on its roster.

At all events, Fuller came to the Court as a man who had had wide experience at the bar, and, what is important, wide experience at the bar of the Supreme Court and with the kind of business that came before the Supreme Court in his day. He was a dapper little man. I remember vividly seeing him for the first time. I was a student at the Harvard Law School and he was president of the Harvard Alumni Association. He was introducing the speaker of the day, none other than William H. Taft, who had just returned from the Philippines to become secretary of war. Fuller had silvery locks, more silvery and more striking, because he was a little man. He was an extremely cultivated man, which is important. He read the classics. He was a student of history. He had felicity of speech.

Fuller came to a Court that wondered what this little man was going to do. There were titans, giants on the bench. They were powerful men, both in experience and in force of conviction, and powerful in physique, as it happened. For myself, I think all Justices of the Supreme Court should be big, powerful-looking men! Certainly those whom he met there, who welcomed him courteously but not hopefully, were as I have described them. (Believe it or not, there is ambition even in the breasts of men who sit on the Supreme Court of the United States. There is a good deal to be said for the proposal of Mr. Justice Roberts that no man should ever be appointed to the chief justiceship from the Court.) At any rate, Fuller met on that Court at least four or five men of great stature. The senior among them was Samuel F. Miller, who had been appointed by Lincoln and whose career, incidentally, is an exciting story of American life. Miller started out as a physician and practiced medicine for ten or twelve-odd years, until he became a lawyer and in very quick order a Justice of the Supreme Court. He had great native ability, and was a strong man in every sense. Fuller, if they had had the expression in those days, might have been called an egghead. He was a blueblooded intellectual, and the contrast with Miller was great. Then there was Harlan, a six-foot-three, tobacco-chewing Kentuckian. You did not have to come from Kentucky to chew tobacco in those days. They did it in Massachusetts too. But Harlan was all Kentuckian. And there was a smallish man whom I regard as one of the keenest, profoundest intellects that ever sat on that bench, Joseph Bradley of New Jersey. And then there were Matthews of Ohio and a six-foot-five- or six-inch giant from Massachusetts, Horace Gray. Those were the big, powerful, self-assured men over whom Melville Fuller came to preside.

They looked upon him, as I have indicated, with doubt and suspicion, but he soon conquered them. They soon felt that the man who presided over them presided over them justly. He had gentle firmness, courtesy, and charm. He also had lubricating humor. Justice Holmes was fond of telling a story. In his early days, he said, "I'm afraid my temper was a little short." (There could hardly have been two men more different than Mr. Justice Holmes, who wielded a rapier, and Mr. Justice Harlan, who wielded a battle-ax. A rapier and a battle-ax locked in combat are likely to beget difficulties for innocent bystanders.) Justice Harlan, who was oratorical while Justice Holmes was pithy, said something during one of the Court's conferences that seemed to Holmes not ultimate wisdom. Justice Holmes said he then did something that ordinarily isn't done in the conference room of the Supreme Court. Each man speaks in order and there are no interruptions, because if you had that you would soon have a Donnybrook Fair instead of orderly discussion. But Holmes afterward said, "I did lose my temper at something that Harlan said and sharply remarked, 'That won't wash. That won't wash.'" Tempers flared and something might have happened. But when Holmes said, "That won't wash," the silver-haired, gentle little Chief Justice said, "Well, I'm scrubbing away. I'm scrubbing away."

Whether you are in a conference room of the Supreme Court, or *en banc* in a court of appeals, or at faculty meetings, or in a law club, the same kind of thing can happen. When men get short of temper, humor is a great solvent. Fuller had that. He presided with great courtesy. He presided with quiet authority unlike Hughes's, of whom I shall speak shortly. He presided with great but gentle firmness. You couldn't but catch his own mood of courtesy. Advocates, too, sometimes lose their tempers, or, in the heat of argument, say things they should not. There was a subduing effect about Fuller. Soon these men, who looked at him out of the corner of their eyes, felt that they were in the presence of a chief whom they could greatly respect. I have the authority of Mr. Justice Holmes, who sat under four chief justices in Massachusetts before he came down to Washington, and under four (Fuller, White, Taft, Hughes) in Washington, that there never was a better presiding officer, or rather, and more important in some ways, a better moderator inside the conference chamber, than this quiet gentleman from Illinois.

Somehow or other the felicity of his pen, more of his tongue but also his pen—read a speech he made on the occasion of the centennial of the founding of this country, reported in 132 *United States Reports*—that charm which he had in occasional writings did not manifest itself, or he did not exert it, in his opinions. You cannot tell the quality or the importance of a man on the Supreme Court solely from his opinions. Mr. Justice Van Devanter, in passing, is a striking illustration of that. And so Fuller's opinions will give you nothing of his charming qualities. He is rather diffuse. He quotes too many cases. And generally he's not an opinion writer whom you read for literary enjoyment, though you can profitably read his nonjudicial things for that purpose.

Fuller was invited to leave the Supreme Court, not to become governor of New York, but because Grover Cleveland was very anxious to have him as his secretary of state. An important document in the history of the judiciary, and I think in the history of the law, is Fuller's letter to President Cleveland stating why a man shouldn't leave the chief justiceship, and, I should add, an associate justiceship, for any political office. He was, as I said, fifty-five years old when he came to the Court. He was Chief Justice for twenty-two years. The difference in functions between the Chief Justice and the other members of the Court, is, as Holmes said, mainly on the administrative side, and there never was a better administrator on the Court than Fuller.

I ought to add one thing that seems to me not without interest and not without pleasure to record. I said Fuller was appointed in 1888. That was, let me remind you, a presidential election year. Like every party out of power, the Republicans expected to be returned, as indeed they were. If mere partisanship had ruled, it would not have been difficult to await the result of the election and give the selection of a Chief Justice to the incoming administration. Instead, the Senate confirmed the Democratic choice of President Cleveland. This broad-minded action reflects honor on all the Senators whose votes confirmed Fuller. Especial mention, however, should be made of Senator Shelby M. Cullom of Illinois, who knew Fuller and his qualifications as lawyer and man, and, transcending party considerations, pressed his confirmation. Now, that is a very gratifying thing to one who, like myself, is out of party politics and party attachments—that politicians did not play for position in relation to such a high office.

I must move on. Fuller died in 1910, and the appointment of his successor is a most interesting episode in American history, because Fuller died shortly after President Taft had named Governor Hughes of New York as an Associate Justice. As a matter of fact, Hughes had not even taken his place when, in the summer, shortly after he was named, Fuller died. President Taft was a great admirer, not unnaturally, of Hughes, who made the decisive campaign speech for Taft in 1908 at Youngstown, Ohio. In offering Governor Hughes the place on the Supreme Court, Taft, with that charming exuberance and forthrightness of his, indicated that Fuller couldn't live forever, and that, of course, he, Hughes, would be the natural choice of Taft for the chief justiceship. He indicated, as much as words can indicate, that he would name Hughes to be Chief Justice. Then, having doubtless reread the letter after he signed it, he scribbled under it a postscript, being fully aware of his delightful and generous indiscretion, "Of course, I do not make this as a firm promise," or words to that effect. (I'm not quoting accurately.) Governor Hughes, in accepting the position, told the president that of course he was as free as a bird as far as the chief justiceship was concerned.

Well, a vacancy in the chief justiceship did occur six weeks after this exchange of letters, and everybody expected Hughes to be made Chief Justice. Hughes took his seat, and it must have been extremely embarrassing for the baby member of the Court to be the heir apparent to the vacant chief justiceship. Some of the older fellows must have disliked the idea. You know, the notion of a freshman runs all through life—younger brother, younger sister, freshman at college, freshman on the Supreme Court.

By that time—1910—the Court had completely changed. Of the men whom Fuller had found when he went there in 1888, only one survived. That was Harlan. There were very strong men on the Court in 1910. It would be a pathetic Court indeed if there weren't always at least some strong men on it. By 1910 there were some new strong men. When Hughes joined the Court he found there, in addition to Mr. Justice Harlan, that nice birdlike creature with a beard, Mr. Justice McKenna of California. Holmes by that time had been on for eight years. There was Mr. Justice White. There was Mr. Justice Day.

They did not like the idea of having this untried New York governor and politician become Chief Justice. They drew up a round robin to present to Taft, who had appointed some of them. They saw President Taft, I believe, and indicated that they did not like to have their junior member made Chief Justice. Mr. Justice Holmes, with his characteristic high honor, refused to join this kind of protest. He was perfectly ready to have Hughes become Chief Justice.

Taft appointed a member of the Court, a powerful member of the Court, Edward D. White of Louisiana. President Taft was glad to appoint—we are so much removed from 1910 in some ways—White as Chief Justice because White had been a Confederate. It was not until the 'eighties that a Confederate southerner had again been put on the Supreme Court. That was Lucius Quintus Cincinnatus Lamar of Mississippi. But to make a Confederate, an ex-Confederate—are Confederates ever "ex"?—Chief Justice was something that could contribute much, even then, so Taft thought, and I believe rightly, to the cohesion of our national life.

We shall never know the full story of what happened, but within twenty-four hours after the Justices called on him there was a change in the mind of Taft, and it was then that White became Chief Justice. There is the most absurdly contradictory testimony of people who think they do know what happened. Within a half hour after Taft had summoned Hughes, probably to tell him he was going to be Chief Justice, he canceled the request that Hughes come. During that time something happened.

Anyhow, White was made Chief Justice. At the Saturday conference following the sending of White's name to the Senate, Hughes, the junior member of the Court, made what I am told was one of the most gracious speeches of welcome to the new Chief Justice.

Now let me tell you about Edward D. White. He looked the way a Justice of the Supreme Court should look, as I indicated a little while ago. He was tall and powerful. I think a jowl also helps a Justice of the Supreme Court, and White had an impressive jowl. He had been a drummer boy in the Confederacy, and that had upon him a very important influence, not only in life, but as a judge—a very profound influence. It is a very interesting thing, but Edward D. White, the Confederate drummer boy, was much more nationalistic, if that phrase carries the meaning I should like it to carry, and was far more prone to find State action forbidden as an interference with federal power, than was Holmes, the Union soldier, who went to his death with three Confederate bullets in his body. White was so impressed with the danger of divisiveness and separatism, with the intensification of local interest to the disregard of the common national interest, that again and again and again he found that local action had exceeded the bounds of local authority, because it might weaken and endanger the bonds of national union. One of the most interesting things is the division between him and Holmes in specific instances, where White was, if one may use colloquial, inaccurate terms, for "centralization" and Holmes was for "States' rights."

White had "read" law. He did not have the advantage that you and I have had, of systematic training in the law in a university law school. He was educated by the Jesuits—another very important part of his life, because for him logic and logical analysis played a very important, sometimes an excessive role. Very early he was put on the Supreme Court of Louisiana, but he was there only two years because he was then legislated out of office, or rather the court to which he belonged was. So that he had had only two years of relatively unimportant judicial experience. During those two years he never had a case of the kind which most frequently came to the Supreme Court after be became a member of it. After his brief State judicial career, White practiced law and in 1891 was sent to the Senate of the United States, on the great issue whether there should or shouldn't be a State lottery. That's a profound question, isn't it? Anyhow, it took him to the Senate of the United States, where he began to play an important part. He was an effective speaker, a man of cultivation, and much respected.

Then comes another one of those incidents which lead me to caution the young in this room not to fix their ambition on becoming the Chief Justice or even an Associate Justice of the Supreme Court of the United States. Mr. Justice Blatchford of New York died in 1893 and there were reasons why the natural thing was to pick a New Yorker for his place. This was in the second administration of Cleveland, after he had come back following Harrison's intervening presidency. But the New York politicians had got into an awful row with Cleveland, and the Democratic party in New York was split wide open. The leader of the anti-Cleveland forces, David B. Hill, was in the Senate of the United States. Mr. Cleveland, who was himself a lawyer of very considerable parts and knew the bar, first sent in the name of William B. Hornblower, a leading member of the New York bar. Senator Hill, exercising a historic prerogative of Senators, said, "I oppose this nomination," (If a Senator from the nominee's State is opposed to him and speaks the traditional words, the nomination fails. This works on the theory of "you scratch my back today and I'll scratch yours tomorrow.") So Mr. Hornblower's name fell by the wayside.

President Cleveland then sent in a second name, Wheeler H. Peckham of New York, another one of the really topnotch lawyers of his day. There was nothing against him except that he was a Cleveland man, but that was enough for David B. Hill. He again rose, swirled the toga about him, and said that he was very sorry but that Mr. Peckham, an otherwise estimable man, was "personally obnoxious." And so Mr. Peckham's name was withdrawn. Cleveland was put to it, and he did what Presidents have done before and since. He drew on that powerful force, the club feeling of the Senate. And he said, "I'll fix you. I'll name a senator to the Supreme Court." (They never reject Senators for anything, almost.) So he named Senator White of Louisiana, and within fifteen minutes Senator White was confirmed.

That's how White came on the Supreme Court in 1894. He sat for sixteen years as an Associate, a very significant member of the Court, until he was made Chief Justice at the age of sixty-five. He had been a judge for sixteen years, but it's important to remember again that when he was made a judge he had only this rather unimportant, not very relevant, not quite two years on the Louisiana Supreme Court. He remained Chief Justice from 1910 to 1921.

An important thing in the work of a Chief Justice which distinguishes him from other members of the Court is that he is the presiding officer, and has guidance of the business of the Court in his charge. It is not what he says in his opinions that is more important than what his brethren say, but what he advises on the mechanics of doing the job—should we give a lawyer extra time, should we hear this case now or later, should we grant a rehearing if the Court is divided? These are things that pertain to the way that the business should be done, things that cannot properly be managed without knowledge of the nature of the business, or, since you deal with eight other human beings, without knowledge of the ways of the other Justices.

It is thus very important that, number one, the Chief Justice should have had some familiarity with the business of the Court before he gets there, and, number two, that he start off on the right foot in his relations with his colleagues, whom he finds there. Of course, influence, in the sense of respect and deference, can be acquired in the course of time, but it makes a lot of difference if the start is a good one. White, when he came to be Chief Justice in 1910, dealt with men with whom he'd been a judge for periods varying in length from sixteen to a few years. But, as sometimes happens, there soon was a wholesale change in the Court. While a number of the Associates remained—McKenna and Holmes and Day—a new lot came on in the other places. A very able lot they were too.

I ought to say something here about the differences in the nature of the business that has come to the Court in different periods. When Fuller assumed office in 1888, the Court dealt a great deal with problems arising from the vast industrialization which the Civil War had set into motion. It was also during Fuller's time that the war with Spain and the acquisition of territory led to new controversies. These events were reflected in the business of the Court—because the Court is a good mirror, of which historians for some reason have little availed themselves, of the struggles of dominant forces outside the Court. Sooner or later the conflicts in the economic and social world result in litigation before the Court. Tocqueville, in 1832, when he wrote his great book, had the discernment to see what later writers have so often not seen, that by the very nature of our Constitution practically every political question eventually, with us, turns into a judicial question. The question may become somewhat mutilated in the process, but come before the Court it will.

One sometimes reads about the Supreme Court and wonders whether anyone ever studies history any longer. One would suppose that dissenting opinions were a recent discovery. In fact, I am sometimes told that they are an invention recently brought down by a Harvard professor. Well, the men on Fuller's Court divided drastically and fiercely on the issues of their time. In the *Insular Cases*,[1] they wrote over two hundred pages of opinions, which were illuminatingly summarized by that great philosopher, Mr. Dooley, when he said that so far as he could make out, "the Supreme Court decided that the Constitoosh'n follows the flag on Mondays, Wednesdays, and Fridays."

1. De Lima v. Bidwell, 182 U.S. 1 (1901); Dooley v. United States, 182 U.S. 222 (1901); Downes v. Bidwell, 182 U.S. 244 (1901). [Ed.]

Beginning about in the 'seventies, the States, not yet the federal government but the States, began to regulate business. And there came before the Court a series of questions as to the power of the States, in view of the Civil War Amendments. With the Interstate Commerce Act of 1887, we enter upon an era where the federal government intervenes. It is the era we are still in, in which I suppose the statistically predominant issues concern the relations between government and business, broadly speaking. During Fuller's period, on the whole, the outlook of the Court was very—what shall I say—inhospitable toward control of business. Restrictions upon the free activities of business came into Court, on the whole, under a serious handicap.

By the time White came to be Chief Justice the federal government had gone in for regulation more and more. Hughes was on the Court, with his great experience, as governor of New York, in regulating business. During White's tenure, Brandeis came on the Court, without any previous judicial experience, but with, I suppose, unparalleled experience in the domain of practical economics, with an understanding of the relations of business to society. Yet, though White came to the Chief Justiceship with full knowledge of the Court's business and with a strong hold on his colleagues, if anybody thought that merely because of that there would be unanimity of opinion and a want of differences, he was bound to be mistaken. Indeed, during White's tenure the divisions became more frequent and not fewer. But he was master of his job. There was something very impressive about him, both in appearance and otherwise. He was also a great personality. He was a master of speech, though sometimes too abundant speech. I should suppose, on the whole, his opinions are models of how not to write a legal opinion. He made three words grow, usually, where there was room for only one.

The Court became more and more divided in opinion during his period, not because of him, but because the issues became more contentious, the occasions for making broad decisions were fewer, and cases came more and more to be recognized, as Holmes early pointed out and for fifty years continued to point out, as presenting questions of degree.

White was Chief Justice for only ten years. When he died an astonishing thing happened, unique in the history of this country and not likely to recur, at least as far as one can look ahead—an ex-President of the United States became the Chief Justice of the United States. That was, of course, William H. Taft.

Now, his case may contradict what I said about not fixing your ambition on a particular job, because William H. Taft, from the time he came to manhood, wanted to become a member of the Supreme Court. His great ambition in life was to be a Justice of the Supreme Court, and he finally not only attained it, but with, as it were, a dividend. He became Chief Justice of the United States. Yet, if I were you, I wouldn't draw too heavily on Taft for encouragement, let alone derive assurance from his case. Let me tell you why.

Taft was a brilliant student, as we all know, at Yale College. I think he would have continued to be even if he had gone to the Harvard Law School, as his son did after him. He went out to Cincinnati and had a quick success at the bar, vindicating the promise of his youth. At thirty-two he was solicitor general, having been on a lower court in Ohio before that. Shortly after the present system of Courts of Appeals, then called Circuit Courts of Appeals, was established in 1891, he became a circuit judge, and he was a notable judge, for eight years, from 1892 to 1900, when McKinley sent him to the Philippines as governor general.

While he was out there, vacancies occurred on the Supreme Court of the United States, and his then bosom friend, Theodore Roosevelt, who knew of his ambition, twice offered him a place on the Supreme Court. To the very great honor of his name it is to be recorded that Taft twice refused that which his personal ambition was most eager to have, because he thought he owed it to the Philippine people not to leave—what's the phrase?—"the plow in the furrow." So twice he put behind him the realization of his personal ambition, because duty commanded him otherwise.

Then he became secretary of war, and after that President of the United States. His heart must have twinged more than once as he had opportunity to put five men on the Supreme Court and fill places that he himself coveted. In 1913 Taft ceased to be President and was promoted to be a professor of law. Well, if any man ever put behind him the thought that he would ever be on the Court, it was William H. Taft, when he went up to New Haven to profess law. If you want to be foolish, if you want your life subject to the hazards of such fortuities as those which determined the fate of William H. Taft, then you can follow his example. Who could have foreseen that the course of events would be such that in 1921 Warren Gamaliel Harding would be President of the United States and would ask William H. Taft to be Chief Justice?

Taft became Chief Justice at the age of sixty-three, having been, as I have indicated, a notable judge, but having been out of the business of judging and out of touch with the Supreme Court, except for having filled five of its nine places, for twenty years. He himself said, and he was very happy to say, with that generosity of his which politicians would do well to, but do not often, imitate, that whatever he did as Chief Justice was made possible by his great reliance on him whom he called his "lord chancellor," Mr. Justice Van Devanter.

Mr. Justice Van Devanter is a man who plays an important role in the history of the Court, though you cannot find it adequately reflected in the opinions written by him because he wrote so few. But Van Devanter was a man of great experience. He'd been chief justice of Wyoming. He was then made a United States circuit judge and in 1910 he became a member of the Supreme Court. He had a very clear, lucid mind, the mind, should I say, of a great architect. He was a beautiful draftsman and an inventor of legal techniques who did much to bring about the reforms which were effectively accomplished by Taft as Chief Justice.

Taft's great place in judicial history, I think, will be as a law reformer. In the characteristic way of this country, various federal judges throughout the country were entirely autonomous, little independent sovereigns. Every judge had his own little principality. He was the boss within his district, and his district was his only concern. A judge was a judge where he was, and although he may have had very little business, he couldn't be used in regions where the docket was congested. This, as you know, was changed, and the change has been highly beneficial.

An even more important reform for which Taft was effectively responsible was the legislation authorizing the Supreme Court to be master in its own household, which means that the business which comes to the Supreme Court is the business which the Supreme Court allows to come to it. Very few cases can come up without getting its prior permission. So that cases which never should take the time, energy, and thought of the ultimate tribunal in the land are allowed to rest, if they come from the federal courts, after those courts have had two go's at them, or, if the cases come from the State courts, after they have received the hierarchal adjudication provided by the State. No longer is it true, as it was before this legislation, that a case would come to the Supreme Court automatically after it had gone through, let us say, four other courts, as though having an endless litigation were one of the God-given rights of the American citizen.

So Chief Justice Taft had a place in history, in my judgment, next to Oliver Ellsworth, who originally devised the judicial system. Chief Justice Taft adapted it to the needs of a country that had grown from three million to a hundred and twenty million.

Taft was, of course, very genial. He did not have to learn to be genial. It is better to learn to be genial than not to be genial at all, but Taft was instinctively genial, with great warmth, and a capacity to inspire feelings of camaraderie about him. When he came to the Chief Justiceship in 1921, the papers had been full, as the papers are from time to time nowadays, of talk about the great divisions on the Court. Laymen are constantly troubled, even as are lawyers, especially when they lose a case, about divisions on the Court. But why should anyone expect nine men, presumably there because of their special capabilities, all to have the same thoughts and views? One would suppose that nine men are put there because you want variety of thought. No one expects such harmony and identity of views among physicists, let alone among professors of sociology or history. Why should they expect nine people to know how to apply in unison and in concord such delightfully vague phrases or concepts as "due process of law," phrases, as a great judge once said, of "calculated ambiguity"? To be sure, there can be no difference of opinion on the proposition that twelve is twelve; and it is clear, therefore, that a jury must have twelve members under the federal system. But when it comes to things like, when does a State encroach upon the right of Congress to regulate commerce, or what kind of limitations may you put upon people who want to speak at Hyde Park, or in Union Square, or on the Lawn of the University of Virginia, that's a different story.

When Taft became Chief Justice there had been this succession of great divisions on the Court—serious divisions on very serious matters. And every once in a while there were five-to-four decisions. Just as the newspapers do not print, "Mr. and Mrs. Jones have been happily married for fifteen years this day," but would print somewhere in the paper that Mr. and Mrs. Jones are getting a divorce, so the newspapers do not often publicize the cases in which the Court is unanimous. I can assure you that there are a great many such—most of them, in fact. What captures the headlines are the divisions: "The Supreme Court divides on child labor. The Supreme Court divides on this and that."

The appointment of Taft gave rise to the hope that all this would end. "He's such a charming man, don't you know?" I like to recall a newspaper editorial printed when Mr. Taft was appointed Chief Justice in June 1921. The present New York *Herald Tribune*, the then New York *Tribune*, commented, as did every paper in the country, on what a delightful man William H. Taft was, how charming, how everybody liked him, and now there would be no more five-to-four opinions. I thought the *Tribune* put it best: "Mr. Taft has such tact and good humor, and has so unconquerable a spirit of fair play, that he is greatly beloved of his fellow citizens. These gifts and this character may not be the first ones sought for in a chief justice, but even the most eminent judges are none the worse for having them. With Justice Taft as a moderator"—now listen to this—"it is probable that not a few asperities that mar the harmony of the celestial chamber, the consulting room, not a few of those asperities will be softened and that not quite so often in the future will the court divide five and four."

I really think that's very funny. The assumption of this serious editorial writer that Taft, C.J., would just smile and then Holmes would say, "Aye, aye, sir," or Justice Van Devanter would say, "For ten years I've been disagreeing with Holmes, but now that you've smiled at both of us, why we just love each other." I suggest a subject for a paper by one of you students. I have never done it, but my impression is strong that a count would show more five-to-four decisions during Taft's time than during White's time, or certainly just as many. Life was very pleasant with Taft as Chief Justice, but judicial conflicts existed because the problems before the Court evoked them. As for asperities during the period between '21 and '30, when Taft left—I think the conference was just as lively a place. I was not there, but the sparks even carried outside of the conference room to singe the pages of the *United States Reports*.

Of course Taft knew the men on the Court well, and he found there two whom he had appointed. That did not prevent those two from disagreeing with him, I can assure you. One of the strongest and most memorable of the dissenting opinions against Taft was written by a man whom he had appointed. What judge would be worth his salt if it made any difference to him that the President who appointed him, whether he was on or off the Court, disagreed with him? What judge worth his salt would have his convictions influenced by whether the Chief Justice is a charming man and a delightful raconteur, or not? That isn't the nature of the enterprise.

In 1930 Taft became ill and retired. He always had the love and affection of his colleagues. He and Brandeis, when Taft was President, crossed swords very fiercely indeed; Brandeis was counsel in the famous Pinchot-Ballinger attack on the administration. But they became fast friends on the Court. One of the things that laymen, even lawyers, do not always understand is indicated by the question you hear so often: "Does a man become any different when he puts on a gown?" I say, "If he is any good, he does."

Taft was followed, of course, by Hughes. Now the last thing that Hughes ever expected to be after he left the Court in 1916 to run for the presidency (I have ventured to say in print that I believe this was the one act of his life which he regretted)—he later became secretary of state, then became a member of the World Court, and finally returned to the bar to, I suppose, as vast a practice as that of any man at the bar in our time, or at any time in the history of this country—the last thing Hughes expected to become was Chief Justice. He was, to Hoover's great surprise, subjected to severe attack when his name was sent in. He finally was confirmed, though it was a nip and tuck business. He took his seat at the center of the Court, with a mastery, I suspect, unparalleled in the history of the Court, a mastery that derived from his experience, as diversified, intense, and extensive, as any man ever brought to a seat on the Court, combined with a very powerful and acute mind that could mobilize these vast resources in the conduct of the business of the Court. There must be in this room lawyers who came before the Court when Chief Justice Hughes presided. To see him preside was like witnessing Toscanini lead an orchestra.

Aside from the power to assign the writing of opinions, which is his by custom, and of which I shall speak, a Chief Justice has no authority that any other member of the Court has not. That really is an institution in which every man is his own sovereign. The Chief Justice is *primus inter pares*. Somebody has to preside at a sitting of nine people, and he presides in court and at conference. But Chief Justice Hughes radiated authority, not through any other quality than the intrinsic moral power that was his. He was master of the business. He could disembowel a brief and a record. He had an extraordinary memory and vast experience in the conduct of litigation, and of course he had been on the Court six years, from 1910 to 1916. And he had intimate and warm relations with some of the men he found on the Court. He was a great admirer of that greatest intellect, in my judgment, who ever sat on the Court, Mr. Justice Holmes. He was an old friend at the bar of Mr. Justice Brandeis. He had been one year in the cabinet with Stone. So he not only felt at home in the courtroom, he felt at home with his colleagues.

I have often used a word which for me best expresses the atmosphere that Hughes generated; it was taut. Everything was taut. He infected and affected counsel that way. Everybody was better because of Hughes, the leader of the orchestra. That was true, too, of Cardozo, when he was chief judge of the New York Court of Appeals. One is told that the same men were somehow or other better when he was chief judge than they were the next day after he had ceased to be chief judge. That is a common experience in life. One man is able to bring things out of you that are there, if they are evoked, if they are sufficiently stimulated and directed. Chief Justice Hughes had that very great quality.

Chief Justice Stone is the antithesis, in the fate that was allotted to him, of Marshall and Taney and Fuller. If you're Chief Justice for only five years, as Stone was, even though you come to the Chief Justiceship after having been an Associate, the opportunities to realize on the moral opportunities that place gives you are necessarily very limited. Time plays a very important part. Stone came to the head of the Court in 1941. He had been an Associate Justice since 1925. Before that he had been a professor of law and dean of a law school, an extensive practitioner in New York, and then attorney general of the United States. He was familiar with the business of the court. He was a very different personality from Hughes. Hughes was dynamic and efficient. That's a bad word to apply to Hughes, because it implies regimentation. It implies something disagreeable, at least to me. I don't like a man to be too efficient. He's likely to be not human enough. But that wasn't true of Hughes. He simply was effective—not efficient, but effective. Stone was much more easygoing. The conference was more leisurely. The atmosphere was less taut, both in the courtroom and the conference room. It has been said that there wasn't free and easy talk in Hughes's day in the conference room. Nothing could be further from the truth. There was less wasteful talk. There was less talk that was repetitious, or indeed foolish. You just didn't talk unless you were dead sure of your ground, because that gimlet mind of his was there ahead of you.

Stone was an "easy boss," as it were. Boss is the worst word to use with reference to a Chief Justice of the United States, because that's precisely what he is not. Anybody who tried it would not try it long. There is one function, however, that the Chief Justice has by virtue of being Chief Justice, other than being the administrator, presiding in open court, presiding at conference, and there opening the discussion on each case. That other function is, I believe, the most important of all that pertains to the office of Chief Justice. I know not how it is in the Supreme Court of Appeals of Virginia. The method of designating the member of the court who writes the opinion for the court varies in the various State courts. In New York, for instance, it goes by rotation. That's a practice very common in this country. Even when it goes that way, a great man can make a dent on the accidental system by which cases come to him. They used to say in New York, until they knew better, "Why is it that Cardozo always gets the interesting cases?" The answer was that no matter what case he got, he made it interesting; he didn't "get" it—it came to him in automatic order. I believe it is a fact, though it is so strange a fact that I shall not identify the State, but I am assured on dependable authority that in the supreme court of at least one of our States, and not the least populous of States, they shake dice to determine who should write an opinion. Having it go in order lacks, for my taste at least, the aleatory aspect that dice have.

From Marshall's time in the Supreme Court the Chief Justice has designated the member of the Court who writes the opinion of the Court. As most of you know, we hear argument five days a week and on Saturday there is a conference. After everybody has had his say, beginning with the Chief Justice and following in order of seniority —and everybody can say whatever he wants to say— there is a formal vote. In order that the junior should not be influenced, everybody having already expressed his view, the formal voting begins with the junior. (How careful we are not to coerce anybody!) After conference, in cases in which the Chief Justice is with the majority, as he is in most instances, he designates the member of the Court who is to write the opinion. If he is in the minority, then the next senior Justice of those in the majority does the assigning. So that in most of the cases the Chief Justice decides who is to speak for the Court. As for dissents and concurrences—that's for each member to choose for himself.

You can see the important function that rests with the Chief Justice in determining who should be the spokesman of the Court in expressing the decision reached. The manner in which a case is stated, the grounds on which a decision is rested—one ground rather than another, or one ground rather than two grounds—how much is said and how it is said, what kind of phrasing will give least trouble in the future in a system of law in which as far as possible you are to decide the concrete issue and not embarrass the future too much—all these things matter a great deal. The deployment of his judicial force by the Chief Justice is his single most influential function. Some do it with ease. Some do it with great anguish. Some do it with great wisdom. Some have done it with less than great wisdom.

No Chief Justice, I believe, equaled Chief Justice Hughes in the skill and the wisdom and the disinterestedness with which he made his assignments. Some cases are more interesting than others, and it is the prerogative of the Chief Justice not only to be kindly and fair and generous in the distribution of cases, but also to appear to be so. The task calls for qualities of tact, understanding, and skill in the effective utilization of the particular qualities that are available. Should one man become a specialist in a subject? Or is it important not to place too much reliance on one man because he's a great authority in the field? Should you pick the man who will write the opinion in the narrowest possible way? Or should you take the chance of putting a few seeds in the earth for future flowering? Those are all very difficult, delicate, and responsible questions.

I must conclude this discursive narrative—this almost absurd attempt in a short talk, to give you some sense of five men who have been at the head of a Court on which ultimately rests the maintenance of the equilibrium between central authority and the constituent States, between the authority of government, whether State or national, and the liberties of the individual.

As I said earlier, when you deal with such few instances, you do not have a statistical basis for generalization. If I wanted to be a little playful, I might say I leave generalizations to political scientists who sometimes think that the crude details are not worthy of high philosophical attention. I hope I have indicated enough, however, to disclose that in view of the functions of the Supreme Court what you want in a Justice is not a specialist in this or that field, not necessarily a man who has been broadened by high office, as was the case with Hughes, rather than broadened by the depth and range of his reading and his thinking, as in the case of Mr. Justice Holmes.

What is essential for the discharge of functions that are almost too much, I think, for any nine mortal men, but have to be discharged by nine fallible creatures, is that you get men who bring to their task, first and foremost, humility and an understanding of the range of the problems and of their own inadequacy in dealing with them, disinterestedness, and allegiance to nothing except the effort, amid tangled words and limited insights, to find the path through precedent, through policy, through history, to the best judgment that fallible creatures can reach in that most difficult of all tasks: the achievement of justice between man and man, between man and state, through reason called law.

The Judicial Process and the Supreme Court

If one is to talk at all before an audience as learned as this, he had best talk about that of which he is least ignorant. And so I have chosen the topic I have, circumscribed as one in my position is to talk about it. But this is not to be a technical professional paper. What I shall say derives from the assumption that I am talking about complicated and subtle problems to those who are not professionally concerned with them, nor professionally trained to their understanding, and yet feel free to make judgments, because as citizens they are deeply involved in these problems. Broadly speaking, the chief reliance of law in a democracy is the habit of popular respect for law. Especially true is it that law as promulgated by the Supreme Court ultimately depends upon confidence of the people in the Supreme Court as an institution. Indispensable, therefore, for the country's welfare is an appreciation of what the nature of the enterprise is in which that Court is engaged—an understanding of what the task is that has been committed to the succession of nine men.

I said I shall speak "circumscribed" as I am in doing so. I am circumscribed not only by the very limited freedom of speech that his position imposes on a member of the Court. I am no less circumscribed by want of those qualities that are not the normal endowment of judges, nor cultivated in them by training. Those who know tell me that the most illuminating light on painting has been furnished by painters, and that the deepest revelations on the writing of poetry have come from poets. It is not so with the business of judging. The power of searching analysis of what it is that they are doing seems rarely to be possessed by judges, either because they are lacking in the art of critical exposition or because they are inhibited from practicing it. The fact is that pitifully little of significance has been contributed by judges regarding the nature of their endeavor, and, I might add, that which is

A paper read at the April 22, 1954, meeting of the American Philosophical Society, reprinted from 98 *Proceedings of the American Philosophical Society* 223 (1954), with permission.

written by those who are not judges is too often a confident caricature rather than a seer's vision of the judicial process of the Supreme Court.

We have, of course, one brave and felicitous attempt—Mr. Justice Cardozo's little classic. I have read and reread, and reread very recently, that charming book and yield to no one in my esteem for it. And yet you must not account it as immodesty or fractiousness if I say that the book would give me very little help in deciding any of the difficult cases that come before the Court. Why should a book about the judicial process by one of the great judges of our time shed relatively little light on the actual adjudicatory process of the Supreme Court? For the simple reason that *The Nature of the Judicial Process* derived from Cardozo's reflections while in Albany, before he came to Washington. The judicial business out of which Cardozo's experience came when he wrote the book was the business of the New York Court of Appeals, and that is very different business from the most important aspects of the litigation on which the Supreme Court must pass.

Let me indulge in one of the rare opportunities for the valid use of statistics in connection with the work of the Supreme Court. The reports of the New York decisions for the year during which Judge Cardozo delivered the lectures which comprise his book show that only about one out of a hundred cases before the New York Court of Appeals raised questions comparable to those that gave him most trouble in Washington. The year that he left Albany for Washington, 1932, only two opinions out of a hundred in the *New York Reports* raise the kind of questions that are the greatest concern for the Supreme Court. Cardozo wrote something like five hundred opinions on the New York Court of Appeals. In them he was concerned with matters that would not have been foreign, say, to Lord Mansfield or Lord Ellenborough, and would have been quite familiar to Cardozo's contemporaries on the English Supreme Court of Judicature.

After Cardozo came to Washington, he wrote 128 opinions for the Court during the tragically short period that fate allowed him there. He wrote 21 dissents. Of these

149 opinions only 10 dealt with matters comparable to those which came before him while on the New York Court of Appeals. No one was more keenly aware than he of the differences between the two streams of litigation; no one more keenly alive than he to the resulting differences in the nature of the judicial process in which the two courts were engaged. Let me quickly add that such were the genius and the learning and, perhaps most important of all, the priestlike disinterestedness of his mind, that, even during his few brief years as a Justice, Cardozo became an outstanding contributor to the history of Supreme Court adjudication. What is relevant to our immediate purpose is realization of the important fact that the problems dealt with in Cardozo's illuminating little book, and in two other little books which played on the same theme,[1] derive from an experience in the raw materials of the adjudicatory process very different from those that are the most anxious concern of the Supreme Court of the United States.

498 It is time for me to be explicit. I am advised by an arithmetically minded scholar that the Constitution of the United States is composed of some 6,000 words. Not every provision of that document that becomes controversial can come before the Supreme Court for adjudication. The questions that are not meet for judicial determination have elicited their own body of literature. A hint of the nature of such questions is given by their fair characterization as an exercise of judicial self-limitation. This area constitutes one very important and very troublesome aspect of the Court's functioning—its duty not to decide.

Putting to one side instances of this judicial self-restraint, de Tocqueville showed his characteristic discernment when he wrote: "Scarcely any political question arises in the United States that is not resolved sooner or later into a judicial question."[2] Those provisions of the Constitution that do raise justiciable issues vary in their incidence from time to time. The construction of all of

1. *The Growth of the Law* (1924); *The Paradoxes of Legal Science* (1928). [Ed.]

2. 1 *Democracy in America* 280 (Bradley ed. 1948).

them, however, is related to the circumambient condition of our Constitution—that our nation is a federalism. The most exacting problems that in recent years have come before the Court have invoked two provisions expressed in a few undefined words—the clause giving Congress power to regulate commerce among the States and the due process clauses of the Fifth and Fourteenth Amendments.

A federalism presupposes the distribution of governmental powers between national and local authority. Between these two authorities there is shared the power entirely possessed by a unitary state. In addition to the provisions of our Constitution making this distribution of authority between the two governments, there is also in the United States Constitution a withdrawal of power from both governments, or, at least, the exercise of governmental power is subject to limitations protective of the rights of the individual. Of the two types of constitutional provision calling for construction from case to case, the limitation in the interest of the individual presents the most delicate and most pervasive of all issues to come before the Court, for these cases involve no less a task than the accommodation by a court of the interest of an individual over against the interest of society.

Human society keeps changing. Needs emerge, first vaguely felt and unexpressed, imperceptibly gathering strength, steadily becoming more and more exigent, generating a force which, if left unheeded and denied response so as to satisfy the impulse behind it at least in part, may burst forth with an intensity that exacts more than reasonable satisfaction. Law as the response to these needs is not merely a system of logical deduction, though considerations of logic are far from irrelevant. Law presupposes sociological wisdom as well as logical unfolding. The nature of the interplay of the two has been admirably conveyed, if I may say so, by Professor Alfred North Whitehead:

> It is the first step in sociological wisdom, to recognize that the major advances in civilization are processes

which all but wreck the societies in which they occur: —like unto an arrow in the hand of a child. The art of free society consists first in the maintenance of the symbolic code; and secondly in fearlessness of revision, to secure that the code serves those purposes which satisfy an enlightened reason. Those societies which cannot combine reverence to their symbols with freedom of revision, must ultimately decay either from anarchy, or from the slow atrophy of a life stifled by useless shadows.[3]

The due process clauses of our Constitution are the vehicles for giving response by law to this felt need by allowing accommodations or modification in the rules and standards that govern the conduct of men. Obviously, therefore, due process as a concept is neither fixed nor finished.

The judgment of history on the inherently living and therefore changing applicability of due process was thus pronounced by Mr. Justice Sutherland, one of the most traditionally minded of judges:

> Regulations, the wisdom, necessity and validity of which, as applied to existing conditions, are so apparent that they are now uniformly sustained, a century ago, or even half a century ago, probably would have been rejected as arbitrary and oppressive.[4]

A more expansive attempt at indicating the viable function of the guarantee of due process was made in a recent opinion:

> The requirement of "due process" is not a fair-weather or timid assurance. It must be respected in periods of calm and in times of trouble; it protects aliens as well as citizens. But "due process," unlike some legal rules, is not a technical conception with a fixed content unrelated to time, place and circumstances. Expressing as it does in its ultimate analysis respect enforced by

3. Whitehead, *Symbolism* 88 (1927).
4. Village of Euclid v. Ambler Realty Co., 272 U.S. 365, 387 (1926).

> law for that feeling of just treatment which has been evolved through centuries of Anglo-American constitutional history and civilization, "due process" cannot be imprisoned within the treacherous limits of any formula. Representing a profound attitude of fairness between man and man, and more particularly between the individual and government, "due process" is compounded of history, reason, the past course of decisions, and stout confidence in the strength of the democratic faith which we profess. Due process is not a mechanical instrument. It is not a yardstick. It is a process. It is a delicate process of adjustment inescapably involving the exercise of judgment by those whom the Constitution entrusted with the unfolding of the process.[5]

This conception of due process meets resistance from what has been called our pigeonholing minds, which seek to rest uninquiringly on formulas—phrases which, as Holmes pointed out long ago, "by their very felicity delay further analysis,"[6] and often do so for a long time. This is, of course, a form of intellectual indulgence, sometimes called the law of imitation. "Traditions which no longer meet their original end" must be subjected to the critique of history whereby we are enabled "to make up our minds dispassionately whether the survival which we are enforcing answers any new purpose when it has ceased to answer the old."[7]

But a merely private judgment that the time has come for a shift in opinion regarding law does not justify such a shift. Departure from an old view, particularly one that has held unquestioned sway, "must be duly mindful of the necessary demands of continuity in a civilized society. A reversal of a long current of decisions can be justified only if rooted in the Constitution itself as an historic document designed for a developing nation."[8] It makes an important difference, of course, if the validity

5. Joint Anti-Fascist Refugee Committee v. McGrath, 341 U.S. 123, 162-163 (1951) (Frankfurter, J., concurring).

6. Holmes, *Collected Legal Papers* 230, 231 (1920). [Ed.]

7. Id. at 225.

8. Graves v. N.Y. ex rel. O'Keefe, 306 U.S. 466, 487-488 (1939) (Frankfurter, J., concurring).

of an old doctrine on which decisions were based was always in controversy and so did not embed deeply and widely in men's feelings justifiable reliance on the doctrine as part of the accepted outlook of society. What is most important, however, is that the Constitution of the United States, except in what might be called the skeleton or framework of our society—the anatomical as against the physiological aspects,—was "framed for ages to come."[9] As to those features of our Constitution which raise the most frequent perplexities for decision by the Court, they were drawn in many particulars with purposeful vagueness so as to leave room for the unfolding but undisclosed future.

At this point one wishes there were time to document these generalizations with concrete instances which would help to define the problem and illustrate generalities from which the Court starts and differences of opinion which naturally enough arise in their application. Such documentation would expose divergencies by which common starting points lead to different destinations because of differences in emphasis and valuation in the process of reasoning. They would also shed some light on the interplay between language and thought. Differences in style eventually may embody differences of content, just as a sonnet may sometimes focus thought more trenchantly than a diffuse essay.

The other major source of puzzling problems is the commerce clause. With us the commerce clause is perhaps the most fruitful and important means for asserting national authority against the particularism of State policy. The role of the Court in striking the balance between the respective spheres of federal and State power was thus adumbrated by the Court:

> The interpenetrations of modern society have not wiped out state lines. It is not for us to make inroads upon our federal system either by indifference to its maintenance or excessive regard for the unifying forces of modern technology. Scholastic reasoning

9. Cohens v. Virginia, 6 Wheat. 264, 387 (1821).

> may prove that no activity is isolated within the boundaries of a single State, but that cannot justify absorption of legislative power by the United States over every activity. On the other hand, the old admonition never becomes stale that this Court is concerned with the bounds of legal power and not with the bounds of wisdom in its exercise by Congress. When the conduct of an enterprise affects commerce among the States is a matter of practical judgment, not to be determined by abstract notions. The exercise of this practical judgment the Constitution entrusts primarily and very largely to the Congress, subject to the latter's control by the electorate. Great power was thus given to the Congress: the power of legislation and thereby the power of passing judgment upon the needs of a complex society. Strictly confined though far-reaching power was given to this Court: that of determining whether the Congress has exceeded limits allowable in reason for the judgment which it has exercised. To hold that Congress could not deem the activities here in question to affect what men of practical affairs would call commerce, and to deem them related to such commerce merely by gossamer threads and not by solid ties, would be to disrespect the judgment that is open to men who have the constitutional power and responsibility to legislate for the Nation.[10]

The problems which the commerce clause raises as a result of the diffusion of power between a national government and its constituent parts are shared in variant forms by Canada, Australia, and India. While the distribution of powers between each national government and its parts varies, leading at times to different legal results, the problems faced by the United States Supreme Court under the commerce clause are not different in kind, as are the problems of judicial review under the due process clause, from those which come before the Supreme Court of Canada and the High Court of Australia.

10. Polish National Alliance v. Labor Board, 322 U.S. 643, 650-651 (1944).

Judicial judgment in these two classes of the most difficult cases must take deep account, if I may paraphrase Maitland, of the day before yesterday in order that yesterday may not paralyze today, and it must take account of what it decrees for today in order that today may not paralyze tomorrow.

A judge whose preoccupation is with such matters should be compounded of the faculties that are demanded of the historian and the philosopher and the prophet. The last demand upon him—to make some forecast of the consequences of his action—is perhaps the heaviest. To pierce the curtain of the future, to give shape and visage to mysteries still in the womb of time, is the gift of imagination. It requires poetic sensibilities with which judges are rarely endowed and which their education does not normally develop. These judges, you will infer, must have something of the creative artist in them; they must have antennae registering feeling and judgment beyond logical, let alone quantitative, proof.

The decisions in the cases that really give trouble rest on judgment, and judgment derives from the totality of a man's nature and experience. Such judgment will be exercised by two types of men, broadly speaking, but of course with varying emphasis—those who express their private views or revelations, deeming them, if not *vox dei,* at least *vox populi*; or those who feel strongly that they have no authority to promulgate law by their merely personal view and whose whole training and proved performance substantially insure that their conclusions reflect understanding of, and due regard for, law as the expression of the views and feelings that may fairly be deemed representative of the community as a continuing society.

Judges are men, not disembodied spirits. Of course a judge is not free from preferences or, if you will, biases. But he may deprive a bias of its meretricious authority by stripping it of the uncritical assumption that it is founded on compelling reason or the coercive power of a syllogism. He will be alert to detect that though a conclusion has a logical form it in fact represents a choice of competing considerations of policy, one of which for the time has won the day.

An acute historian recently concluded that those "who have any share of political power . . . usually obtain it because they are exceptionally able to emancipate their purposes from the control of their unformulated wishes and impressions."[11] For judges, it is not merely a desirable capacity "to emancipate their purposes" from their private desires; it is their duty. It is a cynical belief in too many quarters, though I believe this cult of cynicism is receding, that it is at best a self-delusion for judges to profess to pursue disinterestedness. It is asked with sophomoric brightness, does a man cease to be himself when he becomes a Justice? Does he change his character by putting on a gown? No, he does not change his character. He brings his whole experience, his training, his outlook, his social, intellectual, and moral environment with him when he takes a seat on the Supreme Bench. But a judge worth his salt is in the grip of his function. The intellectual habits of self-discipline which govern his mind are as much a part of him as the influence of the interest he may have represented at the bar, often much more so. For example, Mr. Justice Bradley was a "corporation lawyer" par excellence when he went on the Court. But his decisions on matters affecting corporate control in the years following the Civil War were strikingly free of bias in favor of corporate power.

To assume that a lawyer who becomes a judge takes on the bench merely his views on social or economic questions leaves out of account his rooted notions regarding the scope and limits of a judge's authority. The outlook of a lawyer fit to be a Justice regarding the role of a judge cuts across all his personal preferences for this or that social arrangement. The conviction behind what John Adams wrote in the provision of the Massachusetts Declaration of Rights regarding the place of the judiciary in our governmental scheme, and the considerations which led the framers of the Constitution to give federal

11. Pares, "Human Nature in Politics—III," *The Listener* 1037 (Dec. 17, 1953).

judges life tenure and other safeguards for their independence, have, I believe, dominated the outlook and therefore the action of the generality of men who have sat on the Supreme Court. Let me recall the Massachusetts Declaration:

> It is essential to the preservation of the rights of every individual, his life, liberty, property and character, that there be an impartial interpretation of the laws, and administration of justice. It is the right of every citizen to be tried by judges as free, impartial, and independent as the lot of humanity will admit . . .[12]

Need it be stated that true humility and its offspring, disinterestedness, are more indispensable for the work of the Supreme Court than for a judge's function on any other bench? These qualities alone will not assure another indispensable requisite. This is the capacity for self-searching. What Jacques Maritain said in another connection applies peculiarly to members of the Supreme Court. A Justice of that Court cannot adequately discharge his function "without passing through the door of the knowing, obscure as it may be, of his own subjective."[13]

This is not to say that the application of this view of the judge's function—that he is there not to impose his private views upon society, that he is not to enforce personalized justice—assures unanimity of judgments. Inevitably there are bound to be fair differences of opinion. And it would be pretense to deny that in the self-righteous exercise of this role obscurantist and even unjustifiable decisions are sometimes rendered. Why should anyone be surprised at this? The very nature of the task makes some differences of view well-nigh inevitable. The answers that the Supreme Court is required to give are based on questions and on data that preclude automatic or even undoubting answers. If the materials on which judicial judgments must be based could be fed into a machine so as to produce ineluctable

12. Article XXIX.
13. Maritain, *Creative Intuition in Art and Poetry*,114 (1953).

answers, if such were the nature of the problems that come before the Supreme Court and such were the answers expected, we would have IBM machines doing the work instead of judges.

> How amazing it is that, in the midst of controversies on every conceivable subject, one should expect unanimity of opinion upon difficult legal questions! In the highest ranges of thought, in theology, philosophy and science, we find differences of view on the part of the most distinguished experts,—theologians, philosophers and scientists. The history of scholarship is a record of disagreements. And when we deal with questions relating to principles of law and their application, we do not suddenly rise into a stratosphere of icy certainty.[14]

The core of the difficulty is that there is hardly a question of any real difficulty before the Court that does not entail more than one so-called principle. Anybody can decide a question if only a single principle is in controversy. Partisans and advocates often cast a question in that form, but the form is deceptive. In a famous passage Mr. Justice Holmes has exposed this misconception:

> All rights tend to declare themselves absolute to their logical extreme. Yet all in fact are limited by the neighborhood of principles of policy which are other than those on which the particular right is founded, and which become strong enough to hold their own when a certain point is reached . . . The boundary at which the conflicting interests balance cannot be determined by any general formula in advance, but points in the line, or helping to establish it, are fixed by decisions that this or that concrete case falls on the nearer or farther side.[15]

14. See "Address by Mr. Chief Justice Hughes," 13 *American Law Institute Proceedings* 61, 64 (1936).

15. Hudson County Water Co. v. McCarter, 209 U.S. 349, 355-356 (1908).

This contest between conflicting principles is not limited to law. In a recent discussion of two books on the conflict between the claims of literary individualism and dogma, I came across this profound observation: "But when, in any field of human observation, two truths appear in conflict it is wiser to assume that neither is exclusive, and that their contradiction, though it may be hard to bear, is part of the mystery of things."[16] But judges cannot leave such contradiction between two conflicting "truths" as "part of the mystery of things." They have to adjudicate. If the conflict cannot be resolved, the task of the Court is to arrive at an accommodation of the contending claims. This is the core of the difficulties and misunderstandings about the judicial process. This, for any conscientious judge, is the agony of his duty.

16. "Literature and Dogma," *Times Literary Supplement* (London), Jan. 22, 1954, p. 51.

Mr. Justice Jackson

Such are the paradoxes of life that one with unique opportunities for understanding the operations of the judicial process in Mr. Justice Jackson is by that very fact barred from sharing with readers the adventure of pursuing insight. Not that Brother Jackson and I saw things with a common eye. How could we, if for no other reason than the great differences in our backgrounds. Apart from the influential dissimilarity between our professional training and experience, he was a child of the country before Ford came, while the big city marked me as its own. The first opinion written by Jackson, J., was in characteristically vigorous dissent from an opinion of mine. *Indianapolis* v. *Chase National Bank.*[1] And in the last case in which he wrote, *United States* v. *Harriss,*[2] we were on opposite sides. Our conflicting views in these two cases could readily be used as texts to expound differences of outlook on the larger issues of which the two cases were instances, of differences in evaluation of the clashing factors which had to be accommodated in the two situations. What is more immediately relevant, however, about these two cases at the beginning and at the end of his judicial career and others between them is their proof that what binds men in fellowship is not identity of views but harmony of aims.

That law in its comprehensive sense is at once the precondition and, perhaps, the greatest achievement of an enduring civilization since without it there is either strife or the enslavement of the spirit of man; that law so conceived expresses the enforcible insights of morality and the endeavors of justice; that law is not word jugglery or the manipulation of symbols; that precedents, while not foreclosing new truths or enlarged understanding, are not counters to be moved about for predetermined

The first essay reprinted here appeared in 68 *Harv. L. Rev.* 937 (1955). The second essay is reprinted from 55 *Colum. L. Rev.* 435 (1955), with permission. Both law reviews were dedicated to the memory of Robert H. Jackson.

1. 314 U.S. 63 (1941).
2. 347 U.S. 612 (1954).

ends; that this significance and role of law must particularly be respected in a continental federal society like ours; that the Supreme Court as the ultimate voice of this law must always be humbly mindful of the fact that it is entrusted with power which is saved from misuse only by a self-searching disinterestedness almost beyond the lots of men—these were convictions which Justice Jackson passionately entertained. They were part of him. He scrupulously applied them, though he moved, like everyone else, within the outer limits of his temperament and understanding.

This estimate of his outlook and views is not the private gleaning of a fellow worker. To an unusual degree in the history of the Court, Justice Jackson wrote as he felt. It is my impression that the opinions of most Justices have conformed to what they conceived to be the appropriate form of an opinion. In the delicious classification that Mr. Justice Cardozo made of legal opinions, he emphasized literary style. But I think the style often reflects the writer's notion of the form in which an opinion should be cast or his desire to promote one purpose rather than another. A literary genius like Holmes no doubt writes the way he must. But there have been men on the Court whose conception of the required austerity of a Supreme Court opinion rigorously held in check an otherwise lively pen. Again, it makes a difference whether an opinion writer consciously aims to be understood by the casual newspaper reader, or whether he has a strong sense of the educational function of an opinion within the profession, and more particularly among law teachers, or writes merely to dispose of the case.

While Justice Jackson and I never discussed the art of opinion writing, and so I speak only on the basis of impressions open to every reader of his opinions, I would put him in a different category. He belonged to what might be called the naturalistic school. He wrote as he talked, and he talked as he felt. The fact that his opinions were written talk made them as lively as the liveliness of his talk. Unlike what he praised in Brandeis, his style sometimes stole attention from the substance. He had "impish candor," to borrow one of his own phrases. Candor, indeed, was one of his deepest veins. Even an occasional explosion was a manifestation of his candor. There was nothing stuffy about him, and, therefore, nothing stuffy about his writing. To confess error was for him a show of strength, not of weakness. No man who ever sat on the Supreme Court, it seems to me, mirrored the man in him in his judicial work more completely than did Justice Jackson.

Of all the adjectives that have been used to characterize him for me the most apt are gifted and beguiling. He was ineluctably charming, but his charm was not a surface glitter. It compelled affection and was not marred by passing temper or irritation. Gifted in the case of Justice Jackson does not imply the talent only for brilliant flashes or evanescent displays. His gifts were solid. They were revealed in the Swiftian irony of his famous Alfalfa Club Speech on January 31, 1953, his arresting arguments before the Supreme Court, his impressive opening and closing at Nuremberg. Mr. Justice Brandeis said that Jackson should be solicitor general for life. The function of an advocate is not to enlarge the intellectual horizon. His task is to seduce, to seize the mind for a predetermined end, not to explore paths to truths. There can be no doubt that Jackson was specially endowed as an advocate. He appreciated a good phrase, even his own. But his aims increasingly groped beyond that of mere advocacy. He steadily cultivated his understanding in the service of these aims; the advocate became the judge. Deeper insight made him aware that the best of phrases may be less than the truth and may even falsify it. He had the habit of truth-seeking and faithfully served justice.

To "Administer justice . . . agreeably to the Constitution and the laws of the United States" was the oath taken by Robert H. Jackson when he took his seat on the Supreme Bench. Regard for that oath confined the free play of his personality as it had not been confined in his very active professional life, either in his variegated private practice or during the seven preceding years as lawyer for the Government. That oath was for him not the utterance of a mere formula. It summarized the ingrained conviction that there is such a thing as law and that judges are set apart to define it. The duty of Justices is not to express their personal will and wisdom. Their undertaking is to try to triumph over the bent of their own preferences and to transcend, through habituated exercise of the imagination, the limits of their direct experience. But since the designed or the inevitable ambiguity of language makes the pronouncement of law not a mechanical but a judgmatical process, ascertainment of what the Constitution and the laws of the United States require partly depends on the personalities of the bench. The notion that the text should yield the same meaning to every conscientious member of the Supreme Court is the offspring either of ignorance or self-deception. Contrariwise, to apply Humpty-Dumpty's philosophy to the Constitution and the laws—"when I use a word, it means just what I choose it to mean, neither more nor less"—is to treat law as an ignoble game and to falsify the course of our history. Being fallible, Justices have not always achieved their task of impersonalization. But neither are the *United States Reports* a record of systematic deception.

Inasmuch as the Constitution and statutes, as well as prior decisions, often render unavoidable variant interpretations, not infrequently of considerable range, the individuality of the Justices inescapably enters into the judicial process of the Supreme Court. Not that men before coming on the Court normally have ready-made views regarding substantive issues that are in the air; besides, wholly new issues arise in the quick passage of time. Moreover, vital to the outcome of Supreme Court litigation is the attitude of Justices toward problems of the Court's jurisdiction. This concerns not merely the technical aspects of the Court's power but, even more important, the effective regard entertained for those considerations that the Court has evolved for exercising its jurisdiction. Except in the rare instance of prior preoccupation with them, these are matters to which most members of the Court bring virgin minds. What becomes decisive to a Justice's functioning on the Court in the large area within which his individuality moves is his general attitude toward law, the habits of mind that he has formed or is capable of unforming, his capacity for detachment, his temperament or training for putting his passion behind his judgment instead of in front of it. The attitudes and qualities which I am groping to characterize are ingredients of what compendiously might be called dominating humility.

Every man is the whole of his life, and to assess the driving forces within him, so far as relevant, which Mr. Justice Jackson brought to the Court, and the growth and change of the man while he was on it, is for his biographers, particularly those who will be writing about him in the perspective of history. But a few strong elements in his composition were manifest to his contemporaries. Time is not likely to displace their significance.

He came from a rural background and in his essential feelings remained there. Spring Creek, Pennsylvania, where he was born, was a community of fourteen hundred, and his beloved Jamestown, New York, with all the extensive law practice that it afforded him, had some forty thousand inhabitants when he left it, in 1934, for his spectacular national career. For him the rural background was not a backwash of the great streams of American life. It generated, in his own words, "a way of life much the same all over America." No one can read his delicious review of Judge Arthur Gray Powell's *I Can Go Home Again*[3] without feeling that Mr. Justice Jackson's past left in him not romantic nostalgia but an allegiance to qualities he never ceased to deem essential. Self-reliance, good-humored tolerance, recognition of the other fellow's right to be and to thrive even though you may not think he is as good as you are, suspicion of authority as well as awareness of its need, disdain of arrogance and self-righteousness, a preference for truculent independence over prudent deference and conformity—

3. 30 *A.B.A.J.* 136 (1944).

these were the feelings that shaped his outlook on life. He liked his kind without being sentimental about it; he was gregarious but shy about intimacies.

I said in his essential feelings he remained in his rural background. But not in his mind. The depth and versatility of his culture shamed many of us who have had what is called the advantages of a higher education. He did not go beyond high school, and he was one of the last, as he was by far one of the very best, of office-trained lawyers. No matter how good the Albany Law School may have been in his day, one year at any law school affords a meager systematic legal training. He was a self-educated man and a self-taught lawyer. He had, of course, great native powers. His strength of character developed them into intellectual distinction. Happily he fell under the influence of one of those unsung, inspiring teachers who can profoundly affect a man's life. Miss Mary Willard spotted the voracious mental appetite of young Bob, fed it, and encouraged in him habits of wide and critical reading. This was not only reflected in his felicitous writing but bears on the breadth and depth of his understanding of issues that came before the Court.

His wide reading helped to counteract the powerful impact of the immediate and the concrete, natural enough in one so thoroughly immersed for so long in practice. Undue regard for the so-called practical leaves out of account the fact that a generalization based on it too often works injustice to the practical needs of the future. By keeping the pores of his intellectual interests open, Mr. Justice Jackson was alert against regarding his limited views, as any man's views are limited, as eternal verities and treating them as the commands of the Constitution. In addition to this unremitting effort to extend his understanding through wide and reflective reading, Nuremberg, I believe, had a profound influence on his endeavor to understand the human situation. An essentially good-natured, an even innocently unsophisticated, temperament was there made to realize how ultimately fragile the forces of reason are and how precious the safeguards of law so painstakingly built up in the course of the centuries.

His voice is stilled. His vitality persists. And not merely in the memory of his familiars. His speech breaks through the printed page. He was one of those rare men whose spoken word survives in type.

Mr. Justice Roberts

The dictum that history cannot be written without documents is less than a half truth if it implies that it can be written from them. Especially is this so in making an assessment of individual contributions to the collective results of the work of an institution like the Supreme Court, whose labors, by the very nature of its functions, are done behind closed doors and, on the whole, without leaving to history the documentation leading up to what is ultimately recorded in the *United States Reports.* To be sure, the opinions of the different Justices tell things about them—about some, more; about some, less. As is true of all literary compositions, to a critic saturated in them, qualities of the writer emerge from the writing. However, even in the case of an opinion by a Justice with the most distinctive style, what is said and what is left unsaid present to students of the Court a fascinating challenge of untangling individual influences in a collective judgment.

To discover the man behind the opinion and to estimate the influence he may have exerted in the Court's labors, in the case of Mr. Justice Roberts, is an essentially hopeless task. Before I came on the Court I had been a close student of its opinions. But not until I became a colleague, and even then only after some time, did I come to realize how little the opinions of Roberts, J., revealed the man and therefore the qualities that he brought to the work of the Court. In his case it can fairly be said the style—his judicial style—was not the man.

The *esprit* of Roberts's private communications leaves little doubt that when he came to writing his opinions he restrained the lively and imaginative phases of his temperament. I speak without knowledge, but he had evidently reflected much on the feel and flavor of a judicial opinion as an appropriate expression of the judicial judgment. The fires of his strong feelings were banked by

Reprinted from 104 *Univ. of Pa. L. Rev.* 311 (1955), an issue dedicated to the memory of Owen J. Roberts.

powerful self-discipline, and only on the rarest occasion does a spark flare up from the printed page. The sober and declaratory character of his opinions was, I believe, a form consciously chosen to carry out the judicial function as he saw it. We are told that Judge Augustus N. Hand, in disposing of a case that excited much popular agitation, set himself to writing an opinion in which nothing was "quotable." The reasons behind this attitude doubtless guided Justice Roberts in fashioning his judicial style. Moreover, his was, on the whole, a hidden rather than an obvious nature—hidden, that is, from the public view. His loyalties were deep, as was his devotion to his convictions. Both were phases of an uncompromising honesty. They constituted the most guarded qualities of his personality, and he would not vulgarize them by public manifestation.

In not revealing, indeed in suppressing, the richer and deeper qualities of his mind and character, the Roberts opinions reflect his own underestimation of his work. Partly, he was a very modest man, partly his judicial self-depreciation expressed his sense of awe to be a member of the bench charged with functions, in the language of Chief Justice Hughes, "of the gravest consequence to our people and to the future of our institutions." Above all, the standards for his self-appraisal were, characteristically, judges of the greatest distinction in the Court's history. On leaving the bench, he wrote: "I have no illusions about my judicial career. But one can only do what one can. Who am I to revile the good God that he did not make me a Marshall, a Taney, a Bradley, a Holmes, a Brandeis or a Cardozo."

Roberts was unjust to himself. He contributed more during his fifteen years on the Court than he himself could appraise. His extensive, diversified experience at the bar and his informed common sense brought wisdom to the disposition of the considerable body of litigation, outside the passions of popular controversy, that still comes before the Court. Again, his qualities of character —humility engendered by consciousness of limitations, respect for the views of others whereby one's own instinctive reactions are examined anew, subordination of solo performances to institutional interests, courtesy in personal relations that derives from respect for the conscientious labor of others and is not merely a show of formal manners—are indispensable qualities for the work of any court, but pre-eminently for that of the Supreme Court. Probably no Justice in the Court's history attached more significance to these qualities than Mr. Justice Brandeis. It tells more than pages of argumentation that Brandeis held Roberts in especial esteem as a member of the Court.

It is one of the most ludicrous illustrations of the power of lazy repetition of uncritical talk that a judge with the character of Roberts should have attributed to him a change of judicial views out of deference to political considerations. One is more saddened than shocked that a high-minded and thoughtful United States Senator should assume it to be an established fact that it was by reason of "the famous switch of Mr. Justice Roberts" that legislation was constitutionally sustained after President Roosevelt's proposal for reconstructing the Court and because of it. The charge specifically relates to the fact that while Roberts was of the majority in *Morehead* v. *New York ex rel. Tipaldo,*[1] decided June 1, 1936, in reaffirming *Adkins* v. *Children's Hospital,*[2] and thereby invalidating the New York minimum wage law, he was again with the majority in *West Coast Hotel Co.* v. *Parrish,*[3] decided on March 29, 1937, overruling the *Adkins* case and sustaining minimum wage legislation. Intellectual responsibility should, one would suppose, save a thoughtful man from the familiar trap of *post hoc ergo propter hoc.* Even those whose business it is to study the work of the Supreme Court have lent themselves to a charge which is refuted on the face of the Court records. It is refuted, that is, if consideration is given not only to opinions but to appropriate deductions drawn from data pertaining to the time when petitions

1. 298 U.S. 587 (1936).
2. 261 U.S. 525 (1923).
3. 300 U.S. 379 (1937).

for certiorari are granted, when cases are argued, when dispositions are, in normal course, made at conference, and when decisions are withheld because of absences and divisions on the Court.

It is time that this false charge against Roberts be dissipated by a recording of the indisputable facts. Disclosure of Court happenings not made public by the Court itself, in its opinions and orders, presents a ticklish problem. The secrecy that envelops the Court's work is not due to love of secrecy or want of responsible regard for the claims of democratic society to know how it is governed. That the Supreme Court should not be amenable to the forces of publicity to which the Executive and the Congress are subjected is essential to the effective functioning of the Court. But the passage of time may enervate the reasons for this restriction, particularly if disclosure rests not on tittle-tattle or self-serving declarations. The more so is justification for thus lifting the veil of secrecy valid if thereby the conduct of a Justice whose intellectual morality has been impugned is vindicated.

The truth about the so-called "switch" of Roberts in connection with the minimum wage cases is that when the *Tipaldo* case was before the Court in the spring of 1936, he was prepared to overrule the *Adkins* decision. Since a majority could not be had for overruling it, he silently agreed with the Court in finding the New York statute under attack in the *Tipaldo* case not distinguishable from the statute which had been declared unconstitutional in the *Adkins* case. That such was his position an alert reader could find in the interstices of the *United States Reports*. It took not a little persuasion—so indifferent was Roberts to misrepresentation—to induce him to set forth what can be extracted from the *Reports*. Here it is:[4]

> A petition for certiorari was filed in *Morehead v. Tipaldo*, 298 U.S. 587, on March 16, 1936. When the

4. Mr. Justice Roberts gave me this memorandum on November 9, 1945, after he had resigned from the bench. He left the occasion for using it to my discretion. For reasons indicated in the text, the present seems to me an appropriate time for making it public.

petition came to be acted upon, the Chief Justice spoke in favor of a grant, but several others spoke against it on the ground that the case was ruled by *Adkins vs. Children's Hospital*, 261 U.S. 525. Justices Brandeis, Cardozo and Stone were in favor of a grant. They, with the Chief Justice, made up four votes for a grant.

When my turn came to speak I said I saw no reason to grant the writ unless the Court were prepared to re-examine and overrule the *Adkins* case. To this remark there was no response around the table, and the case was marked granted.

Both in the petition for certiorari, in the brief on the merits, and in oral argument, counsel for the State of New York took the position that it was unnecessary to overrule the *Adkins* case in order to sustain the position of the State of New York. It was urged that further data and experience and additional facts distinguished the case at bar from the *Adkins* case. The argument seemed to me to be disingenuous and born of timidity. I could find nothing in the record to substantiate the alleged distinction. At conference I so stated, and stated further that I was for taking the State of New York at its word. The State had not asked that the *Adkins* case be overruled but that it be distinguished. I said I was unwilling to put a decision on any such ground. The vote was five to four for affirmance, and the case was assigned to Justice Butler.

I stated to him that I would concur in any opinion which was based on the fact that the State had not asked us to re-examine or overrule *Adkins* and that, as we found no material difference in the facts of the two cases, we should therefore follow the *Adkins* case. The case was originally so written by Justice Butler, but after a dissent had been circulated he added matter to his opinion, seeking to sustain the *Adkins* case in principle. My proper course would have been to concur specially on the narrow ground I had taken. I did not do so. But at conference in the Court I said that I did not propose to review and re-examine the *Adkins* case until a case should come to the Court requiring that this should be done.

August 17, 1936, an appeal was filed in *West Coast Hotels* [sic] *Company vs. Parrish,* 300 U.S. 379. The Court as usual met to consider applications in the week of Monday, October 5, 1936, and concluded its work by Saturday, October 10. During the conferences the jurisdictional statement in the *Parrish* case was considered and the question arose whether the appeal should be dismissed[5] on the authority of *Adkins* and *Morehead.* Four of those who had voted in the majority in the *Morehead* case voted to dismiss the appeal in the *Parrish* case. I stated that I would vote for the notation of probable jurisdiction. I am not sure that I gave my reason, but it was that in the appeal in the *Parrish* case the authority of *Adkins* was definitely assailed and the Court was asked to reconsider and overrule it. Thus, for the first time, I was confronted with the necessity of facing the soundness of the *Adkins* case. Those who were in the majority in the *Morehead* case expressed some surprise at my vote, and I heard one of the brethren ask another, "What is the matter with Roberts?"

Justice Stone was taken ill about October 14. The case was argued December 16 and 17, 1936, in the absence of Justice Stone, who at that time was lying in a comatose condition at his home. It came on for consideration at the conference on December 19. I voted for an affirmance. There were three other such votes, those of the Chief Justice, Justice Brandeis, and Justice Cardozo. The other four voted for a reversal.

If a decision had then been announced, the case would have been affirmed by a divided Court. It was thought that this would be an unfortunate outcome, as everyone on the Court knew Justice Stone's views. The case was, therefore, laid over for further consideration when Justice Stone should be able to participate. Justice Stone was convalescent during January and returned to the sessions of the Court on February 1, 1937. I believe that the *Parrish* case was taken up at the conference on February 6, 1937, and Justice Stone then voted for affirmance. This made it possible

5. Evidently he meant "should be reversed summarily," since the Washington Supreme Court had sustained the statute.

to assign the case for an opinion, which was done. The decision affirming the lower court was announced March 29, 1937.

These facts make it evident that no action taken by the President in the interim had any causal relation to my action in the *Parrish* case.

More needs to be said for Roberts than he cared to say for himself. As a matter of history it is regrettable that Roberts's unconcern for his own record led him to abstain from stating his position. The occasions are not infrequent when the disfavor of separate opinions, on the part of the bar and to the extent that it prevails within the Court, should not be heeded. Such a situation was certainly presented when special circumstances made Roberts agree with a result but basically disagree with the opinion which announced it.

The crucial factor in the whole episode was the absence of Mr. Justice Stone from the bench, on account of illness, from October 14, 1936, to February 1, 1937.[6]

In *Chamberlain* v. *Andrews*,[7] and its allied cases, decided November 23, 1936, the judgments of the New York Court of Appeals sustaining the New York Unemployment Insurance law were "affirmed by an equally divided Court." The constitutional outlook represented by these cases would reflect the attitude of a Justice toward the issues involved in the *Adkins* case. It can hardly be doubted that Van Devanter, McReynolds, Sutherland, and Butler, JJ., were the four Justices for reversal in *Chamberlain* v. *Andrews*. There can be equally no doubt that Hughes, C.J., and Brandeis and Cardozo, JJ., were for affirmance. Since Stone, J., was absent, it must have been Roberts who joined Hughes, Brandeis, and Cardozo. The appellants petitioned for a rehearing before the full bench, but since the position of Stone, as disclosed by his views in the *Tipaldo* case, would not have changed the result, that is, affirmance, the judgments were allowed to stand and the petition for rehearing was denied. Moreover,

6. 299 U.S. iii.
7. 299 U.S. 515 (1936).

in preceding Terms, Roberts had abundantly established that he did not have the narrow, restrictive attitude in the application of the broad, undefined provisions of the Constitution which led to decisions that provoked the acute controversies in 1936 and 1937.

Indeed, years before the 1936 election, in the 1933 Term he was the author of the opinion in *Nebbia* v. *New York,*[8] which evoked substantially the same opposing constitutional philosophy from Van Devanter, McReynolds, Sutherland, and Butler, JJ., as their dissent expressed in *West Coast Hotel Co.* v. *Parrish.* The result in the *Nebbia* case was significant enough. But for candor and courage, the opinion in which Roberts justified it was surely one of the most important contributions in years in what is perhaps the most far-reaching field of constitutional adjudication. It was an effective blow for liberation from empty tags and meretricious assumptions. In effect, Roberts wrote the epitaph on the misconception, which had gained respect from repetition, that legislative price-fixing as such was at least presumptively unconstitutional. In his opinion in *Parrish,* the Chief Justice naturally relied heavily on Roberts's opinion in *Nebbia,* for the reasoning of *Nebbia* had undermined the foundations of *Adkins.*

Few speculations are more treacherous than diagnosis of motives or genetic explanations of the position taken by Justices in Supreme Court decisions. Seldom can attribution have been wider of the mark than to find in Roberts's views in this or that case a reflection of economic predilection. He was, to be sure, as all men are, a child of his antecedents. But his antecedents united with his temperament to make him a forthright, democratic, perhaps even a somewhat innocently trusting, generous, humane creature. Long before it became popular to regard every so-called civil liberties question as constitutionally self-answering, Roberts gave powerful utterance to his sensitiveness for those procedural safeguards which are protective of human rights in a civilized society, even when invoked by the least appealing of characters.[9]

8. 291 U.S. 502 (1934).

9. See his opinion in Sorrells v. United States, 287 U.S. 435, 453 (1932); Snyder v. Massachusetts, 291 U.S. 97, 123 (1934).

Owen J. Roberts contributed his good and honest share to that coral-reef fabric which is law. He was content to let history ascertain, if it would, what his share was. But only one who had the good fortune to work for years beside him, day by day, is enabled to say that no man ever served on the Supreme Court with more scrupulous regard for its moral demands than Mr. Justice Roberts.

Mr. Justice Cardozo

Benjamin Nathan Cardozo was born in New York City, May 24, 1870, and after a heart attack and stroke, followed by a long illness, died at the home of his intimate friend Chief Judge Irving Lehman of the New York Court of Appeals, in Port Chester, New York, July 9, 1938. He was the younger son of Albert and Rebecca Nathan Cardozo, both of whom were descended from Sephardic Jews who had been connected with the Spanish and Portuguese Synagogue in New York from before the Revolution. Having been tutored by Horatio Alger, the popular author of stories for boys, he entered Columbia College from which he graduated at the age of nineteen and received his master's degree the following year, while attending the Columbia Law School. He did not stay for a degree in law and was admitted to the bar in 1891. For twenty-two years he modestly pursued what was essentially the calling of a barrister, that is, he was, in the main, counsel for other lawyers. As the practice of law is pursued in the United States, this was an unusual professional activity, even at the New York bar. Quite unknown to the general public, he rapidly gained the esteem of the bar and the bench of New York by his arguments and briefs, as counsel as well as referee, a functionary appointed by judges in specific cases, particularly those of a complicated commercial character, a field of law in which Cardozo especially excelled. His wide experience in arguing cases before the Court of Appeals (the highest in the hierarchy of New York courts) led him to write his first book, *Jurisdiction of the Court of Appeals of the State of New York,* published in 1903.

President Taft offered him a place on the United States District Court for the Southern District of New York. He had two sisters to support, and he felt compelled to decline it because of the then too meager salary. In 1913, as

The biography of Benjamin Nathan Cardozo is reprinted from Volume XXII (Supplement Two) of *Dictionary of American Biography* (© 1958 American Council of Learned Societies) by permission of Charles Scribner's Sons.

a result of one of those occasionally successful anti-Tammany movements in New York City, Cardozo was lifted out of his wholly private life by nomination and subsequent election as a justice of the Supreme Court of New York. This is the court that carries the heavy burden of litigation in New York. He was, however, destined to have little experience as a trial judge. Within six weeks, on the request of the Court of Appeals, the judges of which had long held him in high esteem, Governor Glynn designated him to serve temporarily as an associate judge of that Court. In January 1917 he was appointed a regular member by Governor Whitman to fill out a vacancy, and in the autumn was elected for a term of fourteen years on the joint nomination of both the major parties. In 1927, he was elected chief judge without opposition.

As he had been a lawyers' lawyer, so Cardozo became a judges' judge. For eighteen years his legal mastery, conveyed with great felicity, gave unusual distinction to the *New York Reports*. Joined as his learning was with an uncommonly charming personality, Cardozo exerted such intrinsic influence upon his court as to make it the second most distinguished judicial tribunal in the land. His philosophic temper of mind was nourished on wide reading. Naturally enough, this needed an outlet for freer expression than legal opinions permit. In four volumes, slender in size but full of insight, he set forth his views upon the relations of law to life: *The Nature of the Judicial Process*;[1] *The Growth of the Law*;[2] *The Paradoxes of Legal Science*;[3] *Law and Literature*.[4] Their common theme is the task that confronts the judge, but a candid scrutiny of what confronts the judge must face what confronts the law. By deftly spelling out much that was implicit in the early writings of Holmes and luminously analyzing what others gropingly felt, *The Nature of the Judicial Process* has established itself as a little classic. The essay form chosen by Cardozo was the fit instrument for a thinker

1. (1921).
2. (1924).
3. (1928).
4. (1931).

whose concern was to lay bare the contending claims that seek the mediation of law and to give some indication how this process of mediation in fact operates. An essay is adaptable to the tentative and suggestive, incomplete or even contradictory. It is thus an appropriate vehicle for conveying the zest and complexities and intractabilities of life.

The New York Court of Appeals, with its wide range of predominantly common-law litigation, was a natural field for Judge Cardozo. Barring only Mr. Justice Holmes, who was a seminal thinker in the law as well as vastly learned, no judge in his time was more deeply versed in the history of the common law or more resourceful in applying the living principles by which it has unfolded; and his mastery of the common law was matched by his love of it. His evolutionary adaptation of common-law principles to situations to which our industrial civilization gave rise influenced adjudication of courts throughout the English-speaking world. For example, in *MacPherson v. Buick Motor Co.*,[5] Judge Cardozo's opinion convincingly established the right of a person injured by a latent defect in a car purchased at retail to redress against the manufacturer, for the reason that the defect might have been discovered had the manufacturer exercised appropriate care. The specific instance gave rise to a radiating principle which was so convincingly vindicated that it eventually commended itself to the House of Lords,[6] and has now become an established part of the law of torts.

Not only was the stuff of the litigation before the Court of Appeals of New York congenial to his professional interest, he was wholly happy in his personal associations. It was therefore a severe wrench for him to be taken from Albany to Washington. Probably no man ever took a seat on the Supreme Bench so reluctantly. This he did in 1932, when President Hoover, upon the resignation of Mr. Justice Holmes, named him as Holmes's successor.[7] While his nomination was universally acclaimed, from the point

5. 217 N.Y. 382 (1916).
6. Donoghue v. Stevenson, [1932] A.C. 562.
7. See 285 U.S. iii.

of view of "practical politics" serious obstacles emerged against it before he was named. There was the geographic objection: two New Yorkers, Chief Justice Hughes and Mr. Justice Stone, were already on the Court, and it would make for imbalance for one State, particularly New York, to have a third of the membership of the Court. When this objection was made, Senator William E. Borah of Idaho, one of the Republican leaders and chairman of the powerful Committee on Foreign Relations, told President Hoover that Cardozo belonged as much to Idaho as to New York. As Professor Chafee put it, "President Hoover ignored geography and made history."[8] When the sectarian difficulty was whispered, in that there was already one Jew, Brandeis, on the Court, Senator Borah said to the President (who was himself singularly free from this bias), "The way to deal with anti-Semitism is not to yield to it," adding, "Just as John Adams is best remembered for his appointment of John Marshall to the Supreme Court, so you, Mr. President, have the opportunity of being best remembered for putting Cardozo there." Disregarding all irrelevancies, the President named Cardozo because he was Cardozo.

Fate granted him less than six full Terms on the Supreme Bench. With rare exceptions, the great reputations on that Court have been partly a function of time. It is some measure of Cardozo's qualities that in so short a time he left so enduring a mark on the constitutional history of the United States. With astonishing rapidity he made the adjustment from preoccupation with the comparatively restricted problems of private litigation to the most exacting demands of judicial statesmanship. Immense learning, deep culture, critical detachment, intellectual courage, and unswerving disinterestedness reinforced imagination and native humility, and gave him in rare measure the qualities which are the special requisites for the work of the Court to whose keeping is entrusted no small share of the destiny of the nation.

It bespeaks much for the responsiveness of the mass of mankind to sheer goodness that so shy and sensitive

8. 165 *Harper's Magazine* 34 (June 1932).

a man, so withdrawn a nature as Cardozo, should have communicated his exquisite qualities on so wide a scale. The feeling of respect bordering on reverence which Cardozo aroused was strikingly manifested in relation to a poignant episode in his life. His father was one of the so-called Tweed judges—William M. Tweed, the Tammany Hall boss and corrupt ruler of New York—and resigned under a cloud when Tweed was deposed. By tacit agreement the press kept quiet about this incident when Cardozo ran for high judicial office in New York and on the occasion of his nomination to the Supreme Court. He did not have the common touch, but he was tender and compassionate. Great courtesy, accentuated by the slight stoop of the cloistered scholar, a face, according to Holmes, "beautiful with intellect and character,"[9] a fine head with silken white hair, combined to give him a striking personal appearance. Though he was most at ease with a few familiars talking law, he charmed whenever he ventured forth, on rare occasions, into the social life of Washington. He never married, but he had chivalric feelings about women. When he dedicated one of his books to the "sacred memory" of his sister Ellen, he described precisely what he felt. In his writing generally, he was given somewhat to the heightened language of rhetoric and a tendency toward figurative language dangerous to judicial speech. While pedestrian critics complain that Holmes was unduly incisive, Cardozo may fairly be charged with being elegantly diffuse. His style was Corinthian, not Doric.

Greatness implies uniquity. It is idle, therefore, to compare Mr. Justice Cardozo with other towering figures among American judges. That Cardozo belongs among our great judges—not more, surely, than a dozen—is not in dispute. Indeed, his achievement in Washington merely confirmed and amplified the distinction he made manifest in Albany. He was translated to the Supreme Court, despite all the considerations of narrow expediency against his selection, precisely because of his unique qualifications. Chief Judge Cardozo was the one man, in

9. 2 *Holmes-Laski Letters* 837 (Howe ed. 1953).

the general opinion of bench and bar, fit to succeed Mr. Justice Holmes.

With an accent of reverence, Cardozo always spoke of Holmes as "the Master." Both served the same mistress —the law—with complete devotion. Neither St. Francis nor Thomas More led a more dedicated life than these two men, so different in antecedents and temperament, who applied their great endowments to resolving by law the conflicts between man and man and between liberty and authority—law compounded of wisdom from the past and insight into the future. Cardozo spoke for all great judges when he wrote that the judge must be "historian and prophet all in one." For law is "not only as the past has shaped it in judgments already rendered, but as the future ought to shape it in cases yet to come." The common law, which was Cardozo's preoccupation during his long tenure on the New York Court of Appeals, is a process of constant rejuvenation to meet the demands of a society that is not stagnant. Such readjustments require a proper balance between retaining and changing. Under the influence of his master, Cardozo was second only to Holmes in making of the judicial process a blend of continuity and creativeness.

Like Holmes, Cardozo carried his philosophic outlook on law into the more spacious and more treacherous field of constitutional law. That he should have attained pre-eminence after so short a tenure on the Supreme Bench (where one does not get one's bearing, so Chief Justice Hughes said, for at least three years), is only partly due to the unusual flow of litigation of far-reaching import during his few years on the Court. Mr. Justice Cardozo did not derive distinction from the distorting significance of so-called "great cases." Some cases are born great and a judge shares the great occasion. Other cases achieve distinction through the creative power of the judge, especially when insight is conveyed with felicity. Cardozo imparted intellectual significance to cases great or small, whether of inflamed public interest or of recondite technicality.

To select representative samples of Cardozo's judicial prowess and of his art in manifesting it is an ungracious task. The range and richness of his seven-score Supreme Court opinions could be demonstrated equally well by others than those here named. Of the six here chosen, three are in private litigation, three in public, three are opinions of the Court, three are dissents. They are: *Reed* v. *Allen,*[10] because of its resourcefulness in making the law of remedies an instrument of justice; *Stewart Dry Goods Co.* v. *Lewis,*[11] because of its illuminating analysis of problems of taxation; *McCandless* v. *Furlaud,*[12] because it proves the law of corporate trusteeship can master the skill of individual chicanery; *Ashton* v. *Cameron County District,*[13] because it demonstrates, with a persuasiveness that eventually carried the day, that the distribution of power between the nation and the States does not mean the impotence of both; the *Social Security Cases,*[14] because of the proof that the Constitution does not preclude the federal system from meeting exigent and pervasive human needs; *Palko* v. *Connecticut,*[15] because of its penetrating exposition of the task confronting the Court in the enforcement of the due process clause of the Fourteenth Amendment.

Courage is especially shining when exercised by a markedly gentle nature. This lawyers' lawyer, this man of the cloister, as he faced the application of the Constitution to a rapidly changing world, at times dared to free the future from the tyranny of slogans and outmoded formulas when some of his brethren, who came from the world of affairs, imprisoned themselves in the ephemeral past. The few short years on the Supreme Court of this gentle and withdrawn spirit coincided—such is the sardonic play of Fate—with one of the most tempestuous periods in the Court's

10. 286 U.S. 191, 201 (1932) (dissent).
11. 294 U.S. 550, 556 (1935) (dissent).
12. 296 U.S. 140 (1935).
13. 298 U.S. 513, 532 (1936) (dissent).
14. Steward Machine Co. v. Davis, 301 U.S. 548 (1937); Helvering v. Davis, 301 U.S. 619 (1937).
15. 302 U.S. 319 (1937).

history, the years of its invalidation of much of the New Deal legislation and the consequent proposal by President Roosevelt for reconstruction of the Court, the so-called "Court packing plan." But so dominant was his serene temper that he transcended the heated controversies in which the labors of the Court were enmeshed. Mr. Justice Cardozo's opinions during those troubled years have already come to reflect, not the friction and passion of their day, but the abiding spirit of the Constitution.

John Marshall and the Judicial Function

Two hundred years ago a great man was born who indisputably is the "one alone" to be chosen "if American law were to be represented by a single figure." John Marshall was the chief architect "of a new body of jurisprudence, by which guiding principles are raised above the reach of statute and State, and judges are entrusted with a solemn and hitherto unheard-of authority and duty."[1] Such is the verdict of one whom so qualified a critic as Mr. Justice Cardozo deemed probably the greatest intellect in the history of the English-speaking judiciary.

Unlike other great pioneers in the law, Hardwicke in equity, Mansfield in commercial law, Stowell in prize law, Holmes in torts, the essential heritage of Marshall, because of the very nature of constitutional law, does not lie in specific precepts, definite rules more or less easy of application in new circumstances. Of his opinions it is peculiarly true that their "radiating potencies" go far beyond the actual holdings of the decisions.[2] The tendencies propelled by his opinions give him his unique place in our history; through them he belongs among the main builders of our nation. Although he led an important diplomatic mission and was not an otiose secretary of state, the decisive claim to John Marshall's distinction as a great statesman is as a judge. And he is the only judge who has that distinction. It derives from the happy conjunction of Marshall's qualities of mind and character, the opportunities afforded by the Court over which he was called to preside, the duration of his service, and the time in which he served—the formative period in the country's history.

When Jefferson heard that Hamilton was urging John Marshall to enter Congress, he wrote to Madison, on June 29, 1792: "I am told that Marshall has expressed half a mind to come. Hence I conclude that Hamilton has plyed

A speech at the Harvard Law School's celebration of the two hundredth anniversary of the birth of John Marshall, originally published with all the proceedings of the celebration under the title *Government Under Law* (Sutherland ed., 1956).

1. Holmes, *Collected Legal Papers* 270 (1920).
2. See Hawks v. Hamill, 288 U.S. 52, 58 (1933).

him well with flattery & sollicitation, and I think nothing better could be done than to make him a judge."[3] How ironically Fate outwitted Jefferson in his desire to sidetrack Marshall to what Jefferson conceived to be the innocuous role of a judge.[4]

When Marshall came to the Supreme Court, the Constitution was still essentially a virgin document. By a few opinions—a mere handful—he gave institutional direction to the inert ideas of a paper scheme of government. Such an achievement demanded an undimmed vision of the union of States as a nation and the determination of an uncompromising devotion to such insight. Equally indispensable was the power to formulate views expressing this outlook with the persuasiveness of compelling simplicity.

It is shallow to deny that general ideas have influence or to minimize their importance. Marshall's ideas, diffused in all sorts of ways, especially through the influence of the legal profession, have become the presuppositions of our political institutions. He released an enduring spirit, a mode of approach for generations of judges charged with the awesome duty of subjecting the conduct of government and the claims of individual rights to the touchstone of a written document, binding the government and safeguarding such rights. He has afforded this guidance not only for his own country. In the federalisms that have evolved out of the British Empire, Marshall's outlook in constitutional adjudications has been the lode-star. Unashamedly I recall the familiar phrase in which he expressed the core of his constitutional philosophy: "it is a *constitution* we are expounding."[5] It bears repeating because it is, I believe, the single most important utterance in the literature of constitutional law—most important because most comprehensive and comprehending.

3. 6 *The Writings of Thomas Jefferson* 95–97 (Ford ed. 1895).

4. I am indebted to Professor Julian P. Boyd for calling my attention to this letter as well as for its exact phrasing, based on the recipient's copy in the Madison Papers, Library of Congress.

5. M'Culloch v. Maryland, 4 Wheat. 316, 407 (1819).

I should like to follow James Bradley Thayer in believing that the conception of the nation which Marshall derived from the Constitution and set forth in *M'Culloch* v. *Maryland* is his greatest single judicial performance. It *is* that, both in its persuasiveness and in its effect. As good a test as I know of the significance of an opinion is to contemplate the consequences of its opposite. The courage of *Marbury* v. *Madison*[6] is not minimized by suggesting that its reasoning is not impeccable and its conclusion, however wise, not inevitable. I venture to say this though fully aware that, since Marshall's time and largely, I suspect, through the momentum of the experience which he initiated, his conclusion in *Marbury* v. *Madison* has been deemed by great English-speaking courts an indispensable, implied characteristic of a written constitution. Holmes could say, as late as 1913: "I do not think the United States would come to an end if we lost our power to declare an Act of Congress void." But he went on to say: "I do think the Union would be imperiled if we could not make that declaration as to the laws of the several States. For one in my place sees how often a local policy prevails with those who are not trained to national views and how often action is taken that embodies what the Commerce Clause was meant to end."[7] One can, I believe, say with assurance that a failure to conceive the Constitution as Marshall conceived it in *M'Culloch* v. *Maryland,* to draw from it the national powers which have since been exercised and to exact deference to such powers from the States, would have been reflected by a very different United States than history knows. Marshall surely was right when he wrote, a month after he rejected the argument for Maryland: "If the principles which have been advanced on this occasion were to prevail, the Constitution would be converted into the old Confederation."

Marshall's intrinsic achievements are too solid and his personal qualities too homespun to tolerate mythical treatment. It is important not to make untouchable dog-

6. 1 Cranch 137 (1803).
7. Holmes, *supra* note 1, at 296.

mas of the fallible reasoning of even our greatest judge, and not to attribute God-like qualities to the builders of our nation. Does it not border on the ludicrous that by questioning whether Marshall was an original thinker Holmes nearly barred his own way to the Supreme Court? So deeply had uncritical reverence for Marshall's place in our national pantheon lodged itself in the confident judgment of President Theodore Roosevelt.[8] As though one should look among even the greatest of judges for what Holmes called "originators of transforming thought."[9] I venture to suggest that had they the mind of such originators, the bench is not the place for its employment. Transforming thought implies too great a break with the past, implies too much discontinuity, to be imposed upon society by one who is entrusted with enforcing its law.

Marshall's creativeness has from time to time been discounted by attributing the ground he broke in his opinions to the arguments of the great lawyers who appeared before him, especially Webster. The latter was no mean appreciator of his own performance, but an examination of his argument in *Gibbons* v. *Ogden*[10] hardly confirms his boast that Marshall's opinion "was little else than a recital of my argument."[11] Powerful counsel no doubt have impact upon the strongest Court, and probably never in the history of the Supreme Court has such a galaxy of talent appeared before it as in Marshall's day. Not the least distinction of a great judge is his capacity to assimilate, to modify, or to reject the discursive and inevitably partisan argument of even the most persuasive counsel and to transform their raw material into a judicial judgment. So it was with Marshall.

Again, it is not to be assumed that what Marshall wrote was wholly the product of his own brain, freed from infusion of his brethren's thinking. In his day there was the

8. See 1 *Selections from the Correspondence of Theodore Roosevelt and Henry Cabot Lodge* 517–519 (1925).

9. Holmes, *supra* note 1, at 269.

10. 9 Wheat. 1 (1824).

11. Harvey, *Reminiscences and Anecdotes of Daniel Webster* 142 (1877).

closest intimacy among the Justices. It is inconceivable that they did not discuss their cases in their common boardinghouse. A man of Marshall's charm and power was bound to make himself deeply felt among his brethren. But the assumption that he dominated his colleagues leaves out of reckoning the strong personalities among them. Story had the deepest devotion to Marshall, but he also had views and vanity. Johnson's opinions reveal tough-mindedness, abounding intellectual energy, and a downright character. Likewise, we may be sure that Bushrod Washington was no mere echo. And so one may be confident in inferring that the novelty of the issues, the close social relations of the Justices, the ample opportunities they had for discussion among themselves, precluded Marshall's path-breaking opinions from being exclusively solo performances. Then as now, constitutional decisions are the outcome of the deliberative process, and as such, more or less, composite products. But their expression is individual. The voice of the Court cannot avoid imparting the distinction of its own accent to a Court opinion. In the leading constitutional cases Marshall spoke for the Court. But *he* spoke. The prestige of his office, the esteem, which he personally aroused, the deference he evoked, enabled Marshall to formulate in his own way an agreement collectively reached. Thus, in his exposition of the commerce clause, Marshall indulged in observations not only beyond the necessities of the cases but outside the demands of his own analysis.

To slight these phases of his opinions as dicta, though such they were on a technical view, is to disregard significant aspects of his labors and the ways in which constitutional law develops. There can be little doubt that Marshall saw and seized his opportunities to educate the country to a spacious view of the Constitution, to accustom the public mind to broad national powers, to counteract the commercial and political self-centeredness of States. He was on guard against every tendency to continue treating the new union as though it were the old confederation. He imparted such a momentum to his views that the Court and eventually the country were moved in his general direction, beyond his own time and into our own.

The role that Marshall played in the evolution of our nation ought, I should think, to make it difficult for those who believe that history is reducible to laws, to fit them into their schemata. Surely the course of American history would have been markedly different if the Senate had not rejected the nomination of John Rutledge to succeed Jay as Chief Justice; if the benign Cushing, a Federalist of different composition from Marshall's, had not withdrawn after a week and had continued as Chief Justice till his death in 1810; if Ellsworth's resignation had come later; if John Adams had persuaded Jay to return as Chief Justice; or if some readily imaginable circumstance had delayed Ellsworth's replacement till John Adams was out of the White House so that the new Chief Justice would have been a Jeffersonian. (That it would have been Spencer Roane is an unsubstantiated tradition.) John Marshall is a conspicuous instance of Cleopatra's nose.

This does not make me an adherent of the hero theory of history. If I may quote Mr. Isaiah Berlin:

> Historical movements exist, and we must be allowed to call them so. Collective acts do occur; societies do rise, flourish, decay, die. Patterns, 'atmospheres,' complex interrelationships of men or cultures are what they are, and cannot be analysed away into atomic constituents. Nevertheless, to take such expressions so literally that it becomes natural and normal to attribute to them causal properties, active powers, transcendent properties . . . is to be fatally deceived by myths . . . There is no formula which guarantees a successful escape from either the Scylla of populating the world with imaginary powers and dominions, or the Charybdis of reducing everything to the verifiable behavior of identifiable men and women in precisely denotable places and times.[12]

12. Berlin, *Historical Inevitability* 16 (1954).

Certainly on this occasion it is appropriate to assert with emphasis that John Marshall was not the fated agency of inevitable economic and social forces to make this decisive contribution in the shaping of this country's destiny.

Temperament, experience, and association converged to his outlook in judicial action. Even more truly than Gibbon could say of himself, "the Captain of the Hampshire grenadiers . . . has not been useless to the historian of the Roman Empire" can it be claimed that Marshall's experience at Valley Forge was not without decisive influence in the work of the great Chief Justice.[13] Ties of friendship and effective participation in the struggle for the Constitution confirmed his national outlook. Local government had become associated in his mind with the petty bickerings of narrow ambition and dangerous indifference to rights of property and social cohesion. This revealed the need of a strong central government to whose authority the States must be obedient. Subordination of the States to the authority of the national government within the scope of its powers was the deepest article of his faith, political and judicial. Experience of men and affairs in the Virginia House of Burgesses, in Congress, as a diplomat, and as secretary of state, doubtless reinforced a temperament to which abstract theorizing was never congenial. He reflected the literary tradition of his time in his partiality for abstract language to support concrete results. But he had a hard-headed appreciation of the complexities of government, particularly in a federal system. His deep instinct for the practical saved him, on the whole, from rigidities to bind the changing future. Uncompromising as was his aim to promote adequate national power, he was not dogmatic in the choice of doctrine for attaining this end. And so at times, conspicuously in *Gibbons* v. *Ogden*, his views appear to reflect cross currents of doctrine, ambiguously expressed. In one striking instance, *Wilson* v. *The Black Bird Creek Marsh Co.*,[14] he did little more than decide, stating hardly

13. *The Autobiographies of Edward Gibbon* 190 (John Murray ed. 1896).

14. 2 Pet. 245 (1829).

any doctrine but hinting enough to foreshadow, certainly in direction, the vitally important accommodation between national and local needs formulated more than twenty years later in *Cooley* v. *Board of Wardens of the Port of Philadelphia.*[15]

There is a rather supercilious tendency to speak disparagingly of Marshall's work on the Court when dealing with lawyers' law. In contrast to Jefferson's view, which continues to have echoes, of regarding Marshall's associates as his tools in the constitutional cases, praise of his judicial statecraft is sometimes used to emphasize his inferiority in nonconstitutional adjudications. Story, Bushrod Washington, William Johnson, Brockholst Livingston are counted as his superiors. Joseph Story, to be sure, carried great learning, even if not always lightly. Disregard of Bushrod Washington's judicial qualities bespeaks unfamiliarity with Judge Hopkinson's and Horace Binney's estimates of him, and Professor Donald G. Morgan's recent book on Mr. Justice Johnson ought to bring wider appreciation of one of the strongest minds in the Court's history. But none of Marshall's associates will suffer depreciation by recognizing his performance in cases that are lawyers' law. After all, this constituted nine-tenths of the Court's business during the thirty-four years of Marshall's magistracy. He was not a bookish lawyer, though he was no stranger to books. He could, as wise judges do, make them his servants. He eschewed precedents, such as were then available, in his opinions for the Court. But he showed mastery in treatment of precedents where they had been relied on for an undesirable result. By way of example, I avouch his dissent in *The Venus,*[16] against the strong views of Washington, J., supported by Story. Likewise he was not overwhelmed by the parade of Story's learning in *The Neireide,*[17] when such learning led to a harsh view of neutral rights. Though he respected Lord Stowell as "a very great man"

15. 12 How. 299, 319 (1851).
16. 8 Cranch 253, 288 (1814).
17. 9 Cranch 388 (1815).

he cut free from that master of prize law, deeming him to have a learning strong even if unconscious, in favor of captors.

As good an insight as any into the quality of Marshall's intellect is afforded by Francis Walker Gilmer, a brilliant Virginian contemporary of high promise. Marshall's mind, he wrote, "is not very richly stored with knowledge, but it is so creative, so well organized by nature, or disciplined by early education, and constant habits of systematick thinking, that he embraces every subject with the clearness and facility of one prepared by previous study to comprehend and explain it."[18]

Charged as I have been with opening a conference to commemorate the two-hundredth anniversary of the birth of John Marshall, I surely have been obedient to my duty in speaking of him. But once I leave the secure footing of that well-trodden ground, what else can be pertinent to an opening address of a three-day conference on Government Under Law, systematically planned with definite parts appropriately assigned to learned inquirers into the perplexities of the problems summarized by this great theme?

In so far as I have not already exhausted my function, my further relation to the resplendent show to follow is like unto that of the Greek chorus. In view of the pre-occupation of this conference, of course I want to keep strictly within the law of my assignment. Accordingly, I have briefed myself on the proper task of the Greek chorus. While in early days the destiny of the chorus was "involved in that of the principal characters," when the Attic stage was at its highest perfection the chorus was "thrown much further into the background," and appears "not as a participant in the action, but merely as a sympathetic witness." The chorus was, so my authority continues, "removed from the stress and turmoil of the action into a calmer and more remote region, though it still preserves its interest in the events upon the stage."

18. Gilmer, *Sketches, Essays, and Translations* 23–24, quoted in 2 Beveridge, *The Life of John Marshall* 178 (1916).

This clearly is my cue, rather than the later still more receding role of the chorus, whereby it "begins to lose even its interest in the action" and "sings odes of a mythological character, which have only the remotest connexion with the incidents of the plot."[19]

There is little danger that in my remaining observations I shall be intruding on the fertile areas of inquiry that belong to the distinguished speakers whom we are to hear these three days. I hope I shall be equally successful in not straying outside my confining judicial curtilage. One brought up in the traditions of James Bradley Thayer, echoes of whom were still resounding in this very building in my student days, is committed to Thayer's statesmanlike conception of the limits within which the Supreme Court should move, and I shall try to be loyal to his admonition regarding the restricted freedom of members of that Court to pursue their private views.

Marshall's significance could not be more fittingly celebrated than by scrutinizing, which is the aim of this conference, the state of "government under law," more particularly under the legal system to which Marshall so heavily contributed, 120 years after he wrote his last opinion. Could he listen to these proceedings, nothing would be bound to strike him more than the enlarged scope of law since his day. He would, of course, think of law as legally enforceable rights. For, while he occasionally referred to "natural law," it was not much more than literary garniture, even as in our own day, and not a guiding means for adjudication. He would have sympathized, as other judges have, with Sir Frederick Pollock's remark: "In the Middle Ages natural law was regarded as the senior branch of divine law and therefore had to be treated as infallible (but there was no infallible way of knowing what it was)."[20] Marshall would be amazed by the interpenetration of law in government, because during his whole era he was concerned with the Constitution as an instrument predominantly regulating the machinery of

19. Haigh, *The Attic Theatre* 320–321 (2d ed. 1898).
20. 1 *Holmes-Pollock Letters* 275 (Howe ed. 1941).

government, and more particularly distributing powers between the central government and the States. The Constitution was not thought of as the repository of the supreme law limiting all government, with a court wielding the deepest-cutting power of deciding whether there is any authority in government at all to do what is sought to be done.

Thus, the gravamen of the attack in the Virginia and Kentucky Resolutions against the Alien and Sedition Acts of 1798 was that they infringed on the rights of the States and were promotive of "a general consolidated government." It deserves to be recalled that even Jefferson attributed to the States the power which he denied to the federal government. "Nor does the opinion of the unconstitutionality and consequent nullity of that law [the Sedition Act]," he wrote to Abigail Adams, "remove all restraint from the overwhelming torrent of slander which is confounding all vice and virtue, all truth and falsehood in the US. The power to do that is fully possessed by the several state legislatures . . . While we deny that Congress have a right to controul the freedom of the press, we have ever asserted the rights of the states, and their exclusive right, to do so."[21]

The only two Marshallian constitutional opinions that concern individual rights as such, *Fletcher* v. *Peck*[22] and the *Dartmouth College Case*,[23] rather than the delimitation of power between two governments, are, in the perspective of time, not of great importance. This came to pass partly because of easy legislative correction, partly because the doctrine of strict construction devised in the *Charles River Bridge Case*[24] took the sting out of the decision of the *Dartmouth College Case*. Moreover, insofar as the latter case forbade legislative transfer of the prop-

21. I am indebted for the exact text of this letter, dated September 11, 1804, to the kindness of Professor Julian P. Boyd, in one of whose forthcoming volumes of *The Papers of Thomas Jefferson* it will duly appear in its entirety.

22. 6 Cranch 87 (1810).

23. 4 Wheat. 518 (1819).

24. 11 Pet. 420 (1837).

erty of the College to the Trustees, it is a safe assumption that the due process clauses would condemn such an attempt.[25]

The vast change in the scope of law between Marshall's time and ours is at bottom a reflection of the vast change in the circumstances of society. The range of business covered by Marshall's Court, though operating under a written Constitution, was in the main not very different from the concerns of the English courts, except that the latter dealt much more with property settlements. The vast enveloping present-day role of law is not the design of a statesman nor attributable to the influence of some great thinker. It is a reflection of the great technological revolution which brought in its train what a quiet writer in the *Economist* could call "the tornado of economic and social change of the last century." Law has been an essential accompaniment of the shift from "watch-dog government"—the phrase is George Kennan's—to the service state. For government has become a service state, whatever the tint of the party in power and whatever time-honored slogans it may use to enforce and promote measures that hardly vindicate the slogans. Profound social changes continue to be in the making, due to movement of industrialization, urbanization, and permeating egalitarian ideas.

With crude accuracy I have just summarized the situation in the countries of the English-speaking world, about which alone I may speak. But when these transforming economic and social forces got under full swing in the United States, lawyers and courts found available in the Fourteenth Amendment resources for curbing legislative responses to new pressures. That amendment was gradually invoked against the substance of legislation and not merely to support claims based on traditionally fair procedure.

25. See Chief Justice Doe's opinion in Dow v. Northern R. Co., 67 N.H. 1, 27–53 (1887); Doe, "A New View of the Dartmouth College Case," 6 *Harv. L. Rev.* 161, 213 (1892); and Jeremiah Smith in 1 *Proc. N.H. Bar Ass'n* 287, 302 (n.s. 1901).

I have thus reached the slippery slope of due process. But not even to take a glance at it in a reconnaissance, however sketchy, of government under law, would indeed be to play *Hamlet* without Hamlet.

It has been frequently stated that when a question arises in due course of a litigation, whether a constitutional provision has been infringed, the established courts of justice "must by necessity determine that question."[26] This is only qualifiedly true regarding our Constitution. Thus, the explicit provision requiring one State to surrender to another a fugitive from justice (art. IV, §2, cl. 2) is "merely declaratory of a moral duty" and is not, because of the subject matter, enforceable in the courts.[27] Likewise, the "guarantee to every state" of "a Republican Form of Government," must, because of the subject matter, look elsewhere than to the courts for observance.[28] There are not a few other instances in which judicial relief was barred because "political questions" were deemed to be involved.

It is not for me to find the common denominator of these judicial abstentions, or to give the contour and content of what questions are "political," in the sense of precluding judicial examination. But I do venture to believe that no judge charged with the duty of enforcing the due process clauses of the Fifth and Fourteenth Amendments and the equal protection of the laws clause of the Fourteenth Amendment, can free himself from the disquietude that the line is often very thin between the cases in which the Court felt compelled to abstain from adjudication because of their "political" nature, and the cases that so frequently arise in applying the concepts of "liberty" and "equality."

In his First Inaugural Jefferson spoke of the "sacred principle" that "the will of the majority is in all cases to

26. See Lord Selborne in The Queen v. Burah, 3 App. Cas. 889, 904 (P.C. 1878), quoted approvingly by Lord Wright in James v. Commonwealth of Australia, [1936] A.C. 578, 613 (P.C.); see also Swart, N.O. and Nicol, N.O. v. de Kock and Garner, [1951] 3 So. Afr. L.R. 589, 601–602, 611.

27. Kentucky v. Dennison, 24 How. 66 (1861).

28. Pacific States Tel. & Tel. Co. v. Oregon, 223 U.S. 118 (1912).

prevail."[29] Jefferson himself hardly meant all by "all."[30] In any event, one need not give full adherence to his view to be deeply mindful of the fact that judicial review is a deliberate check upon democracy through an organ of government not subject to popular control. In relation to the judiciary's task in the type of cases I am now discussing, I am raising the difficulties which I think must in all good conscience be faced, unless perchance the Court is expected to register a particular view and unless the profession that the judiciary is the disinterested guardian of our Constitution be pretense.

It may be that responsibility for decision dulls the capacity of discernment. The fact is that one sometimes envies the certitude of outsiders regarding the compulsions to be drawn from vague and admonitory constitutional provisions. Only for those who have not the responsibility of decision can it be easy to decide the grave and complex problems they raise, especially in controversies that excite public interest. This is so because they too often present legal issues inextricably and deeply bound up in emotional reactions to sharply conflicting economic, social, and political views. It is not the duty of judges to express their personal attitudes on such issues, deep as their individual convictions may be. The opposite is the truth; it is their duty not to act on merely personal views. But "due process" once we go beyond its strictly procedural aspect, and the "equal protection of the laws" enshrined in the Constitution, are precisely defined neither by history nor in terms. It deserves to be noted that so far as gaining light from pertinent data on the intention of Congress on

29. The following is the sentence in which the quoted phrase occurs: "All, too, will bear in mind this sacred principle, that though the will of the majority is in all cases to prevail, that will to be rightful must be reasonable; that the minority possess their equal rights, which equal law must protect, and to violate would be oppression." A little later in that address Jefferson included in what he deemed "the essential principles of our Government," "absolute acquiescence in the decisions of the majority, the vital principle of republics, from which is no appeal but to force, the vital principle and immediate parent of despotism." 1 *Messages and Papers of the Presidents* 322, 323 (Richardson ed. 1899).

30. See Jefferson's answers to Démeunier's first queries, reprinted in 10 *The Papers of Thomas Jefferson* 18 (Boyd ed. 1954).

specific issues in formulating the Fourteenth Amendment, the Supreme Court found: "At best, they are inconclusive."[31] This finding of darkness was reached not for want of searching inquiry by Court and counsel.

No doubt, these provisions of the Constitution were not calculated to give permanent legal sanction merely to the social arrangements and beliefs of a particular epoch. Like all legal provisions without a fixed technical meaning, they are ambulant, adaptable to the changes of time. That is their strength; that also makes dubious their appropriateness for judicial enforcement. Dubious because their vagueness readily lends itself to make of the Court a third chamber with drastic veto power. This danger has been pointed out by our greatest judges too often to be dismissed as a bogey. Holding democracy in judicial tutelage is not the most promising way to foster disciplined responsibility in a people.[32]

It is, of course, no longer to be questioned that claims under the Fourteenth Amendment are subject to judicial judgment. This makes it all the more important to realize what is involved in the discharge of this function of the Court, particularly since this is probably the largest source of the Court's business. It is important, that is, fully to appreciate the intrinsic nature of the issues when the Court is called upon to determine whether the Legislature or the Executive has regulated "liberty" or "property" "without due process of law" or has denied "equal protection of the laws"; to appreciate the difficulties in making a judgment upon such issues, difficulties of a different order from those normally imposed upon jural tribunals; and, not least, to appreciate the qualifications requisite for those who exercise this extraordinary authority, demanding as it does a breadth of outlook and an invincible disinterestedness rooted in temperament and confirmed by discipline. Of course, individual judgment and feeling cannot be wholly shut out of the judicial process. But if they dominate, the judicial process becomes a

31. Brown v. Board of Education, 347 U.S. 483, 489 (1954).

32. See AFL v. American Sash & Door Co., 335 U.S. 538, 555–557 (1949) (concurring opinion).

dangerous sham. The conception by a judge of the scope and limits of his function may exert an intellectual and moral force as much as responsiveness to a particular audience or congenial environment.

We are dealing with constitutional provisions the nature of which can be best conveyed compendiously by Judge Learned Hand's phrase that they "represent a mood rather than a command, that sense of moderation, of fair play, of mutual forbearance, without which states become the prey of faction."[33] Alert search for enduring standards by which the judiciary is to exercise its duty in enforcing those provisions of the Constitution that are expressed in what Ruskin called "chameleon words," needs the indispensable counterpoise of sturdy doubt that one has found those standards. Yesterday the active area in this field was concerned with "property." Today it is "civil liberties." Tomorrow it may again be "property." Who can say that in a society with a mixed economy, like ours, these two areas are sharply separated, and that certain freedoms in relation to property may not again be deemed, as they were in the past, aspects of individual freedom?

Let me sharpen these difficulties by concreteness. In *Plessy* v. *Ferguson*,[34] Mr. Justice Harlan floated an oft-quoted epigram, but in a few short years he did not apply it, proving once more that sonorous abstractions do not solve problems with intractable variables.[35] Thinking of "equality" in abstract terms led Mr. Justice Harlan to be blind to the meaning of "yellow-dog contracts" as a serious curtailment of liberty in the context of anti-union strategy;[36] and to be equally blind to the fact that important differences between industry and agriculture may justify differentiation in legislation.[37]

33. Daniel Reeves, Inc. v. Anderson, 43 F.2d 679, 682 (2d Cir. 1930).

34. 163 U.S. 537, 559 (1896).

35. See Cummings v. Richmond County Board of Education, 175 U.S. 528 (1899), and its influence on Gong Lum v. Rice, 275 U.S. 78, 85 (1927).

36. Adair v. United States, 208 U.S. 161 (1908); Richard Olney, *Discrimination Against Union Labor—Legal?*, 42 *Am. L. Rev.* 161 (1908).

37. See Connolly v. Union Sewer Pipe Co., 184 U.S. 540 (1902), and compare with Tigner v. Texas, 310 U.S. 141 (1940).

Take the other side of the medal. It is too easy to attribute judicial review resulting in condemnation of restrictions on activities pertaining to property to "economic predilection" of particular judges. The due process clauses extend to triune interests—life, liberty, and property—and property—and "property" cannot be deleted by judicial fiat rendering it nugatory regarding legislation touching property. Moreover, protection of property interests may, as already indicated, quite fairly be deemed, in appropriate circumstances, an aspect of liberty. Regulation of property may be struck down on the assumptions or beliefs other than narrow economic views. And so we find that Justices who were the most tolerant of legislative power dealing with economic interests have found in due process a protection even against an exercise of the so-called police power. It was true of Mr. Justice Holmes in *Pennsylvania Coal Co.* v. *Mahon*,[38] and of Mr. Justice Brandeis in *Thompson* v. *Consolidated Gas Utilities Corp.*[39]

Let us turn to the much mooted "clear and present danger" doctrine. It is at least interesting that that phrase originated in one[40] of a series of cases in which convictions for heavy sentences were sustained against defendants who had invoked the right of free speech in circumstances which led Mr. Justice Holmes to characterize them as "poor fools whom I should have been inclined to pass over if I could."[41] "Clear and present danger" thus had a compulsion for Mr. Justice Holmes against recognizing Debs's freedom to an utterance that in retrospect hardly seems horrendous.[42] Would it carry equal compulsion with other judges? One can be confident, in any event, that Mr. Justice Holmes would not have deemed his doctrine a bar to the power of a State to safeguard the fair conduct of a trial for a capital offense

38. 260 U.S. 393 (1922).
39. 300 U.S. 55 (1937).
40. Schenck v. United States, 249 U.S. 47, 52 (1919).
41. 2 *Holmes-Pollock Letters* 11 (Howe ed. 1941).
42. Debs v. United States, 249 U.S. 211 (1919).

from being thwarted by intrusion of utterances from without. There is the best of reasons for believing that Mr. Justice Brandeis would not have carried his natural devotion to the place of freedom of speech in a democracy to such a doctrinaire denial of an equally indispensable need—trial in court, not outside it—of a free society.[43]

Concerned as I am with the evolution of social policy by way of judicial application of Delphic provisions of the Constitution, recession of judicial doctrine is as pertinent as its expansion. The history of the constitutional position of the right to strike affords an illuminating instance. After invalidating a law withdrawing the use of the injunction against strikes,[44] the Court came to conceive of the conduct of a strike as an aspect of the constitutionally protected freedom of discussion,[45] but soon retreated from this position and recognized that picketing, as the weapon of strikes, is not merely a means of communication.[46] No matter how often the Court insists that it is not passing on policy when determining constitutionality, the emphasis on constitutionality and its fascination for the American public seriously confound problems of constitutionality with the merits of a policy. Industrial relations are not alone in presenting problems that suffer in their solution from having public opinion too readily assume that because some measure is found to be constitutional it is wise and right, and, contrariwise, because it is found unconstitutional it is intrinsically wrong. That such miseducation of public opinion, with its effect upon action, has been an important consequence of committing to the Court the enforcement of "the mood" represented by these vague constitutional provisions, can hardly be gainsaid by any student of their history.

Much as the constitution-makers of other countries have drawn upon our experience, it is precisely because they have drawn upon it that they have, one and all, ab-

43. See Maryland v. Baltimore Radio Show Inc., 338 U.S. 912 (1950), denying certiorari to 193 Md. 300 (1949).

44. Truax v. Corrigan, 257 U.S. 312 (1921).

45. Thornhill v. Alabama, 310 U.S. 88 (1940).

46. Giboney v. Empire Storage & Ice Co., 336 U.S. 490 (1949).

stained from including a "due process" clause. They have rejected it in conspicuous instances after thorough consideration of our judicial history of "due process."[47] It is particularly noteworthy that such was the course of events in framing the Constitution of India. Sir B. N. Rau, one of the most penetrating legal minds of our time, had a major share in its drafting, and for the purpose he made a deep study of the workings of the due process clause during an extensive stay here.

Is it the tenor of these remarks that courts should have no concern with other than material interests, that they must be unmindful of the imponderable rights and dignities of the individual which are, I am sure I shall have your agreement in saying, the ideals which the Western world holds most high? Of course not. Recognition of them should permeate the law, and it does so effectively even in courts that do not have veto power over legislation. They constitute presuppositions where parliaments have not spoken unequivocally and courts are left with the jural task of construction in its fair sense.

Thus, while the Chief Justice of Canada could say: "We have not a Bill of Rights such as is contained in the United States Constitution and decisions on that part of the latter are of no assistance," he reached the same result in *Saumur* v. *City of Quebec*,[48] as a matter of construction, that was reached under the due process clause in *Lovell* v. *City of Griffin*.[49] Again, only the other day the Supreme Court of Canada rejected the view that the mere claim of immunity by a Minister of the Crown from producing in court a document relevant to its proceeding is conclusive. It deemed such a claim "not in harmony with the basic conceptions of our polity." The reason given by Mr. Justice Rand deserves to be quoted: "What is secured by attributing to the courts this preliminary determination of possible prejudice is protection against executive encroachments upon the administration of justice; and in

47. See Mendelson, "Foreign Reactions to American Experience With 'Due Process of Law,'" 41 *Va. L. Rev.* 493 (1955).

48. [1953] 2 Can. Sup. Ct. 299.

49. 303 U.S. 444 (1938).

the present trend of government little can be more essential to the maintenance of individual security. In this important matter, to relegate the courts to such a subservience as is suggested would be to withdraw from them the confidence of independence and judicial appraisal that so far appear to have served well the organization of which we are the heirs."[50] So, likewise, the Appellate Division of the Supreme Court of South Africa ruled that when an act conferred autocratic powers upon a Minister —it was the Suppression of Communism Act—it must, in the absence of explicit direction by Parliament, be construed with the least interference with the liberty of the subject.[51]

While the subjection to Parliamentary criticism is the only remedy for much in Great Britain that with us becomes the stuff of lawsuits, the English executive is amenable to challenge in court for exceeding statutorily defined legal powers. In construing such authority, English courts enforce the right to a hearing as a presupposition of English law, unless Parliament has clearly enough indicated the contrary.[52] The English courts have also been resourceful, through the use they make of certiorari, in setting aside executive action when based on reasons not justifiable in law.[53] This increasing tendency of courts to scrutinize the legal grounds given by administrative agencies for their actions may well promote greater responsibility in the agencies' exercise of authority and in their justification of that exercise.

If government under law were confined to what is judicially enforced, law in government would be very restricted, no matter how latitudinarian one's conception of what is fitting for judicial examination of governmental action. For one thing, courts have a strong tendency to ab-

50. Regina v. Snider, [1954] Can. Sup. Ct. 479, 485, 486.

51. Regina v. Ngwevala, [1954] 1 *So. Afr. L. R.* 123.

52. See S. A. deSmith, "The Right to a Hearing in English Administrative Law," 68 *Harv. L. Rev.* 569 (1955); so, likewise in Canada, L'Alliance des Professeurs Catholiques v. Labour Relations Board, [1953] 2 Can. Sup. Ct. 140; and in New Zealand, New Zealand Dairy Board v. Okitu Co-operative Dairy Co., [1953] *N.Z.L.R.* 366 (1952).

53. For application of this principle in the United States see Perkins v. Elg, 307 U.S. 325 (1939), and Securities and Exchange Commission v. Chenery Corp., 318 U.S. 80 (1943).

stain from constitutional controversies.[54] Thereby, they may avoid conflict, at least prematurely if not permanently, with the other branches of the government and they may avoid also the determination of conflict between the nation and the States. Moreover, settlement of complicated public issues, particularly on the basis of constitutional provisions conveying indeterminate standards, is subject to the inherent limitations and contingences of the judicial process. For constitutional adjudications involve adjustment of vast and incommensurable public interests through episodic instances, upon evidence and information limited by the narrow rules of litigation, shaped and intellectually influenced by the fortuitous choice of particular counsel.

Mr. Justice Brandeis made a fair estimate in saying that by applying its restrictive canons for adjudication, the Court has in the course of its history "avoided passing upon a large part of all the constitutional questions pressed upon it for decision."[55] This is true not only of our Supreme Court, which cannot render advisory opinions however compelling the appeal for legal guidance even at times of national emergency.[56] Insistence of an immediate, substantial, and threatening interest in raising such constitutional issues is a characteristic of all high courts with power to pass upon them.[57] But even where advisory opinions are constitutionally authorized, tribunals are reluctant to pronounce in situations that are hypothetical or abstract or otherwise not conducive to judicial disposition.[58] It is, I believe, not inaccurate to say that most of the

54. E.g., Peters v. Hobby, 349 U.S. 331 (1955).

55. Ashwander v. Tennessee Valley Authority, 297 U.S. 288, 346 (1936).

56. See Chief Justice Jay's reply to President Washington's inquiry, conveyed by Thomas Jefferson, in 3 *The Correspondence and Public Papers of John Jay* 486–489 (Johnson ed. 1891).

57. See the recent Australian case, Australian Boot Trade Employees' Federation v. Commonwealth of Australia, 90 *Commw. L. R.* 24 (Austr. 1954); see also Musgrove v. Chun Teeong Toy, [1891] A.C. 272, 283 (P.C.).

58. See Lord Haldane, in Attorney General for British Columbia v. Attorney General for Canada, [1914] A.C. 153, 162 (P.C. 1913); Lord Sankey, in In re the Regulation and Control of Aeronautics, [1932] A.C. 54, 66 (P.C. 1931).

occasions when the Supreme Court has come into virulent conflict with public opinion were those in which the Court disregarded its settled tradition against needlessly pronouncing on constitutional issues.[59]

The confining limits within which courts thus move in expounding law is not the most important reason for a conception of government under law far transcending merely law that is enforced in the courts. The day has long gone by when Austin's notions exhaust the content of law. Law is not set above the government. It defines its orbit. But government is not law except insofar as law infuses government. This is not wordplaying. Also indispensable to government is ample scope for individual insight and imaginative origination by those entrusted with the public interest. If society is not to remain stagnant, there is need of action beyond uniformities found recurring in instances which sustain a generalization and demand its application. But law is not a code of fettering restraints, a litany of prohibitions and permissions. It is an enveloping and permeating habituation of behavior, reflecting the counsels of reason on the part of those entrusted with power in reconciling the pressures of conflicting interests. Once we conceive of "the rule of law" as embracing the whole range of presuppositions on which government is conducted and not as a technical doctrine of judicial authority, the relevant question is not, has it been achieved, but, is it conscientiously and systematically pursued?[60]

59. Dred Scott v. Sandford, 19 How. 393 (1857) does not stand alone; see Pollock v. Farmers' Loan & Trust Co., 157 U.S. 429 and 158 U.S. 601 (1895), controlling until the Sixteenth Amendment of February 25, 1913; Adkins v. Children's Hospital, 261 U.S. 525, 543 (1923), overruled by West Coast Hotel Co. v. Parrish, 300 U.S. 379 (1937).

60. In what I have said of course I do not mean to give the remotest support to the notion that the law is "a brooding omnipresence in the sky." I reject it as completely as did Mr. Justice Holmes in Southern Pacific Co. v. Jensen, 244 U.S. 205, 222 (1917) (dissenting opinion). It might further avoid confusion to restrict the term "law," particularly in a judge's mouth, to the commands of society which it is the duty of courts to enforce, and not apply it to those decencies of conduct which should control other branches of government but are without judicial sanction. But perhaps law has so established itself as a portmanteau word that clarity does not require too pedantically restrictive a use of it so long as no doubt is left regarding the circumscribed scope of the judiciary's function.

What matters most is whether the standards of reason and fair dealing are bred in the bones of people. Hyde Park represents a devotion to free speech far more dependable in its assurances, though unprotected by formal constitutional requirement, than reliance upon the litigious process for its enjoyment. Again, widespread popular intolerance of the third-degree, such as manifested itself in the well-known Savidge affair, reflects a more deeply grounded rule of law than is disclosed by the painful story of our continuing judicial endeavor to root out this evil through decisions in occasional dramatic cases.[61] Let me give another illustration. "Crichel Down" will, in its way, serve to summarize the duty of obedience to standards of fair dealing and avoidance even of the appearance of official arbitrariness. As such it will affect the future conduct of English government as much as some of the leading cases which have been important factors in the development of a democratic society.[62] You will note that the instances I have given of manifestations of law responsive to the deep feelings of a people are drawn from a nation that does not rely on a written constitution. I need not add that the distinctive historical development in Great Britain, in the context of its progressive cultural and economic homogeneity, has made possible accomodation between stability and change, defining the powers of government and the limits within which due regard for individual rights require it to be kept, without embodying it in a single legal document enforceable in courts of law.

I hope, however, that you will not deem me unduly romantic in deriving comfort from the undertaking given the other day by the Kabaka, as a condition of his return to his people in Buganda, when he promised that he "will well and truly govern Buganda according to law."[63] I find

61. For the Savidge case, see 220 H.C. Deb. (5th ser.) 805–891 (1928); Inquiry in regard to the Interrogation by the Police of Miss Savidge, CMD. No. 3147 (1928). As to our experience, see e.g., Chafee, Pollak, and Stern, *Report on the Third Degree,* 4 National Commission on Law Observance and Enforcement Reports 13 (1931), and the series of well-known cases in the *United States Reports.*

62. See Public Inquiry ordered by the Ministry of Agriculture into the Disposal of Land at Crichel Down CMD. No. 9176 (1954); Brown, *The Battle of Crichel Down* (1955).

63. *The Times* (London), Aug. 13, 1955, p. 6, col. 5.

reason for my comfort in the fascinating account by Professor Max Gluckman of Manchester University of the extent to which law permeates the lives of the Barotse tribes of Northern Rhodesia, law in the sense in which this Conference is discussing it and not something religious in nature.[64]

If what I have brought you, in my endeavor to give you as frankly as I may the distillation of sixteen years of reflection from within the tribunal peculiarly concerned with government under law, is charged with being an old-fashioned liberal's view of government and law, I plead guilty. For the charge implies allegiance to the humane and gradualist tradition in dealing with refractory social and political problems, recognizing them to be fractious because of their complexity and not amenable to quick and propitious solutions without resort to methods which deny law as the instrument and offspring of reason.

I have not been able to submit to you large generalizations that illumine or harmoniously assimilate discrete instances. Still less have I been able to fashion criteria for easier adjudication of the specific cases that will trouble future judges. They are bound to be troubled, whether they will be faced with variant aspects of old problems—old conflicts between liberty and authority, between the central government and its constitutent members—or new problems inevitably thrown up by the everlasting flux of life.

Believing it still important to do so, I have tried to dispel the age-old illusion that the conflicts to which the energy and ambition and imagination of the restless human spirit give rise can be subdued, even if not settled, by giving the endeavors of reason we call law a mechanical or automatic or enduring configuration. Law cannot be confined within any such mold because life cannot be so confined. Man's most piercing discernment of the future cannot see very far beyond his day, even when guided by the prophet's insight and the compassionate humility of a Lincoln. And I am the last to claim that judges are apt to

64. Gluckman, *The Judicial Process Among the Barotse of Northern Rhodesia* (1955).

be endowed with these gifts. But a fair appraisal of Anglo-American judicial history ought to leave us not without encouragement that modest goals, uncompromisingly pursued, may promote what I hope you will let me call civilized ends without the need of defining them.

In what I have been saying you have no doubt heard undertones of a judge's perplexities—particularly of a judge who has to construe, as it is called, vague and admonitory constitutional provisions. But I am very far from meaning to imply a shriveled conception of government under law. Quite the contrary. The intention of my emphasis has been not on the limited scope of judicial enforcement of laws. My concern is an affirmation—my plea is for the pervasiveness throughout the whole range of government of the spirit of law, at least in the sense of excluding arbitrary official action. But however limited the area of adjudication may be, the standards of what is fair and just set by courts in controversies appropriate for their adjudication are perhaps the single most powerful influence in promoting the spirit of law throughout government. These standards also help shape the dominant civic habits and attitudes which ultimately determine the ethos of a society.

In exercising their technical jurisdiction, courts thus release contagious consequences. Nothing is farther from my mind than to suggest that judges should exceed the professional demands of a particular decision. If judges want to be preachers, they should dedicate themselves to the pulpit; if judges want to be primary shapers of policy, the legislature is their place. Self-willed judges are the least defensible offenders against government under law. But since the grounds of decisions and their general direction suffuse the public mind and the operations of government, judges cannot free themselves from the responsibility of the inevitable effect of their opinions in constricting or promoting the force of law throughout government. Upon no functionaries is there a greater duty to promote law.

Index

Index

Bei Fragen zur Produktsicherheit wenden Sie sich bitte an:
If you have any questions regarding product safety,
please contact:

Walter de Gruyter GmbH
Genthiner Straße 13
10785 Berlin
productsafety@degruyterbrill.com